THE LOST UNIVERSE

THE LOST

UNIVERSE

PAWNEE LIFE AND CULTURE

GENE WELTFISH

UNIVERSITY OF NEBRASKA PRESS

Lincoln   London

Publishers on the Plains

UNP

Copyright © 1965 by Gene Weltfish
Copyright © 1965 by Basic Books, Inc., Publishers

Originally published under the title *The Lost Universe with a closing chapter on "The Universe Regained"*

First Bison Book printing: 1977

Most recent printing indicated by first digit below:
2   3   4   5   6   7   8   9   10

Library of Congress Cataloging in Publication Data

Weltfish, Gene, 1902–
    The lost universe.

    Reprint of the ed. published by Basic Books, New York, under title: The lost universe, with closing chapter on The universe regained.
    Bibliography: p. 480
    1.   Pawnee Indians.   I.   Title.
[E99.P3W45   1977]   970'.004'97   77–7164
ISBN 0 8032 0934 7
ISBN 0–8032–5871–2 pbk.

Bison Book edition published
by arrangement with the author.

Manufactured in the United States of America

TO NEIL, EVAN, ANN, AND DES

AND THEIR NEW *Mundus Novus.*

THE LOST UNIVERSE
Prologue

The Lost Universe *is an account of one year in the life of a six-hundred-year-old American Indian nation that continued its existence within the United States through the Civil War period, retaining its integrity as a nation until it was uprooted and dissolved in 1876.*

This is the story as told directly by the citizens who were part of it in those last years and who, in the course of their lives, saw it become a lost universe.

Nations are even now in danger of dissolution, but they are not lost. The knowledge and wisdom of the six-hundred-year-old Pawnee nation is one of the unknown building blocks that was built into the nation of the United States. In the Pawnee nation was summarized the knowledge of a continent that reached back nearly twenty thousand years in time to when mankind first discovered the New World. In it is embodied our continuity with human history as it developed in this land.

PREFACE

THE LOST UNIVERSE was first rediscovered through the language of the Pawnee people. As a research associate of the Department of Anthropology at Columbia in 1928, it was suggested to me by Franz Boas, its chairman, that I undertake a formal study of the Pawnee language, the best preserved member of the then unknown Caddoan language family. After a week's preliminary work with Henry Moses, the only Pawnee member of the One Hundred and One Ranch Circus which was performing in New York at that time, I went to Pawnee, Oklahoma, bearing a letter of introduction to his father, John Moses, dictated in Pawnee phonetics so that I could read it to him since he was monolingual. The next step took me to the Pawnee Indian Agency where I met Walter Keyes, Agency interpreter, who, taking due note of my impecunious condition, commended me to Stacy Matlock, who endowed our science with my first material on the Pawnee language. Following our usual procedure, he dictated myths and tales in the Pawnee language, which I wrote down in the International Phonetic Alphabet and subsequently obtained from him a more or less word-for-word translation, as well as a free English rendering. As the work proceeded, he felt that a more classic form of the language could be obtained from the few surviving monolingual Pawnees; I was able to record similar myths and tales, getting a translation subsequently by reading them back to Henry Chapman, a man who had a remarkable interest and facility in Pawnee and English and who continued as my interpreter and assistant in analyzing the grammatical categories. As a result of this work three pieces were published—a volume of recorded Pawnee texts, *Caddoan Texts, South Band Pawnee Dialect*; an analyzed text and grammatical sketch, "The Vision Story of Fox Boy," in the *International Journal of American Linguistics*; and an article jointly with A. Lesser, "Composition of the Caddoan Linguistic Stock," in the *Smithsonian Miscellaneous Collections*. This work was supported by the Committee on American Indian Languages of the American Council of Learned Societies, Washington, D. C.

The next step was to record the way of life of the Pawnees of which the language was an instrument, in the interests of semantic analysis; this was undertaken under a grant from the Columbia Council on the Humanities through the Department of Anthropology, the work continuing at Pawnee, Oklahoma, until 1936 at various intervals. The present work represents the main substance of what was gathered for this purpose. The chief narrator was Mark Evarts, a Pawnee of the Skidi Band, whose childhood was spent on the reservation in Nebraska from 1861 to 1875, when Pawnee culture was still very much an integral polity and way of life. His personal identity is embodied in the "Boy Otter" as he appears in the following narrative.

My relationship with Mark Evarts began casually in the course of my grammatical researches. Historically there were four political groups of Pawnees known as bands, the Skidi or Wolf Band, the Kitkehaxki or Little-Earth-Lodge Band, the Tsawi or Asking-for-Meat Band and the Pita-hawirata or Man-Going-Downstream Band. Each of these traditionally pronounced the language somewhat differently, but it was always known that the major difference was between the Skidi and the other three known collectively as the South Bands because of their former more southern location. From linguistic samples I took of each of the four, the distinctions among the South Bands were not clear enough to identify at that time. Only the Skidi difference was clear. Mark Evarts served as my Skidi informant with Henry Chapman as interpreter in my attempt to find any grammatical and pronunciation distinctions. Evarts' English was broken and so heavily overlaid with a Pawnee accent that it was understandable only with considerable difficulty. As my Pawnee vocabulary improved, we developed a Pawnee-English mode of communication that made the interpreter no longer necessary. As I extended my research into the semantic and cultural background of the language, Evarts became a major resource and ally in my investigations and our work extended over seven years and involved the entire Oklahoma Pawnee community.

At this time (1928–1936) Evarts was living with friends and relatives. His wife and child had died tragically only a few years before, and he had lost his little farm to the bank. The crises that had beset his life as a member of his tribe and times were epic in their proportions; as a man in the decline of his years, he had many questions to ask, and I, as a novice in life's ills and trials, had many questions to ask of him. Many of his questions concerned the white culture and its values, and, as a young anthropologist, mine sought answers through the cross-cultural perspective I hoped to find in studying the Pawnee way. Together we established the language of our common humanity and communicated what we wanted to know about the special character of each other's culture as well as of life in general. It was my purpose to understand the Pawnees as people, not as Indians or as social categories and certainly not as historical antiques.

Although in the 1920's only seven hundred Pawnees survived, some Pawnee customs remained among them and at least eight of the older people spoke no other language than Pawnee. The town of Pawnee, Oklahoma, was surrounded by the allotted lands of the Pawnees, the lands of each band being located in a different direction. The bands were still somewhat socially discrete. The mainstay of the diet was largely the traditional corn, beans, and squash grown on their own farm plots and dried and stored as of old. Beef had taken the place of buffalo meat and was prepared by thin slicing and drying for storage or boiled on feast days. Relationships in kin groups continued, and some of the religious ideology survived. A Doctor Dance Ceremony was performed by the last survivors who possessed the arts and the knowledge involved and brought us some welcome rain after a long dry spell. The question was, "How to give these fragments life and place them in their integral context?" We evolved the plan of utilizing one year of Pawnee life in as much detail as possible, covering the round of the year through the four seasons as reconstructed with the help of the surviving Pawnees. Our plan proved to be an effective means of developing vivid recall in Evarts and the other old Pawnees. For a number of reasons we would think of our year hypothetically as 1867; in that year the Pawnee settlement and round of life was sufficiently integral to serve as a base line for our reconstruction. Some of the other surviving Pawnees were in their late teens and twenties in that year. Evarts supplied a normal thread of events in answer to my prodding questions for the details that seemed to a Pawnee all too obvious and we supplemented and checked this with whomever we thought had relevant knowledge concerning one point or another. Most of the old people had worked with me on linguistics before that time.

It was not possible to reproduce the material in the exact order in which I collected it. I have had to reassort the material somewhat so that it falls into some of our own functional categories and at the same time so that it fits within the seasonal round of the year. Under the pressure of time when my notes were recorded I rendered the Pawnee or Pawnee-English in which it was given into the closest normal English equivalent I could muster. Also, this book was compiled a quarter of a century or more after it was recorded. I have avoided altering the original simple declarative language too radically. In some cases I have retained the original language with very little variation, particularly where it is an incident that had often been recounted among the Pawnees, a very familiar situation, a technical account, a speech, a personality sketch. Such passages are indented from the left margin.

In addition to the informant record, I have checked my account in detail with most of the existing material on the Pawnees and in some cases supplemented it from these sources. This is detailed in the Notes and Comments with references correlated with my text. Recently excavated archaeological materials together with eyewitness accounts by contemporary observers of the 1830's and 1840's have overwhelmingly vindicated the accuracy of my Pawnee informants. The most substantial help in this recent phase of the work has been given me by Prof. John L. Champe, author of an important stratigraphic treatment of Nebraska archaeology, *Ash Hol-*

low Cave. As chairman of the Department of Anthropology of the University of Nebraska, he welcomed me to his laboratory where I worked from 1954 to 1958; during this period he gave unstintingly of his time and knowledge, going over my material and taking me to many of the archaeological sites where the Pawnees and their predecessors are known to have lived. He and his wife, Flavia Waters Champe, most generously welcomed me to their home during that time. I also acknowledge with profound thanks the unfailing help and support of my former student and now colleague in the science, Carol King Rachlin.

I received substantial help at all times from the staff of the Nebraska State Historical Society—Mr. Marvin Kivett, Director, Dr. W. D. Aeschbacher, Dr. Donald Danker, Dr. White; Prof. James C. Olson of the History Department of the University of Nebraska; Virginia Faulkner of the University of Nebraska Press; and Mari Sandoz and her sister Flora, who entertained me at the ancestral home and made me really understand the value and the beauty of the Nebraska sandhills. I have also been aided and abetted by the Missouri River Basin Surveys group of the Smithsonian Institution in Lincoln, under the direction of Dr. Robert Stephenson, one of whose Missouri River excavations I was privileged to visit and there enjoyed his cordial hospitality. My friend Mrs. Rella Looney of the Oklahoma Historical Society was most helpful to me during my stay in Oklahoma City recently.

In 1954 I had the opportunity to visit the Pawnee again. My return was gladdened by the hospitality of Blanche Matlock, her daughter, Bessie (now Mrs. Delbert Horse Chief), and the grown-up grandchildren of my now departed first informant and mentor, Stacy Matlock; Walter Keyes, his wife Norah, and their daughter, Alma, who had married Basil Chapman, son of my interpreter, Henry Chapman (recently deceased); and my friends, Andrew and Eulah Eschelman, together with her sister, Pauline Murie, one of my close personal friends now living in Wichita, Kansas, and the Echohawk family. I was also welcomed by Mrs. George Roberts and Dolly Moore and, on a subsequent visit, Mr. Henry Roberts, Chief of the Pawnee Council, and his wife. My return to Pawnee was a deeply moving experience because of the profound effect my work there has had on my life and the warmth with which I was received into the community.

During the years after 1932 I received a great deal of support from my colleagues in anthropology. The late Prof. William Duncan Strong, who did pioneering work in Nebraska archaeology, was a constant source of psychological and intellectual support in his unfailing interest over the years. I owe a special debt of gratitude to Prof. Charles Wagley of Columbia for his many years of active interest and encouragement. In this connection also I wish to thank Dr. Frank H. H. Roberts, Jr., recently retired Director, Bureau of American Ethnology.

From 1958 to 1960, as a Fellow of the Bollingen Foundation, I have been the recipient of a grant that made the writing of this book possible; I would like particularly to mention Miss Nancy Russ and Mrs. M. Curtis Ritter of that organization. To my sister, Florence Goldin, Director and Vice President of the Grey Advertising Company, I want to express my gratitude and deep appreciation for support far beyond the call of sisterhood in all ways, including financial when it became necessary.

During the summer of 1963 I have had substantial assistance in rearranging the manuscript from my colleague at Fairleigh Dickinson University, Prof. Andrew H. Drummond, talented producer and dramatist.

Madison, New Jersey GENE WELTFISH
October 1964

CONTENTS

Contents   xvii

ILLUSTRATIONS

THE LOST UNIVERSE

1

THE LOST UNIVERSE

~~~~~~~~~~~~~~~~~~~~~~~~~~~~~~~~~~~~~~

Modern Problems and Their Relationship to Older Cultures—Archaeological Sites on the Great Plains—Early Recorded History of the Earth-Lodge Peoples—Results of European Settlement of the Land—the Basic Household of the Pawnee—Political Control and Social Organization—Religious Life—the Significance of This Study for Our Own Future Outlook

~~~~~~~~~~~~~~~~~~~~~~~~~~~~~~~~~~~~~~

No ONE KNOWS what our future will be. Shattered are the bounds of our safe universe where the earth met the sky on the horizon and infinity lay beyond, where the rock was the solid foundation of our experience, and where now the particle of a ten billionth of a second will splinter beyond our foreseeing and whirl itself into unknown oblivion. In all things the outer bounds of our lives are broken—in the universe and in the home; in the family and in the nation; in the region and in the uni-nation. Are there more people beyond our planet? In the past people have come from other continents and destroyed many local worlds. When the European invader set out from his continent to explore the oceans, he too broke the secure images of life of the peoples he met and overwhelmed. Fearfully we can imagine that advanced peoples live on the planets, and they may come to us.

But this is not all of our concern. Our problems are more intimate and immediate. What will be the shape of the home and family of the future? What kinds of occupation will people have when machines activate machines? How do we find our way into tomorrow?

It has long been man's custom to look into the past to find a way into the future, but the anthropologist has brought a new dimension to our thinking by exploring the culture worlds of other peoples. This is a delicate task, and it takes a special kind of listening. The wholly different

I

image of life possessed by another people can be acquired only with patience and understanding, for as we do comprehend a different perspective on human experience, one by one our most cherished beliefs of what is basic to humanity are challenged, and we feel at a loss in the face of a need for new horizons.

What can there be of current interest in the life of an American Indian people who lived their way and were overwhelmed by time and events? Their way of life is very different from our own and bears little resemblance to ours even in its fundamentals, and by that very token it opens up a new world of human possibilities that we need to ponder before we can come back to our own problems with a fresh outlook.

During the past twelve years nearly a million and a half dollars has been spent by the United States Government on a special archaeological project whose purpose is to investigate man's life on the Plains. Forty archaeologists are working in the Missouri River Basin trying to uncover the remains of old Indian villages along the river banks. They go about their work with a special urgency, for soon the flood waters of the river, caught up by the new dam, will cover the area altogether, and the ancient history of man's conquest of the Great Plains will be lost.

The archaeological sites are lonely places high along the river banks, but once they were teeming with life. Clusters of circular embankments mark the places where high domed earth lodges formed a Plains Indian village. In the bottoms close to the river were the fields of corn, beans, and squash, each patch carefully tended by the women and their little daughters. Toward evening the men would be coming home with the deer or the elk they had killed, and later their friends would come in to share the feast. The big storage pit outside the house was full of a year's supply of dried vegetables and the dried meat of the buffaloes they had killed during the last summer's hunting expedition. The dried kernels of corn were simmering in the clay pot that hung over the fire, and the family would eat its meal quickly before the guests arrived. When the guests came for the feast of deer meat, they would talk about the three-day tribal harvest ceremony and how much dried buffalo meat would be available for the large banquets they would have. They would talk of the enemies they repulsed, and now in the deserted quiet of the place the archaeologist was gathering up the broken potsherds, the charred kernels of corn, the chipped stone arrowheads, the stone pipe bowl. All these things he carefully catalogued and photographed with a record of just how each thing was found in the ground, and he shipped them back to the museum where they would be kept for further study.

From historical records we know that in the 1700's when our record for this area begins, there were Indians living there in earth-lodge villages, some of whose tribal names we can identify. Is it possible that from their modern survivors we can glean some fragments of remembered custom and old ways of life? Today the ethnologist is hard put to get very much that is significant. Even with the opening of the present century, most of these peoples had so long ago been decimated by disease and war that memory of their past life was extremely fragmentary. Along with whatever fragments of custom were recorded then, the archaeologist must use the written testimony of the chance traveler and trader to give life to his findings.

In the 1700's when the trade and travel records were written, the Missouri River was a main artery of European–Indian trade. Commercial companies centered in St. Louis maintained regular contact with trade centers up the river, and in the 1800's steamboats plied their way upstream with goods and guns to exchange for furs. Trade centers for exchange were an ancient tradition of American Indian life, and now they eagerly made their way to the trade centers of the European where new goods and materials could be gotten. But the price was dear. For besides the new goods, there came new and fatal diseases—measles, smallpox, cholera, and a variety of fevers—wiping out hundreds and even thousands of people at one blow. Whole tribes that had lived in the region for hundreds of years were wiped out or left in such a fragmentary condition that they joined with other tribes and lost the knowledge of their past identity.

The Pawnees who lived outside the mainstream of commercial traffic were less affected than the others by this holocaust. They lived along the outlying tributaries of the Missouri—the Loup, the Platte, and the Republican—that flow eastward across the present State of Nebraska and join the Missouri at their eastern ends. It was only in the 1830's, when the Pawnees were living in the western part of their territory at what they refer to as Old Village, that the direct effects of the many historic pressures of the time began to bear down on them. At that time they numbered about 12,000 and were living a well-integrated native life of a sedentary Plains people such as the archaeological remains indicate— planting crops and hunting buffalo in alternate seasons. Then disease began to do its terrible work, and the large bands of refugee Siouan peoples (some 30,000 strong), pushing in from the east, attacked them with increasing furor in order to gain their territory and their hunting grounds. Finally the Pawnees began to move eastward along the river courses to be nearer the centers of civilization, and by 1859, by agreement with the United States Government, they moved onto a reservation near the present town of Genoa, Nebraska. By this time their numbers were reduced to 3,400, but they still retained their old social forms and independent polity and a traditional rhythm of life throughout the year. Added to their problems had been the full force of westward migration of the expanding United States—the Oregon Trail, Mormon Trail, and Gold Rush along the Platte, and, from 1861 on, a crescendo of Sioux attacks unchecked by a United States torn by Civil War. Then, when the war was over, came the white settlement of their territory and still more conflicts for the land, the water, and the timber. Finally they could stay there no longer; they had to leave their homeland, and they moved south.

The Pawnees were related by language to a people to the south of them, the Wichita, and they often went visiting, some of them remaining for several years in order to learn new ceremonials which they brought home with them when they returned north. As far back as the 1770's a contingent of three hundred Pawnees had gone south and settled permanently there. They were very welcome at this time and every inducement was given to make them stay, as the Wichita were already heavily depleted in numbers by disease and enemy attack; the Pawnee group constituted a much-needed reinforcement.

In the summer of 1870, just a hundred years later, a Pawnee chief led a visiting party of three hundred men to the Wichita. After their return, subsequent parties went down in successive years and were made welcome by the Wichitas and other tribes in the area that is now Oklahoma; in 1873, despite many doubts on the part of their chiefs, two-thirds of the Pawnees finally left their Nebraska home and migrated south. By November 1875 the last Pawnee contingent arrived in Oklahoma. Many met their death as a result of the change. Fevers and starvation took such a heavy toll that by 1879 only 1,440 survived, and, by the U.S. census of 1910, just 633 Pawnees remained alive.

The time of my arrival in Oklahoma to do ethnological and linguistic work was 1928, some fifty years after the time the Pawnees had settled there permanently. We did not know then that Pawnee life with its combined settled village life and migratory buffalo hunting was an old way of life on the Plains.

The general opinion among anthropologists was that in the not too distant past earth-lodge peoples such as the Pawnee had formerly lived in the woodland areas east of the Mississippi and, migrating out onto the Plains, had begun to adopt the migratory life of buffalo hunters and were in the process of abandoning their settled ways.

Archaeology has since shown us that the combination of migratory and sedentary village life is much older in the Plains than we had thought and that, far from being in transition, the ancestors of the Pawnees had probably followed a similar way of life in Nebraska for nearly seven hundred years. Archaeological remains of earth-lodge villages are found along the Republican, Platte, and Loup rivers, a progressive evolution of the houses from rectangular to round appearing with the passage of time. The houses and the remains of objects and food found in the archaeological settlements show such a clear continuity into historic times that their identification as ancestral Pawnee is well nigh inevitable.

In 1867 the four bands into which the Pawnee were politically organized were concentrated along the banks of Beaver Creek, a northern tributary of the Loup River near the present town of Genoa, Nebraska. They had moved to this place in 1859 as a result of their treaty with the United States Government. Each of the bands had its separate location, the Skidi villages in the westernmost position and the three South Bands ranged along the stream to the east about half a mile away. From west to east they were: Kitkehaxki (Little-Earth-Lodge), Tsawi (Asking-for-Meat), and Pitahawirata (Man-Going-Downstream, or East). Each of the bands is said to have comprised a number of villages; for the three South Bands this cannot be documented. From 1700 on, when our historical records are clear, the Skidi were the largest of the four bands and were composed of a number of distinct villages, estimated between twelve and nineteen. In 1867 the Skidi had four distinct villages, Tuwahukasa (Village-across-a-Ridge), Tuhitspiat (Village-in-the-Bottomlands), Tskirirara (Wolf-in-Water), and Pahukstatu (Pumpkin-Vine). The villages were made up of ten to twelve earth lodges, each a high spacious dome-shaped building housing thirty to fifty people. Besides containing thirty to fifty people under one roof, the personnel was likely to change from season to season after each migration to the buffalo hunting grounds. The basic Pawnee household was as different from ours as it is possible for a human arrangement to be. And yet it gave personal satisfaction to its members and within itself produced the whole material and social base for an ongoing community. In fact, this is what we wish our family life would do. Sibling rivalries, partial or total rejection of child by parent or smothering attention, demands on the child for the unfulfilled ambitions of the parents, or overprotection because of resented parental hardships, heavy-handed control of parent over child in a severely restricted social environment—these are ills that are intimately linked with the very physical arrangements of our present family living. There are things about Pawnee life that suggest that an enlarged home environment for our children would improve our lives—a matter to be considered in the concluding chapter.

Even more startling to me than the contrast in home life was the question of political control among the Pawnees. They were a well-disciplined people, maintaining public order under many trying circumstances. And yet they had none of the power mechanisms that we consider essential to a well-ordered life. No orders were ever issued. No assignments for work were ever made nor were over-all plans discussed. There was no code of rules of conduct nor punishment for infraction. There were no commandments nor moralizing proverbs. The only instigator of action was the consenting person. In religion, the regular round of ceremonies that followed the seasons was in charge of a priesthood, but no one of these ceremonies was ever instigated by them. Only when a single person had the call through visions and invited the priesthood to discuss it with him, pledging his support in food and goods, would the ceremony ever be performed. In all his work, both public and private, the Pawnee moved on a totally voluntary basis. Whatever social forms existed were carried within the consciousness of the people, not by others who were in a position to make demands. As I talked to the old men and women I realized that this is what we wish for but do not have. As they described the coordination of their households, I repeatedly asked when they got together and laid the plan they were apparently carrying through and in what exact terms they discussed it. The answer was always, "They didn't discuss it at all. They don't talk about it. It goes along just as it happens to work out."

For example, sentinels were always needed to man the outposts and keep watch for the enemy who might be lurking nearby ready to attack the villages, or in the process of sneaking up on them. Sentinels were neither assigned nor called for by anyone. A number of young men who were friends would be talking together and one would mention that this was about the time the enemy would be attacking. Then one of them would remark, "I think I'll go up to the sentry post early tomorrow morning." Another would say, "I think I'll do that too." Then several others would chime in and word would get around, and other young men would also turn up long before dawn at the different sentry posts. The household coordinated itself in precisely the same way. A remark by one person brought a complementary remark from another, and the plans seemed to shape themselves.

Time after time I tried to find a case of orders given, and there was none. Gradually I began to realize that democracy is a very personal thing which, like charity, begins at home. Basically it means not being coerced and having no need to coerce anyone else. The Pawnee learned this way of living in the earliest beginnings of his life. In the detailed events of everyday living as a child, he began his development as a disciplined and free man or as a woman who felt her dignity and her independence to be inviolate. I was often confronted with the feeling that they expected of me a kind of independence and decisiveness that was not considered becoming to a woman in our society. Men and women expected the same clear and well-defined reaction from me, and among themselves it was evident that it was their accustomed mode of interacting.

The Pawnees had chiefs, but these were the focus of consensus, not the wielders of power. There was no over-all chief of all the Pawnees. The two major political groupings among the Pawnees were the Skidi and the South Bands, distinguished by a slight difference in the pronunciation of the Pawnee language. The main subdivisions within these groupings were villages and households. The village numbered from three hundred to five hundred people in ten to fifteen households. The real administrative officials of the Pawnees were the chiefs of the villages. All people within a village considered themselves kin, and the chiefs were conceived as heads of extended families rather than as superimposed government officials. Although the chieftainship was hereditary in certain families, the individuals selected to fill the post were chosen for their humility and sagacity. An aggressive temperament was considered a barrier to the office. There were definite implicit mechanisms for village coordination and interband cooperation, often by means of emissaries sent between the households of chiefs to express their combined opinions and to learn the wishes of the other parties. Public opinion and consensus were always well estimated. No official conceived that an arbitrary decision was feasible or desirable.

The difference in our expectations is shown in the words of Fray Francisco Casañas de Jesus Maria, first missionary to the Caddo-Hasinai, a related tribe to the Pawnees, in 1691 (Swanton, 1942, pp. 170-171):

> These allied tribes do not have one person to govern them (as with us a kingdom is accustomed to have a ruler whom we call king.) They have only a *xinesi*. He usually has a subordinate who gathers together four or five tribes who consent to live together and to form a province or kingdom, as it might be called—and a very large one too, if all these tribes had one person to rule over them. But such a head they have not, and I, therefore, infer that this province in New Spain is called "Teijias" [Friend]—which really expresses just what they are because each tribe is a friend to all the others—cannot be called a kingdom.

And Robert Lowie says in *The Crow Indians* (1935, p.5):

> How shall we conceive the ancient chief?—a good "valiant" man. He was neither a ruler nor a judge and in general had no power over life and death —he decided when and where his followers should move and pitch camp.

As I studied Pawnee life I often asked myself how far the power mechanisms that characterize our present social life are really indispensable. In our theory of democracy we express a profound desire for the kind of voluntarism that the Pawnee practiced. It is not easily described, for it is implicit in the individual personalities of the people themselves. Their personality pattern only too readily eludes us, and only by attention to minute detail can we come to understand its special quality.

And yet, although very different in all other details, Pawnee life, like our own, was strongly molded by the four seasons. Each of the seasons had its special program of activities that, taken together, made a complete and consistent pattern. The spring and fall of the year were the times of planting and harvesting the crops of corn, beans, and squash. During these two seasons the Pawnees lived in their earth-lodge villages that were ranged along the bank of Beaver Creek. During the summer and again in winter, the whole tribe left their villages behind and set out on a long expedition to the southwestern part of the state where large herds of buffalo followed their accustomed paths of migration. Several thousand men, women, and children with their horses and dogs were lined up for miles as they followed the river courses on their journey south and west, carrying tents, utensils, and other paraphernalia and a quantity of dried vegetables for their food. They killed some thousands of buffalo on each of these expeditions, drying the meat and packaging it to take home to their villages. While they were in the villages, they manufactured everything they needed both for household life and for their life on the march.

But the thing that made life most worthwhile to the Pawnees was their elaborate round of ceremonies. This was based on a complex philosophy of the creation of the universe and of man and of their ongoing nature. The ceremonies were considered as the means for keeping the cosmic order in its course and the continuance of the earth and its life processes. No ceremony could be conducted without a feast of boiled buffalo meat, and a large part of the meat that was gotten on the tribal buffalo hunts was used for this purpose. Rehearsals for the ceremonies, the preparation of costumes and ceremonial objects, and the performance of the cere-monies themselves occupied a large part of the time, attention, and skill of the men, and from the household itself the women contributed not only the dried meat that they had prepared, but also boiled corn, corn bread, and other vegetable dishes for entertaining during rehearsals and for ɹne feasts.

The ceremonies were more than religious observances. They were the whole focus of Pawnee aesthetic life, particularly in the performing arts. The pageantry and the costuming, the dances and the miming were de-veloped for beauty as well as for religious significance. They were opera and ballet, and the songs were appreciated for their technical and aes-thetic value and were sung on many occasions throughout the year just for the pleasure of singing or hearing them. Laughter and enjoyment as well as religious fervor were common experiences of the spectators dur-ing the performances, and the performers tried to get a good audience and to please them.

The same Plains region that brought terrible hardships to our settlers, provided a rich life for the Pawnees. Their way of life on the Plains goes back to a very old tradition. Archaeologically we have reason to believe they were in the same area from about A.D. 1250. They appear in written history in 1540 when Coronado and his Spaniards were trying to expand their territory northward from the Southwest. Marquette, exploring the Mississippi for the French in 1672, carried the calumet down the river as a pipe of peace, a custom attested by other tribes to have been originated by the Pawnees. The Pawnee custom of sacrificing a captive maiden to their god of war, the Morning Star, captured the attention of the people of the eastern United States and Washington in 1820 through reports of a young Pawnee hero, Man Chief, who risked his life to rescue a Sioux girl from the sacrificial scaffold in defiance of the Pawnee priesthood and the other participants in the ceremony. Echoes of Aztec customs that appeared in the ceremony and in other phases of their religion made people wonder how the Pawnees had come to make their home in the northern Plains or in what manner they could have received such customs. In the 1840's as main trails going westward cut directly across their territory, the Pawnee name became a feared byword to the settlers going west.

To many people today the word Pawnee suggests Plains Indian life. They were indeed a people of our Plains, but the nature of their life was very different from the common stereotype of a Plains Indian. They were not the horse-riding, settler-hounding people that we think of as the typical Plains Indian. In the following account the Pawnee will appear in very human terms in the context of organized tribal life. We hope this more realistic setting will dispel some of our static preconceptions and open up new possibilities for change in our point of view about these early American settlers.

But beyond this primary goal, this study has a more general value for us. The portrayal of Pawnee life through the most ordinary situations has thrown into sharp contrast the major qualitative differences in their life-ways which fit none of our familiar stereotypes. As a human mode, it is a New World life and a new and unfamiliar dimension in the human spectrum. Cultural contact with the European and adoption of some of his ways did not change its essential character as even now American Indian groups persist in being not European. It is this persistent patterning that makes this account of Pawnee life an important resource as a control case in our search for a science of society. If we make an effort to enter it sincerely so that we see it whole, we can look at our own life with new eyes and be better able to perceive new paths to our own tomorrow to become the New World people that we really are.

I shall first introduce a number of Pawnee individuals who lived more than a hundred years ago in a Nebraska Pawnee village and the various life circumstances in which they were involved. Then I will place them within a household in that village and tell in full detail how they worked, played and worshipped together over the course of an entire year. Finally I will relate what became of them at the end of the nineteenth century and the beginning of the twentieth, after their village life ended. I will finish my account with a possible life pattern for our own future that my Pawnee studies have helped me to develop.

2

PAWNEE PEOPLE AND

THEIR FORTUNES: I

~~~~~~

*General Introduction—the Pawnee Outlook on
Reality—the Meaning of Courage—the House-
hold of the Pawnee—Marriage and Interpersonal
Relations—the Village*

~~~~~~

I WRITE NOW of the personal arrangements of the Pawnee not so much as
a means of reconstructing our past history but rather as a contribution to
our future. Ours is a time when new nations have been born and old nations must be reborn. Within each nation the people have shared a common self-image, compounded of their evident material circumstances and
the elaborate rationalizations of their administrative sector. Our present
form of nationalism is a new social form hardly two centuries old. It is
dependent on an art and science of communication unparalleled in man's
history. Through this medium, our individual hopes and aspirations have
been cast in a common mold to an unprecedented degree. In this country
we speak of individualism and individuality as our most precious contribution to the human mode. At the same time, manufacturing stand-
ardization has placed us in a mass-designed material environment to an
extent that no people has ever experienced. And as for our thoughts, I
need only mention the mass media. In effect, we are free to think when
we are not assailed by mass-designed thoughts.

Two centuries ago Jean-Jacques Rousseau, Swiss expatriate in France,
had a premonition of this mechanization and mercantilization of the human personality in a growing mercantilist society. He pleaded for a return—return to the land, return to the woods—in effect saying, "Stop,
look, and listen!" But who could then stop the march of humanity to-

ward the material well-being for which it had ever been striving?

The communications revolution in Europe had opened up the New World of available land and resources for the taking—that is, to those that had power to take it. The European, with an atavistic feudal mentality, found the people that inhabited the land no problem. The Spaniard found them a convenient work force, the north European, an obstacle. Through whichever view, the life of the people was forfeit: in the first case through disregard of their dignity and humanity; in the second, through exile and extermination. When it became convenient, we spirited others from their own continent across the ocean. At this date, the revolution of the underdog resounds in our streets, and we are compelled to review all our values. We have no choice. The future American dream must grasp realities that are not yet here.

For this task, neither instant wisdom nor instant answers are available. The mind and the spirit is called on to make a new kind of effort. In common parlance we speak of "stretching our imagination." Whoever of us has knowledge or science must bring it to bear on this problem with which we are so urgently confronted at this time. It is through an understanding of a widely divergent human mode—another world view—that I ask you to begin our quest for a new individuality—a new self-sufficient independent personality, capable of resisting mass thoughts and mass things and of following its own star, of shaping its own hopes and aspirations.

This personality must be self-sufficient but not self-enclosed, for without a free and dynamic interaction with other people it can only dry up and wither away. Such a personality cannot grow in a relationship of dominance and submission. Genuine equality is its only environment. It cannot grow under pressure or the personal war we so blandly call competition. We need no longer hold lengthy debates on whether human equality is possible. It is being fought for now, and it will be won. Our society will change accordingly, and for the first time we will have, not theoretical, but *de facto* democracy. What kind of society will that be?

In addition to the renaissance of the human personality within the general social context, another major aspect of our lives has changed. Historically, society has moved step by step from a food-gathering economy to a hunting economy, and, with the death of the large animals at the end of the Ice Age, to an economy based on plants and agriculture. Then man again mastered his environment and produced his plant food so well that he had time to manufacture more and more of what he wanted, and industrial manufacture became the central theme of his economy. With industrial production came its twin brother, universal exchange—mercantilism. Now we have come to another major turning point in human history, "the point of no return for everybody," that is, automation (*Life,* July 19, 1963). Referred to as "sudden" in the magazine article, it should surely not be sudden to most of us. With the advantage of a clear consciousness of a long past and its major changes, we must accept change and move intelligently into the future. We must prepare for our new needs in a new society by opening to the light of questioning even our most basic institutions—the family, the home, modes and institutions of work, the character of administration, and our whole evaluation of everyday human experience. The Pawnee way is one of thousands of ways of life that mankind has developed. As a springboard for a reexamination of our own way of life it has the advantage of being so different from our own, and in fact from the whole patterning of Eurasiatic civilization, that a study of its ways and social interactions helps us to throw into sharp relief our most widely accepted hypotheses on the nature of "the basic human character" and to test whether some of these assumptions are in reality universal human nature or rather limited modes of learned behavior that we have developed for needs that are now becoming obsolete.

In its very essence, the Pawnee outlook on reality differs from our own. For us the material aspect is primary. On a second level of discourse, we place observed events; on a third level, which we count still less sure, is the "human factor"; and finally furthest removed from solid reality is the realm of ideas. In the Pawnee estimate of the world around him, the primary level of reality is thought. In our own story of creation, the deity shaped man out of clay, but the Pawnee deity—Vault-of-the-Heavens—began the process of creation with thoughts and so created the universe and the stars, and they in turn were to create man in their own image. When a Pawnee individual wanted to organize his life goals, he looked within himself in his thinking and was blessed by Heaven with a vision. In the Pawnee context, the *thinking* man was the essential human being. The universe continued its seasonal round only when man willed it through his thought of Heaven and its creative power. In creating man, Heaven had also created the moving force of the universe. In this order of things, events were an adjunct of *human* ongoing, and all the nonliving things were a fluid manifestation of the universal life process. A thing manufactured was a manifestation of a very personal skill, and a thing used was equally personal. The skill of the priest who kept the universe in motion and that of the arrowshaft maker had an analogous quality which was inherent in the person himself, and both were considered as dedicated public professions. For both living and nonliving things in the time of the creation, there were always two storms—one to build the empty structure and one for its continuity. This estimate of the nature of reality is almost the complete reverse of our own and is one of the many ways in which the Pawnee outlook contrasts rather sharply with ours.

As another contrast in values between the Pawnee and ourselves I would offer a story in the realm of human affairs. In attempting to translate from the Pawnee language in which much of this account was first obtained, we stopped to consider the word "courage." In order to give an example of what the Pawnee meant by courage, Mark Evarts told the following story:

A man became aware that a certain person was making slanderous remarks about him in many quarters. This distressed and irritated him deeply. One day he came to a decision as to what he would do. He had a wagon and a horse, and he painted his wagon and decorated his horse and then dressed himself up in his very best, painted his face, dressed his hair, put feathers in his hair, and then set out for the home of the slanderer. When he arrived he called out, "So and so, I want you to come out. I have something to show you." In the light of his actions, the slanderer hesitated to come out. But finally he made his appearance at the entryway of his lodge. Now the man he had slandered took him by the hand and said, "Do you see this horse and wagon?" "Yes," he replied with increasing trepidation. "Well, I give them to you," said his victim, and then departed. Needless to say, he never talked about him again.

"This," said Mark Evarts, "is a man of courage; that was the only horse and wagon he had."

Our first reaction to this story is one of rejection. How can one possibly call this an act of courage? Let us look at this action through Pawnee eyes. For one thing, by his action, the victim had cleared the society of a disruptive social element that could have grown into a more general network of hostilities and polluted the whole social climate so that they might no longer defend themselves effectively from outside attack nor coordinate their efforts for their mutual survival. It took real courage, from the Pawnee point of view, for a man to curb his anger and to make a material sacrifice as well. How different from our reaction which would lead a man to plant his fist forcibly into the face of the slanderer or perhaps counter with a more devious plan to get back at his opponent. The obvious result must necessarily be a continuation and augmentation of the social irritant.

This instance does not stand alone. In recent years the Fox Indians of Tama, Iowa, told a story about the Pawnees in a similar vein. It was customary for the young men to set out on the warpath in the fall or late summer. A young Fox warrior selected the Pawnees as the object of his attack. He made a rich haul and so decided to repeat his performance the next year. Then he went again a third time. This was decidedly against the recognized code according to which he should have distributed his favors more broadly. Now on the fourth occasion, the Pawnees lay in wait in their village and sure enough the young Fox warrior stealthily crept into the encampment ready to collect and run. This time the Pawnees were lying in wait for him, and they seized him and took him to the tent of the head chief. There the young warrior trembled within himself, prepared for the worst. One by one, the Pawnees began to remove his garments as the chief had ordered. Then they painted up his face, put on a new loincloth, a new shirt, new leggings, and new moccasins and loaded him with additional goods saying, "You have favored us three times already, now go home and don't come back for a while." As the Fox report, he never did return to the Pawnees. In fact, was there anything worse that a people could do to an attacking enemy soldier?

Let us now look at the household of the Pawnee—his home life. Most earth lodges housed from thirty to fifty people. The lodge was a production workshop in which, with few exceptions, everything required for use was produced, including the collection and processing of raw materials. A substantial part of this work was done by the women. The house was conceived as being divided into two duplicate halves—the north sector and the south sector—each of which carried out the essential household functions in alternation. There were two main meals a day, for example, the one being provided by the north side, the other by the south side, both serving all. In operation this meant that the woman who cooked the meal had raised all the vegetables in her own gardens, had dried and preserved them and kept them in her storage pit, and that all the meat she served was dried and packed by her on the buffalo hunt, carried back to the village (formerly on her back or by the dogs she raised), and also stored in the pit. In the past, the clay pot she cooked in would have been made by her (now a brass kettle from the trade store), and she was still making the large buffalo-horn ladle with which she served, the wooden mortar and pestle in which the mush was pounded, and for her "side" alone the wooden bowls and buffalo-horn spoons in which the food was served, the rush mats on which the people sat, and all the clothing they wore. Every day, morning or evening, she would serve twenty, thirty, forty, or fifty people a meal.

The way in which the morning and evening meal was allocated to one or the other "side" was a clear example of the characteristic Pawnee mode of personal interaction. There was no prearranged schedule at all as to which side would take the morning, which the evening meal. This was determined on each individual occasion by the inclinations of the principals most directly involved. From our point of view a plan would be made and the people fitted into it—from the Pawnee view, the plan emerged from the feelings of the people. This difference of approach is so basic that I feel impelled to stress it particularly. The Pawnee individual embraced responsibility; he had no inclination to shirk it. In a sense, the rhythm of Pawnee work life was like a ballet, whereas ours is like a prison lockstep: "You must, you must, you must get to work!"

The day's routine in our Pawnee household began when either Victory Call or Old Bull happened to awaken; this depended on which one decided to get out of bed first. Or else White Woman or Queen Woman might be the first to awaken, and then she would remind her husband that it was morning. From the time one or the other of the two men got out of bed, the day's program was set; the others simply followed the initial cue. When the man had gotten out of his bed he went outside and inspected the horizon and the stars, came in and kindled the fire, and said, "Fire's made." His senior wife then got up and started the breakfast. As observed by one of the contemporary missionaries in 1837, the rest followed with precision. The minor cycles of household operation were also conducted in a similar mode. Someone felt impelled to take care of a needed task and mentioned it and volunteers were forthcoming without further ado. Pressure and compulsion are implicit in our attitude toward work; voluntarism was the Pawnee way.

The functions of the women in the earth lodge were subdivided roughly according to age. The north and south quarters of the circumference of the house were each subdivided into three "stations." The central one of these (due north and due south) was the core position and it was occupied by the mature women of the lodge. They furnished the main provisions and directed the necessary work. At the inner or western station on each side was the place of the immature girls and newly married young women. The outer or eastern station on each side was for the old women, symbolically on the way out and physically nearest to the exit (or entryway) of the lodge. Most commonly each of these stations was occupied by several women who carried out its special functions jointly.

The details of the function of the central station have been mentioned above in connection with general household operations. The other two stations supplemented it in very different ways. At the east stations for the old women, the children past the age of infancy were cared for, the old women being referred to by the children as "grandmothers," regardless of the actual biological kinship. The children slept in the beds with their "grandmothers" and shared a bowl of food with them at meals. Grandma saw that they were warm and well fed and tried to help them in every way. She was a permissive, familiar, kind person to whom the child could always appeal. Between grandma and grandchild there was neither formality nor constraint. Jokes were made about a boy saying, "Look how close he sticks to his grandma; he wants to marry her!" or "There he goes always running to his grandma." Besides child care, the grandmother would give a good deal of assistance to "the senior women of the house." She supplemented their supplies of vegetables from her own garden from time to time, saying, "Daughter, cook this for our supper." She would also have a small private stock of dried meat that she had gotten by helping with its preparation during the hunt season, and she would also offer this at various times when it seemed a good idea. Again there was no regular schedule for this, nor any amount that was standard. Grandma already rendered considerable services to the house and was considered entitled to her "keep." She also gave substantive help with skin working, sewing, getting firewood, special manufacturing, and so on.

The young women and girls at the west stations did minor household tasks, but had a far more significant contribution to make to its ongoing. They were there to please and care for a capable man who would protect the people in the lodge, provide them with fresh meat by his almost daily hunting expeditions for deer, elk, or antelope, participate in the tribal buffalo hunts in the summer and winter each year so that they would all have dried buffalo meat, and carry on the official interrelationships with the community outside the household, including those with the village officials.

An influential and capable man might be given one of these girls in marriage with the understanding that her younger sisters would also be given to him when they came of age. If he were adjudged too old, the family was unlikely to agree to these further marriages. In the case of Old Bull, the family of his junior wife, Clear Day, was unwilling to give him her younger sister on this account. Fifteen years was considered a suitable age for marriage in a girl, and eighteen for a boy. However, the probability is remote that the couple would be of these ages respectively. First marriages for both a boy and a girl were almost always of a "May–September" type. A boy of eighteen was considered altogether incapable of playing a suitable married role in a household. A man contracted a marriage in terms of services he could render to the family of the girl that he married. Normally he was expected to come to live in her household and "take care of them," i.e., render them major services.

The son-in-law, i.e., the man married into a household, was known as *kustawixtsu*," the one that is sitting among [us]." The man on his part referred to his in-laws as *tatutkaku*, "I sit inside for you," that is, "I am in the house for your benefit." The reward he receives is his wife whom he calls *tatiraktaku*, "I own her," and she in turn refers to her husband as *tikuktaku*, "he owns me." These terms are not normally used under informal circumstances, the couple addressing each other by the common term for spouse, *raku*, or if they are on particularly pleasant terms, the man calls his wife *tsustit*, "old lady," and she refers to her husband as *kurahus*, "old man."

Because of the services required on both sides, a young man would have little alternative but to marry a capable older woman, and a young girl who was in no position to carry the responsibilities of a mature woman would normally marry a mature man. The situation finally reversed itself when, after a marriage to an older man, the woman attains maturity and the competence to maintain a household. She is now in a position to choose a handsome young man as a second husband. The young man on his part finally gains maturity at the age of forty and can sue for the hand of a young girl of fifteen and join a household where his capabilities will be appreciated. The father and father's brothers of the girl will look around for such a person for their daughter and will be glad to entertain his suit. In fact, as a young girl gained her maturity, numbers of such men would sue for her hand. The "fathers" might have some scruples about the suitors that already had a wife, chiefly because of the ill feeling it might generate between the households involved. But a man was not compelled to limit his marital relations to one woman or to one household so long as he could fulfill his obligations, i.e., provide meat for all through his exceptional talents as a hunter and horses and other luxury goods through his special ability as a warrior that could bring home booty. There was thus a certain fluidity about the marriage situation, although some marriages did last for many years.

A proper marriage was arranged with considerable formality, with special acts and mutual gift-giving on the part of both families. The element that determined the most binding unions was a substantial gift of horses to the girl's family by the suitor. The amount of the gift was a mark of the esteem in which the bride was held, and, even in the 1920's, one old woman mentioned with pride from time to time that six horses were given for her. As a woman got older, a marriage involved less and less property consideration, although a man suing for the hand of a woman in her prime would be likely to give a horse to her brother or a relative who stood in an analogous relationship as a mark of his respect for her and an earnest of good faith with her family. Everyone felt that an informal liaison without some family arrangements was bound to be a passing thing.

A man's obligations to his children were to some extent independent of these considerations. The Pawnees were very literal about fatherhood. For a child to be accepted in the community with any decent status, its physiological father must be known. In any given month from one menstrual period to the next, a woman had to confine her sexual activities to one man only, and when she was aware through the cessation of menstruation that she had conceived, she was required to notify the man and point out on what occasion of intercourse together the child was conceived. The man was then obligated, until the child reached full maturity of eighteen or more, to provide it with fresh meat in whatever household it might be residing and in other ways to be concerned with its well-being. A woman who departed from this iron-clad rule was unable to convince a man of his physiological paternity, and her child would then be a social outcast. It would be known as *pira-paru,* "hidden child," since the mother would be ashamed and try to hide it when her brothers came to visit. The child would be subject to many insults and humiliations throughout its life. In these terms, whatever the sentiments of the parents for each other, the child always had a legal right to the care of both its parents, clearly identified as its physical progenitors. Children were normally cared for by their grandmothers, and it was quite possible that various fortunes placed the child in one household with its grandmother, its mother in another household, and the father in still another. The obligations for support, however, remained incumbent on both parents.

The household as a working group of coordinated members was precisely organized, and each household had the same general structure. However, twice a year when the tribe set out on its semiannual buffalo hunts, the household work group fragmented itself into many smaller groupings, which reassorted themselves so that an able hunter became the nucleus of each new composite grouping. When they returned to the village the households did not necessarily reassemble with the same personnel as before. This was entirely optional, and there were many reasons why people might decide to join a different household group than the one they had been with before leaving. However, it was not too hard to establish a working household on this basis even twice a year, since the pattern of operation was the same everywhere. The three duplicate stations on the north and south sides of the lodge with their full complement of the young, mature, and old women was a frame into which any individual woman could fit herself in whatever household she entered with little loss of efficiency, since her duties were so clearly defined once she selected the category to which she belonged. And a child with a grandmother to care for it could fit in anywhere. Young men led a more transient existence. They were likely to congregate at different times in one lodge or another, and a bed would be made for them by putting down a mat between the central pillars and providing it with the necessary skin bedding. Old men also moved about rather freely, staying over night in various households whenever they were detained late of an evening telling stories or participating in a ceremony. As for the mature man, his married-in household was not considered his "true" home. In his married-in household he was an outsider with formal obligations, which sometimes tended to weigh rather heavily on him. Then he would go where his home really was—that of his sisters and his mother, where they would gladly feed him and take care of him and where he could relax and feel like a child. When this happened, his wife understood, and she knew he would be back after a few days.

The only stable and fixed unit of Pawnee life was the village with three hundred to five hundred people and from ten to twelve households. The village community centered around the chief who had his sanction through a vision from Heaven. Every person within the village was also under the tutelage of a given star, and the chief held the sacred bundle that represented the supernatural story of its origin and gave the village its continuity. In these terms, all the people in the village were considered as a kindred, but their specific cosmic derivation gave them differing social ranks. According to their star affiliations, some were born as chiefs, some as braves, and some as commoners; their social functions in the community were thus relatively preordained. When a chiefly infant was born to two high-ranking parents, he was wrapped in a wildcat skin, symbolizing the heavens with its panoply of stars and planets. When he married, the priest and his senior errand man impersonated the Morning Star and the sun respectively. High-ranking chiefly families provided the administrators, whereas the families of braves—the next in rank—provided the executive officers. The commoners, known collectively as *akitaru* "the tribe or people," were often reminded by their officials that only their support made it possible to carry out the responsibilities of high office. However, one's life was not entirely cast in this mold. A chief or brave might never be considered worthy of the office, or he himself might not feel capable of dedicating himself to its responsibilities, while a commoner could rise high in the social scale and acquire considerable wealth by becoming a successful doctor and earning high fees from his grateful patients. Some people of commoner rank had little use for prestige positions and would say, "I don't care to be a noted person." Another group would prefer a carefree life of adventure. They would go out on long scouting expeditions, roaming about the country and exploring to see what they could find. They were helpful to anyone in the village who needed them, without considering it beneath their dignity to perform any menial task and gave away what they had rather freely. Such men were referred to as "boys" on the grounds that they were like boys, having no care for accumulating anything or for providing for the morrow. They were regarded with affection and sometimes rose to the rank of brave in recognition of their long public service.

3

PAWNEE PEOPLE AND

THEIR FORTUNES: II

~~~~~~~~~~~~~~~~~~~~~~~~~~~~~~~~~~~~~

*Marriage Arrangements—Chart of Kin Geneal-
ogical Structure—Personal Relationships among
Kin—Individual Aspirations Expressed in Names
—Brief Sketches of Eleven Pawnee Lives—the
Kin System Not a Constricting Mold but a Fluid
System for the Individual Personality*

~~~~~~~~~~~~~~~~~~~~~~~~~~~~~~~~~~~~~

Marriage and Kin

ACCORDING TO PAWNEE theory, all marriages should be made within one's
own village, for to marry outside would be considered a poor risk, contrary to the cosmic plan. The sacred bundle and its ritual epitomized the
special heavenly order under which the villagers lived, and an outsider
would have no place within this order. As a result, the village was in fact
a large extended family, geographically localized.

However, within this general family connection the lines as to whom
one could and could not marry were very sharply drawn. The careful
identification of the physiological father as well as of the mother was an
important aspect of this plan. The kinship system was designed to avoid
the marriage or sexual involvement of close blood relatives. Marriages of
parents and children, brothers and sisters, both half- and full-sisters and
brothers, were definitely excluded. Beyond this rather universal type of
incest ruling, there were other principles which governed these relationships among the Pawnees. The family was primarily matrilineal—that is,
the mother's family was regarded as one's very own family, while that of
the father and his relatives was considered a different order of relationship.

As I have already pointed out, a man always had a home in his sister's household, even though his marriage might lead him to take up residence elsewhere. For this reason, according to Pawnee ideas, the brother owed his sister a special lifelong debt. In recognition of his indebtedness, when the sister had a son, she might send him to live in her brother's married-in household when he was about ten years old. There his maternal uncle would teach him whatever he needed to know in life, and as he reached adolescence he would receive his first sex instruction from one of his uncle's wives. If his uncle had several wives, the boy might extend his attentions to the others from time to time. The term for maternal nephew was *tiwat* and maternal uncle, *tiwatciriks*, super- or real-*tiwat*.

Another basic Pawnee family pattern concerning the man, was the identification of a whole group of brothers. Through the rule of primogeniture the oldest brother inherited all the family property and as senior member of the group was responsible for the well-being of all his younger brothers. A younger brother who availed himself of the sexual favors of his older brother's wife upon occasion was not considered out of order, and theoretically the older brother should act like a gentleman, paying no attention and making no mention of it. This ideal, however, was not always realized. It was fairly usual form for two or more brothers to set up a joint household, sharing their wives and their property. The children addressed them all as fathers and mothers and they in turn addressed all the children as their own. A similar but not identical condition might exist among a group of sisters married to the same man, the children addressing all the sisters as mother. A group of brothers would address each other as *irari*, and the same term was used among a group of sisters. But across the line of sex different terms that were more precise were used: a man's sister was referred to as *itahi* and a woman's brother, as *iratsti*. Under the difficult conditions of Pawnee life, a child gained considerable security from this multiple parenthood. As the Pawnees phrased it: "We think a child should not be too closely bound to its own mother, for should she have to be away or should she die, it would break the child's heart."

As each person was introduced into a child's life, the child was given an idea of how to act toward that person. One of the ways in which this was conveyed was through the kin term by which the child was instructed to address the newcomer. Along with the term of address, a style of conduct was indicated so that the child received a code of manners as he came in contact with one after another of his normal associates.

As the depth of the relationship merits, the Pawnee child was taught to treat his mother with profound respect. The term *atira*, "my mother," carried with it a high degree of reverence among the Pawnees. However, the mode of acting toward a mother was far more formal than it is ordinarily in our society. The mother was concerned at all times for her child. She provided for him and instructed him in how to act in his own

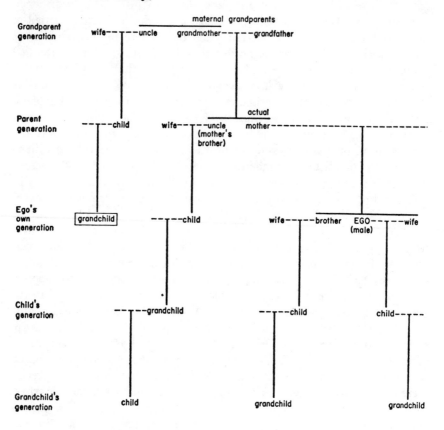

MOTHER'S LINE
(connecting lines indicate siblings,
dotted lines ——— indicate marriage)

Ego has a grandchild relationship in his
own generation through a collateral line
of his maternal grandmother, that is,
through the descendants of her brother.

FIGURE 3-1. Genealogical kinship table showing Mother's Brother's and Father's Sister's lines. Ego has grandparent-grandchild categories in his own generation through descent from the brothers and sisters of his grandparents. These could provide him with marriage partners.

FATHER'S LINE

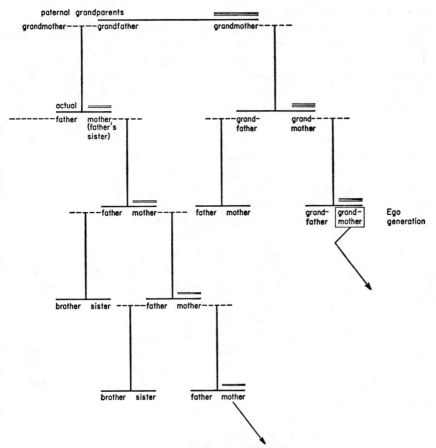

Ego has a grandparent relation in his own generation through a collateral line of his paternal grandfather, that is, through the descendants of his grandfather's sister.

life and in social situations, but there was no easygoing informality. A mother was a mainstay for life, but one did not bother her with petty problems. When the child was weaned, he was given over to the care of his grandmother where he enjoyed a relationship of intimacy, warmth, and informality that made it easy for him to appeal to her for any want he might have, however petty or apparently foolish.

In terms of the conduct associated with them, these two kin relationships, the one to *atira*, "my mother," and the other to *atika*, "my grandmother," stood at opposite poles. These two kinds of relationship might be called a *respect* relationship and a *joking* relationship respectively. The one type of conduct was designed to preclude any kind of sexual involvement or marriage, while the joking relationship implied the possibility of physical familiarity, including sexual relations. This is not to say that a boy was likely to become sexually involved with his own grandmother, but the term was also applied to other relatives in the kin network, in which case sex relations were permissible and marriage (when the individuals were not otherwise attached) was positively encouraged.

A network of kin relationships extended throughout the village for every individual member. The number of actual kin terms employed was very limited, but under each kin term a number of relatives of varying degrees of biological closeness were included. The term, *atira*, "my mother," applied not only to own mother and mother's immediate sisters, but also to the sisters of the father as a mark of special respect. This attitude and the kin term, *atira*, was applied not only to the sisters of the father, but to their daughters, i.e., the daughters of the paternal aunt, and in turn to their daughters as well, going down the generations as long as the relationship could be traced. The object of the extension of the mother term to these women in the father's line was to preclude any possibility of sex relations or marriage with them. At the same time these women reciprocated by answering to this term, *atira*, with the term for child, *piirau*, and treating these individuals as a mother would, but to an exaggerated degree. A person entering the household of a paternal aunt or her female descendants would be welcomed at once with exclamations of concern; he would be spoken of as child, or even as baby, and offered food and care. The person would be given to understand that "they have a home here." One was very careful to limit one's visits to these relatives. You were bound to be quite circumspect, for should you admire something in the house or even show some interest in it, you might well receive it as a gift as a mark of their regard.

The relationship with the father was also highly formalized, involving special concern and instruction in right conduct and maintenance, particularly providing fresh meat and dried buffalo meat which were considered necessary for energy and growth. Strictly speaking, the father and his family were not *own* family as that of the mother was. The mother's sisters were completely identified with the mother, and there was little difference in the attitude toward them. The mother's brother, *tiwatciriks*, was an even more familiar person, who was theoretically ready to share whatever he had with his nephew, *tiwat*. The boy might enter the household into which his maternal uncle was married from the age of ten and assume the role of apprentice husband and eventually, when he came of age, of junior husband. He called his uncle's wives "wife" and the children of his uncle *piirau*, "my child." After adolescence, he might in fact be the physiological father of one or the other of them. On the other hand, some of his uncle's children might be older than he; he would still call them *piirau*, and they in turn would address him as *atias*, "my father," the same as their own father. Thus it might very well happen that a man in his twenties would call a boy of ten, *atias*, "my father," and the boy would call him *piirau*, "my child." Such an age reversal might also happen in the father's sister's line, where a grown man would address a little girl as *atira*, "my mother," and the little girl would call the man *piirau*, "my child." In the first case, the grown man would be expressing his respect for his father, and even more particularly for his father's sister in his treatment of her son. In this role, the boy was in a superior position and addressed the man as "child." The second case would involve the women and girls in the father's sister's line directly. At bottom, both these situations had their basis in the unequal relationship between a sister and a brother, as the brother was the taker while the sister with whom he always had a home was the provider. He owed her nothing in return, but he accorded her great respect, and his children followed suit. They demonstrated their respect by applying to their paternal aunt the most revered term they knew, *atira*, "my mother," and carried it to all her female descendants. The boys in this line they called *atias*, "my father." In this case these terms were used to express not age or parenthood, but respect. The factor of age did not enter the relationship; a small boy might call a grown man, *piirau*, "my child," the man addressing the boy as *atias*, "my father."

Wherever the grandfather term *atipat* was applied or extended, it was a relaxed relationship. Familiar joshing, poking fun, and manhandling were in order. When a girl addressed a man by this term, sex relations were a possibility, and, if the circumstances were right, marriage was favored. In this mode, during the intermissions in the *Awari* or Groundbreaking Ceremony in the spring just before planting, virgins received advice on their prospective sex life from warriors whom they addressed as *atipat*, "grandfather," the girls in turn being addressed as *raktiki*, "grandchild." Under any circumstances other than the joking kin category, the Pawnees scrupulously avoided any reference to the physical person or to intimate relations. To transgress this prohibition would be regarded as a personal insult that could be classed as almost criminal. Even within the joking category, they were very careful not to go too far. Account was taken of the respective personalities involved—some people being considered too sensitive to take "strong" joking while others with more hardy spirits being treated somewhat more roughly. A not uncommon tactic of an actual grandfather was to take his grandson out of bed of a cold morning and dump him into the water or into the snow. This was intended to harden him, and no one else would be in a position to do such a thing. The boy on his part could be somewhat rough with grandpa as well, though an actual grandparent was unlikely to receive such physical manhandling, since regard for age was never wholly out of the picture. At formal meals and official feasts, during the actual eating of the meal, relaxed conversation was in order, and this usually took the form of one of the prominent men's teasing the other, whom he addressed through a kinship classification as "grandpa." The humor was partly in the fact that they were of similar age and status. In this climate of feeling toward the grandparents, the marriage of a young man or woman to an older person was more congenial emotionally than it would be to us. Among the Pawnees, intimacy and grandparent were constantly associated, while the attitudes toward the parents were diametrically opposed. There was a similar prohibition among brothers and sisters, and since there were no strangers as possible marriage partners, the direction of marriage and sex interests was only too clearly pointed toward the classificatory grandparent group. The mastery of kin behavior was indispensable to the Pawnee, and he kept refining its nuances for his interpersonal relationships throughout his life.

The actual number of kin terms involved, except for the relationships by marriage, were limited to thirteen essential ones (see tables 3-1 and 3-2). Their application to other categories appears in the genealogical chart of standard kinship relations of a male (see Figure 3-1). This covers own generation and two generations above (parent and grandparent) and two below (child and grandchild)—five generations in all that the Pawnees regarded as the essential ones to consider. Beyond these generations, parents and child terms were again used, i.e., in the great grandparent and great-grandchild categories. There is a clear logic of reciprocity in the kin terms—that is, anybody who calls someone father is called child by that person and vice versa, anyone who calls a person sister is called in return sister or brother as the case may be, grandparent answers with the term grandchild, and so on.

The form of the Pawnee kinship structure has a direct relevance to our theory of how society evolved. In its crudest form and as rather popularly held, the theory is that man began as a food-gathering group with more or less promiscuous interrelationships of the people and no real social form. According to this construct, when garden culture later

TABLE 3-1. *The Essential Pawnee Kin Terms Except for the Relationships by Marriage*

1.	*atira*	my mother
2.	*atias*	my father
3.	*irari*	sibling of the same sex, viz., brother to brother, or sister to sister
4.	*iratsti*	brother, woman speaking
5.	*itaxri*	sister, man speaking (Skidi dialect, *itahi*)
6.	*piira'u*	child
7.	*tiki*	son
8.	*tsuat*	daughter
9.	*tiwat*	nephew or niece, viz., child of a man's sister
10.	*tiwat-ciriks*	uncle, mother's brother, meaning the super-*tiwat*
11.	*atika*	my grandmother
12.	*atipat*	my grandfather
13.	*rak-tiki*	grandchild, viz., son's child.

The parent and grandparent terms are different from the others in that each has three variants. They contain a ROOT and also a possessive pronoun. Thus:

ati-AS	my father	*ati*-RA	my mother
as-AS	your father	A'*as*	your mother
is-AS-*ti*	his father	*i*'A-*sti*	his mother
ati-PAT	my grandfather	*ati*-KA	my grandmother
a-PAT	your grandfather	*a*-KA	your grandmother
i-PAK-*ti*	his grandfather	*i*-KA-*ri*	his grandmother

Normally people did not indicate that a woman was their biological mother as distinct from her sisters, nor the woman that the child was biologically hers within this grouping, but under exceptional circumstances it could be said that a mother was *irata'u*, "my very own," and that a child was *kutatixra'a*, "my very own child."

became man's way of life, the woman, being the gardener, acquired considerable social power. As an economy depending on herds of domestic animals came into being, the men took power and held the women in check, insisting on a recognition of their individual paternity of their children and therefore on monogamy on the part of the woman. The Pawnee situation casts some doubt on a literal interpretation of this theory. The Pawnee women do cultivate the gardens, run and maintain the house. They can hardly be said to be politically dominant. Kin closeness is considered greater in the mother's line than in the father's, but the incest taboo covers both. One cannot maintain that the political position of the men can be equated with that of the Roman patriarch who had power of life and death over the permanent members of his household, which included captive slaves and the immediate members of his family. Nei-

TABLE 3-2. *Pawnee Kin Terms for Relationships through Marriage*

The kin terms by marriage involved verbal roots and were specifically descriptive of certain functions. They had pronominal elements attached and often varied with the specific meaning of the phrase:

kus-tawex-tsu	sitting-among-the one who	said of a *son-in-law*
tat-ut-ka-ku	I-for you-inside-sit	said by a son-in-law about *the men of his wife's family*, signifying that the son-in-law is at the service of his wife's family
tatira-ktaku	I her-own	*my wife*, husband speaking
ti-ku-ktaku	He me-owns	*my husband*, wife speaking
raku	A term used reciprocally between husband and wife in direct address—*spouse*	

If husband and wife are on good terms, they call each other:

tsustit	old lady	*wife*
kurahus	old man	*husband*
tskurus	is for all female in-laws, used by both men and women in speaking of them. It is unlikely to be used alone outside a verbal context. For example, *ti-kut-tskurus, she-to me-is female in law*, etc.	

ther can one reverse this idea and say the women are the real power, and therefore we have a matriarchate. In point of fact, neither one is dominant, but rather the position of men and women among the Pawnees is decidedly more balanced than in our society. Physiological paternity is known, but this does not lead to a double standard with monogamy enforced for the women. The household is not a power structure of women but a plan for the organization of work, with the personnel being very fluid. One could argue that this was a society in an intermediate stage between matriarchy and patriarchy. No one can deny that change must necessarily occur, even in Pawnee society—or in any other for that matter. But the direction this change will take is less likely to depend on the internal conditions than on the larger forces that impinge on it from outside. One can make a broad leap into the realm of speculation and think of the possibility that had the European not arrived on the scene, the

Pawnees might have improved their horticulture to such a degree that they would have made important advances in industry and thus developed a much more widespread pattern of trade. What the division of labor would have been and the status of different occupational groups in the light of their implicit attitudes can only be conjectured. There is no assurance at all that they would have developed one group as dominant over the others or a permanent power structure of the Old World type. As much as 20,000 years may separate the bulk of New World population from the Old, and the Old World social formulas need not have appeared among them at all. Athough the buffalo have been domesticated in individual instances, suggesting that they may be domesticable, there is no certainty that the North American Indians would have domesticated them. And even had that been the case, it does not mean that the men would have developed the kind of dominant position over women that characterizes most of Old World culture, nor even that empires of the Ghengis Khan type would have appeared. In the light of the development of urban concentrations in Peru, Mexico, and Central America, as the economy became more complex and as a consequence the population more concentrated, urbanlike centers were very likely to occur. Both Mexican and Peruvian native political administrations as we know them from the period of contact were conquest organizations. Conquest need not have been the path of the Pawnee. In fact, intergroup alliance that has gained fame in connection with the League of the Iroquois was characteristic not only of the Pawnee but of the other Caddoan peoples extending all the way south to Texas and the Gulf and north to Dakota.

In the major division of labor between men and women, a man did not feel threatened because he acquired skills possessed by women. On the contrary, it was considered incumbent on the Pawnee man to be a "good Pawnee cook," and men were perfectly adept at slicing and drying meat, shelling corn, and other skills. In the 1930's during the period of my fieldwork in Oklahoma, the men offered to demonstrate for me and, when I looked dubious, they reassured me saying that, after all, they often had to do these things when they were far away on the warpath or on exploring expeditions. While I was in Oklahoma I observed that the men often lent a hand to the women, without the slightest self-consciousness, and if the woman didn't happen to be home when they came in they tended to get right on with the necessary mealtime preparations and attention to the children. Neither the man nor the woman felt threatened or in a position of blurring the sex lines by this procedure. From their point of view it was a matter of acquired skills, not sex. Although homosexuals or lesbians were rare, these relationships were not regarded as a serious social anomaly but as a personal inclination which the Pawnees thought people had a right to have. With their reaction to their primary division of labor, there is no certainty that as greater specialization of labor developed, the Pawnees would have developed a social hierarchy of occupations of which India is a supreme example.

It is all too easy, having analyzed a social structure, to give it a certain rigidity and permanence that it does not have among the people themselves. Definite as the Pawnee kinship system may seem, in operation it permitted a wide area of alternative behavior for the individual.

The question of kin lines came up in a substantive way whenever a marriage was being arranged. As this involved the acquisition of property by some of the relatives and the establishment of social contacts for others, there was always a certain variation in the individual interests. The first question asked in relation to the proposed marriage was whether the partners were so closely related that there was too great biological closeness. If it was decided by the assembled father's brothers that they were definitely outside the incest group, then the degree of distance would be discussed. One man who favored the marriage for his own personal reasons would say, "As I see it, they can be reckoned child and grandchild, and, although the relationship is a close one through the mother's line, it is a good thing for marriages to be kept within the family, as they will share each other's interests." Another, not in favor of the match for his own reasons would state, "True, they are child and grandchild through the mother's line, but it's a disadvantage for marriages to be made too closely within the kin grouping, as any quarrel between the couple will quickly spread to the whole kindred. I think so and so who is more distantly related would be more desirable on this account." Then someone else might counter with, "Well, while one might say the couple are related through the mother's line in such and such a manner, from another point of view, looking further back, there is still another kin category that should take precedence, and I think they are not so closely related that this latter argument should be involved." And so it continued until they came to terms. But these terms were by no means fixed by what the outsider might consider *the* rules.

Another common occasion where the kinship factor came up was at the time of the tribal hunts. While they were on the march, there was an attempt to improve one's connection in a better household or in a more advantageous position, and a request to join such a household when they got home was backed up with a genealogical discussion as to how close the kinship was to an important member of the desired household through various alternative kin lines.

And finally it was also possible to disown one's relatives, no matter how close they might be. Long-standing hostilities might grow up over time and finally give rise to coldness between even the closest kin. A kin tie, in order to be effective, had to be validated in a number of ways or it might in fact lapse. The most elementary condition was the use of the kin term as a greeting. This could be done with more or less enthusiasm or affection, denoting how far one could count on the tie. The use of the kin word on meeting might simply be withheld altogether—an absolute disclaimer of the relationship.

A second cue as to how valuable a person considered a given kin tie could be taken from the manner in which the typical kin behavior was carried out. In the joking grandfather–grandchild type of behavior, the jokes might be mean, sarcastic, or mildly jocular, but if the person showed no reaction at all it was most damaging to the relationship. Careless behavior within the "respect" categories would simply be taken as a personal insult, but no response whatever to the other person that should have a kin status, canceled the relationship entirely as a personal bond.

There were no normal interpersonal relations among the Pawnees that did not carry with them a kin designation. People with whom one dealt as equals had to be placed in some kin category; lack of such a relation could only imply slave or enemy status. In the various trade or gift exchange ceremonials that were conducted between tribes or bands, a whole kin structure was built up so that they could communicate on a peaceful level. The most notable example was the Calumet or Peace Pipe Ceremony, in which the visiting trade party represented Fathers, while the ones they visited were designated their Children. Many of the ceremonial acts were designed to carry out this idea. There was no way of communicating with peaceful strangers unless they were fitted into the kin structure, and it is for this reason that the President of the United States is referred to as the Great White Father and that white friends are adopted into the tribe.

A third aspect of kin reactivity was the exchange of gifts and this too was an index of cordiality or lack of it between two kinsmen. It sometimes happened that a distant relative was so warmly cultivated that the relationship took on a degree of intimacy that was considerably greater than would ordinarily be implied in the genetic tie. Such a case happened with the mother of the boy Otter, White Woman. As was customary, Otter's maternal uncles—his mother's brothers—were frequent visitors to the household. Uncle War Cry and his younger brothers High Noon and Noted Fox would come in often to meals. Uncle War Cry was head brave of the Skidi, and he would often linger to smoke and talk with Victory Call. Uncle War Cry was solicitous for Otter's welfare at all times, and the boy was welcome to his uncle's home at any time. Whenever they passed each other in the village, Uncle War Cry would call out to him, "*Nawa tiwat*," and Otter would reply with "*Nawa tiwat-ciriks.*" The same was true of the other two uncles.

From time to time something would happen that puzzled the boy very much. Two men in particular would insist on greeting him in the same terms as his own uncles, saying, "*Nawa tiwat*," and they came up to him and stated that they were his *real* uncles and that his mother was mean as she was not willing to have them to the house as she should. However, the boy kept his counsel until one day when it came to the attention of his mother. Then she said in a strongly hostile voice, "They're mean. They're no brothers of mine!"

A considerable time passed before the boy found out what had actually occurred. He found out that the men who had approached him were actually his mother's brothers, while his supposedly close uncles, whom he thought were the closest of kin, were in fact relatives classified from a more distant genetic line. The story went back to White Woman's childhood and this is what had happened:

White Woman's father was old Chief Butcher Knife, a prominent Skidi chief. The term Butcher Knife was a contemporary euphemism for American and his real name was Chief Bald Head—in Pawnee, *risax-paks-katsis*. The old chief had two wives of similar age who were not related to each other. White Woman's mother had two girls and a boy, while the other woman had three boys. Once the Poncas came on a raid and White Woman's younger brother was killed. The sons of the other wife remained alive. (These were the men that had accosted Otter and who should have counted as brothers to White Woman.) There must have been bitter rivalry between these two wives of old Chief Butcher Knife, for White Woman carried her anger toward her half-brothers all her life, refusing to acknowledge the relationship, and sought among her more distant kindred for men she wanted to recognize as her brothers in their stead. Mark Evarts summarized her feelings on this as follows:

> The old chief thought more of the boys than of the girls. My mother couldn't get anything. The old man would give it all to the boys even though he was a chief (implying that a chief should be above such favoritism). The girls were hurried off to school in Iowa while the boys were allowed to remain at home. Perhaps the old man had in mind that the boys would go on the warpath when they grew up and bring him horses, while the girls would stay close to their mother and do as she wished. My mother must have felt hurt by the way her father, old Chief Butcher Knife, acted.

But, time passed and things went better with White Woman. Victory Call, a man with considerable resources and ability, after the death of his first wife, had married White Woman's older sister. When she died, Victory Call married White Woman, and they established a new household on the reservation near Genoa and their fortunes prospered. She had a young son who was growing up and a prominent place in the community. Now she felt it was her turn to get retribution for the special privileges that her half-brothers had enjoyed in their father's household. She would deny the relationship, shut them out of her house, and welcome as brothers a group of men that were so classified in a more distant kin line.

These were kin on the mother's side—perhaps further back through the old ladies—but *not on the father's side*. The three that were adopted as uncles were of our own village of Pumpkin-Vine. White Woman called them *iratsti*, "brother," and they called her *itahi*, "sister." They acted like real brothers to her.

There was still another "uncle" who was welcome to their household. His name was Buffalo-Leader, *taraha-kitawiu*. He had been adopted into the family as a surrogate for the brother that was killed by the Poncas. After the raid, White Woman and her sister mourned deeply for the death of their brother. Once White Woman took particular notice of a young man in the village, remarking to her mother that he looked like their own brother that was killed. Then the two mothers (i.e., co-wives of the old chief) invited the young man to the house for a special dinner, giving him a gift and caressing him in blessing. He was given to understand that they wanted him to come to the house at any time and be a brother to White Woman. If he didn't come for a while, the mothers would give him a gentle reminder saying, "You can come over any time." Now that White Woman had a substantial position and a household of her own, he came often and enjoyed her hospitality.

Kin categories, therefore, did not guarantee a fixed relationship. They could only be valid if they were recognized by both parties. This recognition could be of a more or less enthusiastic kind. As with us, poor relations might be treated with a shade less enthusiasm than those of greater wealth or status. Then there were other factors such as degree of common interest or personal liking. One could follow a minimal interpretation of the pattern in order to preserve "the decencies" without actually disowning the people concerned.

Added to the factors of wealth and personal congeniality was the matter of hereditary status and family honor which was at times a very important element in the behavior of relatives toward one another. Brothers in particular were called on to preserve the reputation of the family. Since the Pawnees were especially sensitive on this point, brothers avoided going about together as much as possible, for should one be personally challenged or humiliated, the other would be bound to fight, and the conflict might spread to the several families concerned. On the other hand, if the other brother were not around, the two parties might be able to work out some way so that the incident could be passed over. Even after they had established themselves in different households, brothers were very careful to preserve appearances on behalf of the family. A man noticing that his brother's family did not have enough horses to go on the tribal buffalo hunt in the style to which they were accustomed would tactfully indicate that he had an extra horse that he could make available for the forthcoming hunting expedition.

If a man's supply of tobacco got too low for the necessary social entertaining that he felt he should carry on, he would ask his brother rather than an outsider in order to keep the matter within the family. A man who noticed his brother appearing in a worn-out buffalo robe or blanket would immediately send him a good one, for it would not do for anyone to get the idea that the family was not prosperous. A term of great contempt among the Pawnee was poor, *kapakis*. The worst insult one could hurl at a man was to call him *ruti-kapakis-kawitat*, "the one who is-poor-ragged." As the final insult one might say *kapakis-kuut*, "poor-dead," or in our way of saying it, "dead-poor." Respect for seniority among a group of brothers was preserved throughout life. The oldest brother continued to be the surrogate for the entire family, and the cadet members would make particularly sure that their senior brother made a good appearance. Their personal conduct toward him always continued to be respectful. Even after Victory Call had achieved an important status apart from his older brother Sitting Hawk, he still respected his brother's seniority rights. As senior brother, Sitting Hawk would sometimes come to Victory Call's house and say, "Tomorrow at dawn we'll go hunting. We'll go in this and this direction." Or Sitting Hawk would feel free to ask Victory Call to go far out and find him some medicinal plants for his doctoring practice. He would say to Victory Call, "Before the birds eat it up, I want you to go way over there and get me so and so weed so that I'll have enough for this winter." As a man of prominence in the community, he had plenty of people who would willingly do this for him, but in this case he wanted to keep his medical secrets in the family, and he knew he could trust his brother not to reveal them or use them without his sanction. It was the part of a good father to instill these attitudes in his sons while they were young. For example, if the younger of two brothers had six horses and the elder only one, it would be proper for the younger man to put all seven horses together and say to his older brother, "Brother, take your choice." Original disagreements between parents might lead brothers to quarrel all their lives. It was generally felt that parents should be watchful of growing hostilities among their children and try to remedy the situation before it was too late. In the plural marriage situation there was special danger of this as a co-wife who felt her husband preferred the other woman and her children would set the children against each other as had happened in the case of White Woman and her half-brothers. About their sister, a father would say to his sons, "You boys must take care of your sister. She's a girl and when she grows up she's going to take care of you." And this was indeed the case, for sister's house was a permanent home.

The boy was also taught that his paternal aunt whom he called *atira*, "my mother," would also give him a home. If the relationship were good he would come to her house and say, "*Tatiriraka*, I have a home here," and he could request a permanent or a temporary home with these relatives. He might remark, "*Atira*, I'm hungry," or "mother, I'm tired. I want a place to sleep here." The brothers of these women were called *atias*, "my father," but no fatherly conduct was expected of them as they were married into different households. Formal behavior such as characterized the relation between father and son was the only thing expected of them. The husbands of these kindly paternal aunts were called *atipat*, "grandpa," possibly to denote their unfailing benevolence toward the "child" to match that of their wives. Periodically, while the individuals in this relationship were still children, they would be invited to the house and "grandpa" would feast them on some delicacies that he had bought at the trade store, joking with them all the while.

The boy Otter enjoyed such a place in the home of Eagle Chief. The three wives of Eagle Chief were sisters to Victory Call, who often went there to relax and to enjoy their hospitality. Otter called these women, *atira* and he called Eagle Chief *atipat*. Eagle Chief would decide upon occasion to entertain four or five children who were in this relation to him as a courtesy to his wives and incidentally as a good public relations gesture for himself, for a chief had to maintain the good will of his constituency. He would go to the trade store and get some favorite foods such as dried prunes, flour, sugar, and coffee and then would send his wives to invite the children. The children sat lined up in a row and Eagle Chief began to tease them. He said, "Look at that fellow. He has two heads. See how he's looking all around the room to see what he can find." Then he would speak to the girls, "Look at that girl painting her face. Is that my paint?" Or he would say to his wives, "Don't give this fellow too many prunes. I think I'll eat them myself this evening." The women would answer with mock hostility, "Well, it's *theirs*. You bought it for *them* to eat." "Say," Eagle Chief would continue, "this fellow eats too fast." "Let them eat!" said the women. "The way you go on, the children might choke. Say, let them eat. Now children don't listen to him!" If they had a piece of fried bread left from the feast the children would try to carry it home to their mothers, but most of the time the older children would grab it as they went through the village.

The joking relationship between grandparent and grandchild was an important social resource. At a family meal where they should have light and cheerful conversation, they would prod a small boy into teasing his "grandpa." If no grandfather were available, they would indicate to the boy that he ought to pay more attention to his brother's wife— the "brother" usually being a quite distant blood relative and an older man. Otter was in such a relationship with Old Bull and they called each other *irari*, "brother." Old Bull teased Otter referring to his younger wife, Clear Day, and she would always play along. The relation between nephews and maternal uncles was also considered analogous to that of brothers. As the Pawnees stated it, "They would love each other like own brothers and give things to each other." Gift giving was a special factor in this relationship, and many kinds of mutual help, especially the teaching of skills. After they had moved to Oklahoma and Otter was a young man, he was favored with a nice gift by two boys who called him uncle. One of the boys had cut wheat for Eagle Chief and received $3.00 for his work. He said to Otter, "Uncle, I was working for Eagle Chief binding wheat and he gave me this three dollars. I want to give it to you." The relationship went back to the old earth lodge in Nebraska when the boys were very small. They were the sons of Queen Woman, the older wife of Old Bull, and Otter used to call her *itahi*, "sister," through a distant kin tie. The boys, accordingly, were his nephews or *tiwat*, and Otter had taught them how to make arrows when they were out on the hunt and other skills. Now, long after in Oklahoma, they were expressing their gratitude. This happened in the presence of the actual mother's brother of the boys, the agency interpreter, Deteyr, but there was no resentment at all on his part, for he had been less able to function as uncle to the boys than Otter. It was considered normal that this should be recognized.

In close relationships, failure to visit once in a while was considered a personal slight. White Woman would complain to Victory Call that while he often went to visit his older brother, Sitting Hawk, his brother did not return the courtesy. She would say, "He never comes here. Why go over there so much?" And so the casual visiting between the two brothers stopped. On one of the rare occasions when Sitting Hawk did come to visit, White Woman would caustically remark after he had gone, "What happened that he came to visit us today. I guess we can expect some cosmic event like rain or snow to mark the occasion. A man should come in once in a while just to say, 'brother.'" White Woman on her part avoided visiting Sitting Hawk's wives. Ordinarily the wives of brothers should be close companions. But when Victory Call was invited over there and the usual invitation was extended to include his wife, White Woman would refuse to go on the grounds that Sitting Hawk's wives were given to gossip, something she didn't care to engage in. As a result these women did not visit her either. Nevertheless, they would regularly send each other gifts. They would send and receive from each other moccasins, a blanket, or some dried buffalo meat. This showed that there was good will between them but simply a personal disinclination to go visiting.

An invitation to visit a household was always given through a relative. The person issuing the invitation would come to the house and seek out his relative there and suggest that he bring along his wife, his son, his nephew, etc., as the case might be. A man would feel free to issue the invitation if he had gotten some meat by hunting or bought some supplies at the trade store. Otherwise the invitation would come from the woman, since she would be providing the food. However, when guests came in at the husband's invitation in order to transact some business or political affairs, the husband had the right to ask the wife to cook something for his guests. If one were simply to "drop in" on a relative without a business reason or an invitation, it would appear as a hint that you wanted a gift or some other service. In order to forestall this impression, one came bringing a gift, opening the visit with the presentation and thus making it appear as the ostensible reason for the visit. The nature and value of the gift was to some extent an index of the regard the donor felt for the recipient.

On the whole, kin ties called forth strong emotions, especially in the presence of a stranger. Where strangers and kin were involved, kin loyalty aroused immediate reactions and was very strong. Outside the kin group it was assumed that people must be mean, unreliable, and treacherous. The household and immediate kin was the closest unit and the village pretty much the outer limit. Intervillage ties did exist, however, and occasionally intervillage marriages. As the population began to dwindle in the last years in Nebraska, such intermarriages became more frequent than heretofore.

Personal Names and Aspirations

A person was never addressed by his personal name; a kin term was always used. This served to indicate the expected behavior and, through the mode of its use, the nuances that could be expected within the category. A personal name among the Pawnees was of an entirely different character from our own. It was an honorary title of an extremely personal nature. The significance of the personal name was stated by a priest (see Fletcher, 1904, p. 365) as follows:

> A man's life is an onward movement. . . . If one has within him a determined purpose and seeks the help of the powers, his life will "climb up." . . . Some men can rise only a little way, others live on a dead level. Men having power to advance, climb step by step. . . . the people who desire to have a name, or to change their name, must strive to overtake in the walk of life, an upper level—such a one as reached by the ancient men who are spoken of in the (name-changing) ritual, who threw away the names by which they had been known before (because of new and higher achievements). *Ru-tur-a-wits-pari*, "in a direction-he is actively-moving-to a point or goal-traveling"; this is a call to the Pawnees, bidding them emulate these men and overtake them by doing like deeds.

The personal name was an act of self-recognition for a goal one had set oneself and achieved. One sponsored a special ceremony by making a donation of food to the priests, and in the course of the ceremony one's new name was publicly announced. But the substance of the name was strictly private and reserved to oneself. The name was cited only on the most formal occasions and from the name itself it was not possible to deduce its private significance. A person who had achieved such a name could lovingly bestow it on a son or a daughter in a ritual, or a son might give his name to his mother and then set out to earn a new and still more important one. Each of the people in the household of Old Bull and Victory Call had such a name, and while we cannot reconstruct the esoteric circumstances, a few facts about their lives gives a sense of their significance.

Victory Call was known for short as *Riwahut*, but his full name was *Siti-riwahut*, meaning "they are making the high trilling sound for victory." This sound was made by the women as the victorious warrior returned to the village. Publicly and socially Victory Call had made an important place for himself in the tribe. He was a younger son of a prominent Skidi chief of Old Village, Chief Big Eagle. His older brother Sitting Hawk (*Pia-tiwitit*, "hawk-he-sits-down") held the senior position in the family and occupied the family seat in the chiefs' council. As a cadet member of the family, Victory Call had to earn his social position in the community, and he had succeeded very well. People in the community said of him that he had almost surpassed his older brother by his achievements. Through his prowess in war and hunting, he had been able to entertain the chiefs and influential men at a number of formal banquets, and he had given them gifts of horses. In recognition of his deeds he was accorded one of the vacant seats in the chiefs' council, where he now sat regularly and had a voice in all administrative decisions for the band and tribe. He played the role of chief very well. He was considerate of people and concerned for their welfare. He was known to have entertained old people from time to time and to treat them with consideration and generosity. At one time when he had had a successful deer hunt, he sent Horse Rider to invite a number of old people, and when they were seated around the lodge he personally served them the deer meat and made sure that each had a generous portion. After the meal, as was customary, the guests began to talk and one old man expressed the sentiments of all when he said, "We thank you for having us here for dinner today. It is my wish to you that you will live to see your grandchildren grow up and do you honor, and that your great grandchildren will play about your feet." This was not to be, but perhaps he has gained a different kind of immortality through his son Otter and through the stories he told of their life.

The most creative and socially significant achievement of Victory Call was in the field of religion. It was he who built up the cult of the Deer Dance (*Raris-ta*, "dance-deer"). Taking it over from his predecessor who had obtained it by studying among the Wichita to the south, Victory Call was largely responsible for its reorganization into the Pawnee religious style and for the wide popularity it enjoyed at that time. He had built it up to such a degree that it posed a serious challenge to the monopoly of the long-established Doctor Association, where heretofore all the medicine cults had been organized. The association was under the leadership of Big Doctor and Sitting Hawk; Victory Call's older brother had a prominent place in it as leader of the Bear Cult. The rivalry between Big Doctor and Victory Call was bitter as some young men began to move over from the association to join the Deer Dance. In his dying moments in the 1860's, Victory Call saw a vision of Big Doctor upon whose sorcery he blamed his sickness and his death. The cult lasted under new leadership for a while, but after the tribe got to Oklahoma in 1876, its popularity continued to decline, while the Doctor Association maintained its vigor some time longer. Victory Call was also a skilled rattlesnake doctor and he was able to make a trade with his brother Sitting Hawk for knowledge of the Bear Cult in return for Rattlesnake knowledge. Victory Call's retainer, Horse Rider, had come to serve him in his household in the hope that Victory Call might give him a place in the Deer Dance and perhaps share other cult knowledge with him.

Victory Call had a friend, Chief's Road (*raru-hatur-risaru*, "the one that is-road-chief"), whose name implied that he was going on the road which he hoped would lead to chieftainship. Chief's Road had no hereditary social status, but he was ambitious for administrative advancement. He hoped that if Victory Call gained first place in the chiefs' council, he would appoint him his official brave. This was possible as when a chief retired or died, the new chief did not carry over the former incumbent, but appointed his own brave to assist him. Chief's Road was an excellent arrowshaft maker and supplied Victory Call with all his needs. On the other hand, he was not too good at acquiring horses, and Victory Call often helped him out by giving him some of their wood and other household needs that were more easily acquired when one had horses for transportation. He had built his house immediately adjoining Victory Call's lodge, and there were generally friendly relations between the two households; their children played together.

As a provider for his family, Victory Call was an accomplished hunter, both of individual big game and as a leading member of the tribal buffalo hunt. He also managed to make some extra cash by trapping beaver. He had some income from gifts he received for his religious activities and he maintained a modest herd of four or five horses. He was a good and able husband and father, inclined at times to be somewhat solemn and a little pompous, though not overbearing. He was about sixty years old at the time of our narrative in 1867. White Woman was his third wife and considerably younger than he. He had a grown son, Fox Chief (*kiwaku-risa'a*), by his first wife. Fox Chief was a young man in his twenties and lived most of the time in the home of Eagle Chief, where he was a close companion of Eagle Chief's son, Man Chief. After the death of his first wife, Victory Call had married the older sister of White Woman and then at her death he married White Woman. Besides his boy Otter, he and White Woman were raising an infant they had adopted—the daughter of one of the wives of Leading Chief, head chief of Village-in-the-Bottomlands. The chief believed that the baby was not his own but that of his younger brother, and when it was born he took the infant by the legs and was about to dash its head against a tree, when Victory Call rescued the baby and brought it home. When she was very small, White Woman kept her in her bed, but after she could walk she displaced Otter in grandma's bed. A small bed was built underneath grandma's bed for Otter so that she could watch them both. Sometimes they would put the baby on his back, and he was told to go off and play and to take good care of his sister. Otter addressed his father at all times as *atias*, "my father," and his father called him, *piirau*, "child."

White Woman, *Ts-taka*, "woman-white," was apparently so called because of the lightness of her complexion and the suspicion that she had some European ancestry. Being considerably younger than her husband, she was very conscious of her responsibilities and of the importance of their social position. Victory Call was always pointing out to her what her duties were. He would say, "I have to go off. If the Poncas come here with a gift of tobacco, take it and try to feed them." Or, "You have brothers and they might come to the house and perhaps they will be hungry. So don't go off anywhere because you ought to take care of them. If outsiders from other tribes come visiting bringing horses and tobacco, take it!" White Woman was so diligent in her duties that when her brother Uncle War Cry came to visit he would ask her why she didn't go out once in a while and get some air instead of sitting around the house all the time. Then she would retort, "I'd like to go, but who would be here to meet you fellows when you came? If I went out, they would just have to call me back when you arrived. That's the reason for my staying home all the time!" White Woman tended to be conservative in her social relations, and she was mindful of the common Pawnee observation that "A woman who stays at home never gossips, but just goes about her own business." She sent gifts to the appropriate relatives but made a habit of keeping her distance personally.

Her little boy Otter had a high regard for his mother, but their relations were quite formal. She would caution him, "Before you go out to play, go get something to eat and don't ask anyone for the food they have. Don't call anyone bad names like 'you hungry thing' or say 'you're poor.' That isn't nice. Anyone you play with you can bring in here to eat with you, and then you can go out and play again." At other times she would say, "You ought to be good like your father and take care of old people that are helpless." As he was leaving the house in the morning she would say to him, "Live well (*tsikstit, rakuwari*), well, go about!" When he returned she would say, "You look tired. You must have played hard. Look at your face." The boy would answer, "*Atira* (my mother) I am tired."

Horse Rider, retainer or *tarutsuhus* to Victory Call, was a young man in his late twenties. His name, *T-ur-akikita*, "he-his-riding," means "riding someone else's horse," signifying that it was a horse he had captured from the enemy. Victory Call was glad to have Horse Rider serving him since his own son Fox Chief, who would normally help him with the horses and other strenuous tasks, was away serving as a U.S. Scout with Major North. He was imaginative as well as socially ambitious in wanting to enter the new and growing Deer Dance Cult. One gathers that he was a good-natured, active young man. He had not yet made his mark in life, and he had married a woman considerably older than himself, whose grown daughter by a former marriage was married to a man employed at the agency. His wife, No Corn, had two other adolescent daughters who were away at school. No Corn was badly crippled with arthritis, but they had been married for some time and there was a close personal attachment between them. Horse Rider went to considerable lengths to compensate in extra services for No Corn's inability to contribute substantially to the work of the house.

> He was willing to do anything. His wife was crippled and helpless. He would do the things she ought to do. She had to stay home all the time and when the other women of the household came in from the fields and stretched out tired on their beds they would remark, "Soon we're going to cook, but we have no water!" Horse Rider immediately picked up two buckets and got some, and sometimes he had to go two or three times before they had enough. When he got back he set the buckets down, saying "hi'ya," because his arms were tired but then he would give water to everyone that was sitting on the beds and even to the little boys. At night he carried me through the village to wherever I wanted to go.

Horse Rider was warmly fond of the boy. Otter called him grandfather, and Horse Rider would tease him about his attachment to his grandmother. Horse Rider was related to White Woman who called him *atias*, through her father's sister's line, and thus Otter called him grandfather. Later in Oklahoma, when both his parents had died, Horse Rider and No Corn were very kind to Otter and gave him a home.

No Corn, wife of Horse Rider, had as her formal name *Tstahari-tsa'iwari*, "the kettle-she asks for something to put into it," that is, "she tries to borrow some corn or other food to cook." The name refers to an incident that is too obscure to be inferred from the name alone. She was a mature woman of good family, related to Victory Call through his father's sister's line, and he addressed her as *atira*. As a consequence, Otter called her *atika*, "my grandmother," but he knew better than to try to joke with her in a grandmotherly way. Her arthritis caused her a great deal of suffering. As Otter tells it,

It was considered only right for No Corn to have a good disposition since she was helpless. She was able to do the cooking although she couldn't stand up. She made herself useful in any way she could, lest someone remark that she was cranky since she was a cripple. For example, she might see White Woman measuring Victory Call's feet for moccasins. Then she would say, "Let me do that. You have something else to do." Then White Woman would give her the awl, sinew, rawhide, and other materials and she would make the moccasins. Or when they were out on the hunt, she would say, "Pile all the dishes right here. I can wash them." She would watch and do any little task she could for anyone in the house. But even so, her son or daughter would sometimes say, "You're a cripple. You can't do anything. You ought to be good." Then she would get angry and cover up her head. The daughter would say, "Mother, you mustn't do that." "Well, you folks are the cause of it. You are the ones that make me cranky." "Oh mother, we try to talk nicely to you, but you always get angry so easily." She couldn't help the fact that she was cranky.

Old-Lady-Grieves-the-Enemy, grandmother of the boy Yellow Calf, was a historic character among the Pawnee. She was famous for her heroic defense of the village when it was under attack by the Poncas. This was a time when she was well in her fifties and the tribe was living at Pa-ha-ku near Fremont, Nebraska. Her name commemorates her deed. It was *Ts-tarahux-tu*, "woman-caused them-hurt," signifying that she had caused the enemy to grieve because of those she had killed and put to flight. This is how the story was told:

Once when we were living in the village of Pahaku, near Fremont, the Poncas, perhaps mingled with Sioux, came on the warpath to attack the Pawnee village. They had hay in their pockets and were ready to set fire to the village. When the men saw how heavily outnumbered they were, they stayed inside the houses and resigned themselves to their fate, expecting to be burned up. As the enemy kept approaching, this old lady decided to do something about it. She was more than fifty then—an old lady. She rubbed some soot from the brass kettle and smeared it across her eyes (signifying defiance of any danger, and particularly of fire). She twisted her hair into a knot on the front right side of her head, put on a loin cloth, and with a war club in her hand she went out to face the enemy saying, "We've got to do *something*. You men just sitting here doing nothing!" This got the men excited and they said, "Just look at that old lady! We've got to go out and fight." Then they all ran outside. The old lady had nothing but a club in her hand, while the Poncas and all the men had their bows and arrows. She killed one of the Poncas right next to the house and sure enough his pockets were stuffed with hay all ready to burn down their houses. Because of her bravery, she could say and do anything as she had saved everyone's life and she felt she could do what a man did any time and she was free to say whatever came to her mind. Right after the battle, she came upon Feeling Bear who had been shot in the leg. "That's good, you should protect the people," she said. "Your mother and father are still living and you're young yet." But then Feeling Bear began to cry and sob and she said to him, "You're nothing but a baby. You don't belong out here at all. Only men should be out here fighting!" Then three old ladies came along and said to her, "Let's see that dead Ponca you killed." At that very moment Whitey came walking along with a stick in his hand that he had used to defend himself. The Old Lady calls him grandchild and they all began to tease him. "Turn that Ponca over," they said. But try as he would, the corpse slipped back and he jumped away. Then, giving it a hard push, he fell right on top of it. The old ladies began to laugh, and he ran away as fast as he could. He said that long after, he could still see that Ponca right before his eyes at night. The body was not buried, but was left in the open.

Long afterward when they were talking it over with the Poncas, and they were reviewing the incidents of the battle, the Poncas said, "When we saw that old man, we thought he was the bravest man we had ever seen and that's what held us back." Then the Pawnees told them that it was a woman. When braves were jealous of their wives, they would sometimes beat them up and then Grieves-the-Enemy would come along and say to them in her full deep voice, "Fine brave men you are! Your place is out beating up the Poncas. They came here to burn up our whole village. We women do you no harm. It's the Poncas you should be out fighting with."

The only men to whom she spoke politely were the chiefs. A chief would never beat his wife no matter how he felt. This would be against the whole code of chieftainship, and if he thought he could not control his emotions, he would not accept the office in the first place. When he was asked, he had to seriously consider whether his character was good enough. He must be generous and good and, if he weren't, he would refuse the call saying, "I'm a drunkard and have many other faults. I can't be a chief." To other men, Grieves-the-Enemy was gruff, even to priests, but not to the chiefs. Even her grown son, she ordered about. She would send him off to get a bucket of water and he would feel obliged to do as she said. Not that she was "mannish" in any way. She wasn't. Among the Skidis, this old lady was a person of note.

She was raising her grandson, Yellow Calf, whose mother had died and whose father, High Noon, had married into another household. She contributed many invaluable services to the household, and she and Otter's grandma liked each other and cooperated well together.

Otter's grandmother was Old-Lady-Chase-the-Enemy. Her name, *Ts-ak-ta-hira'as*, "woman-them-chased-ahead," i.e., "chase the enemy ahead of the line of battle," was given to her by her brave sons in honor of a gallant war deed they had performed, chasing the enemy way ahead of the line of battle. All six of them were killed in battle by the Poncas, and she would think sadly of their death, "If my sons had lived they would have taken care of me." "But," said Otter, "in our household we didn't think of her as a burden. She was my own grandma who used to take care of me and we took care of her." Otter's grandmother was a very old woman. In fact, she was his great-great-grandmother, once removed. She was the sister of White Woman's own great-grandmother and accordingly, White Woman called her *atira*, and she was thus a grandmother to Otter. He would call her *atika*, "grandmother," having no consciousness that in fact she was two generations beyond his mother's mother. Marriage at the age of fourteen or fifteen for girls made it quite feasible to be a great-great-grandmother between the ages of sixty-five and seventy. She may have been seventy-five at the time. Being in the mother's line, she was considered a particularly close relative. That she was a satisfactory grandmother to Otter there can be no doubt. When they walked out together, people would say to her, "That's your husband. He always watches his wife. They can't be parted." And Otter would retort, "Well I have to watch her. She might run away!"

Otter said the following of his grandmother:

Grandma was left-handed and they would sometimes speak of her as *Tskusaski*, "Lefty-woman." She would do everything for me—grease my feet when they chapped and cracked, get me food at night. I wouldn't bother others to do these things. She would do anything in the way of work. She was very saving as she knew how hard it was to get anything. She wasted nothing as she felt hard times might come some time. I guess she was like some white women who don't waste anything, putting everything into the kettle. She would cook anything and make it taste good—turkey feet and some field corn that she had made into hominy—she would just put these together and it would be a good soup when you had nothing else to eat. We like to eat however it tastes, but we certainly like to eat a well-cooked dish. In the spring my grandmother went out and collected wild turnips and things to save up for the winter. She never went dancing. Old-Lady-Grieves-the-Enemy had a very different personality from my grandmother. She was not at all bashful like my grandmother, who was very good at doing all sorts of things, but didn't do much talking. The reason my grandmother was bashful in this way was because she was humble and sad on account of the death of her sons in the battles with the Poncas.

The little boy Yellow Calf, grandson of Old-Lady-Grieves-the-Enemy, was six or seven years old and the constant companion of Otter. His name *Ari-pahat*, "calf-red," referred not to a red color, but to a tawny yellow. The name had an important sacred reference—the calfskin wrapping around the Evening Star bundle, and it must have been given to him in the course of a ceremony to which his family contributed. His father, High Noon, was the middle one of White Woman's three brothers who always came to the house. Otter called High Noon *tiwatciriks*, "uncle," and as the nephew, Otter called Yellow Calf *piirau*, "child." High Noon sent meat to the house on behalf of his son. Otter describes him in the following terms:

> Yellow Calf was a bit livelier than me. We played together. He wanted to fight sometimes but I didn't want to. He wasn't rough though. When we got to Oklahoma we separated, and we never did get together again.
>
> His family was unfortunate for even when they succeeded in getting horses, the horses died. But afterward Yellow Calf had good luck. First he married an old lady who had no relatives of her own and he inherited all her land. Then when he married a younger woman, his wife got some land of her own. They had many daughters, all of whom married and went all over to live. When he died, he left a large family.

The occasion of Yellow Calf's first marriage is an interesting story. When he was about eighteen, Yellow Calf was seized with hysteria. He imagined he saw a kind of Pawnee Lorelei—a little deer called *tatatsiks* that turned into a woman. The family did all they could to cure him but everything they tried was in vain. Then a medicine woman of about fifty said she could cure him, providing they could get married (Old Lady Tsitawa—see pp. 294-295, 305). They did marry and the cure was successful, and Yellow Calf prospered after that. Otter's mother White Woman remarked at the time that it was a pity Yellow Calf's mother wasn't alive when he was having all that trouble or she could have told him to jump into the water and stay under, and when he came out, some deer hair would have come up out of his throat and he would have been well at once. The lesson was not lost on Otter, though he seems never to have needed it.

The case of the old medicine woman is also of interest. Her son, a boy of fourteen, had recently committed suicide. He had resented her second husband and finally shot himself. Otter's older brother Fox Chief had taken the occasion to point out to him that suicide solved nothing and that all the boy had accomplished was to leave his mother all alone.

Old Bull was the leading man of the south half of the house. He was a man of good-natured jocularity, about fifty years old. He was a highly skilled buffalo hunter and on occasion he was known to outrun a buffalo. His full name was *Hikuts-tarus*, "Old Buffalo Bull"—"Scabby" or "Itchy." He was a man of good family who had begun life with a number of advantages. His father was a prominent chief, and he was sitting in his family's hereditary seat in the chiefs' council. In his boyhood he had struck up a friendship with a poor boy named Small who was serving in a chief's household. The poor boy had a vision and he had chosen to share it with his wealthy friend, Old Bull (see pp. 322-335). Then, while he was out tending the horses of his wealthy patron, Small was killed by the Sioux and Old Bull continued with Small's teachings and rose to prominence in the Doctor Association. He was currently a leader of the Deer Cult of that body. Not only his skill as a buffalo hunter, but his rise in the medical profession were notable personal achievements.

Old Bull and Victory Call had a kin relationship that went back to past family history. It was usual for every prominent man, particularly among the important chiefs and doctors, to draw around him numbers of young men who would come to live in his house and serve him in various ways as apprentices or dependents. Chief Big Eagle was such a man with a large household in Old Village in 1838. He had three sons of his own of whom the oldest was *kax-kuutu*, "Rotten-House," the second Sitting Hawk, and the third, Victory Call. Among the other young men who were in the house it was always possible to find some kin line that would make them brothers to the children of their host. Old Bull's father was one of these young men and he had called Victory Call, *irari*, "brother." Now that they were settled together in a common household, Old Bull properly addressed Victory Call as *atias*, "my father," since Old Bull's father had been counted as Victory Call's brother. Accordingly, Victory Call addressed Old Bull as *piirau*, "my child." Otter, who also called Victory Call father and was called by him *piirau*, was as a brother to Old Bull, Old Bull assuming the role of older brother to the boy. As younger brother, Otter would wait until his older brother Old Bull addressed him before presuming to open any conversation with him, and Old Bull on his part was bound to take the initiative in instructing the boy. Old Bull, referring to his younger wife Clear Day, would say to Otter, "This is our wife. Call her *tsustit* (old lady). Say to her, 'I'm starving. Get me something to eat.'" The young woman would answer, "What have you been doing that you're hungry?" Then Old Bull prompted him, "Tell her, 'Well, I've been playing.'" Then the woman answered, "That's all you're good for." A certain amount of teasing went back and forth from time to time after that. Then when Otter got older, he was again prompted by Old Bull to ask his younger wife to cook for him and she would reply, "Well, I have no water. I can't cook if I don't have any. Take two buckets and get me some. If you take only one, one of your arms will get long." "Well I could change about," the boy would answer in all innocence. "No you can't, you must take both at the same time." When he got back, water had splashed all over him from both buckets and Clear Day would say, "That's good. You got water. Don't ask me to cook if you have no water around." Old Bull would praise him then and say, "I have a smart little brother. He can carry the water," and the wife would add, "That's a good little boy after all. He brought the water." Old Bull would also express big-brotherly concern for him in another way. He would ask, "Well, who were you playing with?" "I played with so and so," Otter would answer. "That's good. Just play with those children and with no one else. I don't want you to play with those other boys. They're mean." "We played with the girls. They made a horse of me in our play," Otter related. Even though Otter's older brother Fox Chief was staying in another household the extended kinship system gave the boy the opportunity to learn the rules in his own home while he was small. Later this knowledge would stand him in good stead.

Clear Day, the younger wife of Old Bull, whose name in Pawnee was *Ts-takur-riwax,* "woman-day-clear," was inclined to be the "sporty" type, laughing and joking all the time and spending a good deal of her time out gambling. Her disposition was in marked contrast to the other women of the lodge. Old Bull had married her after he had been married to Queen Woman for quite a while. She was not from their own Pumpkin-Vine Village but from Village-in-the-Bottomlands, and Old Bull had married her because "she had taken his fancy." When the Pawnees moved from Fremont to the reservation village near Genoa, Old Bull brought in Clear Day's mother, Blue Calico, to take up the grandmother place in the new earth lodge that he and Victory Call had established. Clear Day was an assiduous player of the plum-seed game. This was the most popular gambling game of the women, played with plum-seed dice tossed in a round coiled basket. The betting was always heavy and the habitual gambler was likely to lose her blouse, her shawl, or her earrings. A man who noticed a crowd of women playing together like that would have to move along and mind his own business.

Clear Day had her own basket and plum seed dice with which to play the game—tossing up the marked plum seeds in the tray basket. Even when she herself didn't think of going out to gamble, the others would come in and get her. She would go out early in the morning and come back late in the evening, betting whatever she had, i.e., calico, a necklace, or her earrings. Old Bull didn't get angry. He was a chief and it wouldn't have been right for him to express any strong disapproval of his wife.

Sometimes a man whose wife was out gambling would get angry because he got hungry. When the woman came home feeling badly because she had lost, there would be trouble. She would say to her husband, "It was because of you. You were thinking about your hunger and then I lost the game." She gave no thought to her home—only to her playing. Sometimes she would win a nice piece of calico so that she could make her husband a new shirt. Then the reaction at home would be quite different. The husband would say, "That's good. But don't go so often. You might lose your luck." But try as she would to obey her husband's injunction, she would be caught up in it eventually. When the gamblers came around, she would make some excuse and say, "No, I have such and such to do. Why don't you go and ask so and so?" But eventually the other gamblers knew she would succumb. That was the way of Clear Day, Old Bull's younger wife. She was an habitual gambler.

Clear Day had two little daughters with Old Bull. The youngest was a very small child and was in the care of Clear Day's mother, Blue Calico. The older girl, New Queen, was five or six years old and had a bed of her own near the west on the south side of the lodge, adjacent to that of Clear Day. This was in anticipation of the time when the little girl would be fifteen and old enough to marry and her husband would join the household. It was considered desirable to give a little girl a bed of her own as soon as possible. With a little boy it was quite different. He might sleep with his grandmother until he was ten and then have a bed made for him between the central houseposts near the fireplace.

Queen Woman, senior wife of Old Bull, was of an entirely different temperament from Clear Day. Her name in Pawnee was *Ts-taru-ri'u*, "woman-merely-by herself," signifying "one does something great by oneself, single-handed." One translation was "self-made queen," signifying that although not born a queen or woman of chief's rank, her social accomplishments were so creditable that she deserved this high rank. Her marriage to Old Bull was apparently a case of a more mature woman taking a younger man for her second husband. Her children by her first marriage were growing up and were off at school, and she had started a second family with Old Bull. With him she had two small boys, one three years old and one still younger. She carried the whole responsibility for the household since the gambling habits of the younger wife left her with very little help. Blue Calico, the mother of the younger wife tried to compensate for this situation by being especially helpful to Queen Woman, giving her extra supplies to cook for all of them and a great deal of extra help "beyond the call of duty." Queen Woman was of French-Pawnee extraction, the French ancestor being relatively recent as reflected in her rather light complexion and mixed features. She was related to the family of the interpreter, Frank Deteyr, who was killed by the Sioux in the fall of 1861. She was quiet and conservative in her social approach and sometimes Old Bull would jokingly remark, "Why don't you talk once in a while?" "Well," she replied quite literally, "I have nothing to say." Most Pawnee women countered such remarks with a more lively retort. Her character was described in the following terms:

> She just went about her work. If other women came to visit, they would tell her stories about what was going on, but she would never repeat them. She never went out except to get a bucket of water with White Woman. People said of her, "She's a nice woman. She doesn't say much or gossip about anyone. You might tell her something but she doesn't repeat it or make any remarks about it." The two wives got along nicely together. Queen Woman never did any gambling herself, and she never made any remarks to Clear Day about her gambling.

Old Lady Blue Calico was the mother of Old Bull's younger wife Clear Day and grandmother of the south half of the house. The Pawnee name of Blue Calico was *Ts-tapit-tarius*, "woman-bought goods-blue," referring probably to a time when her uncle was portioning out a government allotment of goods or the spoils of a profitable trading expedition of his own and gave her a particularly nice piece of blue calico in the process.

> Her personality was more lively than Grandma Chase-the-Enemy but less so than the rough and ready Old-Lady-Grieves-the-Enemy. Her joking remarks and her general activity were a little more conspicuous than Otter's quieter grandmother. Blue Calico always went off to the Village-in-the-Bottomlands where she had come from to visit a special old lady friend there. The two old women on the north side had their own friends in Pumpkin-Vine Village. If Blue Calico wanted to

go off and gather wild turnips, she went with some other old lady
from Bottomlands Village. Only if it were necessary once in a while,
would the three old ladies of the lodge go together to get a little wood
for fuel.

Old ladies were great ones for visiting one another and talking over
old times—about when they were young and when they got married,
prepared buffalo robes and many other such reminiscences. Whenever
Blue Calico came back from a visit to her own village, she would come
in with stories of what was going on there. "That man went hunting and
didn't bring home anything," she would say, or, "He brought some
game—a deer."

Contrary to a common conception of tribal life, the personal interrelationships of the Pawnee were not fixed within a kin mold. For example, there was a marked difference in temperament between the two
wives of Old Bull, Queen Woman, the senior one, and Clear Day, the
younger of the two. Two factors combined to make the approach to Otter
of these two women different. Through a relatively distant kin line, the
older wife Queen Woman counted as a sister, *itahi*, to Otter and accordingly their relationship was formal. As noted above (page 36), Queen
Woman's two little boys regarded Otter as a mother's brother, *tiwatciriks*,
and he treated them as nephew, *tiwat*. Under these conditions, the kind
of joking Otter was encouraged to carry on with Clear Day was not in
order. On the other hand, Queen Woman had another role as wife of Old
Bull and consequently "wife" to Otter. Two conflicting roles presented
themselves and the sister role was chosen. The likelihood is that this
was an adjustment to Queen Woman's conservative temperament which
tipped the balance in favor of the more formal of the two possible kinship categories. When people used to marry almost exclusively within
the village, the wife of an uncle or of a brother was bound to be some sort
of relative to the younger boy. This was apparently conveniently forgotten or raised as the circumstances happened to warrant.

Neither personal relations nor the personnel of the household were
cramped within a fixed kin structure. The individual personality was not
trimmed down to fit the kin structure, but the structure was used to realize
the individual personality. The Pawnee social structure was written into
no statute book, nor did it have the status of doctrine, and there was no
chain of command to enforce it. Therefore it was not frozen and
clamped onto the people, but carried implicitly by them to serve them
as they saw fit. No built-in guilt, acting as a surrogate for dominant
power, forced them to narrow the scope of their personal lives. They
were socially creative in every personal interrelationship they had. The
world was raw and their life was hard, but it was also freer than ours.
No religious or supernatural sanction enforced the social forms. The only

possible penalty for transgression of kinship forms was adverse public opinion. This was a very important deterrent, but it was of a quite different quality from religious, military, or political sanctions, for it was within the network of the contemporary community, not in a specialized sector of it, and it was therefore possible for a person to cope with it in the course of daily living. Pawnee life was certainly not a Utopia. The time and the place in which it existed could allow no such hope, but in its freedom from dominance it had something we now can afford and don't know how to take.

4

PAWNEE PEOPLE AND
THEIR FORTUNES: III

*Personal Relationships beyond Kin Ties—Love
between Men and Women—Friendships of Girls
to Girls, Women to Women, Boys to Boys, and
Men to Men—Friendly Interband Kicking Match
—the Pawnee Personality Compared with Our
Own—Our Loneliness*

Love and Friendship

THE EMOTIONAL LIFE of the Pawnee was not channeled exclusively
through kinship categories, but the concepts of love and friendship for
their own sake were well recognized. They had a song that stated: "If
even worms are inclined to be in love with one another, how can we expect people not to do so?" The statement was starkly simple and left the
implication to be understood. It said:

tsasiri pirus	Even worms
he	(Pause indicating a comma)
witi-tirak-tap-pirihuru	each other-they them-love.

Their love songs were also in a similar vein, nakedly literal and entirely
free of metaphor.

A man sings:

1. *tsapat tiwakuhu*	Woman she is saying,
2. *wetatatsiksta*	Now I love you.

52

3. *arisit   kustiwu*   Of my own accord   I will go (to
                                                 you)
4. *wirakukuwatu*   when I am lonesome.
5. *hiru hira hai ira'*   (Sung syllables)

A woman sings:

1. *ha   ku   ahaku* (repeat 3 times)   See! There   he is sitting,
2. *tisiratuutara   (ha   i)*   this is the one I did it with.

Another woman's song:

1. *taku hiru kuu iia'*   Someone here I wish he were
                                                 coming.
2. *titaku hawa hiru kuu iia*   Right here again here I wish
                                                 he were coming.

And finally, the nostalgia of a man:

1. *atsiksu tatuuta*   My thoughts are
2. *tihi rarux kusaaru*   upon the other bed.

Friendships among women were much more limited than among men,
as there was little opportunity to form them. Women were closely confined to the home base from an early age and spent a great deal of their
life there. While the boys were quite small, boys and girls played in
groups in the village but when the boy was ten or twelve he began to go
to pasture with the horses and thus separated himself from the girls who
were more closely attached to their mothers at this time and were taking
the first steps toward learning the techniques of planting and the household routines. Just before sundown, from each of the villages, people
would be walking down different paths to the water about a mile
away. This was an opportunity for meeting. Little girls when going for
water would stop each other and talk. The first overtures in courtship
were often made here. Once the girl was married at about fifteen, she
no longer had time for her girl friends. The mature woman was so preoccupied with all the work she had to do that she had no time at all
for such activities. Women addicted to gambling formed a group apart
in a sense, but their association was not so much in the nature of friendship as a common "affliction." Old ladies were a little more free to develop "cronies." John B. Dunbar (1881, p. 740), missionary to the Tsawi
Band 1835–1836 and 1846–1847, describes the Pawnee woman at work in
the following words:

They were given to assembling in little groups: while busily plying their
tasks, their gossiping volubility found unrestrained freedom and was to all
appearances inexhaustible. Their conversation was often quite interesting

and facetious. Displays of wit were quite common with both sexes, and often descended to mere *double entendre*. . . . Still the grotesque grouping and application of ideas was often quite entertaining: A nickname for a tall, slender person, *asu-katu-has-tawiu* ("shoe-shadow-string," shadow of a shoe string), or *karastiat* ("I will not go out"); *kusatsua* ("it will rain"). In reply, *A* ("well"), *uksawatsatsua* ("even if it were to rain"), *kaiit* ("salt"); *karas* ("are you?").

The boy had a more complicated social life in the community and types of friendship were likely to be more varied and more numerous than a girl's. The parents supervised the associations of the little boys in early childhood. The parents in prominent families did not allow their boys to play with children who had no mother or father to imbue them with right ideas, or whose parents were too ill-informed to do so. It was said of a poor boy who had no supervision that he played around the trash pile. Children that moved to a different part of the village seldom retained their former friends. In these early years, children were not very well versed in the use of kin terms, and if they were in a small group they would either use some kin terms for one another or no term of address at all. If the group included ten, twelve or more, they would use the simple names of childhood—Tiny, Little Eyes, Blacky, Whitey, etc.

From the ages of twelve to fifteen, the boys began to take the horses out to pasture and linger for some hours on the banks of the stream. Here more lasting friendships developed. When they reached the age of nineteen or twenty they began to do voluntary scout duty, watching for the enemy from the heights around the village and looking around the countryside for evidences of an attacking enemy. Then came war expeditions into enemy country and finally admission to one of the various Doctor Cults and in some cases, to the chiefs' council. In each of these contexts, special friendships developed or were cemented from previous occasions.

Sometimes a man would awaken in the night and start to sing, and the song would be taken up from house to house for a good part of the night. Scouts keeping watch would make a practice of singing through the night to let the enemy know that they were awake and watching. Some of these songs were religious, some from stories. One of these songs that was popular concerned the friendship of two young men. We do not know the story context from which it came, but the song itself concerns the thoughts of a young woman who noticed that there were two young men who went around everywhere together, traveling, hunting, and going on the warpath, and she wondered, "Will they always be true to each other? Will their friendship endure?" The following (Dunbar, 1881, p. 747) is the text (the first line being repeated six times):

sirawari i	They two who are traveling,
tskara, sirawari i-a-a-a-a	Alone, they two who are traveling,
tsapat-i witiwaku	A young woman, it is said that she says:
sikatasiwaktiks-a	I wonder if they two are true (to each other).

tskara, siraαwari-i-a-a-a-a-a

By the time the boys had reached their teens, it was impossible for their parents to keep close watch on their associations, and friendships not uncommonly grew up between boys of different social status. At this time, a young boy of a chief's family might gain a retainer or a lifelong ally from among the commoners. There is a story told (Dorsey, 1906, pp. 46-50) of the rise of a poor boy who made friends with two boys of wealthy families: A poor boy came down from the north and met the son of a chief and the son of a medicine man. The two wealthy boys liked the poor boy very much and followed his leadership. The poor boy suggested that they each learn all about his father's ways, and finally the three set out traveling over the country. In the course of their travels they came upon a small group of Sioux tents which they attacked, killing the men and sparing the women. It appeared that the women were not too well satisfied with their late husbands, so they readily acquiesced to be taken over by the three boys. Eventually the women and children were taught to speak Pawnee, and the boys continued with similar exploits until the group had increased in numbers considerably. Then one of the boys stole into the village and got seeds for planting the crops. At last the poor boy induced the other two to declare him chief of them all, while the former chief's son was to assume the role of priest of their sacred bundle and the son of the medicine man was to minister to their health. Thus, the story goes, through the friendship of these three boys a new village was founded. It is not clear whether this story is told to induce boys to follow a similar course or whether it actually had some historical basis. Opinions differ on this issue and some think the story accounts for the founding of one or the other of the bands, others believe it refers to the founding of the Arikara, while still others hold that it is simply a mandate for boys to form firm friendships so that they may work together for their future.

Within the group there was little room for comradery among the mature Pawnee men. Their visiting back and forth was formally structured within the house even when only two were sitting together. First there would be the offering to the powers above and below with the pipe, then a smoking together, and—only then—either a simple conversation or business. This sequence of events was inevitably followed by a woman serving some food, in which case it became mandatory for the conversation to become light and mildly humorous. This skeleton plan was applied to any larger gathering as well as to more casual encounters. The seating was aways according to relative social status and the right of priority in conversation was always determined by rank. There was little room for simple, spontaneous, social contact in the life of a mature man. Except for the intimacies of marriage, there was no opportunity for easy conversation between mature men and women either. Missionary Dunbar (1881, pp. 745-746) describes the conduct of the men:

> [The Pawnees] were . . . among themselves very sociable. With the men there was apt to be perhaps, an excess of formality in their formal gatherings, but this is a natural consequence of their oft-recurring feasts and councils. It was quite common for several men in the evening to meet in some house where tobacco was to be had, and there sit smoking and recounting their exploits. One of the party kept up a monotonous thumping upon a drum. Another would dance for a while, make a speech, and sit down. Another would follow with the same role, etc. At certain seasons such gatherings were of nightly occurrence, lasting usually well-nigh till daylight.
>
> Akin to this trait of storytelling, was their delight in discussion. They were extravagantly fond of debating what might be termed questions of general principle, often exhibiting considerable tact in their manner of sustaining an argument. Their principal efforts of this kind were reserved for public occasions, such as councils. It was impossible to attend a tribal council where any important matter was pending and not be impressed with the power and cogency of their eloquence. The reputation of being an orator was coveted, and a man, when once recognized as such, was sure to wield great influence. An orator when addressing a council upon a question in which he was thoroughly interested, seemed to appreciate fully the dignity of his position, and identifying himself with the cause he advocated, and addressing himself directly to the person he was attempting to answer or convince, his speech would become vividly dramatic.

Tribal Fun and Games

Theoretically, friendships were best formed within one's own village for beyond that was a kind of social "No-Man's Land." Sometimes, however, the wall of suspicion broke down, as in one story we heard related:

> The members of the different bands didn't like each other as a rule. We would say, "Don't bother with them (referring to people of another village or band), they're mean."
> But some nice evening the Man-Going-Downstream Band and the Meat-Beggars would join the Little-Earth-Lodge Band and the children

of the Skidi villages of Village-across-a-Ridge and Pumpkin-Vine would join the Wolf-in-Water and Bottomland Village, and they would play rough and kick one another.

The location of the four bands was along the west side of Beaver Creek and the Skidi were in the westernmost position, the other three bands about half a mile away to the east. While according to past tradition, they always lived south of the Skidi and were referred to generally as "South Bands," they were now actually located to the east:

> "The Skidi chief would sit on a high bluff and the Eastward (*tuhawit,* "Settlement-east" chiefs sat on a bluff near their home and they would watch the boys. They said, "When we were boys we used to play like that and kick."
>
> It would begin in the evening when the boys would call out, *hu-hu-hu.* Then the boys would hear and come outside. Folks would say to the small boys, "Don't go there, you'll get hurt," but some would steal out and join the fight anyway. When one side would be chased back, the older people would laugh and say, "Go back again. . . ."
>
> When it got darker the little boys were told to go back and run home because the big boys were going to fight now—the sixteen-to-eighteen-year-olds. Then in the moonlight sometimes, the men of about thirty years old would fight, and then afterward the old men forty and over. The men would take blankets from one another and kick one another, but afterward they had to return the blankets.
>
> This game was never played with the Skidi villages alone opposing one another, only between the Skidi Band as one party and the South Bands as the other. They never kicked hard—just for fun. If the South Band boys met the Skidi boys, there was always a kicking contest."

A similar game is reported between different divisions of the Comanches.

The Pawnee Person

There is no simple formula for describing the intricate logic of the Pawnee people's lives. One thing is clear—that no one is caught within the social code. Against the backdrop of his natural environment, each individual stands as his own person. The Old World design for the human personality does not apply to this New World Man. The Pawnee child was born into a community from the beginning, and he never acquired the notion that he was closed in "within four walls." He was literally trained to feel that the world around him was his home—*kahuraru,* the universe, meaning literally the inside land, and that his house was a small model of it. The infinite cosmos was his constant source of strength and his ultimate progenitor, and there was no reason why he should hesitate to set out alone and explore the wide world, even though years should pass before he returned. Not only was he not confined within four walls but he was not closed in with a permanent group of people. The special concern of his mother did not mean that he was so closely embedded with her emotionally that he was not able to move about.

Other people also were clearly concerned with him in a variety of ways. There was no mistaking the constant concern of Old Bull for the boy, Otter, in the earth lodge. And as for his grandmother, this was of course patently clear. There was no mistaking the affection felt for him by Horse Rider. Even from the earliest time the Pawnee knew there were differences in kinds of affection. He knew he should go to his grandmother for intimate care but he also looked up to his mother as his provider and protector. His father he regarded in the same way wherever he might be, and, as we saw (p. 41), his mother had pointed out to him that he should emulate his father. Otter's Uncle War Cry and his other uncles came to the house and again showed affectionate concern, and one winter when he broke his leg his uncle stayed home and nursed and protected him. He knew very early that he "had a home" in the house of Eagle Chief which had been literally demonstrated to him in special feasts and visits. His older half-brother Fox Chief was there for him even though not in the house. The breakup of the household and travel on the hunt did not dismay him, even when his grandmother stayed behind one winter, for his community traveled with him. This bringing of the community's concern to the child's attention from an early age was deliberately carried out.

The wide application of the kin terms gave the family relationships a much wider reference. It made him realize that there were shades of closeness with his immediate kin and that many varying factors determined this just as they did in his outside attachments. The case of his mother's half brothers was a graphic example. He found out that, in the last analysis, one made one's own relationships with people and that none was absolutely given.

The intensified family togetherness of our present society stands in sharp contrast to these arrangements. The very physical plant of our family household fosters this intensity. Within this century, the apartment or family dwelling has become more and more isolated. In the past ten years, the isolation has become absolute and we have become the loneliest people that ever existed. Mechanical elevators, mechanical shopping, mechanical transportation, and other mechanical devices preclude almost all casual social contacts. At the same time, within the apartment or household the sexes are thrown together in an incest-breeding welter of physical familiarity. Simultaneously a demand is made for personal detachment, so that we require intensive psychological reorganization to heal us from the ordeal of our childhood. This emotional turmoil is implanted so early that we are convinced it is inevitable. In the outside world a further kind of isolation has been set up. We have developed a series of age shelves so that each age becomes a segregated universe of its own. We must desegregate the ages and remingle as persons. There can be no complementarity of experience in such a plan. Retirement is now a shelf for social discard, while the younger age levels are left to their conformities and magnified rivalries. Individuality can be too costly if it does not have a flexible society within which to operate. It is our task to design such a society.

It is not easy for us to perceive the wide gap in kind between Pawnee society and our own, and yet in the face of all the terrible events of the past and the pressure to destroy his personality, surely it must mean something that the American Indian has maintained his identity among us. It was 20,000 years ago in the latter part of the Ice Age that the buffalo hunters of the Old and New Worlds parted company. What communication they might have maintained over the Bering Strait or even the wide Pacific could have been only a trickle compared with the maximum cultural osmosis of Old World peoples. Thus unwittingly the American Indian has furnished us with our major control case in the study of human society and the processes of its growth.

Historically, the control of masses of people has been an important element in the building of Old World civilization. For millennia, people have been grouped into ruling classes and ruled masses. Setting aside the practice of applauding this approach to human affairs as an advance in history and therefore a human benefit, the emergence of mechanization in its most refined form, i.e., automation, has made this social device obsolescent. But we cannot readily free ourselves of this habitual approach to the human being. It is therefore important for us to find a model of a human being who has never been pressed into a mass mold, no matter how different his physical setting may have been from ours. The Pawnee Indian is such a person. For our present and future society, we will need to develop a society composed entirely of creative individual personalities, and for this it is important that we look carefully into the detailed circumstances of the life of a Pawnee individual and study his actions and reactions within them.

The fact that Old World civilization for several millennia has been based on masses of people reflects itself in our view of the individual as a function of the statistical average. The process of statistical generalization involves a disregarding of the very characteristics that make a man an individual, i.e., his uniqueness. Therefore, no matter how objectively the statistical average is compiled, it becomes impossible to rederive the individual from the statistical norm, even when some distribution of the selected traits is given. The Amerindian who has never been subject to mass organization in the North American setting preserved an understanding of the individual personality as the keystone of society rather than as a function of it. His society is therefore fluid and creative, albeit within limited technical resources, rather than inhibiting of the person as an integral entity. He does not require doctrine in order to develop formal social structures, and the structures he does develop are currently functional rather than frozen.

It does not matter what sort of empires the North American Indians would or would not have developed had the European not disrupted his society. What does matter is that in examining his society as a total functioning social organism we have a contrast situation through which we can throw into relief our most stubbornly held social biases.

Although the Pawnee home is at opposite poles to our own, there are suggestions to be derived from it that can be applied concretely to our own mode of living. Within the home, the Pawnee has personal and social mobility and a diverse circle of contacts; within his kindred he has a wide latitude of personal interrelationships. His aspirations are his own. He sets his own goal, which is his personal secret. His aspiration is not to surpass someone else, but to go beyond his own past achievements. He gives himself a name to serve social notice on people that he is on his way. Love and friendship, though less stable than kin, are also honored.

I think I have given enough detail of Pawnee life to show that it was in no sense a Utopia. The struggle for survival and for the maintenance of personal dignity was great. Leaving aside the survival question, the challenge to the individual to develop himself was much greater than our own, for it was not only an avowed, but a literal purpose in life. For those individuals who are concerned that the transition from a mercantilist to a humanist society which we are now perforce making will leave the human being without incentives and challenges, Pawnee life should serve to dispel his doubts. A society built on the basis of the objective of personal fulfillment will not be a lazy or an insipid society. It will be full of strength and dynamic movement. Today for the most part the intellectual and the artist carries this mode. For the future it will belong to us all, for everyone has something to contribute to such a society by the very fact that individuals are different. We need no prima donnas—only people as they are. As a social scientist I owe a tremendous debt to the Pawnees for the fidelity with which they have communicated their culture to me, for it has given me an abiding faith in the individual human being. I hope that this account will be studied and similar value be derived by others. In concluding this work I will outline some of my personal projections for our society that I have derived as a result of the years during which Pawnee life has been part of my thinking.

5

THE WORLD OF A PAWNEE BOY:

SPRING 1867

〰〰〰〰〰〰〰〰〰〰〰〰〰〰〰

*The Day Begins in the Earth Lodge—Breakfast
Preparations—Seating at the Meal—Daytime Ac-
tivities of Women—Chiefs' Council—Supper and
Evening Conversation—Plan for Deer Hunt the
Next Day—End of Day's Activities*

〰〰〰〰〰〰〰〰〰〰〰〰〰〰〰

IN THE YEAR 1867, the villages of the Pawnees were strung along the
west bank of Beaver Creek. (Beaver Creek flows southeastward into the
Loup River that flows east to join the Platte which continues eastward to
the Missouri. In the Skidi village of Pumpkin-Vine was the house of
Chief Victory Call and his friend Old Bull with their families.)

It was a morning late in March, and the high dome-shaped earth lodges
were huddled together in the predawn darkness. On this as on other morn-
ings, Otter was wakened by the sound of his father's voice saying, "Fire's
made." The dawn had not yet broken, and it was still cold; Otter bur-
rowed down deeper under his little calfskin cover. He hated to leave the
warmth of his bed that he shared with his grandmother. Just as the dawn
began to break, Victory Call went outside through the long vestibule
that was the entrance to the house to look at the position of the stars and
to see what kind of a day it would be. Meanwhile his wife, White Woman,
had gotten up to prepare breakfast. She would be cooking for twelve people and an extra guest, and the preparations would take at least an hour.

On both sides of the house along the low circular walls, the people
were still asleep in their beds. There had been a long storytelling session
the night before and Old-Man-That-Chief, who was one of the principal
raconteurs, was too feeble to go home late at night, so a temporary bed
was made for him near the fireplace where the fire was now burning
brightly in the center of the room. High above the fireplace a shaft of

light came in through the smokehole and, as the day broke, the long
radial ribs of the slanting roof stood out clearly like the frame of a huge
umbrella, reaching out from the central ring at the top to the edge of
the low circular wall.

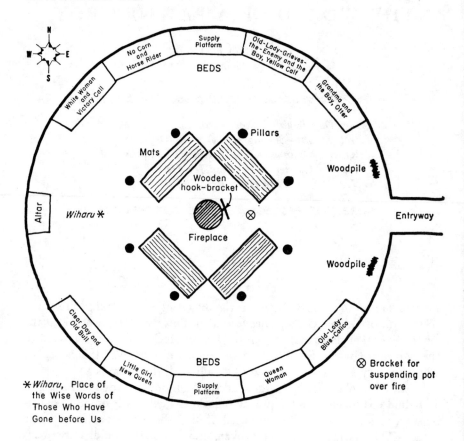

FIGURE 5-1. Groundplan of the house where the boy, Otter, lived with his
father, Victory Call, and his mother, White Woman.

About halfway between the fireplace and the walls stood a series of
stout pillars made of whole tree trunks with the bark removed, forked at
the top and connected together by crosspieces so that they gave support
to the heavy slanting roof. The tall pillars made a convenient division between the sleeping quarters around the outer edge of the circle and the
eating and living quarters around the central fireplace. Here near the fireplace the earthen floor was covered with large reed mats where they sat,
using pillars as a backrest.

Around the outside, each bed platform was divided from the other by
a series of skin curtains that hung at the head and foot of each bed; a reed

screen stood in front of the beds of the mature women to give them privacy. The series of beds was interrupted by an open platform at each side to store current food supplies and household articles.

The long vestibule that gave entrance to the house projected outward from the eastern side of the circular walls. Inside, on both sides of the door to the house, was a working area in each of which a woodpile was braced against the walls. The rear or western wall of the house was the sacred area, the beds being ranged along the north and south walls. There were five platforms along each wall, the middle one for supplies and the four others fitted out as beds.

The boy, Otter, and his grandmother were sleeping on the north side of the house in the easternmost bed nearest the entranceway. The second bed next to theirs was occupied by another little boy, Yellow Calf, and his grandmother, Grieves-the-Enemy. Then came the supply platform for the north side and beyond that the bed of Horse Rider and his wife, No Corn. Horse Rider was an assistant to Otter's father, Victory Call, a prominent chief and religious leader. Victory Call and White Woman had the bed that was in the place of honor near the west.

Along the south wall of the house was another family. The head of that family was Old Bull, friend and associate of Victory Call and also a chief and religious leader. He occupied the west bed with his younger wife, Clear Day, and the next bed was occupied by the little girl, New Queen, their daughter. Then came the supply platform for the south side, and beyond that the bed of Queen Woman, Old Bull's senior wife with her little boy of three, and finally the easternmost bed on the south side for the grandmother, Blue Calico, who was the mother of the younger wife, Clear Day, and had the youngest child sleeping with her.

Everyone in the house knew his appointed place and where he could go and where he could not go. In the sacred area at the west was an earthen platform with a buffalo skull resting on it and above it hung a long, skin-wrapped bundle containing their most sacred objects, including two specially bred ears of corn. Between the fireplace and the buffalo altar, there was a sacred spot that was invisible—the *wi-haru*, "the place where the wise words of those who have gone before us are resting." Rather than step over this place in order to pass from one side of the house to the other, everyone walked around the entire house by way of the east. When the heads of the household sat down to rest or when they entertained important guests, it was near the west that they sat and no one would want to pass in front of them.

The house was a microcosm of the universe and as one was at home inside, one was also at home in the outside world. For the dome of the sky was the high-arching roof of the universe and the horizon all around was the circular wall of the cosmic house. Through the roof of the house the star gods poured down their strength from their appropriate directions in a constant stream. In the west was the Evening Star, a beautiful woman, Goddess of Night and Germination, and in her garden the corn and buffalo were constantly being renewed so that the people could eat; and in the western part of the house the sacred buffalo skull and the bundle with its ears of corn symbolized this power. In the eastern sky was the Morning Star—god of light, of fire, and of war. As he rose every morning he sent his beam into the long entryway of the house and lit the fire in an act of cosmic procreation, symbolizing his first union with the Evening Star in the times of the great creation when he had had to fight off the guardians of night with which the Evening Star surrounded herself. Finally the conflict was won and Morning Star mated with Evening Star and fathered the girl that was the first human being to be placed on earth.

The house was at the same time the universe and also the womb of a woman, and the household activities represented her reproductive powers. The beds of the women along the circular walls were appropriately ranged by age to represent the main stages in a woman's life—the youngest women near the west where the garden of the Evening Star was located, the mature women in the middle of each side (due north and due south) and the beds of the old women near the exit to the east, for at their age they were "on the way out." Being at home was spoken of as being "inside"; ti-ka, he is-*inside*; the house, a-ka-*ru*, the *inside*-place; the universe, ka-*huraru*, the *inside*-land.

The supreme god and First Cause of all was *Tirawahat*, The Expanse of the Heavens. Beyond all others, he directed everything and to his power there were four direct paths leading from the house to the sky in the four semicardinal directions—northwest, northeast, southeast, and southwest; offerings were made from these positions in the house so that they would be readily received.

Everyone in the house, including the boy, Otter, had a clear consciousness of these things as they moved about within it. Now secure in his bed, the boy was also secure in the world. Outside there were a hundred houses like his, clustered close together on the high banks of Beaver Creek, and on the hills the sentinels were watching for the lurking enemy. The round houses with their high-domed roofs were covered with thatch and then with tamped-down earth. As the fires began to be lit, smoke rose here and there from the smokeholes. Inside, the women were cooking breakfast as White Woman was now doing.

White Woman went over to the supply platform, loosened the drawstring of the skin sack that contained dried corn kernels, and removed the skin cover. She poured a handful of dried kernels for each person into a large wooden bowl about 15 inches across and 3 inches deep. She washed the kernels at least twice to remove any dirt and chaff, then dumped them into a tin bucket of cold water that she hung over the fire to boil. Three double handfuls of dried kernels were the product of eight ears of roasted corn. She needed nearly twice that amount for their breakfast. Other dried foods might be added. These were always washed first before including them. Dried beans, dried strips of pumpkin, or dried strips of the inner lining of the buffalo stomach or intestine, made a welcome addition and improved the flavor of the soup.

Sometimes large thin sheets of dried buffalo meat and a sheet of fat were cut up into portions and boiled to make a strong soup for their breakfast. The individual portions of meat were seven inches long and varied from 3 to 6 inches wide.

The rest of the meal consisted of a bread course and some hot black coffee boiled with sugar. Sometimes the soup was served instead.

When they had it in the house, wheat flour from the trade store was made into "grease bread" fried in a pan in lard. This was a good deal quicker and easier to make than bread made from home-made corn flour. Each person should have a whole piece of grease bread and any leftover pieces were torn in half and given to the most important men. A handful of wheat flour made two round pieces of bread. White Woman mixed the flour with baking powder and a little salt in a wooden bowl, and after the ingredients were well mixed she added a little warm water to make a dough. If there was no baking powder, White Woman used ashes instead. Now she took a lump of dough and rested it on a piece of hide placed against her thigh, slapping it with her palm and turning it round and round until it was the right size. She put it in a pan with some lard and leaned it against the rim of the fireplace on some glowing coals, tilting the pan so that the bread was exposed to the heat of the fire. As each round disc was done she set it aside on a piece of tanned hide until they were ready to eat their meal.

Sometimes she made bread out of corn flour baked in ashes. Beans might also be mixed with it. The dried kernels were pounded fine with a heavy pestle in a wooden mortar. Meanwhile the beans had boiled, and after the water was discarded they were mixed well with the flour. Enough warm water was added to make a batter, then the ashes were parted and the batter poured in and spread to make a large cake about 3 feet long by 1 foot wide. The dough was covered with ashes, coals, and earth and allowed to bake. It was tested by exposing a small part of the ash layer and striking it to see if the bread underneath was solid. Then the bread was turned over and allowed to bake on the other side. When it was done, the ashes were brushed off and it was washed with a little warm water, then wrapped in a skin and set aside to cool. Sometimes slices of cold cornmeal mush were served instead of a bread dish; the kernels being pounded and boiled the night before so that the mush would be solidified by morning. Sometimes they would simply eat hot cornmeal mush for breakfast.

After the other foods were ready, the coffee was cooked in a bucket with sugar to be served later in small bowls. This was a task that No Corn was likely to undertake. She would mix a handful of ground coffee with a handful of sugar and boil them together with water in the bucket. The meal would be finished off with sweet coffee served hot and black.

While all these preparations were going on, the people began to get up one by one and sit down in their places around the fire. Now only the boys were still in bed. Grandma warmed her hands over the fire, went over to the bed, put them on Otter's warm nose and "took it off" remarking to Old Bull, "Here's his nose." Then she offered it all around to the assembled company. Sometimes it was his ears that she offered instead. With things about done, Victory Call said, "Boys, breakfast is ready, you can go to bed again later if you want to."

White Woman removed the bucket of corn from the fire and put eleven bowls around it to serve the family. The grandmother–grandchild pairs each got a bowl together and everyone else got a bowl for himself. With each bowl there was a buffalo-horn spoon and two spoons in the bowl for grandma and grandchild. White Woman, who was sitting east and slightly north of the fireplace, dished out the corn with a large buffalo-horn spoon 8 inches long with a bowl that was 4½ inches across and 1½ inches deep. A ladleful or one and a half ladles of corn along with the liquor was a serving, the grandmother–grandchild bowls receiving an extra large portion. For feasts, large wooden ladles were used for serving.

The order in which the members of the household sat at their meal was pretty much in the position of their beds. Old Bull sat at the southwest and Victory Call at the northwest position. Ordinarily a man's senior wife sat next to him, and his junior wives sat beyond. Old Bull and his wives sat in this order, but White Woman had moved down to the east end of the north side so that she could do the serving. The grandmothers and their grandchildren sat at the east end. Old-Man-That-Chief, although a guest, took up the southeast position of humility, for he was old and nearly blind. The bowls were passed around to the people from hand to hand, unless the circle was too large, in which case a young woman would be asked to do the serving. The men were served first in order of importance, the "guest side" always being given priority. In this instance the order was Old Bull, Victory Call, Old-Man-That-Chief, Horse Rider, Queen Woman, the senior wife, then Clear Day, the junior wife, Blue Calico, the grandmother, on the south side; then the women on the north—No Corn, Yellow Calf and his Grandma, Otter and his Grandma, and finally White Woman herself.

Before they began their meal, White Woman made an offering of corn at the west. She took some kernels of corn in a spoon from Victory Call's bowl and offered them to the nose of the buffalo skull that rested on the altar there. Out of delicacy, she did not offer corn to the sacred ears in the bundle; if they had had buffalo meat she would have offered it there but not to the buffalo skull.

Now the meal began, and it was proper that they have light conversation while eating. Their conversation turned to getting water for the household and wood for fuel, the care of the horses, and the food pit. White Woman remarked to Clear Day, who was sitting on the other side of the fireplace, "After breakfast, let's take two kettles and get some water." The other women talked about opening up the food pit and sorting out the good corn from the rotten and about exposing dry meat to the wind and sun. Victory Call talked to Horse Rider, who was sitting at his left, about the horses. He said, "Right up near where the horses are you might find some mushrooms and milkweed so that the women can cook the tops." Then the women chimed in, "I wish you could get some milkweed. That's good mixed with corn." Then Victory Call spoke of the horses: "If there's a good runner among them, get on him and give him some exercise so that we can train him as a buffalo horse. You must look around meanwhile and see if you see some deer tracks. We might go hunting. In the evening take the horses to a safe hiding place and hobble them so that the Sioux won't steal them. Look way off in all directions and if you see anyone lurking about bring them right home and put them in the corral. They won't starve for one night. In the morning we'll turn them loose and they can make up for it." "All right, I'll look around," said Horse Rider, "I'll be home late." Victory Call had some further reminders for him. He asked him if he had any parched corn with salt so that the horses would get thirsty and drink. He also reminded him that he should wet the sides of the horses and then they would rub themselves on the grass and shed their old hair. This was a necessary precaution, as they had no curry comb. Horse Rider actually knew all this, but he listened respectfully.

The meal now over, White Woman cleaned up the dishes and started out with Clear Day to get the water. It was a mile to Beaver Creek, and it was necessary to go at least twice a day to get water for the household. Horse Rider usually helped by making at least one of these trips. The two women now set out with two buckets hanging on a seven-foot-long stick which rested on their right shoulders, one woman walking in front and one behind, with the buckets between. The stick, ordinarily used as a digging iron, had one end fire-hardened and sharpened to a point, the other end being forked. At this time after breakfast and especially just before eating supper, many people were walking toward the creek for the same purpose.

Horse Rider left the lodge to take care of the horses, and Old Bull and Victory Call remained seated in their place, smoking their pipe and continuing their conversation. The old ladies who were left behind looked around their stores to see what they might contribute to the family larder. When the women got back with the water they would say, "Daughter, I want you to cook this." If they were going to have mush for their next meal, the old lady might busy herself pounding the corn in the mortar. Or the old women would go out and look for a little kindling wood.

Now a messenger arrived from Eagle Chief, asking Old Bull and Victory Call to come to a chiefs' council at Eagle Chief's house. They were to plan a mass expedition to get wood in order to store up a plentiful supply of fuel. With the heavy demand upon the wood supply in the immediate neighborhood of the villages, they had to go five miles or more to get any appreciable quantities; for this they had to plan their itinerary and provide military protection against the constantly lurking enemy. The messenger stated: "I've come for the two of you to invite you to to Eagle Chief's house. Take your bowl and spoon with you when you go" (indicating that there would be a feast). Both men got up and set out at once for Eagle Chief's house. By eleven o'clock all the chiefs had gathered there.

The men would be gone until evening, and the women began the household routines at home. When the two women got back from Beaver Creek with the water, they cooked a casual lunch of scraps of dried buffalo meat that they kept in a buffalo paunch bag for the purpose. They made some soup with parched corn and a little salt.

The main business of the women of the household that day was to give the food pit a good cleaning—to remove the large skin bags containing the dried corn and other supplies, examine all the seeds for bad ones and for worms, sweep the thatch-covered walls of the pit, clear off the mold, and take out three weeks' supply of dried foods so that they could keep the pit closed for a while to reduce the danger of rain water leaking in; besides, they liked to let the ground settle down so that the location of the pit would be concealed from lurking enemies. The Pawnee name for food pit, *tahaksu*, means hidden, concealed, or covered up. The women all knew that they were pressed for time as the entire job had to be completed between lunchtime and sundown, since the pit could not be left open for the night. While lunch preparations were under way, one of the old women remarked to the other, "Since it is such a nice day, let's make a start by opening up the pit and letting out the moldy, musty air. Then we can go on after lunch."

Having eaten their meal, the two old women came out again directly and spread a skin on the ground, dipping the dried corn out of the large skin sacks with a pan or bowl and spreading it out to dry. All the corn had to be removed and examined and the walls cleaned thoroughly—moldy spots in the grass lining being rubbed off and thrown away. Sometimes they were lucky enough to find that none of the corn had spoiled at all. After the lunch dishes were cleaned, the other women joined the old ladies, and as they were busily working an old neighbor woman came by and offered to help them. "You've got a lot of corn to attend to there." "Yes I do," said White Woman. Although there were some general stand-ard varieties, each woman had her own special breeds of corn and of the other crops. As she sat down to join them, the old lady remarked, "I don't have seeds like that!" indicating that she would be very glad to have some. They cleaned and winnowed the seeds for several hours, working diligently together. Finally the other women went in to prepare the supper, and White Woman remained outside with the old neighbor woman to finish up the work. When they called out to announce that sup-per was ready, White Woman called back that she and her friend would be in later and to please set something aside for them. Meanwhile she had indicated to the old woman that she wanted her to stay and that they would eat later. As they filled each sack, White Woman put aside a little pile of each kind of corn and other seeds, remarking that she was going to give her some seeds and that she might go home and get herself a sack to hold them. When the woman returned she pointed to the piles of seeds and said, "This is yours. Tie it here. I'm going to put corn of another color on top. Do you have anything to tie it with?" "No, I'll use my garters," said the old woman. Then White Woman said, "Let's put the bag back in the pit," and climbed down into it, using a tree trunk with branch stubs as a ladder. When she got to the bottom, the old woman handed her the large skin bag that contained all the smaller bags of the different kinds of corn and beans. White Woman punched it down to settle the load and came up out of the pit and began to close it up. First she covered everything with a skin cover, then a layer of thatch grass, then she wedged some sticks across the opening into the side walls, then another layer of thatch grass and then earth that she trampled down hard to keep out the rain and to conceal the place of opening. "Let's go eat now," said White Woman. Inside they sat down and ate the food that had been set aside for them, while the others, particularly the older women, sat by to converse with their guest. "How are the folks in your lodge?" they asked, "Oh, they're all right," said the old woman. Meanwhile, White Woman was feeling very friendly toward the old woman for helping her out, and as they sat there she noticed that the old woman's moccasins were worn out. She had a nice piece of black-dyed tanned skin that was ordinarily used for holiday moccasins, and she said, "I'm going to give you a piece of black-dyed skin so that you can make yourself some moc-casins." "Oh, I thank you, I thank you. Oh, daughter, thanks. You have taken pity on me. I'll wear it. Now I've got to go, daughter." When the old woman left, the rest of the people in the lodge would say, "That old lady is always good, always trying to help other people out." When the old lady got back to her own lodge she reported where she had been all afternoon and that she had received a big bag of corn and her dinner besides. "Oh, you got good pay," they said. Then she added the news about the gift of black tanned skin, and her husband teased her and said, "Let's see that. Just right to make me a pair. You can patch up yours."

Back at the lodge, the old ladies said they were tired and went to bed, and White Woman waited for her husband to come home.

While the women were busy with the minor household work and the storage pit, Old Bull and Victory Call had been at a meeting of the Skidi chiefs at the home of Eagle Chief. There were representatives of each of the four Skidi villages—chiefs, subchiefs, and their attendant braves. Eagle Chief yielded his place at the west to the two most important guests and took the southeast position. At the southwest was Lone Chief of Village-across-a-Ridge and in the northwest position, Leading Chief of Village-in-the-Bottomlands. The subchiefs and braves of each of these chiefs sat next to them in a line extending toward the east. At the southeast position, sat Eagle Chief of Pumpkin-Vine Village with his subchiefs and braves extending inward toward the west along the side of the lodge. On the north side in a symmetrical arrangement was Chief Feared-by-the-Enemy of Wolf-Standing-in-Water Village sitting in the northeast position with his subchiefs and braves extending inward along the northside. (See Figure 5-2 for the positions of representatives at the council meeting.)

Eagle Chief was the first to address the company, stating the purpose for which he had called them together: "The Sioux are likely to come around any time. Don't each go individually to get wood. We must all go at a stated time when we can have our scouts on the lookout and bring in enough wood to be piled up while the planting is begun, that is at least four days' supply." Discussion from the others present followed, and then Eagle Chief announced that they would have another meeting in about two weeks or more to discuss the matter of clearing the fields in preparation for planting. He now turned over the conduct of the meeting to the chiefs at the west, and Lone Chief took charge, stating that if anyone had anything to say about the business at hand they should do so at this time as they were to have a feast and then talk of other matters. After everyone had spoken his mind they waited two or three minutes and then Lone Chief said, "Now we are going to eat." At the entrance near the east were the two errand men of both presiding chiefs at the west, and they had prepared the food and were ready to serve. The bowls were piled up near the kettle in which the food had been boiling, and, while one of the men dished it out, the other served. He carried two bowls to the west, one for each of the presiding chiefs. Then he returned to the east, carried the next bowl to the next chief on the south side, then returned to the east and gave the next bowl to the next chief to the north side, and so on in alternation, one by one on each side. Then the braves were served, one on the south, one on the north, until everyone had received his food, whereupon the errand men served each other.

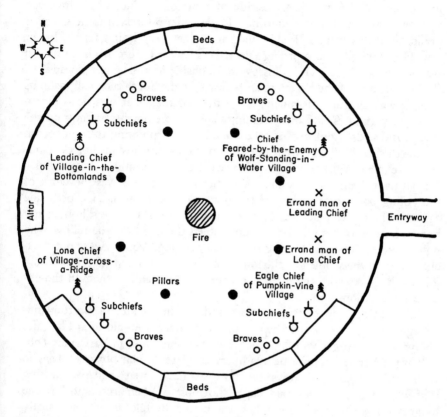

FIGURE 5-2. Administrative feast at Eagle Chief's lodge in the spring. Mats are placed in the outer circuit against the beds to accommodate larger numbers. Of the supposed twelve villages that formed the Skidi Federation in the past, four villages remained in 1867. Villages must have combined as their numbers were decimated. The original twelve sacred village bundles remained, and some of the subchiefs probably represented these assimilated villages.

This was the time for joking "so that everyone could laugh during the meal." The jokes were of a somewhat slapstick variety as they wanted to be sure that no one's feelings were hurt in any way. Ordinarily, while the social relationship with one's parents was quite formal and restrained, the relationship with the grandparents was in sharp contrast. It was a relationship of lively familiarity. Physical handling was rough-and-tumble, a grandfather sometimes pulling his grandson out of bed of a cold morning and dumping him in the snow to harden him; jokes were often leveled at the grandchild and answered in kind. The mode of kin reckoning often involved an extension of the immediate kin terms to more distant blood relatives, and it worked out so that people of similar ages might address each other by the kin terms of grandfather and grandchild—thereby permitting a great deal of free-wheeling slapstick behavior. This was incongruous because of the social position of some of the individuals involved and was considered quite humorous. Eagle Chief addressed Lone Chief as grandson in this way, and he would say, "That's the laziest fellow I ever saw. He sleeps till mid-morning every day. I wish I were at his house. I'd throw him in the water." This evoked considerable laughter because of the incongruity of the situation, and, now that the South Side had made its joke, it was the turn of somebody on the north side. It was decorum to wait a few minutes, and then Leading Chief at the northwest took up the thread and said, "Look at that fellow over there," pointing to someone on the north side. "When I went out with my horses, I saw his horses standing there in a terrible condition. They were turning round and round with flies all over them and they must have been thirsty." (It was the work of the young boys to take care of the horses.) The man on the north side against whom the joke was leveled replied with, "I always hobble my horses, but he took my lariat and unhobbled them. That's the fellow who unhobbled my horses!" During the actual meeting, women were not present, but now the women of the lodge began to return and they too would join in the jokes with the men who happened to stand to them in the appropriate relationship.

This was the end of the meeting, and Leading Chief of Bottomlands Village sitting at the northwest presided over the closing. He said, "Now we are to get wood. Some of you, Lone Chief in particular (object of the last joke), must be in a hurry to go tend their horses. Any who wish can stay and tell stories, but now we have eaten [and the meeting is at an end]." Everyone said *nawa* and most of them rose and left the lodge. A few lingered. Enough extra boiled buffalo meat was usually portioned out at such a feast so that everyone had a substantial piece to take home to the family. Food from a chiefs' council was thought to have the special virtue of conveying a blessing of plenty to the women and children, and some of the men were eager to get home and share what they had with their wives and children. It was for this reason that they had been requested to bring their own bowls when they were invited that morning.

The decisions reached by the chiefs at their councils were always announced to the people soon after the meeting was over. One old man for each village with a somewhat resounding voice usually acted as the village crier. He would stand on the roof of his earth lodge between the smokehole and the entrance passageway facing east and call out:

"Day after tomorrow, we're all going for wood—the whole bunch of us. You young men—after breakfast take your bow and arrows. Go up on a high hill and be on the lookout to picket for Sioux or any other kind of danger. Women have to fix up their packstraps and everyone should sharpen up his axe, fix up the ropes, borrow a horse to haul the wood if you need one. If two or three lodges are going afoot together, they must keep in line so that we know where you are." (Those with horses were in less danger and might go in any order.) There was another thing he warned them against—that is, taking young girls along. They were just the ones the Sioux would be trying to capture, and the old man remarked, they weren't really strong enough to carry wood anyway! Another danger was a magical one. The spirits of men who had been scalped by an enemy were very much feared. They were thought to lurk all around, trying to capture women or steal whatever else they could get their hands on. So the old man cautioned, "If a woman hasn't kept up, the line must wait for her until she arrives. She might be captured by one of the scalped men. This is the time you have to look out for that."

When the young men heard the crier's announcement, five or six of them would gather together at a favorite rendezvous and say, "Let's go together with our bows and arrows real early before the others and stay up there until everyone comes home." According to their plan, on the appointed morning they would go out before the others and disburse over the area to see whether the enemy was lurking about. They would leave the villages about 7:30 in the morning and stay out all day.

The chiefs' meeting had come to an end that afternoon while it was still full daylight. Old Bull had gone off to tend his horses. Victory Call, having nothing in particular to do since he had Horse Rider to help him, wandered over to the gaming grounds where some of the men were clustered about making their bets on the outcome of the hoop and spear game, while others were just watching on the sidelines. Victory Call sat down at some distance from the game and two of the spectators came to join him. The man who sat down at his left filled up his pipe and offered it to Victory Call, lighting it for him. Victory Call offered the mouthpiece upward for the first puff to the cosmic powers in the heavens saying, "Greetings, all of you spread out up there." Then he offered the mouthpiece to the earth and said, "Greetings, my mother." Now he took two puffs on the pipe and began to share it with the men on each side of him in the alternation: first to the right, then himself, then to the left, and so on. When the pipe was smoked out, Victory Call was feeling in a genial mood. He made a special arrangement of his robe that had up to now been carelessly draped around his shoulders. He drew it down to his waist and, crossing his legs with the robe folded in a certain order, showed by this token that he was ready to tell a story. The men who had sat down with him were anxious to hear what the chief had to say, and particularly what had gone on in the meeting he had just attended before the crier got around to announcing it. Several more men joined the party with the same idea in mind. Victory Call might begin directly, or one of the men would suggest it obliquely saying, "I heard you had a feast."

"Yes, we had a feast. It was about having the whole tribe go out for wood." "Yes," one of the men would say, "springtime is coming now and it's about time we got the wood ready. Womenfolk have to go to the fields." Now they would exchange stories until sundown—about war exploits and the horses they had succeeded in getting from the enemy, in which direction they went when they got them, about scouting in the U.S. Army and other similar topics. After about half an hour, the man on his right filled the pipe, but Victory Call ceded it to him. He made the offering to heaven and to earth, and the pipe was passed between them back and forth until they had smoked the tobacco in it. While the storytelling was going on, one of the men decided that he would entertain the chief at his house for dinner and sent a little boy with a message for his wife to prepare a meal for their honored guest. When he was notified that the meal was ready he said to Victory Call, "I want you to come up to my lodge. We're going to have a little bite." The host would call over one or two more and invite them to join the party, saying "I want you to come up. We're going to have something to eat."

Victory Call was seated in the place of honor at the northwest and the host at the southeast. The women of the house dished out the food and passed it around. After they had eaten, Victory Call got up first and left walking out by the north 'side of the lodge. After he had gone they would say, "He's a good chief. He goes about and sees what's going on."

When Victory Call got home that evening, he found White Woman waiting up for him. "I've already eaten," he said. White Woman retorted by way of banter, "I didn't ask you if you had eaten." Then he sat down by the fire and she brought him his tobacco pouch. Guests were likely to come in soon and join him for the rest of the evening for a smoke and some talk. Before the guests arrived, they divided into very small pieces the meat that Victory Call had brought home from the chiefs' meeting so that everyone could have a taste.

When the first guest arrived, Victory Call offered him his pipe and said to White Woman, "Cook something." The guest had just had his dinner and said, "No, no, I've already eaten." Then a little time passed and another guest wandered in. He happened to be hungry and he remarked, "I'd like something to eat," and then White Woman had to get to work and prepare something. By this time all the others who were sitting around would have worked up an appetite and Victory Call would say, "Maybe those fellows are hungry. Maybe they can eat." And so the cooking started up again.

They talked about hunting, trapping, the warpath, chasing the buffalo, and some other incidents that they had seen or heard. Sitting Bull would begin by telling a story on himself. He told that once he had killed a deer and his kinsman came along. Ordinarily he would be expected to give him half the kill, but he had diverted his attention saying, "Go follow the track, the deer went that way. I shot at him and missed." Now he told of how he had hidden the deer so that he wouldn't have to share it. Now Riding-In joined in and said, "I did the same thing once. I killed a buck and put him in a trough and when my kinsman came along I said, "I shot at that deer and missed him, but you're on horseback, so you can go after him." If either of the aggrieved kinsmen were present the guilty hunter would remark, "Now I wish I had given you half." There would be no hard feelings on anyone's part as they would feel that bygones were bygones. The talk went on for some hours and finally all the women had gone to bed. Midnight was the customary time to stop. Someone went outside and looked at the stars. He came in and remarked, "It's midnight. We're all sleepy. We'd better go to bed." They would all go out together and look at the stars and the guests would leave for their own homes. The men of the lodge went out together to tend to their needs before going to bed. This was for their mutual protection, as there was always the possibility of a Sioux lurking in the shadows ready to attack an individual alone. Before going to bed, the women would also go in a group with a man along for their protection.

Victory Call planned to go deer hunting next day. He made lead bullets, cleaned his gun, and loaded it with shavings along with the bullets so that they would ignite. He filled his horn with powder and now he was ready for the morning. Old Bull took note of his preparations and planned to be near the house that day for protection in case of attack. Next morning, Victory Call got up way before down. He made the fire and left before breakfast. White Woman would get up later and prepare the breakfast for the lodge.

6

A DEER HUNT

~~~~~~

Victory Call Goes on a Deer Hunt—His Kinsman Helps—They Return with the Meat—the Division of the Kill—Guests Are Served a Feast— Conversation Follows

~~~~~~

WHEN VICTORY CALL LEFT the house, it was still well before dawn and the stars were clear in the sky. He was carrying his six-shooter, and just as he went out he had called out the direction in which he would be going. This was done so that if a kinsman should come in and inquire, he could join Victory Call and help him butcher, thus earning a share in the kill.

He set out toward the sandhills to the north. Up the ravine near the river, the grass was about an inch high. Now the deer came out into the open and picked the new grass. In the colder weather the deer stayed in the hollow places where the timber grew and where a man did not prowl. The sun had not yet risen and he tied his horse in a hollow and climbed up one of the sand hills and sat down to wait. Victory Call liked to sit there in the peaceful quiet with the breaking dawn. Finally as the sun came up he could see the deer on the hilltops outlined against the sky. In another two or three weeks, when the grass was four inches high, the rains would come and wash away the last of the snow, and then they would begin to clear the fields.

After he had made his first kill, his kinsman came crossing his path saying, "You out hunting?" Victory Call remarked, "That's good, I did want company to help me butcher." They butchered the deer together and the kinsman got approximately half. They divided the spoils in the following order: Victory Call got the hide, the meat along the backbone, head and two "quarters" (a quarter was an arm, leg, or flank). The kinsman got three quarters and the entrails which, whether he received them or not, it would have been his task to clean.

While they were looking about for the second deer, they were also

76

keeping on the alert for mushrooms and milkweed, whose tender tops were relished when cooked with corn. Some of the mushrooms were yellow or green under the head, and these were known to be poisonous. The edible ones were solid pure white. Any with worms were discarded. Some men became so absorbed in this search that they wandered too far out and would be killed by the Sioux. This was particularly likely with men whose food at home was in short supply.

If Victory Call and his kinsman had the good fortune to track down another deer and Victory Call killed it, he would assign the major portion to his helper. Legally, the entire kill belonged to Victory Call and the division was entirely at his discretion. Sometimes he would be planning to have leggings made out of the skins and then he would apologize and say, "Excuse me. I can't give you the hide." His helper would reply, "That's all right. I just came around to help you. You gave me meat anyway."

The meat was all packed and the two men set out for the village. It was nearly sundown and they had to pass the village gaming ground where the men gathered watching the hoop and pole game. The players and spectators would remark, "Look at those fellows. They have a lot of deer meat. I'm going up there to get some soup."

The two hunters separated and each went to his own house. As soon as Victory Call approached, a hide was spread inside to receive the meat, and Horse Rider was waiting outside to unload the horse and bring it in.

When Victory Call arrived inside, the first thing he said was, "The folks down there saw me coming. Hurry up and fix our dinner so that we can eat before they all get here." The family had barely finished eating when the people began to crowd in. If it were the first fresh meat of the season in the village, some women would come and say to White Woman, "Daughter, I am begging some meat." "That's good," Victory Call would say, indicating that they were welcome. White Woman and the other women of the house were cooking the meat in large kettles, and men and women were sitting around waiting to be fed when the meat boiled. Some people preferred strips of meat roasted in the coals, and they were sitting around roasting it for themselves.

Then the fire began to burn up brighter and someone remarked, "How about getting to work and roasting the ribs?" Horse Rider then took the ribs and leaned them on stakes around the fire. These would be served at a more formal feast after the casual guests had left. Otter was sent to invite the guests. Each of the men would invite two honored guests. Victory Call inquired of Old Bull whom he would like to entertain, and he requested that Chief White Eagle be called with his brave, Bringing Trophies, with whom Old Bull was associated in his doctor practice. Victory Call invited Eagle Chief, head chief of his village, Pumpkin-Vine, and his principal brave, War Cry. Meanwhile the women were cooking coffee and frying bread to supplement the meat course for their guests when they arrived. In the old days they would be baking corn bread in the ashes to be served with the soup.

Four buckskin cushions were placed at the west for the guests of honor, and the rest sat around along both sides on the mats. By the time the guests came in, the ribs were cooked and the two largest ones were carried to Eagle Chief and his brave War Cry, who were sitting at the northwest. The next two went to Chief White Eagle and his brave in the southwest seats. The rest of the ribs were carried two by two, first to two guests on the north side, then to two on the south side, and so on until all had been served. A very small top rib was given to any little boy who might be visiting or to the boys of the house, Otter or Yellow Calf.

The food served, Victory Call began to talk to his guests. He told of the highlights of the hunt and that after he had gotten the deer the other fellow came and found him. His horse began to move around and he thought a Sioux was coming, but then he saw who it was and called him over. On such occasions an old man usually invited or just wandered in, knowing he would be welcome. Horse Rider had invited That-Chief, and the old man told them stories of war and old customs continuing after the feast was over. Anyone who wanted to leave right after eating was free to do so. He would get up and say, "I have to go. I have something to do." The old man would stay all night and get his breakfast there. Except for the four guests of honor, there was less protocol required than in the more formal feasts. After the dishes were cleaned and put away some of the women would go to bed, while others would join the men and listen to the conversation. Sometimes boys and their grandmothers would sit on the sidelines, keeping themselves warm with a pan of coals. When everyone had gone, they would come up close to the fire and warm themselves. The session went on quite late. By midnight everyone would leave, and they all went to bed. In the home of Victory Call's helper on the hunt, the same kind of entertaining would have gone on. Past midnight and everyone would be sleeping. Tomorrow it would begin again—the fire lit, the man at his work and his leisure, the women busy, the children playing.

7

THE SPRING AWAKENING

Creation Ceremony—Sacrifice for Creation to Morning Star—Ceremony of Sacred Corn Seeds —Ground-breaking Ceremony—Pawnee Ceremonial Acts Discussed—Planting Cycle Ceremonies Discussed—Significance with Seasonal Progression Noted

THE PAWNEES HAD MANY TASKS to accomplish in the early spring before the time of planting. Some of them were practical and some ceremonial, but to the Pawnees who believed that nothing on earth could move without the heavens, no practical task could be undertaken unless the appropriate ceremony had preceded it.

The first ceremonial act of the year was to awaken the whole earth from its winter sleep. After their long and arduous travels over the plains on their winter buffalo hunt, the Pawnees returned to their villages at the end of February or the beginning of March. The year began about the time of the spring equinox with the ritual recitation of the creation by the five priests, repeated for each of the twelve sacred bundles of the original villages that formed the Skidi federation. The position of the stars was an important guide to the time when this ceremony should be held. The earth lodge served as an astronomical observatory and as the priests sat inside at the west, they could observe the stars in certain positions through the smokehole and through the long east-oriented entranceway. They also kept careful watch of the horizon right after sunset and just before dawn to note the order and position of the stars.

The round of spring renewal ceremonies was heralded by the appearance of two small twinkling stars known as the Swimming Ducks in the northeastern horizon near the Milky Way. They notified the animals that they must awaken from their winter sleep, break through the ice, and come out into the world again. At this time the Pleiades began to take a certain position. When these signs were seen, then they must listen for the thunder that is low, deep, and rumbling, starting in the west and rolling around the entire circuit of the heavens. Sheet lightning gave warning that this kind of thunder would soon appear. This thunder was the voice of Heaven, and when it came from the south they knew that it was the signal for the creation ritual to be performed.

The ritual was part of the sacred lore of the Evening Star bundle which at this time was kept in the earth lodge of Old Lady Lucky Leader. As soon as the thunder was heard, the five official priests gathered there and began their preparations for the ritual. The same ritual would be repeated for each of the twelve major sacred bundles, the Evening Star which they were about to perform, then Morning Star bundle, then Big Black Meteoric Star and nine others. At intervals all during the month of March the priests went in succession to the different households where each of the bundles was kept, performing the ritual to renew their powers. The order for the first three performances was as given above; the other nine, simply as each of the households happened to be ready to pause in its work and to provide the necessary food for the priests.

Now the five priests were sitting at the west in the lodge of Old Lady Lucky Leader, the Evening Star bundle lying open before them. The sacred objects were spread out on the skin of a tawny yellow calf representing the herds of buffalo. Two sacred ears of corn represented their staple food, two owlskins the watchfulness of the chiefs, hawkskins the ferocity of the warriors, flint for fire and sweet grass for incense; paints symbolized the powers of the different directions of the universe. Each of the priests held a gourd rattle in his right hand, and they sang together of the first creation. Their responsibility lay heavy upon them, for they and they alone must bring the world back to life again. Would they now be able to bring back the abundance of summer—the green grass, the trees, the animals reborn, the waters flowing free, the warmth of a summer day? Loud and insistently they recounted each minute step of the creation and in the trancelike depths of their thinking, the events rolled by before them.

In the beginning Heaven sat in the unassorted universe and thought. He sent his thoughts out over space. Then he created the celestial gods to bring his thoughts to fruition. First he made the gods of the cardinal directions—the Evening Star at the west with the moon as her helper, the Morning Star at the east with the sun as his helper, in the north the North Star and in the south, Canopus, the South Star. Then Heaven placed four stars in the semicardinal directions—Black Star in the northeast, Yellow Star in the northwest, White Star in the southwest and Red Star in the southeast. Heaven said to them, "You four shall be known as the ones who uphold the heavens. There you shall stand as long as the heavens last, and although your place is to hold the heavens up, I also give you power to create people. You shall give them the different bundles which shall be holy bundles. Your powers will be known to the people, for you shall touch the heavens with your hands, and your feet shall touch the earth."

Now Heaven spoke to Evening Star in the west. So that they might do her bidding, he sent her clouds, winds, lightnings, and thunders, and these she was to place between herself and her garden; then they would assume human form, appearing in the dress of priests, each with a gourd rattle in his right hand. With these arrangements in order, Heaven was now ready to create the world:

It was the storms that carried out this mission, one great thunderstorm to create the lifeless structure, and a second to endow it with life. All this took many eons.

Heaven told the Evening Star to tell her gods to rattle and sing. As they sang, the clouds came up, then the winds blew the clouds and the lightnings and thunders entered the clouds. The thick clouds gathered over open space and into them Heaven dropped a pebble—a quartz crystal. The pebble rolled in the clouds and as the storm passed over, the whole world below was water. Now Heaven sent out the four semicardinal-direction gods, each armed with a war club of hemlock, the wood known to the Skidi as *atira*, my mother. As they approached their appropriate stations, they were to strike the waters which would cause them to part and expose the earth. Each of the four semicardinal-direction bundles is said to contain such a war club of hemlock that was actually used in the original creation.

Now the lifeless structure of the earth had been formed. A second great storm was needed to put life into the earth. Heaven instructed Evening Star to have her four gods (impersonated by the priests in the ritual) rattle and sing, and, while they sang, clouds came up, winds, lightnings, and thunders, and, while the gods sang of the formation of the earth, "the storms passed over the earth, and as the winds blew, it rained, the lightnings striking in the ground to put life in the earth. The thunders now shook the earth so that in parts where it was not level, the dirt slid down into the valleys." In these two great storms, the earth, *uraru*, was created and then life put into it.

Next were to be created the timbers and the underbrush *tuharu*, that make the land gray. The gods sang, and with the first great storm, the structure of the timbers was created. There was a second great thunderstorm in which the lightning struck them and the thunders sounded over them to put life into the *tuharu*, the timber.

Fourth in the great creation were the waters, *tsaharu*, and two great eras of storm were needed—one to give it its structure and a second to make it a living reality. The bottoms of the creeks, rivers, ponds, and lakes were cleared as "the wind passed over the streams" and it rained. Then the waters filled the stream, *tsaharu*. Then the lightnings struck the streams and the thunders sounded into them and the sound of the streams flowing through the land was heard to reply, and Heaven knew that they were sweet.

The fifth creation was of cultivated seeds, *kaki·u*. In a first storm, the seeds were dropped on the earth by the gods. Then in a second storm, Evening Star sent winds, clouds, thunder, and lightnings over the earth so that the seeds had life and sprouted. "After all this was done, Heaven was glad and hid himself for a time."

To the stars, Heaven had assigned the task of creating people in their own image. Now Morning Star called them all into council, but in the course of their proceedings, a great conflict developed between him and the Evening Star. Now in order to bring light and life into the world, Morning Star had to set out from his home in the east to conquer Evening Star and mate with her. Evening Star was ready for him. In the four semicardinal world quarters she had placed four fierce animals—wolf in the southeast, who had the power of the clouds; wildcat in the southwest, with power of the winds; mountain lion in the northwest, with lightning power; and bear in the northeast, with his power of thunder. While the other male gods had come from the east trying desperately to overcome the powers, they had all died in the attempt. Now Morning Star with his helper, the Sun, had succeeded, but he had one more obstacle to overcome. Evening Star had provided herself with vaginal teeth "like the mouth of a rattlesnake with teeth around," and these Morning Star had to break with a meteor stone in order to mate with her. As a result of his success, a girl was born to Evening Star. She was the first human being that the stars had created. She stood on a cloud and was carried to earth by a funnel-shaped whirlwind. Now Moon and Sun mated, and they created a boy who was also carried to earth.

The gods now held two more councils to make further plans for humanity. In the first council, the Big Black Meteoric Star presided, in the second, the Evening Star. Heaven now came out of his retirement to help them. He told Evening Star to call her four storm priests to rattle and sing, and it rained on the two children, lightning struck around them, and the thunders roared. At last they understood, and they lay together and a child was born to them. Heaven instructed Evening Star again, and through further storms each young person was instructed in his respective role in life—the girl in the fruitfulness of the earth, the form of the earth lodge, the nature of speech and of the land outside. The man got the clothing of a warrior and was shown the way to travel over the earth, how to make war and how to hunt; he was also taught his role in the act of procreation.

The people began to increase and Evening Star came many times in visions to the first man. She came night after night, bringing along her four storm gods who rattled and sang the sacred songs so that he learned of the creation and could give this knowledge to the people. Then the people went hunting far and wide over the land and they discovered that there were villages scattered everywhere in which there were people just like themselves. First Man now decided to call them all to a great council. He sent his messenger to the villages to invite them. Meanwhile he moved his village from south of the Platte to a more central location northward on the Loup, and it was henceforth called Center Village. From the west came Old Village which was actually four villages in one, each representing one of the semicardinal directions and each with a sacred bundle of its own that contained a different color of corn. They came carrying packages of dried buffalo meat on their backs, since it was a time before the Pawnees had gotten horses from the Europeans. The leader of the four was Big Black Meteoric Star bundle, and the head of this village insisted on being "Master of Ceremonies" for all of them. The Chief of Center Village who had called them together was now faced with a problem, and that night Evening Star came to him in a vision and told him what to do. He would divide the functions of priest and chief, stepping aside and allowing the leader of Old Village to be the priest while he himself took over the functions of chief. He kept the Evening Star bundle intact, but made a special ceremonial bundle to denote his chieftainship. In order to commemorate his creative intellectual powers, he directed that when he died his skull was to be attached to the outside of this bundle. Thus it came to be known as the Skull bundle, although it was also referred to as the bundle of the Wonderful Person, *Tsahiks-paruksti*, "person-wonderful." This bundle presided over the meeting of the chiefs late in the spring as well as over other rituals. When the original skull was accidentally broken, it was replaced with another.

This story of the creation embodies two things. On the one hand it is an allegory of cosmic creation, and on the other a thinly veiled recounting, in symbolic form, of all-too-human intervillage conflicts of the past which were resolved by the formation of a political federation. In Pawnee thinking, these were appropriately combined, for peace and ongoing life came always from Heaven. In the ceremonial cycle of the year there was a careful alternation of ceremonial authority, the first ceremony being that of the Evening Star bundle—the creation; the second, a ceremony directed by the Morning Star bundle, and the third a ceremony under the aegis of one of the four semicardinal-direction bundles. (See Table 7-1.) In this way a balance of ceremonial responsibilities was maintained among the leading villages of the past which had joined together in the Skidi Federation.

After the priests had completed their rounds for the creation ritual during the month of March, the second ceremony in the cycle involved the sacrifice to the Morning Star of a young girl that had been captured from the enemy. This was compensation to the Morning Star god for his struggle during the creation. The last girl to be sacrificed to the Morning Star was a young Sioux girl named Haxti in 1838, after which the practice was abandoned. This ceremony symbolized fertility in general.

TABLE 7-1. *Chart of Sacred Bundle Ceremonies in the Spring and Fall*

The several ceremonies of the spring planting and fall harvest form a parallel series, the six ceremonies in each showing a recurrent alternation of the powers of the Evening Star and the four semicardinal-direction bundles. The first four pertain to planting, fertility, and war, the latter two to buffalo hunting and migration.

Spring	*Fall*
I. Spring Renewal—ceremony of the creation at the first thunder from the south; Evening Star sponsorship.	I. Green Corn Ceremony. Evening Star sponsorship.
II. Distributing sacred seed corn of the special breed of corn included in the sacred bundles. Semicardinal-direction bundle sponsorship. Changeover to one of the summer-direction bundles —southwest or southeast.	II. Harvest of Mature Corn. Mature corn from sacred seeds installed in the sacred bundles, replacing the sacred ears of last year's planting. Semicardinal-direction bundle sponsorship. Changeover to one of the winter-direction bundles— northwest or northeast.
III. Ground-breaking ceremony, *Awari*, movement, activity. The Skull bundle of the Wonderful Person, an affiliate of the Evening Star in charge of the ritual as sponsor.	III. Four-Pole Ceremony—symbolizing political federation and control of the country through war expeditions so that they could go out into the country on the hunt. The Skull bundle of the Wonderful Person, an Evening Star affiliate in charge of the ritual as sponsor.
IV. Birth and growth of Young Mother Corn through adolescence to young womanhood; known as *Kurahus*, "Priest." Semicardinal-direction bundle in charge of ritual as sponsor.	

BUFFALO HUNTING AND MIGRATION

Spring	*Fall*
V. Ritual Chiefs' Meeting. Chiefs personify Heaven and acknowledge their sole responsibility to lead the people to a successful conclusion of the buffalo hunt. Skull bundle of the Wonderful Person in charge of the ritual.	V. Ritual Chiefs' Meeting. Chiefs acknowledge their sole responsibility to lead the people to a successful conclusion of the buffalo hunt. North Star bundle in charge of the ritual.
VI. Great Cleansing Ceremony of the ceremonial objects. Big Black Meteoric Star bundle, the Northeast bundle of the four Semicardinal-direction set, in charge. Tribe leaves the village to go off on the migration and summer buffalo hunt.	VI. Great Cleansing Ceremony of the ceremonial objects. Big Black Meteoric Star bundle, the Northeast bundle of the four Semicardinal-direction set, in charge. Tribe leaves the village to go off on the migration and winter buffalo hunt.

The next ceremony concerned the corn itself. The sacred corn included in all the bundles was of a specially cultivated breed that was ordinarily not eaten. At this ceremony these seeds were distributed to each of the sacred bundle owners so that the sacred ears of corn could be grown for their bundles. The two "north" bundles of the semicardinal directions took charge of this ceremony in alternate years, one year the northeast, the next the northwest, etc. This ceremony was held late in April.

During the first week in May the ceremony that immediately preceded the planting of the common varieties of food corn was performed. Until it was carried out, no planting could be done. It was under the sponsorship of the Skull bundle, thus maintaining the principle of alternation of sacred responsibilities, since it was an Evening Star affiliate. The outstanding feature of the ceremony was a pantomime of breaking the ground preparatory to planting. The ground was customarily broken with a hoe made of a buffalo shoulder blade tied to a short wooden stick that served as a handle. During the ceremony, the women went through the motions of breaking the ground with sacred hoes that were kept in the four semicardinal-direction bundles and borrowed for the occasion. The action was very vigorous and the ceremony was appropriately called *Awari*, "Motion." The planting was done the very next day after the ceremony.

The final ceremony of the spring planting cycle was called *Kurahus*,

"Priest"; it was performed when the sacred corn plants were about two inches high and had four good leaves. This ceremony was in charge of one of the two "south" bundles of the semicardinal directions—in alternate years, the southwest and the southeast. The crux of the ceremony was the uprooting of one of the young sacred corn plants, in which the act of birth was symbolized and the young plant carried as an infant on the visionary's back from the field to the ceremonial lodge, where it was attached to a stick fashioned by an arrowshaft maker and painted to represent a person. The plant was now carried through a cycle of childhood and young girlhood and breathed on by the priests to give it life. It was now Young Mother Corn, watching over the tribe. Only when this ceremony had been performed were the women permitted to go out into the fields and weed the corn plants and hill up the earth around them to protect them as they grew. A second weeding and hilling process in the latter part of June was the last attention the corn plants received before being "laid by." The people were then ready to leave for the summer buffalo hunt.

Without this ceremonial cycle, the coordination of the people in their orderly round of life could not go on. While it was primarily a religious frame, it was also of basic practical value since it was based on the seasonal progression. Without it it would have been almost impossible to coordinate people's lives with one another and with external events.

Some of the activities that were necessary during the spring season were fitted into the cycle rather than being part of it. This was particularly true of the manufacturing and maintenance functions, while the ceremonial cycle referred especially to the planting of the crops.

All winter while the people had been wandering over the country on the tribal buffalo hunt the house had stood idle and their clothes and equipment had taken heavy wear. These had to be put in order and repaired before planting time.

The average life of a house was twelve years, but before the end of that time water might leak through the roof and rot some of the radial roof beams. These would have to be replaced, and in order to do this the whole roof covering of thatch and earth had to be removed and reassembled. This task would require more than the personnel of the household. Where the men of the house had little social status they would have few social contacts to draw on, but men like Old Bull and Victory Call were in a much better position to get help from the community. Because of their status as chiefs many more people were likely to volunteer to help. The following section shows some of the social mechanisms involved in the process. However, it should be noted that the assistance given was neither on the basis of power authority nor fundamentally for the sake of gaining social status by association, but rather in appreciation of the role of the chief in public service. For the house of the chief was the place where administrative activities were carried on for the benefit of the people, as we have seen in the meeting described above in the home of Eagle Chief.

8

REPAIRING THE ROOF

OF THE HOUSE

~~~~~~~~~~~~~~~~~~~~~~~~~~~~~~~~~~~~~

Repairing the Roof a Spring Task—Cooperative Nature of Work—Detailed Description of Repairing Roof—Project Is Completed with Wide Cooperation from Villagers

~~~~~~~~~~~~~~~~~~~~~~~~~~~~~~~~~~~~~

ALL WINTER LONG the house had stood unoccupied, the roof covered with snow while the people were away on the hunt. By spring, when the snow began to melt, the water seeping through the hard-packed earth and the thick layer of thatch might reach some of the radial timbers and rot them. Each household had to come to a decision as to whether to rebuild the whole house or just to mend the roof. This depended on the age of the house and the extent of the damage. They would count only on fifteen years as the maximum life of the house, and, when they anticipated a need for rebuilding they had to plan at least two years in advance to locate, process, and season the timbers, grass, and other materials. (See Figure 8-1 for an architect's plan of the earth lodge.) A man who was influential in the community could count on extra help from his fellow villagers who would gladly volunteer, while a less important person had to depend on whatever labor force was available in the house itself.

It took eighty-six to ninety man-woman days of labor to repair the roof of an earth lodge. It was a construction job that was accomplished with no overseer and no commands. A great deal of individual labor was consumed in preparing the materials, and this was done mainly by members of the household over a period of time. The actual construction work took only three days and was accomplished with a large number of volunteers. By way of compensation, the women of the household had to feed from thirty to fifty people for at least three meals.

One day in the fall of the year, Victory Call had been observing the

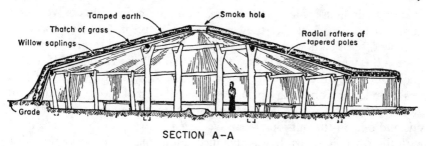

SECTION A–A

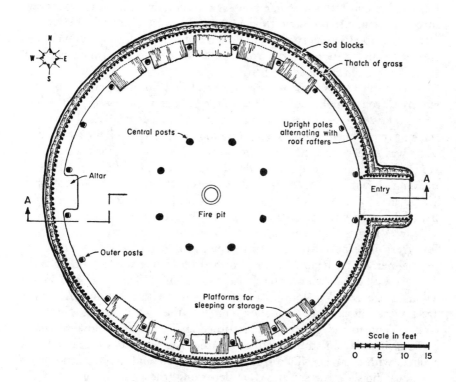

PLAN AT GRADE

PAWNEE EARTH LODGE

FIGURE 8-1. Architect's plan of a Pawnee earth lodge.

Drawn by Alice Dockstader, licensed architect.

roof of their house. He noted that seven of the radial timbers were rotting, and he remarked that they needed replacement. Old Bull made no comment, but he knew that they would carry on this enterprise together. During the winter buffalo hunt, each of them killed a buffalo bull so that they could keep the hides to make rawhide strips for use when the roof was rebuilt the following spring. Around the smokehole, fastening the radial roof rafters together, were two stout willow hoops, one on the inside and one on the outside. These were tied in place on the radial rafters with the rawhide strips. It was this mechanism that gave the symmetrical form and strength to the whole cone of the roof, and the tying was therefore important. At the same time as the hides were obtained, the women made sure to dry plenty of buffalo intestine so that they would have enough to make soup for the volunteers. While the bison hide was still fresh, the women removed the hair.

Now during the spring Victory Call and Old Bull kept an eye out for elm trees from which they could strip the bark to use in tying on the willow circuits around the roof frame. A cut was made near the bottom of the elm tree so that the bark could be loosened; a strip about two inches wide was ripped upward from the bottom. Five or six strips were taken from each elm. The strips were dried and stored until the actual time of building, when they were soaked in water and used wet so that they would make a tight bind when they dried in place. It took a large number of these elm strips to fasten the circuits in place around the roof.

Now Victory Call went into the timber to locate seven suitable willow trees. The next day he returned with his wife, White Woman, and his retainer, Horse Rider. The trip to the Loup River was five or six miles. Victory Call cut down the trees with his axe, and Horse Rider and White Woman proceeded to lop off all the branches with a hatchet. After the trees were cut and the branches removed, they went home. Next day White Woman and Horse Rider returned and began to remove the bark, hacking it off from stub end to point; the man worked with an axe, the woman with a hatchet. Two trees were debarked, and they returned until they had finished the seven. After debarking, the poles were left in the timber to season for three days.

Meanwhile, without further discussion, Old Bull had gone off to look for willow withes to make the circuits. When he got home he remarked to his younger wife, Clear Day, "There are some nice willows down at Beaver Creek. Tomorrow we can go out and cut them." In the evening when Victory Call and the others got home from the Loup where they were fixing the radials, Old Bull remarked that he had been looking around and had seen some willows and that the next day they were going to cut them. Queen Woman and Old Lady Blue Calico of the South Side decided that since the women of the North Side were working so hard on the construction work, they would take over all the cooking for the family. Hauling in the materials was a considerable task. The two families were fortunate in having enough horses so that two could be used to transport the seven radials over the six-mile journey in one day. These radials were leaned outside the house against the roof until needed. It required a wagonload or four large double armfuls of the willow saplings to make the circuits. These had to be hauled in from Beaver Creek about a mile away, a task carried out by Old Bull and his wives.

With these materials in place, Victory Call went out prospecting for thatch grass. He had to travel five miles southwest of the village near the Loup River where the grass grew near the edge of the timber in a little hollow place with some sand hills. Nearer the villages, the horses had eaten it up. That night the women on the North Side, White Woman and the two grandmothers, sharpened up the edges of their buffalo shoulderblade hoes so that they could cut the thatch grass next day. No Corn, Horse Rider's older wife, was crippled with arthritis and was unable to do that type of work. She remained at home and did necessary household chores. Meanwhile, the women on the South Side continued to provide the meals for all of them. Next morning the two men and three women went with their two horses to the grass patch. The women cut the grass and the men saw that it was properly piled up. The grass was gathered into five bunches, each 3 feet high, the layers being laid down, one layer with stub ends one way, the next layer with pointed ends in the same direction so that the bundle would be even in thickness. The grass was tied into tight bundles and loaded one on each side of the horse. The two horses were loaded, White Woman packing one of the bundles, and when they arrived home the grass bundles were placed next to the bundles of willow withes and weighted down with sticks so that they didn't scatter in the wind. The materials were now ready and they could arrange for the actual construction.

Arrangements were now made to move in with other families until the roof was fixed. Old Bull spoke to their neighbor, Coming-Downhill-Bringing-Trophies, whose house was located just across from theirs, and Victory Call made arrangements with Chief's Road whose lodge was right next door. There was a friendly relationship between the households of Victory Call and Chief's Road. Chief's Road had the social rank of commoner, but he was a very successful warrior and hoped that someday his ambition to be an administrative officer would be realized through his friendship with Victory Call. He hoped that should Victory Call become head chief of their village, he would select him as his official brave. He was the most skillful arrowmaker in the Skidi Band, and he often made arrows for Victory Call and rendered him many other services. Victory Call returned the courtesy with gifts of wood for fuel and portions of meat from his hunting. The children of the two lodges also played together. Chief's Road had the lodge with his brother, and both their families lived there together and were glad to offer their hospitality to Victory Call and to the North Side family.

The first step in the process of roof repair was demolition, the earth and thatch having to be removed. The North Side worked on its half and the south side on the south half. There were seven women for removing the earth on the north side. White Woman and the two grandmothers, two women from Chief's Road's household and two women who were the wives of White Woman's brother, Uncle War Cry. Uncle War Cry, as he was known to the boy Otter, was a frequent visitor to White Woman's house, often dropping in for meals, as was appropriate to their relationship. He was the head brave of the Skidi Band, assisting Eagle Chief. He was a huge man of brusque and forthright temperament as befitted his station as executive officer. Victory Call and all the others in the lodge liked him very much, and there was a very relaxed relationship between the two households. He had three wives and a large number of children from whom he often sought relief in White Woman's household. Now two of his wives came to help out, and he was also on hand to watch the proceedings.

From the South Side, Old Bull had four women available to do the work of removing the earth—his younger wife, Clear Day and her mother Blue Calico and two women from the household of Bringing Trophies where they were staying. His senior wife, Queen Woman, was unable to do this work as she was crippled with arthritis, a common affliction among the Pawnees. Each side had a number of important men who stood around and supervised the proceedings, giving advice to the women; it was beneath their dignity to climb up on the roof themselves. On Victory Call's side on the north stood, in addition to Uncle War Cry himself, his younger brother Brave Shield (also known as High Noon) who was a prominent member of the Skidi Doctor Association. Also present was the head of the association, Big Doctor, and their neighbor, Chief's Road at whose house they were staying.

On Old Bull's side stood Eagle Chief, head chief of the Skidi Band, White Eagle, another prominent Skidi Chief, Bringing Trophies, at whose house the family was staying, and Rider, who was keeper of the sacred bundle of Wolf-Standing-in-Water Village.

Assistance with the work itself was given by a group of young men in their twenties who came as volunteers. They had varying social connections with the people involved. When Eagle Chief got home one evening, he remarked that they planned to fix up the roof at Victory Call's house. On hearing this his son, Man Chief, got together a group of young men and they were glad to go. As Mark Evarts remarked, "They didn't have to be told. They just did things willingly. Such people should not have to be asked. The older men would say, 'When I was a boy, I used to do such things without being asked,' meaning that one hears of something of this kind that has to be done and one simply volunteers." A person who acts in this way is referred to as "A-Person-Whose-Ears-Are-Standing-Erect," viz., an alert person. Living in Eagle Chief's household was the older son of Victory Call by a former marriage, Fox Chief. He was also helpful in gathering in the young men to help out his father. Fine Horse, son of Victory Call's older brother Sitting Hawk, also came, and a younger brother of Chief White Eagle, who was standing on the south side with the influential men.

A number of older men who were also referred to as "boys" came. They were men who had little interest in having a prominent social status. They preferred to go hunting, to go on the warpath, to be free and easy in their manner. They were helpful to anyone who needed help and had little interest in social dignity or administrative functions. They freely gave away what they had and had no interest in accumulating anything or in having a well-appointed home. Because of their manner and attitude toward the social formalities, they were somewhat affectionately referred to as "boys" whatever their age might be. They commonly took over the responsibility of dangerous scouting assignments when these were called for. Four of these men came, and they climbed on the roof and helped out with the work. They were: Advance Scout (also known as Skidi Jake); Horse Finder; Riding-ahead-Coming; and Wants-the-Enemy.

About eight o'clock in the morning the women were stationed on the roof near the top and they began to scratch off the earth with their buffalo shoulder-blade hoes. They scratched around one circuit down to the thatch grass and then began on the next one, pushing the earth down each time to the lower course. Finally the earth accumulated close to the sod collar at the bottom, where it was left so that they could pile it up again after they had repaired the frame. The men stood around giving advice, telling the women to scratch here or there; it took until nearly noon to get all the earth off the roof. Meanwhile the young men were removing the thatch grass and cutting the bark tyings that held the willow withe circuits and removed them while the women were scraping on the lower circuits. The thatch grass was placed around the outside of the circle of earth and the willow withes in a circle outside the thatch. Then the young men examined the radials and removed the rotten ones, and the men standing below handed up the new radials which were put in their places.

Horse Rider had been preparing the elm bark strips that he had soaking overnight so that they could be tied on the new circuits of willow withe. They also had the bison hide that Old Bull and Victory Call had gotten on the winter hunt for making the rawhide rope needed to tie on the hoops around the smokehole. War Cry inquired whether they had been cut into strips, and, if this was not already done, Brave Shield, War

Cry's younger brother, would immediately set to work and do it. The young men climbed to the top and fastened the two hoops in place.

Meanwhile White Woman had been cooking a meal for all of them in the house of Chief's Road where they were staying. She entertained the family of the house and everyone who had helped on the North Side. The meal consisted of grease bread and soup made of dried intestine. Some of the women had brought their own bowls out of consideration for the number she needed to feed. Old Bull's senior wife, Queen Woman, was cooking and serving a similar meal in the house of Bringing Trophies, to entertain all who had helped on the South Side. No one lingered over the meal, as they were anxious to get back to work.

The women took their bowls home and came back. They rested while the young men tied on the new circuits of willow withe to the radials with the moistened elm strips. They began at the bottom circuit and proceeded to the next circuit upward. When they reached the higher circuits, the "boys," Advance Scout and the others, began to fasten the thatch grass to the bottom circuit. As they got further up, the young men now took up this work, while the older "boys" began to pile the earth on the lower circuits, the women filling up their pans with earth and handing them up to the men on the roof. In households of less social status, the women would have had to do a good deal of the work on the roof themselves; in this case they were spared any need to climb up further. When the work was completed, there was usually a dinner meal for a large number of people, including some who had merely come to watch the proceedings. Each of the hostesses usually had a party of about fifty to feed. Everyone was tired and they waited until the following morning to sweep out the house and move back in. Now the time for planting was drawing near and they began to think of the immediate preparations that remained.

In the whole course of this large construction job there was no foreman to oversee the work; not a single order was issued nor a command given; the work was performed with precision, and no inspection was needed to check its quality or workmanship.

9

THE PLANTING
OF THE CROPS

*Ground-breaking Ceremony—the Women's Role
—Explanation of Ritual—Songs of the Ceremony
—the Process of Preparing and Planting the Crops
Explained—Cooperation in Fields Discussed—
Dangers of Attack—the Swim at the End of the
Planting Day*

THE CORN WAS THE FIRST CROP to be planted and then came the beans, squashes, and melons. But before any planting could be done, the *Awari* or "Ground-breaking Ceremony" had to be performed. The four special ministers of the Skull bundle of the Wonderful Person kept watch along the creeks for the first leaves to appear on the willows; then they knew the time was right for the ritual. They also had to wait for the dark of the moon that signified darkness and germination. Now the four ministers met together in the lodge where the Skull bundle was kept to make a plan for the ceremony. The actual inception of the ceremony was during the past winter while they were on a buffalo hunt, when a woman had had a vision that she was the one to see that it was performed. She called on the help of her brother, who killed a special buffalo for her, and then she invited the four ministers and told them of her vision. Then she dried and packed the rest of the buffalo meat and kept it in her storage pit to be used when the ceremony was performed in the spring.

This was the only Pawnee ceremony in which women played a major role, and the original visionary through whom the ceremony was instituted for the season was also a woman. But the ceremony itself was directed and carried through entirely by the men. Now with the sprouting of the willows it was time.

The woman of the house where the Skull bundle was kept got up

early in the morning after the ministers had met, took the bundle from
the west where it was hanging, and placed it outside on a tripod. She
cleared the lodge of all the bedding and swept it with hyssops, while the
four ministers each went to his separate house and sent boys out to collect willow sprouts to be delivered to the ceremonial lodge. There they
were piled in two piles, one to the north and one to the south, and the
woman spread them around the lodge radially with their pointed ends toward the fireplace, their stub ends outward toward the wall. She placed
the floor mats on top of them, two on each side of the lodge and one
at the west in front of the altar. The ministers seated themselves and
sent for the woman visionary after inquiring if she had the bundle of
consecrated dried buffalo meat ready. They also invited four prominent
women—daughters of chiefs, warriors, or medicine men—who were
wealthy enough to furnish a parfleche of dried buffalo meat and a kettle
of corn and who would play a major role in the ceremony. The woman
visionary was seated at the north, the four guests at the south, and the
ministers then announced that they were about to conduct a ceremony
so that the women could go into the field and plant their corn and that
they had selected them to be leaders of the dance. Their acceptance of
the role meant they were ready to make the necessary contribution.

That evening they all rehearsed their part in the forthcoming ceremony. The woman visionary was anointed by the ministers and the
significance of the ritual explained to her. The four women who were to
assist her were seated two to the south and two to the north. Other
women who were attending were seated behind them. The descendants
of the original Skull bundle owners were seated on the north side, other
men scattered around the lodge.

The four ministers sent for the four gourd rattles that were attached
to the Evening Star bundle, and when they were brought in they began to rattle and sing while the woman visionary practiced her dance.
The spectators went home, and the four ministers, the woman visionary,
and Skull bundle owners remained and had a dinner of corn and meat
together, talking about past customs and the origin of the Skull bundle.
At midnight the brother of the woman visionary came to escort her home
while the ministers remained sleeping near the altar, the head minister
remaining awake to watch for the dawn when the proceedings would
begin.

The ritual was in three parts, one session from dawn to breakfast time,
the second from breakfast time to ten in the morning, and the third in
which there was major public participation, from ten till six-thirty in
the evening. About seven-thirty in the evening there was a meal for everyone including the spectators to close the ceremony.

The dawn-to-breakfast part of the ceremony celebrated the original
coming together of the villages, commemorating the special creative

achievement of the original visionary of the Skull bundle. This was celebrated by decorating the four pillars of the earth lodge that were in the semicardinal directions. To each of them was tied a bundle of willows and some dried buffalo meat and fat—tied on with buffalo-hair ropes. On each pillar under the offering was painted a colored stripe in the color appropriate to its semicardinal direction. The woman visionary was not invited, but was asked to send the consecrated buffalo meat which was set down at the south side of the fireplace. The Skull bundle owners were sent for and four selected to go out and gather the willows. Then they went in procession around the houseposts, one line on the outside, one on the inside, proceeding in a counterclockwise direction, (southeast, southwest, northwest, northeast) tying on the offerings to each post in succession and then painting them.

The sacred objects were next suffused with incense from burnt sweet grass mixed with fat, and the buffalo skull that usually rested there was removed from the altar and the skull of Wonderful Person put in its place. This was the first object to be "incensed"; then came the other objects in the bundle, then the ministers themselves, and then the errand men. After the incensing, all went home except the ministers and errand men, who had their breakfast there of meat and corn.

After breakfast and for the next four hours the lodge was prepared for the public ceremony. The major feature of the public ceremony would be a pantomime of hoeing to break the ground for planting, and the woman visionary was now called in to take part in the preparations. She came in with her brother, who was dressed in his best because he was to go through the village asking for gifts on behalf of their undertaking. He would walk through the village calling upon their relatives and saying that Wonderful Person needed wood and his sister needed help in her enterprise—would they please cook something? In answer to his request, they would bring gifts to the ceremonial lodge.

Meanwhile the errand men were sent out to borrow four sacred shoulder-blade hoes that were kept in the four direction bundles. When they brought these in they were placed in pairs on the north and south of the altar. From the Skull bundle itself were taken two deer necks placed at the south and two loon necks placed at the north of the altar. These symbolized the fact that loons fly high against the sky and bring us messages from Heaven, which Wonderful Person would now be representing in the ceremony. A pure young man who had shed no blood would be selected to decorate the skull for this role. He first painted the face red and on it a line design in blue, bow-shaped and extending across the forehead and down the cheeks, representing the vault of the heavens, and a blue line down the center and along the nose for the breath of Heaven descending from the zenith, passing down the nose to the heart and giving life to the child (see Figure 9-1). The minister now dressed the skull in a black skin turban with a knot on the forehead. Inside the turban were soft down feathers mixed with red paint (to represent the visionary's brains), and on top, a soft feather as a plume.

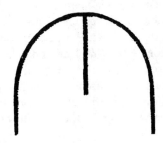

FIGURE 9-1. Representation of face painting symbolizing the vault of the heavens and the breath of Heaven.

Gifts began to come in: kettles of corn and meat were placed at the south, buffalo robes and other offerings between the fireplace and the skull.

The woman's brother and a young man were sent out to all the lodges to invite the people. They dressed in their best and everyone that came brought a gift. Soon they crowded outside the door of the ceremonial lodge, and after the brother had made a smoke offering with the pipe toward the heavens and the skull the people were allowed to come in. They piled their gifts in front of the skull.

The paraphernalia were handed out to the women who were to do the dancing, and a special coiled basket was handed to the woman visionary and one to her assistant. This basket, especially made by a woman under the direction of the minister, symbolized the container ordained by Heaven to carry earth from which the world was created and the germs of life. At the time of the creation, Heaven caused this basket to move of itself through space.

The four ministers of the Skull bundle now took up their rattles and sang, "Now we are going to start to dance. Everyone wants to dance and shake the earth."

At the first song the women stood ready to scrape the earth with their hoes, right foot forward, arms extended. They were followed by the woman visionary and her partner, who now got up and danced with the coiled baskets. Next followed women with loon necks and then young women with deer necks. These had to be chaste young women. Now the hoes were taken over by the old women, for they were early risers and good workers in the fields. When these got tired, other women came over and took the hoes, carrying out the motions of hoeing all the time:

The visionary moves her basket back and forth—dishing out. The four ladies with the loon necks swing them as if digging in the earth. The two girls with the deer heads dip them up and down, swinging back and forth.

As the women danced with the hoes, a few men danced among them with their bows and arrows poised as if aiming at something. If the women seemed to be getting tired, the men rubbed against them like buffalo bulls. After the dance was over, the minister asked if everything was all right, and when they looked around at the ground there were rolls of buffalo hair scattered all over. They knew that everything would be all right then, that they would succeed in the buffalo hunt, and that there would be plenty of corn.

There were eight song episodes in the entire series with three intermissions. In the intermissions, a special type of byplay took place that had nothing to do with the order of the ceremony itself. The special characters comprised four young virgins and four warriors on each side of the ceremonial lodge. As the women were dancing with their hoes, these virgins and warriors stood up and joined them, and at the time for intermission each virgin got a pipe filled with tobacco that was at the altar and gave it to a warrior. The connection between war and fertility is a leitmotif that runs through much of Pawnee sacred ceremonialism as elaborately exemplified in the human sacrifice to the Morning Star. In this byplay between virgins and warriors this theme is also represented. In the kin system, familiar behavior is characteristic of grandparents and grandchildren only; otherwise people must maintain a formal position with each other. Since familiar remarks are going to be made, the virgins address the warriors as grandpa and the warriors address them as granddaughter. Each virgin having handed a pipe to a warrior, the byplay began:

Holding his pipe in his left hand, he flexes his arm and moves it back and forth in jerky movements as if running and stamping his right foot three times and then his left as if on the run. He might say, "I was east on the warpath and I killed a Sioux," or he might tell how he stole horses on the warpath. Now the warrior makes a smoke offering and addresses his "granddaughter." He is going to give her advice on how to conduct her sex and marital relations. "Don't let your husband kiss you unless he gives you a horse." "All right," the girl answers, "I'll do that." A warrior on the south side says to his girl partner, "Granddaughter, give me the pipe and I'll tell you what I did. On the Republican river I killed a Sioux and I left him there." Then everyone will say, "Well, why didn't you bring him home?" Then he makes a smoke offering with the pipe the virgin has given him and says, "Granddaughter, when you get married and your husband leaves you, don't go after him. Let him go." The girl takes the pipe from him and says, "I thank you grandpa, I'll do that." The girl returns the pipe to the four ministers of the Skull bundle and the warrior gives her a gift.

TABLE 9-1. *Some Songs of the Ground-breaking Ritual, the* Awari.

The term *awari* is a compound stem, the first part, *a-* signifying "being" or "living" and the second part, *-wari*, to go actively about, such as traveling. The Pawnee used this stem as we do "up and about" meaning to be in good health. The combination *awari* indicates the principles of life and motion *par excellence*, the vigor of life.

Like all the songs of the sacred bundle ceremonies, each song is repeated in at least ten stanzas or "steps." The stanzas are identical except for the substitution of a single word at each repetition: These substitutions are the words that symbolize the basic realms of the universe in their order of creation, *uraru*, "land"; *tuharu*, "natural vegetation"; *tsaharu*, "waters"; *kakiu*, "seeds"—the four major realms of the women—and *asuru*, "moccasin"; *kstaripiru*, "string of moccasin"; *rawitat*, "robe, covering"; *waruksti*, "something holy"; *atira*, "my mother" (corn); *kiriki*, "thunder"—the six major realms of the men. In each case, the word is substituted for *huraru*, "land," in the version given here.

EIGHT SONGS OF THE GROUND-BREAKING *Awari* RITUAL

Song I

1. *huraru   wirahawati*
   the land   now the one that plucks it (clears)

Song II

1. *huraru   katit   witasikaru* (sung as *-rau*)
   the land   black   now you distribute them

2. *awari   katit   rasikara'u*
   movement   black   you that distribute them

The significance of Song II is that the Evening Star as it appears sparkling and wavering is the power that animates the earth when it generates in darkness. The dancers try to flit about like the sparkling stars.

FIRST INTERMISSION

Song III

1. *wirahuraririwisisa*
   now the earth sidewise comes

2. *hatira   rahuraririwisisa*
   my mother   earth that sidewise comes

Song IV

1. *huraru   ra·a*
   earth   the one that is coming

2. *hi   awari   ra·a*
   there   movement   that is coming

In the third and fourth songs, the earth comes sidewise from the basket and is endowed with life.

Song V

1. *wirispixkawi'*
now you aim

2. *i   huraru   tasiwixkawi'u*
there land   you aim at it

The act of planting is compared to a kind of shooting with the bow and arrow into the earth.

SECOND INTERMISSION
Song VI

1. same as (1) of Song V.

2. *wirahuraraxkawuhu   atira*
when she is putting them in the earth   my mother

3. *huraru   awari   atira'a*
earth   movement, life   my mother corn

Song VII

1. *kutihawaktu'*
Now it is budding

2. *huraru   ti'((u))*
the earth   it is

Second Episode of Song VII

1. *rahawaktariwata*
sprouts come out (peeping)

2. *i   huraru   rawakararuahu*
there earth   the one that is giving forth sounds, implying that the earth
                is shouting, viz., that the plants are calling for life

THIRD INTERMISSION
Song VIII

1. *huraru   (ta-)   sutiriku*
earth   you are   looking at it

2. *i·ri   atira   i·ri   huraru*
here it is   mother   here it is   earth

3. *awari   rahu·ka*
movement   that comes in

4. *i·ri'i   atira*
here it is   my mother

Second Episode of Song VIII

1. *huraru   sirirua·hu*
earth   they two are tossing it about

2. *kaixtsu   hu   siriraruahu*
coiled gambling basket   see   they two are tossing them about

3. *awari   hi   siriraruahu   awari*
movement   there   they two are tossing them about   movement, life

4. *siriruahu   awari*
they two are tossing it about   movement. life

After a whole morning and afternoon of dancing and singing, the feast was served to all, including the spectators and everyone went home except the four Skull bundle ministers and the woman visionary, who had to return the four sacred hoes to the four direction bundles with a gift of meat and calico to their owners and pack up the other objects. By this time the ministers were hoarse from all the singing, and by the next morning the old women who had participated in the dancing were very stiff.

Early next morning the visionary woman's brother took the willows that had been tied to the four house posts and carried them to some clear water west of the lodge. Then he deposited them under the water in the semicardinal directions they had occupied in the lodge.

The ground being ritually prepared, they would begin to plant. Early next morning everybody went into the fields. Men and women pulled up the weeds by hand and occasionally a man would use his axe to remove some sumach that happened to be growing there. All the weeds were burned up on the spot and one could see the smoke of the fires everywhere. Only the sunflower heads were saved, in anticipation of the harvest when they would need fuel for roasting the ears of corn.

According to a missionary report of the 1850's, the time was May 8th and everyone felt impelled to hurry, for the time was short before they would be leaving their villages for the summer buffalo hunt. With everyone cooperating, the entire planting would be done in about six days. By mid-May they could begin preparing their clothes and equipment for the summer migration.

That night, after they had cleared up the fields, they soaked their corn kernels in a pan to be ready for planting next morning. Some people soaked special "medicine" with the seeds to promote their growth. The next morning they went into the fields, carrying their corn kernels in a bucket or sack to keep them moist. Each carried enough for twenty corn hills, five to seven kernels to a hill. The first thing they did when they got to the field was to hoe up the ground with a buffalo shoulder-blade hoe to a depth of about 2 inches. Having removed the roots and sprouts, they replaced the loose earth and began to build up the corn hills. A corn hill was 1–1½ feet in diameter. There was a small circular excavation like a miniature fireplace with loose earth all around it. Four to six seeds were inserted around the sides and one in the middle on top. Some made a number of hills and then inserted the kernels, and some completed the planting of each hill as it was made. After the seeds were inserted, the earth was hilled up all around into a smooth little mound. The corn hills were irregularly distributed over the field about a man's step apart, and the women made sure that there was an even number by analogy with their own breasts, a metaphor that was not uncommonly cited.

Next they planted the beans, sometimes in the same hills with the corn so that the vines could entwine themselves around the cornstalks. If they planted them in separate hills, they set in willow sticks for the vines to cling to.

Last of all, they planted pumpkins, squashes, and watermelons [*Citrullus, citrullus* (L.) Karst., indigenous variety—Gilmore, 1919, pp. 120–129.]. These were planted in separate patches and served to separate the different varieties of corn in order to preserve the breeds. There would be a planting of blue corn, then a pumpkin patch, then spotted corn, then a melon patch, and so on in this order.

Between two adjacent fields, there was a hill or ridge where the sunflowers grew by themselves without planting. Some women surrounded their fields with a fence built of stakes connected with rawhide ropes. Disputes about the boundaries of their fields sometimes occurred among the women. Some women would pile the earth further and further on the far side of the field and encroach on the field of a neighbor. Some women stole crops, whereupon arguments would ensue and they would curse one another and call one another names. The woman from whom the corn had been stolen would strike the other woman with her hands or with a stick. The informant said that stealing was actually unnecessary, as a poor women could easily get some corn by appealing to her neighbor directly, saying, "I want you to take pity on me and give me some corn."

Women always went to the fields in groups for their own protection; the Sioux made a particular point of attacking and scalping them as they were going into the fields or coming home. This was presumably to exert sufficient pressure to chase the Pawnees from their territory and induce them to abandon it entirely. The mortality among the women from this cause was heavy. In 1861 in one such attack eighteen Skidi women were killed. One group of women would say to the other, "We're going to clear our fields, how about you?" Then the two groups would set out together, any woman who finished first helping the others so that all would be ready to return at the same time. The young men, without being told, knew that this was the time to picket around the fields.

In the household of Old Bull and Victory Call, each of the mature women had at least one field. Clear Day, the younger wife, and her mother, Blue Calico, worked one field together, as was customary with mother and daughter until the younger woman was considered responsible enough to manage her own. Fields were located along the bottomlands on both banks of Beaver Creek, and some women had a closer and a more distant field. The ones that were closer to the villages were, of course, the more desirable both for transport and for military reasons. An individual field was from half an acre to one and a half acres in area.

Patterns of cooperation were well developed in each household so that the women would get through quickly. Queen Woman would say to

Clear Day and Blue Calico, "I can take care of the housework myself. You two go plant your field." On the North Side, White Woman had a double role to play and was hard pressed for time. She had "to take care of her husband" and was also the main provisioner of the North Side of the household. She was responsible for repairing her husband's moccasins when they wore out; when he went to the trade store to trade in a buffalo robe for supplies of flour, coffee, sugar, prunes, or dried apples she would accompany him to do most of the carrying. Whether he went on horseback or on foot, he would carry only small items, being poised for any threatened attack. When she became overburdened with work in this way at the crucial time of planting, the two old women on her side, Grandma Chase-the-Enemy and Old-Lady-Grieves-the-Enemy, would come to her aid. "Let's get through with our 'daughter's' field first. She has to do the cooking for the whole family and take care of her husband." The three of them would then go out together and finish up White Woman's field and then the two old women would work each other's fields in turn cooperatively.

On the way home from the fields they all washed their hoes and took a swim in Beaver Creek. Heads would be bobbing up and down all over as they swam back and forth. When they finished their swim and cleaned their hoes, they would pick up whatever driftwood they could find and take it home. High water sometimes left good sticks at the bend of the creek. This moist wood was piled way at the back of the woodpile, since unless it was left to dry out it would smoke and hurt the eyes. The young women sat on the banks of the creek and slapped the surface with their feet to see who could make the loudest noise. This was considered quite a trick, and sometimes they tried it with their hands. It was like the sound of the dried corn kernels when they were threshed at the time of harvest, and expressed the hope that the corn might ripen.

Sometimes a sweat bath was preferred to a swim in the creek. When they got home tired and dirty they would then build a sweat lodge inside the earth lodge on the north side. All during planting time an old man would sit on the roof of his earth lodge in the evening and call out various items of advice. He would particularly recommend a sweat bath. He would say, "If you're tired it's best to sweat. Then you will feel better next day. If you should have a headache, you must sweat. When you get in from the fields, take a sweat bath. It cleans you up better than the creek." There were many other things the old man had to say, particularly complimentary remarks to the women to bolster their morale. After some general praises, he would cite some particular women specifically, saying how industrious they were and what fine crops they raised. Presently a little boy or girl would come and invite the old man to a little treat in the home of the woman he had mentioned, usually some bread and coffee.

The following is a simplified translation of an old Pawnee woman's statement of her experience of planting when she was a little girl in Nebraska, and a more exact statement of the old man's speech:

> An old man sitting on top of the earth lodge would be talking to the women at the time when they were going into the fields. He would say, "Now dear ladies, now you are disfiguring your bodies (getting them all muddy). Heaven has placed the wonderful bow and arrows in your hands. Heaven made it for you to be wonderful. You are wonderful! You repeatedly keep 'swelling me up.' When you put the corn in and it comes peeping out, that's what you fatten me with, my dear ladies."
>
> Then we women began to cut the grass, that is, clear the field. And when I was not yet mature, they would get me up early in the morning while it was still dark, and we two, my mother and I, would be in her field. She would have some porridge there for me. When mother was planting, oh, the corn mound would be big! Then she would dig a hole in the top and place inside the mound, seven seeds—not bunched together, but separately spaced. Then she covered it over with earth and the mound would be smooth.

One of the only common instances of group planting was "planting for the daughter-in-law." The women relatives of the newly married groom would plant, cultivate, and harvest the bride's first crop. As many as twenty-five women would be gathered in her field and they would go to her house and get her seeds and line up in the field ready to plant. The field, about "half a block" long was hoed and planted by the women more or less in unison while two old women sat at the far end singing a song from one of the sacred bundle ceremonies:

> You are just hoeing around,
> Big ground, lucky ground.

They were ranged in rows and while the women sang they made the mounds. Then they put in the seeds and then they all went to the home of the daughter-in-law where they were entertained at a feast of corn and dried buffalo meat. They repeated this performance when the corn sprouted, when they cultivated the field, and again at harvest.

10

THE CAPTIVE GIRL

SACRIFICE

AFTER THE CREATION CEREMONY in times past, the Pawnees had an awesome rite that they believed would ensure the fertility of their soil and the success of their crops. In the creation story, fruitfulness and light had come into the world because Morning Star and his realm of light had conquered and mated with Evening Star in her realm of darkness. Out of that contest, the first human being was conceived—a girl. From time to time the Morning Star demanded a girl in return.

He came as a vision to a warrior in his dreams on a night in the fall of the year. In the vision, Morning Star appeared as a man anointed with red paint, wrapped around with a buffalo robe, his leggings decorated with scalps and eagle feathers. There were soft down feathers in his hair and a single eagle feather stood upright in his scalplock. Holding his war club he spoke to the warrior in his dream: "I am the man who has power in the east. I am the Great Star (*Upirikutsu*). You people have forgotten about me. I am watching over your people. Go to the man who knows the ceremony and let him know. He will tell you what to do." When he awoke and went outside before dawn, the warrior saw the Morning Star in the sky and he knew he had been chosen for the heavy burden of making the sacrifice. He ran crying through the village to the house of the Morning Star priest, singing as he went, "When he comes, when he comes, father, I am seeking for you." When he arrived at the priest's house, they embraced and wept together, and then the priest filled a little pipe with tobacco and asked the warrior to tell of his dream.

After he had heard his vision, the priest filled the pipe and went outside where he lit it and offered it to the Morning Star so that he would bless the young man. When the pipe was smoked out, the priest returned, emptied the ashes, and sat for a while talking with the warrior. The priest again filled the pipe and handed it to the warrior who lit it in the fireplace and carried it outside offering the first puff to the Morning Star, begging his pity and his guidance. Then the priest told the warrior to go home and to return when he was ready. He thought deeply of his forthcoming task as the priest had instructed him and at last asked the people in his lodge to make him several pairs of moccasins for the journey, filled with balls of pounded up sweet corn and some parched corn for his food. Everyone in the village was watching him, and some experienced warriors who had decided to go with him also asked their families to make similar preparations.

The visionary returned to the priest's lodge where they sat together for four days. When he came on the fourth day, the priest took the Morning Star bundle down from where it was hanging over the sacred altar and removed the holy objects that the warrior would need, lighting the pipe from the bundle and offering smoke to each of them in the required fashion. The objects were an otterskin collar, Mother Corn, a hawkskin, an extra pipe from the bundle, some soft down feathers, and the skin of a wildcat, its legs filled with native tobacco and paints. These things the warrior would need for his costuming when he impersonated the Morning Star so that he could set out on his fateful journey. The ceremony took four days, and then the warrior went through the village to call on the men he knew were ready to come with him. He also chose a number of assistants—a younger man, four scouts from among the volunteers, and helpers and errand men. While the priest instructed him, the others went to their lodges and got their things. At midnight the priest went outside waiting for the Morning Star to rise and then went inside and costumed the warrior to impersonate him—a buffalo hair rope around his waist, an otterskin collar around his neck with a hawkskin fastened on and suspended from his right shoulder, the ear of Mother Corn from his left shoulder. He painted his face with the red ointment— two streaks on either side of his face and a bird's foot on his forehead (astronomically unidentified; "right on the Milky Way"). He gave him the pipe to carry in his left hand or in his robe with the stem pointing upward. As the Morning Star was rising the priest said, "Here is your man. He is wearing your clothing. Protect him and make him successful." Then he led the warrior around the fireplace, faced him toward the entrance, his assistant beside him and the others following behind in the order of the procession—the four leading scouts, firemakers, cooks, and messengers.

After traveling 15 or 20 miles, they lay down to sleep among the thick weeds, resuming their journey through the afternoon to a timbered spot where they made camp. The errand man cleared the ground, made a little fireplace in the middle, and the leader took off his costume and put it at the west end of the fireplace where the altar would be in the earth lodge. They all sat around the fireplace in order of their rank and cosmic affiliation, ate a meal, and talked a while; then the leader told them to lie down while he watched the sky and from time to time smoked his pipe. Just before the Morning Star rose, the scouts went out; when the star came up the leader began to recite the ritual, and hearing it everyone awakened and they continued on their journey. At noon they stopped, the scouts joined them and reported what they had seen; in the afternoon, they continued with their journey. Every day they traveled this way until the scouts reported that they had seen signs of the enemy. When the village was sighted, the scouts went all around, counting the tipis and generally taking stock of the situation. They made a final camp in the timber, making a large circle as if for an earth lodge, a fireplace in the middle with the excavated earth from the fireplace in a little mound to the east outside the circle. At the request of the leader, the warriors placed their gifts at the west, and taking some tobacco from the feet of the wildcat skin, he filled the sacred pipe and one of the men was chosen to do the ceremonial smoking to the celestial powers. The scouts made a final check of the enemy camp and when they got back, the leader ordered a large fire built and the ritual dancing began. The leading members of the party sang the songs of the creation: "The power of the *earth* goes through the enemy's country; the power of the *timbers, waters, seeds.* . . ." Others all sang and danced, "This is the way I do when I am imitating him (the Morning Star), when I become angry, when I am imitating him," and as they sang and danced, they attacked the fire as if it were the enemy. At the rise of the Morning Star, the leader also danced, put on some of his regalia, and got his pipe ready, and they set out for the enemy village, the scouts in the lead. In his prayer to the Morning Star he asked that he lose none of his men. At the enemy village, the leader was stationed at the east facing the Morning Star; he sent his assistant to lead a party around by north and another man by south to surround the village. At the southeast the man representing the Fools-the-Wolves Star was to alert them with his first wolf cry, and then at his second wolf signal everyone would attack the village. They were reminded that they were not to kill unless it was necessary, but only to locate a thirteen-year-old girl and pronounce her holy for the Great Star. The one who found her was assisted by the others to bring her to the leader. No one else in the village was to be harmed. The four scouts were to drive the horses from the village toward their encampment so that they could leave in a hurry. The enemy would not immediately attempt a pursuit as there was a feeling that this was a kind of cosmic destiny. Retribution would be visited upon the whole tribe later on in a regular war party. The girl was placed on a pony behind her captor, and they rode all day, sleeping only three hours during the night until they approached the village. As they approached, the leader set the prairie on fire to let them know that they had been successful. The warriors smeared their faces with soot. The Morning Star priest came out and led the captive girl to the village and to his lodge.

Now that the girl had been captured the first stage of the warrior's mission had been accomplished. The sacrifice would not take place until the following spring. The whole tribe would go off on the winter buffalo hunt, taking the girl with them. When they got back to the village and the creation ceremony had been performed, the priest of the Morning Star would watch for a sign from the cosmic god that the time for the ceremony had arrived. Meanwhile, the returned war party settled back in the village. The visionary warrior went to the lodge of the Morning Star priest and returned the costume which was replaced in the sacred bundle. Warriors told how many of the enemy they had touched and the war counts they should receive because of this and the number killed. The women danced the victory dance. The keeper of the Wolf bundle was called to the Morning Star lodge to take over the care of the girl who would remain in his charge until the time of sacrifice, throughout the period of the winter buffalo hunt and the spring that followed. He was to watch over her at all times and was to take her for her meals to the home of the visionary warrior. According to the creation legend, the wolf was the first creature to suffer death; he was murdered by the people because of his perfidious conduct and as a result from that time on all living things must die (see below, pp. 328-329). The Wolf bundle commemorated these incidents and its keeper was thought to be a descendant of the original owners. Sirius, the southeast star, was the Wolf Star and it was connected with death. The Wolf man now entered the lodge of the Morning Star priest who bathed both him and the girl in incense from the smoke of burning sweet grass—first the girl and then the man. Then the girl's costume was taken from the Morning Star bundle. She was rubbed with red ointment made of pigment and buffalo fat and dressed in a calfskin skirt tied around the waist by a rope, an overblouse, a warm buffalo robe, some black moccasins, and a soft down feather to wear in her hair. She was given a special wooden bowl and a buffalo horn spoon for her exclusive use at meals, that was also taken from the bundle. It was dangerous for others to use her utensils as the supernatural beings might then consider them part of the sacrifice.

While they were on the winter hunt, the warrior visionary would have to kill a fat buffalo cow whose tongue and heart would be dried and used in the sacrifice ceremony.

Returned from the buffalo hunt, the diligent search of the Morning Star priest was rewarded when one morning the Morning Star arose ringed in red, giving the signal for the ceremony to begin. The warrior visionary was notified to clear out his lodge as the ceremony would be held there. The lodge was prepared, the warrior was dressed in a special costume for this role and the girl was brought in and dressed for her role. Then the scaffold was built and the sacrifice carried out. These proceedings occupied five days from the time the Morning Star gave the signal.

In the visionary's house all the beds were cleared out and a new fire of cedar logs was built. The Morning Star priest brought in the bundle in order to costume the visionary: around his waist a long belt of otterskin with sixty-five scalps taken in war, symbolizing war, death, and also the renewal of life, as the otter is the first animal to come up from the water after the winter ice and take the first breath of life for the year; a feather to place in his scalplock; and a war club to hold in his hand. So dressed he ran through the village calling on his relatives for contributions of new mats, food, and wood for the ceremony. The women came bringing mats, wood on their backs, cooked corn, and buffalo meat. Four long poles of special kinds were obtained to place radially in the fireplace extending outward in the semicardinal directions and meeting at the middle. They would last for the four day ceremonial period, being pushed inward as they burned down. Each was a different kind of wood appropriate to the semicardinal direction in which it was pointed: elm, northeast; boxelder, southwest; cottonwood, northwest; willow, southeast. The willow stood for death like the death star and at the same time the renewal of life in the spring. At the altar of sacrifice, willow and otter would be fastened together to express this symbolism.

The ceremonial lodge in order, they were now ready to begin the first day's ceremony. The chief of Village-across-a-Ridge (*Tuwahukasa*) that owned the Morning Star bundle, entered and seating himself at the northwest, inquired whether they were ready to receive the Wolf man and the girl. On the south side of the lodge there was a large buffalo bull robe with two cushions on it for them to sit on. As they entered, the man suffused the girl with smoke from the burning sweetgrass and then he "incensed" himself. The Wolf man sat on the southeast of the two cushions, the girl at his left with her bowl and spoon before her, the visionary at the south. Others came and seated themselves according to rank and the direction of their celestial bundle powers in the firmament, and there were several old men who were to talk to the girl and the Wolf man whenever there was a pause in the proceedings. Each one had suffused himself with sweet grass smoke as he entered and painted himself with red buffalo-fat ointment. Four circles were made on the ground one in each of the semicardinal directions to symbolize the four quarters of the universe that the Morning Star had to pass as he approached the Evening Star. The circles were made by a man who stood in the middle and extended his toe as far as possible, drawing his foot on the ground as he turned. The tracks were filled with soft down feathers from the bundle. The priest smeared himself with red buffalo-fat ointment and suffused himself with sweet grass smoke. The actual ceremony could begin.

The priest of the Evening Star bundle sang the first part of the ritual and after a pause, the Morning Star priest took charge. He sang two songs. Then they had their meal. The Wolf man opened the next phase, bringing the girl to the altar where she was anointed by the priest with red ointment given to him by the war leader. They returned to their seats and the ceremony continued all night. The second day's ceremony was of the same kind. On the third day they continued to sing and dance, the war leader beginning the dance and then being joined by the others. The war leader took up the northeast pole from the fireplace with the fire still burning on its end and pointed it at the girl without touching her, first toward her right side then toward her left. Next he took first the southwest pole following the same procedure, then the northwest pole and then the southeast pole, following the prescribed order. Now, on the third day, the crowd of spectators became heavy and began to push into the lodge and tear holes in the roof so that they could witness the proceedings.

While the ceremony was going on in the lodge the priest gave directions for the preparation of the sacrificial scaffold. He sent men to find a suitable location a mile or two east of the village with a ravine or a series of dips in the ground to the east of it where the attacking warriors could hide during the ceremony. Wood for each part of the sacrificial frame had to be of special kinds: cottonwood for the two uprights; the four crossbars near the bottom serving as steps, each symbolizing one of the four semicardinal directions, the bottommost elm, then box elder, cottonwood, and willow, each associated with an animal power. Elm represented the bear and the northeast; box elder, the mountain lion and the southwest; cottonwood, the wildcat and the northwest; and willow, the wolf and the southeast. When the men reported back to the priest that they had located the wood, he gave them four strips of animal skin, each one of the appropriate animal with which to tie the crossbars to the frame. Near the top of the two uprights was another crossbar of willow, symbolizing Heaven, which was tied on with otter-skin to symbolize the renewal of life. They were instructed by the priest to dig a rectangular pit under the scaffold in area about the size of a buffalo robe commonly used to wrap a sacred bundle and 5 inches deep, the bottom to be covered with soft down feathers. The pit symbolized the Garden of the Evening Star from which all life originates. The pit was called *Kusaru*, which in Pawnee simply means bed.

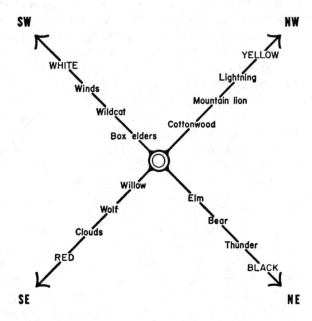

FIGURE 10-1. Association of symbolisms for the four semicardinal directions: colors, natural forces, animals, trees.

In the ceremonial lodge, the dancing and singing continued on the fourth day. Whenever they ate during the ceremonies, the girl was served, and once in a while she was taken out to walk around, always accompanied by Wolf man. The main theme of the fourth day was the destruction of the four semicardinal circles in the appropriate order as Morning Star had done in the creation as he warred on the Evening Star. The priest, impersonating the Morning Star wore leggings decorated with scalps. First he arose and sang and danced around the north side, then the south side, then back to the altar. He danced around the lodge again and when he arrived at the east he whirled around suddenly and destroyed the northeast circle scattering the white feathers around the lodge, then the southwest, the northwest, and the southeast circles, making a grunting sound each time as if attacking an enemy. Then all sang the fifth song and the girl was taken to the altar to be costumed for her last role.

Her body was painted, red on the right side, black on the left, the red to symbolize day, the time of the Morning Star, and the black to represent night, the time of the Evening Star. She wore a skirt and a painted hide robe around her shoulders. Now they sang of the origin of the Morning Star itself that they thought had come from a meteor. They sang to the girl, "You are now wearing the covering of meteorite grandfather," and in the next song, "You are now wearing the covering of the meteorite father," and then, "You are now wearing the covering of the meteorite brother." They completed her costume with a row of feathers standing up erect along the median line of her head. Her costume complete, she sat down in her place next to the Wolf man. They sang until midnight and then they paused, awaiting the time of the Morning Star. Meanwhile they placed a pinch of tobacco before the altar and sang about flint, the meteorite grandfather and other Morning Star symbols. Thereafter they would have to address their songs to the Morning Star in the sky. During the pause, once in a while the visionary took up the four direction poles from the fireplace and pointed them at the girl as he had done before in the prescribed succession: northeast, and so on.

Now the procession to the scaffold would begin. All the men and boys and even male infants were to participate in the sacrifice. During the day, one of the priests had climbed up to the roof of the earth lodge and called out, alerting them to be prepared with their bows and arrows. In the ceremonial lodge, the priest gave the war leader the braided elk-hide ropes to tie on the girl's wrists. He took up the gourd rattles. It was almost daylight. The four priests of the four direction bundles had gone out to dress, each being assisted by a specially designated person to adjust their costumes and to get ready. The Northwest man (Yellow Tent) wore two owlskins on his back that he had taken from his bundle; in his hand he held the bow he took from the Skull bundle and a red arrow that he had added to it. The Southeast bundle man (Red Tent) also had two owls and took a stick with coals on the end. The Southwest bundle priest (White-Mother-Born-Again) had two owls also and he took a war club. The fourth priest, representing the Big Black Meteoric Star (black, northeast) who also wore two owlskins on his back, took the flint knife.

Now all sang and started on the procession, the girl and the Wolf man in the lead followed by the visionary-war leader dressed in his otter collar, his otter belt with sixty-five scalps, his pipe, and other regalia and the four direction priests in their costumes.

The dawn was coming and the scaffold was ready. Slowly the procession went toward it. As they went they sang four songs. The girl looked around and wondered. The first song said, "She was looking around for just a little time." Then they sang of Heaven and of the powers of the bear, the mountain lion, the wildcat, and the wolf as the girl approached the scaffold. The Wolf man urged her to mount and as she climbed each rung, a song was sung about the appropriate animal. Singing they tied her on and then left her there facing east.

The war leader and four direction priests were hiding in the ravine; now the four priests came out one by one. The Southeast bundle man with the burning stick ran out of hiding and barely touched the girl on the arms and loins. The Northwest bundle man came out with his bow and arrow and shot her through the heart. Now the Northeast man of the Big Black Meteoric Star rushed up with the flint knife and made a small cut over her heart. Taking some of the blood, he painted streaks on his face. The southwest man came with the warclub, and he made a gesture at her. The blood of the girl was allowed to drip on the dried tongue and heart meat of the consecrated buffalo, and the priest made a new fire at the southeast, the burnt offering of the sacred meat being made by the priest of the Evening Star bundle. Now all the men and the boys of the Skidi Band, singing war songs, riddled the body with their arrows. Then the priest told them to leave the sacrifice.

The priests now made a final disposition of the body. It was full daylight, and four men who had been chosen to assist, untied the body and took it about a quarter of a mile to the east, placing it on the ground face down. They sang, "The whole earth, she shall turn into. The whole earth shall receive her blood." Then they spoke of nine things in turn: "She will turn into a bunch of grass; the ants will find her, the moths will come and find her, the fox shall come and find her, the coyote, the wildcat, the magpie, the crow; buzzards will come and find her, and last of all will be the bald-headed eagle who will come and eat her."

All the people who participated in the ritual went to the ceremonial earth lodge and there ate a meal of consecrated buffalo meat. The public dispersed.

In the village there was general rejoicing. Men and women danced, and there was a period of ceremonial sexual license to promote fertility. Some women dressed themselves in their husband's war costumes, dancing around and making fun of the men. They mimicked what they did in war and ceremony.

They carried the Mother Corn. . . . They would go to the secret lodge, and standing outside of it would tell the story of how they came to go on the pretended war party and what they did while they were gone, what enemies they struck—the whole long story. The people stood around laughing as they did these things. Imitating the warriors, the women changed their names also. One of the leading old women once took the name "Mud on Meat" another "Skunk Skin Tobacco Pouch" another, "Sitting Fish Old Man," another "Stepping on the Heart." The old men standing around joked with the old women and they all joked and made fun of each other.

(Grinnell, 1925, p. 368)

So the ceremony had ended. The Morning Star had received back the first girl to be placed on earth, and he would again look after the people in peace and in war. In the way of the Morning Star, death and life, war and fruitfulness were one process.

When the news of this dramatic rite first reached the eastern seaboard of the United States in 1820–1821, it created something of a sensation, especially in the light of the obvious Mexican analogies. In 1816 an Ietan (Comanche?) girl was captured by a Skidi warrior in preparation for sacrifice to the Morning Star in the spring of 1817. The chief of the Skidi at this time was Knife Chief (*Ritsirisaru*) of Pumpkin-Vine Village. In 1811 he had been on a delegation to see William Clark in St. Louis who was then Superintendent of Indian Affairs for the region and they had had a long and serious talk in which Clark impressed Knife Chief with the fact that the white people were coming in ever-increasing numbers "like the waves of the ocean—in, in, in. . . . It's coming; every year more people come over here," and that the Pawnees must prepare to adapt themselves. Knife Chief was impressed with the validity of his argument and he realized that their ceremonial practice of human sacrifice was a serious barrier to their relations with the whites. He talked to the people in an effort to get them to abandon the custom, but the warriors of the tribe and the priests, always suspicious of the political motives of the chiefs, were hostile and defiant. The ceremonies were continued and on the appointed day the girl was led out and tied to the scaffold.

On the trip to see Clark in St. Louis, Knife Chief had been accompanied by his son (or possibly paternal nephew) Man Chief (*Pita-risaru*), and, now in his early twenties, he was an outstanding warrior and universally respected. With the crowd gathered and the warrior ready to shoot the fatal arrow, Man Chief rode before them and told them that his father disapproved of what they were about to do and he had come to rescue the girl or die right there. By Skidi belief, anyone who touched the consecrated girl during her captivity would soon die, for they would be taken by the Morning Star in her stead. From the point of view of those assembled there, Man Chief was thus offering his life as forfeit for hers. The crowd now held off in awe, and Man Chief was able to cut the girl down from the scaffold and place her on a horse and send her south to rejoin her people, which she succeeded in doing.

The next year, 1818, a Spanish boy of ten was captured in Oklahoma and dedicated to the Morning Star. This time Knife Chief managed to call a chiefs' council and he was able to ransom the boy with his own store of goods to which was added that of the trader and interpreter, Papin, and Manuel Lisa. The boy was returned to Lisa's trading post on the Missouri north of Omaha, Nebraska, by the middle of June 1818. Notice of the escape of the boy, along with an account of an additional sacrifice, appeared in the *Missouri Gazette* of St. Louis.

By 1820–1821 the story of the conduct of Knife Chief and his son Man Chief had come to the attention of Edwin James and Jedidiah Morse, and through them it became known. In the fall of 1821, when Man Chief went east to Washington with a delegation of chiefs, the detailed story of his bold rescue had been published, and the girls at "Miss White's Select Female Seminary" contributed enough money to have a large silver medal made which they presented to the handsome young Pawnee hero at a public ceremony. The medal bore the inscription "To the Bravest of the Brave." The medal was later excavated in an Indian grave near Fullerton, Nebraska, on the Loup River by Alonzo Thompson. It is illustrated in Hyde's book. The portrait of Man Chief was painted in Washington by Dr. King and later included in the McKenney and Hall volumes on Indian tribes. As Man Chief accepted the silver medal, he said that when he had done this thing he had not known it was brave. But now that they had called him brave and given him this medal, he thanked them and would always think of them. After the delegation left Washington, they continued on to Baltimore, Philadelphia, and New York and wherever they went they were greeted by large crowds and showered with gifts. Originally the delegation had left the Pawnee village in October 1821 under Major O'Fallon and was undertaken with the purpose of impressing the Pawnees with the power of the whites. A chief from each of the four bands had gone.

But despite these efforts, by May 1833 news of a plan to sacrifice a Cheyenne woman reached the Indian agent, John Dougherty at Bellevue, who took five men with him and rode out to the Skidi village. Chief Big Ax received him and promised to try to help him ransom the captive. The Chief called a council of the other chiefs and leading men and exhorted them to abandon their plan. The crowd in the village was hostile, but nevertheless the woman was brought into the chief's lodge. Big Ax was opposed by all the chiefs but one—Black Chief, of rather swarthy complexion. Finally Dougherty, seconded by a few friendly Pawnees, tried to ride through the angry crowd with the captive woman. The people had gathered in the narrow spaces between the earth lodges to try to block him, and, as he passed the lodge of a prominent brave named Soldier Chief, a priest who was standing in the vestibule drew his bow and shot the woman. The warriors took the dying woman out onto the prairie and carried out the sacrifice.

In 1837 an American Fur Company boat came up the Missouri. Some of her crew were down with smallpox and, despite the captain's warning, the Mandan insisted on boarding. Of the 1,600 remaining Mandans, only 31 survived the ensuing epidemic. Meanwhile the Arikara who lived in a neighboring village in the same locality returned there from the summer hunt and they lost half of their population of 4,000. The Dakotas also contracted the disease. Now the Skidi priests insisted that the Morning

Star must be placated. An Oglala Sioux girl of about fifteen whose name was Haxti was captured, and on April 22, 1838, she was sacrificed to the Morning Star.

This is the last reported case of a Pawnee sacrifice to the Morning Star. Grinnell and others feel that there must have been further incidents that did not come to attention. However, when our ethnological narrative takes place (1867) it seems pretty certain that no further sacrifices were being carried out. About two hundred Pawnees, many Skidis among them, were organized into four companies of regularly registered U.S. Cavalry in Major North's Batallion. As part of their activities, they protected the crews working on the Union Pacific Railroad from attack by the nomadic Indians. After an attack on Plum Creek on the Platte, the Pawnees followed the Cheyenne to their camp and there captured fifteen Cheyenne women and children. In the subsequent negotiations, they exchanged these captives for two white women, the Martin sisters, and three small white boys, captives of the Cheyenne camp on the Medicine Creek branch of the

FIGURE 10-2. *Codex Porfirio Diaz* representing scaffold sacrifice; in National Museum, Mexico City, accredited to the Cuicatecan tribe of the State of Guerrero. From Clark Wissler and Herbert J. Spinden, "The Pawnee Sacrifice to the Morning Star," *American Museum Journal*, XVI (1916), No. 1, p. 54. See also illustrations on pages 52, 53, and 49 of the article. Photograph courtesy of the American Museum of Natural History.

Republican River. It seems unlikely that the Pawnees carried on any further sacrifices of captives to the Morning Star after that time.

Aside from the obvious resemblances, there is some documentation of detailed Mexican analogies. Wissler and Spinden would place the time when a direct transfer through the Aztec could have occurred, between 1506 and 1519. In an article (1916) on the subject they give clear parallels in illustrations from the codices (see Figure 10-2).

Within the Pawnee system of theology, it certainly had an organic place.

11

VARIETIES OF CORN,
BEANS, AND SQUASH

〰〰〰〰〰〰〰〰〰〰〰〰〰〰〰〰〰

American and Indian Corn Varieties—the Planting Ritual—Comparison of Corn Varieties to Present-Day Classification—Squash and Pumpkin Varieties—Bean Varieties

〰〰〰〰〰〰〰〰〰〰〰〰〰〰〰〰〰

THE PAWNEE WOMEN were skilled horticulturists. They had ten pure varieties of corn, seven of pumpkins and squashes, and eight of beans. According to our classification, all American Indian corn is one species, *Zea mays*. Columbus reported that he found cornfields that were 18 miles long; when he returned to Spain, he took seed corn with him. It was soon diffused all over the world so that today corn has surpassed wheat as a world crop and is only exceeded by rice and potatoes. Corn has six subspecies, of which three are major and three minor. The first three are flint, flour, and dent, each adapted to different climatic conditions. When the Indians were first contacted, flint corn was the characteristic variety of New England, dent corn of the Southeast, and flour corn of the Southwest. Flint is suitable for cold moist climates, flour for dry climates, and dent for warm moist climates, the dent being heaviest in yield when the climate is favorable. Botanically these three varieties seem to represent a certain evolutionary sequence. In the flint, the oldest, the whole kernel is occupied by horny starch except around the germ; it is high in gluten. Flour corn lacks the horny starch altogether and is made up entirely of the softer starch except for the germ, while dent is a combination of the softer starch in the interior with horny starch on the sides, thus giving rise to the dent or dimple on the surface end of each kernel. The three other subspecies of corn are more occasionally used: sweet corn, with a high sugar content, and pop corn, two very primitive varieties, and the rare pod corn.

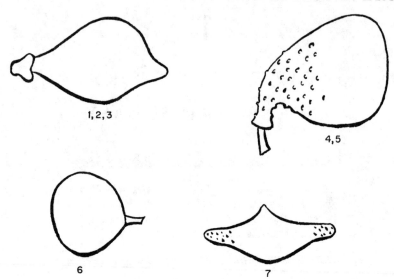

FIGURE 11-1. Seven varieties of squash and pumpkin known to the Pawnees generically as *Pahuks*: (1) *rus-kirius*, "soft-buttock" (as soft as the buttocks); pointed at both ends; a little more than 1 foot in length and 9 inches in diameter; yellowish in color; "as sweet as sugar." (2) *pahuks-tarahi*, squash or pumpkin-grooved; yellow in color; a kind sometimes seen in white men's stores. (3) *pahuks-katit*, squash or pumpkin-black; same size, shape, and taste as (2), the only difference being the black color. (4) *ri-katsu*, "lower half of body, white," *ri'u*, being the lower half of human body from the navel all around to the bottom of the feet. (The rest of the body is called *kisikitu*, upper half of body from *kisikiit*, "alive," and *-katsu*, "dead white." Sometimes the ordinary word for white, *taka*, is used instead.) The shell is as thick as a board and so hard that it needs to be cut up with an ax, but it is very sweet tasting. It has a crooked neck and is knobby or pimply around the neck end and very smooth on the body. (5) *ri-kats-katit*, same as (4), but black (*-katit*, "black") (6) *pahuks-kata*, "pumpkin-dry"; dry near the stem, sometimes a little pointed; somewhat dry inside when cooked; real round and smooth; color, light green. (7) *pahuks-tarahi-kiripaxki*, "squash-grooved-small"; in a variety of colors—green, white, yellow, and dark green, also a rather dark blue and some very blue.

The Indian groups of the Missouri River Valley of which the Pawnees were one, raised mainly flint and flour corn, but not dent. They also raised sweet corn. Flint and flour corn apparently both did equally well among the Pawnees. Mark Evarts named ten breeds of corn for the Pawnees, one of them borrowed from the Osage. There were two flints, one yellow, and one varied in color, five or possibly six flour corns in five different colors—blue, speckled, white, yellow, and red; and one sweet corn, reddish-yellow in color. In addition, there was an archaic breed of corn known as Wonderful or Holy Corn which was never eaten but was raised only for inclusion in the sacred bundles. Two ears were placed in each bundle, each wrapped up and sewed into a covering—the winter ear in a tanned buffalo skin and the ear dedicated to summer in a buffalo-heart skin. Each individual ear of these holy corns in the bundles had a different name by which it was addressed. Early in April before the *Awari* or planting ritual, a ritual was held in which the seeds of the holy corn were distributed to the keepers of the sacred bundles so that their wives could plant them in their fields. At harvest time, when these sacred ears were mature, the old ears were removed from the bundles and replaced with ears from the new crop. Fine examples of some of the best ears of the more common varieties were also placed in the sacred bundles at harvest time, particularly those with a male spike. Compared with the white flour corn, the holy corn, which was also white, had small kernels that sometimes covered the cob to the very tip. "Sometimes it has something like a soft feather at the tip of the ear." This is apparently the male spike at the point end; archaeologically it appears very early, 4,445 ± 180 B.C., in the tiny ancestral corncobs taken from La Perra Cave in northeast Mexico. Such an ear is also shown in the headdress and hands of the Maize God on a prehistoric Zapotec funerary urn from Mexico (Mangelsdorf, 1958).

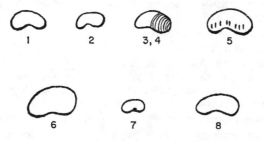

FIGURE 11-2. Eight varieties of beans, generically known to the Pawnees as *atit:* (1) *ati-pahat,* "bean-red"; a large sized bean. (2) *atik-taka,* "bean-white." (3) *ati-paks-katit,* "bean-head-black"; black-head beans. (4) *ait-paks-pahat,* "bean-head-red"; same as (3). (5) *ati-pirari,* "bean-spotted"; color of a spotted horse, spotted all around, some with red, some with black spots; a somewhat large-sized bean. (6) *ati-katus,* "bean-flat"; large, flat bean. (7) *atit-tiwats-katit,* "bean-navel-black"; spotted where it joins the stem; navel, *-riwat,* phonetically altered in the context. (8) *ati-taxkata,* "bean-yellow"; a rather large yellow bean.

Our classification of the species of corn is based on the starch content, but when a Pawnee was asked to name the varieties of corn they had, he or she would enumerate them in terms of color categories—black, spotted, white, yellow, and red. It is interesting that these represent the varieties of flour corn that they had. However, in classifying their corn, they subsumed the flint, sweet, and sacred varieties under these color categories. When asked to name the varieties of Pawnee corn, Mark Evarts named ten, one being Osage. George F. Will, nurseryman and anthropologist of North Dakota, experimented with planting Indian corn from various tribes of the Missouri River region and managed to isolate nine pure strains of Pawnee corn. These correspond with considerable accuracy to those named by Mark Evarts. I have placed his classification as it appeared in his publication (Will and Hyde, 1919) in a parallel column alongside that of Mark Evarts. (See Table 11-1.)

TABLE 11-1. *Classifications of Varieties of Pawnee Corn.*

As Named by Mark Evarts	As Named by Will and Hyde, 1919
1. *Blue* corn—*uraax-katit*, earth-black, referring to very dark blue	Blue *flour* corn, No. 40
2. *Spotted* corn, *rikis-tipiku*, corn-spotted (*ripiku*, egg)	Black-eyed and red-speckled corn, p. 308
3. *White* corn, big kernels, *rikis-taka*, corn-white	White *flour* corn, No. 36
4. White with small kernels, *rikis-paruk-sti*, corn-holy	Not identified by authors
5. *Yellow* corn, harder variety, *rikis-taxkata*, corn-yellow	Yellow *flint*, No. 38
6. A yellow corn, softer than No. 5, called *parus-arut*, rabbit-soft	Yellow *flour* corn, No. 37
7. Hard corn, *kitsirit*, flinty, hard, translucent; real smooth, with different colored kernels on the same cob—white, spotted, yellow	Red *flint*, No. 89, flinty mixed colors with red predominating
8. *Red* corn—*rikis-pahat*, corn-red	Red *flour* corn, No. 45
9. Sweet corn—*rikis-karus*, corn-sweet, somewhat reddish yellow and sticky	Sweet corn, yellow sugar corn, No. 41
10. Osage corn—*rikis-pasasi*, corn-Osage, gotten from Osage, grows 9-10 feet high and can have 8 or 9 ears on one stalk	

From the experiments of George Will, it is evident that the Pawnees were quite capable of producing pure strains of corn and maintaining the breeds. And yet when asked to list the classes of corn that they had, they did so in terms of a certain order of colors rather than by a horticultural classification. Consistent with the Pawnee belief that the Heavens are the first cause of all things, this is a cosmic rather than a botanical classification. In Pawnee theology, the four semicardinal directions are associated with the four color designations—northeast–black; southeast–white; northwest–yellow; and southeast–red. In the creation legend it is stated that in the western part of the ancient territory there were four villages, each representing one of the semicardinal directions; each had a different-colored ear of corn in its sacred bundle, as cited above. The order of the colors of corn followed by Mark Evarts in his classification if translated into directions are northeast, southwest, northwest, southeast. This diagonal succession forms a simple cross, the Pawnee symbol for a star. What star is implied is not known. Typically of Pawnee thought, there must be deeper theological meanings and references than are apparent. The order of naming the varieties of corn is clearly connected with these religious implications.

For the Pawnee, there is very little that does not have some direct connection with the cosmos. But in sharp contrast to the corn, the other two crops, squash and beans, have no religious connotations whatever. This lack of ideological involvement seems strange, as we know archaeologically that first squash and then beans were the earliest domesticated crops in the New World, followed after a considerable time interval by the domestication of corn. Among the Pawnees the whole horticultural cycle was conducted in terms of the corn. In the spring the corn was the first of the three crops to sprout, and in the fall it was the first to mature. There were seven common varieties of squash and pumpkins current among the Pawnees at that time and eight of beans. (See figures 11-1 and 11-2.)

12

CLOSING EPISODE OF
PLANTING PERIOD

THE CLOSING EPISODE of the planting period was the carrying through of the young corn plant from a seedling to its "adolescence," when it could be "laid by" for the summer until they returned in the fall from the buffalo hunt and it would be ready for harvest.

The four semicardinal-direction bundle priests kept careful watch, and when the sacred corn seeds had sprouted to about two inches and had four good leaves, they knew that it was time to conduct the ceremony of the young corn plant. In this ceremony the priests prepared the young corn plant for her role as Mother to all the people. The young corn plant was carried through a series of ritual steps symbolizing the birth, infancy, and growth to first motherhood of a young girl. The corn could then mature and become Mother of the people.

The practical steps, as always, were preceded by a ceremonial preparation. The conduct of the ceremony was under one of the south semicardinal-direction bundles—either the Southwest or the Southeast in alternate years. As always, although the ceremonies were seasonally oriented, they were initiated by a visionary who received a mandate from the cosmic power involved, instructing him to see that the ceremony was performed. In this case the vision always came to a man who was an outstanding buffalo hunter and eagle trapper. The vision would have occurred while they were out on the winter buffalo hunt; as soon as possible he would kill a buffalo and pronounce it holy. Then he called in the five official Skidi priests, who were the ministers of the four semicardinal-direction bundles and that of the evening Star, and entertained them at a feast of buffalo ribs, telling them of his vision. His wife sliced, dried, and packaged the rest of the consecrated buffalo meat and kept it in her storage pit at home until the spring, when the ceremony was to be performed.

The visionary became a principal actor in the ceremony and made a major contribution of buffalo meat to the ritual feast, while his wife contributed a considerable amount of the boiled dried corn. He considered it a great privilege to participate in the ceremony and to receive instructions from the priests concerning the cosmic traditions. During the ceremony he would impersonate an important god of the creation, *Paruksti*, the Wonderful, the personified Thunderstorm with its four aspects of cloud, wind, lightning, and thunder. After the Star Gods had created man in their own image, they combined the powers of the storm into one great person, *Paruksti*, the Wonderful, and sent him to earth to inspect their handiwork. In him were embodied all the self-renewing powers of earth. In the course of his travels he acted as scout, found the buffalo, and taught the people how to hunt them. The visionary was to impersonate the god in two roles—one in the symbolic acting-out of the male role in procreation and later as the guardian of their fortunes in the buffalo hunt.

In this ceremony of the young holy corn plant, the keepers of all the twelve sacred bundles had assembled in the lodge of the Southwest (or Southeast) Semicardinal-direction priest. The Evening Star priest and the four semicardinal-directions priests sat at the west and the other bundle ministers were ranged along the sides in positions appropriate to the place of origin of their legendary villages and their cosmic affiliations.

The visionary stood before the Evening Star priest, who arranged the buffalo robe that he wore and tied the buffalo hair rope around his waist so that he was dressed as a priest. The Evening Star priest now instructed the visionary in what he was to do. He gave him a small pipe filled with tobacco from the sacred bundle. The visionary then led the procession that was to go into the field where the sacred corn plant was growing. It was the field of the wife of the Southwest (or Southeast) bundle priest. The procession lined up on the north side of the ceremonial earth lodge, the visionary in the lead, the four-directions priests following behind him and an errand man following after to serve them, carrying a lighted brand with which to light the visionary's pipe. The Evening Star priest remained in the lodge at the west and the ministers of the other sacred bundles continued to sit in their places. As the procession emerged from the lodge everyone in the village was standing on the rooftops to see the priests get the young plant of the holy corn. The priests were wrapped in their buffalo robes with the hair side out and were rattling their gourds and singing. They felt it to be a long journey symbolically signifying the eons of the creation, and the song was sung to recapitulate all its stages—the stages that pertained to women (the land, the vegetation, the waters and the cultivated seeds), and the stages that pertained to men (the moccasin, its string, the robe, the power of the universe, Mother Corn, and the thunder). These stages of the men symbolized conception and birth—the moccasin, a pocket-like covering into which something is thrust; the moccasin cord, the umbilical cord; the robe, the enveloping membrane of the foetus; the creative power of the universe, the sacred nature of conception and birth; Mother Corn, germination; and the thunder, the fertilizing principle. The little corn plant they uprooted in the field would symbolize all these things.

When they arrived at the sacred corn hill, they ranged themselves around it, the visionary to the west, the four semicardinal-directions priests in their appropriate stations. They again sang the steps of the creation as they sat in their places, and then the priests remained seated while the visionary rose and prepared to smoke his pipe with the powers above. He walked to the north side of the hill, where the errand man lighted his pipe, then proceeded around it, pausing to offer the mouthpiece to the powers in the order directed by the Evening Star priest before they had left the lodge. He offered it to Heaven, the Evening Star, the Morning Star, the Big Black Meteoric Star in the northeast, the North and Lucky Wind, a great legendary hero *Pahukatawa*, then southeast to the Sun and southwest to the Moon. Next he emptied the ashes on the corn hill and gave the pipe to the ranking priest. Then he sat down at the west and in counterclockwise order beginning at the northeast he pressed into the cornhill a gift of little pellets of buffalo-heart fat and tongue fat wrapped around with some tobacco. He alternated his offerings, beginning with tongue fat at the northeast and heart fat at the northwest, and so on.

Now the most solemn part of the ceremony was to be enacted. They were to uproot the sacred corn sprout in a symbolic act of birth. The visionary stood at the west and instructed the Southwest (or Southeast) priest to ease the plant out of the ground very gently so that he would not disturb any part of the delicate roots. The roots symbolized the moccasin strings and the seeds, the moccasin or covering for power. The priest wrapped the "newborn" plant in buffalo wool and handed it to the visionary, who placed it on his back in his buffalo robe as a woman carries her child. Now they began again to sing the steps of the creation and lined up preparatory to returning to the ceremonial lodge. Everyone in the village was watching and listening as they sang on their way back.

In the lodge, the Evening Star priest unwrapped the plant from its wool covering and placed it on the ground before him, offering his pipe to it to smoke.

The next steps involved the transformation of a dogwood stick into a "body" for the plant, by an expert arrowshaft maker, for whom tools were ready in the sacred bundle—a new knife, an elkhorn arrowshaft straightener, a grooved sandstone smoother, some sinew, and different-colored paints. After the shaft was made, red and white paints were applied, and it was anointed with milk from the breasts of a young nursing mother who was called in to volunteer this donation. In their proceedings, they were symbolically creating a young mother out of the corn plant which was tied onto the head of the shaft. The shaft was painted with a little red groove near the top to signify the face, and a red line drawn down the length signified the windpipe, breath, and the principle of life. First the priest spoke to the new young mother corn, after which it was passed around among the other bundle ministers in the lodge who spoke of it as "the voice." Then it was passed around a second time and all breathed upon it—the Evening Star priest first, followed by all the others.

Now the errand man went through the village crying out that the new mother needed a robe, a cowskin in the hair, and a buffalo hair belt. The donor brought them to the lodge. The last act of the ceremony consisted in wrapping Mother in her new robe with her face exposed so that she might watch over the people. She was tied to the outside of the Southwest (or Southeast) bundle.

Just before this final step, the visionary was dressed up by the priest for his second role that he would carry throughout the summer buffalo hunt until they arrived back at the village. He would now impersonate *Paruksti*, Wonderful Power, the Thunderstorm. He was wrapped in a buffalo skin that he had specially prepared, and wore special moccasins and a buffalo-hair rope belt tied in the back in four loops to represent the rain. His duties would be very trying, for all summer while they were on the march he would have to remain wrapped tightly in his robe, refrain from washing or bathing, handling knives, scratching himself, or participating in any acts of violence. He must think only gentle and noble thoughts. If his feet were allowed to touch water, there would be violent thunderstorms. In his person he held the great force of the creative power of all the universe. When they reached the buffalo herd, as the hunters stood lined up ready to surround it, this holy man would have to kneel facing the herd and pray to the cosmic powers, naming the buffalo and the eagles that he had consecrated to them in the past. Should anyone be injured in the course of the attack on the herd, the people would blame him and feel that he had had evil thoughts and had not been sincere. Throughout the hunt one or the other of the prominent old men would stay with him, talking to him and seeing that he did not transgress any taboos. He was always fed first before the others at every meal so that his mood would remain pleasant. He lived and moved in the encampment of the chief who was leading the hunt during that season.

In the previous ceremony, when the seeds of the sacred corn had been distributed to the ministers of the various bundles for planting, the visionary of that ceremony had been constituted a holy man for the well-being of the corn crop. He also had to remain wrapped in his buffalo robe all summer and to observe similar taboos until the harvest was in. Presumably, as he remained wrapped in his robe, he was impersonating the ear of corn itself in its husk.

In the final stages of the young corn ceremony, the priest went through the village, praising the donor of the cowskin and buffalo-hair belt in which they dressed the young Mother Corn, referring to the robe as the symbolic wrapper into which a germ of life could be thrust and the buffalo-hair rope as the string.

The ceremony of the Young Mother Corn was concluded with a feast in which all who had participated shared in the meat of the buffalo that the visionary had consecrated on the previous winter hunt. His wife usually added a donation of boiled corn to round out the banquet.

Until this ceremony was completed, no woman could go into her field and begin to weed and cultivate it. Now the women all went into their fields carrying their hoes. First they would pull out the weeds one by one from the corn hills by hand and then pile up the earth around the young growing plants. The corn was hilled up so high around the plant that the leaves barely stuck out at the top; they were compared with an earth lodge with the smoke issuing out of the smokehole in the roof.

It was early morning and the dew had fallen, and as the women worked around and around the corn hills their bodies would get soaking wet. After they had hilled up the earth around the plants, the women would kneel close to the hill and pat it all around with their hands to make it smooth and even. The woman's left side, as well as her face and hands, would become covered with mud. To mention this fact to a woman on her way home from the fields would be the height of presumption. On the way home everyone took a swim in Beaver Creek and washed off their hoes. Again the young women splashed with their feet on the surface of the water and tried to make as loud a report as possible by slapping the surface of the water with their hands. The old man again sat up on his earth lodge and addressed the community at large. He reminded everyone that the women were now "disfiguring themselves" for him, getting all muddy, and that while their hoes were still full of mud, all of them would be eating the food that the women had raised. Some of the women went in groups to cultivate the previously planted fields of their new daughters-in-law, singing while they worked together and again enjoying a festive meal at their daughter-in-law's house afterward.

Now at the beginning of June everyone's mind was turned to completing the preparations for leaving on the summer hunt. They would weed and cultivate the corn plants and hill up the earth once more just before leaving, when the plants were about 3½ feet high. The present Nebraska farmer says, "Knee high by the fourth of July" and the Pawnee said, "Tall enough to tickle the horse's belly."

The corn and the buffalo that sustained the Pawnee placed heavy demands upon him. Only by carrying out his year's round with great precision and by careful coordination of his activities with other people of the tribe could he combine these two major food resources. The administrative activities of the priests and the chiefs were as vital to his enterprise as the physical resources themselves. Few administrative structures have commended themselves so directly to the people as that of the Pawnees. Respect for the chief was a cardinal tenet of every Pawnee's life, in return for which the chief demonstrated a dedicated concern for his people.

13

CEREMONIAL PREPARATIONS
FOR SUMMER BUFFALO HUNT

Ritual Meeting of the Chiefs—New Responsibilities of Chiefs—Mythohistorical Significance of Skull Bundle—Development of Original Village Federations—Ceremony Described—Chief of Hunt Is Chosen—Banquet Follows—People of Village Informed

WHEN THE CORN WAS LAID by in the beginning of June, a new phase in the Pawnee year's round began. Everyone turned their thoughts to the long migration out onto the prairie. The mass hunt of the buffalo herd that was the next phase in the Pawnee year's round would last all summer until time for the harvest in the beginning of September. Would they find the herd, would they get a plentiful supply of meat for their ceremonial banquets, would they be attacked by the enemy, would they live in health and at peace with one another—three thousand people in four Skidi villages and four Pawnee bands—each with its own ways and interests on a journey of 900 miles over the land and across the rivers?

As was their practice, it was the chiefs, priests, and medicine men that took the first formal steps toward initiating each new round of activities through the year so that the people were taught and reminded of what lay ahead. In the village, priest and chief shared almost equally in keeping life on an ordered course, but on the march it was the constant vigilance of the chief that determined the achievement of this goal. And so this season opened with a ritual meeting of the chiefs, validating their cosmic sanction and soliciting the confidence of the people.

The whole meaning of this ceremony was that the chiefs alone were taking responsibility for the welfare of the people on the hunt and that the sacred meat they were about to get was a great and Heaven-sent blessing for all the people. These thoughts and feelings were expressed in a characteristically Pawnee idiom: the chiefs were costumed as Heaven itself and were told by their old leader, That-Chief, that they could not look to Heaven for their decisions as *they* were now Heaven and were carrying all its responsibilities for the well-being of the people. In this role they walked from house to house and received a gift of firewood from each.

As no ceremonial could be conducted unless there were a donation of dried buffalo meat, the buffalo hunt signified the entire ceremonial life as well. Lying on the ground in the ritual lodge there was the long buffalo steak that was the customary donation, and upon it the chiefs all blessed themselves. After the ceremony the chiefs blessed their children with what was left of the donated meat as Heaven had blessed their people.

Amid these ceremonial significances, they also took the practical step of choosing one of their number to assume leadership for the forthcoming hunt season.

The chiefs met twice a year just before the tribe planned to leave for the buffalo hunt. The summer meeting was under the direction of the Skull bundle, the winter meeting under that of the North Star whence the buffalo came at that time, driven southward by the cold. In view of the historical events, priests were excluded from this ritual, only chiefs being present, and there could therefore be no ceremonial procedure. It was said that like their cosmic counterpart, the Corona Borealis, the chiefs simply sat around in a circle and talked.

We do not know how many villages joined the first federation, but at the time of our account (c. 1867) there were sixteen chiefs' places in the council, four for each of the Skidi villages. At the northeast was a place for Old-Man-That-Chief whose voice was final in all matters relating to chieftainship. Closest to the exit, one on the north and one on the south side, were the chiefs' errand men, *tarutsuhus*. The chief's errand man had a very important role to play, as he was the chief's envoy at all times. Like the chiefs, he held his position by heredity. He carried messages back and forth between the villages and to the other bands, and while the council was in session he kept carrying its decisions to the other bands, returning with their reactions to them. Both of the chief's errand men were mature, experienced men; the one, Heavy-Trophies, was also head sacred priest of the Skidi, while the other, Know-His-Face, was also a man of some social consequence. Old-Man-That-Chief carried the main direction of the ritual.

The ritual was held in rotation through the years in the lodges of the different chiefs who were members of the council. On this occasion, Eagle Chief of Pumpkin-Vine Village was the host. On the morning of the council he had sent the errand man, Know-His-Face, to issue the invitations to the other chiefs and had the lodge prepared for their arrival. The sacred buffalo meat lay to the south of the fireplace about three feet away. Eagle Chief sat at the southeast with three other chiefs ranged along the side to his left. They each had different materials needed to help the chiefs costume themselves in their role as Heaven. Each chief would bring his own eagle feather that he would wear on top of his head to represent Heaven itself during the creation. Eagle Chief had a quantity of soft white feathers, *kiskuskawiu* (not down), placed on the head at the base of the eagle feather to represent the clouds on which Heaven traveled while the creation was in process. The chief who sat at the left of Eagle Chief had a knife and a supply of sticks to which the chiefs could fasten their eagle feather in order to put it through their scalplock. The chief who sat next on the left had some elk sinew to tie on the feather. The fourth chief had a supply of paints for painting the faces with the bow-shaped vault-of-the-heavens design. Each chief was expected to wear his best clothes so as to be worthy of his role.

Each chief entered with his tobacco pouch in his right hand and went directly over to where the sacred meat lay on the south side of the fireplace. The meat was the long muscle steak that lay along the backbone of the buffalo, dried and processed for preservation. It was called *kis-atsu*, "bone-lying along." It now rested on the south side of the fireplace, lying at a slant with the "head" or neck end pointing northwestward. Facing in this direction, the chief straddled the meat at this end and placed his tobacco pouch down near his right toe. He rubbed the end of the meat and then rubbed himself in blessing and, retrieving his tobacco pouch, went to his traditional place. As soon as two or three chiefs had entered, they filled their pipes which errand men lit up for them. When they were all in their places, Old-Man-That-Chief began to talk.

He explained to them that in their ritual smoking of the pipe they were to remember that they were now impersonating Heaven itself and therefore they were not to offer the mouthpiece upward, but only down to the powers of the earth, for they were occupying Heaven already. He also mentioned the donor of the buffalo meat that had made the ceremony possible, Lone Chief. He stated that they were to costume themselves properly so that they could go among the populace, *akıtaru*, and receive from each household two well-dried sticks of firewood that the people had been saving for the purpose so that they could denote their allegiance to the chiefs.

The ritual pipe from the Skull bundle was then filled and brought to him at the northeast where he was sitting and lit up by the errand man. Then Old-Man-That-Chief smoked and pointed the mouthpiece twice downward and passed it to his neighbor to his right, who in turn did the same thing and passed it to his neighbor until it had gone around the lodge in a counterclockwise circuit. After the pipe had been returned to the owner, That-Chief spoke again. He reminded them that they were to undertake their task of chieftainship with humility, for all they had was their own human frailty. He said: "People think we are big men, but we're no bigger than poor men. Look at yourself and see this. Look down at the earth. Power is there."

The chiefs now lined up for the procession that was to go through the villages. Eagle Chief was in the lead, carrying the main pipe, with Lone Chief about two feet behind him, also carrying a pipe. All the other chiefs that were to take part in the procession were lined up behind them. They would carry the sticks as they received them—about six or eight each, carried in their arms. As the procession moved along, they would complain jokingly about the weight. Newly inducted chiefs followed behind, as this was a good time for them to be seen by the people. Before they left, they all had to pass the inspection of Old-Man-That-Chief, who gave them instructions as to their procedure: "Now you're to go out through the village and although they already know when you enter anyone's lodge you must say, '*Rakis* (wood), *tatihaa*' (I came to get), *tatitska* (I want), *rakis* (wood).'"

They had to visit all the lodges in turn. As Eagle Chief led them in, the women would be sitting on the beds along the sides. When he made his request, a woman in the lodge who was chaste would get up and give him the sticks. If it was the lodge of an important man, before the donation was made, he would have lit his pipe and offered it first to Eagle Chief and then to all the others, and each would thank him. In other less important lodges, the wood would simply be given. Sometimes in the lodge of an old chief, the old man would reminisce about his own experiences when he was in such a procession and how some important men had "smoked" him when he went the rounds, and how a woman had given four sticks so that she might have a good word from the chiefs and be doubly lucky. The chiefs in the procession would ask for cottonwood sticks because they were light, complaining that their arms ached and bantering with Eagle Chief about lingering too long over the smoking. "How far must we go yet?" they would ask. "I don't know how many houses!" Eagle Chief would say.

When they arrived back at the ceremonial lodge, they dumped the sticks at the southeast and went back to their places complaining about the fact that they were hungry. "My stomach's way in—I'm hungry! That fellow Eagle Chief is too slow." That-Chief would have directed the errand men to take a little dried meat and cook up a soup in a hurry so that they could refresh themselves. This was just an impromptu meal. The official banquet would come at the end, after all the ritual and business had been transacted. That-Chief would again remind them that in offering some buffalo fat to the powers they were not to raise it upward to the Heavens but only to the earth, and that they were to eat directly without waiting for anyone else.

After they had finished, the most sacred part of the ceremony was held. They would smoke the pipe and talk of the creation. The old man instructed them and pointed out that they were not to be too eager, but to be measured in their devotions for they might otherwise tempt fate and use up their luck. He said: "This is the time for you to smoke, and anyone can talk on whatever serious subject he wants to—the creation or any other matter. Don't talk too long. Just say what you want to say if you have a notion. Just say a few words. You can talk again. Don't talk too fast. If it's Heaven's will, you will live long. If you talk out your words too fast, you wont live long; that is what we all believe. When we go visiting the Wichitas for example, if they don't give you a gift, that's all right. If they give you too much too often, you might not live long. If you get horses on the warpath, don't go again too soon. You might get killed. Conserve what you have. Do everything in a measured way. Heaven wanted us to live on this earth and here we are. These are the things that Heaven gave us—the corn and other things—and we must take care of them. We can't throw away or waste anything. We can't know what is going to happen in the future. *Raru* (merely, just), *kakirarakurararat* (don't waste anything)!"

The serious part of the ritual was now over and the old man instructed the errand men to begin to cook the main banquet which would be served about four in the afternoon. During this time they would converse on more practical matters, finally leading to the choice of the chief who was to lead the hunt during the forthcoming season, after which the banquet would be served. The old man led off: "This is your time to talk. We're not in a hurry. We have nothing else to do but talk. If you have a story to tell, tell it. We come here twice a year, as chiefs— once in spring and once in the fall. If you want to say anything, say it. I would like someone to volunteer to help the errand man cut the meat into portions." The talk by the others now concerned their leaving on the hunt. One would say, "This time of year the buffalo are not quite fat enough. How many days will it be after we leave the village before we see them? Perhaps so and so many. What do you think?" "Corn isn't big enough yet. Maybe it will be ready the latter part of the month." "Perhaps when we get out on the move, we can travel eight or ten miles a day."

Now after each one had made some remark on these matters, Lone Chief of Village-across-a-Ridge who was sitting at the west and who had donated the meat, proposed that Eagle Chief be made administrative chief of the forthcoming hunt. Eagle Chief replied that he had only recently performed this role, and proposed that White Eagle be chosen in his stead. White Eagle, after due expressions of humility, addressed them. He stood up and said, "Now you have selected me. I'm going to call a meeting in a few days to decide when to go buffalo hunting. When we (Skidis) have decided this, the other three bands will be looking to us to find out when, and we must send them word."

The main banquet was now ready to be served and Old-Man-That-Chief said, "This is what Heaven gave us. We must take care of it. Now we're going to eat." The food was passed out in formal order and ordinary conversation went the rounds. One said, "Let the horses race now. Whoever has a good horse will get a good buffalo. This fellow has a horse that never gets fat because he races it. He feeds it all the time and it never gets fat." Someone else would remark about the state of the corn and the pumpkins. Then again, someone would say, "When we get to the Platte River, we will see big grapes and plums and chokecherries. There will be good plums where we're going." Another one would remark, "How are you fixed for the equipment for your horses? I guess you have to fix your saddle so that you can pack things on it." Then again, "I have to get some arrows. I have to get someone to make the shafts. I still have time yet." "I have to get an iron barrel hoop at the store to make the points, and a file to trim them down. First I have to get the blacksmith to rough them out for me. I have to get a lot of them." In this way they reminded one another of some of the practical things they had to do before leaving on the hunt.

It was now early in the evening and Old-Man-That-Chief made the closing speech and summarized some of their findings: He reminded them that they had been occupying the seats that the older chiefs had occupied before them; they had talked over whatever they wanted to say and what they knew of the past, and now they must look toward the future. That they had heard White Eagle who had been selected as leader of the forthcoming hunt upon his selection by Eagle Chief, and that they as chiefs could only reply upon their own judgment, for representing Heaven itself, there was no supernatural power to depend upon. He thanked Lone Chief for donating the meat for the banquet and then instructed them to get up and go. Before his final dismissal, That-Chief reminded them that the meat which they were carrying away from the feast was to be entirely eaten up as soon as they got home, and that it was not to be left overnight, as it might become infected with sickness or bad luck and endanger the well-being of the tribe. They were to bless their children with the meat and then see that it was eaten up directly. When the meat was handed to the wife, as she blessed her children she said, "I want you to grow up to be worthy of this chief's meat. Your father has come home with this meat for us to eat. This is the food that Heaven has promised to provide for us. Now we're going to eat it and Heaven is going to bless all of us. I'm going to bless you; we're going to eat this food from the chief's lodge there. Now we're going to eat it and I hope it brings good luck to our house and that you grow up to be better children through Mother Earth." Then she blessed the children and she blessed herself by rubbing her hands upon them and herself.

As was customary, as the meeting was drawing to a close, an old man had climbed on top of the earth lodge, and facing east addressed the people, informing them of what matters had been discussed and what decisions had been reached in the council. He said: "Now the chiefs have had a meeting. Now their business is nearly over. Everyone must go into the fields and try to get things ready. Get the corn laid by as soon as you can. If you have not already gotten your tent fixed up as I have reminded you before, get it fixed up now. From now on, try to get everything done in a hurry." With this exhortation, everyone in the village accelerated their pace in preparing to leave the village and migrate out onto the plains.

14

PRACTICAL PREPARATIONS
FOR THE BUFFALO HUNT

*The Arrowshaft Makers—the Problem of Horses
—Patterns of Cooperation on the Hunt—the
Value of Horses to the Pawnees—the Tent Skin
and Implements Needed with the Tent—Furniture—Household Utensils—Household Grouping
for the Hunt—the Stay-at-Homes*

BEFORE LEAVING ON THE HUNT, one of the Pawnees' primary considerations was the weapons they would need for hunting and for their protection. Guns were expensive and sources of ammunition were not
readily available while they were on the march. And so they used the
bow and arrow, which could be made from local materials. Every
hunter made his own bow of ashwood and his own sinew bowstring, but
the making of the arrowshaft was a highly specialized craft. The shaft itself fashioned of dogwood sticks had to be carefully shaped and the
feathering skillfully applied so that it would shoot true. In 1867, there
were only five arrowshaft makers for the whole Skidi Band. Everyone
who needed arrows had to place his order with one of them and arrange
to compensate him for his work. They also had to bring the craftsman
the dogwood sticks well seasoned. They had collected them some
time beforehand and left them in the rafters of the house so that
they would be ready. When Old-Man-That-Chief stood on the roof of
the earth lodge and reported on the chiefs' ritual meeting and exhorted
them all to hurry, the arrowshaft makers were the first to feel the pressure. The arrow point required a different kind of negotiation. In the
past they were made of chipped flint that no doubt had to be traded for
at some distance. At this time they were using iron barrel hoops that
they got from the trader in the tradestore, which they had rough-shaped

by the blacksmith. They would sharpen them to their taste with a metal file that they also obtained in trade.

The arrowshaft makers had a monumental task to keep everyone supplied. They considered it a social service and made sure everyone had them whether they were compensated or not. The Pawnee community was always more or less in a state of siege, and the arrowshaft makers felt that their work was essential to their common survival. As Mark Evarts expressed it, "Sometimes the arrowmaker made up his mind himself to make some arrows for someone. They want to supply the whole camp with arrows out of public spirit so that if the enemy comes on the war-path, everyone will have arrows. Even if they don't get any special compensation, they will do it to protect their children and others."

Practically the entire supply of arrows that they needed for the summer had to be made while they were still in the village as there was no time for such work while they were on the march or attacking the herd. A craftsman could produce about ten a day and he usually made them in lots of twenty, working them all in successive stages for the whole lot. With the limited leisure they had on the march they could barely finish one in a day, and this would only be done in case of emergency. They did take some dogwood sticks along for such a contingency. A hunter would consider twenty to forty arrows a reasonable number to keep in his arsenal. In 1840 the Skidi population was estimated to have 469 males over the age of ten years. If 200 of these were adult hunters, this would mean that each of the five craftsmen would have 40 of them to take care of, and supplying each with 20 arrows would mean that he had to produce 800 arrows to keep his group supplied once around. This was eighty full days of work.

When a man decided he needed to replenish his stock, he took the dogwood sticks that he had seasoning in the rafters of his house and went to the arrowmaker and asked him to make him twenty. It would be tacitly understood that if in time he got a buffalo, he would make him a gift of a buffalo robe, or perhaps a blanket, some dried buffalo meat, leggings, or a pair of good moccasins.

Sometimes, without having a special order on hand, the craftsman would ask a young man to get him forty to sixty dogwood sticks and would compensate him when he had finished, with a gift of ten completed shafts. He wanted to make sure that everyone was supplied whether they made a special request or not. They had to get their own feathers—turkey for the most part, but if they could not get one, a buzzard or a goose was a substitute.

In the latter part of May just before the chief's council, they were likely to accelerate their efforts. One of them would be sitting at the gaming grounds watching the hoop and spear game, and then another would be likely to sit down and join him. They would begin to talk about arrows. Presently all five would have congregated there and they would continue the conversation. People at the gambling grounds would remark, "See those fellows over there? I guess they're talking about arrows and who makes the best ones." Meanwhile the arrowmakers would be talking about how many arrows they had made during the spring and how many more they would have to make. They would talk about how many they had given as gifts. With the younger men, arrowshafts were a favorite item for gambling; the older ones played for higher stakes, like horses and dried buffalo meat. One of the makers would remark, "I gave one fellow so and so many, but he's a great gambler and he's already lost them." "I gave that fellow arrows too," another would say, "and I'm sure he'll also lose those!"

The most skilled arrowmaker of the group was Chief's Road, who shared the lodge next to that of Victory Call and Old Bull with his brother, Horse Thief. His shafts were slender and graceful and had black feathers on the ends. He was jealous of his skill; when someone tried to approach him when he was working, he would turn and conceal what he was doing. He had probably learned the craft from his father. He was a commoner in hereditary rank, but ambitious to rise in the social scale. He would supply Chief Victory Call, Otter's father, with arrows and do other services for him in the hope of gaining status. The arrowshafts made by his brother, Horse Thief, were also of fine workmanship.

Two other craftsmen were also grouped and made shafts that were similar. Path-of-the-Enemy made arrowshafts that tended to be large and not as fine as those of the two brothers. He had been born as a brave, the rank second to that of chief, but he had little interest in validating his public position. He was good-natured, with a pleasant disposition, and well liked. He had taught New Young Dog his craft, and he also made rather large shafts. He was a man of great courage and was always off on hunting and scouting expeditions that at times took him far from the village.

The fifth arrowmaker was Careless-of-the-Enemy. He would go off long distances by himself on hunting and scouting expeditions. He had no interest in public recognition or status problems.

Besides the characteristic shape of the shafts that each of these men made, they each put a slightly different-colored marking on his shafts. The distinctive character of the shafts were confined to the makers, not the owners. Everyone knew who got shafts from which maker and when and how many. While out on the buffalo hunt, everyone was conscious of who chased which animal, and when they came up to a fallen buffalo and examined the arrowshaft, they put together the circumstances and knew who had killed that particular bull or cow. Nobody needed a personal property mark for this purpose.

Horses were a second major problem. It is a well-known historical fact that horses were introduced to this continent by the Spaniards in the early 1500's, and whatever use was made of them by American Indians had to develop after that time. Even though it was a considerable length of time, the Pawnee practices in connection with the use and care of horses were not as advanced as those of the Spaniards. As regards the buffalo hunt, at the time of our narrative horses were used in the chase when they were attacking the herd in a group and also to carry their food and camping equipment. The strategy of the mass attack upon the herd was to develop a "surround" by the mounted hunters who had been lined up behind a hill out of sight. No doubt they had previously used a similar technique on foot. As to carrying the food and equipment, a good deal of it was packed on the backs of the women and girls. However, the women had dogs who were trained to drag the tent poles behind them, the heavy ends of the poles tied to a harness on the dog's back. The tent poles were grouped into two sets, one on each side of the dog, and connected by two cross sticks toward the lower ends. Upon these a skin cover was wrapped where other luggage was placed. A dog could drag as much as 70 pounds. The custom of dog traction and extensive carrying on the back by the women was in full operation as late as 1837 when a famous painter, Alfred Jacob Miller, portrayed the Pawnees in this manner. After 1850, however, dogs were no longer used for this purpose, and it was mostly the men who kept them around so that the puppies could be sacrificed and eaten at a special ceremonial. Some, of course, were kept by the women as pets. By 1867, the horse had taken over the carrying function almost entirely except for a few poor single or old people who had to do some packing of their dried buffalo meat on the way home. The packing of the horse resembled that formerly used in connection with the dog; the horse travois or carrying frame was also the same as that of the dog. All the leather trappings for keeping the luggage in place had now to be carefully prepared before they left for the hunt.

The Pawnees were relatively poor in horses compared with other Plains tribes at this time. This may have been due to constant attacks by the Sioux and the other nomadic tribes, although this is not certain. At any rate while among the Blackfoot or the Kiowa twenty-five horses at least were considered an average number for a family on the move, Eagle Chief, who was head of the Skidi Band, had only ten, and a reasonably comfortable family like that of Victory Call had only four or five. Some families had only one or two horses and it was with great difficulty that they went on the hunt at all. Even in their war practices, the Pawnee retained some of their prehorse habits. It was well known that they set out on their war expeditions on foot and they were known to the Kiowa as "Walkers." The rationale given for this by students of the subject has often been that they kept themselves free to take the horses of the enemy and ride them home. They did gain in stealth of approach, but this is no doubt a secondary explanation of what was probably a survival of older custom. The fact that the men looked for booty or various kinds of valuables in the places they attacked and carried them home on their backs is indicated in some of the well-known names that were current, such as He-Comes-Carrying-Sitting-Down-from-Time-to-Time-Coming—implying that the things brought home as war trophies were so heavy that the bearer had to sit down from time to time and rest. Another such name is He-Brings-Many-Trophies-from-Over-the-Wide-World, or again, He-Comes-Bringing-Them-Down-a-Hill, or still another, He-Comes-Carrying-His-Trophies-Today.

It is clear that the actual pattern of cooperation on the migration and hunt was established long before they had horses and present practices were adapted but not substantially changed. In 1540 Coronado's expedition met a party of buffalo-hunting Indians on the Plains who were using the dog travois and carrying dried buffalo meat. Mark Evarts describes some of the traditions remembered by the Pawnees at the time of our narrative, when they had no horses:

> Near Old Village there was a hill called Calf-Against-Upon-Standing. The calf referred to was a certain kind of yellow calf with a long body and the people knew that when they saw him standing on the hill, the herd would be right beyond him. The people would line up on each side and surround the herd and make the buffalo circle about inside. They would kill them and butcher, and carry the meat home on their backs. They had no horses. There was no trade store.
>
> The North Wind was called Lucky Wind because when it blew it sent the buffalo. In winter in deep snow, one could chase the buffalo into a hollow where the snow was deep, and some of them got their feet stuck in the snow, and could readily be killed. This was particularly the case before we hunted with horses.
>
> In summer the buffalo went scattered in small bunches and this was difficult, but in winter they traveled in closer formation when we could also drive them onto the ice.

The Pawnee surround is described by George Bird Grinnell (1925, pp. 249-250):

> Choosing a still day, they would surround a small bunch of buffalo, stretching out in a long line whose extremities would gradually draw together, as the hunters, disguised as wolves, stole from hill to hill around the unconscious prey. When the circle was complete some man would shout and startle the buffalo.

From some of these accounts of the hunt without horses, it is clear that the social patterning of the buffalo hunt was probably quite ancient. Yet by 1867 horses had become a necessity for the hunt.

If a man had only one horse, only the man and one of his wives could go on the summer hunt. He would have to leave his other wife and all the children at home and any old people or other dependents. The couple that were going would pack their one horse with food and goods and join someone else's tent, taking just their covers along by way of household equipment. If a family had no horses at all, they could not go. Unmarried or widowed individuals who had no horses could join a household where they could work their way, simply getting their board and keep "for going." They would go on foot wearing a double blanket for their covers. It was said that they went "just to eat."

If a man had two horses, he would also be able to take only one wife along, leaving the rest of the family home. She would go along to process the meat.

There were some rough-and-ready characters who, even though they had two horses, would decide to go alone, leaving their wives behind. They were men who were not averse to doing all kinds of work, including the hunting and preparing the meat besides. Such a man would say to his wife, "You'll only be in my way." No insult was intended. For example, Mad Bear would team up with his friend Many People who had a small tent and two or three horses. Together they could bring back a great deal of dried meat in this way. Two men of this kind were friends and equal partners. Sometimes two men would team up, one of whom was the senior buffalo hunter of the two. Then the more prominent hunter would ride the buffalo horse to the hunting grounds while his assistant rode the pack horse. During the chase the assistant stood back, holding the pack horse, while the hunter went after the buffalo. The assistant then helped him butcher and they packed the extra horse with the meat. The senior hunter rode the hunting horse back to the encampment and the assistant rode the pack horse on top of the meat. If they got two buffalo, both horses were packed with meat and they both rode on top.

A man with two horses and no assistant could manage by riding the pack horse and leading the hunting horse by a rope. When he got to the herd, he hobbled the pack horse on the sidelines. When he got the buffalo, he rode over on his fast horse and led his pack horse to where the buffalo lay. Then he loaded the pack horse and led it by a rope, riding to the camp on his fast horse.

The possession of three horses made it possible for a man to take his whole family along, while four horses made it possible to manage easily. Ordinarily he would not have a guest traveling with them, but if he did he would assign him one of the horses so that he could pack his things on it. A man like Eagle Chief who had eight or nine horses and whose son-in-law had a similar number, could afford to lend two or three to outsiders, although this did not mean they would also share in the family tent, as his administrative functions required that he take his entire family along.

In the Pawnee language, the word horse means "super-dog," the only pack animal the Pawnees had before the impact of European culture. With all due respect to the capacities of the dog, however, it was the people themselves that did most of the carrying on their own backs. They had to pack not only the things they needed for camping—food, tents, and equipment—but they had to carry back the dried buffalo meat and the large hides. Every able-bodied person they took along with them could earn his way by carrying things on his back. The men, whether first-rate hunters or not, could play a useful role in the surround of the herd. The only people they would leave behind in the villages were the old and disabled. But the horse had made quite a difference in the social economy. A horse could be packed with the dried and packaged meat of four buffalo while a person could not carry more than one—about 80 pounds. If need be the horse could carry still more goods on his back. Unless they could be of substantial assistance in the work of the camp, a person would only be an extra mouth to feed. In the case of a chief or a man who was socially ambitious, there would be a great deal of entertaining to do in the camp; women, in addition to their work in preparing the meat and skins would also assist with the entertaining. In a family which had no social ambitions, like that of Mad Bear cited above, two men in partnership taking a minimum of housing and utensils and a maximum of horses could return with a great deal of buffalo meat and hides, to the general benefit of their families. The wife left behind under these circumstances could hardly resent it.

The horse also represented a unique and highly valuable item of capital that had the unprecedented value of not having to be carried, but of moving itself. In the past, differences in wealth would depend on a much more direct kind of personal skill. The man who was swiftest on his feet and the most skilled with the bow and arrow got the best buffalo, and his wife could produce the finest packaged meat and the best skins. These in turn could be traded for other valuable things—valued ornaments or participation in the sacred ceremonies. Now skill in horsemanship, which had become an indispensable factor in hunting the buffalo, implied also major successes on the warpath and the capturing of horses as well as their subsequent care and protection. The horse thus provided a material basis for a greater degree of social differentiation. The horse was an item of personal property, but unlike property in our society it was by no means as much of a factor in developing differential status as other aspects of experience, chiefly knowledge of man, the world, and the universe. The Pawnees had great contempt for extreme poverty and raggedness, but no great desire or awe for wealth in large quantities. Historically the likelihood is that the cooperative social patterns of the Pawnees go back to a time when practically every person had an important function in the material economy, while a person of outstanding value was one who had special insights and knowledge.

But for all the value the Pawnees placed on knowledge and the things of the spirit, a tent was an absolute necessity as they traveled over the country. The making of the tent skin was one of their most complex technical achievements. It was a major enterprise to get one made, which had to be anticipated at least two years in advance. Eight skins had to be accumulated over four successive hunting periods—a summer hunt, a winter hunt, and on the following year again, a summer and a winter hunt. Sinew of eight buffalo for sewing the skins together also had to be saved. As signs of wear would appear in their tent skin, a woman would remind her husband of their need. Then he would set aside two good skins in each of the four seasons. The average life of a tent skin was no more than ten or twelve years.

Seven buffalo hides were used to make the body of the tent; an eighth was cut up for gussets, loops for the pegs at the bottom, and a double thickness at the door. In order to fit the skins together in the smoothest and most economical way and to arrange the pattern of the applied parts, a woman specialist in this field had to be called in to supervise the work. There were only a limited number of women with such knowledge in the tribe. In addition, it would take four or five women working pretty steadily for three or four days to do the actual sewing of the skins. The workers all had to be compensated with gifts of dried buffalo meat, skin clothing, and trade store goods that had to be purchased with buffalo products. In the course of the hunt, the hunter had to anticipate these needs as well as the need for the skins and the sinews. Payment for the work of planning and sewing amounted to at least the sale value of a good buffalo robe.

The same tent skin was used for both the winter and the summer hunts, but the framework was different. In winter they used the standard pointed skin tipi, supported by a frame of thirteen tall and heavy rigid poles that were leaned against one another at the top to form the conical frame. With its fire burning in the middle, this tent provided an excellent protection against the winter cold, but it was too warm for summer. For the summer frame they used a series of flexible saplings to make an open-faced shelter. The making of the heavy tipi poles was a long and difficult process and had to be planned well in advance, whereas the saplings for the summer framework could be gathered near the time of leaving for the summer hunt. Elm or willow saplings were available near the creek in the late spring or early summer and at this time the bark came off easily. They were considerably lighter to carry than the rigid tipi poles. For the summer shelter they also needed two upright posts forked at the top and a cross piece to connect them to form a frame, onto which the saplings would be tied and through which the summer tent was entered. Wooden pegs were needed for both summer and winter tents to hold the skin tight by driving them through the loops at the base of the cover. They were usually gotten at the last minute.

A very necessary implement for these operations was a long 7-foot stick to be used as a digging iron. It was forked at the top and had a strong fire-hardened point to make holes in the ground for the poles of the frame.

Furniture for the tent included five large mats finely woven of bulrush to be used as floor covering. These were carried rolled up and tied with a string in the middle that had been provided for the purpose.

A wooden mortar was also needed for making mush and corn flour and for other cookery. It was made of a section of elm log, the bottom whittled into a point so that it could be stuck upright into the ground. There was a hole drilled through this part of the mortar so that it could be tied onto the horse with the other baggage. The working end at the top was excavated by charring and scraping into a deep bowl shape. With it they had to carry a long pestle made of a small tree trunk with both ends left intact and the middle portion cut down for a handhold. This was carried grouped with the long tent poles and the digging iron; the poles were tied at one end to the horse's back with the other end dragging on the ground.

Other household utensils were six or seven wooden bowls made by the women as were the other wooden objects for the household, a string of buffalo-horn spoons for tableware and perhaps some small enamel bowls gotten at the trade store for their coffee. Also included was a larger wooden ladle for serving.

All the cooking vessels in Mark Evart's time were of metal replacing the older pottery and they had to be gotten from the trader. As late as 1835–1856, a few clay pots were being made, but by 1867 there were none at all. By 1928 almost all memory of how they were made was gone. Metal came into use among the ancestors of the Pawnees by 1650 or before, when sheet metal was being cut up to make some of their arrow points. In 1833 the Pawnees had an extensive trade with the Kiowas in brass buckets. For the present expedition, they needed a large brass kettle for cooking corn, soup, or mush, two standard metal buckets—one for water and one for coffee—and a metal frying pan to make grease bread.

In order to get these latter items, Victory Call rode up to Bishop and Matlock's trade store on his best-looking horse to establish his credit, saying to Mr. Bishop, "Grandpa, come out and take a look at my horse.

Do you think it can get a good buffalo? Well, you can have a buffalo robe when I get back and my wife can tan it." Mr. Matlock would then join them and the traders would say, "Sure." "Well, I need two buckets," Victory Call would say. "And what else do you need?" the traders would ask. At the same time there would be an old lady in the store trying to establish some credit so that she could get some sugar to make sweet corn pounded up with sugar. She would promise that when they got back from the hunt she would bring in a sack of pounded-up dry meat. This was the equivalent of the better-known pemmican and was bought by travelers at the trade store for emergency rations. When warriors went on the warpath they took extra pairs of moccasins filled with pounded sweet corn and sugar and some of the pounded-up dry meat as concentrated supplies.

Not everyone had the skill or the diligence to accumulate all this equipment. Every man or woman who did not have it yet wanted to go on the hunt had to try to attach themselves to someone who did. This practical consideration had an important effect on how the individual encampments were set up. Sometimes a family had enough horses but no tent. The man would send his mother-in-law or his wife to inquire of a woman who owned a tent whether they could join her encampment. If it was agreed that they·should camp together they would discuss how they would combine their needs for equipment—a mortar, a kettle, dishes, etc. Sometimes a woman would make such arrangements, only to find at the last minute that her husband had already committed them with someone else, and then one of the families would have to remain behind.

The general rule was that a man had to take care of his father-in-law and the family into which he was married. It was understood that he would travel with his father-in-law and his wife's family. This is what his marriage implied—that he was to serve and care for the family of his wife. The son-in-law was called by the family into which he married *kustawixtsu*, "he who sits among (them)." The son-in-law would refer to himself as *rat-ut-ka-ku*, "I-for-you-inside-sit," meaning that it his function to serve their house. This was an obligation greater than that to his own parents. If his parents were old and alone, he would give half of his kill to them after his wife had picked out what she wanted. When they first married, the couple normally lived in the girl's house and went out on the hunt with them. As they got older, the young man might want to set up a tent of his own and hunt separately and his father-in-law might consent, but he would send a gift of a leg from whatever buffalo he killed. When they got back to the village, they would rejoin the girl's family. If the girl's father was getting very old and his tent was worn out he would say, "Son-in-law, I want to go with you. You came here to take care of us." "Certainly, that's good," the younger man would say. This marriage responsibility sometimes got on a man's nerves, and if he wandered over to his parents' tent and asked his mother to fix a bed for him it was accepted as a normal thing. His wife would understand that "he felt like being childish for a while" and that next morning he would be back with them. Sometimes the sounds of fighting would be heard inside a tent—a father-in-law and a son-in-law in conflict.

Although he might live elsewhere in the village, an unmarried younger brother was likely to join his older brother for the hunt. This was his obligation. When he married, however, he would be impelled to go with his wife's family. Sometimes two brothers and their families lived in an earth lodge jointly and they might very well also go jointly on the hunt.

The household of Old Bull and Victory Call broke up into three groupings. Each of the four villages of the Skidi Band had a separate section of the encampment. Old Bull and Victory Call both camped in the Pumpkin-Vine Village section in the west, but each had a separate encampment and ran their households entirely independently. The camp of Old Bull included his two wives and the grandmother and their young children. In Victory Call's camp were his wife White Woman, his assistant Horse Rider, his wife No Corn, Grandma Chase-the-Enemy, and the boy Otter. The old lady Grieves-the-Enemy and the boy Yellow Calf went far over to the east section where her son was encamped in Village-in-the-Bottomlands with his father-in-law, Path-of-the-Enemy. The two little boys did not see each other all summer, as there were hundreds of tents between them. When they returned to the village in the fall, it was optional whether they rejoined the household or not.

In the past, the people who were left behind in the village were in great danger and they all cried bitterly as the expedition departed. The Stay-at-Homes were usually the sick and the old. Some men would stay longer to give a little more protection to an old grandmother or someone of whom they were fond. The Stay-at-Homes would congregate in a few earth lodges in the village, knowing where to find food in the storage pits. Leaving the slow and the sick at home was a necessary step, as the line of march had to move with precision because other tribes were also pressing in on the buffalo herds. They might move entirely out of reach, whereupon the tribe would be faced with the danger of losing all of the effort they had invested in the expedition. Nevertheless, sometimes a soft-hearted chief would say, "Let's all go, even if we have to camp every five miles!" Others would demur, saying that was too slow; finally the old people themselves would say, "No, we can't go along. We're old anyhow," and having made this concession of their own accord, they would be permitted to return to the village. Sometimes noticing that a perfectly able-bodied family he liked was not coming along, Eagle Chief would inquire and, finding they were staying behind because they had no horses, would lend them two of his own.

Some men stayed behind in the village because they wanted to be alone for a while to think and make peace with themselves. They would plan to catch up with the party in five, six, or even ten days, living on limited rations of dry meat as they were accustomed to doing when they went scouting over the country for days and even weeks.

Such a man would sit quietly on the roof of his lodge and sometimes go inside and lie down. Not uncommonly he would have a vision. The vision is the Pawnee's introspective device for organizing his wishes, goals, and purposes. Mark Evarts expressed the mood in the following terms:

One man was left there alone. He just wanted to stay. He thought he could go any time—in five or ten days. He might even not go at all. He just felt like staying. He didn't think of any danger. Early in the morning before sunrise, he sat on the roof of the earth lodge looking about, way off. He goes into the lodge and lies down; he doesn't even make a fire. He has a little dried buffalo meat to eat. He has gone three or four times on the war path and has experience in how to be hungry. He is thinking about how far they may have gone in the ten or fifteen days that have passed. He can't quite make up his mind to go and join the people on the march.

One evening while he was sitting on the roof and it was getting dark, he heard a woman crying in east village (Village-in-the-Bottom-lands). As he listened to the crying he decided to go where it was coming from. When he arrived he found a woman sitting wrapped in a buffalo robe and crying. "Where do you come from?" he asked. "Right here," she said. "I am crying because they have all gone hunting and I had my children (litter of mice) in that sacred bundle. In five or six days they will be getting buffalo and sacrificing the meat. A priest will untie the bundle and when they open it, there will be a nest where my children are. Maybe the priest will have to give up my children to them. That's why I am crying. I am poor. I wish you could go and get my children before they open the bundle. Get my children and come back with them." "I'll go right now," the man said. The woman thanked him and he got up and went directly to get his quiver, bow, and arrows and left that night.

He knew how to catch up with the line of march through a short cut and starting out in the morning he traveled all day. He stopped a little while and smoked and then trotted on his way, hurrying to reach the group. In the camps everyone had been wondering why he had not come along. They thought perhaps he had been killed. He arrived about nine o'clock in the morning, just as the priest was taking down the bundle.

The people in the camps called to him as they saw him approach, but he walked right through until he stood before the priest as he was untying the bundle. The five priests were ranged at the west and he went to the one in the middle and rubbed his hands on him in blessing and then the others in turn and then whispered to the leading priest, "Untie it gently because in the north side of the bundle there is something." The priest understood and after all the bundles had been unwrapped, the four little mice were found alive in a nest inside one of them. "These are the ones I came for. I must go back now. She said they might be starving." He returned at once by the way he had come and on the evening of the fifth day, got to the village where the woman was sitting. "Here they are now," he said, and after she had fed them she said to him, "I am a woman and can take care of my children. I can get any food I want. Now I am going to predict for you, for I had my children in that bundle and it was only you who saw them, and because of that I have something to tell you. I am a woman and I don't have much power, but now everything you do will be successful. We mice are all over the world and we can talk to you anywhere." Her prediction came true and he became an important man. Sometimes two or three men might stay behind in the village after everyone had left on the hunt and catch up later. They would sit alone, scattered out in widely separated lodges. Sometimes they would have a vision.

By 1867 there was a class of Stay-at-Homes who were able to remain behind in comparative safety from attack because of the proximity of the white town of Columbus, about 22 miles from the village. They would set out from the villages with the others, traveling to the first stop on the Platte River and then part company and go toward the town. They were mainly men and women who were unmarried and unattached, though more rarely a couple or a whole family would have to remain because they did not have horses or because their arrangements for joining a tent had fallen through. In the past all of them that were able-bodied would have gone along, but now many more remained behind. For people who had no tent or no horses, going along would have meant attaching themselves to a family and receiving board and lodging in return for performing minor services. They felt they might be open to humiliation if someone seemed to be giving them orders or telling them to hurry with what they were doing. When plans were being made for leaving, a group of women in this position would get together and talk among themselves; "If I go I have to work for someone else. I'll have to haul wood and help the other women and they might not give me enough dry meat in return." Another would say, "That's what I think. It might be hot. And they might not get many buffalo." Some single men would congregate in a similar way and say, "I don't feel like going." "Look how far they have to go. I think what you say is right. We have legs and can get plenty of fresh meat by hunting deer and antelope right nearby. Let's go to Columbus."

Near Columbus they were reasonably secure from Sioux attack and they would build a big lodge of tin or sheet iron, and a man and his wife who happened to stay would take over the direction of the party, while the others would assist, running it like a village household. They would run a common commissary and the men would go out hunting for antelope and deer while the women would supply the dry vegetables and cook the meals, alternating on the north and the south sides.

Once the seventeen-year-old son of White Eagle decided he didn't feel like coming along. "He might decide that it was a good thing for him to get used to being by himself. This was an idea that their grandfathers would inculcate into them saying, 'Now you're old enough to go on the warpath, be a horse thief, and be independent.' White Eagle tried to talk to him saying, 'Now we're going hunting. You come along.' 'No,' the boy said, 'I'm going over there to my uncle.' 'All right, if you want to, but now they're going to talk about me and say that White Eagle didn't take his boy.' 'Well, I'm going to stay with my uncle anyway.' So White Eagle would take a poor orphan boy who had been staying in his earth lodge along with him on the hunt instead of his recalcitrant son." It seems that adolescent protest was not unknown to the Pawnees. On the other hand, his father was in no position either to force him or to exert pressure for him to go. He was considered entirely within his rights to make his own decision.

· 15

THE GREAT CLEANSING
CEREMONY

~~~~~~

*A Summary Ceremony—a Symbolic Washing of
All Ceremonial Objects—a History of the Ceremony—Celestial and Doctors' Symbolism Combined—Ceremony Explained—Participation of
People in Ceremony*

~~~~~~

THE GREAT CLEANSING CEREMONY that was held before leaving on the
hunt was, in effect, a summary of all the Pawnee religious beliefs and
practices. In Pawnee ideology, the sky was one realm and the earth and
the waters another. The priests were in charge of the cosmic ceremonies,
and the medicine men, or doctors, were in charge of the animals that
were connected with the earth and the waters. In this last category, the
physical structure of man and his physical health were included. But ultimately, according to Pawnee thought, the sky was the first cause and
the continuing source of power in both realms. The doctors conducted
a separate cycle of ceremonies from the priests, and in the fall, at the gala
ceremony that was held after the harvest was in, they acknowledged their
celestial origin by hanging buffalo-hide cutouts of the Morning Star and
the other sky gods from the ceiling of the ceremonial lodge. During the
forthcoming summer hunt, a specially selected doctor would kill a buffalo bull and a cow to provide the skins for this purpose and another bull
and cow to build up the images of their own special gods.

The central feature of the ceremony they would now conduct was the
carrying of all the sacred objects to the stream, there washing them
symbolically. Then the people would clean up the whole village and wash
themselves in the stream. This great cleansing ritual was under the direction of the Big Black Meteoric Star bundle, the northeast of the semicardinal-direction bundles. In mythohistory this god was a sort of master

of general ceremonial procedure. He was also the patron of knowledge as indicated in the star chart attached to his sacred bundle, and also patron of the knowledge of the earth and the waters and the doctors, who took care of this aspect of man's life. He controlled the coming of the night, the animals, and, particularly, the buffalo.

The Great Cleansing Ceremony was conducted under his tutelage twice a year just before going out on the hunt. It combined the symbolisms from both the celestial and the earth and water realms. In the creation ritual held after the first thunder in the spring, the systematic theology of the cosmos was given. The doctors also had a systematic ideology of their own. While many of their curing practices and behavior had much in common with other individual North American Indian shamans or medicine men, all their animal cults were organized into a unified association outside of which no one was able to practice lest he be accused of witchcraft operations. Traditionally, this was founded in the Pumpkin-Vine Village where all the men were doctors. This village was anciently supposed to have been associated with Village-Lying-across-a-Ridge. The association of the doctors was attributed to a single founder who experienced a series of visions that formed an integral system, paralleling in a sense the formation of the political federation of villages. The visionary had a series of visions in an animal lodge that was located under the water, where he learned the true nature of the animals and illusionist techniques of sleight of hand and other arts of suggestion as modes of curing and of influencing events. He was also taken over the country by the animals in his subsequent visions and taught the value of different roots and herbs. Eventually he invited a few other men to his house and shared the mysteries with them. After the harvest and the summer buffalo hunt, still others were invited and learned from these new doctors. They constructed little lodges of willows and cottonwoods inside the earth lodge, and to each the leader gave the skin of an animal that was to characterize his cult. Within his individual booth, the animal would instruct the new recruit in a dream. Then calling each in turn, the original visionary, through a process of hypnotic transfer, taught each head doctor the songs and dances of his special cult. Dressed in their animal-skin costumes, these men danced and were taught the arts of suggestion and sleight of hand. First they practiced hypnotizing one another and then, going out of the lodge, made a public display of their powers. After the ceremony they deposited in the water of the stream, the little lodges they had built and the images they had made. When they got home, they were told to hold their dances in winter and spring after the first thunder, but not to display their hypnotic and sleight-of-hand powers until the fall, when all had returned to the village after the summer hunt. A great public ceremony was to be held for the benefit of the people, lasting two or three months. Thereafter, whenever a man had an animal vision, he applied to the Doctor Association and was given a place in the lodge.

All during the summer hunt and the hard work of getting in the harvest that followed, the people looked forward with great anticipation to the elaborate performances that the doctors would put on all during the month of October. It was a Grand Opera with a connected series of episodes, combining animal mimes, displays of sleight of hand, and illusionist performances of different kinds, hypnotic acts, songs, and dances. In that summer the people contributed the dried meat of eighty buffalo to the Doctor Association for the forthcoming ceremony and in former times as many as 140 were given. This was one of the prime motivations for going on the hunt.

In the Great Cleansing Ceremony now to be held before departure, both the celestial and the doctors' symbolism was combined, one connected with crops and the other with the wild animals.

As soon as the chiefs had determined the date for the departure on the hunt, they notified the priest of the sacred bundle who was in charge for that season, and he in turn got in touch with the other four priests. They all came to his lodge, beating on their bundles to signify that they were now going to conduct a national ceremony. They took their appointed places at the west, putting their bundles down in front of them and sending the errand man to summon the other bundle keepers to come with their mats and food bowls. They spread their mats and sat in their traditional places, hanging their bundles on the wall behind them. They remained in the lodge for three days and nights, feasting and talking together. Meanwhile the four main priests went through the village calling on the people to bring gifts to Mother Corn. They were being asked to bring the clothes that would costume the chief who was to lead the procession when they took the sacred objects to the stream. Only men of sterling character were privileged to make such a contribution—those who were public spirited enough to initiate public ceremonies, were courageous in defense, volunteered frequently for public service, were generous in helping the less fortunate, did not harbor malice, did not engage in any kind of violence or loud conduct, did not gamble or indulge in sexual adventures in unsanctioned social categories. They were to bring a buffalo robe, moccasins, a buffalo-hair cord as a girdle, and dried buffalo meat and fat that had been consecrated on the previous buffalo hunt. The donors would paint themselves red, carrying their gift through the village for everyone to see as they took it to the ceremonial lodge. After the gift was presented, two messengers went through the village announcing the gift and publicly thanking the donor.

The actual ceremony in the lodge was performed on the fourth day after the bundle keepers had assembled there. Very early that morning the four priests dug a rectangular pit west of the fireplace to represent the Garden of the Evening Star. The bottom of the pit was covered with soft downy feathers and was referred to as *Kusaru*, "bed." All the bundles were now opened and the two sacred ears of corn, one attached to a stick (representing the male), were placed in the "Garden," with the other ear (representing the female) leaning against it.

Now another model was made representing the waters and the animal life that pertained to them—the waterfowl, swan, and loon, and a garfish to represent the Great Sea Monster that had guided the original visionary of the doctors and a turtle. These were placed around a wooden bowl containing some water with a clamshell in it to represent the running waters.

Next came some ceremonial procedures that pertained to the specific tradition of the Big Black Meteoric Star. The principal objects involved were the star chart which was attached to the bundle. This was placed on a stick, carried outside, and fastened on top of a little mound of earth in front of the door. Then four smooth stones, thought to represent both meteorites and buffalo maw stones, and to have come down to them from the beginning of the world, were each attached to a stick; four men were assigned to carry them to the mound outside. The "northeast" man of the group was given the sacred pipe and a long strip of buffalo fat. When they got outside, he placed the strip of dried buffalo fat on a little fire, built to the east of the little mound of earth for the purpose. As the procession filed out of the lodge, the priests were singing a song about the men scanning the heavens and the earth all around. They continued to sing as the steps of the ceremony were performed outside. The melting buffalo fat was rubbed on their hands and faces by the four men who were outside; these men also greased the four sacred stones. As they smoked the sacred pipe they slowly surveyed the sky in all directions.

When they got inside, the priests stopped singing and the men performed their devotions around the bowl of water with the skins of the waterfowl and the turtle.

The next two episodes were acts of sympathetic magic for success in the buffalo hunt. The leading priest said, "Priests, the men whom we have sent to look around have returned. They will tell us what they have seen." The man on the northeast arose and said, "We went out before daylight. We found the buffalo—so many of them that they have almost drunk the river dry." The other three men each replied in the same way. A famous warrior was then selected by the priest to carry the sacred pipe and a chief to carry the strip of the buffalo fat. As they went around the room, first along the north and then the south, everyone reached out to try to put his hands on the pipe and to seize a piece of the buffalo fat, tearing off as much as he could to symbolize that he was starving and was desperate to kill the buffalo.

Finally they had the formal procession in which all the sacred objects were carried down to the stream. The chief who was to lead the procession was called by the priest and dressed in the clothes that had just been donated. The sacred pipe from the Big Black Meteoric Star bundle was placed in his hands. The bundle keepers retrieved the sacred ears of corn from the "Garden" and placed them next to their bundles. A prominent warrior who had ownership rights to the Big Black Meteoric Star bundle led the main body of the procession bearing the star chart. Immediately following him were to be three men with quivers from the sacred bundles. These four sat near the entrance, lined up one behind the other, while arrangements were being made for the bearers of the rest of the objects. Meanwhile men from different villages had come in and seated themselves in front of their respective village bundles. Two men from each were selected to carry the "Mothers" or sacred ears of corn, others to carry the hawkskins symbolizing warriors and owlskins symbolizing chiefs that were also contained in the bundles. And last of all, the leading chief who was to head the procession went out and rounded up all the little boys he could find—an act signifying his watchfulness over the people. The little boys were given minor objects from the sacred bundles to carry, particularly the raccoon bones attached to the sticks with which meat was removed from the soup during the ceremonial banquets, or the arrowshafts used as pipe tampers and sticks to tend the fire.

Now there was a race to the river; the priests singing and shaking their gourd rattles while the objects were being given out. When they got to the fourth song, the warrior with the star chart jumped up and began to run toward the river as fast as he could, the quiver bearers close behind him. As they pushed out through the long entryway of the lodge, everyone tried to follow, and anyone who overtook the man with the star chart on the way to the river took it from him and ran on until he came to the bank where it was returned to him.

The crowd standing along the river bank now grouped itself into four symmetrical rows. In the first row, front center, was the warrior with his star chart. He was flanked on both sides by the men with quivers, who were in turn flanked by the men with the sacred ears of corn. In the second row were the men with hawkskins and owlskins. In the third row were people with less important bundle objects such as braids of sweetgrass usually burned as incense, buckskin pouches containing red, black, and white paints, pieces of enemy scalp, and other objects peculiar to the particular sacred bundle. Finally, bringing up the rear in the fourth row were the little boys with their raccoon bone forks, arrowshaft fire pokers, and pipe tampers.

The group now parted ranks. Down the middle came the chief carrying the sacred pipe to the water. He waded in and symbolically washed himself by dipping his right hand and then his left into the water, each time touching it to his mouth, nose, forehead, and down his face, alternately first with the right and then with the left hand. Then he went back through the group and stood facing the village ready to lead them back. The others followed suit, the men of first rank pretending to wash their objects and their bodies, then walking through the line to stand behind the chief and the others in order. The chief led them back to the village and the objects were replaced in the bundles in the ceremonial lodge. The little boys ran away at once, and the other men retrieved the robes they had left behind in order to race to the water before they went home. The priests and bundle keepers tied their things and had a meal of cornmeal mush that had been donated by one of the women. Then they all took their mats, pillows, bowls, and sacred bundles and went home.

The town crier went through the town telling all the people to clean their lodges and the streets and to carry all the dirt far away. The next step was for everyone to wash and clean themselves. The priests who had led the ceremony had a sweat lodge built, and one of them stood outside shaking his rattle and singing. All the people assembled there and raced to the river as fast as they could go. They waited there for the priests who waded in and came out at once and went to their sweat lodge to take a steam bath. All the rest of the people—men, women, and children—stayed at the river, swimming and playing in the water.

16

FINAL PREPARATIONS
IN THE VILLAGE

The Chiefs Sit in Council—Announcements to the
People—Personal Needs: Tobacco, Foods, Clothing—Estimates of Food Taken for a Family

FOUR DAYS MORE and they would all be gone on their summer journey.
All the chiefs of the different bands were sitting in council to plan their
strategy. White Eagle, who was to lead the hunt, had called in representatives of the four villages, and now as they reached their decisions he sent
his errand man, Know-His-Face, to Curly Chief of the Little-Earth-
Lodge Band to inform him of their plan. Curly Chief would relay the
message through his errand man to the council of the Begging-for-Meat
Band which was gathered in the lodge of Man Chief. Man Chief in his
turn sent his messenger to Many Trophies, Chief of the Man-Going-
Downstream Band, in whose lodge their council was meeting. Meanwhile Know-His-Face had returned to the Skidi council and reported
what reaction Curly Chief had had to their plans. If the council were still
in session they would get the message directly; otherwise they would
hear indirectly. This was the usual form by which the four bands coordinated their administration throughout the year in the settlement and
this continued in the same way while on the march. When an errand man
or envoy came to a chief with a message from another chief, he was received formally and entertained as an emissary of the chief who had
sent him, offered a smoke and a meal, before it was proper for him to
state what he was sent for. If the chiefs' meeting should break up too late
in the afternoon, the council would wait to send out their errand man
until the next morning so that he could be received with due formality
and the rest of the chiefs would have a chance to send out their envoys to
the other bands in a suitable manner.

Just as the meeting was drawing to a close, as in all chiefs' meetings, an old man would climb up onto the roof of the lodge and cry out to the village what had been decided. In this case he did so early next morning. His wording was in a precise telegraphic style so that it could be clearly understood by everyone. He said:

This was what was decided in the chiefs' meeting. White Eagle decided we are going to hunt in four days. Anything you have to do, get finished in that time. On the fifth day, we'll go out of the village. We'll camp on the other (south) side of the Loup River (*its-kari*, "potatoes-many").

We'll camp there a whole day so that any of you that aren't quite through can join us any time that day and up to the evening of the sixth day. On the seventh day we are going to be moving upstream (westward).

The old man, having completed his announcement, went back into his lodge.

Toward evening any old man who felt impelled might get up onto the roof of his house and talk to the people. He would say whatever was on his mind—about events in the past and their lessons for the future, or any other matters that seemed pertinent. Reviewing past events that were successful was considered a kind of sympathetic magic as well as of practical value. At this time the old man might talk about the fields and of how they were in the past. "All that," he would conclude "is in the past. But today we may have the same luck." Then he would continue in a different vein: "Try to help one another and take care of the children. The little ones like to swim and one must watch that they don't drown. I hope we come home well and find everything in good order."

Such an old man was likely to speak gently and phrase his thoughts diplomatically and people listened carefully and thought about what he said. However, at the gambling grounds the gamblers had other matters on their minds. They were thinking about the good places they would come to along the way that were nice and smooth, with good buffalo grass growing on them—such a fine playing field for the hoop and pole game. They would discuss the different sites they were going to camp at where these would be found and agree between them that one would take along one stick and one the other so that they would have the equipment they needed for playing. For the inveterate gambler, this subject was always uppermost in his mind.

Other men were thinking about how to get enough smoking tobacco to fill their needs, and the doctors were occupied with the herbs and medicines they would need to take along that were available only in this area. The tobacco was needed for ritual as well as for social purposes.

The tobacco was always mixed with the inner bark of the red dogwood (*Cornus amomum* Mill, pictured in Gilmore, 1919, plate 22.) The outer bark was removed and the fragrant inner bark scraped and dried for smoking, mixed with the tobacco. The red color of the bark appeared in winter. In 1867 the tobacco the Pawnees used was all gotten at the trade store, but in former times the men raised their own in specially prepared patches. The native tobacco, formerly cultivated by all the tribes of Nebraska was *Nicotiana quadrivalvus* Pursh. For the summer hunting expedition the men had to be sure to have plenty of tobacco in their pouches, and they took along the dogwood while it was still unripe so that it would cure along the way. A man would take a sackful about 1½ feet high and a foot in diameter included with their other supplies.

They had to be sure that the horse gear was all in order as much would depend upon it, particularly for packing the luggage. If a new saddle had to be made, they would have to scrape a deer hide and get a horn. A saddle for packing had to have four long rawhide strings, two in front and two in the rear, for tying on the packages. The packages that were tied to the sides of the horse were of standard size. They were large rawhide envelopes, 2½ feet long by 1½ feet wide and a foot deep, designed to hold the thinned and dried meat of a whole buffalo, but were also used to carry other types of luggage, particularly foods. The soundness of the rawhide straps on the saddle was vital as should these break while they were crossing the water, the food would be ruined. They checked the stirrups and provided themselves with plenty of rawhide rope for hobbling the horses.

For clothing, they had to take along blankets and some broadcloth for the women—possibly some dresses. Moccasins wore out frequently on the march. A sewing bag with sinew, awl, and moccasin patterns was an essential item of luggage.

Sacred objects had to be carefully carried and tended by the women. Sometimes a woman would carry the sacred bundle she was caring for on her back, and sometimes it would be placed on top of the other luggage on the horse. Depending on their particular tradition, some of the bundles had to be placed on top lying the long way and some lying across.

The bulkiest item was the food. This consisted of dried vegetables, dried buffalo meat, and some trade-store items—flour, baking powder, coffee, sugar, and dried prunes, apples, and peaches—all highly concentrated foods. These were included in the standard rawhide envelopes. The journey to the hunting grounds took about twenty days. By that time many of the vegetable foods were used up and the envelopes would now be available to pack the newly dried buffalo meat. The main vegetable provisions were dried kernels of corn that had been removed from the cobs. The corn was treated in two basic ways during the harvest: One batch was gathered early while still "in the milk" and the ears were roasted in the husks. The kernels were then cut from the cob with a clam-shell and dried. Corn prepared in this way, known as *rawaritu*, "roasted," required little soaking and could be boiled in an hour. When the camp was moving along quickly, this was the corn they depended on for the basic staple. While some of the corn crop was thus gathered early when it was "in the milk," the rest of the crop was allowed to mature and dry on the stalk, *rikis-tahis*, "corn-dry." After the cobs were snapped off the stalk and carried in, the kernels were pried off with a pointed stick. Any of the nine varieties might be treated in either way, but the blue flour corn was particularly favored for maturing on the stalk to be processed as dry corn. Dry corn took considerably longer to prepare than roasted. It had to be soaked for some time before it could be boiled, and they used it when they stayed over at a place, arrived early, or stayed at camp late one morning. Although it took longer to prepare, this kind of corn was heavier and more satisfying. The sticky, yellow sweet corn pounded with sugar was taken along as a kind of sweet meat or served when they had no time at all to cook a meal. This was most commonly prepared by the old ladies who had more time to pound things in the mortar. Thin sheets of dry buffalo meat were also pounded in the mortar with a little fat and served as an alternative uncooked meal. Old women who some-times started very early and went ahead of the line carried these foods in a skin bag as rations. Dried spotted corn was particularly preferred for parching, to be eaten like popcorn or with soup. In addition, they took along several varieties of dried beans to be boiled with the corn and some dried pumpkin and buffalo intestine for the same purpose, in order to add a variety of flavors. Dried buffalo meat from the previous winter hunt was also included. Each of these foods was separately packed in a tanned skin bag with a piece of skin on top to cover the opening and

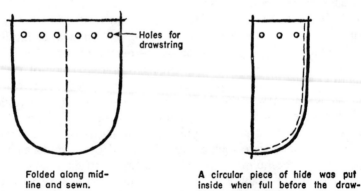

Holes for drawstring

Folded along mid-line and sewn.

A circular piece of hide was put inside when full before the draw-string was pulled.

FIGURE 16-1. The small sack, *asa-karusu*, "dog-sack." Slightly larger than our 50-pound flour sack, it is used for carrying pounded-up sweet corn, dried pieces of meat, scraps, and so forth.

closed up with a drawstring before placing them together in the rawhide envelope or in a larger sack. The tanned hide sacks were of two sizes, the smaller known as *asa-karusu*, "dog-sack," standing 3 feet high and 1½ feet in diameter when full and containing about a bushel or 50-60 pounds of dried corn kernels (see Figure 16-1); the other "almost twice the size," standing about 3 feet high and 2 feet in diameter when filled, containing 1½ bushels or more.

The camping household of Victory Call comprised five adults and the

TABLE 16-1. *Two Months' Supply of Dried Food Carried on the Hunt.*

White Woman's Supplies, Including Grandma's Contribution

Corn, roasted, quicker cooking variety.	2 small sacks
Corn, dried, longer cooking variety, mostly blue flour.	1 large sack
Corn, dried, spotted, mostly for parching.	1 small sack
Sweet corn pounded with sugar.	2 small sacks
Beans, done up in small bundles, each containing a different variety—spotted, red, black-head.	2 or 3 sacks
Pumpkin, dried, cut into circuits, the strips braided into simple checker-plaited mats about arm's length and 2 feet wide.	1 or 2 mats
Dried buffalo meat, a slab of dried meat, 1½ feet long and 4 inches thick, comprising thin sheets of buffalo meat alternating with layers of dried fat, most of the family supply being left in the food pit.	½ a package
Trade-store goods: in the package with the slab of dried meat, ½ sack of flour, sugar, coffee, baking powder, dried fruits; if there was any room left in the package, little bags of corn, beans, or a pumpkin mat were included.	

No Corn's Supplementary Supplies

The corn was all in small sacks and there was no meat, merely dried buffalo entrails:

Corn, roasted.	1 sack
Corn, dry.	1 sack
Corn, dry, spotted.	1 sack
Pounded sweet corn with sugar.	1 sack
Pumpkin.	1 mat
Beans, two or three kinds, a bundle of each.	1 sack
Dried buffalo entrails:	
Buffalo paunch, similar to pumpkin cut into strips and made into a checker-plaited mat.	1 mat
Intestine, cut into sections, dried and plaited into a mat about 2 feet long and 1 foot wide, both adding flavor to the soup when cooked with corn.	1 mat

boy Otter. Victory Call was assisted by his retainer, Horse Rider, and there were the three women—White Woman who carried the main responsibility for the encampment, assisted by No Corn, Horse Rider's wife, who because of her affliction with arthritis was less able to contribute, and Grandma Chase-the-Enemy, who helped whenever she could. The food supplies these women carried were fairly standard and were estimated as shown in Table 16-1. (Grandma included hers with White Woman's.)

These dried foods were very concentrated and swelled many times their size when boiled with water. For their bulk, they were economical to carry. Victory Call's family of six took six to eight rawhide envelopes, packing the food and certain small objects that happened to fit in, also a few skin sacks, and half a sack of food for immediate use. In addition, during the twenty days en route to the main hunting grounds, Victory Call went out regularly, as he did in the household, and hunted for a deer, an elk, or an antelope to supply them with fresh meat, although a good deal of it did go into social entertaining as it had in the village. The fresh deer bones were cooked along with the dried corn for the family. On the return journey lasting twenty-seven days, or more, the dried vegetable food was supplemented with partly dried buffalo meat known as *kiparu*, "moist," processed so that it would keep for a short time.

Normally two meals a day were eaten, one before they broke camp in the morning and one in the late afternoon. It seldom happened that they had a chance to eat a lunch in between as they were mainly on the march through the day or extremely busy processing the meat and hides that the hunters brought to the camp. A good breakfast was mandatory to sustain them on their day's journey, and corn was the most satisfying food. The pattern of meals was much as it was in the earth lodge and included fried bread of commercial wheat flour and coffee mixed with a generous amount of sugar. The value of sugar as a quick source of energy was well appreciated, and a man would ask his wife to put some sugar in the fried bread if he was going to have a hard day.

17

THE RENDEZVOUS CAMP

*They Leave the Village for the Hunt—Packing
the Equipment—the Order of March—Crossing
the Loup River—Setting Up the Camp—Raising
the Tent—Supper and Afterward*

THE MORNING FOR LEAVING THE VILLAGE had finally arrived. Victory Call
got up early and made the fire, and White Woman cooked the breakfast.
Meanwhile Horse Rider had gone out to get the horses and put them in
the corral so that they would be ready for loading. They had been hobbled nearby where there was plenty of good grass available at this season. Right after the horses were in, White Woman served the breakfast.
After the meal, saddles and saddle blankets were gotten and the loading began. It was important to systematize the process of loading at this
time, for it would set the pattern for the rest of the journey.

Three of Victory Call's four horses were to be loaded; he would ride
the racing horse. One of the horses was loaded with four of the rawhide
containers and another with two. The mare took the heaviest load, consisting of the softer bundles with the tent cover on top to keep it from
rubbing. She also dragged the tent poles and other items behind her.
First one of the horses was loaded with the four rawhide containers. Four
long rawhide strips were hanging down from the saddle, to tie them on.
As Horse Rider brought out the first container, Victory Call and White
Woman lifted it up against the right side of the horse and tied it in place
with the rawhide straps, then quickly turned the horse around, tying
on the other container so that it would be evenly balanced. The other
two containers were laid flat—one on each side resting on the first two
against the saddle horns—and were tied in place with the remaining
lengths of rawhide. The second horse was similarly laden, but with only
two containers, one against each side to leave room for a rider on top.

This was the place for No Corn, who was too disabled with arthritis to walk.

The mare, in addition to all the large soft bags, carried the long elm saplings to be used for the framework of the tent, divided into two bunches and tied across her shoulders by the stub ends, the thinner ends dragging on the ground behind her. The two cross pieces that kept them from splaying out were used as a carrying frame by wrapping them around with a large tanned hide cover. Here small children might ride and sometimes drop off to sleep; an old woman always followed to keep them from falling off. It was said that in the past when the poles were dragged by the dog instead of by the horse, the dogs would sometimes run away, carrying the children with them. The digging iron, almost seven feet long, was grouped on one side of the horse where the smaller number of poles were. The mortar was tied on by a string which was drawn through a hole in the pointed end and could be seen swinging near the ground under the tent poles. The tent cover was tied in place over the saddle horns with the rawhide strings and with what was left of the strings, the kettles were tied on the sides of the tent cover—unless one of them happened to be black with soot and had to be tied to the back. Finally they were very happy if they could get a gunny sack to hold all the extra things. In it they would put the big brass kettle with the wooden bowls inside. They might wedge in other things if they fitted—spoons, plates, frying pan. "Oh, that's handy," they would say, "you can put anything that's left over right here." "Now is that all? Well, look around. Is it fixed all right? Well, now we're going to move!" "We can tell how well it's packed after we start off." They put some brush across the door of the lodge in such a fashion that they could tell when they got home whether it had been disturbed.

Grandma had left for the encampment much earlier. Horse Rider helped his wife No Corn up onto the less heavily laden horse, and Victory Call said, "Let's go," mounting his horse and helping little Otter up by using his foot as a stirrup; behind him was a blanket where the boy sat. The procession consisted of:

   (1) White Woman leading the horse packed with the four rawhide containers;

   (2) No Corn riding the horse with the two containers loaded on the sides;

   (3) Horse Rider leading the mare all loaded up; and

   (4) Victory Call on his racing horse with little Otter sitting behind him.

Their destination was about five or six miles to the south of the villages. The villages were strung along the west side of Beaver Creek, a small southeastward-flowing stream that joins the Loup River some miles down. The Loup is an east-flowing river, and the camp was to be set up on its south bank. Groups of people from each of the four bands were moving southward to the river. The villages of the Skidi were furthest westward and the line going southward was west of the others. The villages of the other three bands were located downstream on Beaver Creek about half a mile east of the Skidi. There the three bands stretched eastward with the Little-Earth-Lodge Band nearest the Skidi, the Beggars-for-Meat Band beyond them, and the Man-Going-Downstream Band in the location furthest east. In former times these three bands were located south of Skidi territory and were still referred to as the "South Bands."

The Loup River could be seen far off, with a few white tents in the distance already set up. The chiefs, particularly White Eagle who was to lead the hunt, had gone ahead very early and set up camp. If others happened to be prepared before the chiefs, they waited until they had set out. Victory Call's party, after making sure that everything was securely packed, moved along through the villages and then southward at a leisurely pace, arriving at the north bank of the Loup in about two hours. As they moved along the bottom bench of the embankment, the South Bands people kept coming along to the east of them and were crossing at their regular crossing place further downstream.

Both banks of the Loup were lined with people to watch them and help them get across safely. Some of the young men had put stakes in the water to mark out the boggy places where they might get stuck. People shouted to them, "Hello there, it's kind of boggy in the sand here. Go on this side, not there!" "All right, thanks." The water was quite deep and people had to take off their moccasins even if they were riding on horseback.

When a horse got stuck, everyone would come and help get him out. Even quite close to the bank there were some very muddy places. As Victory Call's party was crossing, everyone was shouting, "Look out, look out. Pull the horse to the right side. You're getting into boggy sand!" But before they could get out of the way, No Corn's horse got caught and she fell off. Everyone called out, "Don't let her drown!" "Look out," they shouted, "there's a baby on horseback. Take that baby off. It's muddy here." "No, it's all right. It's tied on."

When No Corn got to camp she might spread her clothes out to dry or simply let them dry on her. Tanned hide can be dried after it's been wet, but it gets somewhat wrinkled.

At last Victory Call's family arrived on the south side of the Loup, White Woman and Horse Rider fording the stream and leading their loaded horses and the others riding in. Eagle Chief and White Eagle had set up camp for the Pumpkin-Vine Village at the western part of the encampment, and Victory Call found a little hilly place in the area for their tent that would be dry. (See Figure 17-1 for the plan of encampment.) "Here's a place," he called and got off his horse, removing the bridle and allowing the animal to graze. He left the saddle on, going over to help unload the other horses. Horse Rider helped No Corn to dismount and at once began to unload the mare. They untied the straps and removed the tent cover first and then the buckets so that Horse Rider could go and fill them with water from the river. Everyone was thirsty and wanted a drink.

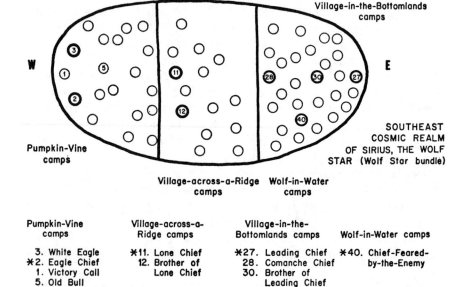

WESTERN SKIES (Evening Star bundle) MILKY WAY (Morning Star bundle) EASTERN SKIES (Morning Star satellite bundle)

Village-in-the-Bottomlands camps

W

E

Pumpkin-Vine camps

SOUTHEAST COSMIC REALM OF SIRIUS, THE WOLF STAR (Wolf Star bundle)

Village-across-a-Ridge camps Wolf-in-Water camps

Pumpkin-Vine camps	Village-across-a-Ridge camps	Village-in-the-Bottomlands camps	Wolf-in-Water camps
3. White Eagle	*11. Lone Chief	*27. Leading Chief	*40. Chief-Feared-by-the-Enemy
*2. Eagle Chief	12. Brother of Lone Chief	28. Comanche Chief	
1. Victory Call		30. Brother of Leading Chief	
5. Old Bull			

Figure 17-1. Pawnee plan of encampment while on the hunt, following a cosmic pattern as in the Skidi earth-lodge villages.

Now Victory Call and White Woman untied and took off all the raw-hide containers, and Victory Call removed the saddle from his horse and let him go. The next job was to remove and tie up all the rawhide ropes that were hanging from the saddles of the packhorses so that the saddles could be removed and the horses set free. White Woman began tightening the first rope on the front right side of one of the horses, then the rear right, then the rear left, and finally the front left. No Corn was helping her, and, if Horse Rider was back, he would pitch in and help too. The men removed the saddles and set everything out so that the sun would strike them where the horses had sweated and they were damp.

When Horse Rider had arrived with the buckets of fresh water, he said, "This water is still cold. Better take a drink." Everyone was thirsty and they were all glad to get it. Then Victory Call would say, "Go hobble the horses," and Horse Rider went directly. It was important to hobble the mare, especially since all the horses were likely to stay around her. On his way out Horse Rider saw some sand cherries among the sand-hills, and as he turned back toward camp he gathered them up in his blanket. They grew on low bushes, and those that were covered up with sand were yellow while the ones that had been exposed were a rich dark red like big ox-heart cherries sold commercially today. They would make a nice dessert for supper.

Meanwhile White Woman and No Corn were busy putting up the tent. (See Figure 17-2.) This was harder to erect than the pointed tipi, but the open front made it cooler in the summer weather.

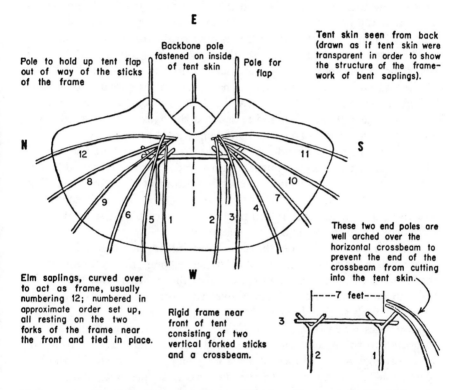

FIGURE 17-2. Curve-roofed summer tent. The front is open and faces east. An oblong fireplace is excavated somewhat to the north of the entrance.

The first step was to set up the frame in front. Two forked sticks were set vertically in the ground about 7 feet apart. Before each stick was inserted, White Woman punched a hole in the ground with the long pointed stick that she used as a digging iron. When the sticks were in place she joined them with a horizontal cross stick that rested in the forks. Now twelve sticks were stuck in the ground to form the outer frame. They were set in the form of a long half-oval. Before each stick was inserted, White Woman grasped her digging iron and punched a hole in the ground in front of her. Then the stick for the framework was inserted. These sticks were long flexible elm saplings about 2½ inches in diameter. She set all twelve of them in place. The tent must be so oriented that the entrance faced east and the rear was at the west. The first two sticks were set up at the west, the next two alternately on each side until the curved outline was complete with six uprights on each side. White Woman threw the far ends of each two sticks she inserted onto the entrance frame, fastening them with rawhide rope onto the fork, those on the southside onto the south fork and those on the northside to the north fork. She was careful to draw them over the fork so that they protuded well beyond it in order that the horizontal stick of the entrance frame would not cut the tent skin. The curved framework was now ready for the tent skin.

The first step was to spread out the skin on the ground to the west of the frame. A long elm sapling was placed upon it to act as the "backbone" of the tent and to raise the cover. The cover was provided with rawhide strings at the top and bottom to tie the stick in place. She then raised the stick with the tent skin on it and rested it at the back of the curved framework. Now No Corn would come and help with the next steps.

White Woman went inside and stretched the skin over the frame, while No Corn fastened it on the outside with wooden pegs. The rawhide loops for the pegs were all around the outside bottom of the tent cover about 1½ to 2 feet apart. The tent cover was pegged down at both sides to stretch it, then in the middle and then in the intervening spaces. The pegs were driven into the ground with an ax-head.

In the front of the tent, the skin hung rather loosely on both sides. There was a hole in each side into which a long stick was introduced that held the skin stretched out neatly. In the pointed tent, this part of the skin controlled the smokehole over the entrance and was held open or closed with similar long sticks.

Sometimes when they arrived White Woman discovered that she had forgotten to bring tent pegs. She would have to get three or four dogwood saplings in the timber, about 2 or 3 inches in diameter at the base. She would cut them close to the bottom. Each peg was about a foot long, and she might get three pegs out of a sapling. Each peg was sharpened at the thick end. If she happened to see a man anywhere around, she would remark, "Say, we have no pegs." Then he would simply go off and get them for her. If they thought of it they would get them beforehand and allow them to season. But in an emergency they could be used green.

Finally, the tent being set up, the rawhide containers were carried in and piled in twos at the rear of the shelter close together all around. The woven bulrush mats were brought in, unrolled, and laid down. Then a fireplace was made on the outside a little to the north of the entrance. It was made in oblong form about three feet long and a foot and a half wide, with its long axis running north–south.

The next step was to get everything in order for cooking. They had enough water, and now they needed wood for fuel. As she was pegging down the tent, No Corn remarked to her husband, Horse Rider, "We're pretty nearly finished now and we have no wood." Then he would go off carrying a long rope. He used the rope as a kind of lasso: attaching a stick about a foot long to the end, he would throw it up around a dry cottonwood limb and the cord would wind itself around the limb so that it could be pulled down. It would take considerable skill to pull it down without having it fall on your head, which sometimes happened despite the best of care. Horse Rider tried to get enough wood to last them for that evening and the next day while they stayed at the rendezvous camp. Some of the wood he gathered from the ground, tied it up with his cord, and came into camp carrying it on his back. As soon as he got in, he made the fire and White Woman began to cook. They had a simple meal of bread and coffee and some sand cherries for dessert. No Corn volunteered to make the coffee. While the cooking was going on, the old ladies were stretched out resting, and Victory Call was doing the same. Everyone was very tired. It was proper to joke a bit while the food was being prepared and during the meal. Horse Rider began to tease No Corn about how she had fallen in the water.

Immediately after supper the women cleared up the dishes and sat down to rest—tired from all their work. Horse Rider went off to see how the horses were getting along and Victory Call went up and sat on top of one of the sand hills to have a smoke and to look around and at the encampment below. Presently five or six men joined him for a smoke and some conversation.

The boy Otter ran off at once to the river to go swimming with the rest of the children. On the way he saw some other little boys leaning over a pond. "See the sunfish. Let's 'choke' them!" They tied some bread to the end of a string and let it down into the pond and as the fish bit, they pulled them up and 'choked' them. Then the boys went off and gave the fish to an old woman who was living alone in a shelter she had built for herself. Her relatives gave her something, but would not take care of her and she had no other place to go. "Here, grandma," they said, "Here's some fish." "That's fine," said the old lady. Later that summer while they were setting up camp one day, the boys came to give her fish and she was dead. They dug a hole in the embankment against which she had been leaning and buried her there. Man Chief, who was Eagle Chief's son, and a generous young man, gave a red blanket to wrap her in. There were only one or two old women alone like this. Sometimes while they were on the hunt, such old people would say, "Just give me enough to eat and go on."

Some old people just walked off because they were tired of living. "I'm old. I don't care what becomes of me," they would say. In this case, people thought it was a shame for the old lady's relatives to leave her all by herself like that.

Most of the women and children were swimming in the river. By sundown they began to wander back toward their encampment. When little Otter came in after his sun-fishing adventures they all said, "Minwu, you smell of fish. You'd better go wash your hands." There was no soap so he had to rub his hands with sand and then wash them with water. Horse Rider had been looking after the horses, and again he passed through the sand hills and gathered in some sand cherries. Victory Call was still sitting and smoking on top of the sand hills with his friends and they looked down contentedly upon the women and children swimming in the river. By sundown all had gone home; the men would go swimming late in the evening by themselves.

Now at evening the crier went through the encampment and made his announcement. He said, "We'll be here all day tomorrow. If you have any business at the store, attend to it, because day after tomorrow, we'll be moving on." It had been a long day and everyone went to sleep.

Next morning Grandma got up earlier than anyone else, before dawn, saying everyone must practice getting up early. They passed the day pleasantly, swimming in the river or doing whatever they liked. For breakfast they had a modest meal of fried bread and coffee and for lunch a good soup of roasted corn mixed with braided intestine. At supper, they had boiled dried buffalo meat with bread and coffee.

When evening came, the crier went through the encampment calling out, "They have decided to move tomorrow. We're going about ten miles from here."

The next morning their travels would begin in earnest. They would travel and encamp this way for the next twenty days before they reached the main herd of buffalo.

18

THE MIGRATION TO THE
BUFFALO HUNTING GROUNDS

~~~~~~

*Geographical Orientation—the Routes of the
Four Bands—Platte River a Major Landmark—
Trip Made in Ten Encampments—Four Mass
Attacks Planned on Buffalo Herds—Cooperation
during Hunt—Enemy Attack—Bad Weather—
Death*

~~~~~~

THREE RIVERS CUT ACROSS the state of Nebraska, flowing eastward into
the Missouri which forms the eastern boundary of the state. They rise in
the foothills of the Rockies and are sometimes deep and sometimes de-
ceptively shallow, but the water when it flows is always swift, and they
have shifting sandy bottoms even when the river bed seems almost dry.
The northernmost of the three is the Loup and south of it the Platte,
which it joins toward the east. The Platte almost bisects the state in an
east–west line. On the southern border is the Republican, which for the
most part cuts through northern Kansas.

The Pawnee migration followed the river courses progressing westward and southward in successive stages, west along the Loup, then south
to the Platte and for some distance west along that river, and then south
to the Republican, where the migrating buffalo herds were to be found.

The westward journeys along the river banks were relatively easy, but
in turning southward the overland travel took them over deeply scarred
irregular surfaces that were slow and hard to cross. North and south of
the Loup the land surface consists of glacial loess blown into tall sandhills
that look like dunes. To conduct a march across this terrain, especially
loaded with baggage, is extremely difficult. Moreover, there are no identi-
fiable landmarks, and it is easy to get lost. The land between the Platte
and the Republican is of a different character. The entire land surface is

covered with a deep, compacted layer of sand. Both rivers have changed their courses numbers of times in the past and the marks of their winding fossil beds are deeply carved into the sandy layer, forming a series of shallow but sharply defined canyons and troughs. Reaching north and south between the two rivers, the curves and canyons of the two fossil beds almost meet, cutting up the whole land surface so that there is no level land and the trip across has to be made over a few narrow land bridges. The later pioneers who tried to cross this area going southward aptly named one of the best of these land bridges "Devil's Gap" (southwestern Nebraska between Lexington and Arapahoe).

The Pawnees had a detailed knowledge of every aspect of the land they would traverse. Its topography was in their minds like a series of vivid pictorial images, each a configuration where this or that event had happened in the past to make it memorable. This was especially true of the old men who had the richest store of knowledge in this respect. Their journey out was about ten miles a day and eight on the way back when they were more heavily laden with the dried meat. Anticipating these distances, they had to plan on stopping places where there was enough level land, wood for fuel, and available water for their whole large encampment of several thousand people and many more animals. They estimated the journey out as twenty days and the return journey twenty-seven days.

Each of the four bands had different routes that they preferred. From their rendezvous camp south of the Loup, the Skidi preferred to go several camps westward along the south bank, before turning south to the Platte. The South Bands preferred to leave the settlements and go directly south to the north bank of the Platte River where they made their rendezvous camp. When they were ready to go west, they would cross over the Platte and proceed along the south bank all the way west until they came to the place where they turned and crossed the country south-

FIGURE 18-1. Approximate campsites of the Pawnee summer hunt in Nebraska. Starting from Genoa on Beaver Creek, X is the first rendezvous camp south of the Loup. Camps 2, 3, and 4 proceed west from Camp 1 along the south bank of the Loup. Camp 5 turns southward toward the head of Grand Island in the Platte River. They camped overnight between the Loup and the Platte because the sandhills between the rivers make the journey hard. Camp 6 was made on the south bank of the Platte after crossing Grand Island and Fort Kearney. Between camps 5 and 6 a small reconnoitering party went south of the Republican to sight buffalo; they brought meat to Camp 6. Camps 7, 8, 9, 10—four camps west of Fort Kearney along south bank of the Platte, arriving at Plum Creek near Lexington, Nebraska. At camps 7, 8, and 9 individual hunters went after deer, elk, and antelope. Setting out from Camp 9, the chiefs and braves hunted small herd in order to "feed the people." They brought meat to Camp 10. They went along Plum Creek and then southeast overland to find Turkey Creek. Camp 11—the hunting camp, where the main herd was attacked by all the hunters of the tribe. The people moved south along the west bank of Turkey Creek and encamped at its confluence with the Republican River. X near Trenton is Massacre Canyon.

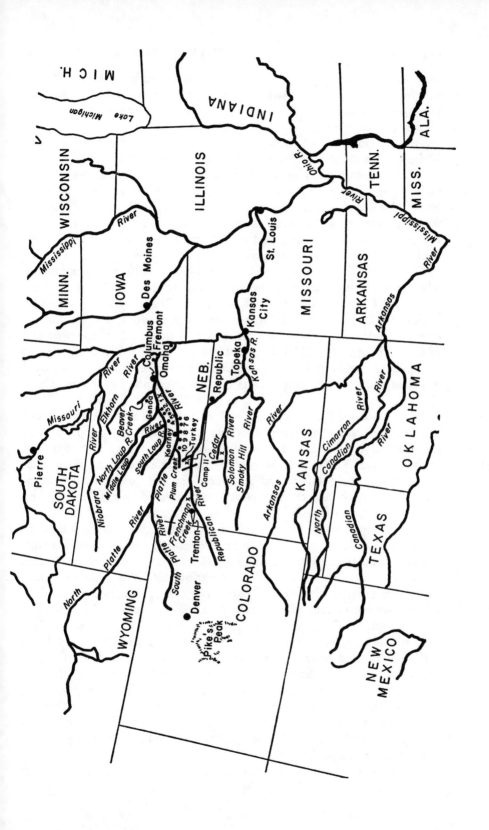

ward to the hunting grounds on the Republican. Each of the bands had
its own well-known landmarks. As White Eagle was leading the four
bands on this hunt, they all had to follow the south bank of the Loup for
the first part of their journey in the Skidi tradition.

A major landmark of the trip was Grand Island in the Platte River.
There were a number of long, sandy islands in the Platte, some of them
covered with lush grass and grazing animals and with trees growing on
them. Grand Island is one of the largest of these (more than twice the
size of Manhattan Island). It is about 20 miles long and 5 or 6 miles wide,
with a narrow channel on the north and south sides between the island
and the mainland. On the island the United States had established Fort
Kearney, where there was also a trade center.

The trip to the hunting grounds was usually made in ten encampments.
The hunting camp, not uncommonly within sight of the migrating herd,
was called Camp 11. By the Skidi route traveling west along the south
bank of the Loup, they would make three camps beyond the first one and
arrive 32 miles out. This would put them just due north of the west end
of Grand Island over which they planned to cross the Platte. Because of
the sandhills between the Loup and the Platte, the crossing southward
was slow and they would make one camp between the two rivers (Camp
5).

Camp 6 was made on the south bank of the Platte and two miles westward of the place of crossing. This was done so that the camp could be
set up on high ground to avoid the mosquitoes and bugs that abounded
in the lowland. This was the stop they usually referred to as "Fort Kearney" because the chiefs would go over there and collect their government allotments while the line of march continued two miles west and
set up camp.

Continuing along the south bank of the Platte, they made four camps
"west of Fort Kearney," viz., camps 7, 8, 9, and 10. At Camp 10 they
reached another important landmark, Plum Creek, a small creek that
was a southern tributary of the Platte (near present Lexington, Nebraska).
Up to this point the individual hunters went out privately and got deer,
elk, or antelope to supply fresh meat for their own camps. While the line
was en route to Camp 6, a small group of independent hunters made a
long trip southward to the Republican to scout around and they killed
three buffalo and brought the meat to Camp 6. As the line of march
was moving toward Camp 10, the ablest hunters of all four bands went
out and surrounded a small herd of about twenty buffalo, bringing in the
meat to Camp 10. This group of hunters included all the chiefs, other administrative officials and prominent men. The meat they obtained was
widely distributed in the form of gifts and symbolized the fact that "the
chiefs feed the people buffalo meat."

The next stop was Camp 11 on the Republican. While the previous buffalo surround had been made exclusively by the elite, now while they were en route to Camp 11, every able-bodied hunter in the entire tribe would make a concerted attack on the herd. To guide the line of march overland from Camp 10 to Camp 11 took considerable skill. They left the Platte by following southeast and upstream along Plum Creek almost to its source, and then headed somewhat in the same direction overland to the head of another small stream, Turkey Creek, that flows due south into the Republican. They traveled southward along the west bank of Turkey Creek, and the line of march halted about midway and combined all the baggage they could so as to free as many horses as possible for the hunters. The line of march proceeded to the confluence of Turkey Creek and the Republican, where they set up Camp 11 in preparation for the arrival of the hunters with the meat and hides. They would remain there for some days as they would have a great quantity of meat and hides to process. This was about the end of July. The place is west of the present town of Naponee, Nebraska. Four mass forays would be made by all the bands in concert, after which the bands would separate and follow their own fortunes.

Officially, White Eagle was in charge of all the bands. However, he chose to make a number of diplomatic gestures in this connection. On two occasions he deferred his leadership of the hunt episode to chiefs of the other bands, with whom the Skidi had a special kind of political relationship. This was a relationship established through the calumet or peace pipe. The calumet was not so much a treaty-making symbol as an elaborate ceremonial through which interband and intertribal trade was carried on, the pipe, therefore, being a sign of peaceful intention and thus a safe-conduct pass through alien territory. In 1672, Marquette carried one down the Mississippi and was able to establish peaceful relations with all the tribes along the way. Other tribes agree that the ceremonial originated with the Pawnees. The ceremony was always carried on in terms of a visiting party bringing gifts. The visitors, who were called "fathers" by their hosts, brought with them dried vegetables, bowls, and cooking utensils; decorated clothing, and blankets; "jewelry" and ornamental objects; and—most valued of all—the highly decorated pipe stems that were symbolic of the male and female eagle. The visiting party might number a hundred or more. An earth lodge was set aside by the hosts for the ceremonial and for the leaders of the party. The rest of the visitors had brought their own tents and camping equipment as well as all the food supplies and utensils that they would need. It took almost a year for a man to initiate such an enterprise. In the party were always included a chief, a priest, and a doctor. The hosts who received the party were called "Children" by the visitors, who assisted the hosts with their planting and other work so that they would be free to attend the ceremonies. When the ceremony was over, the guests, in addition to the gifts, left all their equipment behind, and also the two sacred pipes. The "Children" on their own account gave their parting "Fathers" a large number of horses they had elaborately decorated for the occasion. In the past they had given quantities of dried buffalo meat. Only people of some prominence and wealth could participate in these operations. At this time the Skidi Band were the "Children" of the Begging-for-Meat Band, while the Skidi were "Fathers" to the Man-Going-Downstream Band having recently paid them a trading visit. In view of the mutual courtesies involved, for the Chiefs' Hunt and the first major hunt episode, White Eagle deferred his leadership to his "father," Man Chief of the Begging-for-Meat Band. The fourth episode he placed in charge of his "child" Many Trophies, chief of the Man-Going-Downstream Band.

They stayed north of the Republican River for the first two mass attacks on the herd. By this time the herd on the north side was pretty well scattered, and the hunters had to cross over the river for the attack and bring the meat back over the water into camp. For the fourth mass attack on the herd, under the leadership of Many Trophies of Man-Going-Downstream Band, they moved their camping location from Camp 11 to a place on the Solomon River to the south, a branch of the Kansas. This was a site preferred by the Man-Going-Downstream Band. It was a difficult overland journey for which they had to carry water with them. They would finally locate a small south-flowing stream, the Cedar, which led them directly to the Solomon. They made their camp in the angle where the Cedar joined the Solomon, hunting the herd further up the river. When the bands parted, they mainly went to separate locations further to the west along the Republican as the herds in the more eastern location would have been scattered. This territory in the west was dangerous as the nomadic tribes, Sioux, Cheyennes, Comanches, and others were constantly poised to attack for what they considered to be an encroachment on their hunting grounds. In 1873 the Sioux attacked the Pawnees while they were on such a venture, butchering their kill in a canyon near Trenton, Nebraska. The death toll was so severe that this event tipped the balance in their decision to leave their traditional territory and migrate to Oklahoma.

On the way out and the way back from the buffalo hunting territory they moved their camp in fairly regular succession one day after another. But sometimes it rained and they had to remain where they were for several days, or they might be delayed by the sickness of a prominent man. Rain, of course, was an inevitable factor. It could delay the camp for several days. If they were caught in a rain while on the march, everyone had to spread his things out to dry and this operation might require the next day or even two before they could resume their journey. Tanned hide becomes hard and has to be tanned again with grease and rubbing after it gets wet. If the tent cover was folded when wet it would get moldy. The sinew bowstring also would be ineffective when wet. Rain had very serious consequences when they had sliced a quantity of buffalo meat and were drying it on the rack. If it should be wet by a sudden storm, the meat throughout the encampment would be spoiled. There was nothing that could be done with this meat. If one tried to eat it, it tasted like dead wood. It fell to pieces in one's hands. Even if one tried to cure it over a fire, it simply rotted. Meat once exposed to rain, even after it had been cooked, became moldy next day. A rack of meat that had been rained on was called *kariks-kutu*, "rack-dead, spoiled." The meat had to be thrown away.

Accommodation and adjustment to rainy weather was therefore very important and a nice distinction had to be made between the problem of delay and the risks involved.

One day word was sent to White Eagle that an important man of the Man-Going-Downstream Band was so ill that he could not go on. White Eagle had to consider very carefully whether they would go ahead and leave him or delay the entire group. A day's delay might mean the difference between reaching the full herd on time or finding only stragglers left after the herd had passed. Considering, however, that the Man-Going-Downstream Band was in a "Child" relation in the Peace Pipe ritual to the Skidi and was in the process of giving them a return gift of horses, White Eagle diplomatically decided to delay the march so that the sick man could be treated by a doctor. It was also felt that if inter-band relationships were not solidified from time to time, one or the other of the South Bands might conceivably be induced to collaborate with the Sioux on some occasion. Then everyone would consider that White Eagle had failed in his administrative functions and in his diplomacy. The death of an influential man in another band would also be the occasion for delay until after the funeral. If the wife of a prominent man were about to give birth, the whole family of this tent and a doctor would stay behind and wait, and White Eagle would assign one of his principle braves to see that things were all right with "their Child" (in terms of the calumet), while the rest of the camp moved on. In the case of an expected birth to one of the wives of White Eagle himself, he would request Eagle Chief to lead on and say, "My wife is going to be sick." But Eagle Chief would refuse to go ahead saying, "I might spoil your luck. We can go on when she's well again." Ordinarily a woman would have to go aside while traveling and have her child in the open aside from the line of march. Also, in the case of death, the own family would usually stay behind and bury the person, then come on and join the rest. After a day's delay, everyone would be glad to be moving along.

19

COMMON CAMPING ROUTINES

Description of Camping Routines—Starting the
Day—Breakfast—Loading the Horses—Striking
the Tent—the Camp Crier—Entertainment

THE ROUTINE OF CAMPING and decamping followed the same pattern throughout the summer. Advance scouts left the encampment about four in the morning to survey the route and to protect the old women who preceded the line of march in order to be sure to keep up with the group. As dawn was breaking, everyone had had breakfast and was under way. The families of the chiefs got up earliest in order to lead the line of march.

In Victory Call's camp, Grandma got up before anyone else—she made a low fire and put the bucket of corn to warm up on the glowing embers. Then she brought in an armful of wood and put it down next to the fireplace and went to the creek to get a bucket of water.

Now Horse Rider would begin to grunt and growl and say, "It's morning now," so that everyone would get up. The horses were hobbled and picketed around the encampment; he got into his moccasins, picked up his lariat, and went off to tend to them. He watered them since he wouldn't have a chance after breakfast, bringing them close to the tent and hobbling them there so that they would be ready for loading.

By the time the old lady was coming with the bucket of water, White Woman had gotten up, washed her hands and face, and begun to prepare breakfast.

Now Victory Call arose, went out, and looked at the sky to see if there were clouds far out over the hills. He came in and took a little basin of water and washed his hands and face, drying them on the hairy part of a buffalo robe—the leg and arm parts, and then shaking off the water. Some men went to the creek to wash, gargled with some water, and blew it out. While doing this, one had to face west toward the Evening

Star. If during the night one had dreamed a bad dream, one might swallow a great deal of water and regurgitate it before eating.

White Woman was making the grease bread and No Corn was making the coffee. During these preparations, Victory Call sat by smoking his pipe.

By the time Horse Rider was through bringing in the horses, breakfast was ready. After they had all eaten, the women cleaned the dishes, using the plant known as water string or "false indigo" (*Amorpha fruticosa*, Gilmore, p. 93) to rub on the dishes and buckets to sweeten them while washing. This plant grew close to the creeks with its roots in the water; the leaves and stems were used and the roots discarded. In winter, strips of the bark were taken from the dry stalks. False indigo was invaluable, particularly on the march; you might find nothing but boggy water in a depression and the plant would freshen it. It could also be used to make palatable meat that had a gamey flavor like wildcat, by boiling it in two waters with the plant and pouring off the water each time, after which it could be cooked in the ordinary way and tasted good. The plant was spread on the ground while butchering to keep the pieces of meat clean.

The dishes having been cleaned, they were ready to dismantle the camp and load the horses. Two or three old ladies were waiting nearby for Grandma to join them. They would set out at once to get an early start, carrying a little ration of pounded up sweet corn and sugar to sustain them on the way.

As soon as they had eaten, the two men saddled up the horses while White Woman prepared to dismantle the tent. She shook the tent pegs loose and pulled them out, then began to fold over the tent cover while it was still on the frame, first pulling one side around to the back and folding it over and then the other side; pulling down the "backbone" pole with folded cover on it, she untied the stick where it was attached at the top and bottom and put it aside. The tent skin was then folded down the middle lengthwise and evenly rolled from the bottom end toward the top, then tied around the middle with the string that was there for the purpose (see Figure 19-1). Additional ropes were used to tie the roll securely across the ends. Now White Woman dismantled the wooden frame, and the poles were divided evenly so that they could be tied to the horse's back in two even bunches.

Only the oblong rawhide containers were now left standing, as they had been placed next to the back wall of the tent. Meanwhile No Corn had been rolling up the bulrush mats that were on the ground and tying them in the middle with the strings that were provided there. She was also rolling up the blankets.

Now that everything had been dismantled in the camp, the next job was loading up. The horse was brought around close to where the containers were. Horse Rider and No Corn stood on one side and Victory Call and White Woman on the other. While the women held up the containers, the men tied them on. Now everything was loaded and they could join the line of march.

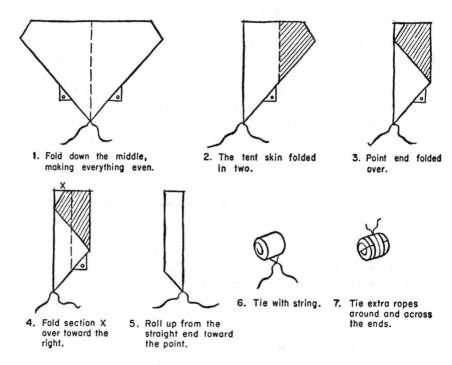

1. Fold down the middle, making everything even.

2. The tent skin folded in two.

3. Point end folded over.

4. Fold section X over toward the right.

5. Roll up from the straight end toward the point.

6. Tie with string.

7. Tie extra ropes around and across the ends.

FIGURE 19-1. The method of folding the tent skin.

Every morning the crier would go through the camps to repeat the instructions he had called out the night before. He would tell how far they were going and where they expected to camp. Until after Camp 9, individual hunters would ride off from the line of march as soon as their families were packed up and go hunting by themselves to get some fresh meat. While they were out, the group would have arrived at the designated camping place and set up camp, to which the hunters would come with their kill, usually in the late afternoon.

In the evening each hunter entertained his own friends at a feast with the meat he had gotten that day. This was parallel to the household routine for the man in the villages. The administrative procedures were also similar to those in the settlements. The chiefs of each of the bands more or less kept open house, and every evening there was an informal council where notable happenings of the day were recounted. The official braves, who policed the villages on behalf of their respective chiefs, now performed the same service while they were on the march.

20

HUNTING THE FIRST BUFFALO

AND BUTCHERING IT

*Five Scouts Decide to Hunt the First Buffalo—
They Ask and Receive Permission for This Hunt
—Description of Hunt—Butchering the Buffalo—
Return to Camp*

WHEN THEY REACHED the fourth encampment, White Eagle began to be very worried. His hunters were bringing in nothing but deer, elk, and antelope. Not a single buffalo had been sighted. They were now 32 miles west of the rendezvous camp, having traveled an extra two miles beyond the customary ten that day. This placed them in the position for leaving the Loup and traveling southward toward the Platte. The difficulty of crossing the sand hills made it necessary to set up Camp 5, at a halfway point, before completing the journey south to the Platte.

That night the crier went through the camp to notify them of their itinerary for the next day. Since the camp was none too comfortable, they would get up especially early and proceed southward to the Platte, cross over to Grand Island, and proceed two miles west on the south bank, where they would make Camp 6 or Fort Kearney camp on some high ground—much better than the boggy camp they were now occupying.

In the Skidi encampment, five scouts made up their minds they would get up well before dawn the next morning and ride 12 miles south to the Republican to find out for themselves whether there were any signs of buffalo there. The leader of the group was Roaming Leader of Village-in-the-Bottomlands. This expedition would be of material assistance to White Eagle, who was much concerned about their failure to find buffalo so far. White Eagle, a subchief of Pumpkin-Vine Village, was "married into" Bottomlands Village, and his in-laws gave him substantial assistance throughout the hunt.

In Camp 5 that night, when the crier was calling out their next day's itinerary, Roaming Leader was on his way to hobble his horses when he met his friend Running Scout. He said, "I have it in mind that we could go far south to the Republican river to see if there are some buffalo there. This time of year the bulls always stand over there. What do you think?"

"That's just what I've been thinking about. I'd certainly like to do something like that."

"I've got to hobble my horses right now," said Roaming Leader, "but if you see Mad Bear, tell him to come to my tent and we'll talk it over— also New Young Dog and Wants-the-Enemy. About sundown, you people must come to my tent."

These five men had grown up as a group of friends since they were boys. They used to meet when they took the horses to pasture while they were very young. Some of these groups would break up after marriage, if a man's wife tended to disapprove or if he was jealous and afraid that his friends might try to share his wife's sexual favors. But in this case the group had stuck together and had many adventures together. Roaming Leader, between forty and fifty years old, was the leader of the group and tended to take the initiative. At this time they came to his tent for supper where his wife had prepared a meal of corn, bread, and coffee. After the meal, Roaming Leader asked them to wait while he went to see White Eagle to ask his permission for their expedition. After his return they would continue with their plans.

When Roaming Leader arrived at White Eagle's tent, he found that the errand man of the Little-Earth-Lodge Band was also there. He had come on the same errand, as there was a group of men in each of the other three bands that wanted to go south next morning and try their luck at locating the buffalo. After some discussion, White Eagle granted permission, and they talked about how they would coordinate the activities of these four scouting parties. It was planned that they were to fan out in different directions so that they could make a survey of the country and they would get some idea of where the herds might be. Each party had a different assignment.

After the Little-Earth-Lodge Band envoy had left, White Eagle inquired of Roaming Leader who would be in his party. When he mentioned who they were, White Eagle commented that they were a good bunch. He wished him good luck and said, "Don't forget the *kawis*." This was a sort of sausage they made by washing the intestine and turning it inside out and putting a long piece of buffalo meat inside with a little water and tying it at both ends. The *kawis* could then be boiled in water or, if the hunter were alone, broiled over the fire. It was a favorite delicacy that could only be made of fresh intestine and White Eagle's remark was a reminder for Roaming Leader to be sure to bring the intestines home.

When Roaming Leader rejoined his friends in his tent, they continued their planning in the light of what White Eagle had said. Their assignment was to go toward the southwest. New Young Dog said, "That's a good place to go. It's hilly there. Last year about this time we saw three or four buffalo over there." Roaming Leader reminded them to hobble their horses next to the tent so that they could get an early start; he told them to meet at his place so that they could leave together. He also said they should plan to leave very early so that no one would try to follow along and join the party.

Roaming Leader was the first to awaken next morning, then New Young Dog, who was so anxious to get off that he had hardly slept. After that Mad Bear came, half running, and then the other two, who were a bit slower.

It was still somewhat dark when they left, but they had a long way to go—five or six miles to the Platte, and then the crossing. When they got to the crossing place, the scouts from the other bands were also there. They greeted one another, and after they had crossed over, each scout announced the direction his band was traveling.

If any of the parties saw the buffalo massed together, this was a sign that the Cheyenne and Arapaho must be lurking around somewhere near the Platte. They would keep right on until they saw two or three bison or buffalo standing alone, with no others to be seen anywhere around as far as the eye could see. Then they knew it was safe to hunt them.

There were five scouts in Roaming Leader's party and three buffalo to be attacked. All five could not chase the three buffalo at once, so they split up into two groups of three and two respectively. The three bison stood next to a pond. The men were on a little hill and they approached cautiously, going down into a trough where they would be concealed. Then they removed their saddles and rode out bareback. The party of three would chase two of the bison and the party of two, the third one. The man on the fastest horse headed off the two bison and led them to the place where they had left their saddles. "Hurry up, hurry up and try to shoot," he called to the other two men. The other party of two would head off the third bison and try to kill it.

Now they were in a hurry to butcher. It was a hard trip back over the sand hills, especially with the horses loaded, and they wanted to reach the encampment before dark. For the butchering, the five men divided into three parties—two each for two of the buffalo, and one man to butcher the third buffalo by himself.

The procedure in butchering a bison was different from that of butchering a cow in the way the hide was removed. The cow was placed on her back and the whole skin removed from the belly out. The bison hide was heavy and they placed him on his belly and removed the hide in two sections, dividing it along the backbone and making two skins out of it. After they had made a cut along the backbone and divided the robe in two, they would flap open the cut edges and split the hide down the forelegs and hind legs to get the two halves off.

The next step was to remove the meat. This was the same for both bull and cow. They removed the meat first from one side and then from the other. The carcass was turned over on its side and the long piece of meat that lay along the backbone was cut loose and turned aside. Then the flank over the ribs and forelegs was flapped back. Now the foreleg could be removed and the lower portion with the hoof on it discarded. This part would find use as a hammer. The most important meat was the long steak extending all the way down the length of the backbone. Its name, *kis-satsu*, "bone-lying against," was also the generic name for meat, *kisatski*, the *-ki* being a diminutive, i.e., "small meat." The long steak was the ideal part for thinning and drying as it could be cut into a long continuous sheet. It contained important sinews that were removed before slicing.

When the meat had been removed from one side, the carcass was turned over onto the other. Although the meat had been removed from the underside, the carcass was held up off the ground by the fact that the paunch was still inflated. They decided that in butchering this side, they would leave intact a large slab of meat that was ordinarily considered to be two parts, one covering the windpipe, and the other the part that lies below it, the *awahu*, the "spread out." This was a large, very fatty slab of meat. After the backbone steak, the flank, and the foreleg had been removed, they would take off this piece. This fatty layer was needed since in storing the thinned-out dried meat, they would alternate each thin layer of meat with a layer of dried fat.

Now they had to clean the internal organs; the paunch, liver, lungs, and intestines. If they had no water for cleaning the paunch, they simply shook it out. When they took care of the entrails, they also removed the tongue and brains. To get the brains from the braincase, they used the hind leg with the hoof on it as a hammer and broke off the skull cap just below the brow ridge, taking the brains out of the cover or membrane. In order to determine the best place to aim the blow, they had first to take off the scalp lock.

After all the meat had been removed from the bones, they had to get the ribs, which were a main delicacy for cooking and eating right away. Most of the rest of the meat was dried and preserved. The ribs were consumed mainly by the men in their feasts. To crack the ribs off the backbone, they lay the carcass on its side and cut up the front where the cartilage was with a knife. Then they used the discarded foot with the hoof on it as their hammer and struck along the ribs where the rib bones were jointed at the back. They made two slits between the ribs to get a good fingerhold and pulled the ribs so that the bones cracked at their joints near the back. They turned the carcass over and removed the ribs from the other side in the same way. Then they removed the collarbone and first rib.

This whole process was accomplished with a single knife. As far back as 1540, Casteñeda gives an almost identical description of butchering with a flint. "They cut the hide open at the back," he writes, "and pull it off at the joints, using a flint as large as a finger, tied in a little stick, with as much ease as if working with a good iron tool. They give it an edge with their own teeth. The quickness with which they do this is something worth seeing and noting."

The butchering completed, there was a pile of meat; it remained to portion it out among them. The initiative in this distribution belonged entirely to the man who had actually killed the animal. Legally the animal belonged to him. However, it was the custom to give half of the meat to any who had been present at the kill and helped with the butchering. A generous man—in Pawnee terms, "a good man"—would give something to a person who arrived after the killing but helped with the butchering. Late arrivals could expect no such courtesy. The rule also held in this case. The bison was readily divided in two, including the skin, with two doing the butchering. If three had butchered, "the nonkillers" would have had to divide the half between them. Such a quarter bison skin could be used for moccasin soles or a small rawhide envelope-shaped container. Out of an undivided half skin of the bison, a robe might be made, or a water package. This was a skin folded like an envelope with sticks fastened underneath to be used to float things across the stream in high water.

After the butchering and distribution, the horses were packed with the meat so that they could return to camp. In order to load, they saddled the horses and put the meat on top; the skin, which had been too slippery, had been allowed to dry somewhat and was now put across the saddle, hair side down, with the flaps hanging down on both sides of the horse. The long backbone steaks were placed on top of the hide, and upon this the flank meat from over the ribs and forelegs. In order to balance the load on both sides of the horse, the thighs were cut across in two, each threaded with an eyeletted piece of rawhide drawn through a hole in the meat and tied to the back of the horse so that they hung down against the sides. Each rib cage was tied in a similar way with a string through it so that it hung down on each side toward the rear. The sharp edges were up so that they did not cut the sides of the horse. The brains were tied inside the rib cage to protect them. The other entrails were tied together with a rope and placed on top and tied near the back. A person taking a whole buffalo by himself couldn't take the backbone but could take the back of the neck. He had to leave "the hips and backbone" behind. Everything now being in place on the horse, the skin was folded over to make a cover. First the back half was folded forward toward the front and then the front half folded backward and lapped over it. It was possible to ride on top of such a package, as was necessary whenever they had a considerable distance to go. A man who had not received a hide had to use his saddle blanket in the same way. Entrails and paunch were always tied near the back so that they would not get in the way.

The five hunters now set out for Camp 6, the Fort Kearney encampment on the south bank of the Platte. They rode in close formation, the leader in front, with one man on each side of him and two in the rear. As they rode they would look around to see if they could sight any more buffalo so that they could make their report when they got to camp.

21

CROSSING THE RIVER AND
THE RETURN OF THE HUNTERS

〰〰〰〰〰〰〰〰〰〰〰〰〰〰〰

*Crossing the Railroad and the Platte River—
Hunters Arrive at the New Encampment—Leader
of Hunt Gives Thanks for Buffalo*

〰〰〰〰〰〰〰〰〰〰〰〰〰〰〰

WHILE THE FIVE SCOUTS were off hunting the buffalo, the people broke their fifth encampment among the sand hills between the Loup and the Platte and started south. As they were taking down their tents, the people noticed that these men were absent. Realizing what they had gone for, the people would give their wives a hand in packing up, offering to help by taking some of their baggage for them. They would say, "You can't keep those men home. They're always off somewhere— that whole bunch!"

The line of march was usually in four parallel columns, the chiefs of each of the bands in the lead ranged from west to east—westernmost, the Skidi, then Little-Earth-Lodge Band, then Meat-Beggars, and Man-Going-Downstream furthest eastward. When they had gotten about three miles out, someone would yell, "Oh, my, we've got to cross the railroad!" This was a great nuisance as there was an embankment and ties and sometimes a freight train or a passenger train would be coming. They called the freight train *mule*, "long ears," and a passenger train, "These-Chiefs-Traveling," referring to the fact that each passenger was so wealthy that they were all chiefs.

Three miles more and they arrived at the Platte. As the first group got there the word would go down the line, "The water isn't high. The sand bottom is hard." "That's good," everyone said, for it meant that the crossing would be easy. Sometimes they got to the bank and found there was deep water in the river. It was seldom deeper than a man's knee or thigh, but if it were chest-high they could not cross, as the pack-

187

ages tied to the sides of the horses would get wet. Then the question was, "Was the water on the rise, or was it going down?" People said if it were warm on Pike's Peak in the Rockies, the water level would soon be low. In order to find out whether the river was rising or subsiding, the women would set up a stick in it; if the river was rising, it would soon be covered over, or vice versa if falling. They also knew that if the river was muddy soon after getting a bucket of clear water, it was rising. The men, on the other hand, were inclined to be more impulsive and didn't bother with such observations; they simply forded the river. If the river was rising, they would have to change their plan and continue west along the north bank of the Platte until it subsided. This time they were able to cross directly. The crossing was over the western end of Grand Island, the largest of the "sand-bar islands" in the Platte. In winter it was a good place to camp, but in summer it was full of mosquitoes. Grandma would have arrived long ago and gone onto the island to pick plums and grapes. The channel is wider and shallower on the north side of the island and deeper and narrower on the south side. The island itself is five or six miles wide.

When they were ready to cross, some young men volunteers who were from eighteen to twenty years old would go ahead and stake out the path with willow sticks to show where the deep holes were. If there was a steep sand bank on either side, they would chop at it with a buffalo shoulder blade and kick it down so that there would be a sloping path for the horses. Sometimes on the return journey in August the river bed would be dry, and in this way they came to know the best way to ford the river. A group of young men of this sort would volunteer for all sorts of services, including picket duty. They always carried their bows and arrows and were constantly on the alert to see if the enemy were coming on the warpath. Sometimes as the years passed, they would continue in this way, remaining as a group even after they had become mature men. Such a group was that of Roaming Leader and his friends who had gone out on the buffalo-scouting expedition that day.

When the line of march finally got across the river, they climbed ashore and up the first bank which was relatively steep and then the second bank that had a more gentle slope. They continued west along the high bank for about two miles until they came to the place where they planned to camp.

By about four or four-thirty in the afternoon they were all encamped. A man was out taking care of his horses, and as he looked onto the horizon he happened to sight Roaming Leader and his party, silhouetted against the sky, coming over some sand hills about two miles off. From their outline against the sky, he could see that the horses were all bulging out with meat and the legs of the riders were sticking far out as they sat on top of the packs. As they rode he could also see the hides swinging back and forth a bit. He was a considerable distance from the camp and he called to someone who was within closer shouting distance that he had seen them, and that the scouts had had a successful hunt and would soon be there. The message was relayed to the camp and everyone heard about it and was on the alert. Finally, as they got nearer, people began to see them, and someone called out to the wives of the men, "They're coming, bringing meat!" Excitement ran high, for this was the first fresh buffalo meat of the year. Chief White Eagle saw them too and he said a heartfelt "Thanks to the Great Powers!" For as leader of the hunt, he was held most of all responsible for it.

22

THE RETURN OF THE HUNTERS

AND THE BANQUETS

OF BUFFALO MEAT

Meat Is Cooked—Account of Hunt Given—
Hunters' Families Entertain—Conversation during
the Meal—Other Hunting Expeditions Formed—
Family Relationships

As THE FIVE HUNTERS came in, each of their families began to prepare for the family meal and the feast that would follow in their respective camps. In each case, a brother or a brother-in-law was waiting at the hunter's tent to take care of his horse. As the hunter dismounted, he took off his quiver and bow sack from his back and handed it to his wife, asking her to bring out a skin spread for the meat. The brother who had come to help came out of the tent and put the meat on the spread, took off the saddle, and took the horse to water. The hunter said to his brother, "When you water it, wash the blood off his sides." The brother went off to tend the horse and hobbled it in the place where the hunter was accustomed to keeping it. The hunter had gone inside the tent where he sat down to rest and smoke while his wife began to cook for him.

Roaming Leader, because he was leader of the expedition, had been given the heart and tongue by the man who had had charge of cleaning the entrails. Now his wife was cooking them for their meal. The tongue was first put in the coals until the rough outer covering had blistered off. When it was puffed up, the covering came off easily and the tongue was then boiled. This made good soup and the tongue itself was "smooth eating." To prepare the heart, it was first cut around the rim and the outer skin carefully peeled off so as not to tear it. This little sack could

190

be used for water or dried as a tobacco container when they went on a Peace Pipe expedition.

While the cooking of the meal was in process, the brother returned from tending the horse and Roaming Leader motioned him to sit down at his left. The place at his right was reserved for his wife. Roaming Leader was sitting on the north side. He told his brother how far they had had to go in order to get the bison, how fast the horse was, and other details of the chase—of how three of them had chased two of the bison and the other two, the third animal—of how they butchered and divided up the meat and who got which pieces.

Before he had quite finished with his account, his wife announced that she was through with the cooking. He had to interrupt his story, as they must eat at once because the buffalo meat was still lying outside on the spread. His wife's mother, Lady Lucky Leader, had come in meanwhile and her son, Dog-Sitting-at-the-West (also known as Frank Leader), and they joined the family for dinner. The tongue would have been adequate to feed the three of them, but with five they also needed to use the heart. Each one received a small piece of each kind of meat. The Pawnees believed that the first meat of the season should be cooked rare so that the digestive system could become accustomed to it. Roaming Leader remarked this to his wife, "Cook it a little rare. Don't overcook it—it's easier to digest that way." The meat was cut into long thin strips at this time so that it would boil quickly.

As soon as they were through eating, Lady Lucky Leader went outside to tend to the meat. She gave some to the Meat-Askers and at Roaming Leader's instruction, prepared half of the backbone steak as a gift for White Eagle. First she removed the sinews and cut the steak in two. Since her daughter was busy with the dishes, she carried it to White Eagle's tent herself. As she approached, an old lady from White Eagle's tent noticed her coming and came out to meet her. She said, "I'm bringing meat," and the old lady replied, "Oh, thank you, thank you." As she handed over the meat she said, "Oh, they got three of them—three bison." As White Eagle's mother-in-law entered the tent she told him the news. "They found three bison so and so far." "That's all right!" he said. Some of the meat was cut into long strips and boiled right away, White Eagle making the usual remark about cooking it rare, and the rest of the steak was sliced up by the old lady preparatory to making it into dried meat for storage.

After the families of each of the hunters had eaten their meal, they would prepare for their several banquets. Each of the five invited friends and prominent people from his own village—Mad Bear from Pumpkin-Vine, Running Scout from Village-Lying-across-a-Ridge, and Roaming Leader from his own Village-in-the-Bottomlands. New Young

Dog was a Pumpkin-Vine man, but under the circumstances, since this village was already invited by one of the hunters, he invited people from the fourth Skidi village, Wolf-Standing-in-Water. The fifth hunter, Wants-the-Enemy, chose other personalities that he felt should be included in the feasting. Each guest would take some of the meat home after the banquet for his family and friends, and in this way a great many people in the encampment shared in the first buffalo meat of the season.

Roaming Leader, who was entertaining the prominent people of his own Village-in-the-Bottomlands, had as his guest of honor White Eagle, who had married into their village. He was given the seat of honor at the northwest. In the southwest seat sat Comanche Chief, an outstanding chief of Bottomlands Village, and a man somewhat older than White Eagle. Next to White Eagle on the north side was the head brave of Bottomlands Village, Strikes-the-Enemy, and beyond him, Horse Thief, a man prominent in the Peace Pipe Ceremony and an outstanding warrior. Along the south side next to Comanche Chief sat Dog-Sitting-at-the-West, who was Roaming Leader's brother-in-law, and another man well known for his bravery.

In his opening speech the host, Roaming Leader, said, "White Eagle, Comanche Chief, Horse Thief, my brother-in-law here, and . . . (citing each one). Here we have something to eat. I wanted to have you people with me. I give you this little food that I have; it is yours. We're just going to eat." After this first speech, everyone remained silent for about five minutes, thinking that White Eagle, as leader of the hunt, would speak. White Eagle for his part was sitting with head bowed in deference to Comanche Chief, as an older man, hoping he would take the cue and speak first. He also felt that Comanche Chief as head of the host village should take the lead. Finally, since he was his kin, he simply leaned over and remarked, "I want you to hurry and speak so that we can eat our food." "All right," said Comanche Chief, "I was waiting for you." Now he mentioned them all by name, first along the north side, then on the south and especially the host and his wife. "You have been cooking and your hands and face must be hot. You have been doing the cooking for us." To Roaming Leader he said, "This is not the first time you have done this—given feasts to our different groups of people. You got up early in the morning to go out and look for some buffalo and now you have accomplished it. I know how it is. The horse is tired from chasing the buffalo and after that, the hardest thing is to do the butchering. And you have done this for me. Now here is the food before me and here are these fellows. This is what White Eagle wants and so far White Eagle has had good luck in leading us. I don't want to talk too long as someone else might want to say something."

White Eagle had been waiting for him to say this and as Comanche Chief turned to him he said, "That's what I wanted. Thank you for your talk, Comanche Chief. You have helped me a lot. I wanted someone of ex-perience to talk to Roaming Leader as you did. I could not have done anything by myself. Only if Heaven is willing can we have good luck. The other four hunters are sitting and feasting as we are. I can hardly speak for I am so filled with joy. My food is right here and I am going to eat these ribs here, and I thank your wife for doing the cooking. That's all I want to say." Comanche Chief had an idea that his brave, Strikes-the-Enemy, might want to make a few remarks and he nudged him to get on with it. Finally Comanche Chief concluded the predinner speeches and asked one of the men from his own village to serve. The old lady, Roaming Leader's mother-in-law, had gone outside to tend to the meat that was lying there and after the guests had received theirs, and the host and his wife had their portions, meat was carried outside for her.

During the meal, pleasant conversation was always the order of the day. Stories were told and the events of the hunt recounted again in detail. Then Comanche Chief made the closing speech, again men-tioning them all by name and thanking the host and his wife. "As you and your wife intended, we have now partaken of this feast. White Eagle has spoken and good luck may come to you. Now we have eaten. Now we are going to go." As they got up to leave, Roaming Leader's wife made a bantering remark to one of the men to whom she had a kin re-lationship for which relaxed behavior was appropriate. She said, "What's your hurry? Maybe you're in a hurry to go gambling." "No, I forgot to hobble my horses. They're just about to go back to the last camp where we came from." Roaming Leader told them to leave the rib bones right in their places and his wife would tend to that. As they filed out, each one stopped before Roaming Leader and said, "Thank you for hav-ing us to dinner."

This degree of formality was by no means the general rule among the less status-conscious members of the tribe. After this episode, any of the hunters who chose to could go out without special permission from White Eagle. A man who had a gun was likely to go by himself, while those with bows and arrows would go in small groups. They hoped to find a stray buffalo or perhaps an antelope that had strayed from the herds that were gathered on the plains like sheep. Young men twenty-eight to thirty years old would be inclined to go together on such in-formal expeditions. Very much like young white men who say, "Let's go fishing," they would just go for the sport, and they would sit around the fire and eat up whatever they had caught. Sometimes an older man would feel in the same spirit and he would join in with them. "Never mind about the chiefs and big fellows," they would say, "they won't invite us. Let's eat." Then they would hold a mock feast and say, "I'll eat like Comanche Chief." "And I'll eat like War Cry." "Here's your meat,

Comanche Chief. Here War Cry, here's yours. Here Eagle Chief, here's your meat!"

Sometimes this group of happy-go-lucky young men were unable to get anything and then they would curse one another saying, "Why do we have bad luck? It must be because of you!" One man called *Rawihu'u*, "The Go-Getter," which also means "Warpath," was their favorite scapegoat. It seemed as if he always did something at the wrong time to spoil things. As a man was about to shoot a buffalo, he would look over the man's shoulder and the buffalo would see him moving and run away. Once when they were stalking a deer, approaching on their bellies, Warpath coughed at the crucial moment and the deer ran off. One of the men said, "I wish I could shoot you." "I couldn't help it. I had to cough. My throat was dry," said Warpath.

Some men went after antelope and took the meat home to their families. They would call in three or four of their more intimate friends to share it with them.

Such a man was Fearing-a-Bear, an able hunter and warrior, a mature man but a rough-and-ready type. He had little interest in social status and public affairs and when he was successful in his hunting he would say, "I'm tired. I think I'll just eat this up myself with my friends." He and his wife lived in a tent with his father, his sister, and her husband. Theoretically the brother-in-law should take care of them, but the brother-in-law in this case was from the Omaha tribe, and the father-in-law did not find it a very congenial arrangement. Relations between them were strained.

As they sat at dinner one night, as the host of the occasion, Fearing-a-Bear sat in the southeast position. Next to him sat his wife who was doing the cooking. On the other side of the entrance, in the northeast position, sat his father and beyond him on the north side the Omaha son-in-law. But the two women, Fearing-a-Bear's wife and his sister, were worried about this close proximity of the two hostile men and so the sister seated herself between her Omaha husband and her father. Ordinarily she would have sat at the east end beyond the two men. She had separated them, for trouble might arise, or the old man, being shaky, might accidentally spill some soup on his son-in-law and then there would be a flare-up. The adjustment they had made in seating arrangements, however, was very awkward for the hostess. She could not pass the food to the old man who was sitting on the end, as it was absolutely forbidden for a daughter-in-law to have any contact with her father-in-law. So she had to get up each time and give the food to her sister-in-law who was sitting between her Omaha husband and her father, in order to pass it to the men. Then the sister-in-law was in a dilemma. Should she serve her husband first or her father? Either way, she was bound to offend one or the other of them.

The other guests at Fearing-a-Bear's dinner all had somewhat distant kinship ties to him, but according to the logic of the Pawnee kin system they all called one another brother. They were seated in order of seniority. The hostess, sitting at the southeast, dished out the food for them, and her husband passed it to his neighbor on the left, stating who it was intended for, whereupon it would be passed along to the designated party. There were no speeches, and people were not obliged to wait for anybody else but could eat as soon as they were served. When they were through, if they were in a hurry they would just pick up the bread and meat that they had left over and go directly out, taking the leftover food to their wives and children. The manners of the common people were far simpler than those of the socially elite, or the socially ambitious, although the customary forms were similar.

As they continued on the move, pressures might build up between individuals because of the closeness of the living conditions in camp and the strain of constant migration. This was particularly true between father-in-law and son-in-law. Theoretically, it was the first duty of the son-in-law to serve his wife's family, but when his father-in-law was quite old, the son-in-law often felt put upon by the arrangement. Sometimes in the camp one could hear people calling out, "Fight, fight!" and father-in-law and son-in-law would be grappling with each other in a tent. People all came running and a roughneck in the crowd would call out, "Who's underneath?" Someone who was close to the tent would say, "Son-in-law." In general the crowd would approve and say, "That's good," the sentiment being with the underdog, the old father-in-law. Such a quarrel would be ended when a brave or other person of high social rank put a hand on each of the combatants and said, "I want you to stop." Out of respect for his rank and eminence, they would separate at once and go in different directions. Should they not respond it would be a major insult and he would say a second time, "Didn't you hear me?" This would certainly end the fight. Any person known to be sensitive and to dislike violence could perform this same good office. Violence of this kind within the village or band was considered a serious social malfunction and people made every attempt to avoid it or put a stop to it. The effort to anticipate and prevent such situations from arising can be seen in the efforts of the wife and sister of Fearing-a-Bear to keep a hostile father and son-in-law apart.

23

THE TENTH ENCAMPMENT

*Prominent Men Plan a Scouting Party—They Kill
a Small Herd of Buffalo—Holy Ritual in Connection with Hunt—Gifts of Meat Symbolic of
Chief's Promise to Get Meat*

AFTER WHITE EAGLE LEFT the feast at Roaming Leader's tent that evening, he called in the errand man, Know-His-Face, and sent him to Curly
Chief of the Kitkehaxki to announce the place of Camp 7 for the next
day, six or eight miles west of Fort Kearney. On the way they planned to
make a brief stop while the main chiefs and braves went over to the fort
on Grand Island to get the government provisions that had been assigned to them. Then they rejoined the line of march which continued
to the seventh camping place. At the fort, Eagle Chief and Lone Chief
represented the Skidi Band, Curly Chief, the Kitkehaxki, Man Chief, the
Tsawi, and Many Trophies, the Pitahawirata. When they rejoined their respective groups, they divided up the provisions they had received before
proceeding on their way.

Before they had left the villages, the chiefs in their ritual meeting had in
effect promised to lead the people and see that they had buffalo meat to eat.
They were literally now going to make good that promise. Every day
as the people were on the march, scouts had gone out well before dawn
to survey the country and see where the buffalo were. The scouts were
men drawn from the ranks of commoners who had little interest in social status or public prominence. As they were leaving for Camp 9, a
scouting party drawn from the upper ranks of the population, mainly
braves and prominent doctors, particularly from Village-in-the-Bottomlands into which White Eagle was married, went out to look for a small
herd of ten to twenty buffalo. The objective was that they would plan
their strategy so that they could surround and kill all of the small herd.
Only men with the fastest hunting horses could undertake this task—the

chiefs of the several bands. With them would go their braves and other prominent men of their bands who were sufficiently wealthy to own fast horses and could give them the assistance they needed.

The scouting party had been led by Stolen Horses, and when his party had sighted the small buffalo herd they were looking for they returned to camp and notified Brave Chief, White Eagle's brother-in-law, who in turn got in touch with White Eagle, telling him where and how the herd had been sighted. The next morning they would go after it, and everyone was on the alert for this news that evening. White Eagle called in Roaming Scout to ask him to direct the attack on the herd next day. He was to climb a hill and survey the position of the herd and motion his instructions to the hunters, who would be waiting below.

Now that all arrangements had been made, White Eagle sent out the official chief's errand man, Know-His-Face, to go through the camp, calling out the announcement and then to carry it to the other bands. He announced the following message: "They saw ten to twenty buffalo out there about twelve miles out. Tomorrow while we move the camp, let's try to chase those buffalo." Then after giving the location of their next encampment, he continued with his instructions for the hunters:

There by the schoolhouse—on the other side—on the northeast—there is a hill. You stop right there at this big hill, on this side of it where we'll all meet, and White Eagle will get there to meet us. All of you are to wait there, and one of us will go up on top of the hill to see if the herd is still in the same location as previously sighted or in what direction it has gone.

Early next morning Camp 9 broke up and the outstanding hunters from all the bands went to meet at the appointed place, while the line of march moved westward toward Camp 10, the last camp south of the Platte. There were fifteen to twenty hunters from each of the four bands, sixty to eighty in all. By contrast to the later hunt episodes, they were dressed in plain working clothes. For the formal hunt, they dressed in decorated leggings and they decorated their horses, but in this instance they all wore plain leggings and moccasins, a brief, simple loincloth, and for the horse a blanket to ride on and other equipment—a whetstone, a knife, and some rope—one of buffalo hide to bridle horses that were rough, and one of buffalo hair for those that were easier to handle. Some because of a special vision experience or exploit had a right to wear a red or white cloth about their heads, while others went bareheaded. Some were privileged to wear a skin shirt because of special war exploits. Some took their bow and quivers and others carried six-shooters. They brought no food, but would eat something raw after the kill. Meat was never eaten raw but they would eat the entrails—some raw liver, kidney, or tripe—

the lining of the second stomach well washed and eaten with some raw fat.

The people on the march tried to double up their goods in the morning in order to free the horses for the hunters. It was most desirable for the hunter to have two horses, one to ride and one to load with meat. If he had two horses, he would hobble his loading horse on the sidelines during the chase or leave it with a boy who had come along for the purpose.

When the hunters arrived, the small herd was to the south of the appointed hill. The scout Roaming Leader was on top, surveying the situation. The herd was a small one, gathered in a kind of trough or depression. The hunters were lined up on the north side of the hill, facing it, entirely out of sight and hearing of the herd which was on the other side. The hunters of the four bands had arranged themselves in the line from west to east, the several bands in the usual order with the Skidi westernmost and the Man-Going-Downstream furthest east. As the hunters on horseback sat facing the hill, a brave from each band rode back and forth in front of his group to keep them in order. They had to be controlled and kept in line while the strategy was determined and a ritual performed.

On top of the hill, having surveyed the country and its configuration, Roaming Leader had come to a decision as to their plan of attack. He descended the hill a short way down and signaled with his blanket to give the waiting hunters an idea of the position of the herd. If the buffalo were more to the east, Roaming Leader threw up his blanket and swung it over along the east horizon. Swinging it in the opposite direction along the west horizon meant the buffalo were further to the west and the main force of the attack should come from that direction. If the buffalo were straight ahead, he would throw his blanket straight up and release it, indicating that they could ride directly over the hill and need not approach by stealth from the sides, since the herd was in a hollow and could not see them coming. In this particular case, Roaming Leader had given an east signal. Now one chief from each band rode up to consult with Roaming Leader and he came down to meet them halfway. Roaming Leader said to White Eagle, "You saw me standing there throwing my blanket around the east side. There are about ten or twenty buffalo there and if they are approached cautiously by two parties, first one from the east and then one from the west, we may be able to surround them and get them all. If we are careful, some of the buffalo may still be sitting down and before they can get up, our hunters on horseback will be upon them." White Eagle then summed up what Roaming Leader had said and put it up to the four chiefs, which would go to the east and which to the west. He gave the first choice to Man Chief of the Meat-Beggars Band as a diplomatic gesture for the sake of their Peace

Pipe trade relations. As the east party would have a prior advantage, he was leaving it open for Man Chief to take it for his own group. "All right," said Man Chief, "I'll take a group around east," and Curly Chief of the Little-Earth-Lodge Band said, "I'll go with him." White Eagle then agreed to take a group by way of the west and Many Trophies of the Man-Going-Downstream Band agreed to go with him.

Having decided, the different chiefs motioned to their hunters waiting lined up below. In each case the individual hunters were free to join either party as they wished. The various hand motions made by the chiefs graphically indicated their plans. As each chief motioned, his brave went down to the hunters and again told them what the motions were about. The extra pack horses were hobbled right there and the boys taking care of them were nearby.

The next step was a ritual, performed by a holy man known as a "hand-waver," named for the manner in which he made his vow. White Eagle chose He-Sees-the-Sky because he had consecrated five or six buffalo to the sacred bundle ceremonies in the past and in general seemed to be lucky in whatever he did. He had established "credit" with the supernatural powers. Now he knelt down on both knees facing toward the hill with his back to the lineup of hunters. One of the men from the line was selected by White Eagle to keep watch on the holy man and signal them immediately when he was through. The watcher stood about ten feet back, leading his horse while the prophet was kneeling, settling himself comfortably with his open hands resting on his thighs. Now he extended his right arm and as he was moving it outward he said, "This time of year I sacrificed a whole white eagle and that is what is going to lead you (west)." Then he made a similar motion with his left hand and mentioned a wildcat hide and a whole buffalo and the fact that this would lead those going east. Then he repeated each direction with an Otter and Buffalo (west), and a young spotted deer and buffalo (east). The watcher, seeing the holy man's hands back in his lap and his head down, signaled that that was all and as soon as he turned around, the line formed into two parties, the watcher coming down to join them. The holy man started for home, being required to remain as quiet as possible so that nothing should disturb the good fortune of the hunters, for he would be blamed for any accidents that occurred. White Eagle or one of the successful hunters would see that he got half a buffalo for his service. The hunters rode to the chase from both sides of the hill so that the herd was surrounded and all were killed. Then they butchered and distributed the meat according to who had actually killed the animal and who had assisted with the butchering.

As soon as they were through butchering, they packed their horses and waited until they had a group of two of three so that they could travel together for protection from attack. The horses were lightly packed and everyone could ride home on top of the load. Gifts were generously sent by everyone, and everyone that had gone on the hunt got some meat. In their turn the hunters shared it so that every tent had some. The chiefs had fed the people as they had promised in their ritual.

The next move was to the Republican River and their main buffalo hunting grounds, where everyone would join in getting the meat.

24

CAMP 11—AT THE BUFFALO
HUNTING GROUNDS

*Camp Established—Formal Precision Necessary
for Hunt—Religious Considerations—the Council
Tent—Plan of Attack—Sympathetic Magic*

〰〰〰〰〰〰〰〰〰〰〰〰〰〰〰〰〰〰

AT THIS TIME OF YEAR the main buffalo herd was moving eastward down
the Republican River. When they had set up camp at the confluence of
Turkey Creek and the Republican, they would be within two miles of
the north bank and often within sight of the herd itself. The whole operation now took on a much more formal turn involving the whole encampment. At the council tent of each of the bands that night, a special group of military police was set up to make sure that no hunter went
out individually and disturbed the herd, and that absolute quiet was maintained in the camp itself among the women and children as well as the
men. Children must be soothed and prevented from crying, dogs muzzled and wood chopping done only when the herd was not within hearing distance. The individual hunter who violated these rules and went
among the herd was beaten over the head with a heavy club and sometimes severely injured. The attack upon the herd was their main objective and it had to be accomplished with precision, for they had to be
back at the villages by September first when the south star Canopus was
in the sky—the signal for the beginning of their harvest.

In addition to these practical considerations, there were religious factors that gave form to their operations. A large part of the preserved
meat, particularly the long steaks along the backbone of the buffalo,
would be pledged to the performance of their sacred ceremonies. Feasting on the meat was an essential phase of every important ceremony.
This was the food that Heaven had sent, and it was fitting that sharing it
in a feast should be part of their devotions. The creation story that was

often reviewed in these ceremonies told them how this had come about. The number four had a sacred significance in connection with the four semicardinal directions, and the combined hunt of all the bands together was conducted in four major episodes.

At the council tent in Camp 10, during their last evening on the Platte, White Eagle and the other Skidi chiefs planned out the strategy of this major phase of the hunt. The chiefs of the other three bands were also meeting in council. White Eagle as the leader of the hunt was to take the initiative. For diplomatic reasons he had decided to give over the management of the first hunt episode to Man Chief of the Asking-for-Meat Band, who were currently "Fathers" to the Skidi in the Peace Pipe trading relationship. Man Chief was formally notified and he appointed the necessary religious and technical personnel, including three scouts who would go out long before dawn to survey the country and locate the herd. Long before the camp broke up that morning they had gone out, and when they found the hill beyond which the herd was located the chief scout crawled up cautiously on his belly, imitating the motions of a wolf so that he would not be detected by the herd. As long ago as 1540 the account of Coronado's expedition reported that white wolves ranged all over the plains, living peaceably in the presence of the buffalo cows, so that the bulls as well as the herd as a whole were obviously well accustomed to having wolves nearby. They would not detect humans unless the scouts stood in the direction of the wind so that they could be scented. After the head scout had surveyed the situation to his satisfaction, he invited his fellow scouts to come up, each in turn crawling up like a wolf and taking a look around. In a war party one wrapped oneself in a whole wolfskin with bow and arrows concealed under the arms and tail, but a blanket was sufficient to fool the buffalo.

Meanwhile the people in camp had awakened, broken up camp, loaded up and set out across the country for Camp 11. Following along Plum Creek almost to its source, the line of march continued overland in a southeast direction until it reached the head of Turkey Creek, continuing southward along its west bank. When the people were about midway along, one of the scouts came riding up to inform them of conditions in connection with the herd. As he approached, he signaled with his blanket, throwing it up twice to show that there were many buffalo. When he reached the line he told them that the herd was coming up from the river and wasn't very far, but that nevertheless the line of march should continue slowly along the west bank of Turkey Creek rather than crossing to the east side in an attempt to avoid disturbing the herd, and then crossing back again to make their camp. He told them that Turkey Creek was muddy near its confluence with the Republican, as some of the herd had already crossed over and were moving eastward.

Taking account of these factors, the plan of action was as follows.

Every available hunter would get a horse if he could and leave the line of march to go to the hunting grounds. Even if the horse were not fast, there were enough buffalo for everyone to hunt. In order to free as many horses as possible, the people were to combine and reload all their baggage, doubling up with their neighbors if necessary for the balance of the journey into camp. Man Chief and White Eagle, the first to be ready, rode off a little distance to await the others. The scout now rode all along the line telling all the hunters to get their horses and go where Man Chief and White Eagle were waiting to start.

As the scout turned back to rejoin the waiting chiefs, an old doctor of the Asking-for-Meat Band began to go among the people to perform a pantomime of sympathetic magic. He followed the path that the scout had taken and, impersonating a buffalo, he went in a trot with his arms flexed at his sides, chanting:

> Now you are going to trot
> Buffalo who are killed falling.

As he went among the people of each of the four bands, he sang his song each time. The children would try to trip him and make him fall down. When the boy Otter tried this, the old man asked, "Have you any tobacco to give me?" The boy shamefacedly answered no, but the old man fell down for him anyway.

Man Chief had appointed his prophet or "hand waver" who was to make the incantation to the powers as the hunters were poised ready to make the attack on the herd. Now this man was holding back, reluctant to ride out to the hunting grounds, worrying whether his luck would be good. Finally he joined the hunters, as they were in a hurry to get started. Then Man Chief called out, "Now we're going ahead!" and with White Eagle he started off a little ahead while the others followed in a bunch. They all galloped their horses as they hurried on. The scout went on ahead to guide them to the place. As soon as they got in sight, the head scout signaled with his blanket from the hill where he was stationed. If he threw his blanket up leisurely and caught it, there was no hurry, but if he threw it up and pulled it down quickly to his left, they had to hurry because the buffalo would be close and coming on.

25

THE FIRST MAIN

HUNT EPISODE

Beginning the Attack—the Intricacies of the Hunting Process—the Butchering and Return of Meat to Camp—Recounting of Stories

〜〜〜〜〜〜〜〜〜〜〜〜〜〜〜〜〜〜〜

THE SERIES OF STEPS before the charge on the herd was always the same as that described above for the "Chiefs' Herd." The head scout, coming a little way below the top of the hill, signaled with his blanket how the herd was disposed on the other side. The scout continued down the hill about half way, while the main chiefs rode up to meet him and hold a further consultation about the matter. He first spoke directly to the chief in charge of the hunt episode—in this case Man Chief. The other chiefs stood by, holding their horses, impatiently resting their heads in their hands, until they would be told the message. The crowd of hunters lined up below was also impatient and everyone was saying, "Softly, softly."

Man Chief told the other chiefs their plan and each motioned to his band in the line below. They went back to their line as soon as possible, as the buffalo in this instance were very close and they had to try to keep their hunters in order. The hand-waver or prophet had not yet arrived; he was coming on slowly, having been held back by worry over his responsibility. The Skidi hunters were saying, "Why do we have to wait for him? We could all be hand wavers!" But finally the old man arrived and knelt down facing the hill, making his prayers, calling upon the powers and saying that they should try to get the whole herd, although in this instance it was clearly not possible. The head scout stood holding his horse in readiness to join the attack as soon as he was able to notify Man Chief that the incantation was over.

Man Chief now signaled the waiting hunters below, motioning how they would attack. In effect his motions stated: "Any of you want to go east or any want to go west, just go ahead. There are lots of buffalo. As for me, I'm going right over the hill." Only those with the best horses could go right over the hill. One could see the buffalo in the distance here and there as they were coming up from the water to graze on the other side of the hill. Some of the Man-Going-Downstream Band decided to go eastward across Turkey Creek, even though the creek was muddy to cross, as there were many buffalo there and less hunters to attack them. The holy man, who had to remain still in order not to disturb the effect of his magic, sat at the base of the hill and waited. He could not go back to camp, since it would not be set up until the attack on the herd was over.

As soon as the signal was given, the hunters all rode to the chase. The herds were very scattered and had to be chased by men in small groups. In the past they chased the buffalo on foot and there was still a man, Charley Buffalo, who was such a fast runner that he could overtake a buffalo on foot and shoot him.

Now each hunter selected his own buffalo to chase, depending on his skill as a hunter and the speed of his horse. There was little value in trying to get more than one buffalo or at most two—though a good hunter could conceivably get more—as there was no help to be gotten with the butchering and he would not be able to haul in the extra meat in any case. A second animal might be consecrated to a sacred bundle, in which case as the hunter shot it he would say, "It is sacred!" The South Bands designated such a sacred animal by crossing its forelegs and tying them together as the animal lay on its back, then tying the hind legs, but the Skidi did not follow this practice. A man who had the misfortune to fall off his horse and could not get back on in time would be enlisted to help butcher and receive half an animal, although the ribs would not be given him at this time.

The chase was carefully timed to the habits of the buffalo. At this season the buffalo spent most of the time scattered about in the uplands where the buffalo grass was. (In winter they stayed closer together in the timber.) In the morning, the buffalo went down to the water and between ten-thirty and eleven o'clock they were back in the pasture grazing. At noon they were all sitting down resting and by evening had gone down to the water again before returning to the uplands.

The hunters usually lined up for the attack about ten-thirty in the morning and by eleven rode to the chase. Everywhere a cloud of dust would rise as they rushed forward except after a rain when big clods and mud would hit them in the face. They never hunted when it was actually raining, as the sinew bowstring stretched and was ineffectual when wet.

It was easy to tell which were the most desirable buffalo. Those with their bellies still swollen with water had been the last to get down to the water and get a drink and were therefore the older and slower animals. The fatter and faster animals had been down and returned to the pasture to graze by the time these animals had gotten there.

The better the horse, the faster the animal one could try to chase. As two men sighted a good buffalo, one would remark, "That's mine," and his neighbor would observe, "When your horse gets there it will be yours!" The fat buffalo knew he was going to be chased and a contest began between the hunter and his prey. The hunter would test the metal of his horse by baiting the buffalo with "hae, hae, hae!" a sound that made the buffalo angry so that his tail stuck up and he shook it. Only a fast horse could get an angry buffalo. When the shot found its mark the hunter would say, "ex' hau!" or "uhe'e, ahe'e!" As soon as he saw blood coming out of the buffalo's mouth, he knew that the animal could not go far and he would go get his horse nearby to be convenient for loading and begin at once to butcher. If they were at any distance from camp and two were close together, they would save much needed time by butchering cooperatively, first the animal of one, then of the other.

If they were far from camp it would be best to drive the animal toward the water before killing it for convenience while butchering. Most desirable, however, was to drive the animal close to camp where they wouldn't have far to haul the meat. When they chased an animal close to camp, the women came out asking for intestine or kidneys. They would yell, "Here comes one over here!" Another advantage of killing the buffalo close to camp was that they, could bring in the bones which would be too heavy to carry otherwise, especially the backbone. Then they could make marrow fat by boiling the bones and skimming off the grease. The fat was stored in a paunch and used to eat with pounded-up dried meat.

Some of the hunters of the Man-Going-Downstream Band had gone over east across Turkey Creek. After the camp was set up, two bison, apparently having escaped the hunters, had come across the creek and trotted right through the encampment. As the bison came through, there was great excitement in the camp. Women grabbed their babies and put them onto their backs, old people tried to get out of the way, and the dogs were barking as the bison tried to hook them. The men that remained in camp lined up two deep along both sides in their path saying, "Hah! e, hah!'e" to bait and anger the bison, but no one would do them any harm as it was felt that they had been brave and had some supernatural purpose in coming through the camp. When the hunters got home for their dinner, this incident would be recounted in great detail and similar incidents in the past recalled. One of the more "slapstick" types of story was told of an old man named Crazy who once decided he would be brave and would shoot one of these buffalo with his rifle. He only succeeded in being hooked by the buffalo and tossed up in the air so that his loincloth broke and he landed on his face in the grass calling for his wife who came bringing his buffalo robe to rescue him from indecent exposure.

The hunters got into camp sometime between two and four in the afternoon. Those who wanted to stopped outside the council tent as they rode in and dropped the ribs as a contribution for the evening meeting. It was a great honor to be the first to arrive and drop the ribs there; this was mentioned later during the feast. The first ribs were made into a sort of archway, leaning against each other, while the others were laid chevron fashion piled up next to it. The hunters hurried with their butchering in order to be the first. Then they went to their own tent where they rested, ate a meal, and left the meat and hides to be processed. After that they could return to the council tent and recount the incidents of the hunt and sit around telling "tall stories" during and after the evening feast. The only exception was the evening of the first big hunt, when they would install the military police after they had had their conversations, as described in Chapter 26.

26

THE MEETING IN
THE COUNCIL TENT

〰〰〰〰〰〰〰〰〰〰〰〰〰〰〰〰〰〰

*Selection and Installation of Military Police—
Description of Council Meeting—Duties of Military Police—a Second Meeting after Second Attack on Herd—Stories Told*

〰〰〰〰〰〰〰〰〰〰〰〰〰〰〰〰〰〰

WHILE HIS FAMILY WAS BUSY slicing the meat and processing the hides,
Victory Call went to the council tent to meet with the other chiefs,
braves, and prominent hunters. His usual practice was to set out about
three-thirty in the afternoon after he had eaten and rested and go to
White Eagle's large council tent where others would be congregated.
On the first night the camp was set up on Turkey Creek, the council
meeting was of a more formal character. It was for the selection and installation of the military police.

White Eagle's wives had set up an exceptionally large curve-roofed
tent to accommodate the council. They had to rush with their work for
the family when White Eagle arrived with the meat in order to be ready
to leave when the council came in. On this particular evening White Eagle
sent for his chief errand man, Know-His-Face. He was to go to the head
chief of each of the four Skidi villages to ask him to come in the evening with ten of his prominent men. Each chief in his turn called his
subchiefs, braves, and "boys" to his tent. When they were all there, they
lined up in order of rank and walked over to the council tent, where
they seated themselves formally in their appointed positions. The tent
was open to the east, and had a sacred area at the west. The four chiefs
sat in the semicardinal positions, their respective braves ranging inward
toward the cardinal positions at the north and south. At the northwest
was Leading Chief of Village-in-the-Bottomlands, his braves ranging in an
arc from northwest to north. At the northeast was Feared-by-the-Enemy

of Wolf-in-Water-Village with his braves ranging inward from northeast to north. On the south side were Lone Chief at the southwest, his braves ranging from southwest to south, and finally Eagle Chief in the host position at the southeast with his braves reaching inward toward the south station. In front of the braves in a sort of inner arc were the "boys" of their respective villages. No one could properly be seated in front of a chief. Outside the curve-roofed shelter to the north of the entrance, was a long oblong fireplace and a small token fire was made in the middle of the tent with a few coals for the ceremonial offerings. Forty people were in the council tent that evening, ten from each village.

Eagle Chief of the host village of Pumpkin-Vine spoke first and addressed Leading Chief of Bottomlands Village who sat at the Northwest. After he and some prominent men from his village had spoken the initiative passed to Lone Chief of Village-across-a-Ridge, who also spoke as well as his brave and others of his village. Then Feared-by-the-Enemy at the northeast, of Wolf-in-Water Village, who passed it back to Eagle Chief in the host position at the southeast. The final responsibility was given to Leading Chief of Bottomlands, who was bound to accept— for White Eagle, who was leading the hunt, was married into his village. He now took up the directive and passed it to his head brave Strikes-the-Enemy, who, to everyone's relief, accepted the difficult post as head military policeman.

The paraphernalia of the appropriate military society, the Two Lance or Horse Society, was in the Wolf-in-Water Village, and the chief, Feared-by-the-Enemy, called on Chief's Road who had the lances and lance covers in his tent to send for them, and Angry Horse to send for the crow-feather belt with the sleigh bells on it that the head policeman was to wear. The two lance covers in their rawhide cases were brought in and the two long sticks on which they were to be placed. If there was still enough daylight, the covers would be taken from their cases, put on the sticks, taken outside the tent, and planted in the ground in front of it so that the wind could strike the feathers and they could be seen by Heaven. By sundown, Chief's Road would instruct the chiefs at the west how to fold up the covers with their feathers into their cases for the night.

The head policeman selected his second brave to assist him, along with two from each of the other three Skidi villages. When the people in camp saw the feathered lances outside, they knew that the council tent had been officially established and they wanted to know who had been selected as chief of police and who the others were. Some thought Strikes-the-Enemy was too severe, others not.

Very early next morning, just before sunrise, the lances were reinstalled outside the council tent. The new chief of police, Strikes-the-Enemy, donned his crow-feather belt with the sleigh bells on it and, armed with his special club, rode back and forth in front of the council tent waiting for White Eagle to lead off the hunt. His club or whip (see Figure 26-1) was of hickory, 3 feet long, 4 inches wide and wedge-shaped, with the thick back edge about an inch and a half wide, sloping down to the thin edge that had teeth cut into it. Through a hole in the handle end was a rawhide strap so that the club could be hung over the wrist and another hole near the head held several strips of rawhide for whipping.

FIGURE 26-1. The whip or warclub, *tahipirus-tax karax-kitawa*, "whip-teeth-upon it," carried by the "Hunt Police." Made of hickory it is 3 feet long, 4 inches wide, with the back of the unserrated edge being about 1½ inches thick, sloping to the thin toothed edge. The rawhide loop allowed it to be hung on the wrist. The strips of rawhide at the top for whipping were usually plain, but sometimes striped or covered with white clay. (The dimensions and the drawing were supplied by informants.)

A group of Tsawi once tried to anticipate the tribal attack on the herd and were severely whipped. The leader of the party was beaten over the head with the club until he lay unconscious and his head was bleeding. When he appealed to Man Chief, he was told that it was "the law" and that he had to submit to his punishment. At a later time, the Tsawi police had a chance for reprisal on some Skidi hunters who were struck across the mouth with the rawhide whip, as their infringement was not at such a critical phase of the hunt. The only escape from such a beating was to take sanctuary on a buffalo wallow—if the culprit could find one in time.

After the four major hunt episodes, the four bands went their own ways, but within the bands the military police continued their power until they were actually on their return journey. The sending of the scouts early in the morning and the plan as to where they should go was now assigned by White Eagle to the chief of the police, a similar plan being followed in each of the other two bands when their chiefs took the lead.

The next afternoon, after they had made a second major attack on the buffalo herd, there was a very large meeting in the council tent. At least five sets of ribs were donated by each of the four Skidi villages, and five or six buckets of boiled corn kernels by wives of the leading men in their names. Two women, one in front and one behind, would come with the long "digging iron" stick resting between them on their right shoulders with the kettle of corn hanging from it, bringing it to the council tent and saying, "This is so-and-so's."

After proper offerings had been made to White Eagle's sacred Left Hand bundle, they ate roasted ribs and then corn, and told in detail all the happenings of the hunt. Some of the men then began to go back to their own tents while the prominent citizens remained, the older men beginning to tell "tall stories" of times gone by. They lingered so long in the Skidi council tent that night that Many Trophies of the Pitahawirata Band had to send his errand man to find out what the plans for the next day were to be, and then trot off to tell the chiefs of the other two bands.

As they sat in the tent, one old man said, "When I was young, I came close to a buffalo once and shot it with my arrow and the arrow went right through and came out the other side." Another old man now tops that one and says, "I did that once and when my arrow came through it shot a jack rabbit sitting on the other side." Old Man Pitsu'u (Arrived) now adds his tale, "I chased a bison, and you know they have long hair and as I chased him I saw something shiny on his neck. I thought it was a rock, but after I killed him and tied my horse to his leg, I looked and saw that he had a chief's medal around his neck. 'I wonder how he got that medal,' I thought, 'that bull must have been to Washington!' It wasn't on a ribbon though, but on a buckskin string. Now how do you think that bison got that medal around his neck?"

Different answers were posed one of which gave an account of a chief who had been killed and the bison rolling nearby, thus acquired the medal. "Now," said That Chief, "tell us Eagle Chief what you think?" "I'll tell you what might have happened," says Eagle Chief, "A Cheyenne or Comanche might have roped this bison while he was young and maybe he wanted to be blessed and put his medal on the calf. He might say, 'I'm giving you this medal. I want you to bless me. I'll let you free.'"

It appears that no one was ready to top this, so this story rested. Then Charley Buffalo began to tell of his fancy exploits somewhat embellished until it got very late and the old men fell asleep where they were sitting while the rest went home.

From now on they would meet in the council tent, especially the most prominent men, throughout the hunt.

27

PRESERVING THE MEAT AND

PROCESSING THE HIDES

〰〰〰〰〰〰〰〰〰〰〰〰〰〰〰

Women Slice the Meat for Preserving—Preserving of Flank, Legs, Internal Organs—Boiling and Drying—Processing the Hides—Grease from the Bones—Ultimate Use of the Meat

〰〰〰〰〰〰〰〰〰〰〰〰〰〰〰

As soon as the men got in from the hunt, each tent became the scene of busy activity. The time was usually between two and four in the afternoon. In Victory Call's tent, from the first killing, they had two buffalo, one by Victory Call and the other by Horse Rider. As they came in, the women spread a tanned hide on the ground for the meat that was taken off the horses, and Horse Rider then went off to hobble the horses nearby. Victory Call went into the tent where No Corn was cooking a meal of grease bread and coffee; she called out that Horse Rider was to come right in as the food was ready.

While the men were resting and having a meal that No Corn had prepared, Grandma and White Woman began at once to work on the meat, coming in for a quick snack whenever they felt they could pause in the work. Grandma devoted herself entirely to this work. She built herself a small sunshade of three willow branches on which, later in the hunt, they sometimes left some roasted buffalo ribs for anyone who wanted a bite between meals. The most highly skilled work was the thinning of the two long backbone steaks. After removing the fat and the sinews, they would make a series of cuts in the meat with a sharp knife. Holding the long column of meat in the hand, they made a series of short cuts into it, first on one side and then on the other in alternate order. The cuts were so made that they did not quite sever the slice, and the meat could be stretched out into a broad continuous sheet 3 ¾ feet long by 2 ¾ feet wide and half an inch thick. After drying, these large sheets of meat were each covered with a slab of dried fat that was not quite as large—3¼ feet long by 1½ feet wide and an inch thick. The edges of the meat were folded down over the fat like an open-faced envelope, first the top edge, then the bottom edge, and then the two sides (see Figure 27-1). Folded in this way, they were just the right size for the rawhide

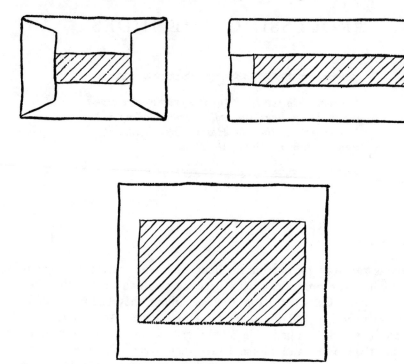

FIGURE 27-1. The manner of folding dried buffalo steak from along the backbone, *kisatsu*. A layer of dried fat (diagonal shading) is placed on top.

container in which they would be stored. The two steaks with their layers of fat were placed one on top of the other on the rawhide with other pieces of dried meat and fat on top of them, and the container was folded over them, first the top edge, then the bottom edge and then the two sides which met in the middle where they were tied together, laced with hide strips. The surface of these two short ends were painted with large designs in bright colors, but unlike the usual angular designs of the other Indian tribes of the Plains, the Pawnee painted cosmic symbols on these containers—the moon and its rays, the sun, the dawn, and the stars (see figures 27-2–27-3). Such a container held the dried meat of a whole buffalo. When the meat was fully dried and packed, it was 2½ feet long by 1½ feet wide and a foot deep. The "neck" end of the long backbone steak was thicker than the tail end, and the dried pieces of the other parts were piled more thickly near the tail end, each layer covered with a layer of dried fat to keep the meat soft. The meat of a whole buffalo dried and packed in this way, was reduced to a weight of 80 pounds. A live bison weighed about 2,000 pounds.

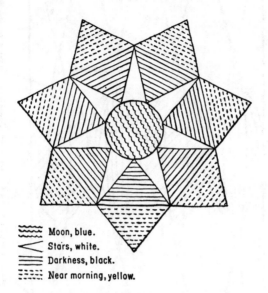

~~~~~ Moon, blue.
< Stars, white.
≡ Darkness, black.
⋮⋮⋮⋮ Near morning, yellow.

FIGURE 27-2. A cosmic design painted on a rawhide container for dried buffalo meat, to be painted only by a person with the necessary religious qualifications.

Other parts of the meat prepared were:

The flank. The sinews were removed and the membrane being taken off to be used in packing up the raw marrow that they took out when they cracked the long bones.

The foreleg and hind leg. The limbs were disjointed and the meat removed from the bones for drying.

The internal organs. These included the intestines, the lining of the stomach, the tripe (likened to the leaves of a book), the heart from which the membrane was carefully removed by cutting around the top for use as a tobacco pouch or for other treasures. The heart was split so that it would lie flat in drying. The tongue was blistered in the coals and the rough outer covering removed. Heart and tongue were boiled in water before being hung up to dry. Lungs were sometimes sliced like the backbone steaks and then dried. They made good pulverized dry meat. The stomach lining was washed in cold water and cut into long strips after it had dried, the strips woven into a checker-plaited mat, in which form they were stored in the rawhide container.

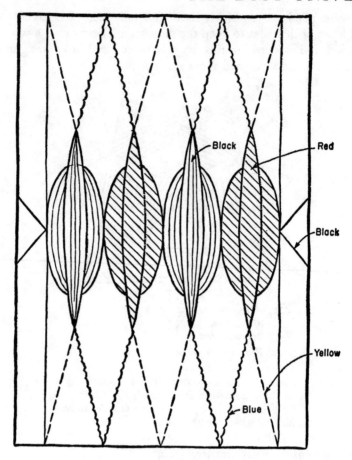

FIGURE 27-3. A design painted on a rawhide container for dried buffalo meat, the significance of which is unknown.

Intestines were turned inside out and boiled in the kettle. Then they were hung on the rack so that the water ran out and they would dry. After they were dried, they were broken into a number of pieces and woven into a checker-plaited mat for storage. The intestines of two buffalo were used for one mat. Each intestine was 12 to 15 feet long and was broken into four pieces. The pieces hung over a stick to a length of about 2 feet on each side. The mat was ten strips wide with cross pieces woven in. A mat would sometimes be given to a little girl as a special gift. For this purpose, they would leave the stick in the mat and fasten a boiled buffalo eye at each end. When they broke camp and a little girl was seen carrying her gift mat on her back, people would remark, "Look, that's hers! Are there eyes on it?"

The tripe was boiled at the same time as the intestines. It was not otherwise treated, but simply hung on the rack to dry.

The internal organs, particularly the tripe, took several days before they were dry enough for storage. They had to be hung on the rack on several successive days, while the rest of the meat usually cured in a day or so. These dried internal organs were used for mixing with dried corn kernels to make soup.

The drying rack had been completed and ready to hang up the meat by the time the men got in from the hunt. It had three upright forked sticks planted in the ground, with three cross sticks, one resting in the forks at the top and two tied on at intervals below with strips of inner bark or of hide. A double-length rack was sometimes made to accommodate all the meat prepared in their camp. The rack was erected with its broad side facing east so that the sun would strike the meat directly. The meat was hung on the rack with the two long steaks in the center and the other parts out toward the ends, pieces of kidney fat and other parts of the fat in between.

As soon as the camp was set up, they brought in plenty of water in anticipation of the fact that the intestines and other parts would have to be boiled. When the men had arrived, Grandma set them to boil at once and began slicing the meat. White Woman was helping and when No Corn had fed the men, she came out and joined them, while Horse Rider got to work disjointing the limbs and removing the meat from the bones. Having joined forces, the meat began to pile up and White Woman hung the meat on the rack while the others sliced. With three women and Horse Rider working together, the meat of each buffalo took about an hour and a half to get on the rack, and from two-thirty to five-thirty they had prepared the meat of both buffalo that the men had brought in. Thus it would take a single worker five or six hours for each animal.

The hides had to be pegged out onto the ground and defleshed simultaneously with the slicing of the meat as they had to be stretched out while they were still fresh. After they had made considerable progress with slicing the meat, Grandma suggested to White Woman that she would continue with the meat and that White Woman might go and tend to the hides. This was the most strenuous part of the work and since No Corn was crippled, White Woman had to process both the hides. No Corn continued to help Grandma slice the meat, and while White Woman was pegging down one of the hides, Horse Rider offered to peg down the other. White Woman then proceeded to deflesh both of them. The fleshing tool was made of the shaft of a buffalo tibia, the small end cut to a fine-toothed edge and the thick end with a hole through which a rawhide strap was drawn to go around the wrist. White Woman bent over from a standing position, striking the fleshing tool downward and toward her against the hide. Some women avoided bending over by not pegging down the hide. They put a stick or tree trunk about 3 inches in diameter at a slant in the ground. Laying the hide over it, they tied it at the top with rawhide and supported the hide underneath with the palm of the left hand, applying the fleshing tool to this spot and then moving successively down the length, shifting the position of the hide over the log for the next section. This method was particularly useful when they had to work inside the tent in winter. The small scraps of meat removed in the defleshing were also placed on the drying rack.

When the meat was dry on one side, they took it off the rack piece by piece, and each piece was set on an open rawhide container with the dry side up, pounded with a pestle to remove some of the moisture, turned over and pounded on the moist side and replaced on the rack so that this side could now be exposed.

Just before the half-dry pieces of meat were again removed from the rack and placed on a rawhide, each piece was trampled with the moccasined feet to remove as much of the moisture as possible. At this stage the meat was called "moist dry meat" and while it was not fit for long-term storage, it could keep well for several days. In this form it was cooked for their more immediate use. For permanent storage, after the meat had been trampled on, it was stacked up on a skin spread and carried inside the tent to protect it from the dampness that came up from the water after sundown. Inside the tent, they covered it up by lapping over the edges of the skin spread and covering it up with an open rawhide container. They would go out just before sunrise in the morning and hang the meat on the rack again so that it could continue to dry.

Grease from the bones was another important commissary item. After the third killing, the herd was pretty well scattered in this locality and they were going to move the hunting camp to another location a considerable distance away, to the Solomon fork of the Kansas, south of the Republican River. Before they left their old hunting camp, White Eagle allowed them an extra day in camp to finish up with some of their work. In most of the camps they were glad to have an opportunity to make use of the larger bones that were lying around from the first two killings, particularly the backbones and the large knuckle bones. Some men, having nothing else to do, went out to the place where the bones lay and, tethering their horses nearby, dug out the chunks of meat and fat that adhered to the backbones and brought them home for their wives to boil for soup. These small chunks of meat were known as "small meat." Most of all they wanted to take the opportunity to make "bone grease" which they called "bone water." This was eaten particularly with the pulverized dried buffalo meat, by biting off a piece of the solidified fat to eat with the dry fluffy pounded-up meat. This was probably their last chance of the season to make bone grease, as they were unlikely to stay long enough in any one place and be so close to the hunting grounds as to have all these large bones around and the time to treat them. The bone grease was made by cracking up the backbone and boiling it in a large kettle of water along with the knuckle bones. The grease, skimmed off with a spoon, was kept in a buffalo paunch, prepared by peeling off the inner lining, which left a smooth surface on the inside. The paunch, with a wide slit cut into it for an opening, was placed in a depression in the ground and the opening flaps spread out at the top. In summer it was hard to get the grease to solidify, but in the evening when a cool breeze came up from the river it became solid enough to transport. Though they seldom did so, if they wanted to make bone grease en route they put it into the large intestine and tied it up at both ends for transportation. The winter was a more propitious time for making bone grease as it hardened more readily; sometimes they would stay up at night and work by the light of a burning brand while on the winter hunt in order to make it. The soup was spilled out at some distance from camp along with the boiled bones. Before they got rid of the soup, Horse Rider liked to eat a bowl of it with a handful or two of parched corn. Sometimes when it cooked for a long time, certain soft parts from the bones around the lower part of the foreleg were also eaten.

Now as Horse Rider was coming into camp with a backbone for Grandma to boil up for bone grease, she set him to work first picking off the small pieces of meat and fat. He sat down directly with his legs extended and wedged the backbone between his feet and got to work digging out the meat. They used the meat for soup at supper. The long bones were cracked and the marrow removed and wrapped in a membrane taken from the flank. The marrow was eaten raw with dry meat.

They now had the partially dried buffalo meat to supplement the supplies of dried corn, beans, and squash and the dried meat they had brought with them from the previous winter hunt. For the camping family of six, they would use a thin sheet of dried buffalo meat with its covering layer of fat. The dried piece of meat was 12 inches wide by 30 inches long and would be cut into eight portions, 6 inches wide, 7 inches long and ⅜ to ¼ inch thick. The fat was a little thicker and with each portion went a piece of fat—2½ by 5 inches. The portions of meat and fat were washed with cold water and then put in the kettle which was placed on the coals to boil. The fat tended to disintegrate into the soup. When they were cooking dry meat for supper, a guest, usually a close friend or relative, was very likely to drop in. In Victory Call's camp, Uncle War Cry, White Woman's brother, was the one most likely to appear.

For feasts at official or ceremonial occasions, the backbone steaks were used, a number being donated for each occasion (see Figure 27-4). A

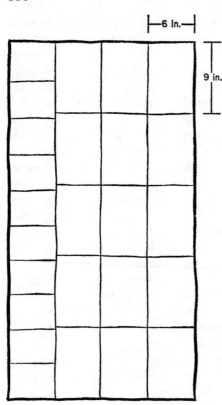

FIGURE 27-4. The manner of cutting and setting out portions of the layer of dried buffalo meat made from the backbone steak, *kisatsu*, at a feast. (1) Preparatory to cooking, the steak is cut into four long strips. The three strips at the right are each made into five portions. The fourth long strip at the left is made into as many additional portions as is deemed necessary. The large portions are for the honored guests sitting in the special positions, the smaller portions, for the rest of the guests. The slab of dried buffalo fat is cut up in the same way. (2) The portions are set out on a tanned hide, ready to be served. (The dimensions and the drawing were supplied by informants.)

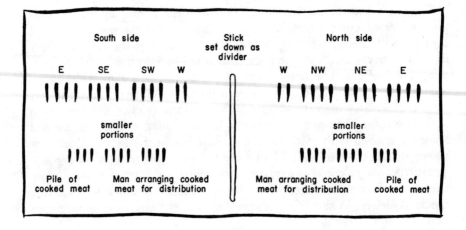

tanned hide was spread out and formally divided into sections, a right section for the guests on the north side and a left section for those on the south side with a stick lying on the spread between them to mark the divisions. Two backbone steaks were opened out, one on one side and one on the other and separated from their layer of fat. This operation was carried out at the southeast of the earth lodge or tent with the two steaks pointed with their "neck" or head ends toward the northwest. Each steak was cut down the length into four strips, each about 6 inches wide. The three strips on the right were made into five large portions each, about 9 inches long, and the fourth or leftmost strip was cut into a whole series of smaller portions depending upon how many people needed to be served. The larger portions were for the important guests at the main "positions," while the smaller pieces were for the others. The layer of fat was cut up in the same way, but this disintegrated in the soup. For a feast of sixty people, four steaks would be cooked. Each potful took about twenty minutes, about fifteen for the meat and a few minutes more for the fat to be thoroughly cooked. For this amount they cooked three or four batches, spearing out the pieces of meat with a stick each time and placing them on the spread in the appropriate position for serving. Sometimes while the errand man was doing the cooking he would observe that the steaks were unusually small, viz., from a small animal, when additional meat would have to be added. When additional steaks were received, the important guests received double portions or more. This was the only direct compensation for administrative services.

Most of the meat preserved during this summer hunt would be used during the following fall and winter, while the succeeding winter hunt would provide the additional meat for the spring. From the summer hunt, the hides were processed as rawhide or tanned hide with hair removed, while on the winter hunt they got hides with fur and wool for warm robes.

The drying and preserving of the buffalo meat along with their crops was one of the major technical achievements of the Pawnees. This ancient art of preserving food by drying was almost continent-wide in America among the food gatherers as well as the food producers, and the method contrasts markedly with the general Old World approach of fermenting, pickling, and spicing for food preservation.

Each household had its own estimate of the amount of dried buffalo meat required to carry on its social and religious obligations. Four formal attacks on the herd by all the able-bodied hunters of the tribe were considered sufficient to provide for most of their needs. The first mass attack had taken place as the line of march was slowly making its way southward along the west bank of Turkey Creek. When they had gone about halfway, the scouts had located the herd, and the hunters left the line of march to attack and make the kill. While they were butchering, the line of .march arrived about two miles north of the confluence of Turkey Creek and the Republican and set up Camp 11 to which the hunters came with their meat. The second and third formal hunts were conducted from this encampment. For the fourth formal attack they had to move overland to another location to the south as described in the following chapter.

28

THE FOURTH MAJOR
ATTACK ON THE HERD

〜〜〜〜〜〜〜〜〜〜〜〜〜〜〜〜〜〜〜〜〜

*Decisions Made for Further Hunting—the Camp
Heads South to the Republican River—the Attack
—the Blessed Meat*

〜〜〜〜〜〜〜〜〜〜〜〜〜〜〜〜〜〜〜〜〜

AFTER THE SECOND VERY SUCCESSFUL attack on the herd, the animals north of the Republican River were pretty well scattered and the scouts located the herd south of the river. It was decided that they should remain at Camp 11 on Turkey Creek, but the hunters would cross over for the hunt and bring the meat back north over the river to the camp. They would have to leave the "rumpbones" and backbone behind and bring the rest of the meat that could be more readily transported. As the buffalo appeared to be getting scarce in this location, White Eagle decided to give over the leadership of the fourth hunt episode to Many Trophies of the Man-Going-Downstream Band. There was some complaint on the part of the council members, as they knew he would lead them far to the south along the Solomon River, but White Eagle reminded them that they were "Fathers" in the Peace Pipe trade relationship with the Downstream Band, who, as their "Children," had given them many horses which even now were carrying them to the hunt. White Eagle gave them an extra day to prepare everything and to get ready to move camp, to which the chiefs of the other bands were agreed.

After they broke camp next morning the line of march would set out in formal order, all except the old ladies who had gone ahead long before. Chief Many Trophies of Downstream Band had instructed his military police to see that scouts were sent out before dawn. In the Skidi 'camp, Strikes-the-Enemy, as Chief of Military Police, was riding back and forth in front of the council tent wearing his official belt and carrying his club. The errand man was going through the camp repeating his announcement and waking everyone.

Finally the tents were all folded and the police moved back and forth among the camps. They would head south for the Republican River and cross it. In the Skidi camp, Strikes-the-Enemy led off and behind him Chief White Eagle. Then the two lance bearers following on foot, one on each side, the feathers of the lances flying as they went. Behind these came the other chiefs and then the rest of the people. The leaders advanced for fifteen or twenty minutes and then stopped, waiting for the others to join them.

Each band had its own officers in the lead as they proceeded in parallel columns, stopping at their special crossing place in the river and lining up to go over. The men with lances rode over first, followed by the other leaders on horseback, in order to pack down the sand. Those that were walking across took off their moccasins and leggings and rolled them in their blankets which they were wearing on their backs. By this time most of the people were walking, leading their horses which were heavily loaded.

It was the lance bearers that gave the signal for the line of march to proceed. They would move ahead and, when they came to a stopping place, plant their lances upright in the ground. Then when they were signaling to move ahead, one would pull out his lance and say "ru," and in rapid succession the second man would pull out his lance and say "ru," then the line would again move forward. The south side of the river has a "bench" or step and then above it a high bank. When the lance bearers got to the first bench they planted their lances and sat down to smoke and wait for the others. Then when they caught up, the lance bearers pulled out their lances calling "ru, ru," and hurried up to the high bank, where they again repeated the procedure. The line of march proceeded southward and overland until they reached the head of Cedar Creek which flowed southeastward into the Solomon River in the Kansas drainage. The scouts had reported that the herd was moving eastward along the Solomon and as the line of march traveled south on the west bank of Cedar Creek, they halted within five or six miles of the herd, consolidating their baggage in order to release as many horses as possible to any effective hunter. The lance bearers tied their lances to the saddles of their load mares and rode off to the chase with the rest of the hunters.

Crossing southward over the hills, they could see buffalo from the hilltops when they were within three or four miles of the river. The Head Policeman had sent two or three of his men to find a suitable hollow in which the whole line of hunters could conceal itself. This was found two miles short of the herd, and there Chief Many Trophies asked his prophet to make his devotions. The military police of the several bands were busy restraining the hunters from anticipating the attack of the group. The herd was very widely scattered over the land and they were coming up from the river to graze. They could not manage the usual surround, so the hunters dashed ahead over and around the several hills that lay between them and the herd.

Meanwhile the line of march had been holding back, proceeding very slowly so that they would not interfere with the hunt itself. When the men had completed their attack on the herd, the encampment was set up in the angle of the confluence of Cedar Creek and the Solomon.

The hunt having been successful under the leadership of Chief Many Trophies, an old priest of the Downstream Band came walking through the camps. He represented the tradition of the sacred bundle under whose auspices the hunt had been conducted. He wore a war bonnet with feathers all around his head, possibly symbolizing a comet, and around his waist a buffalo robe that hung down about his legs. In his right hand he held the sacred pipe and over his left arm he was carrying some breast meat and some fat. All along the way men and boys from the four bands were trailing after him.

When he stopped at the west of the encampment, everyone lined up. He placed the pipe against the meat and fat, then raised the latter up toward the west four times in offering. Just as he was about to put the meat and fat on the ground, the whole crowd pounced on it and tried to grab a piece of meat and fat to bless their homes. They grabbed from one another on all sides, with the little boys scampering out of the way for fear of getting hurt. The old man, meanwhile, picked up his pipe and went north around the camp to his own tent. The other two South Bands also had their special band bundles, the Asking-for-Meat Band had a very sacred Ant bundle, and the Little-Earth-Lodge Band, a Raccoon bundle.

29

THE ADDITIONAL
HUNTING EPISODES

〰〰〰〰〰〰〰〰〰〰〰〰〰〰〰

*The Less Formal Part of the Hunt—Scouting for
Enemy and Buffalo—a Sioux Attack—the Herd
Sighted and Attacked—Final Attack and the
Start Home*

〰〰〰〰〰〰〰〰〰〰〰〰〰〰〰

THE MAIN FOUR EPISODES of the hunt were now completed, and the rest
would be undertaken on a less formal level. In the last one at Cedar
Creek, it was felt that they hadn't gotten much and White Eagle decided
that it would be best for them to move their camp westward. They
would move eight miles west and upstream (Post Hunt Camp 1). White
Eagle sent his errand man to Curly Chief of the Kitkehaxki Band to
notify him, and Curly Chief in turn sent his errand man to announce it
all through the South Band camps, while the Skidi errand man came
back and announced it in theirs. The meat was nearly dry and they carried it along. When they got to the next camping place, the women
simply finished drying the limited amount they had by spreading it out
on the ground on a hide.

The afternoon before, scouts from each of the bands had gone out
over the country to look for signs of the enemy and the buffalo. From
the Skidi, a party of three led by Roaming Leader went off to the southwest. Scanning the landscape from the top of a hill, they were unable to
see anything. Sometimes one could make a mistake when enemies dis-
guised themselves by wearing buffalo hides, but if you looked carefully
you could see the robe flapping at the sides and other men similarly
dressed, joining the first one. The Sioux, Cheyennes, or Arapahos
would do this, sitting on a horse with a buffalo robe draped over their
heads with the sides hanging down. Roaming Leader had come especially
to this area to get some sweet cicely (*Washingtonia longistylis*) called

kats-taraha, "medicine-buffalo," because it is found only in areas where the buffalo are. It is like quinine. It is also called *kats-taxkata,* "medicine-yellow," because of the color of the long root. Even on a hot day it has a cooling effect when chewed. It makes one salivate and relieves thirst when there is no water available. The men tied their horses to the grass and collected what they needed. Cicely was hard to get except in this area. They also collected quite a lot of sand cherries. They started home when it was nearly sundown and when he had taken the saddle off his horse at his own tent, Roaming Leader went to report at the council tent. There he told the Chief of Police, Strikes-the-Enemy, what they had seen and that there were no buffalo anywhere. The scouts of the South Bands had gone east and north over the land the people had traversed to see if the enemy were tracking them from the rear. From the report that no buffalo were to be seen, White Eagle decided that they had best move anyway. They all started out very early in the morning. By about sunrise all the horses were loaded up and the old ladies were already on their way. The advance scouts had gone ahead to protect them. Others had gone out to locate the herd. The place of encampment was on sort of an embankment with the water at the foot of it. The timber was a little distance away. Of the Skidi villages, Bottomlands and Wolf-in-Water were near the edge and the children could jump right into the water; the other two villages were located a little to the south.

The young men who had been out scouting all day came directly to the council tent. They had a bad report to make. They said, "You want buffalo. Well they must have gone east. We're getting to Sioux country. As far as we could go, we saw no buffalo." White Eagle decided to enlist supernatural help. He called in the four official scouts of the sacred bundle, the *periksu,* and he called in the priest, old man Angry Horse, to come very early next morning while it was still dark, to smoke the ceremonial pipe with them and give them instructions. Meanwhile White Eagle also decided that the camp had better move still further west to a place about nine or ten miles away on the other side of where the stream, *Kitsa-waku,* "Stream-Noisy," empties into the Republican (Post Hunt Camp 2).

"This is a fine place to swim with clear water," said White Eagle. "It is a wide, rocky stream, the water making noise on the rocks." They followed a buffalo path, the line of march crossing over where the buffalo had made a path leading down to the stream and up on the other side. The South Bands camped as soon as they got across; the Skidis had to go further west.

Very early that morning the old priest Angry Horse had gone through the camp and assembled the four official scouts in the council tent and sent them off on their mission. There were three other men who decided to do some scouting on their own and possibly locate a lone buffalo. They were Mad Bear, White, and Old Man Beaver Tree. While the camp was moving to Noisy Water, these three men had gone to the south and west. Mad Bear was sure he saw a Sioux, but White tried to make light of it. Old Man Beaver Tree thought they had better go and see. The Sioux scout was about a half a mile away and as they approached he turned back down the hill. When they got to the top he was riding away far to the west. They made various plans and then decided to cross the creek and as the old man said, "If anything happens, we can go into the timber." This party ended in disaster as they were surrounded by a Sioux war party and White and Old Man Beaver Tree were killed. Mad Bear and the old man shot point-blank at the approaching enemy, but the old man was struck in the leg and simply sat down in the path and piled his bow and arrow before him to await his fate. Later his body was found by the Pawnees on their way to their encampment. Of himself, Mad Bear said,

I could see the old man sitting there. As I got among the willows along the creek, they shot me in the right shoulder blade. My bow and arrows dropped. I couldn't hold anything. My arm was just swinging. I held my bow and arrows in my left hand. If they had seen it, they would have killed me, but when I got among the willows they thought I was all right. After a while I heard some growling. Then the Pawnees were coming singing. I got up and saw a great many passing by. The Sioux had gone quite a way off.

They put his arm in a sling when they found him and later managed to heal him.

Old Man Beaver Tree lay dead on the other side of the creek. They never found White. It was suspected that he had been scalped, and even if he had survived this harrowing experience would have been ashamed to come home, as "he had no hair." He would have to make himself a dugout to live in.

The official scouts had seen these happenings from a distant hill where they were and suspected someone had been killed. When they got to the camp at Noisy Water, the scouts were very discouraged. They said, "We ought to go the other way. It's going to be that way. This time of year the Cheyenne, Arapaho, any tribe, go running around on the warpath." They decided they would move one more camp west and then go back to the north bank of the Republican River (*Kiraruta*). The new camp was a short distance, about seven miles along (Post Hunt Camp 3). The night before it was decided that the official scouts had done them no good and the head policeman, Strikes-the-Enemy, appointed three young men. They climbed a tall hill and all along the valley below they saw the buffalo. It was somewhat to the northwest and ten miles or less from where they were camping. "That's what we want," they said, and sat down to smoke together. They went close and saw a big lake. When they got to the Post Hunt Camp 3, about four in the afternoon, they went directly to the council tent and made their report. They said, "We went about ten miles from here." "Well, sit down. Have you good news?" "Yes, we have." "Errand man," said White Eagle, "go through the village and call grandpa Angry Horse and the other men of the village. Have them all come in. Three men came in with good news." After due ceremonies and greetings from the chiefs and important men the leader of the scouts described the place. He said, "The buffalo can't get away because the lake is in a valley between two steep hills and they must come for water." The older people recognize and know of the place. They refer to it as *ru-ti-wa-tatar-ariks*, "there-it-hill-down-standing." Now White Eagle, realizing that they were all thinking about the two who were killed by the Sioux, said, "What happened we must stop thinking of. Remember that we are still living. Here are these men. They have good news for us, for our tribe and for our women and children. I hope we will have no more such disasters. When a day comes and something like that happens we can't help it. Sometimes you may be walking along and just simply fall over. Remember, that's the way things are. But now we are still living."

A message was sent to Curly Chief of the Kitkehaxki and the other Bands and the announcement made through the Skidi encampment. They decided to attack the herd early in the morning at seven o'clock. Insofar as they could, they would chase the buffalo toward the camp. Now people were in a good mood and began to joke. They said that the three scouts probably had "scared eyes," *ti-kiriki-tiruut*, "it is-eyes-frightened." Perhaps they had seen *pakuts* grass and thought they were buffalo!

Early next morning they made the mass attack on the herd as planned. Back at camp, some of them left ribs at the council tent. Among the South Bands, when they leave ribs, they line up one behind the other and say bird names. Here and there in the different tents where there were sacred bundles someone would give consecrated meat and the priest would be called in to perform the ceremony.

Some people left meat and ribs at the Society of Lucky Children, *Pirakawaharu*, "child-lucky." They have no sacred bundle. They simply sit and recount lucky events that have happened to them or to their predecessors from whom they had inherited their place. The headquarters of this society was in the tent of Old-Lady-among-Queens, *Ts-tawi-ku*, "woman-among-sits," signifying that she always associates with queens or influential women. She had inherited the place from her grandmother. The Old-Man-That-Chief also belonged, and he conducted the proceedings. He tells of how the society came to be, though he says he only surmises—doesn't really know. He says, "One might be thinking, 'Luck, come to me, kawaharu, *rakuwaxtsa!*" and luck actually did come. For example:

> It had snowed four days. Some men who had gone out on the warpath were starving. The men put up a grass house, for they didn't want to go out for fear of being detected by the enemy through their tracks. An old man among them went into the timber and saw three deer. The snow was hitting the deer in the face and blinding it. "We were starving. Nawa, akaa, kawaharu! Now, oh, luck! Then I aimed my bow and arrow and shot one through the shoulder. The others ran but the big buck fell over. Then I called the others and we all took the buck into the grass house. That was the time we had kawaharu. Kawaharu (luck) came to us."

These were the kind of stories they told, but someone decided to lighten the atmosphere and told the following:

> They were hungry and on the warpath. One of the party was a fine shot. Suddenly they saw two or three buffalo sitting there. Then we all put our hands up and said, "Nawa, Kawaharu." The man who was a good shot got angry, thinking to himself, "I do the shooting and here they're saying, 'Kawaharu.' " So he got up and frightened the buffalo away and said, "Well, let kawaharu shoot it now." So they all had to keep quiet after that.

Most men felt that they had enough buffalo meat for their needs and as much as they could transport. They did not go out to hunt on the lake but stayed behind to protect the women and children from the enemy. In Victory Call's family, it was agreed that Horse Rider should stay while Victory Call went out. They also decided that they would eat the roasted ribs that evening in the family instead of contributing them to the council tent, as this would be the last time they had a chance to get them.

At the council tent, White Eagle decided they would stay over one more day and then go on directly north and across the Republican. It was fifteen miles and a very hard journey. The other bands were notified. They arrived by night, having set out very early in the morning. Water had to be carried in a buffalo paunch. When they had gone half way they stopped, unloaded the horses, and let them graze while each little family camp group sat down in the open and had an informal lunch. Victory Call came and joined his family; White Woman took some pounded dry buffalo meat, *tapaharus*, from the tanned hide she had packed it in. Each one put a clean cloth or piece of hide in front of him, and she placed a little pile of the meat there and a piece of bone grease to eat it with.

They were very tired but when the policeman called out, "Get ready," they had to pack and go on. They arrived at the river about five in the evening and then began to cross preparatory to camping on the north bank. All along the line, word passed that the water was low—a foot or less on the average. Here and there were deep holes with large fish swimming in them which could easily have been taken; they liked fish but they were much too tired and busy crossing to bother with anything. As soon as they got to the north side they all camped. Fishing was often done in Beaver Creek with a decorticated willow stick mat. Some men used a gunny sack as a fish net. They preferred catfish, but also took buffalo fish and the boys sometimes got sunfish. Boys took turtles and brought them home to make soup. But on this occasion not only were they too tired to pay attention to the fish but they also had to have corn husks to wrap them in in order to boil or roast them, and these were unavailable.

When they were camped on the north bank, a few small parties went out and hunted buffalo, but when this camp was broken up they were officially headed for home. The night before, the military police had officially resigned their office and White Eagle had stepped down from his leadership of the hunt. He thanked them all and reviewed the events of their expedition, and then Lone Chief of Village-across-a-Ridge proposed that Leading Chief, of Village-in-the-Bottomlands, now lead them all back to their settlement for the rest of the way home. This was appropriate, as Leading Chief and Village-in-the-Bottomlands had given White Eagle, their son-in-law, many kinds of special cooperation and helped to make their venture a success. Young men would bounce a buffalo leg bone along the ground to see how many camps along the Republican they would have to make before they could start north for the Platte. The bone might bounce end over end five or six times.

Various donations of dried buffalo meat had been pledged for the sacred bundles and the cults, but of special interest to everybody was the Grand Opera that the associated doctors would give after the harvest, lasting thirty days. At their next encampment, Big Doctor, head of the association, called for his two errand men to go to all members, apprentices, and any who aspired to enter and ask for their donation to the forthcoming ceremony. As they set out through the camp each errand man would pick a dry weed, *hawastatu*, with a stem as thick as a pencil, and when a doctor reported that he had a parfleche of meat to contribute, the errand man broke off a piece of the stalk and placed it in his hand to keep count. The two errand men arrived back at Big Doctor's tent, dumped out the small pieces of weed stem before the doctor and proceeded to count them, the sum in this case coming to sixty parfleches. At an earlier time, when the Skidis were more numerous, one hundred and forty parfleches had been pledged. After the pledges were counted, the word went from tent to tent and everyone was full of anticipation of the color and excitement of the ceremony. In addition to this big medical association there were a number of private cults that the people generally took an interest in.

30

THE RETURN HOME
FROM THE HUNT

"Village Scouts" Return to Village for Reports—
Main Body of Encampment Moves Homeward—
Their Diet—Young Men Leave for Warpath and
Horse Stealing—Village Scouts Return to En-
campment—Tell of Stay-at-Homes and Crops—
Releasing the Holy Man of the Hunt—Chief's Re-
marks at End of Hunt

EVERYONE WAS LADEN with meat and hides, and now that they had completed a successful hunt, all thoughts were turned toward home—particularly toward their crops and the people they had left behind. A group of young men decided they would ride ahead and see how the *Kakusu,* "Stay-at-Homes," had fared and how the crops were doing in the fields, and then come back and meet the line of march halfway, about two camps west of Fort Kearney (Camp 8), and report back to the people. These young men took up their mission on a purely voluntary and spontaneous basis. They were called *kitkehax-wiriksu,* "village-scouts." Sometimes one of them had a grandmother left behind that he wanted to know about or a girl. People were also anxious about the children who had been left at the school. The young man would tell his mother or grandmother of his plan and she would make him some pounded-up dried meat and some slabs of dried meat to take along with him. The boys took a short cut, going in a group and getting quickly back to the village.

Meanwhile in the encampments, the women were packing up the meat in the parfleches for permanent storage and strapping them up. Others were thinning buffalo robes by scraping them down—for barter at Fort Kearney in exchange for flour, coffee, sugar, and other trade goods. **In** this area now, north of the Republican, they were in Pawnee territory and were less concerned about danger of attack. As the South Bands had their villages to the east of the Skidi on Beaver Creek, they moved ahead while the Skidi lagged behind. They ate mainly dried buffalo meat at this time and a little parched corn in soup. If anyone happened to have any roasted corn kernels on hand, they boiled them and ate them, but most people had used up their supply by now. The old women were always busy when they stopped, pulverizing dried buffalo meat in the mortar with a pestle. They made a flat package, *tsat-katus*, "package-flat," of tanned hide (see Figure 30-1) and filled it up with the pounded-up dried meat. The package could be carried on the back with a strap that ran across the chest. It was 2 feet long by 1½ feet wide, and was often carried on their backs by the old women. It was a good trade item. Sometimes they also included some dried meat. Both kinds could be eaten without cooking as they were already thoroughly cured. One could simply break off a piece of the dried meat and eat it.

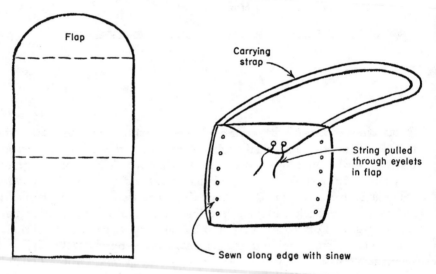

FIGURE 30-1. The pattern of a skin knapsack, *tsat-katus*, "package-flat."

Some old women made a *hu-tsaku*, "water-package," of half a buffalo bull hide made into rawhide, with sticks fastened underneath and the baggage wrapped inside envelope-fashion, to be floated across a swollen stream. Most of the women were busy tanning buffalo robes and scraping hides all the way home.

Some young men were saying that when they got to the Platte River they would set out on the warpath. There were plenty of Sioux around from whom they could well steal horses, and some young men thought they would like to go to the Osage country. The women of their household would outfit them with three or four pairs of new moccasins, tanning some hides especially for the purpose. Each pair would be filled with supplies—pulverized dried meat, parched corn, and dried meat. The young man would have a large flat package, especially wide to carry on his back with straps across the chest to carry his baggage. Under his belt he carried his tobacco and his pipe, and every time he sat down while he was on the warpath he must smoke. When he went off to steal horses he hung his flat-package on a tree and sometimes did not get a chance to retrieve it at all.

In Victory Call's household, they had gotten eight hides. A small one would be tanned by White Woman to get supplies at Fort Kearney. One was reserved for Mr. Bishop, the trader near home, to whom a good one had been promised before they left in payment for supplies Victory Call had obtained at his store for their journey.

While they were going east along the Platte River after their arrival two camps west of Fort Kearney (Camp 8), the village scouts came back with their report of how things were back home. They came in directly to the tent of Leading Chief who now had charge of their return journey and reported:

We went down to the village. We couldn't go in, it was full of fleas. Toward evening we went to the different corn fields. The corn is pretty ripe in some places. The pumpkins are hard yet. There are lots of beans of all different kinds. One fellow got on a freight and went to Columbus to see how the Stay-at-Homes were. Everything looks good. From there we went to the school. We gave the children some pulverized dried meat and some plain. We told them you folks were coming home. We stopped in Bishop and Matlock's store for the night and said it would be about eight or ten days before we got to the village. Everyone looks all right.

Now Know-His-Face went through the encampment, announcing this message to all. In one of the other bands a rougish old lady called out "And how about the sunflowers? How are they doing?" The boy said, "The sunflowers are way high!" The byplay is that the sunflowers were the place where clandestine affairs were carried on. These grew as weeds in the boundaries between the fields.

One of the scouts brought five or six ears of corn that were ripe from different fields, and gave them to the ones to whom they belonged. One ear had come from the field of Otter's grandmother, and before she took off the husks she blessed him with it four times. Then she removed the husks, roasted the ear in the coals, and broke it into three pieces, one for

White Woman and Victory Call to eat, one for No Corn and Horse Rider to eat together, and one for herself and her grandson, Otter.

When they got to the top of the hills eight miles west of Genoa they could sight the school house. Everyone called out, "There it is—*kax-karit-pahat*" (house-stone-red). It was red brick. Along the north and south side of the Loup is a deep valley and from the hills on either side of the river, one could see a considerable distance.

No one could camp anywhere near the earth lodge village itself. It was infested with fleas. They camped in the bottomlands within reach of their fields where they stayed for three weeks while they treated the crops and cleaned out the earth lodge so that it became habitable. In the open, they could more readily dispose of the husks, cobs, and other wastes that resulted from processing the crops. The Stay-at-Homes came along to meet them starting out from near Columbus 22 miles away and following northwestward along the Loup River. "Here come the Kakusu, the Stay-at-Homes," everyone would call out as they approached.

There was one more item of formal business that they had to attend to before they could get down to the activities of the harvest. To his tent, White Eagle called representatives of each of the four villages and the five old priests. In White Eagle's tent and in his charge at all times had been *taxpiku*, the holy man, who symbolized the luck of the whole tribe on the hunt. It was during the spring, when they had the ceremony of the Young Corn, *Kurahus*, that he was charged with this holy office. He was a man of exemplary character who was favored by the supernatural powers through the generous offerings he had made to their ceremonies. He had to keep his buffalo robe wrapped around him at all times. There was an absolute taboo against his bathing. He was not allowed to cut his fingernails or comb his hair. The other old men went along, one or the other of them staying alongside all during the hunt. His food was fed to him in a special bowl and he was always served first, for it was recognized that he was under a severe strain. Should he take a bath or his feet touch water, there would be severe thunderstorms. It was at this ceremony that he was praised for his courage and diligence and dismissed from his office. Now he was able to laugh and joke. "Oh my, I'm lousy," he said, "and my feet stink!" He tossed off his blanket and ran down to the creek to take a bath as soon as he could. He was no longer an official and no longer needed to be on his dignity.

They still had one more holy man, *taxpiku*, who was holding in the luck of the crops. He had been appointed early in the spring when they distributed the first seeds of the sacred corn. He would not be released until after the harvest. This man had been appointed when the Young Mother Corn was installed, and carried through the summer buffalo hunt and was then dismissed. These were men who had proved themselves devoted to the supernatural powers by their offerings to the sacred bundle ceremonies, and for them the success of the venture was a token of the favor they enjoyed with the powers above.

In his closing speech in the council tent, White Eagle had thanked his chiefs, braves and young men of the tribe who had helped him in every way to get all the dry meat that they now all had. For, he said, the horses were all heavily laden and every old man and old woman had some meat too. He spoke of the fact that they should now look to the future tasks that were ahead—their crops of corn beans and squash that they had left growing in their gardens and would harvest and preserve. There was no delay when they got to the village in getting to work on the drying and processing of the crop for storage. The star Canopus had risen in the southern sky and the harvest month of September was upon them. The Pawnee felt himself fortunate that by his work he could ensure himself so many of the good things of life.

31

HARVEST TIME IN

THE VILLAGE

EVERYONE'S THOUGHTS were now upon their gardens and their corn. In the sky, the South Star, Canopus, had appeared and they knew it was time for harvest. By our calendar it was about the first of September. The time of the hunt was over; the time of the harvest begun.

Before they left the village at the end of June, the corn had grown about knee high and the earth was hilled up around the young plants so that they looked like little earth lodges with smoke issuing from their smokeholes. Now the stalks were ten feet tall and the ears were not quite mature but "in the milk." The corn harvest was in two stages: some of the corn was treated at once in this early stage by roasting and drying, and some left to mature completely on the stalk before being dried and processed. Between the first and second corn drying, they harvested and dried the beans and then the pumpkins.

When they camped in the bottomlands near the fields, they set up a commodious tent as they knew they wouldn't have to move it for at least three weeks, and they needed room to keep their meat and dried crops under cover. Their earth lodges were infested with fleas and they couldn't spare the time to clear them up until they had gotten on with the work of the harvest. However, they did go up to the villages and open up and inspect and clean their storage pits that they had left with considerable quantities of dried corn, vegetables, meat, and some skins and clothing, and they took out some of the dried corn and beans for current use, until the green corn would be ready.

As soon as the encampment was set up, Grandma had a visit from Old-Lady-Grieves-the-Enemy who was camping way over east with the Village-in-the-Bottomlands group where she had been all summer with her son. She came to talk to Grandma about going up to the cache pit the next morning, cleaning it up and getting out a few supplies. Old-Lady-Blue-Calico who was the grandmother in Old Bull's family that occupied the south side of the earth lodge, also came with a similar proposal and early next morning the three old ladies went up there and got to work. White Woman and No Corn said they would join them later after they had finished the household chores in order to get a few supplies of dried corn and pumpkin.

When they first opened the pit, the air smelled moldy and they had to let it air a bit before anyone could enter. Then they put down a tree ladder, and Old-Lady-Grieves-the-Enemy, who was the tallest, went into the pit to look things over. The ladder was a tree trunk with stubs of branches left on for a foothold and two extra notches at the bottom. The pit was 10 feet deep. The moldy smell might have come from the thatch grass that lined the pit or from the actual supplies. When she got down inside, the old lady discovered a moldy place in the grass which she proceeded to rub off with a broom and throw out of the pit. The women had each brought along a small sack, *ritsakusu*, in which to carry home their supplies. This was about 8 inches high and a foot in diameter when full (compare with sack carried on the hunt, *asakarusu*, 3 feet high and 1½ feet diameter when full). In the pit each woman had a very large sack of tanned hide in which her provisions were stored, and each one asked Grieves-the-Enemy to dip out some from her store into the small sack. No Corn who had arrived with White Woman by this time, asked for some green roasted corn kernels (*rawaritu*) and a half a checker-plaited pumpkin mat. White Woman asked for the same. Grandma reminded them that they shouldn't take too much at this time, as they would very soon have fresh roasted green corn from their current crop. Since the other women in the household had taken roasted corn, Grandma asked for a different kind—mature dried blue flour corn, *uraaxkatit*, that she could pound up and make into mush with buffalo soup, *u-taraha* "mush-buffalo." She also asked for dried sweet corn, the rather sticky yellow variety, *rikis-karus*, "corn-sweet," that she intended to pound up in the mortar with sugar which could then be eaten without further preparation.

The younger women carried their supplies back to camp and the three older women lingered a while to close up the pit securely and to talk over their plans. They had decided that each of the old women would stay in her own field and completely process her crop there. The younger women whose husbands had horses for transportation would often go out together with another couple and bring the crop back to camp, where they would do the processing in a coordinated group. Victory Call and White Woman along with Horse Rider and No Corn formed such a work group, first in White Woman's fields and then in those of No Corn, carrying the crops into camp on their horses. The old lady sat in her field all day and brought the finished product back to camp when it was completely prepared for storage. Families with only one horse or with no horses also processed the entire crop in the field before packing it into camp.

While the women were at the food pit, the men had been out piling wood in the fields and in camp so that it would be ready for roasting the green corn. They preferred to get dead willows and driftwood; Horse Rider was at the creek piling up the driftwood while Victory Call was bringing the willows into the camp. Some men would say, "I don't care —that's women's work," but a good man would help his wife.

At this time of year they gathered a plant, *parus-asu*, "rabbit-foot," used for making a brown tea that they drank if they didn't happen to have coffee (*Lespedeza Capitata* Michx.) At the top in a cluster are some fruits looking like tiny rabbit feet. The plant grew on a bush about 3 feet high. They brewed the tea by breaking up the dry twig with the leaves on and steeping it in a coffee pot. Now everything was ready for harvesting and roasting the green corn.

Very early next morning Grandma went out to her field and there prepared a place for her work. She built herself an ample shade, *kipasiu*, of willows—a circular enclosure, open at the top with an entrance at the east. The leaves were a bit interlaced to make the fencing solid, the side branches beginning about a foot from the ground. When she left for the night, she put a willow sapling with leaves at the top in the doorway so that the shelter was closed in and well protected from horses. People who did not work in the field sometimes built themselves a more temporary shelter by arranging four or five willows in an arc. In her enclosure Grandma roasted all her corn and would leave it overnight in bags to be husked there next day and the kernels removed before bringing it to camp. During the harvest she cooked all her meals there. She left before breakfast and ate whenever it was convenient. She had a kettle along and a small mortar and pestle for preparing her meals. She would pound some of the fresh corn kernels from the roasted cobs and wrap them in corn husks, putting them in the boiling water to make dumplings. After she removed the dumplings she would add some dried meat scraps that had been scraped from the hide at the hunting grounds, *kstasi'u*, to make a good soup. Sometimes she took her grandson, Otter, into the field and shared her meals with him.

Grandma built herself a corn-roasting pit inside her shelter. It was an oblong pit with an embankment along each long side or a log for the ears to rest on—the pit lying across the shelter with the long dimension running north and south; the back of the shelter being west and its entry east.

Before putting up the shelter, on the way to the fields she had looked for some wood so that it would be ready for the roasting. If she was unable to find wood, she used sunflower stalks. Now with the shelter all prepared and the pit ready, she fixed up a parfleche as a container for the ears she picked by closing one end and leaving the other open, and since it was of stiff rawhide, she stood it up ready to throw the ears of corn in. When it was full, she carried it on her back with a packstrap which she had fastened to it. The ears of corn from one parfleche-full make a pile about 3 feet high by 2½ feet in diameter. She would gather about two parfleches of corn at a time which she would roast before gathering the next batch.

Now she built a fire in the pit. If it was morning, she would sit near the west edge facing east, the raw corn piled at her right (at the south end of the pit). The corn was set in the pit resting along the near side with the stub end down and the point end up—the ears lined up one next to the other. While they were roasting, she had to keep turning the ears, and it was hard to keep her hands from getting burnt while this was going on. With one woman working alone she could utilize only one of the long sides of the pit at any one sitting, because of the need to turn the ears. In the morning she worked along the west edge and in the afternoon after the sun went down she worked along the east edge, sitting with her back to the door, facing the rear of the shelter. She again piled the raw corn to her right (the north end) and proceeded to roast it. When two women worked together they could use both sides of the pit simultaneously.

The husks of the corn were considerably charred after the roasting, but the corn inside was not burnt. The ears were left in their husks in a pile to cool off, and this very much improved their flavor. Only if the woman was in a great hurry would she begin to husk the ears before they had cooled off.

After all the corn was husked, the kernels were cut off row by row with a fresh water clamshell. Some of the ears had such small kernels that they could not be cut off, and these ears were left aside in a pile for any guests who happened to come in and visit.

While the roasted corn was cooling, Grandma would pick the ripe beans. She swept the place clean and spread them out to let them dry in the sun and as they dried, you could hear them pop. She also went to the pumpkin patch and got two or three pumpkins that were hard enough. Like the beans, she would gather these up in her skirt. She roasted them in the fire and when they were burned all around, she scraped off the burnt places with her clamshell. So as not to waste it, she ate some of this burnt pumpkin rind and sometimes gave some to the little boy and his mouth would get all black and ashy. The next step was to cut the roasted pumpkins in half and scoop out the seeds with the pulp, removing the seeds and spreading them out to dry for next year's planting, since these were the first of the season to ripen. If she felt inclined to, she could cook the pulp with some fresh corn in her kettle; otherwise she would simply throw it away.

After the six half pumpkin shells had cooled off, she cut them into rings about 1½ inches wide. She kept cutting the pumpkin shells all around (*tihakaratsarahaku*) until she had cut them all. The bottom disks, about 4 inches in diameter, were also saved. One or two of these she wrapped in corn husks and roasted them in the ashes covered up with the hot coals so that the little boy could eat them. Then she prepared a rack for drying the strips and the bottoms were spread out on the ground on some corn husks in the sun. The drying rack was two forked sticks set in the ground with a long cross stick resting in the forks. The rack faced east so that the sun could strike it better. Hanging the pumpkin rings on her left arm, she took them one by one and hung them on the cross stick, pushing them up against the fork. When the stick was about half full, she lifted the cross stick and added rings, and when the space between the forks was full, she continued to hang them up on both ends of the stick. The three ordinary-sized pumpkins filled a little over half a cross stick.

The first corn picked were the small-kerneled varieties—the *rawarit-kiripaxki*, "roasted-small." After she had worked a little on the beans and pumpkins she went into the field and picked the larger kerneled corn, *rawarit-kutsu*, "roasted-large," particularly the blue flour *uraax-katit*, "earth-black." These she also roasted in the pit and left aside any with kernels so small that they could not be cut off with the fresh-water clamshell, for any casual guests to eat that might come to visit her in the field.

Both in the previous gathering and now with the larger-kerneled ears, after roasting, Grandma selected about a dozen or two ears that were particularly good specimens, leaving them in the husk and removing just the charred parts. These she would not husk or remove the kernels, but when they dried, braid them together into a long continuous chain that she joined together at the ends. When the ears were dry, the husks were drawn up toward the butt ends and joined together in a braid, *ki'u*, making a string some 2 feet 9 inches long about two dozen to a braid, and then the ends tied together and hung up to dry in the sun on the south side of the shelter. Some people made braids of only a dozen. Strings of spotted corn, *rikis-tipiku*, "corn-egg," were braided in a double row with more ears to the string. Most of all they braided the sweet corn, *rikis-karus*, "corn-sweet." Later when they gathered the mature corn that had been left to dry on the stalk and not roasted, they also selected some prime ears and braided them together. In the earth lodge on each side leaning against the wall was a sapling with lopped-off branches on which they hung some of these corn braids. Even if this corn was not cooked until December or January, it tasted as fresh as if it had just been plucked. From a braid of mature dried corn, anyone who wanted an occasional bite could break off an ear and roast it. Those braids that were not hung up in the lodge were put in the storage pit along with the dried kernels and other dried crops.

All day Grandma worked in the fields, and in the evening she loaded her parfleche container of roasted corn kernels on her back and carried them to the camp. She would bring six or seven corn stalks with her that had been stripped of their ears for the little boy to chew on "like sugar cane." The old lady said, "Here, that's good for you!" He bit between the joints and twisted the stalk to get out the sweet juice. While he was enjoying them, some boys would come along and say, "Give me one." At camp an old tent cover had been spread on the ground so that the corn kernels could be spread out to dry. The next morning she said to White Woman, "Tsuat Tstaka, Daughter White Woman, here's some corn. Spread it out to dry." On the way home from her fields, Grandma always took a swim in Beaver Creek.

Back at camp, they had a team approach to the harvesting that involved somewhat different steps from Grandma's. The two fields, White Woman's and No Corn's, were harvested in succession, at least two going into a field at a time, while the others might remain behind for the processing. Also all the crops were loaded on horseback rather than being packed on the back from the field to the camp as Grandma did. Husking was also done in a group, people from other camps joining them from time to time.

The team of four—Horse Rider and his wife No Corn and Victory Call and his wife White Woman—worked in the following way:

Morning of the first day, White Woman and Horse Rider went out to her field and brought in eight parfleches of corn ears that they had picked. They took along two horses and loaded them with four parfleches each. It was estimated that in our terms, eight parfleches of corn ears amounted to a wagon load, level and without the side boards up.

When they got back to camp, White Woman and No Corn immediately set to work roasting. The two men, Horse Rider and Victory Call, went back into the field and brought back two more horseloads— eight parfleches full of corn ears. In one day they had gathered in two wagonloads as stated above.

In the *afternoon*, they kept on roasting all day. The men shucked the corn. They worked fast and had no time for refinements like picking out the ears suitable for braiding as Grandma had done. They kept at it all day, and if anyone was hungry he ate some roasted corn. Sometimes one of the women stopped and made bread and coffee while the others kept right on working. They allowed the problem of cleaning dishes and other household chores to rest for the time being.

In the *evening* Uncle War Cry came along and observed, "What are you folks doing? Oh, roasting corn!" Then he sat down and lent a hand, husking away until he found an especially good ear that he would eat up on the way. Soon his younger brother, Brave Shield (also known as High Noon) joined the party. Victory Call said to Grandma, "Old Lady, go to sleep. You must be tired. You don't have to help us. We have two boys to help." Grandma went to bed and the men sat up husking together and telling stories until quite late. Moonlight nights were particularly likely to invite such husking parties.

For the next three weeks their pattern of work continued in the same way. The four would go out into the fields for the morning, come home at noon and the women set to work with the processing, the men going out again returning in the afternoon, and helping in the evening with the processing. Grandma came in, in the late afternoon or evening, and set down her processed material in a pile next to the rest.

The crops were gathered in the order of their readiness, first from White Woman's fields, then from No Corn's, and the various processing was carried on while other gathering was taking place. The *first green corn* was gathered for two days from White Woman's and then another two days from No Corn's fields. For the *first bean crop,* a day each was spent in each of the fields. Now a *final load of green corn* was gathered with the team splitting up two and two to each field on the same day. For the *second bean crop* all four worked one day in White Woman's field and then another day in No Corn's field. This was tedious work, as one had to bend down and search for the beans all along the vines. Now all four spent a day each gathering the *pumpkins,* bringing them back to camp. Then the pumpkins were roasted and cut into circular rings the next day. After the pumpkins, for which about three days had been spent, the team of four spent two days getting in and husking the *mature corn* that had been left to dry on the stalks from each of the two fields, and prying the kernels from the cobs with a pointed stick. The next step was to gather in the small *nubbin ears* to be fed to the horses so that they would get fat; Horse Rider gathered some and chopped them up and fed them to a horse that was thin and then let them loose in the field to find and eat them. Poor families sent their boys into other people's fields to glean these small ears to supplement their meager supplies. Finally the *sticky sweet corn* that was left longest on the stalk to dry was gathered, one day by Victory Call and White Woman in her

field, and then next day by Horse Rider and No Corn in her field, the two
teams staying alternately at home and watching as well as processing the
crops. Sweet corn was mainly made into double braids. Quantity production depended on team work, of course, but the women had to sort
out the eight varieties of beans after everything was done, as the men
would not bother with such a detail and would pay no attention to the
selection of the best ears for braiding. When all the corn was in, the
blackbirds began to fly over the fields, presaging the cold weather.

The following are some of the processes used in preserving the crops,
together with a breakdown of how these were coordinated with the activities of gathering.

The green corn was gathered from the stalk "in the milk" and roasted
in a long roasting pit in which a fire was built. It was allowed to cool
off and the husks removed. The kernels were cut off the cob row by row
with a fresh-water clamshell and spread on a tanned hide to dry. At night
the kernels were first winnowed to remove any chaff, gathered up and
put in a flour sack, and then taken into the tent. They were put in a
wooden bowl and spilled out from a height so that the wind would
blow the chaff away. Next morning they were again spread out on
the tanned hide. After several days, as they were being spilled for winnowing in the evening, they would make a tapping noise when they
hit the hide, showing that the kernels were completely dry.

When the beans were picked off the vines and brought into camp,
they were dumped onto the spread and allowed to dry in the sun. As
they dried, one could hear the popping of the pods. At night they
were left outdoors, covered only with a spread of tanned hide, and in
the morning uncovered and allowed to dry again. Then they were
flailed with a peeled willow rod about 4 feet long and 1 inch thick to
remove the pods as much as possible. Some of the beans had to be
picked out by hand—a small pile of beans was always picked this way.
If there was a large pile the woman would strike them with the stick,
then stop and pick out the loose pods and pile them to one side, push the
beans together again and further beat them with the stick. The beans
were winnowed by spilling from a height from a wooden bowl, in
this way loose pieces of dry pod blew away and the pods still containing
some beans fell to the ground and were opened by hand—an operation in which someone usually gave her help if they were available.
After winnowing, the beans were spread out to dry thoroughly. When
all the other work had been done, the beans were sorted into their
eight varieties.

After the beans, they brought in the pumpkin harvest. The women
spent most of one day hauling them from the field. First they brought
the largest, then the next largest, and so on. One parfleche in which
they were transported carried five large pumpkins, or seven to eight

middle-sized pumpkins, or twelve to fifteen small ones. A horse could carry in only two parfleches filled with pumpkins at a trip. Using two horses, they made five trips to the field, some in the morning and some in the afternoon, carrying about twenty parfleches in all of the different sizes. This represented the crop of White Woman's field and amounted to about a wagon-load and a half, perhaps a little more, with the wagon being level without sideboards.

The pumpkin rinds were removed by roasting them in the fire until they could scrape off the outer rind with a fresh-water clamshell. Each individual pumpkin was roasted and set aside to cool, then scraped. Some people peeled them with a knife, but this was time-consuming and was considered wasteful. Small pumpkins 4 inches or less in diameter were neither roasted, peeled, nor halved—they were simply cut into blocks, laid out on a tent skin and dried. They could be cooked any time now with the large roasted corn to add flavor. The standard-size pumpkins were cut in half, the pulp and seeds taken out, and the halves cut into a series of circular rings each about 1½ inches wide. These were hung on a rack and when they had dried somewhat were pressed underfoot to express some of the water as was done with the sliced buffalo meat, then hung up again to dry further. At night the pumpkin rings were left on the rack covered with an old tent skin. By the time the mature dried corn crop was coming in, the pumpkin strips would be dry enough so that they could be woven into checker-plaited mats. They would alternate the processing of this corn with the making of the pumpkin mats, *ri-katsitu,* "braid-woven."

The plaited pumpkin mats were arm's length and 2 feet wide. The individual strips had shrunk in the drying to an inch in width. It took about two hours to weave a pumpkin mat. In an afternoon, each woman would make two mats before supper. The dried pumpkin was used by cutting off a number of the 2-foot strips in the width with small portions of the cross pieces adhering to them. The very smallest pumpkins about the size of tomatoes were boiled fresh and eaten in the morning for a breakfast during this harvest period. They were very much relished.

The preparation of the mature corn that had been allowed to dry on the stalk, was somewhat different from the ears that were gathered "in the milk." No roasting was necessary. The ears were snapped off the stalk, taken to camp, and husked that evening and the following day. The ears were then spread out and allowed to dry until evening and after supper the women began to remove the kernels. They used a small pointed stick to pry them off, pushing it in between two rows and along the cob from stub end to point so that in spreading the rows of kernels they were readily pried off. In the evening the corn was winnowed and taken into the tent. The next day the removal of the kernels continued. They were spread out to dry along with those removed the day before. In the late afternoon they were again winnowed and kept in the tent for the night, and again spread out to dry further. When the kernels made a tapping sound on the hide during winnowing they were judged to be dry.

These were the technical steps taken to process the crops. The general scheme of events among the household personnel was as follows:

First day. White Woman and Horse Rider went into her field and brought in the corn loaded on two horses. White Woman and No Corn stayed and roasted the corn. Victory Call and Horse Rider went back into the field and got a second load. In the afternoon women kept on roasting and the men removed the husks. In the evening two more men came in and helped with the husking while the women went to bed. The four men stayed up doing the husking and telling stories.

Second day. In the morning two men continued husking until eleven A.M.; the two women continued cutting off the kernels. After this time the two men spread out the kernels to dry. The two women continued to cut off the kernels from the cobs.

If Victory Call was tired, he rested and White Woman took over the spreading of the kernels while No Corn continued to cut the kernels from the cob. Horse Rider might have to go and tend the horses.

In the afternoon, Grandma came in with her parfleche of shelled corn, having crossed Beaver Creek and stopped for a swim. She dumped her corn kernels on the skin spread in a separate heap and spread them out to dry.

In the evening, having gathered in most of the green corn that was ready from White Woman's fields, they made a plan to go into No Corn's field the next morning. All four would go off into the field and they needed someone to keep watch over their corn against stealing. Also, should anyone need Victory Call for official business, it was necessary to tell them where he could be reached. White Woman asked her brother War Cry to send over one of his three wives as "Room-Watcher," *ratut-kihar-atsiksta,* "I that am for him-room-watcher." She could also spread out any corn kernels that still needed to be dried while she was there.

Third day. They go to No Corn's field to get the green corn. Victory Call, White Woman and No Corn set out on foot and pick whatever was ripe in No Corn's field, leaving it here and there in little piles. Horse Rider meanwhile had gone out to get the horses and saddle them up; then he joined them in the field. When one load was ready they went back to camp and the two women stayed there, beginning at once to roast the ears. Horse Rider went back to the field and brought what was left in the several piles, loading it onto the horses and bringing it back into camp. The women continued to roast and the men began to do the husking.

That evening Sun Chief and Leading Fox, older sons of Victory Call by a previous marriage, came in to help with the husking.

Fourth day. Men continued to husk the corn, while the women now cut the kernels from the cobs with a clamshell. They all helped to spread out the kernels to dry. All the green corn from both sets of fields that was ripe enough, had now been gathered, roasted, and set out to dry. It was usual to finish this task in the first four or five days.

Fifth day. This was the time for the first bean harvest in White Woman's field. This was hard work as most of the vines didn't climb on anything but grew close to the ground. Sometimes they grew in separate patches and sometimes in a patch with the corn. The women gathered the pods in their skirts; the men threw them in whenever they got a handful. All four worked in the field until late afternoon. On the way home, they stopped and took a swim in Beaver Creek. Again as in the time of planting, they slapped the water with their feet, making as loud a noise as possible. As the women slapped the surface of the water with their soles, it resounded all along the creek like the report of a gun. "They are slapping the water with their feet" (*tutastaxkitspiru*). The girls used their hands for this (*tutikstaxkitspiru*), and Otter had a hard time learning the trick from them. Possibly it was a kind of sympathetic magic for the tapping of the dry beans and corn on the threshing floor. They went home about 4:30 in the afternoon, having gathered about four parfleches of the beans in the pod in a good year. At home one of War Cry's wives or daughters had been serving as Room Watcher for their tent. It was five o'clock by the time the pods were all spread out to dry. Everyone was tired and took a rest. Inside the tent, Horse Rider and No Corn were wrestling playfully together and saying, "Now we have some roasted corn" (*rawaritu*).

In the evening the beans were covered up where they lay and the corn kernels were winnowed and taken inside for the night in flour sacks. Now grandma came in carrying her sack of corn or beans that she spread out. White Woman offered to come out and help her in her field but she refused saying, "Oh, no. If you help me I'll get through too soon and I won't have anything else to do. So I'd just like to do it myself."

White Woman made the fire and cooked some grease bread and No Corn prepared the coffee and dried apples for their supper. Uncle War Cry came to join them and began to tease Grandma about how tired she was; Grandma asked to have her dinner brought to her. War Cry then began to talk about the trade store and Victory Call remembered he owed them a buffalo robe, but War Cry observed that he was sure they would wait until the harvest work was done. He promised to mention it to them. Everyone went to bed early, for next day they would be picking the beans in No Corn's field and this meant another day of back-breaking work.

Sixth day. All during this time young men would go out very early in the morning with their bow and arrows to act as sentinels, watching particularly for the Sioux, who lurked about to attack women going to and from the fields. Victory Call always took along his bow and arrows should there be a surprise attack. The Skidi fields were located northwest of the villages. Going out early in the morning, one could see the boys picketing about on the high bluff to the west. That morning as they looked up at a big hill west of Genoa, they would also see someone stationed, scouting around for the enemy. The night before Mad Bear and another man had made up their minds to do this. Before dawn they climbed the high bluff west of Beaver Creek and sat down and looked toward where they were roasting corn. "Look at that smoke. Afterward, we can get some corn," they said. Their legs were hanging over the bluff. There was a little creek that ran from the southwest into Beaver Creek running parallel with the edge of the bluff where the two men were sitting, and a Sioux had been hiding in a trough and watching them. The two men were talking about the cherries on the side of the bluff and the big yellow plums in the bottom and how they would eat them next day. As they were talking, they heard the Sioux making a noise like a crow.

Later Mad Bear told his story. "I got frightened and I never thought of my bow and arrows. I was transfixed with fear when I saw all of them. But all at once I got over it. The other man didn't get over it. We ran down the bluff to the creek. The other man left his bow and arrows there." Mad Bear continued: "I don't see why the other fellow left me and ran away to get under the brush. The Sioux caught him. As I ran down the bluff, I felt a shot through my back. It came out of my chest, but I got into the water anyway and they let me go. The other fellow had disappeared." We looked in the water for him but couldn't find him. Long after when someone came back to Nebraska, they thought they saw him and he had been scalped and was ashamed to come back.

The Pawnees took Mad Bear over the creek and he was doctored by Heavy-Trophies and Herd-of-Horses. As Mad Bear described it, "The doctor put his mouth against mine and blew some water with some medicine in it into my mouth and made me swallow it. I had been sleepy all along, but this woke me up. Then they gave me some medicine to chew and water to drink and I felt better and never worried about it again. I sent the doctors home." Finally the Pawnees came out and killed a big tall Sioux. His bones remained there a long time afterward. One Sioux was killed and one Pawnee killed or scalped. This is why Mad Bear was known as a brave man, heedless of any danger to himself, like a boy, a *piraski*.

All the time that this struggle was going on, Victory Call, White Woman, and No Corn were in No Corn's field picking beans. Horse Rider had had to go quite a way to find the horses and when he got back to camp to saddle them, they had left him a bite of breakfast and then he joined them in the field. First he inspected the pumpkins and then they all went around picking up the vines, and when a vine wrapped around a cornstalk, they had to look all around for the ripe pods. This took until noon and on the way home they took a swim in the creek. Arriving at camp, they prepared a modest lunch of bread, coffee, and bits of ready-cooked meat saved in a sack for such purposes—pieces of dried heart, leg muscle, pieces of paunch, fat, etc. They called this *tsuspakahu*. They opened the sack and dumped the pieces of meat on a spread and simply picked up one and ate it with the bread and coffee. Sometimes they had pulverized dried meat, *tapaharus*, with some bone grease instead of the meat. They decided to have the same kind of meal in the evening, as their backs ached from picking the beans. After the meal, the newly picked beans were spread out to dry, and about three in the afternoon White Woman decided that her beans were dry enough to thresh with the long willow stick to get the beans out of the pods. Victory Call wandered up to the store and Horse Rider either went to the gambling grounds or just sat on a bluff smoking and looking around. The women kept working with the beans.

That evening, Victory Call came in with supplies from the store for supper: prunes, dry apples and some candy sticks for Otter—a gift of the trader. People had seen Victory Call coming in while they were at the gambling grounds watching the game, and they decided to come over and have some dinner there. War Cry's younger brother, Brave Shield, and Wants-the-Enemy dropped in for a visit. Some decided to visit with Misery (*Akapakis*) instead, and White Woman felt slighted because the youngest brother of War Cry, Leading Fox, had decided to go there as also had Sun Chief, Victory Call's older son. She scolded Leading Fox saying, "Why don't you come in. People will think I don't take care of you." "Well," he said, "the boys wanted me to come with them." She remarked about Sun Chief to Victory Call who reassured her saying, "That's nothing. You have to watch girls, but you can't keep boys home like that."

At dinner, Brave Shield mentioned that some of the Kitkehaxki doctors were preparing to go back into the earth lodges to prepare for the forthcoming doctor dances. Victory Call said that it was a bit too early. It was better to finish the work so that they didn't have all this rubbish in their yards at home and then go up to the village. He said the leading doctors would wait until people got all through before beginning as "They liked to have a good crowd to attend the dances." At the gambling grounds the talk was about the same subject. Presently two or three men came in from the South Bands and joined them at supper and talked about how things were going with them. "What are your folks doing over there?" they were asked. "We are working hard making roasted corn. The village is full of fleas. You have to clean it out two or three times before you can get in," said the South Bands men. "Same with us," the Skidis said.

Next morning Victory Call went to the field to see if there was much of a load of green corn left to be gathered and roasted. The following day they went to the two fields and brought them in.

After that a second bean crop was picked from each field on successive days—the vines being almost entirely cleared with this picking. Then the pumpkins were hauled in by all four of them and roasted: one day from White Woman's field, the next from No Corn's. They were all roasted and cut into rings.

About the *eleventh day* they got the mature corn from White Woman's field in two double horse loads—one in the morning and one in the afternoon. They got home about two o'clock in the afternoon, and being very tired dumped the load of dry ears and rested till supper time. Then Old-Man-That-Chief joined them for supper and talked of the old days in Old Village. He said:

In the old days, an old lady like grandma would see an ear of corn or a single bean lying on the ground and she would be half-crying to see it lying there. Nowadays it's different. They leave things to waste on the ground. If they were roasting corn and they scraped an ear and left the kernels on one side, they would pick it up from the discarded pile again and clear it off. For if you didn't, the corn would talk about you. It was like a person. But nowadays they don't care.

Horse Rider and Victory Call listened with respectful attention to what the old man said. He continued, "You Horse Rider, are two steps behind me, but Victory Call—he is nearly on top (in the middle of life). He will be able to look around in all directions to see how he has come up there.

"A story is like a little seed. From it all sorts of other stories branch off for you. A story gives you life. Now that I am old, people invite me to come and eat good things with them and then they ask me to tell stories. So these stories keep me alive."

Now he told another story of the past. He said: "I heard that once way back when corn first came to our village, a good ear of corn had been thrown out with the rubbish and swept aside. The

people went on the hunt and still the corn lay there. A man going
through the village heard someone talking. He thought there must be
another man in the village. But he followed along to where the
voice was coming from and got to the sweepings. There lay the good
ear of corn. He stopped and picked it up and began to talk to it.
He asked it to bless him and send him good luck for this corn is our
Mother. He kept that ear of corn. That's how it was in the old days.
Now since you've been wasting, the corn will become scarce."

That evening they husked the dry corn and continued next day until
about two in the afternoon. Then it was left spread out to dry on the
cob until evening and pried off after supper with a stick. Some men
joined them and helped and after the women had gone to bed they
continued to pry off the kernels, telling stories while they worked until
late in the evening. The next day the shelling of the dry corn continued and that afternoon the men just wandered about the camp for a
little recreation. Horse Rider had gone down to the grounds to watch
the gambling. The women were tired and lay down to rest; their hands
felt cramped from prying off the kernels.

After they had collected the dry corn from No Corn's field, the
women alternated work on it with making pumpkin mats as the strips
were now dry enough. Then they proceeded to get the small nubbin ears
for fattening the horses and collecting the sweet corn and braiding it to
finish off the work.

While they were doing the pumpkins, the old ladies had already
made a plan to go up and begin the process of clearing the earth
lodge in anticipation of the time when the harvest was done. They had
to go up at intervals of four days successively and burn out the fleas
with torches. "These fleas bite worse than bedbugs!"

The three old ladies met at the lodge in the morning as planned. They
removed the brush that had been placed across the door to seal it before they left on the hunt. They took off their clothes and put on an
old petticoat. They made a brush or short broom of dry *pakuts* (thatch)
grass and tied it to a stick. Then each woman took her brush inside the
lodge and lit the grass, each one going around one side of the room
and being careful to stay near the floor as the dry grass in the roof
thatch might catch fire. When the grass was burned up on their broom,
they put some more grass on it and repeated the process throughout the
day. They repeated this four days later, and then on subsequent days.
They built a little fire in the fireplace and burnt some wild sage, kiwaut,
(*Artemisia gnaphalodes* Nutt.) as incense to clear the air and make the
room smell good. They would also burn some of the sage on their
brooms along with the other grass. After the final smoking, they left
the lodge empty for a day and on the following evening the lodge was

quite habitable. Each of the old ladies brought in her dried corn and put it on her side of the lodge. They slept over and talked that night about the events of the past summer. They had a good deal to tell one another.

Grandma began: "The first time we got buffalo, we had two, and my, I was slicing away to make the dry meat and White Woman was busy at the drying rack. Then we made bone grease. We had a hard time getting the flesh we scraped off the hides to dry." Grieves-the-Enemy commented: "I went out and got lots of intestines from the men after the kill." Grandma said, "I never got a chance to get out there, but Horse Rider brought in plenty of entrails. When we were south across the Republican, three of us old ladies found some wonderful turnips. Oh, I wish we had them now! We were shouting to each other, 'Here are some!' and everyone said the officers should have punished us for yelling like that (the buffalo might have been frightened), but they finally decided to let us alone to have our good time." They talked about how they would get Indian potatoes after they were well settled and what else they might do then. Old-Lady-Blue Calico then talked of her hunt experiences: "Oh my, we didn't get a chance to eat ribs very much. My very public-spirited son-in-law, Old Bull thought he should give White Eagle his support so that nearly every day that they got buffalo, he would leave the ribs at the council tent and sometimes the backbone steak too. Once in a while Old Bull brought home two or three ribs from the feast for the family to eat. My daughter Clear Day and I made dry meat. Queen Woman, who isn't too strong, we gave the job of hanging up the slices to dry and turning them over. Clear Day had to wash the paunch after she sliced the meat. I tried to make bone grease, but I barely got it made. It was too hot." Grandma now chimed in with, "I have mine all right. I made it the first night we got to the Republican River. Horse Rider brought in the bones." "My, that woman knows how to do everything," Blue-Calico remarked. They might sit up most of the night talking until they got too sleepy. In the morning they came down to the camp and joined the family for breakfast. Even before the family finally moved in, they took the corn and beans up there to protect them from rain. They were not worried about stealing as everyone had plenty of the same kind of supplies at this time.

32

THE CEREMONIAL OBSERVANCE

OF THE HARVEST

〰〰〰〰〰〰〰〰〰〰〰〰〰〰〰

*Holy Significance of the Mother Corn—Pawnee
Logic of the Universe—Three Harvest Ceremonies—Green Corn Ceremony—Mature Corn Ceremony—Four-Pole Ceremony—Ceremonial Rituals
Explained—Symbolic Significance*

〰〰〰〰〰〰〰〰〰〰〰〰〰〰〰

To THE PAWNEE, the ear of corn was his daily food and also the object of
his most profound reverence and worship. In every sacred bundle that
represented the cosmic powers there were two ears of corn of an ancient
breed, cultivated exclusively for its role as a holy object—their Mother
Corn. The leader of a war party that went afoot far out onto the Plains
to capture horses and booty wore an ear of sacred corn on his left shoulder so that Mother Corn might guide them to victory. It was an ear that
had served in a sacred bundle for one year from harvest to harvest. The
calumet expedition for peace and trade with another tribe, besides the
two symbolic eagle-feathered pipes, carried an ear of sacred corn representing the universe. It was painted blue around its bottom half with four
blue lines leading up toward the point representing the semicardinal-
direction pathways of prayer to Heaven, while on the point of the corn
stood a single white feather to represent Heaven itself.

Each sacred ear of corn in the sacred bundle was sewn into a skin
cover: the ear for winter in a tanned buffalo skin, and that for summer
in a heart skin. At every meal the wife or sister of the chief in whose care
the bundle was kept addressed each ear of corn by its own name to give
thanks for the food they were about to enjoy. If it were buffalo meat
they were having, she would point some of it toward the sacred bundle
hanging at the west in order to give Mother Corn the first portion. When
they ate corn it was of course not offered to her but the bowl of the spoon

was pointed toward the nose of the buffalo skull that rested below on the altar platform, and a few kernels dropped there so that Father Buffalo might eat.

Few ceremonial acts of the Pawnee were so obscure that they could not be understood in terms of his "logic of the universe." A rhythm of alternation of cosmic powers was a very important phase of that logic. The winter and the summer, the night and the day, succeeded each other in a never-ending round. The powers of the south succeeded the powers of the north and the powers of the east followed those of the west. As these two rhythms were combined, the semicardinal directions ran their biennial course—northwest, southwest, northeast, southeast—and for each of these a sacred bundle took charge of the tribe in its turn through the alternate seasons. In many functions of his life, including the household, the Pawnees followed this alternating principle. As he valued these alternating rhythms of the universe, he also followed a pattern of rotation of power and responsibility in all phases of his life, particularly in his political life and in his appeal to the cosmos.

Three ceremonies celebrated the harvest, each representing a different aspect of the sacred tradition. The first for the *Green Corn* was under the Evening Star bundle that embodied the tradition of the original creation of the universe and its yearly renewal.

The second was the main harvest ceremony and was celebrated when the *Mature Corn* was gathered. It was under the authority of the four semicardinal-direction bundles that carried the theme of the progression of the seasons and the growth of the sacred corn into their major deity, Mother Corn.

The third ceremony celebrated the alliance of the Skidi villages in their political and religious life. Appropriately, it was conducted under the aegis of the Skull bundle of the Wonderful Person. This represented the cult of the visionary chief who in past times had gathered them all together and established their organization. It was known as the *Four-Pole Ceremony*—signifying the four semicardinal directions, which taken together, represented the whole world. In the course of the ceremony warriors went out symbolically in all directions to see that their land was safe.

The Pawnees had a marked preference for complex ceremonial symbolism, and each of these cosmic authorities had a somewhat variant "ceremonial vocabulary" that was systematically organized in the lore of its sacred bundle, which also contained the paraphernalia for its performance.

The ceremonial pattern of the green corn ceremony under the Evening Star bundle was ritually quite simple. No songs were sung by the priests and no dances carried out. When the people were getting ready to settle back in the village, the Evening Star priest called in the other four priests of the four direction bundles. They were representing the four aspects of the primordial storm given by Heaven to the Evening Star to assist her in the process of creation. The Evening Star priest also invited a number of noted warriors and old men and had a quantity of green corn cooked for their feast. The sacred bundle was opened and its pipe smoked and shared with the Evening Star and the other great western powers by pointing its mouthpiece toward the west and then in the same way with the other celestial gods who took part in the ongoing of the universe. The contents of the sacred bundle were passed through an incense of burning sweet grass smoke, and an offering of the corn was made to the gods. Then the invited guests had their feast of green corn. After the Evening Star bundle had completed its ritual, all other sacred bundles followed suit, offering green corn to the bundles and having a corn feast.

The main harvest ceremony which centered around the Mature Corn was a continuation of the symbolic theme of the life cycle of Mother Corn carried by the four semicardinal-direction bundles. Its connection with the progression of the seasons was also part of the ritual pattern.

In the spring, after the Evening Star priest had performed the creation ritual for the renewal of all things, the four direction priests began their ritual cycle in anticipation of the planting time by a ceremonial distribution of the seeds of the sacred corn to the twelve owners of the sacred bundles whose wives planted them in special hills in the fields. Pursuing the theme of seasonal succession, the four sacred bundles of the group took charge of their ritual in turn. For the winter season, a North bundle was in charge. At the ceremony when the sacred seeds were distributed, the North bundle gave over its sacred mission to one of the South bundles of the group. A number of cornstalks symbolized this transfer of power, and these were now handed from the North to the South bundle. After the ground-breaking ceremony which belonged to a different cult (Skull bundle—Evening Star), the second ceremony of the Four Direction series concerning the Mother Corn was carried out. In this case the birth, infancy, and adolescence of Mother Corn were symbolized by uprooting the new little shoots of the sacred corn plants and providing one of them with a shaft on which a mouth and windpipe were painted to represent its life. The Young Mother Corn had carried them through the summer attached to the outside of the sacred bundle. Now the maturing Mother Corn had attained her full power to look after the people. The ceremony of the Mature Corn represented her installation to this office. It was also the occasion when the four-direction-bundle group shifted the ceremonial prerogative from the South bundle to the North bundle for the forthcoming winter. Some of the cornstalks of the sacred corn from the current harvest were given to this bundle to signify its mission. In addition to the principle of the succession of winter and summer seasons followed by the four-direction-bundle group, another principle of alternation of powers was carried through as a means of assuring complete cosmic protection. This was the alternation of the powers of the western and of the eastern skies in successive years. There was, therefore, a fourfold alternation of bundles in the four-direction-bundle group over a cycle of two years: North*west*-South*west* in one year, and North*east*-South*east* in the subsequent year. The west and east each dominated a year, while north and south moved in half-year seasonal cycles for winter and summer.

As they were returning from the summer buffalo hunt when they had gotten about half way home, the priest of the summer direction bundle had sent a young man to the sacred corn hill to make an offering to it of buffalo tongue and heart meat. He pressed alternately into the corn hill a strip of tongue and a strip of heart in the four semicardinal directions.

Now with the harvest in, the priest asked his wife to clear out their earth lodge so that the ceremony for the Mature Mother Corn could be held. The women removed all the beds and other furniture and swept it out well, and the priest took down the sacred bundle from where it had been hanging at the west and placed it on the altar. Before dawn he sent four men to the sacred corn hill in the fields to bring in four stalks of the holy corn with the ears still on them. In the course of the ceremony, these would replace the old Mother Corn ears in the sacred bundles. In this way the sacred bundles always contained some fertile seeds.

The priest now invited a number of other people to participate. He called the other four high priests—his three colleagues of the four-direction-bundle group and the Evening Star priest. He also called in the holy man who had taken office when the sacred seeds were distributed in the spring and who had lived under severe taboos from which he would only now be released. All summer while they were on the march, this holy man had been living under the watchful eye of the priest. Also invited was the young woman who had contributed milk from her breasts at the ceremony of the Young Corn Plant in order to symbolize conception and the other owners of the sacred bundles.

When everyone was assembled, all went down to the camps where the women had piled their mature corn and other crops. The priest announced that Mother Corn was about to be installed and asked them to bring their harvest offerings. They came with their best ears of corn, and as the women entered the ceremonial lodge they put the corn on the north side in piles according to the color. Any of the ears that had the male spike at the tip, a feature that was regularly found in the holy corn, might be included in the sacred bundle in the course of the ceremony that was to follow. The women also brought beans and squash for the harvest offering. Then the women left the lodge and the ceremony was carried on entirely by the men. Now a man was sent to the sacred corn hill to uproot any stalks that remained there with the ears still on them. They were tied to the northwest post of the lodge, which symbolized the Garden of the Gods. When the new winter direction priest was installed at the end of the proceedings, he would receive these as a sign of his office.

The priest was now ready to conduct the ceremony. He sat at the west with his bundle open before him. He put aside the stick with the Young Mother Corn Plant tied to it that they had made in the spring and the two sacred ears in their respective wrappings. He also had before him the four new sacred ears that were brought in that morning. The new sacred ears had been cut with the first section of the stem left on to symbolize the windpipe and the voice of the Mother Corn which was the "breath of life." After singing four songs mentioning the different colors, black, red, yellow, and white for the semicardinal directions, he sang a fifth song and cut off the stem. Then he sang another song welcoming the new Mother Corn. He embraced the new ear, passing it to the other priests who were sitting to the south and to the north of him, and then passed it down the south side and then the north of the lodge, everyone in turn embracing the new Mother Corn. When the ear was returned to the priest, he sang a seventh song stating that the voice of the corn was raised to the heavens.

At the close of the songs, the pipe was filled and the mouthpiece pointed toward Mother Corn as an offering to share in the smoking. Then the ear was passed to the people on each side of the lodge and each person blew his breath on it four times, symbolizing its new life in the world.

The next symbolic act was to concentrate all the power in the world into Mother Corn herself. The priest took a buffalo-hair rope about a yard long from his sacred bundle. It was said to have been made of "hair from beneath the waters." Taking one of the new Mother Corn ears in each hand, he knelt before the altar holding the ends of the rope against the ears. Then moving his hands, he made the rope circle around into a loop to represent the horizon as it had circled out from the gods in the west during the original creation. He now made movements as if he were throwing the rope over objects and drawing them to his breast. This was spoken of as "trapping the powers of the Heavens" for Mother Corn and all the sacred objects.

The ears of sacred corn whose "lives had been ended" were now given over to a distinguished warrior, who would carry them on the warpath to guide him to success, or to the entrepreneur of the Peace Pipe Ceremony, who would carry them on his expedition to give him success in trade and international relations.

With the installation of the New Mother Corn accomplished, steps were taken to shift the cosmic power to the North Direction bundle for the winter. The priest announced that the change was at hand, went to the northwest house post, and took down the sacred stalks that were tied there, giving them to the chief who was in charge of the newly appointed North Direction bundle. He addressed the chief briefly upon the import of the procedure and formally charged him with the office. The new chief replaced the stalks on the post and then divided the harvest offerings that the women had brought among the chiefs and priests present at the ceremony.

Following this ceremony, all the sacred bundles changed their ears of Mother Corn for those of the new harvest. This ceremony was conducted very simply in each case, the usual smoke and meat offerings being made to the appropriate powers and a feast shared. In all the sacred bundles the pipe was turned so that when the bundle hung on the west wall of the house over the altar the mouthpiece of the pipe would be pointing north, so that the winter powers located in that direction could smoke.

The Pawnee year opened in the spring with a ceremony celebrating the creation of the universe and within it the uniting of all the people under one religion and society. Now as the harvest was done, a closing ceremony commemorated their unity and the common defense of their land. The four house posts in the semicardinal positions symbolized the entire world and its peoples. It was under the aegis of the Skull bundle of the Wonderful Person and its four special ministers.

The setting for the ceremony was a special circular structure—a low circular embankment opening to the east. First the priests marked out the circle with a compass consisting of two sticks with a long string between; they also marked out the fireplace in the center in the same way. The fireplace was 3 feet in diameter and the excavated earth from it was dumped outside the east entrance to form a small mound. They dug four holes about a foot deep in the semicardinal positions within the circle to receive the posts that would be planted later on. All around the inside of the circular embankment saplings were set up in the ground, forming a screen that shaded the participants as they sat around during the ceremony. The chiefs who were the owners of the sacred bundles sat along the north and along the south side of the circle, each representing one of the villages that was a member of the original federation. Most of them sat on the north side, as the original villages were mainly on the Loup River, only one having come from the Platte to the south. At the west sat the keepers of the four direction bundles as they had originally come from Old Village in the west.

The ceremony itself comprised two major episodes. One was the getting of the four poles, a war party setting out in a different direction for each one. The second part of the ceremony consisted in the recitation by a chief of certain events in the creation ritual that represented the essential nature of the world.

In the first episode, the four war parties went out for the poles. When everyone was assembled, four warriors took positions at the semicardinal places. Each was dressed in full regalia. He wore an otter fur collar, a sacred ear of corn on the left shoulder, and a hawkskin on the right shoulder. On the head, each wore a ball of white down feathers and, transversely in the scalplock, an eagle feather. Each element of their costume had a symbolic meaning—the otter collar, awakening of life in the spring; the ear of corn, Mother Corn to guide them over the world; the hawk, to symbolize strength and fierceness; the eagle feather in the scalplock, Heaven during the creation; the white downy feathers, the clouds on which he rode. Their faces were painted with red streaks along the sides and a bird's-foot mark on their foreheads which was also the name of a constellation in the Milky Way. Each warrior carried a war club and a pipe from one of the leading sacred bundles.

While the warriors were being costumed, four scouts had gone in four different directions to locate the trees for the posts. The White Pole was located in the southwest direction and was a cottonwood. The Yellow Pole was found in the northwest and was a willow. The Red Pole of the southeast was a box elder, and the Black Pole of the northeast, an elm. The warriors came outside the enclosure and danced in their appropriate positions and a group of people gathered around each of them. The warriors now led their parties in their different directions and were met by their respective scouts who reported that they had located an enemy standing among the timber. Each warrior now led his party as if stealing upon an enemy. When the tree was sighted, they rushed in and the first man to reach the tree acted as if he were touching an enemy in battle, meriting a special war honor.

Standing at the east, the warrior made a smoke offering to the tree. Then he carried the smoked-out pipe to the west where he deposited the ashes. Then another man, in similar fashion, made an offering of buffalo meat. Then a virgin took up her ax and symbolically cut down the tree. She motioned four times in each of the four directions, cutting off a chip in each. The tree was then actually cut down by her uncles and brothers amid the shouts of the people. As the tree fell they made as much noise as possible.

Now the warriors took up the tree and started toward the village, the crowd following. On the way in they stopped to rest at four different intervals when they were beset by old women who encircled them making suggestive remarks referring to sexual intercourse and speaking of sexual acts as deeds of war. None of these remarks were personal. When the party tried to bring the pole into the enclosure, someone blocked their way and touched the tree as if it were an enemy, claiming war honors and stating that they were entering the territory of the enemy. Then they brought it inside.

While the war parties were out, the priests had prepared the postholes. In each they placed a cake of buffalo fat sprinkled with some tobacco, the fat representing the earth and the tobacco the people. A similar cake of fat sprinkled with tobacco was placed in the center of the fireplace. These cakes were then taken outside and buried under the little mound outside to the east of the enclosure.

As each war party came in with its pole, the priest of that semicardinal-direction bundle offered it the pipe to smoke and sang the song ritual while the warrior danced four times and planted the tree in the posthole. All the branches had been trimmed from the posts except the very top ones. The priests sang songs referring to the appropriate colors connected with the semicardinal directions and each post was painted its proper color.

The next phase of the ceremony was considered its most vital part. The chief who was keeper of the Skull bundle of the Wonderful Person now recited certain acts of the creation by Heaven. The skull, fastened to a stick, was costumed to represent Heaven as in the first episode of the ground-breaking (*awari*), ceremony in the spring. The paraphernalia for decorating the skull, including the paints, was kept inside the bundle in a bladder bag when not in use.

Another symbolic object was a wooden bowl filled with water to represent a primordial pond or the waters in general. In the water was a shell to represent running water and the continuity of life. On the shell was placed the jaw of a gar pike, the head of a (thunder?) bird and the image of a turtle, all symbolizing the denizens of the water and the rains. The skull rested to the west, and to the east of it the bowl of water with the objects connected by a framework of sticks on which the turtle was placed with a clamshell over his middle. There were four smooth stones that were either meteorites or buffalo maw stones which came from the sacred bundle of the former Village Partly-on-a-Hill. The turtle and the shell were from the Southwest Direction bundle. The four smooth stones stood for the four quarters of the world.

The chief who had charge of the Skull bundle now stood up with the skull in his hands and, facing the bowl, recited the acts of the creation that had been performed by Heaven. The main part of the ceremony was now complete.

During the following night there were additional dramatic acts. Certain doctors appeared dressed in the skins of bears, loons, wildcats, and wolves, each connected with one of the four semicardinal directions. During the creation, as the Morning Star went out to conquer the Evening Star, he had to overcome each of these primordial animals who were also aspects of the storm and who guarded her domain. They thus symbolized all war and conquest. Dressed in these skins, the doctors charged about the camp, symbolically fighting the people.

The final act of the priests was the "opening of the road to the enemies' country and to the buffalo." The chief who was keeper of the Skull bundle danced with the skull and made certain movements with the skull in the four directions in turn as the priests sang the appropriate songs. Then with loud shouting the people joined in the dance. The way was now ceremonially open for war parties to set out and for the chiefs to make plans for the tribal migration and buffalo hunt for the winter season.

Now everyone moved back into their houses, stored their crops and buffalo meat from the summer hunt, and awaited the time they had all been looking forward to for so long—the thirty-day Grand Opera of the Wild Animal Cults that would be put on by the Doctors' Association. But first the crops and meat had to be stored in the food pit and everything connected with the harvest put in good order.

33

THE HOUSE REESTABLISHED
AND THE FOOD STORED

~~~~~~~~~~~~~~~~~~~~~~~~~~~~~~~~~~~

*The Move into the Earth Lodge—Final Meal in
the Tent—Beds in the Lodge Are Repaired—Bed-
ding Explained—South Side Family Moves In—
Storage Pit Opened—Harvest and Meat Stored—
List of the Contents—Importance of the Storage
Pit*

~~~~~~~~~~~~~~~~~~~~~~~~~~~~~~~~~~~

OVERHEAD THE BLACKBIRDS were flying south and everyone knew that it
would soon be cold. The tents were crowded with parfleches of dried
buffalo meat and tanned skin bags of corn kernels and dried beans. The
harvest ceremonies were done and the cosmic powers had received their
thanks. All over the encampment people began to think of moving back
into the earth lodges where they would have better protection for themselves and their stores. The men were thinking about the forthcoming
Grand Doctor Ceremony and their part in its thirty-day round of ceremonies and performances. The needed food supplies would have to be
gotten ready and their paraphernalia gotten in order.

Victory Call was one of the early ones in the encampment to plan to
go back into the village. One morning he announced, "Tomorrow we're
going to move into the earth lodge." "Well," said Grandma, "it's ready
for us. Grieves-the-Enemy, Blue-Calico, and I got it all cleared out."
White Woman, going on with the plans remarked, "We'll need two
horses to do the hauling. The parfleches must go in first. You men will
go up first and pile them up outside."

Horse Rider, who got up that next morning before anyone else, announced to his wife, No Corn, "Fire's made"; directly she got to
work boiling some buffalo meat for their breakfast and preparing the
grease bread. Horse Rider went to the creek for more water and then

White Woman got up and joined in, making the breakfast coffee. The cooking was going on near the long oblong fireplace somewhat to the north of the curve-roofed shelter that opened to the east. Across the front of the tent and just inside, the long twined-woven rush mats were lined up. Now Victory Call got up and sat near the south end and began to smoke his pipe. He remarked, "Now leave the tent here for last. We can take everything into the lodge first." With that, Uncle War Cry looked over from his tent and, seeing the activity, thought he would wander over and see what it was. "Nawa," he greeted them. "Nawa," answered Victory Call, "sit down over here" (viz., to his left). "Looks as if-you're-about to travel" (*kura-tas-takuhu'u*), said the visitor. "Oh, yes, we're going to try to move in this morning, that is rather—today." "That's what we've been thinking too. But I think we'll go in tomorrow." Now Horse Rider arrived with the water and after greetings of "Nawa, nawa," were exchanged, he sat down and joined the men. War Cry repeated his observation about their moving in and Horse Rider made his acknowledgment, War Cry adding, "Now you're going to make-us-feel-lonesome" (left behind, *wi-tas-kurak-atsiks-awahu*). "Oh, just one day. Just this evening, that's all," said Horse Rider.

Now Grandma began to sit up on her bed and White Woman handed her a small basin of water. "Mother wash your face," she said and Grandma poured some of the water into her hand and washed up.

Everyone arranged themselves on the mat—White Woman at the south end, Victory Call next to her, War Cry next to him, Horse Rider next, No Corn who was doing the cooking and serving, and on the northern-most end of the line Grandma and then Otter. The dishes of food were passed first to Victory Call, then War Cry and then Horse Rider, and now the boy Otter was given a dish to carry to his mother at the south end. He got up and made a wide circle so that he wouldn't pass too close in front of the men. Dishes were next passed by No Corn to Grandma and through her to Otter, and then they all began to eat.

As soon as breakfast was over, Horse Rider went to get the two horses that would be needed for the hauling and War Cry went back to his tent, remarking as he went off, "Tomorrow we must move in, too." White Woman and No Corn began to bundle up their things. Grandma had already taken most of hers into the lodge. The mare and the horse were loaded up with parfleches of corn, pumpkin, rolled-up mats, and dishes. The two men went up and piled the goods outside the doorway and came back directly for their next load. As they began to load up, the women were saying, "Our men don't know how to load these things." The men on the other hand were likely to say, "When we first came home, we had hardly anything. Now look at that pile we've got around to fix up." The children were running back and forth among the piles of goods.

It took three trips to get everything back to the lodge and, on the last one, White Woman piled some of the remainder on her back and admonished Horse Rider to bring up whatever wood they had around as someone else might appropriate it. The women went into the lodge and at once removed the grass padding from the bed platforms to see how the willow sticks of the frame were. Next day they would get some new willow sticks to replace any that were found to be rotted.

Each low bedstead was made of three forked uprights stuck in the ground between the central pillars and the wall of the housepit; a long sturdy willow rod rested on the forks of the uprights to form the edge of the bedstead. Shorter sections of willow sapling were laid on crosswise, at 3-inch intervals, one end resting on the outer rod and the other end on the shelf all around the housepit, which was actually the ground level remaining within the circular collar or sod wall inside its sloping radial skeleton. This low slope-roofed area was called *ti-ka-ka-wi'u*, "it-lodge-inside-sits." Upon the bed frame with its cross sticks was placed another layer of willow saplings in the length, and upon this in the width, a layer of thatch (*pakuts*) grass. Each bed was built between a pair of the short outer houseposts that were placed in the ground at an outward slant and 7 feet apart. These were the permanent bedsteads, and when they left on the hunt these were left intact. The only time they were dismantled was when a ceremony was to take place in the lodge when all the sticks were pulled up and carried outside until the ceremony was over.

The bedding was designed to keep the occupants warm and to ensure a certain amount of privacy. The basic bedclothes comprised two layers of tanned hide. At the head were skin pillows stuffed with turkey feathers or deer hair. Sometimes a roll of discarded skin clothing was used instead. At the foot was also a roll of worn out skin clothing against which one could rest one's feet. A skin curtain hung at the head and the foot of every bed, suspended from the roof for privacy. These were tucked in underneath before putting down the bed clothes to keep anything natural or supernatural from coming into the bed at night. In the more luxuriously appointed beds, an extra skin curtain was suspended against the wall so that should any mice living in the thatch loosen any earth, it would fall behind the curtain. The curtains were usually made of discarded pieces of tanned buffalo-hide tent skin. When they went to bed, everyone disrobed. In the warmer weather they covered themselves with a tanned skin—preferably elk or deerskin for really soft tan. This was commonly dyed black and was worn as a wraparound garment during the day. At the time of this account most people used trade-store blankets instead for this purpose. In winter they used a double-purpose buffalo robe with its hair and wool left on for warmth. In the morning when they got up the covers were folded up toward the head or foot end of the bed so that one could sit on the bed during the day or lie down without disarranging the bedding. In the warmer weather, a mat might be placed on top of the skin as a "sheet." In addition to these appointments, some of the beds had an additional screen of willows built in front of them to make them especially private. Some married women preferred these— in this household for example, White Woman and Old Bull's older wife, Queen Woman. These screens, *kawiriwisisu*, were a permanent part of the bed structure. Six tall uprights were fixed in the ground, reaching from floor to ceiling, and across them close together were tied on with willow bark, 6-foot-long horizontal willow saplings. The horizontals were laid in alternate order, one with the stub end to the left and its point end to the right, and the one above it in the opposite position to ensure evenness. These were gathered in spring, peeled, and the irregular stems or knots cut off. Before they could be fastened to the uprights, they had to be briefly seasoned for a few days so that they would be neither too green when they would shrink too much and leave the fastenings loose, nor too dry, when they could not be properly straightened out in place. For decorative effect, six black were alternated with six natural horizontals, the peeled saplings being passed through a decoction of sumach that had been boiled to make a black dye. After all the horizontals were tied in place, they were trimmed off on both edges to make the screen even. The entrance through the screen was made by cutting a low narrow opening in it at bed level, the vertical for this portion being hung from the roof.

As for the rest of the furnishings of the house, the buffalo skull had been left resting on the altar at the west and above it they now hung whatever sacred bundles they had. To the east of the fireplace they set up the bracket from which the pot was hung over the fire to boil. This was a forked stick stuck in the ground at a slant or having a natural curve; to one arm of the fork a wooden hook was suspended by a rawhide strap that could be raised and lowered by winding, depending on how close to the fire they wanted the pot to hang.

Against each side, on the east wall, was a woodpile supported by two tall forked sticks stuck in the ground. A little farther along the wall, leaning against it was a tree trunk with lopped off branches from which strings of braided corn were hung.

Now as the women were through with their cleaning, examining the beds and generally getting things in order, they brought in the parfleches of meat and the bags and placed the twined-woven rush mats on the floor. Two mats were put down on their "side"; the better one near the west end and the more worn-out one near the east. Some pumpkins were stored on the intervening platforms between the beds, some were placed under the beds and others on the floor near the doorway. One of the parfleches had been placed in a handy position and left open as it contained current supplies. The rest were all closed up.

Toward evening, Horse Rider made a fire in the fireplace and went to get water. Then No Corn cooked some dry meat for the family and began to prepare the "grease bread" when White Woman said, "Give it to me. I'll make it. You get the coffee ready." The South Side family had not yet moved back in, and White Woman sat in the southeast position to do the cooking and serving, passing the food around to the north. When they returned, she would take her place northeast of the fireplace for this purpose. After they had finished with supper, Horse Rider went out to get some water for the morning and then everyone went to bed, as they were all tired.

It took about a week to get the earth lodge warm and lived-in. When they first moved in, it was cool like a dugout. During the first week, in the evening about every other day, they made a small fire near the doorway and burned sage weed (*kiwaut*) so that the draft would carry in the fragrant odor and sweeten the air in the lodge. It was also a protection against evil spirits that might have entered while they were away on the hunt.

The day after they had moved in, Uncle War Cry had moved his family up from the camp. He came in and joined them for supper while his house was being set up by the women. He sat down next to Victory Call near the west and while White Woman sat down at the southeast doing the cooking, he said, "When we started out, we didn't have much. But now we've accumulated a lot of stuff—old moccasins and whatnot—old pots and pans. They're still trying to arrange things at home. A man just picks up his bow and arrows, but a woman always has all sorts of stuff she gathers up, like old horns. She says she'll make spoons of them." "Same thing here," said Victory Call. White Woman did not let these remarks remain unanswered. She said, "Of course you men don't know how to load things up. That's why you're always complaining of the amount of stuff we accumulate. If you could pack right, you wouldn't talk that way." War Cry, undeterred, went right on talking. "A woman picks up everything she sees. The women are working in my home. I don't want to get mixed up in it. Now I'm going, nephew (*tiwat*)." "All right," said Victory Call, and just after he had gone, he added, "He always has something to say to make a man laugh." The women comment, "Tomorrow we must pick out those beans we pulled up in the pods with our fingers. If we use sticks to thresh them, it'll make dirt outside the lodge. We ought to pick them by hand."

In the next day or so, Old Bull met Victory Call and said they wanted to move back into the lodge next morning. "That's good," said Victory Call, "you ought to be in by now. There'll be something going on soon." (He is referring to the Doctor Dance Ceremonies.) Victory Call tells his folks at supper that Old Bull is moving in next day.

The following morning the South Side family rode up to the lodge,

dumped their goods outside, set up the beds, and laid the mats. Then
they brought in the rest of their things, and the house was crowded
with parfleches of dry meat, corn, beans, and everything they had gathered. The women talked of storing them in the cache pit. Grandma and
Old-Lady-Grieves-the-Enemy told about how they had looked over the
pit when they first got home from the hunt and cleared off some mold
that had developed on the grass lining and that it was now clean and
ready to be filled. After the pit was filled this time, it would not be open
until the middle of November when they were ready to go off on the
winter hunt. It did not do to open the pit more than once a month at the
most. Otherwise, if one opened it often, a storm might come up and
water might leak in. In the wintertime there was less danger of this.
From time to time one would hear that a certain woman had not put
enough earth on the lid of the pit and water had leaked in, with the resulting tragic consequence that all her corn was destroyed—the bags and
everything having turned moldy (us-kutu, "hair-rotten," viz., mold).
Two years of hard work and the security it could bring destroyed by
one careless oversight. In the Pawnee way of life, vigilance could seldom
be relaxed!

The storage pit was built nearby when the earth lodge was constructed.
It was an indispensable part of the earth-lodge economy. The usual size
was about 10 feet deep. It was bell-shaped, with a narrow neck and a
round bottom about 10 feet in diameter. The north side of the pit was for
the use of the people who inhabited that side of the earth lodge, and
the south side for the South Side families. In the case of an exceptionally
important public figure, the household might have two cache pits. The bottom was covered with clean sand and on top of this some sticks as a sort
of grating and these covered with grass. The walls were lined with thatch
grass fastened in place with sticks that were shored up against it.

Tanned hide sacks of various sizes were used to store the corn and
beans in the pit. The largest was the hax-kaitu, made by sewing two
buffalo hides together, folding them over and sewing them along the
bottom and the long side. It was 6 feet high and 3 feet in diameter when
full and was used only to store the mature dried corn kernels known as
rikis-tahis, "corn-dry," that had been pried off the cob after the corn had
matured on the stalk.

The second size was the "large sack," about 3 feet high and 2 feet in
diameter when filled, containing 1½ bushels or more. The next size, "the
small sack," asa-karusu, "dog-sack," stood about 3 feet high and 1½
feet in diameter when full, holding about a bushel or 50 to 60 pounds of
dried corn kernels. In size, it was approximately equivalent to the 50-
pound flour sack. A still smaller sack was called rits-a-kusu, "intestine-of-
sack," standing about 8 inches high and a foot in diameter when full.

Sometimes the supplies were simply wrapped around with a piece of tanned hide or old tent skin.

The most pressing matter was to get the stores into the food pit. This was the last time they would open it until November in preparation for leaving on the winter hunt. It was fifteen to twenty days since the corn had been harvested, and it was good and dry and ready for storage. A great many calculations had to be made before the storage pit could be organized. The forthcoming month of performances would require everyone's support, and food would be taken from the pit and held in readiness in the lodge to feed the many performers and other participants. Meat from the hunt had been pledged and this too would be held in reserve. Some people made it a policy to remove all of last year's crops that were still in the pit and contribute the excess over current needs to the performance. They would keep it in the lodge in the east sector in very large skin bags which were tightly closed at the top to protect the food from mice and snakes. Some of the held-over dried buffalo meat in the rawhide containers would be so hard that it could only be prepared by being separated into sheets and pulverized with a pestle in the wooden mortar. In this form it was quite tasty when eaten with bites from a lump of solidified buffalo bone grease.

The new supplies were placed in the pit in a traditional order. Before the bags were put in, the grass lining of the pit was carefully checked and also the bottom which had a layer of clean sand and some sticks laid across to keep any moisture from reaching the skin bags. At the very bottom some sacks of the mature dry corn were placed. These sacks were laid so that they pointed radially inward from the wall. The layer above this consisted of sacks of roasted green corn which were placed crosswise upon the lower layer so that they were parallel to the wall. The third layer was sacks of beans again in radial order, pointing inward from the wall. Finally, they put in the oblong rawhide containers of dried buffalo meat crosswise on the beans lying parallel to the wall.

An attempt was made to set the various layers steady one upon the other so that when the woman went down into the pit she could step down from one layer to the other. On top of the material laying all around the pit in packages and sacks they piled pumpkin mats and braids of corn on the cob. Sometimes instead of piling the corn braids in this fashion, they put a stick with stubs of branches in the pit leaning against the wall and hung the corn braids on it. Also leaning against the wall were rolled-up buffalo skins that they had not yet tanned, which they planned to process just before going on the winter hunt so that they could be taken to the trade store for the groceries and other equipment they might need for the expedition. Odds and ends were put in the space that was left in the middle—pumpkin rings that had not been braided,

TABLE 33-1. *A Few Summary Figures of the Produce of the Women of the North Side of the Earth Lodge.*

Corn, sacks of dried kernels:

White Woman	9	Stored 5
Grandma	13 (8 to White Woman)	
No Corn	7	Stored 3
Grieves-the-Enemy	8 (4 to daughter-in-law outside the household)	Stored 2
TOTAL	37 sacks	Stored 10

Corn, braided:

White Woman	4 braids	Stored 2
No Corn	3 braids	Stored 2
Grieves-the-Enemy	6 braids (4 to daughter-in-law outside the household)	Stored 1
TOTAL	13 braids	Stored 5

Available for current use in the household—23 sacks of dried corn kernels (10 in pit, additional as reserve); 4 braids of corn for current use (5 in the pit, additional as reserve).

Pumpkins and Squashes:

White Woman	3 plaited mats	Stored 1
Grandma	4 mats (2 to White Woman)	
	1 50-pound sack of dried pumpkin seeds stored)	
No Corn	3 mats	Stored 2
Grieves-the-Enemy	5 mats (3 to daughter-in-law outside the household)	Stored 1
TOTAL	15 mats	Stored 4

Available for current use in the household, 8 mats; 4 additional in the pit.

Beans, dried and in 50-lb sacks:

White Woman	4 sacks	Stored 2
Grandma	4 sacks (2 for White Woman)	
No Corn	3 sacks	Stored 1
Grieves-the-Enemy	5 sacks (3 to daughter-in-law outside the household)	Stored 1
TOTAL	16 sacks	Stored 4

For current use in the household, 9 sacks of dried beans, and 4 additional in the pit.

some dried meat that wouldn't fit into the rawhide containers, some dried intestines folded up, and perhaps some clothing they wanted to store.

The work of arranging the pit took a group of women in a household from about ten in the morning until about three in the afternoon, with a brief recess for lunch. There was no time in the household when the women were not fully aware of their capital in provisions and goods and the rate at which they were using them. Practically every meal was a large-scale operation and portions were carefully calculated. The men had to be aware of this too as it was their major resource for public and social relations. Except for horses, or perhaps even more important, the main current capital they had was the preserved food. In the forth-coming round of ceremonies, the doctors calculated with great care their donations of meat and how they were going to apportion them.

It was in the light of a knowledge of the amounts they had produced and accumulated, that the men now planned their forthcoming extensive ceremony—the Grand Opera of the Doctors that would last for thirty days and involve the feeding and the giving of gifts to a large corps of performers and participants. For these ceremonies, the cooking and ap-portioning was done by the errand men, *tarutsuhus*, who were regularly constituted officers of the societies, and the chiefs, priests, or doctors had to keep exact account of the amount of food pledged and make their plans according to what they could afford. The food was their most im-portant current capital for the support of their program.

While the implications of this great annual festival were certainly re-ligious, deliberate showmanship was not neglected and the production was well planned and highly organized as such. It was remarked by the informant that they waited until the harvest was entirely complete "as they liked to have a good crowd."

34

PREPARATION FOR

THE GRAND OPERA

The Doctors' Profound Connection with the Animal World—Hypnotic Powers—Organization of the Doctor Lodge—Animal Cults—Construction of Images—Ideology of the Doctors—the Ceremonial Mode: Fighting and Sleight of Hand—Gaining Animal Knowledge—Getting the Cedar Tree for Ceremony

THE DOCTORS' OPERA had to do neither with the ordered cosmos nor with the well-regulated world of the cultivated plants, but with the mysterious realm of the wild animals and their wild plant environment. The chief and the priest to whom the cosmic powers spoke in visions, were men of reason who spoke out clearly on what they thought, while the doctor who communed with the animal world had a slow, deliberate, introspective mein, seldom if ever making clear pronouncements. The animal cults all had their origin in the experience of an individual man who in despair had reached out to the universe at large and received a vision from an animal who was ready to intercede for him and help him work out his problems. He had received special knowledge that would help him cure the sick through the properties of the plants and other curative procedures. In addition to this kind of knowledge, the animal also transmitted to his protegé the power of hypnotism and suggestion that gave him control over animals and other people and, if he was skillful enough, over the enemies of the tribe. The Pawnee animal cults were the result of traditions that had been handed down from one person to another and elaborated in the course of time. People who wished to share in the cult knowledge apprenticed themselves to a doctor and gradually learned his lore, adding their own variations in the course of time. Each of the different cults held their own special ceremonies at least twice a year—in the spring before going out on the summer buffalo hunt and in the fall before leaving for the winter hunt. In addition, all these cults were organized into one big "Doctor Lodge." It is said that in the past there were two separate doctor lodges within the Skidi Band that would stage big hypnotic contests between them. They were called "East Doctors" and "West Doctors."

At the time of this narrative in 1867 there was one combined Doctor Lodge with two major leaders, one for the south side, Pipe Offering of Pumpkin-Vine Village, and one for the north side, Big Doctor of Village-in-the-Bottomlands. Despite their location in the lodge, they were still referred to as West and East Doctors respectively, coinciding with the relative location of their villages in the settlement. Big Doctor was considered the more authoritative of the two, which may have been due to personal factors rather than formal or ceremonial ones. Each of these leaders had an assistant from his village to help him manage his side. Sitting Hawk of Pumpkin-Vine assisted Good Pipe and Wonderful Old Bull of Bottomlands Village assisted Big Doctor. These men were both prominent in their own right—Sitting Hawk, for example, being a prominent member of the Bear Cult and a senior member of his family in the chiefs' council. The apprentices to these prominent doctors acted as errand men and cooked and served the meals. They were stationed on each side of the entrance at the east. Theoretically the head men should be willing to give them any information they wanted in return for their services, and eventually they would move up to a position in one of the animal cults in which the doctor had a vested interest. Several subapprentices sat next to them waiting to assume the position of errand man when they should move. Venerable old men who were not currently members of the cults sat in the northeast and southeast positions, further in the lodge than the apprentices. Chiefs who were invited to witness a performance were seated next to the old men still further in.

The bed platforms had all been uprooted and put outside on the roof of the entry way and along the sides a series of booths had been built for the animal cults. The booths were constructed with partition walls of willow saplings and main outer posts of cottonwood logs. Each booth was completely screened in, with a tiny entranceway cut near the bottom of the front wall so that the doctors could crawl in and out. Each cult was directed by a leader who had a series of apprentices and subapprentices with different degrees of knowledge of the cult tradition.

At this time eight cults were represented in the different booths, four on each side.

On the South Side	On the North Side
A *reindeer* cult in charge of Old Bull	An *eagle* cult
A *black-tailed deer* cult led by Old Lady Tsitawa (see p. 45)	A *fish hawk* cult
A *buffalo lodge* led by Wonderful Old Bull	A *coyote* lodge (including wolves and foxes)
Another *buffalo lodge* led by Leading Buffalo	A *bear* lodge jointly lead by Sitting Hawk and Angry Horse

The origin of the Associated Doctor Lodge was said to be in Pumpkin-Vine Village where they would conduct a twenty-day ceremony. When they joined the Skidi Federation, they incorporated the other doctors and extended the term to thirty days. The formation of the association was attributed to an original visionary and images were constructed to commemorate various aspects of his vision. The most elaborate was one that represented the serpentlike water monster that led him to the earth lodge of the animals under the Missouri. The body of the serpent, which was nearly 60 feet long, curved around the outside of the houseposts with its head at the southeast, a forked tail at the northeast, and its body curved toward the west. The body was constructed of a framework of pieces of ashwood tied with sinew, covered over with a layer of grass and plastered with clay, smoothed and painted in different colors. Its mouth, large enough for a man to crawl inside, was built of two rawhide containers, covered over with a black-dyed buffalo robe and painted and decorated with white downy eagle feathers. The open mouth was provided with large wedge-shaped cottonwood teeth and on each side of the mouth long slender willow rods to represent feelers or antennae.

They also had to model the figure of the witch woman who was in the visionary animal lodge under the Missouri. First they built up a willow frame and then covered it with grass and clay. They provided the witch with a realistically modeled face and pumpkin-seed eyes, blackened in the center to represent pupils. On her head they put a buffalo scalp to which they attached two long braids of human hair; for clothing she wore a buffalo-hide dress.

Next they modeled the fireplace into the shape of a turtle, with its head pointing east, its tail west and the four legs in the semicardinal directions. They scooped out the back for the fire pit.

It took twelve of the leading doctors two nights running to build these figures, for which large quantities of clay had to be brought in. They worked at night so that they would not be observed. These were the main figures that represented the vision in the animal lodge.

The next task was to represent the star gods from whom everything came, including the animals. For these, two consecrated buffalo skins were shot with a special bow and arrow during the preceding summer. The gods were represented as cutouts suspended from the roof of the lodge. Each was hung approximately where it appeared in the heavens. The female gods of the western skies were cut out of the buffalo cow-skin. The bull hide was used for a large cutout figure of the Morning Star fastened to a stick and raised above the smokehold outside just before the star rose in the sky.

The tasks of the doctors in preparing the ceremonial lodge were summarized by my informant as:

> Now that the booths, the drums and gourds (rattles) were done, the pictures hung, the serpent, witch, and turtle modeled, there was one more thing to do—to get the cedar tree.

Each one of these elements of ceremonial furniture represented an involved ideological network of religious beliefs. The theology of the celestial gods and the creation has already been sufficiently elaborated on. The ideology of the Doctor Spirits concerned chiefly the waters as the primordial source, followed by the earth, the plants, and the animals —all however, ultimately subject to and derived from Heaven as denoted by the cutout figures of the cosmic gods.

The ideology of the doctors was greatly valued from a humanistic as well as from a practical point of view. Theoretically, chiefs with hereditary status should not want to be doctors as to some extent we might not expect a Grand Duke to want to go to medical school and set up an office for general practice. The degree of apprenticeship and subordination to an established practitioner seemed hardly consonant with the dignity of a chief from the point of view of the Pawnee, but nevertheless some of the chiefs did seek out doctor knowledge and participated actively in the apprentice roles. When a chief applied to a doctor to become his pupil, the doctor would try to dissuade him saying, "You're a chief. I don't sleep at night. I am always working. You don't want to be that way. I have to watch the sick at night." But if the chief is determined his wish will finally be granted. The doctor again would test him, saying, "You're good-looking. You don't want to have mud all over your face!" At last after all these probing questions, if the applicant said, "That's what I want," the doctor, convinced of his sincerity, would bless him and receive him under his tutelage. White Eagle, who had led the previous summer hunt, and his brother Charley Box were both chiefs and also deer doctors. Old Bull and Victory Call were both chiefs and practicing doctors; Victory Call's senior brother Sitting Hawk had an important place in the chief's council and was also a leading doctor in the lodge.

The kind of experience involved had a profound personal value. The way in which this knowledge was conceived is perhaps indicated by the personality attributed to the doctor—slow, deliberate, thoughtful and, to a considerable degree, introspective. As a more practical measure of social esteem perhaps was the fact that during the previous summer buffalo hunt, 60 parfleches of dried buffalo meat had been pledged in support of the performance, and in former times, before the population had been so heavily reduced, 140 parfleches were donated in one season.

The mode in which the doctors operated during their ceremony was of two kinds. One was the inducing of a trance state in the other doctors: utilizing the motions of the animal that was their special cult mentor. This was called *patsaku*, "shooting," and was also metaphorically referred to as "fighting." The second kind of activity of the doctors was a highly skilled sleight-of-hand performance, *tawaruku*, so expertly carried out that the illusion was completely convincing to the spectators. The metaphor for this kind of performance was "playing" or "romping," as of a child. The skill of the illusion in both cases has been attested to by the most hard-headed outside observers and this required extensive preparation and a long process of learning. The props were carefully designed to achieve the desired illusory effect and the strategy was planned with great precision, involving accomplices in the audience and special lighting effects developed by regulating the fire in the fireplace.

In view of these deliberate and extensive preparations for illusion, the question has often been raised of how these ceremonies could be regarded as religious in character. From my long experience with my informant, who retained a good deal of his old belief, it was the success in creating the illusion that was the mark of favor of the supernatural mentor, and therefore the performance was sincerely believed to be a religious experience. He would say, "If one does not have faith, he will fail." He cited examples where people of insufficient faith caused injury to themselves and to others while trying to perform. The success of the illusion depended upon the dexterity and agility of the performer and his ability to deflect the attention of the spectator just long enough for him to make the necessary shifts. There may possibly have been some measure of self-induced trance such as occurred to the priests incidentally in the course of the creation ceremony. (Our own knowledge of the subject is too elementary to identify the situation psychologically.)

A major difference between our experience and theirs should be especially noted. The Pawnees as well as many peoples who practiced these arts were in constant association with wild animals in their natural habitat, an experience which is entirely absent in our own world. They lived within a world of wild animals in their hunting and even in defense of their settlements, they had to have an intimate knowledge of the emotional as well as the physical structure of these animals. The device of animal impersonation by dressing up in animal skins and imitating their sounds and motions is universally reported for hunting peoples and must go back to the very dawn of man's history. It may be that some degree of self-induced trance or control of the prey in these terms may have been involved in these operations. In any case, an intense rapport with the animals was involved.

Each doctor developed his own "animal repertoire." We may be able to gain some insight into the relation between the doctor and his animal mentor from an actual case of a transfer of animal powers between two brothers who decided to make a fair exchange of their different knowledge.

Victory Call was anxious to get Bear knowledge from his older brother, Sitting Hawk, who was a leader of the Bear Lodge in the Doctor Association. One day when they were alone together he broached the subject. Sitting Hawk, however, was not willing to part with what he knew for nothing. He said, "I want something there on your side. We're going to trade." "You're my own brother," said Victory Call, "and you won't teach me for nothing?" "You're my own brother, too, and I know you won't teach me for nothing either," said Sitting Hawk. We should explain that Victory Call was the leader of a private doctor cult the *Raris-ta*, Dance-Deer or Whistle Dance involving the mescal bean that had become so prominent among the Pawnees that it was developing into a feared rival of the Doctor Association itself. Two generations before, this cult had been borrowed from the Wichita, the Caddoan-speaking kinsmen of the Pawnees to the south. Among other kinds of knowledge, rattlesnake power was involved in the teachings. It is hard to know what plants were involved in connection with the curing of snakebite or the control of the snakes. Members of the *Raris-ta* could handle a weed that was thought to be poisonous to other people, though there is no proof that this was the case. It was undulating in form like the snake itself. People were warned not to touch the plant unless they were members of the society. It was said of them that they had "snake-shot" or power, *rut-patsat-kuriraru*, "snake-shot-to-possess-or-own." Weeds associated with rattlesnakes have variously been identified from other tribes—a Mexican mentioned Dodder or Love Vine (*Cuscuta paradoxa* Raf.), saying that snakes took it into their dens for food; from the Dakota Indians there is a report that Bittersweet (*Celastrus scandens* L.) was known as snake food. The botanical identity of the Pawnee plant, however, is not known. In the cosmic mythology it was said that the jealous Fools-the-Wolves Star (Sirius) who had felt himself excluded from the original Council of the Gods, was angered when people told irreverent stores about Wolf or Coyote. Although in winter he couldn't control the situation, in summer he could enlist the aid of the Snake Star (Scorpio), who would send the snakes on earth to bite the teller. There are many other indications in Pawnee mythology of the fear and respect the Pawnees held for the power of the rattlesnake.

Later in the course of our account of the doctor performances, we shall see that Victory Call did receive Bear knowledge from his brother, but first he taught him rattlesnake knowledge.

One day Victory Call said to Sitting Hawk, "Well, let's go." If luck were with them they would find a rattlesnake right away. Sure enough, there sat a snake curled up with his head sticking up in the middle. Victory Call said, "Go ahead and catch it." Sitting Hawk thought, "It's going to bite me." The snake knew that Sitting Hawk was afraid of him. His fangs were sticking up and he was getting ready to bite. Sitting Hawk grabbed him by the neck. The snake felt cold on his arm. Sitting Hawk put the snake down and began to talk to him. He said, "That's what I wanted to know. That's what I wanted to find out." The snake said to Sitting Hawk, "I'm just like you. But you whip me and kill me for nothing. That's why, when you come in my path, I rattle to you to let you know I'm here. If you get out of my way then, I don't have to poison you. But when you come and abuse us, we must do something about it."

Sitting Hawk now caressed Victory Call in blessing. The two men sat down and smoked a pipe together, offering puffs of smoke to the snake and talking to him. Then they went home and Victory Call gave Sitting Hawk some medicine to cure snakebite and showed him the weed it was prepared from.

Long after this time, when Sitting Hawk and Victory Call were dead and the tribe had moved to Oklahoma, Otter's older brother Fox Chief tried to transfer some rattlesnake power to him. But Otter failed from fear and hesitation:

We two were walking along and we saw a big rattlesnake. Fox Chief told me to get hold of it, but I was afraid. Because of this, I would never have another chance. Fox Chief always had a little bundle of medicine in his buttonhole with fringes that hung down about four inches. He took a twig and chewed the end of it, dipping it in the medicine and then putting it near the end of the snake's nose. The snake relaxed and lay stretched out. He picked it up and put it in the crook of his arm so that it rested against the sheet that Fox Chief was wearing as a blanket. In this way he carried the snake home.

When we arrived at his earth lodge, his wife was sitting in front on a mat making a pair of moccasins. He said to her, "I've brought you something to eat." She was very pleased until she saw what he had brought. She yelled, "Take that away!" "He's all right," said Fox Chief, "You people are foolish." "But he'll bite someone if you set him free in the village," said his wife. "No, he knows we live here. He'll go straight off to that rocky place over there." Then he released the snake and the snake went directly away without disturbing anyone. And so I lost my chance to learn—by not believing.

This story, told in Oklahoma in 1936, sixty years later, was sincerely believed.

With this confident knowledge of the herbs and roots connected with it, the doctors did cure the sick, combining what must have been some empirical observation of physical efficacy with personal influence and suggestion. It was this latter aspect that was the subject of their ceremony at this time and an affirmation of their faith in their calling.

Last of all they had to get the cedar tree that would stand just outside the Bear Booth to the west of its entrance. The bear and the cedar were associated together, and both belonged to the northeast direction. Their celestial affiliation was with the sun and moon. All the trees that were used in setting up the Doctor Lodge were brought in with a great deal of ceremony. The six cottonwood trees that had been used to build the animal booths symbolized the beaver, and the waters and were consecrated accordingly. To get the cedar, twenty doctors set out before sunrise for the Loup River where the cedar tree had been located the day before. The leader of the party carried a bearhide rattle.

On the return journey, they stopped halfway and practiced hypnotism on one another. The doctors who had remained behind in the lodge would try to prevent the incoming party from entering the village. One of the doctors was stationed at the top of the lodge to sight them as they were returning. The incoming party stopped in the timber and painted themselves so that they could rehearse in order to "put on a good show for the people of the village." They were sighted approaching from the southwest by the doctors in the lodge who went south through the village to meet them as they were about to enter and managed hypnotically to drive them back. The leader of the incoming party was sounding his bearhide rattle and the people climbed onto the roofs of their lodges to watch. The approaching party dropped the cedar, and, in their hypnotized condition some began to impersonate wolves, some deer, all imitating the motions of the different animals. As they came, one of the deer tumbled over, and the wolves tumbled on their noses and lay there kicking. Then they got up looked around dazed as they recovered from their trance. People came and threw offerings of calico and black handkerchiefs on the cedar tree as it lay on the ground.

Inside the lodge, Big Doctor stood ready to receive the cedar tree which was ceremonially treated and set down east of the fireplace while they ate a feast together. That evening, with a special ritual, it was stood in the ground next to the Bear Booth.

At the feast that afternoon, Big Doctor had given an accounting of how their meat supplies were holding up. Sixty rawhide containers of dried buffalo meat had been donated and these had to last for the whole proceedings. Including the present meal, they had used up fifteen. The doctors had been working for nine days. Two more were used cleaning the lodge of fleas, and, for the two days used in building the serpent, the turtle, and the witch woman, they had used up four containers.

The question of wood for fuel also came up at this time. As the meal was coming to a close, the north errand man whispered into Big Doctor's ear that he should mention this matter in his closing speech, particularly as a number of chiefs were present at the session. Getting wood was normally the function of the women and now they would have to enlist the help of a considerable party of women to lay in a supply. The two chiefs present would tell the various members of their families asking the women to get wood for the doctors and then word would readily get around. Old Man High Water was also instructed to go from house to house soliciting volunteers, saying, "The doctors want you to go for wood for them." He was cautioned not to mention any particular amount lest the women feel they were being pressured into going. The chiefs would arrange to have scouts go out with the women to protect them. Other young men would go voluntarily and picket on the hills.

35

ORGANIZING THE EARTH LODGE

FOR THE CEREMONIAL

PERFORMANCE—REHEARSALS

AND CONSTRUCTION WORK

〜〜〜〜〜〜〜〜〜〜〜〜〜〜〜〜〜〜

Work Corps to Prepare Earth Lodge for Cere-
mony—Fleas Burnt—Drums Repaired—Practice
Sing—Meat Served the Singers—Building of
Booths in Lodge—Building the Images

〜〜〜〜〜〜〜〜〜〜〜〜〜〜〜〜〜〜

OF THE FOUR LEADERS of the Doctor Lodge, Sitting Hawk had the largest
and most conveniently located earth lodge, and it was in his lodge that
they decided to conduct the ceremony. The following are the details of
the way in which they managed to get the work done and the ceremonial procedures connected with it.

As soon as they got back from the hunt and set up camp, the three
other doctors called on Sitting Hawk and discussed the matter; two
weeks later he made arrangements to begin to get the lodge ready. Like
all the others in the village, his lodge was infested with fleas that had to
be smoked out. He organized his work corps, first calling in the two
doctors' errand men and then sending each of them in turn to bring in
another young man to assist. The five had dinner at Sitting Hawk's
camp, then met next morning at the lodge and got to work. They
pulled up the beds and piled them outside on the roof of the long entrance passageway. Sitting Hawk supervising, two of them got to work
with burning torches to smoke out the fleas on each side. The floor was
carefully swept and the dust carried far from the lodge to be dumped.
Dusty and tired, their legs red with flea bites, about five o'clock they

took a swim in Beaver Creek and set out for Sitting Hawk's tent where they would be served dinner. Meanwhile, since word had gone all around the camp of what they were doing, other doctors decided to join them for supper. From this point on, all activities connected with the Doctor Lodge would be charged to the "Doctor Fund" of sixty parfleches of buffalo meat that had been pledged for the purpose. At each event the leader stated how much was being used for the current proceedings and how much of the total. At this meal, half a parfleche of buffalo meat was used up and it was so stated by Sitting Hawk.

The fleas would have to be burnt out one more time, and Sitting Hawk had told them that they would allow a day to pass in between and then do it on the subsequent day. As they were leaving the dinner that night, two other young doctors decided to join the work corps. The other two assistants, Man Chief and Fox Chief, decided to relax and do some gambling in the interim, before resuming their work next day.

When people in camp heard about what the doctors were doing, they all talked about speeding up their harvest. Someone would say, "Oh I'd like to see Bear!" Old ladies would say, "Oh, so they're cleaning the Doctor Lodge. Well it's high time. There ought to be a session in there already. When I was younger I used to be a good singer. When they went through the village, I used to sing." Other old ladies would reminisce about old times and about how many doctors there used to be in Old Village, Kitkehax-pakuxtu.

Now the men gathered at the lodge for the second bout with the fleas. Again Sitting Hawk supervised and two smoked them out on each side. The two additional young men cleared off the spider webs near the roof, for they were going to hang the cutouts up there; since they would have a large fire all during the sessions, the sparks might ignite the webs. Sitting Hawk wanted to keep them all busy so that during that day they didn't go off and gamble. They proceeded at a leisurely pace, sitting down for a smoke and telling stories every now and then. He sent his son Misery down to the Loup River to check the condition of the cedars and to locate a straight one about 4 inches in diameter. By late afternoon they took a long bath in Beaver Creek and then went to Sitting Hawk's tent for supper. On this occasion, the second half of the parfleche of meat from the Doctor's Fund was used up.

When everyone moved back into their earth lodges, Sitting Hawk's family had to divide up and move in with others. The women and children moved in with Chief's Road whose house was immediately to the west of theirs, and the boys went to the earth lodge of Comanche Chief into which Sitting Hawk's oldest son, Misery, was married.

While the others were cleaning the ceremonial lodge, the three other leading doctors had been working on the drums and other things. This had been mentioned among the guests at the dinner. Sitting Hawk had said, "Now while we're cleaning, it's only right that Big Doctor, Wonderful Old Bull, Pipe Offering, and Old Bull should be fixing their drums and other things so that the boys can go into the lodge and practice as soon as it is fixed up. We'd like the drums to sound good when we get in there." "That's right," some one else would say, "I've been wanting to sing even now, but the drum isn't fixed yet. It doesn't sound good."

At last everything was in order and the four leading doctors moved into the ceremonial lodge for the duration of the ceremony with the two errand men to do the cooking. That night they would have a practice sing with all the doctors who wanted to participate. The two leading doctors sent the two errand men out to invite them. They saw that the two men were appropriately clothed to go through the village, providing each with a buffalo robe which they wrapped around themselves with the hair side out, and an eagle-wing fan to carry. They filed out of the lodge one behind the other at a trot, and as they entered a lodge where a doctor lived they sat down one behind the other at the east with their eagle-wing fans in front of their faces. The appropriate response was for someone in the lodge to whisper into their right ear the question as to what they wished. They would answer also in a whisper that the doctor was to come right away. Then the two errand men would get up and trot out again, moving on to the next lodge where a doctor lived. Their mission did not always proceed with dispatch. Sometimes the two errand men got to a lodge where everyone was sleeping and the occupants would say, "Oh, I hate to get up," but they had to get up anyway and whisper their question and receive the whispered reply. In some lodges there were just young girls about and they said to each other, "You go and do it." "No, you go." Finally one would sit down next to the errand man and ask the question. He would whisper his reply, but not knowing the proper decorum, the girl would call right out loud, "Oh, I'll tell him." All these incidents were recounted in detail when the two men returned to the Doctor Lodge. In some places the people were eating and they made the errand men take a few bits of food before they would let them go. If the doctor happened to be home and was smoking, he would make them smoke with him a while before whispering his question and receiving his reply. Should the errand men meet a man outside the lodge on his way somewhere or toward the house, they would not discuss their business with him but would proceed to his lodge and notify the people there. As soon as the doctor was notified, he went straight to the Doctor Lodge. Everyone knew that on that night they were going to start by singing the doctor songs.

Twenty-six doctors came to the ceremonial lodge and Big Doctor opened the evening with a speech. He said, "Tonight we are going to practice our first songs so that we can send the birds, the winds, and everything on their way south for the coming winter. I have sent men out to see about willows for our booths. They report that there are good trees for us. I wanted you to know that in a few days we are going to start to set up the lodge. Now the leaves are turning yellow and they are falling. This is the way the year goes round and that's why I wanted to tell you so that you can get ready. In two or three days you can come up here and get the wood to build your booths. Meanwhile you must fix up your paraphernalia, your whistles, and anything else you will need. I don't want to take up too much time talking this evening, as we have a great deal to do."

Now he instructed the errand men to go to two of the men who had pledged meat and to bring it to the lodge. They went, carrying a piece of tent skin between them, and when they got to the lodges the meat was removed from the parfleches and placed on the skin, then carried by the errand men to the ceremonial lodge where it was set down near the southeast pillar. Now Sitting Hawk stated how their account stood. He said, "We used half a parfleche of meat cleaning up the lodge the first time, then the rest of the parfleche when we did the second cleaning. Now with these two, three parfleches will be used up."

Now the first song was begun and men, women, and children crowded in around the outside doorway to listen. They would say, "Oh, I like a good song." "Oh, I wish I could sing that song." A woman would remark, "I wonder when they'll put in the booths. I'd like to see the Bear." Inside the singing and dancing continued. The men were not costumed but simply painted, as this was a practice dance.

After the first round of singing, the spectators were told they had to leave. Big Doctor said, "It's all over." This was because they were now going to make their ceremonial smoke offerings to the powers and outsiders could not be permitted to witness this. Some doctors refrained from singing in the first round altogether because they wanted to keep their songs from the public.

At the west were sitting the four leading doctors with their wives sitting directly behind them. On each side, along the north and south, the rest of the doctors were ranged. At the east ends on each side were eight chiefs, two from each of the four villages, viz., at the southeast, two from Village-across-a-Ridge and two from Pumpkin-Vine, and at the northeast, two chiefs from Bottomlands Village and two from Wolf-in-Water. Beyond these at the southeast were the old men, and an errand man at each side.

In the interim between the first and second round of singing, one of the eight chiefs got up and spoke on behalf of all of them. The doctors on their part spoke and said, "The echo of the drum drives back sickness when it comes."

The singing alternated between the sides, first on the north and then on the south. When they had gone halfway down the line, Big Doctor appointed someone to get up and cut the meat into portions while the errand man put up the water to boil. As the singing continued, the errand man finally announced that the meat was all cooked and a spread was laid down east of the fireplace and 43 portions were set out for the singers. It was midnight or later when the singing was over and the four drums and a number of gourd rattles were brought back to Big Doctor. He made a brief speech: "Now in three days we are going to get the wood for our booths. We must look to the future and make our plans. Now we are going to eat." Then he appointed two men for each side to do the serving of the meat. One portion was sent to the house where Sitting Hawk's wife was staying, "for the lodge." Before they could eat, an offering of meat and fat was made to the spirits in the significant directions of the universe. When the offering was completed, all said, "Nawa."

One more matter had to be attended to before the meat could finally be served. The meat was arranged on the spread according to where the people were sitting, and a stick was placed in the middle to act as a divider between the north and south halves. The pieces of meat were of two different sizes, some particularly large and some of ordinary proportions. Big Doctor asked Sitting Hawk to see that the special portions were placed in position so that they would be properly assigned. There were to be special portions for the four doctors at the west and their wives, for the eight chiefs, the two errand men, one each for the person sitting at the north on behalf of the North Star and at the south on behalf of the South Star, and for the four men who had been specially appointed to do the serving. Three or four extra pieces were set aside for possible mistakes in the count; if no mistakes had been made, these extra portions were placed on top of those that had already been set out for the chiefs. The smaller-size pieces were set out for the rest of the people. The meat was passed out in formal order and then the soup, in the same way. The feast this time consisted of meat and soup only.

By now it was extremely late and Big Doctor made some very brief closing remarks. He said, "Now we know what we have to do (viz., come back in three days and get wood for the booths). Now we have eaten. Now we can go." All got up and went home. It would take six or seven days more before the dance preparations were complete.

The next stage in their preparations was the building of the booths and other structures in the ceremonial lodge. As announced, this would be three days after the practice sing. On the appointed morning before daybreak, Big Doctor told the errand men to go to certain specified lodges and get four parfleches of dried buffalo meat that had been pledged so that they could have their feast that evening. The four donors had already been alerted at the previous meeting.

The doctors came in very early wearing only their moccasins and a loin cloth and carrying an ax. Before sunrise they were to go into the woods and get six cottonwood trees and a quantity of willow saplings to build up the booths. The cottonwood trees were symbolic of the beaver, and the trees were cut down with an involved ceremonial procedure. When the doctors had all assembled, Big Doctor, dressed in his buffalo robe with the hair side out and carrying an eagle-wing fan and a gourd rattle, said, "Now get ready!" They sang four songs, four rounds each, and then Big Doctor appointed Sitting Hawk to lead the men into the timber. He also wore a buffalo robe with the hair side out and carried an eagle-wing fan, gourd rattle, and a pipe that had been filled with tobacco by Good Pipe so that he could perform the ceremony when they cut down the first cottonwood. Pipe Offering instructed him: "Go by the east agency road. Before you get across Beaver Creek, all along the north side, you will find good willows and cottonwoods and also some very small thin willows. Cut a good many of those. Now go!"

They all filed out behind Sitting Hawk, and when they got to the timber they found a good cottonwood and sat down around it to perform the ceremony. Sitting Hawk, who was seated at the west, pointed the unlit pipe toward the tree—first toward the top, then the middle, and then the bottom. Now he moved to the north side, again offering the unlit pipe to the top, the middle, and the bottom of the tree and so similarly at the east and at the south. The next step was an offering of the smoke from the lit pipe in the same manner. Squatting at the northeast of the tree he lit the pipe with a flint and proceeded by north to west where he directed puffs of smoke to the top, middle, and bottom of the tree and then at the other stations as before. After the pipe was smoked out, he made the same offering with the ashes, rubbing first his right hand along the stem up toward the top of the tree, then his left hand, then the same to the middle, sitting at each of the four cardinal directions— west, north, east, and south. He now handed the pipe to the man at his right (south) and instructed him to find a cottonwood just like the one before them and to treat it ceremonially in the same way. These two cottonwoods were to stand near the western end of the lodge on both sides (north and south). He now instructed Bringing Horses to take his men and get two more cottonwoods, one to stand in the north position and one to the south as representatives of the beaver. (The ceremony was performed only for the two cottonwoods that would stand at the west.)

Finally, two other men were sent to get two cottonwoods that would stand one on each side of the lodge near the east. These men simply cut down the trees and sharpened them at the stub end so that they could be stood up in their appropriate positions in the lodge. Meanwhile, Sitting Hawk went on with his ceremony for the two trees that were to stand at the west. After the smoke offerings, he made a series of cuts in the tree at the four cardinal points in the standard order—first at the west, then north, then east and then south, cutting it so that it would fall gently to the east where two men were standing to catch it so that the limbs would not break. They sharpened it at the stub end so that it would stand up in the lodge. All chips were gathered and either thrown into the creek or carried home and burned in the fire. After gathering as many willow saplings as they could carry, the procession for the Doctor Lodge set out with Sitting Hawk in the lead and two men each carrying the six cottonwoods, one at each end of the tree.

Halfway home, they stopped. They began to make animal motions and to try to hypnotize one another (*patsaku*, "shoot one another"). Some of them had their buffalo robes on, some did not. They made peculiar motions with their eagle-wing fans, touching the ground. Then some were knocked down and got up growling and grunting. One of them "hypnotized" another by trying to put a corn cob in his throat, making his mouth all bloody. Another attempted to put fish bones in someone's throat, with the same result. The victims vomited up these things without too much damage being done and continued to move along with the cottonwoods. When the little boys saw this they got excited and said, "Look at those fellows! Look at that big bear over there!" As they arrived at the village, they made a second stop and again hypnotized each other. Then they took up the trees once more and went toward the ceremonial lodge. As they were arriving, Big Doctor took up his gourd rattle and began to sing. They came in and when the singing was over, Sitting Hawk gave the pipe back to Pipe Offering at the west. The cottonwood that had been ceremonially gathered was carefully placed to the east of the fireplace with its stub end pointing west and the head end eastward toward the exit. The second "west" tree was placed in the same position beside it and the others in any order on the ground, nearer the entrance. Now Big Doctor, getting the pipe from Pipe Offering, smoked all the trees ceremonially, treating each one in turn as in the woods.

They could now proceed to build the booths. Meanwhile, the errand men did the cooking. First the six cottonwoods were erected, three on each side. Then the willow partitions and fronts were added. Everyone was arguing—"This is our lot; move over a bit." "Well, we have a lot of buffalo!" "Well, we have a lot of deer too!" The leaders stood on the inside directing the apprentices who were doing their work. The willows were all piled up on the north side of the entrance while they proceed with the job. At the southeast the errand men were preparing the kettle so that they could cook their meat. They had had nothing to eat all day. The wives of the four leading doctors had brought in four buckets of boiled dried corn kernels and set them down on either side of the southeast lodge pole. Sometimes a woman would come in and give the "boss" of one of the animal booths a gift of corn bread so that later on during the performance they would be permitted to sit near the booth and get a better view instead of crowding in at the entryway.

When the food was ready, Big Doctor spoke and told them they were going to interrupt their activity and eat now, and that they could resume their work later. He said that he himself would make the offering to the powers with the corn and save time. The errand men were instructed to distribute the food.

The meal over, Big Doctor said, "Now we have eaten. Now you can go and tend to anything you want to. But after that, return here and get back to work!" They went off home to take their extra dry meat to their families, to tend their horses, and to take a little rest before going on with the work in the evening. The four main doctors did not linger long away from the ceremonial lodge. They had to fix up the gourd rattles, drums, and other things. Old-Man-That-Chief who has elk (*pax*) power was too old to wander about. If he should want to go home, someone must lead him. Most of the time he remained in the lodge throughout the ceremonial period.

That night and the next they built the serpent, the witch, and the turtle. They worked at night when they would not be observed. The serpent would take a whole night, the witch and the turtle perhaps another night. They had to bring in quantities of clay from the river bottom to do all this modeling. Twelve of them did the modeling—the four doctors at the west, and Old Bull and also the son of the subleader at the north, Wonderful Old Bison; the son of Sitting Hawk, Misery; also Angry Horse of the Bear Lodge. Bringing Horses was called in by Pipe Offering to assist him. On the next night, after the serpent was done they divided up, six working on the witch woman and six on the turtle-fireplace. Then the skin cutouts of the celestial powers were hung in place and the two loon skins put before the altar. Finally they were to set out for the cedar tree. They followed the same kind of procedure as for the cottonwoods, except that only one tree was obtained on this occasion.

A suitable cedar had been spotted by Misery and Strikes-the-Enemy on the Loup River, and before sunrise the next day a party of twenty doctors led by Strikes-the-Enemy set out to cut it down and bring it back to the lodge. Symbolically the cedar represented the Bear whose celestial affiliation was with the sun and the moon. The cottonwood symbolized the Beaver and the waters of the earth. Strikes-the-Enemy led the party, carrying a bear-hide rattle. On the return journey, they stopped half way and had a hypnotic contest as described in Chapter 34.

When the party reached within four feet of the lodge, they halted and

Big Doctor prepared to receive them and the tree on behalf of the Doctor Lodge. At his signal they came inside carrying the tree, stub end forward, and walked around the fireplace four times through south, west, north, and east where they stopped and placed the tree with its stub end touching the rim of the fireplace and its head end pointing toward the entrance at the east.

Pipe Offering made the offering of tobacco, smoke, and ashes with the sacred pipe to the three vital parts of the tree—the base, the middle, and the top as they had previously done with the cottonwoods. Meanwhile the errand men were sent outside to start to boil the dried buffalo meat for their feast.

All this time the other doctors had remained inside their respective booths, only the officials of the Doctor Lodge conducting the smoke offering ceremony. These included the four doctors at the west, one doctor each at the north and at the south, one old man (*kurahus*) each, at the northeast and the southeast, and the two errand men, one on each side of the entrance way.

Now that the cedar tree had been brought into the lodge and received, it was time for all of them to eat. The doctors all came out of their booths and sat right down on the serpent as there was no other place to sit between the booths and the fireplace. Three buckets of boiled corn kernels had been donated and these constituted the first course of their banquet. As always, they had to share the food with the supernatural powers before it could be eaten by the people, and the serving followed an order that was determined by the particular powers they had called on for the occasion. After eating, the ceremony to stand the cedar in its place was performed and then anyone who wanted to could go home.

36

THE WOMEN GET WOOD

FOR THE DOCTORS

Women Volunteer to Get Wood—Women Invited to Entertainment and Feast at Doctor Lodge—Quartz Crystal Sleight of Hand

WHEN OLD-MAN-HIGH-WATER went around the village notifying the women, he told them to meet outside the village and that two men would go along to protect them. Meanwhile Eagle Chief had sent one of his wives to ask Running Scout and Won't-Run-from-the-Enemy to take over this task. They knew they would be asked and they were all ready to go. They were given instructions to lead the women south of the creek rather than to the west where the enemy was likely to be lurking. As the women started for the appointed meeting place, other men set out for the surrounding hills to picket.

Twenty women had volunteered. There was a standard backload of wood that the women usually carried (¼ cord or 2 cubic feet—2 armloads; eight armloads = 1 cord or 4 backloads). For each night that the doctors performed, they would need four backloads. Besides their preparations during the current week, the doctors were likely to give five performances, so that the women have to go on three more such expeditions to keep them supplied.

While the women were in the timber cutting the wood, the two scouts were standing on a hill watching them closely. Some women were saying, "Don't take too much. Take a light load. There are a lot of us." As one woman would get loaded up, she would stand aside and wait for the others. Finally when most of them had gathered, the men called out, "All of you here yet?"

One was found to be missing and when she finally emerged they all lined up one behind the other and set out for the village. As they approached, people were watching from the housetops, saying, "They're coming with wood." A ridge ran east and west above the village and the women sat down there to rest before coming in. They were wishing they could take a bath in the lake beside the road. "Have you rested enough?" asked Roaming Scout. "Yes." "Come on, then." When they had gone halfway into the village, their scouts left them and went home and the women proceeded to the Doctor Lodge where they dumped the wood, some of it inside and some outside to the north of the door. Big Doctor said, "Now you ladies go home and change your clothes. Dress up in your best. Paint your cheeks and then come back because you are going to have a feast. Tell those two men who went with you to dress up and come. Who were they?" "Running Scout and Won't-Run-from-the-Enemy?" "All right."

By about three or four in the afternoon, the children who were waiting around to see everything sighted the line of women with the two men in the lead going to the Doctor Lodge. The women were carrying their wooden bowls and buffalo-horn spoons. They were seated along the north side of the lodge, the two men at the western end of the line. Wonderful Old Bull of the north side was doing the honors for the four main doctors. The wives of the doctors had contributed four buckets of boiled corn which were now brought in and the meat was given by one of the designated donors. An offering of corn was made to all the objects in the lodge, and it was served to the guests. After the second helping some of the women were patting their stomachs and saying, "My, I ate too much!" Those with more foresight had brought a bucket along to take the extra food home.

All the doctors except the four at the west remained in their booths. In anticipation of the forthcoming entertainment, some were calling out, "I'm going to take a quartz crystal out of that good-looking woman over there!" The women, who were apt to be shy on such occasions, were whispering among themselves instead of speaking out as the men usually did. The three big doctors at the west supplied the talk. "That one—I'm going to take a quartz crystal out of her!" "No you won't. That's the one I want." While they were eating the corn, twenty-two pieces of the cooked meat were spread out on a tent skin ready to be served, and as the women finished their corn they were served soup in their bowls. Wonderful Old Bull, representing all the head doctors, served them with the meat. Finally the dishes and pots were cleared away, the women put their bowls behind their backs, and the entertainment began.

At the west, Wonderful Old Bull and Sitting Hawk began to drum and sing doctor songs, while the doctors in different booths made all sorts of animal sounds. The little boys ran in to see what was going on. They were saying, "Now they're taking their quartz crystals." At this juncture, the two head doctors got up and danced facing the booths—Big Doctor down the north side and Pipe Offering down the south side. Each doctor carried a gourd rattle in his left hand, an eagle-wing fan in the right and as they went along the side they said, "Hu', hu', hu'," to signify that they were bent on hypnotizing. They passed along their booths from west to east and then back again.

Now the two doctors set out from the west again, Big Doctor in the lead and Pipe Offering behind him. They moved very carefully inside the serpent, making sure their feet did not touch it. When they arrived in front of the women sitting along the north side, they made odd motions and Big Doctor fell over. When he came out of his daze he patted his hand on his stomach, passing it up toward his throat and the quartz crystal came out of his mouth. Then Pipe Offering did the same and the two doctors went back to their place at the west. Now the other doctors all came out of their booths in a bunch, rolling and writhing, and they took the crystals out of the women. Old-Man-That-Chief who was blind asked to be led in front of an old woman and he took a crystal out of her.

By this time it was five-thirty and Big Doctor made his closing speech, stating that they had seen their "romping and playing" and now the show was over. They had shared a feast together and now all got up and left, including the spectators. On the way out everyone was laughing at Old-Man-That-Chief taking a crystal out of an old lady.

The doctors put away their "quartz crystal" paraphernalia and discussed plans for the forthcoming performance. Big Doctor said, "The day after tomorrow, in the evening, Good Pipe and I are going to put on a regular performance. Tomorrow evening we doctors are all going to parade through the village. Anyone who wants to take part in the performance to be given the day after tomorrow, ought to get everything ready!" The big public performances were now about to begin.

37

THE BIG DOCTOR

PERFORMANCE

~~~~~~~~~~~~~~~~~~~~~~~~~~~~~~

A Combination of Theater and Ceremony—the Form of the Performance—the "Scalped Ones" Mime—Swallowing a Deer Head—the Mud Duck —the Parade through the Village—the Round of Ceremonial Activities—the Sleight-of-Hand Performances

~~~~~~~~~~~~~~~~~~~~~~~~~~~~~~

IT MUST BE REMEMBERED that the doctor performance was both ceremony and theater and so regarded by the doctors themselves. The whole organization of the acts, the costuming, and the stage effects were designed to impress and entertain the people while at the same time supporting the confidence of the doctors. While for us in analogous situations, a trilogy or three-act play is considered most satisfying, with a five-act performance secondarily acceptable, for the Pawnees the four-act or fourfold organization is fundamental and based on their cosmic ideology. For more complex organizational forms he would develop four units with a final unit added, an introduction with four basic units less often, or two double-fours, one four following the other with an interim unit between them. During the twenty-day period in which the actual performance would take place, the sequence of acts on subsequent days had a "double-four" character with an interim unit of a different kind, and an introductory unit to the whole series and one in closing. The sequence of the kinds of acts presented might be summarized as A-B A A B—C A C—B A A B-A conceived by the doctors as four B's with at least four-day intervals between each of them filled in either with A's or blank days, with the interim C A C being a special elaboration of the four-day interim theme between the second and third B. The B unit was a large-scale animal mime performed in the late afternoon in the outdoor plaza before the Doctor Lodge with the crowd watching from the roofs of the surrounding earth lodges. It was called Big Dance, *Kihax-kutsu*, dance-big, and the doctors were in a greater or lesser degree of trance while they carried out their performance.

The A's, the secondary acts between the Big Dances, were indoor performances comprising a series of sleight-of-hand feats including trance induction in one doctor by another. They were held in the night from about eight o'clock until midnight and included a sequence of acts by four different doctors with drumming, rattling, singing, and dancing in the intervals. All during the day the doctors who were to perform in the evening prepared themselves and their paraphernalia and refrained from eating until the following morning. The performances were interspersed with blank days during which they all rested and made other preparations for the Big Dance as well as for their subsequent performances. The entire series of performances was introduced by an initial indoor performance and ended with a finale that featured a lively battle between the Bears and the Buffalo Clowns, whose theme was, "Who's afraid of the great big bears? They're only little puppies after all!"

The C units were a special type of mime also given outdoors, featuring the "Scalped Ones," the *Kitsahuruksu*, who were thickly plastered with mud "so that they looked like mud banks approaching" and acted in weird and fearsome ways. It was a Pawnee belief that should a person who had been scalped survive, he could never return to his people. It was reasoned that if anyone did survive the process of being scalped by the enemy, he would become so malevolent that he could not live in society. Such a man would make himself a dugout in an embankment and live by attacking people and stealing what he needed. Frank North in his autobiography tells of a young woman who had been scalped by the Sioux in one of their raids in June 1861 while she was returning from her cornfield. Found to be alive, she was apparently buried up to the neck in an old Mormon cellar with a straw matting over her head and face and left there to die. She was rescued and nursed back to health by the schoolmistress, Mrs. Platt. There is of course, no proof that this was the work of the Pawnees themselves, nor can anyone substantiate the subsequent report that she was dispatched with a tomahawk after her return to the tribe and sunk in a deep eddy in Beaver Creek. It does indicate, however, that a person could survive scalping. A tribal belief was universally maintained that a scalped person could never return to the tribe. Children were constantly warned about these mischievous spirits and alive or dead they were considered a threat to adults also. They lived by stealing whatever they could get and sometimes seized women and young people. Because of them people were afraid to go about in the dark, especially near the banks of streams.

One of the principal actors in this mime was Old Lady Tsitawa, who was the leader of the black-tailed deer cult and the only woman leader in the lodge. She appeared wearing a short black skirt of tanned hide and a tanned hide shawl. Sometimes one and sometimes two of these "Scalped Ones" outdoor performances would be given in the interval between the second and third Big Dance, an indoor performance (A) intervening between the two Scalped Dances, so that at least four days would pass between the two Big Dance episodes.

The night before each indoor performance (A), the doctors who were to perform on the next evening paraded through the village in costume, stopping in as many earth lodges as they could and singing their songs. The general sequence of the sessions was as follows:

A. Introductory performance indoors, to open the proceedings.
I. B. Outdoor Big Dance the following day in the late afternoon.
A. Indoor performance the next night.
   Interval of one day.
A. Indoor performance the next night.
   Interval of one day.
II. B. Outdoor Big Dance, late afternoon (second big dance).
C. Dance of the Scalped Ones, *Kitsahuruksu*—outdoors.
A. Indoor performance the next night.
   Interval of one day.
C. Dance of the Scalped Ones, outdoors.
III. B. Outdoor Big Dance (third big dance).
   Interval of one day.
A. Indoor performance next night.
   Interval of one day.
A. Indoor performance next night.
IV. B. Outdoor Big Dance, the fourth and final one.
A. Indoor performance at night, to close. Grand Finale with the Buffalo Clown warriors attacking the Bears and conquering them.

After the women who had gotten their advance fuel supply had gone home, Big Doctor announced to the other doctors, "Good Pipe and I are going to put on a regular performance the day after tomorrow in the evening. Tomorrow evening, we doctors are all going to parade through the village." He also reminded them that any doctors who were going to join the two head doctors in giving a performance would have to make their plans for the parade and for the performance the following evening.

As usual, there would be four acts. Big Doctor planned to demonstrate how he swallowed a deer head whole. Pipe Offering was going to make a mud duck come alive. The third on the program would be Brave Horse, whose son would succeed in locating a horse's tail that would be carried away during the performance by one of the audience and hidden in an earth lodge in a place known only to himself. The fourth act was to be by Brave Shield or High Noon, who was a buffalo doctor. He would shoot an arrow into the chest of his young son, Yellow Calf, who would be impersonating a young buffalo.

The Pawnee doctor, wearing nothing but his loin cloth, was apparently a highly successful illusionist, as attested by the number of hard-headed white spectators who were thoroughly mystified. Among them was Major Frank North who early became a clerk in the trade store on the Pawnee reservation and later rose to be the leader of the U.S. Battalion of Pawnee Scouts that were regularly inducted into the U.S. Army. North, having a good grasp of the language and being familiar with the personalities involved, on witnessing the act where "the Bear" rips open the abdomen of a boy and eats part of the liver, could only conclude either that a dummy had been used or that the boy had actually been murdered on the spot. George Bird Brinnell of Yale, who had been among the Pawnee in Nebraska, after their removal visited a medicine man in Oklahoma and he too was at a loss to explain what he had seen in broad daylight. Luther North, young brother of Frank, who was with him on this occasion said that while he was on duty with the Pawnee scouts in Nebraska some of his scouts would practice their illusionist feats while they were out on campaigns with him. "One man hid among the tall grass and appeared as a deer, then the next moment as a man," he reported. Another would simply take up a handful of mud and, rubbing his hands together, produce a live turtle, reconverting it into mud again. North asked him what would happen if he released the turtle and let him go. The man said he would die. North returned to the spot after such an episode and found the dead turtle there. There are also eyewitness accounts of such feats as cutting off a foot during the course of a performance, reattaching it backward and then restoring it to normal.

My informant who had participated in some of these feats from the operational side was by no means mystified. The illusions were carefully planned, with assistants planted in the audience and all the practical details organized with great precision. The methods for convincing the audience that are familiar to us, such as allowing the spectators to examine some of the objects involved, were freely used. Various lighting effects produced by lowering or brightening the fire were also employed. Knowing all this, Evarts continued to believe in the divine intervention in the process, while a friend of similar age, David Gillingham, remained an unbeliever from his boyhood on into later life.

Now on the first evening before their performance, the doctors got ready for their parade through the village, *wi-ti-kihar-rar-itsax-ka-wu,* "now-it-dance-they-through-the-village-among-going." The first contingent comprised the four leading doctors at the west. They made an extensive tour of the village, going into each earth lodge as far as they could manage it and stopping east of the fireplace where they stood and sang. Then they went around the fireplace from east, by south, west, north and then out of the lodge and into the next one, where they again sang and walked around the fireplace, continuing until they had visited a considerable number. The next contingent was the Horse Doctors who would perform next evening, led by Brave Horse, making a similar tour, followed by their wives or any other women that wanted to join them in their songs.

Finally the Buffalo Doctors went through led by Leading Buffalo (*Taraha-rakitawiu*, "buffalo-outstanding"). As one of their number Brave Shield was going to demonstrate how he would shoot an arrow at his son Yellow Calf's chest and leave the boy unharmed. Brave Shield was also in the procession followed by Yellow Calf's grandmother Grieves-the-Enemy, who had given his father a gift so that he would teach the boy. All over the village there were abandoned cache pits, and, although the women tried to throw their old sweepings into them in order to fill them up, they never quite succeeded and from time to time someone that was not very familiar with the particular part of the village fell in. On this occasion as Brave Shield's group was going along they came to an old cache pit and the group separated, walking around it. But Grieves-the-Enemy was so preoccupied with her singing that she fell straight in. She yelled as loud as she could, but everyone was singing so loud that no one could hear her. Finally when the next party came passing that way and the men began to walk around the pit, they heard the old lady yelling and got a ladder so that she could climb out. "I was singing for Brave Shield when I fell in and they never heard me," she said. The men asked her, "Are you hurt?" "No, I just hit my knees," she said. "That's good!"

Now those doctors who were not performing the next evening were free to go home. The others remained in the Doctor Lodge all night and the next day, fasting until the following morning after the performance. That night in the ceremonial lodge, each leader talked over their strategy with his assistants. Brave Horse said to his son, "They're going to hide the white horse's tail and I'll tell you where (so that you will be able to find it when the time comes during the performance). It will be in the house of Leading Chief, right in his bed, where his wife sleeps—the bed over which his small bundle, *tsatki*, hangs. During the performance at the appointed time, you go in there and whistle around and put your hand right there and get it." In this manner, Brave Horse briefed his young son. The plan was that the man in the audience who offered to hide the tail would be in league with them.

The two leading doctors simply talked over the specific feats they would perform without discussing any of the mechanisms involved in their performance. Big Doctor said, "I have a whole deer head with antlers on.

I'm going to swallow it." Pipe Offering told them that he would bring a mud duck to life in some water.

Yellow Calf was to have four sharp arrows shot at him. When everyone had arranged what they would do and all their paraphernalia was in order, they all went to bed. Some of the doctors who were not performing that next evening decided not to remain at home, but to sleep in the ceremonial lodge anyway.

The next morning they all had corn for breakfast that had been supplied by Big Doctor's wife. At all times, there had to be at least two doctors in each booth, regardless of whether they were going to perform or not. Now they all concentrated into one booth on each side and the serving man placed one large bowl of corn in each while they all sat around and ate from it. One bowl was given to the two errand men which they took aside and ate together. This had all been directed and arranged by Big Doctor. About three in the afternoon, the other doctors began to wander in and each was in turn served a bowl of corn that had been donated for the purpose. Only those who were going to perform that evening did not eat at this time.

Just before dark, all the doctors came out of the ceremonial lodge dressed in their costumes and stood outside and sang and then went in again. After the last group, everyone crowded into the vestibule to watch. In the procession were Brave Shield followed by the boy, Yellow Calf, dressed in a buffalo-calf robe. The side of his body was marked with white feathers where he was going to be shot that evening; his grandmother followed behind singing.

There were four or five bird doctors. One of them was dressed in feathers with a whistle in his mouth. All imitated birds and then went back into the lodge. They circled around and the crowd stood around them at a little distance; some people were on the top of the earth lodge.

On each side of the door, a brave was stationed to keep order and keep the crowd out while the final preparations were being made inside the lodge. As soon as the errand man signaled that things were ready, the people rushed in and packed the entranceway. The boy Otter pushed his way to the front of the crowd and the brave tried to persuade him to go home, saying, "You ought to be home, little boy. Nothing but big men in here." But the boy persisted and was finally allowed to stand next to him.

Finally the braves went inside and sat down, one next to the northeast booth and the other next to the southeast, the little boy following after.

Now the drums began to sound and the two leaders started off. Big Doctor went down past the booths on the north side facing them and Pipe Offering down the south, and after each had retraced his steps they arrived at the west where the two doctors crossed paths—Big Doctor going down the south side and back and Pipe Offering down the north side and back, arriving at the west, where they stopped. The drums stopped beating and meanwhile Sitting Hawk and Wonderful Old Bull had risen and all four leaders remained standing at the west.

Big Doctor now moved forward from among the leadership and began his act. He was to swallow a whole deer head with the antlers on. He was assisted by his son, He-Kills-a-Person (*Tsahiks-ti-ki*, "person-he-kills"), who now handed his father the head. With Big Doctor in the lead, his son following and three other doctors behind them, they moved around the fireplace at a half trot by north, east and south and stoppped at the west. Before placing the deer's nose into his mouth as a first step, Big Doctor allowed the spectators to examine the head to show them that it was real. Then he put the deer's nose into his mouth and when the head was about halfway in, the procession again started around the fireplace, by north, east, and south; when they had nearly arrived back at the west, Big Doctor swallowed the entire head—the men behind him motioning with their eagle-wing fans down along the back of his body in order to help him swallow it. After he had swallowed it, he stopped at the west of the fireplace and gave thanks, first by putting his hand on the rim, then on his mouth and then on his abdomen where the deer head should now be contained since he had swallowed it. Then he made a very brief statement to the doctors, declaring, "Now doctors, I am going to keep it (viz., the deer head he had swallowed). That's all." Then he went back to his place.

Next on the program was Pipe Offering, the leading doctor of the south side of the Doctor Lodge. He would convert a mud duck into a real live one and then back again to mud. He had no special assistants as the other three main doctors helped him. He had a duck modeled out of mud and a large wooden bowl of water. All four doctors began to sing and he put the bowl of water west of the fireplace. The errand man was told to make the fire bright. Then Pipe Offering stood at the west and he raised his mud duck, and as he brought his hands down, all four doctors were singing. Just as the mud duck touched the water, it said, "Quack, quack, quack," and ran all around. Now the three other doctors raised their voices and sang as loud as they could, and when Pipe Offering picked the duck up from the water, it was a mud duck again.

The other doctors removed the bowl of water while Pipe Offering addressed the assembled company. He said: "Now spectators and doctors, now you have seen me." From among the spectators, Roaming Leader walked up to Pipe Offering and, taking his new blanket from his own shoulders, placed it on Pipe Offering in gratitude for his performance. As he received the blanket, Pipe Offering said to Roaming Leader, "You will have good luck wherever you go. This is what I depend on and also on my Mother Earth." Now Roaming Leader rejoined the crowd of spectators and Pipe Offering said, "You spectators and doctors have witnessed what I have done. It was with great difficulty that I performed this feat." Then he went back to his place at the west and rejoined the other three doctors there.

The third act of the evening was that of Brave Horse, whose son would find a horse's tail after it had been hidden by a spectator in one of the earth lodges in the village. As soon as Pipe Offering sat down, whistling was heard. This was Brave Horse's son, blowing on his whistle. Now Brave Horse said to the spectators, "I want one of you to volunteer to take the horse's tail off the boy and hide it in an unknown place. No matter how obscure the place is, as you will see, the boy will find it easily." Leading Horse soon volunteered from among the spectators, but in fact it had all been prearranged—"the volunteer" going straight to the place agreed upon beforehand. Returning to the Doctor Lodge he said, "It's hidden." The boy was sent on his way, blowing his whistle, and his father went around and around in the lodge also blowing his whistle, in order that his boy would succeed. The boy made straight for the lodge of Leading Chief where his father had told him it would be the night before. As he entered, the occupants asked him what he had come for and he said, "My father told me the tail would be in here where the bundle is," thus giving away the whole subterfuge to the people in the lodge. When he got back to the ceremony, his father was still whistling triumphantly for his boy's accomplishment in finding the tail. He addressed the assembled company, saying, "You see what my boy did!" Long afterward the story came out. The boy in his defense said that he could not deceive Leading Chief for he called him by the kin term, brother, *irari*, and it would be unethical not to be truthful with him.

The fourth and final act for the evening was that of Brave Shield, a buffalo doctor. He was to shoot four arrows at the chest of his son, Yellow Calf, at close range, but the boy would remain uninjured. The four doctors at the west were singing and rattling with their gourds. Brave Shield was holding four arrows. He brought the boy from the booth. On his ribs Yellow Calf had a round disk of soft white feathers where he was to be shot. He was imitating a buffalo calf and he went around the lodge four times, by west, north, east and south, with his father Brave Shield following after him. As they went, Brave Shield shot with his arrows into the ground around the fireplace, once at the north, once at the east, once at the south, and once at the west. On the final round Brave Shield pulled up the arrows one by one, and stopping at the east where the spectators were, gave them the arrows to examine so that they could see what sharp points they had. The arrows passed from one end of the line to the other and were then returned to Brave Shield. Yellow Calf was standing at the south side of the fireplace facing west, with his arms extended so that his ribs were exposed. Brave Shield went to the north side opposite him and with the four doctors at the west rattling and singing with all their might, he made a running jump over the fire, landing right in front of Yellow Calf on the south side where he released his arrow. The arrow jumped back over the lodge with its head mashed and bent. Now the boy proceeded through the west to the north side, facing eastward with his arms extended, while his father remained on the south. Again Brave Shield jumped over the fire close to the boy and shot his arrow and again it glanced off and flew across the room—the point all bent and broken. The buffalo dancers now instructed the boy to stand at the west facing north, while his father was at the east, and the same performance was repeated. Finally the boy stood at the east with his father at the west—the father jumping over the fireplace and making his final shot. The shooting being over, the father led the boy to the south position and, warming his hands over the fireplace, placed them on the boy's chest where he had been shot, repeating this four times. Then he shook the boy out of his daze a bit and sent him off to the Buffalo Booth. Brave Shield moved around the fireplace by west, north, and then east where the spectators were and showed them all how the heads of the arrows were broken and macerated. On inquiring of my informant how this was done, he said he thought that someone had been planted among the spectators to help change the arrows before they were passed around, or they might have been changed when they glanced off the boy's side and flew all the way across the room, either before they began their journey through the air or when they were picked up.

By this time it was midnight or one o'clock in the morning and the doctors all sang:

> *Tatix-kusisari*, I am-playing (like a child)
> *Witi-ratku-tawaki*, myself-for-me-to enjoy

Big Doctor made a final announcement to the crowd: "There'll be no performance tomorrow night. After that we'll have one again. Well now that's all!" Everyone left. Late the next afternoon they would have a big dance on the plaza outside the ceremonial lodge.

38

THE FIRST BIG DANCE

~~~~~~

*Procession of Doctors Impersonating Animals—
the Bears Fight the Rest of the Animals—Victory
Call's Participation—the Doctors' Meal*

~~~~~~

EVERYONE MADE SURE TO COME home early that evening so that they would be in time to see the show. By five o'clock there was a large crowd gathered around the space in front of the Doctor Lodge, including many little boys and people visiting from the South Bands.

One could hear the drums inside the lodge and then the doctors came out. In the lead were the two errand men, Good Eagle on the right and Big Bear at the left, each one holding a loon (*kuhut*). Right behind them came the four leading doctors, two by two—Big Doctor and Pipe Offering and then Wonderful Old Buffalo Bull and Sitting Hawk. Behind these came the drummers and then the other doctors two by two. As they circled the dance grounds, the two drummers sang, while the men ahead of them kept step to a dance, the two errand men swinging the loons forward.

Now as one looked in the doorway of the ceremonial lodge, one could see a "deer" jumping up inside. Different kinds of deer came out now; a black-tailed deer (played by Brave Bow), a reindeer (played by Fox Scarf), behind him an elk (played by Might-Be-a-Chief, son of That-Chief and trained by him). Each of these deer blew on a different kind of whistle. The next contingent to emerge were the horses led by Brave Horse with his boys following after him. They were running around here and there blowing their whistles when the black horse came. Next there were two wolves, one played by the son of Big Doctor, He-Kills-a-Person, and the other, *Hatuxka*, Won't-Flee-from-the-Enemy, who played the white wolf.

The procession was completed with the two men dressed in bearskins, one of them Misery, son of Sitting Hawk, and the other, Sitting Hawk's brother Victory Call, who was Otter's father. The two bears blocked the entrance so that the other animals would not be able to get back in. Finally they moved aside just long enough for the doctors to get in and then closed ranks again. As the doctors went inside, one could see smoke, dust, and ashes coming out of the smokehole of the ceremonial lodge, and one could hear noise inside. This was because the doctors were in there.

Now all the animals tried to get in too, but the bears blocked their way. The deer stood by pretending to be grazing casually, while the bear sat around looking equally casual. When the deer got close, he again had to jump away. The deer, horses, and wolves all wanted to get in but the bear stayed close to the door. The horses blew their whistles to get in, but the bear remained stationary. He tried to catch the colt, but the colt jumped back. Finally the bear looked the other way for a minute and some of the animals managed to run in. The deer got in but the white wolf had a hard time. The bears tried their best to catch him and they both blocked the way, but finally he squeezed in and only the other wolf was left. If the bears managed to catch him, they would rip open his abdomen and eat some of his liver. He huffed and puffed and tried his hardest to get into the lodge. White smoke (viz., clay) came out of his mouth with the effort. This got the bears angry and one could see the bristles of their hair standing up on the backs of their necks. Finally the wolf jumped right over the bear and got into the lodge, and this made everyone laugh.

At one of the later Big Dance episodes Sitting Hawk had instructed "the two bears" to try their best to catch a deer, a horse, or a wolf. Misery had all his implements ready inside his bear robe. Misery sat at the north side of the entranceway to the lodge looking toward the inside, and Victory Call at the south side somewhat away from the door looking around outside. The animals circled around the dance grounds four times, then tried to get back into the lodge but were prevented by the bears. The horses had buffalo-hair ropes that they were dragging along the ground. The deer managed to skip in, but the white horse, blowing his whistle, was blocked by Misery, who looked very angry with the hairs on his bear neck bristling. Twice the horse approached and managed to escape, with Misery just missing catching the rope. He began to puff and blow. Everyone was yelling to the horse, "He might catch you yet!" Finally the horse made a quick turn and Misery grabbed him too. Everyone on the housetops yelled, "There old man, I told you they'd get you." Both bears laid him down on his back and held him with his arms and legs spread out. Then Misery stuck in his bear claw and made a slit downward, laying open the whole stomach. He pulled out a piece of liver and Victory Call came up and got a piece. Everyone was shouting, "Just look at that old man there. Now old man you can never get enough to eat to fill you up any more!" (They meant that now that his liver was gone his stomach had lots of room to expand.) After the two bears got through, they jumped on their victim and healed him up. They had medicine in their mouths for this purpose which they rubbed on the victim's stomach to heal him up. When they got off, the people could see that he was all right again. Then they shook him a bit and as he came out of his daze, he got up and thought there was nothing wrong with him. He just blew on his whistle and ran into the lodge. But the people knew better. They said, "He can whistle away all right, but he won't ever be able to get enough to eat to fill himself up now!"

This was the first time that Victory Call had participated in this act and he went over to his older brother, Sitting Hawk, and caressed him in blessing. "This is what I wanted to know," he said. From now on, Victory Call could don his bear suit and go through this performance on his own. In return, he had taught Sitting Hawk how to handle rattlesnakes.

After all the animals had gone into the lodge, the public show was over. Inside the errand men would be busy cooking the meal. All sixty doctors would be there and they would use up three parfleches of meat to feed them all.

39

THE DANCE OF
THE SCALPED ONES

〰〰〰〰〰〰〰〰〰〰〰〰〰〰〰〰

*Impersonate Scalped Warriors Instead of Animals
in This Dance—the Song That Is Sung—the
Dance Explained*

〰〰〰〰〰〰〰〰〰〰〰〰〰〰〰〰

THE DAY AFTER the first Big Dance there was to be an indoor performance in the evening like the first one but with four different acts. The
men who were to participate would start to prepare themselves in the
morning after they had finished their breakfast, refraining from eating
till the next morning. Just before dark they circled about before the lodge
and sang as an announcement of what the performance was to be. A
granddaughter of one of the performers, meeting him the night before
his way home, inquired where his booth was located as she and her
mother wanted to have the privilege of watching the performance sitting
comfortably inside his booth. That evening before the performance she
came to the lodge with corn bread, coffee, and dry meat. The errand man
directed her, going past the first, second, and third booths on the north
side and entering the fourth. (He made careful note of what food she
would bring to see if he wanted to claim a share after the dance.) Now
the girl and her mother were seated inside the booth as the crowd packed
in to the rest of the lodge. After this performance the doctors would have
a free day, then another performance and still another free day and then
a second Big Dance outdoors. After this second Big Dance, instead of
just the nighttime performances and free intervals, another kind of outdoor performance was introduced—the Dance of the Scalped Ones.

Instead of animals, the actors in the Dance of the Scalped Ones were
the spirits of those who had been scalped by the enemy. Everything was
done to develop a mood of weirdness. Old Lady Tsitawa, head of the
black-tailed deer lodge, wore a short skirt of black tanned hide and a

tanned-hide shawl. The other actors impersonating the *kitsahuruksu*, the scalped ones, were plastered all over with mud, including a thick plastering of mud on their heads and all over their faces. As they approached they looked like a veritable mud bank.

A big crowd had gathered outside the lodge in anticipation of the performance. The two drummers ran out first and putting their drums between their knees, sat facing each other. As they began to beat the drum, a crowd of scalped ones ran out of the Doctor Lodge. The drumming was in all sorts of irregular beats and the little boys were frightened when they first saw the scalped ones approaching. They motioned erratically and jumped every which way in scary ways. The drummers were singing "Scalped-Ones-Speech":

> *Hiru-rihi*   here-is
> *Hiru-rihi*   here-is, *wakarawi* (speech)
> *Hiru-rihi, hiru-rihi, wakarawi*
> *Kitsahuruks-pakarawi*   scalped one-speech
> *Kitsahuruks-pakarawi*

The song was sung to an irregular tune and as soon as the drummers had finished the song, they all ran suddenly into the lodge and just as suddenly out again, the drummers again coming out and sitting facing each other, singing the Scalped-Ones-Speech with the crowd of actors running out after them. This running in and out was repeated four times and on the fourth round the actors all came out dancing backward, making peculiar motions and finally falling down. Even the drummers fell and kicked over their drums (water drums made of a hollow log.) At last they looked up dazed and as soon as they became aware of the people around, they jumped up and ran back into the lodge.

No one would provide a meal for "Scalped-Ones." As everyone knew, "They were the biggest thieves and stole anything they could get a chance to!" They ate in their booths whatever donations of corn had been made. "As for dry meat, they would provide it for themselves if they could steal some."

Between the second and third Outdoor Big Dance, there were one or two of these special outdoor Scalped-Ones dances with a performance in the night indoors intervening. Afterward the third Big Dance was given, and then after that the two nighttime performances with free days intervening.

40

BREACHES OF THE
DOCTORS' RULES

~~~~~~~~~~~~~~~~~~~~~~~~~~~~~~~~~~~~~~~

*The Young Doctor Decides to Eat Food at Altar
—the Hypnotizing That Follows—the Younger
Men Hypnotize Big Bear—This Power of Pawnees Discussed*

~~~~~~~~~~~~~~~~~~~~~~~~~~~~~~~~~~~~~~~

AFTER THE THIRD Big Dance, everyone was getting tired, especially the errand men. The individual doctors had various matters to attend to at home, and even the main doctors had to leave the lodge at some time during the day. One day the main doctors were all off resting and had left one of the younger doctors sitting in Big Doctor's place so that he could watch the things at the altar. While he was sitting there, a donation of corn and soup was brought in. Some of the other doctors in the lodge decided they would like to eat some of it right away. The young doctor at the west decided that, after all, since they were hungry, they should eat some of it. He asked three of the others to join him at the west and ordered the errand man to serve them and also the other doctors that were in their booths. They made a small offering of the corn to the powers and then proceeded to eat.

Finally, when some of the other doctors came in and found they had eaten some of the food that was donated for all of them, they became indignant. They went about the fireplace, quivering and waving their eagle-wing fans and hypnotized the offenders. Brave Shield who was the first to come in, hypnotized the man who had been left in charge of the things at the altar. He caused him to come around the north side of the fireplace and made him fall so that he hit his head against the pillar of the lodge. Then he made the offender get up and come outside and fall down, where he was left on the ground with blood coming out of his mouth. The other two doctors who had come in at the same time as Brave Shield, spirited out the others who had been eating the corn and also the errand man who had served them. They fell down outside in the same way as the first man. When the first recovered from his trance, he came inside and sat down in Big Doctor's place at the west. The other three also came out of their trance and resumed their places next to him. The others who had eaten the corn also began to recover and to run into their booths. Those at the west had not yet been dismissed by the angry doctors.

Brave Shield and the other doctors went back to their booths, but the young doctor at the west was angry in his turn and decided to take out those who had hypnotized him. He picked up the eagle-wing fan from among the sacred objects at the west and, going about the fireplace, spirited Brave Shield outside. He did the same to the other two. He then went back into the lodge and again sat down at the west, telling his three companions they could go back to their booths if they wanted to. The three he had spirited out now went back to their booths and the whole affair was ended. When Big Doctor heard about it on his return, he simply laughed at the whole affair.

Big Bear who was the errand man on the south side was absent from the lodge for about three days. Three of the younger men decided to get him to come back. The enterprise was initiated by Might-Be-Chief, son of Old-Man-That-Chief. He was about fifteen or sixteen years old at the time, and he was sent around on so many errands in Big Bear's absence that he began to resent it. "Big Bear ought to be doing this," he thought, "I'll get him back." Big Bear, on his part, was pretty tired by this time and wanted a rest. Might-Be-Chief tried to enlist help from two young men, Fox Chief and Man Chief, but Fox Chief demurred, saying, "He's our uncle. We can't do that to him." But they were finally persuaded by Might-Be-Chief's argument that he ought to be there, and they all went to Big Bear's lodge.

Big Bear was sitting on top of his lodge when they got there and they said, "Look at him—the way he sits there as if he had nothing to do!" Then all of them walked back and forth before his eyes and then all three waved fans in front of him until he rolled off the earth lodge. When he got up they made him follow them as they ran, pushing and twisting him around any way they wanted to. Finally when they got to the water they caused him to roll in and wet his buffalo robe and all his clothes. When he got home, he gave his clothes to his wife and dressed in whatever dry clothes he had and went back to the Doctor Lodge. He was furious and went straight to the Elk Booth spiriting Might-Be-Chief outside. Then he went to the Bear Booth and first took out Fox Chief, then coming back again for Man Chief. The three young doctors didn't mind, as they had succeeded in getting Big Bear back to his post in the Doctor Lodge.

Sometimes when a doctor went home at night he went to asleep with his wife and then the doctors might go after him in this way. They would spirit him out onto the dance grounds outside the Doctor Lodge; then he would go home, get his buffalo robe, and return.

From these instances it should be clear that the Pawnee preoccupation with illusionism, hypnotism, and suggestion was neither mere theater nor pure ritual. The power of trance induction was regarded as a threat and a means of control. Possibly the hunter found in it a method of communication with the wild animals and control over them. It is very evident that it was considered a way of immobilizing the enemy. Trance induction was called "fighting" or "shooting at the image or shadow," and illusionism by sleight of hand as a milder form of psychological control was called "playing" or "romping" as of children. Our present preoccupation with psychology and psychosomatic problems should point the way to its connection with healing. The cultivation of these psychological states in the Doctor Lodge was obviously something more than pure supernaturalism.

The final episode in the Opera was a contest between the Buffaloes and the Bears in which the Buffaloes reduced the Bears psychologically to mere puppies, and in this way the Buffaloes are no longer afraid.

41

THE CLOSING EPISODE OF
THE DOCTORS' GRAND OPERA

Contest between Bears and Buffalo Clown Warriors—Description of the Ceremony—the Closing Speech by Big Doctor—the Dismantling Begins

THE MONTH-LONG GRAND OPERA of the doctors ended with a closing performance inside the ceremonial lodge after the fourth Big Dance. Its main feature was a contest between the Bears and the attacking Buffalo Clown Warriors, dressed in mock war costume and led by members of the Buffalo Cult, with John Buffalo, Heavy Trophies, and others playing the several parts. They wore war bonnets made of corn husks and carried spears made of sticks decorated with corn husks to represent feathers. Their shields were also of corn husks, and they made a "chief's medal" for their chief Clown out of the round cover of a tin can. Everyone knew that on that evening the Clowns were going to stab the Bear with their sticks and "make a man of him." The young Bears were released from trance by their leader, Angry Horse, who had also "to awaken" himself. This was the final act.

On the last night the crowd surged into the entryway to see the performance. At the southeast near the wall stood a crowd of Clown-warriors wearing their corn-husk war bonnets with their chief standing proudly at the head of them with his spear. On the north side stood the party of the Bears. Angry Horse was the leading figure of the Bear Party. His face was blackened and he wore a wreath of cedars around his head. In his hand he carried a big rock tied to a string. (My informant did not know what he represented, but people said that his blackened face indicated that he knew everything.) Next to the leader were the two Bear Doctors of the second grade—Strikes-the-Enemy, lieutenant to Angry Horse, and Misery, Son of Sitting Hawk. These men had no other costume than a long pole in the left hand of each and a cedar branch "fan" in the right. The two junior members of the Bear Lodge, Fox Chief and Man Chief, were to be the direct object of the attack and they remained inside the Bear Booth dressed in their bearskin costumes.

The show began with the Clowns. John Buffalo addressed the Clown chief who stood there proudly oblivious of anyone or anything that was going on around him:

> "Say Chief, I heard that other tribe say the Bear is going to come around. Over there, there's a bluff, and a Bear is coming there." "I know that but they're nothing but raccoons," said the chief. Then another fellow addressed him saying, "The other tribe is excited there because they say the Bears are coming." "Bear—talk about Bear—I could ride right on it any time I want to!" Next one of the Clown-warriors went and sat down next to the witch woman. He told her what was going to happen "over there" and he made everyone laugh. He said to her, "I heard the people over there say the Bear is going to come. Do you believe it? But the chief says he was up there and there is nothing but a raccoon in there—not a Bear. Are you afraid of Bears? Well, I guess if they come, I'm going to get one."

After this byplay with the witch, the Clown-warrior rejoined his group.

Now the action moved to the Bears. All the other doctors came out of their booths. The Bear subleaders, Misery and Strikes-the-Enemy, pushed their long poles into the Bear Booth to tease out the two Bears who are still inside. When they started to come out of their booth, the Wolf (played by He-Kills-a-Person) came around and got between the two Bears so that their way was blocked. They tried to catch him, but he jumped away with a quick motion and this made them all the more furious. In their anger, they came out of the booth, one at a time. First one came backing out and then the other one emerged head forward. All the doctors began to move about to blockade their escape. The Bears were very angry and they blew and puffed and the bristles on their necks rose straight up.

The Clowns way over on the other side said, "I got hold of his foot now!" John Buffalo said, "I'm holding their legs. They're nothing but raccoons!" Another clown chimed in with, "Oh, they're puppies—nothing but puppies!"

The Bears tried to escape and the crowd tried to blockade their way. The Clowns got caught between two groups of them. Then the doctors, Clowns, and everyone ran out of the lodge except one Clown that got stuck between the two Bears. He didn't know where to go so he looked around and saw that the serpent's mouth was big enough to get in. So he crawled in there, breaking all the teeth. Then he stuck out his head, looking all around. When the two Bears finally left the lodge, he got out of the serpent's mouth.

Outside the Clown-warriors were all yelling, "They're over here. There're nothing but little bits of puppies." Soon Angry Horse, the chief Bear Doctor, came staggering into the lodge, circling the fireplace as if he were drunk. He was carrying a rock tied to a string, and every now and then he would hit one of the house posts with it as he went around the fireplace. Next his lieutenants, Misery and Strikes-the-Enemy, entered singing and holding their long sticks and cedar-branch fans. Next came the four main doctors who went to their place in the west and stood there holding their eagle-wing fans. In front of them at the west of the fireplace facing toward the east, stood Misery and Strikes-the-Enemy, making sweeping and jerky movements with their cedar-branch fans. They were calling in the members of their own Bear Lodge who were still outside, with the assistance of the two main doctors who were standing behind them to reinforce their efforts with their eagle-wing fans.

Now one Bear comes backing in and the other comes in head foremost, one going around the north side of the fireplace, the other around the south side. The doctors, including those at the west, all try to get out of the way of the Bears, while Big Doctor reminds Pipe Offering to fill his pipe to get ready for the smoke offering.

Angry Horse, the Bear leader, was still staggering back and forth around the fireplace carrying a big stone on a string. When the Bear that was approaching from the south arrived at the west, Angry Horse was waiting for him there. The Bear fell down and he jumped over him and smashed him on the forehead with the big rock he was carrying. As soon as the prone Bear had been hit, Big Doctor told Pipe Offering to light up his pipe and offer the mouthpiece to the forehead of the prostrate Bear twice, then once to his chest (windpipe), then to his right palm, his left palm, and one to each of the soles of his feet. The whole procedure was repeated with the Bear that was approaching from the north side and the two Bears lay facing each other at the west. As soon as he fell, Pipe Offering had also "smoked" the second Bear in the same way as he had the first. Angry Horse was signing, "This is the way I do when I get angry!"

As the two Bears lay limp and lifeless at the west, the two main doctors assisted by Misery and Strikes-the-Enemy carried first one and then the other into the Bear Booth.

During this special act of the leader upon the two junior Bears, the rest of the doctors and spectators had remained outside. Now first the doctors, followed by the spectators and the Clowns in the rear, filed back into the lodge. The Clowns talked about what they did out there. They were saying, "Oh, I got hold of him by the leg and just shook him around a little bit." "Oh, I got on him like a horse. He's a good run-ner."

By this time the Bear leader, Angry Horse, was all crumpled up and quieted down. Standing at the west of the fireplace facing east, he warmed his rock over the fire and then went to his seat near the Bear Booth at the northeast of the Doctor Lodge. There he removed his whole costume, including the cedar wreath, leaving only his blackened face. Now the two ex-Bears, Man Chief and Fox Chief, also came out of the booth without their Bear costumes. Man Chief went to the north of the fireplace, extending his right hand over the fire, then putting it on top of his head. Then he did the same with his left hand. He went through the same procedure with his abdomen and also his knees as he stood up. At the south of the fireplace, Fox Chief did the same thing. Now both men returned to their Bear Booth, Man Chief directly from his station at the north and Fox Chief from his south station around the west and north.

This was the closing act of the whole show, and now Big Doctor made his final address to them all. He said, "Now spectators, young men, women, now you have seen, during these several nights, this, 'our play-ing.' Young men, tribespeople, now I am through with this playing of. ours." (He included the audience as well as the doctors in his statement, expressed through the grammatical first person, plural inclusive form, *ti-wi-rikuhuritsa-witsat*, "this-now-it us all-complete." He thus acknowl-edged the help of the spectators in examining the paraphernalia when offered to them to affirm that they were authentic.) "Now that's all." This was the signal for all spectators to leave.

That night the doctors would take the first step toward dismantling the ceremonial appointments of the lodge. Each of the doctors would bundle up the sacred objects he had used in carrying out his performance and wrap them in a skin cover to form a long-shaped bundle. These must be taken to their respective homes that evening. The four doctors at the west would wrap up everything pertaining to the Doctor Lodge in general—the loons and other birds, etc. That night only the four leading doctors would remain in the lodge, sending home their bundles with the errand men.

Very early next morning all the doctors would return so that they could remove and dismantle all the special ceremonial figures and structures they had built. Insofar as possible these would be carried intact to the wa-ter where they would be deposited in a certain position, approximating their position in the ceremonial lodge. The serpent figure, the witch woman, and the cedar would be carried out as they were and the sticks of the booths used to make them into a booth in the bottom of the creek. While the Bear ceremony was going on, some men had been delegated to find a suitable place for this.

42

DISMANTLING THE
CEREMONIAL DOCTOR LODGE

〰〰〰〰〰〰〰〰〰〰〰〰〰〰〰

*Ceremonial Objects Are Dismantled—All Things
Carried to Creek—Serpent Placed in Water
within Curved Fence—an Additional Hypnotic
Contest—a Banquet Given—the Final Details Settled*

〰〰〰〰〰〰〰〰〰〰〰〰〰〰〰

THE FINAL PHASE of the Doctor Lodge was the removal of the figures
they had built and the animal booths. All these things had to be deposited
at the bottom of Beaver Creek in an appropriate order and fastened in
place. It took about a hundred people, including the sixty doctors, to do
this work. For the final banquet that they would share, they used six or
seven containers of dried buffalo meat and an equal number of buckets of
corn.

The night before, while the Bear ceremonial had been going on, a number of men were sent to choose the place in Beaver Creek where they
would set up their things.

During the ceremony and as the figures were being carried out, people
offered them gifts. These were placed in the water with the figures.
Once, while the performance was going on, a woman made up her mind
to give a gift to the serpent on behalf of her son. She took a piece of calico
and as she entered the lodge, opened up the cloth and dragged it across the
floor, placing it on the inside of the serpent's neck. The errand man
came over and took the calico to one of the four doctors at the west. The
doctor set the material aside and came directly to where the woman was
standing, walking along the outside of the serpent and jumping over it to
where the woman was standing. Now he said, "You have a boy. Maybe
someday he will grow up to be a big man and everybody will notice
him." The woman left and the doctor returned to his seat.

When the doctors got in that morning, they detached the figures so that they could be carried to the water. The serpent went first. It was simply pegged to the ground and was freed by pulling up the pegs. The men ranged themselves along both sides of the 60-foot length—the head being pointed conveniently southeast toward the exit. The men waited, ready to lift it up when the signal was given. The witch woman was lifted up and set down on a spread of tanned hide so that they could carry her out on it. The turtle that had been modeled on the fireplace, was crumbled up and also placed on a skin spread.

It took a lot of men to carry out the cedar gently, as it was loaded with gifts that had been placed on it when it was first brought into the lodge. The birds and cutouts suspended from the rafters were left there, because they did not belong in the water. After everything else had been detached, the sticks of the animal booths had to be uprooted, and any woman that wanted to help would carry these things out.

Now the process got under way with the four main doctors leading. Most of the men were dressed only in their breechcloths, although some doctors were foolish enough to wear their buffalo robes and to carry their eagle-wing fans despite the strenuous work they had to do. They made two stops along the way to rest—one about halfway toward their destination and then another one further along. The four doctors had gone ahead and were already in the water, building, out of sticks from the doctor booths standing upright in the bed of the creek, a kind of curved fence open at the east. This was the beginning of a whole structure that would enclose all the objects.

As the serpent lay along the shore waiting to be deposited in the water, people came up and made offerings to it. One person who hoped for long life said, "I give you this. I hope to see you this way a year from now." A mother, giving a gift on behalf of her son said, "I hope to see my boy grow up and be a great man." A mother hoped her two daughters would grow up to be married and have many children. Each girl carried a gift of calico to give and the mother said, "You, serpent, are going to rest here under the water. I want my children to grow up and have many children when they get married." Some people thought the serpent should be identified as a whale and some as an alligator. The latter seems the more likely from the word for it, "dry-tongue." The forked tail somewhat interferes with this latter identification. In this instance the mother was thinking of the fecundity of fish who have many eggs which hatch in large numbers.

Now they placed the serpent in the water, its head resting inside the curved fence the doctors had prepared. The head was pointing upstream (westward) the direction in which all the fish swim. The body extended eastward or downstream. Everyone got into the water and pegged the serpent and its various gifts to the bed of the stream. All the gifts of goods—

calico, shawls, and blankets—were also fastened to the bottom. The whole thing was encased in a wicker frame of willows under the water. The stakes from the doctor booths were stuck all along the sides of the serpent and bent over across it and interlaced at the top.

Now that the objects were all in the water, the people stepped aside to permit the doctors to engage in one more hypnotic contest. One after the other, as they stood by the water, they caused one another to fall in.

Then the whole group of doctors and any others who had given them assistance repaired to the Doctor Lodge for the banquet. The lodge was empty and they could make a big circle sitting close to the outside walls. The groups of doctors were ranged in from the west. Beyond them along the sides were the general public who had helped them. And last of all to the east were the chiefs, two each from the four Skidi villages. Furthest toward the door of the guests, were two old men, That-Chief at the southeast and Good Land at the northeast. Finally there was one errand man stationed at each side of the entrance. As they were assembled there, some of the people expressed regret that the whole thing was over, for they had had such a good time.

It took eight people to prepare and serve the meal including the two regular errand men. Each of these was provided with an assistant to do the cooking and serving. They had to borrow two of the largest brass kettles they could get, and after they got the water they put in the meat and set them to boil, one at the northeast and one at the southeast of the fire. While the meat was cooking, the donated corn was served after the appropriate offerings had been made, then soup and then the meat. Extra large pieces were set aside for the guests of honor and one for "the house" —that is, for Sitting Hawk's wife to whom the lodge belonged.

During the meal the doctors made conversation about the happenings of the morning—about what had occurred at the river, and so forth. Then Big Doctor made his closing speech, addressing them all. He said, "Now young doctors, doctors, and all members of the Doctor Lodge and the animals that we have imitated here, and you chiefs sitting here watching over your people, and Heaven that has taken pity on us so that we could successfully complete our performance, and you head doctors here who have helped carry out our performance, now we have had our feast— now the Doctor Lodge is over."

A number of business details remained to be attended to. The head doctors had to apportion the meat that they had kept for the final arrangements. The owners of the house would have to fill in all the holes and set up the beds and then entertain the members of the families among whom they had been staying while the lodge was in session. They would need a quantity of dried meat for this. What was left would be divided among the doctors. The errand men and their assistants received gifts of calico.

The Doctor Lodge was one of the most intensive group ceremonies of the year, extending to all the people. In the three South Bands at this time, each had a similar twenty-day Doctor Ceremony that they referred to as Big-Sleight-of-Hand. Apparently they only lacked the serpent or water monster of the Skidi, which was the special feature of the federation of the Skidi villages.

After the Doctor Lodge, the separate animal cults that had been represented there should each have a three-day ceremony of its own—the general one constituting a mandate for this. The ceremonial calendar was so crowded that it was extremely difficult to find three days when all the members would be free of other ceremonial involvements. The Bear and Buffalo cults were large organizations with thirty to forty members, and there were many overlappings in the personnel.

There was one private cult, however—the Deer Dance—that was entirely outside the association. It had been imported a generation before from the kindred Caddoan-speaking Wichita to the south and adapted to the Pawnee ceremonial pattern. It had no obligation to the Doctor Association and was fast presenting a challenge to it for membership. Its ceremony was held at a time that overlapped the Doctor Lodge, and sometimes members were spirited away from one to the other, causing considerable bitterness between the leaders. The Deer Dance, also known as Whistle Dance from the whistles the dancers blew at frequent intervals, celebrated the maturing of the wild sage and the mescal bean. Rattlesnake power was also part of the cult. The over-all pattern was of a Deer Lodge in the timber. In some ways it represented a quite different system of thought from the Doctor Association, and through it new and important developments might have occurred in Pawnee ceremonial thinking. But before this could be realized, its life was ended by the holocaust that overtook the Pawnee people and their culture and their wild animal world as white contact intensified (see p. 3).

Victory Call was the director of this cult and he was largely responsible for its growth and success among the people. On his deathbed he accused his arch rival, Big Doctor, of causing his death through sorcery.

43

THE DEER DANCE

INVESTIGATORS HAVE LONG REALIZED that the Pawnees had a culture that
was unusually rich in ceremony and metaphor. It was particularly in the
theater arts connected with their ceremonies that their aesthetic culture
had its main expression. In the ceremonies, the sustained patterning of
the episodes, the costuming, and the underlying ideology and symbolism represented an aesthetic composite of great richness, which was as-
siduously cultivated and appreciated by the people for its beauty.

The Deer Dance was a comparatively new addition to the Pawnee
ceremonial repertoire. For more than a century certainly, and no doubt
considerably longer, Pawnee men had gone south on extended visits to
the several tribes of their Caddoan-speaking kinsmen. While they were
there they commonly participated in the ceremonies as well as in other
activities. Some remained there permanently such as the brother of Eagle
Chief, Noted-Tent (*Iseru-rikariku*), who became a distinguished Wichita chief. A man of the Kitkehaxki Band, *Tiraritaka'as*, became a chief of
the Kitsai. For a rich source of new ideological and aesthetic material
the Pawnees were conscious that they must go south to the Wichita,
the Wichita probably looking south to the Caddo and the Caddo in turn
to Mexico. It is probable that in this manner, passing from group to

group, Aztec and other Mexican type cultural forms filtered northward to the Pawnees.

Sometime before 1842, while they were living at Old Village (Kitkehax-pakuxtu), Kind Warrior (*Tirarira*) who was still a young man then, used to go visiting the Wichita quite often and on one of these occasions, when his host was going to a Deer Dance he requested that he be taken along. When they arrived at the ceremonial house, he was asked whether he would like to participate and he said he would, as he liked to dance. He was then costumed like the others, painted all over with white clay, a feather worn crosswise at the back of his head, in his right hand a whistle and in his left a bunch of wild sage which had white seeds. A bowl contained white clay with some of the white seeds so that the dancers could paint themselves.

His friend told him to follow him around during the dancing so that the other Wichitas could see him and when the members had gone, the chiefs sitting at the head of the room called over Kind Warrior and asked him whether his friend had told him anything about the dance. When he answered that he had just painted him up, the chiefs said, "When you get home, say to your friend, 'Now my friend, I don't want people just to see me painted up. I want to know what I am painted for.'"

The next evening, when Kind Warrior and his Wichita friend were in the grass house together, he caressed his friend in blessing and said, "I don't want to simply be painted up. I want you to take pity on me and tell me what it means. I will stay with you as long as you want me to. I will take care of your horses, haul water for you, and hunt the buffalo. You don't have to get the buffalo. I'm the one that will get them for you." The Wichita said, "All right my friend. What you want I can tell you." Then Kind Warrior went over to the Wichita's wife and placed his hands upon her in blessing too. "From now on," said the Wichita, "whenever the dance comes, we'll go in together." Kind Warrior stayed two or three years in order to learn. The dance was held almost any time of year and lasted for four days.

The next time the dance was held, the Wichita taught Kind Warrior as he had promised. He said to him, "You must know something more than just the singing. The Wichitas are watching us now. Now I'm going to get up and you get up and follow me around." They were ready to perform their sleight-of-hand feat. Kind Warrior was told to hold the whistle in his left hand and the sage plant in his right. Now they began to encircle the fireplace. At the northwest corner, the Wichita struck the ashes with the sage and the dust arose. Then they went on to the other three semicardinal "corners" in counterclockwise succession (northeast, southeast, southwest) and at the west facing east, burned the ends of the sage in the fire. Then they made another counterclockwise circuit and at the west about a foot from the fireplace, hit the ground with the sage. Kind Warrior did the same and out of each of their sage plants, four beans rolled down. The Wichita now addressed the different "animal stations" where the members were seated and said, "Now you see what I did with my brother. I told him to do whatever I do. And now I'm going to give him what I do so that he can perform it at home." The Wichitas were all glad to see him do this. He continued to address them: "Now if he goes home and you hear that the Pawnees have started to do the Deer Dance, you can all know that I told him to do it. I also told him to listen to how the singing goes and what the singing is about. I told him that the singing was not just done for its own sake but to study how the animals go and what they do. And I told him that some of the songs are about smoking and that smoking is the main thing. And since he was not willing merely to be painted up for the dance, but wanted to learn what it means, I have taught him. And I'll be more than glad if you at the other places will help me with your performance so that he can learn." The Wichitas said, "That's good. We will try to help this man." "Kind Warrior," said his friend, "you ought to be glad that these different people are going to teach you for nothing."

As the doctors went through their performances, one of them would call him over and whisper to him the meaning of his performance. He would turn around and embrace the man, clasping him about the neck and rubbing his hands upon him from the head and down the arms in blessing, for he had taken pity on him and given him what he most wanted. As the dancing continued, another would call him over, and then another, and so he learned many of their different ways. One of the members had a black bean. He said to Kind Warrior, "You see this?" "Yes, I see it." Then the performer went around the fireplace four times and at the four semicardinal "corners," put ashes on the bean at each corner. After he had done this and gone around the fireplace four times, he stopped at the west and threw the bean down and a black spider was seen running around on the ground. "Now," said the Wichita doctor, "when you go home and have a Deer Dance, you can do this." And then Kind Warrior turned around and blessed him and so he learned many ways among the Wichita.

When he got home, it was the fall of the year and the Doctor Dance was just over and they were preparing to leave the village and go on the winter hunt. Some of the men while they were out, had noticed that the wood had been bitten by beaver and they thought this would be a good time to set a few beaver traps and make a little money by selling the skins. Two or three traps would yield a man a good profit. He would mention to a few friends, "Why stay around the village? Why not set out to trap beaver? And those who had guns could chase deer, moose, or elk." Some of their families would want to go along and some old women to collect wild potatoes and the wild beans that were stored by the wood rat. The women could help with hauling wood and cooking and boys could make themselves useful hauling water and tending the horses. Eventually ten to fifteen tipis in two or three bunches would set out in this way, traveling five or six miles a day and staying two or three days in one place. Individual men would join tents with families, going out during the day with their horses and joining the camp at night at the appointed place. Every evening an old man would walk among them announcing the next day's plans. They camped on the north side of the Loup where they could get wood as it might snow at any time. Those who trapped beaver would clean their traps in the evening and set them from the north side of the river, while the deer hunters went either north or south. Whenever anyone caught anything, they would have a big feast all through the camp. Eagle Chief and War Cry who excelled in buffalo hunting did not care for shooting with guns and trapping, but Victory Call, and his older brother, Sitting Hawk, and also Old Bull were good hunters and trappers. They did not believe in exposing their families to enemy attack in this way and so they would come along by themselves. After they had made five or six camps, someone would come from the village and tell them that they would soon be setting out for the winter buffalo hunt and then they would all return and prepare.

It was such an informal hunting and trapping group that Kind Warrior joined when he returned from the Wichita. In his tipi he was singing his Deer Dance songs in Wichita, and when Victory Call, who was feeling lonesome, heard him, he went into the tipi where Kind Warrior was lying on his back and singing as he beat time on his thigh. Kind Warrior got up and welcomed Victory Call and after he said he was attracted by the singing, invited him to lie down and join him. Lying to the left of Kind Warrior he sang along with him and whenever he had nothing to do, he would just go in and sing. Others came in too and sang with them. Back at the village these men would sing together in the lodge and as others heard them, they also came in. These were men who had also been among the Wichita and had learned only individual songs but not the whole ritual. Some had learned polecat teaching, others buzzard, etc., and as they sang together, they taught one another. While Kind Warrior knew the most, he also learned new things from them. When there were about ten members, Kind Warrior could set them out in a formal arrangement (see Figure 43-1). He assigned two to each of the four semicardinal positions, two at the west as *rixkita*, leaders, and one errand man for the north, one for the south. More people came in and filled in the places. They made four rattles of wild squash with green and white wavy stripes to imitate the Wichita version. They also got four bows in accordance with the original version. Kind

Warrior had Victory Call's help in all this and the two men liked each other. Victory Call gave Kind Warrior a horse, a beaver when he trapped it and other gifts to show his appreciation for what Kind Warrior had done for him. Kind Warrior told the members that Victory Call was to lead them when he died.

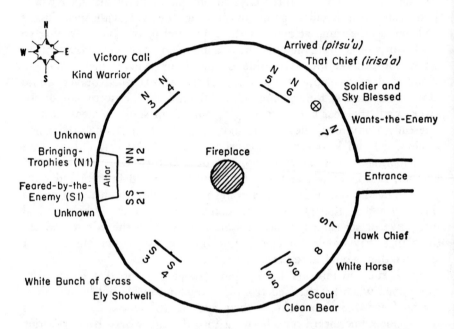

FIGURE 43-1. The first form of the Deer Dance, *Raris-ta*, "dance-deer," a simple gathering of members. The northern half were Pawnees, *Isati*; the southern half, the various southern Caddoan tribes—S3 Kitsai; S4 Kitsai; S5 Tawakaru; S6 Wichita; 8 Kitsai, a bad one; and later Weco, representing the tribes from which the members had learned. The northwest leader on the Pawnee side would say, "The Kitsais, Wichitas, and others are coming on the warpath," signifying one or the other of the south-side people. This was a challenge to a shamanistic contest.

The singing was carried out in four sets. There were four men at each of the semicardinal stations. There were four gourd rattles and four bows. These were carried first to the four at the southeast who would rattle and sing a set of songs and then the paraphernalia was passed to the next station at the southwest, then to the northwest and then to the northeast, each group rattling and singing a set of songs. The four successive semicardinal stations represented the course of a man's life—southeast, youth; southwest, maturity; northwest, getting old; and northeast, old man. As the singing proceeded, whichever of the members felt moved, would get up and give a sleight-of-hand performance. Spectators (*rariwaatuksa*) crowded in, and seeing what they were doing became interested, and began to fill up the membership ranks. Others now went to the southern Caddoan-speaking tribes—the Wichitas, Kitsais, Tawakaru, and Weco—learned their sleight-of-hand tricks, and returned to join the Deer Dance. The ranks thus became full.

In the south half of the lodge, at the west and in the semicardinal positions, each of the men had a tribal name according to where he had acquired his teachings. The north side that represented the Pawnee was called as a whole, *isati* (a noted one, or northerner in the Wichita language). The leader from the Pawnee side at the northwest station would say (mentioning one or the other of the southern Caddoan tribes), "The Kitsais [or the Wichitas, etc.] are coming on the warpath!" This would be a challenge to a shamanistic contest.

The year after the Pawnee moved from Fremont (*Pahaku*) to the reservation near Genoa, Kind Warrior died (1861). Victory Call survived him by seven years and during this time he controlled the Deer Dance and it had many members with performances going full force. Many new features were added to the ceremony, particularly two—the contest between members on the north and those on the south and the addition of two women members, one near the north entrance and one near the south. (See Figure 43-2.) This latter feature came about after someone reported that the Wichita included women, who took part and also gave performances. Then someone dreamed that they had been right in admitting the women and that they should have special duties of taking care of any corn that was donated and sweep the floor of the lodge every morning during the ceremony. Every morning during the ceremonial period, the old ladies would get up very early and tell the boys to get up. Then they gave the room a good sweeping. There were songs that told of this aspect of the ceremonial life in the Deer Lodge.

As Kind Warrior brought the Deer Dance to the Pawnee, most of the songs had Wichita words and reflected Wichita experiences. But in time the Pawnee dancers made new songs that were based on their own experiences and sung in the Pawnee language.

One war experience was of a war party of the Pitahawirata Band to Fort Scott, Kansas, led by Tikarahisat. They stayed on a high tableland for more than a year, hunting the buffalo and making a buffalo robe for their leader. They saw the ducks flying south in winter and then in spring when they flew north again, they flew in triangular formation with their leader at the apex and at the ends of the arms, the two errand men. Children used to ask these ducks, as they flew over the village, to give them moccasins or red bows and arrows. These experiences became the basis for a Pawnee song in the Deer Dance. Another song they sang was about two eagles that they saw, first one with a large log in his claws, then another with another log; they were building a nest. As they built, the eagles would whistle.

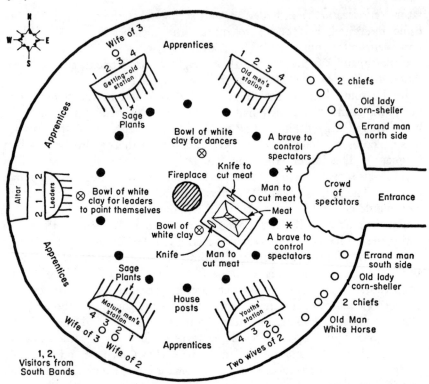

FIGURE 43-2. The developed form of the Deer Dance. It took place in a large ten-post earth lodge. There were sage plants all around to sit on with root ends pointing outward; the thickest bunches were at the stations and the thinner layers between. The circuit of singing is clockwise—southeast, southwest, northwest, northeast, as the circuit of the stars around the North Star. Note the development of specialized personnel.

Then one of the eagles sat on the eggs while the other flew around. The deer dancers of the several Pawnee bands would invite one another to their dances and in this way, the Skidi acquired some of the songs about the Fort Scott expedition, while Skidi experiences found their way into the repertoire of the other bands. One Skidi song concerned a time when the Comanche came to attack. They could see them coming a long way off, and they came down and hid and stole many horses.

Another song was composed by Warrior. He was an old man who had been highly successful in his war expeditions. Most people wondered why such a man would join the Deer Dance, since one of its major interests was success in war. But Warrior had another purpose. He was particularly interested in learning the sleight-of-hand feat in which a wonderful rabbit could turn into a human being. The story was that once when they were moving camp, a rabbit came in and out among the tents, threading his way here and there. However close the people were when they aimed at him, no one could hit him, even when the dogs joined in the chase. So a song was made about this wonderful rabbit who eluded all human pursuers. This was what Warrior wanted to learn.

The author of the original song was an old man, Arrived, who had a place at the northeast station. But instead of approaching him directly, Warrior went to his old friend, That-Chief for his advice as to how to go about it. He was told to come in next day when they had a practice meeting and address his request for membership in the lodge to all the members assembled and particularly to New Young Dog at the northwest. When Warrior entered the ceremonial lodge where the members were assembled for their practice sing, he stood at the east of the fireplace about halfway out to the door and facing west said, "All you Deer dancers, and New Young Dog at the west, I want to learn your Deer Dance. I will give a horse, some blankets, and some meat." New Young Dog, as was the usual practice, tried to deter him. He mentioned that, as Warrior was a successful warrior, everyone would laugh at him smearing himself with clay and participating in their ceremonies when he had no need for further luck either in war or in the hunt. But he remained determined, and finally New Young Dog led him to the old man's place at the northeast station where he took his place.

That evening Warrior went in quest of the rabbit learning that he wanted. New Young Dog had learned it from the original author, Arrived, and it was to him that Warrior went. When he got to the lodge, the people knew the two men wanted to be alone together so they all went to bed. The two men sat and smoked and talked and in the course of their conversation Warrior told New Young Dog about an experience he had had that impressed him deeply. Warrior always wore a white feather and once when the village was under attack as the war party struck, he felt like a feather floating in the wind so that no one could hurt him while he was aloft in the air. New Young Dog advised him that he could make a song about that when they were at the meeting. At the practice meeting, Warrior began slowly and then the next day he sang the song he had composed:

1.	hiwiri	witikuuwia
		Now I feel as if I were flying
2.	"	"
3.	"	"
4.	"	"
5.	"	
6.	"	hia
		feather flying

1.	hiwiri	Wiwitawia
	————	Now it comes flying
2.	"	"
3.	"	"
4.	"	"
5.	"	
6.	"	hita
		feather-coming

The two men continued to talk together that night in the lodge and New Young Dog told Warrior about the rabbit learning that he wanted to know. Should anyone come in and see the sparks from their pipe and hear the whispering, they would know that the two men were to be left alone and would go straight to their beds as they were talking of something important. The next time the dance was held, Warrior followed after New Young Dog. After he had carried out his performance, New Young Dog addressed the assembled company saying, "What you have seen me do here today, I am giving to this fellow here, Warrior. This is my teaching." From this time on Warrior was able to do the rabbit dance and could make a rabbit skin come alive and be a rabbit.

In this way, the original Wichita Deer Dance took on its Pawnee form. By 1867 it had become a typically elaborate Pawnee ceremony. Sleight-of-hand performances and trance induction were both modes in which they operated as they did in the Doctor Lodge. But unlike the Doctor Lodge where animal costumes and animal impersonations celebrated their communion with the animals, in the Deer Dance, war was the predominant theme and each of the members at the stations bore the name of a tribe, the opposing north and south sides representing attack and counterattack. The ceremony was carried through ten consecutive sessions, nine in the night and a tenth in the daytime with a number of rest days between. Technically, they conceived that the all-day tenth and final episode was the actual ceremony and the nine night sessions simply preliminary to it. The nine night sessions comprised several different phases. In the first five, there was a program of four or more sleight-of-hand performances, chiefly in sequence. As in the Doctor Dance, sleight of hand was referred to as "playing." Following these "playing" sessions, going on very late into the night was a series of "fighting" or hypnotic episodes. But these differed from the Doctor Lodge "fighting" which was simple trance induction; in the Deer Dance, the fighting consisted of hypnotic interference with a sleight-of-hand performance while it was in progress, confusing the performer and making it impossible for him to complete his feat. The difference between the two kinds of "fighting" was recognized in the names they were called—the "fighting" of the Doctor Lodge was "I shoot at him," *wi-tatix-tsaaku*, "now-I at him-shoot" (abbreviated as *patsaaku*) while for the Deer Dance they said, "They shoot at his *image*," wi-tit-ir-*awi*-tsaku, "now-they at him-*image*-shoot." This distinction is significant as it reflects the difference in emphasis between the two ceremonies. The emphasis of the Doctor Lodge is on the alliance of man with the animals so that they give him confidence, enabling him to cure the sick or carry out whatever his purposes may be including war expeditions. In the Deer Dance, power over the enemy is a major leitmotif. The use of shamanism as a kind of psychological warfare against the enemy is a known device among other tribes. That the Pawnees were quite successful in this regard is attested by an account collected by a French visitor, Tixier, from their enemies, the Osage, in 1839–1840. He states:

> The Maha (Skidi Pawnee) do not lose courage; their warlike virtues are so great that one brave is often seen setting out by himself to go five and six hundred miles away to steal horses at the hazard of his life, for all the nations are at war with this tribe.
>
> Dark stormy nights are the ones the Pawnee choose by preference to attack. They can warn one another by imitating the cries of wild animals, and also create anxiety among the horses and cause them to stampede; so the Osage claim that the Pawnee are sorcerers whose medicine can make nights darker, attract storms, put the warriors to sleep, and stampede the horses. . . . One of them enters the camp of the enemy alone and without trying to hide his coming into it. He strokes the horses and, of course, does not arouse any suspicion; he cuts the tethers and the reins; then, suddenly jumping on a fast horse, he gallops away uttering his war cry, while the horses scatter on the prairie, where the Pawnee will soon capture them. On other occasions, if all the warriors are asleep, he crawls into a lodge and silently kills and scalps a brave, whose horses he steals away afterwards.

When they were living at Pahaku, near Fremont in 1850 and the Ponca attacked and were about to burn up the Pawnees caught inside their earth lodges, Old-Lady-Grieves-the-Enemy dressed up like a medicine man, came out and succeeded in thoroughly frightening the enemy so that they were repulsed; she was also able to kill one of them near the lodge, armed simply with a stout stick. There seems some likelihood that there was some actual functional value in the hypnotic powers of the medicine men, even in war. If this is the case, the preoccupation with this type of performance in the Deer Dance ceremony can better be appreciated.

The long series of illusionist feats and hypnotic exercises, however, was carried on within a characteristically complex Pawnee ceremonial structure.

In the first five nights of performance, during each night there was an earlier session of sleight-of-hand performances, followed by a "fighting" session that lasted late into the night. The successive fighting sessions on subsequent evenings were installments of a single fight in which a "magically produced" mescal bean is spirited away from its "owner" by various members of the Dance in turn until he finally succeeds in retrieving it and "swallowing" or rubbing it into his side so that it disappears from the scene "in possession" of the rightful owner. The mescal beans are referred to as "horses" and when carried by a man on the warpath are supposed to assure him of success in capturing them. In the course of the hypnotic contest, the contestants are referred to as hostile tribes by their different tribal names according to the semicardinal "stations" where they belong. The rules of the game are that a person can only be attacked by someone who is in the diagonally opposite semicardinal station to the victim. This means that the *Northwest* possessor of the bean can have it spirited away from him only by an enemy of the *Southeast* and if he in turn passes it on to his ally on the *Southwest* then it will be retrieved only by the enemy on the *Northeast*. If the *Northwest* wants its bean back again, this can only be accomplished by a complicated maneuver in which the bean gets to the *Southeast* from which the *Northwest* can finally retrieve it. The Pawnee pictograph of a star is what to us is a simple equal-armed cross. The pattern of "fighting" described above is called "Making a Star," the complete operation of the diagonally opposite pairs, forming the pictographic "star" or cross. This star reference has an important cosmic significance. It symbolizes the Wolf Star, Sirius. As far as one can speak of such a deity at all among them, the Wolf Star is the Pawnee god of death and war. In the story of the creation legend, the gods forgot to invite the Wolf Star to their council, and he continued to harbor deep resentment against all of them, particularly being jealous of the Evening Star in the west and of Paruksti, the personified storm out of the west that the gods sent to inspect their handiwork when the earth was complete. On his journey of inspection to earth, Paruksti carried the people in a whirlwind bag. Whenever Paruksti was tired or lonesome, he set down the bag and the people came out, set up camp, and had a buffalo hunt. Then he gathered them up again and went on his way. Wolf Star in his anger placed a wolf on earth to follow after Paruksti, and, one day while Paruksti was asleep with his head pillowed on his whirlwind bag, the Wolf, thinking he would get something good to eat, gently lifted his head and dragged the bag out onto the open prairie. The people came out and set up camp, but were unable to get any buffalo in this barren place. They entertained the Wolf at a feast of dry meat, not realizing his identity. When Paruksti awoke and came over the hill they realized that the Wolf was an impostor and chased him, succeeding, as a result, in surrounding and killing him. But this did not please Paruksti. He told them that they would have to take the Wolf's skin, dry it, and make a sacred bundle of it and ever after be known as the Skidi or Wolf People. Moreover, that while the gods had intended that they were to live forever, since they had killed the first animal on earth, they had brought death upon themselves and also the men with their lances to make war. The Wolf Doctor played the major role in the sacrifice of the girl to the Morning Star (see Chapter 10). The actual name of the star was *Tskirixki-tiuhats*, Wolf-He-Is-Deceived. It was said that the star appears at times in the southeast just before the rising of the Morning Star and "deceives the wolves" who thus prematurely begin their howling to greet the morning when Sirius appears, without waiting for its true beginning with the rise of the Morning Star.

A further celestial connection of the Deer Dance is the control of rattlesnakes attributed to its members. Fools-the-Wolves Star has a celestial ally, the Real Snake (Scorpio) particularly during the summer time. Stories that the people told about the wolf or coyote were likely to be decidedly irreverent, and they refrained from telling them in summer because in that season Wolf Star would enlist his friend, Real Snake, to send the rattlesnakes on earth to bite the people.

The first five sessions of the Deer Dance ceremony have thus been occupied with a combined program in each session of "playing" and "fighting." The sixth night was given over entirely to "fighting," a second "star" battle ensuing over the mescal bean, in this case a bean belonging to the *Northeast* station, while the former combat originated at the *Northwest*.

With the end of this sixth session the first phase of the ceremony is completed. Here an apparently quite different motif enters the picture. Instead of war, we get a preoccupation with the growing crops. Until the fighting session is over, the members have been forbidden to eat green plant foods. At the banquet of the sixth session, they now have a vegetable stew of green corn, green beans, and pumpkins, all cooked in a kettle, which they ate with great relish, "the dry meat being hard to bite and the green stuff tasting good after being away from it." The corn and beans they had been permitted to eat up to this point were all dried and from last year's crop. While these two themes of war and the growing crops might seem opposed, the fact that the lifting of the taboo against eating the current crop is dependent on a session of intensive "fighting" is an indication of the basic connection in Pawnee thought between war and the fructification of the plants—a motif that also appears in other aspects of the theology and ceremonialism. Apparently the idea of fructification, as it came from the Wichita, pertained to wild plants rather than to cultivated crops, involving the maturation of the wild sage plant and the mescal bean, as well as the wild squash that was originally used for the rattle for which the Pawnee substituted the cultivated gourd rattle. The wild sage plant continued to be a major feature of the Pawnee Deer Dance ceremonial in the performances, and the entire floor was carpeted with the plant placed radially all around with the stub ends outward and the head ends pointing inward. The symbolism of the deer was maintained in the course of the performances when the performer would jump over the fireplace, from north to south and back again, and from west to east and back again, impersonating the deer in this way. Also in his closing speech, the leader told them that their Deer Lodge was now over and they were to follow their tracks home to the timber. They left, blowing their whistles all the way home, and the blowing could be heard all over the village so that the dance was sometimes referred to as the Whistle Dance.

After the sixth session, the "fighting" was entirely ended and the seventh, eighth, and ninth evenings were given over to illusionist sleight-of-hand feats of considerable intricacy, and the calendar eventually became so crowded that several performers might be performing simultaneously or with their performances overlapping. The rattling and singing would be begun at the southeast station, and sometimes no one would be inspired to get up and perform until the gourds and bows had reached a subsequent station in the clockwise round. In any case, if the spectators had not yet accumulated to a sufficient degree, some of the performers felt they wanted to wait "until they got a good crowd." The ceremony of the tenth day is entirely composed of a considerable series of sleight-of-hand performances.

At the time when Kind Warrior was its leader, the membership of the Deer Dance was becoming so considerable and the interest so great that the leaders of Doctor Lodge felt that it might develop into a rival organization to theirs. Sometimes when members were absent from the Doctor Lodge, others would go after them and finding them in the Deer Dance, would spirit them out, causing them to bleed at the mouth and desecrating the ground of the Deer Dance Lodge which had to be spotlessly clean and fresh. This almost developed into an open contest of power, which was finally averted when the doctors sent their apologies to the Deer Dance leaders admitting they had been wrong. At that period, the two ceremonies overlapped somewhat. Kind Warrior had taken a group of his members down to the pond where he summoned up a turtle, stating that if it came to an open fight he would go into the Doctor Lodge and, locking the entryway, make their turtle fireplace come alive. A report of this threat, finally brought the apology from the doctors.

The conflict was resolved at a later time, when Misery, son of Sitting Hawk, took over after Victory Call's death as leader of the Deer Dance and entered into an agreement with the leaders of the Doctor Lodge to hold his ceremony early, right after they arrived back from the summer hunt and before the Doctor Lodge should begin.

As to the public at that time, when the conflict was imminent, some felt a test of power would be welcome between the two organizations, while others felt strongly that it should be avoided.

How much of the ceremony was basically a Wichita plan and how much Pawnee innovation cannot be entirely resolved, as a number of Wichitas came among the Pawnees and stayed for some time, one of them, Atskiri, remaining for three years and coaching Misery for his role as future leader of the organization. Whatever the details, by 1867, the Deer Dance had become an intricate Pawnee ceremony, following the characteristic pattern with complicated histrionic as well as conceptual features.

44

SORCERY

〰〰〰〰〰〰〰〰〰〰〰〰〰〰

*The Vision of a Poor Boy, Small—His Fate—
Rivalry between Old Bull and Behaille—Male and
Female "Witched" Members of the Community—
Suspicions of Witchcraft in Sexual Affairs—Con-
nection to "Fighting" in Doctor Performances—
Fee-Splitting Ventures—Causes of Disease Re-
garded as Anxiety and Hostility—Interpersonal
Hostility in the Community—Deadly Witch Mis-
siles—the Treatment*

〰〰〰〰〰〰〰〰〰〰〰〰〰〰

RIVALRY AND HATRED as well as love and community were as much a
part of Pawnee life as of our own, and the animal lore of a doctor
could be turned to ill as well as to good. In many cases the original
dream vision of the future doctor consisted of being taken to an animal
lodge under the water where the animals sat in council and judged
the visionary. Others were terrestrial or cosmic, but the lodge under
water was a common one. Such a vision came to a poor boy named
Small (*Patsaa*) when he was about twelve years old. The Pawnee were
living near Fremont, Nebraska, in the village they occupied just before
going onto the reservation. It must have been around 1850. The Pawnee
name of the animal lodge settlement was Pa-ha-ku, "hill-in water-sit-
ting"; it was located near the edge of a rather sheer bluff on the south
side of the Platte River. The animal lodge was thought to be located somewhere under water in the side of the cliff and it was reliably attested
that lights were seen and noises heard in this location. It was also said
that the wind was sometimes so strong there, that attempts to examine the
spot closely were always foiled:

> Right on the sheer bluff of the high bank was a cedar tree. This is
> the doorway to the animal lodge of Pahaku. Sitting on the tree are

all sorts of birds—particularly eagles—black, bald, spotted and also the chicken hawk. White people say it is that way yet. They say the wind is too strong there so that when you want to look, it pushes you back. At this bank, right under water is a big fish, the *tawakiiks*. In the night, one can hear drumming and sparks fly right on top of the water. This fish opens its mouth and one can see fire come out. This is Pahaku, the animal lodge.

Small was a poor boy who served in the household of an influential man, hauling water, helping with the household tasks, and tending the horses in return for his keep. One day he was lying at the edge of the bluff under a tree with his bow and arrows, hoping to catch some birds to eat. His friend, Old Bull, who was the son and heir of an influential chief, came along and joined Small and since there was a cool, pleasant breeze blowing, they fell asleep. When he woke up Small was gone and so Old Bull went home, thinking that Small had awakened before him and gone to his lodge.

But Small was on quite a different mission. While they were lying there, he had had a vision and had gone to the animal lodge. The animals had taken him in. When he awoke he was sitting east of the fireplace with his bow and arrows. There were different kinds of animals all around. Near the door was a big snake. Near the altar at the west was a Scalped Man, Kitsahuruksu, who was the boss of them all. He addressed Small saying, "Nawa, greetings, now I leave you to the animals. Now you fellows sitting around here—you brought him in. What are you going to do with him?" At the northeast near the cedar tree was the bear who said, "Let's eat him up." The rest of the animals laughed, but the weasel chimed in, from his seat at the northwest, "That's right. We'd better eat him up right away." Then the big snake at the southeast side of the door said, "He's right. We'd better try to eat him up."

But the elk (moose, *pax*) at the southwest said, "Now you wait. Since you folks could eat him and I can't, I have something to say. I'm the one that supports him and helps him to live." Just as he got through talking, someone about halfway south, the Beaver, spoke up. "He's right. I can't eat him either. I also support him and help him live." Near the southeast the reindeer said the same thing. He also added, "You folks don't try to do anything to help him stay alive. You just want to eat him up. Right now I'm going to allow Scalped-Man to decide what should be done since we disagree." They all said, "Nawa!" Several on each side had spoken up. Now reindeer said, "Who brought him in?" But everyone was silent for no one was willing to admit to having done it. So the Scalped-Man was given the problem of deciding.

He said, "All the animals know how we have to depend on our two errand men. We send them long distances traveling on our errands and they get tired because of it. They work so hard for us that it is only right that we give them the right to decide. Now you two errand men, you can go outside and make a decision." The two went out. They were duck (*kiwakski*) and a bluish bird with a wide stripe around its neck (*kis-katararaxka*, "neck-stripe around-upon"). Meanwhile everyone inside the lodge was getting impatient. Snake mumbled, "I want to eat him up."

Outside the lodge the two errand men were discussing what the boy's fate should be. One said, "He just went out hunting birds to get something for himself to eat and now they brought him in here and want to kill him. I don't think that's right. Now that they brought him in, let's take pity on him and teach him something. Let's reveal the nature of the animals to him." Said duck, "I guess I do have to take care of him. He kills me when he is hungry, but when I want him to starve I can very well fly off, for I know when he is coming. I think I must do something for him."

With this decision, they went back into the lodge and Striped-Neck spoke up first. He pointed out that the boy had gone out intending to kills birds in order to get something to eat. At this point Small was frightened as he thought they would surely kill him for it was Striped-Neck he originally intended to hunt for. But the bird pointed out that as he was a bird that was always along the edge of the creek, he could go into the water and escape so that the boy would be unable to kill him if he himself were unwilling. "Now I'm going to leave it to this fellow, Duck, to decide."

Now duck got up and addressed the group. "Now Boss, bears, weasels, snake, elk, beaver, and reindeer, I have decided this about this fellow here: Today when you brought him, he had no thought about the fact that we also like to live. But still this fellow was hunting up the creek because he was hungry. Right now, he's starving. He has nothing to eat. Let's take pity on him instead of eating him up. After he gets out of here, if we help him, he can tell people that we treated him kindly and they might have respect for us. So now let's do something for him. When you send me way off on your errands, I get tired sometimes. Now in return, I am asking you to do as I suggest. Let's bless him."

For four nights the animals put on a sleight-of-hand performance, and each animal taught the boy a different way. After all had performed, the mole told of his power: "If a man is sitting there, I could come up through the ground and hit him from underneath so that all his insides bounce up and kill him right there." The weasel said, "While he's looking at me, I can eat up a man's liver and other entrails so that he falls over." In this way Small came to know that these two were bad animals and because of what he had learned about them, he was also able to practice sorcery, as well as to cure sickness.

Being friends and small boys together, Small gave freely whatever knowledge he had to Old Bull. Small never lived to carry out the mandate of his vision, but Old Bull did. One day while Small was out tending the horses of the man he served, the Sioux came and took all the horses, shooting Small in the abdomen. He begged his sponsor to throw him in the water so that he could be healed through the animal lodge, but his sponsor, who was very angry because of the loss of all his property, refused to do as Small requested. He cared nothing for the poor boy who was his servant, and having disregarded the boy's request, Small died of his wounds. People felt that the man had been short-sighted as well as cruel. If he had allowed the boy to avail himself of his supernatural powers, he would have been cured of his wounds and grown up to go on the warpath and gotten horses for his sponsor. By being mean, people said, the sponsor had lost everything.

Old Bull grew up and became a prominent man with his teachings. He was the son of a chief, as well, and readily got a place in the chiefs' council. There came a time when the chiefs decided to include in their council the official interpreter of the United States Agency, Behaille, who was of Spanish, French, and Pawnee descent. No doubt this was a politic move, but Old Bull was not satisfied. In the council he referred scornfully to Behaille as "the Mexican." Behaille was not unaware of his hostility and opposition. When they went out on the buffalo hunt and arrived near Grand Island, Behaille stopped off at a small town and drank some whisky, which he immediately vomited up. He thought that he recognized what he had brought up, viz., a witch pellet of a bundle of buffalo hair painted red and containing the sole skin of a corpse's foot. He said, "I know who the sorcerer is. It is Old Bull. Throw the pellet in the fire and burn it up so that it can do no further harm." Then Behaille decided on a further course of action:

Next day he asked his wife to make grease bread and coffee and invited several of the chiefs to his house for an informal feast, including Old Bull. When they had all come in, Behaille said, "Now I want you to eat this food. Old Bull, I don't want you to do that again! You tried to witch me and you nearly killed me." Old Bull was ashamed and he just hung his head. As they went out after the feast, people said, "This feast was given because Old Bull witched Behaille. Some fellow would remark, "Well, so Old Bull wanted to witch the Mexican!"

Of course, we don't know how many people he had witched before this, or whether there were any, but now that he was exposed, he would never be able to do it again. Everyone knew that Old Bull was a witch and he was ashamed.

The majority of the doctors and the ones that "witched" among the Pawnee were men, but there were also women who had both kinds of power. Most commonly they had gotten these from their husbands and begun to practice after their husbands died. When a doctor had a woman patient, he had to take his wife along to assist him; in this way she was bound to learn. If she had a son or a daughter, should they show an interest in the bundle, she would teach them. Among the Wichitas, along with the men doctors, there were a great many women, some of them also witches. They could make rain and by witchcraft cause the rain to stop. Among the Pawnees, Lone Chief's mother, War Leader Woman (*Ts-tixkitawi-ra-wa-hu'u*, "woman-give-leader of a warparty-she-distributes them-gives away"), had learned from her husband and it was said that she slept with a rattlesnake under her pillow and could practice witchcraft. In her witchcraft activities she would more or less confine herself to the affairs of women. Sometimes women fought over the boundaries of their land or the stealing of corn and if the quarrel continued over some time and they came to blows, one might be inclined to "witch" the other. But once it happened that Lone Chief was involved in a quarrel and his mother took it over and got into hostility with another woman on account of it. The issue was something about the distribution of horses after a war raid. A man, Frank Leader, felt that Lone Chief's group had obtained an extra horse in the distribution, unjustifiably. Although Frank Leader was not in the party, he was heard to remark that had he been there, Lone Chief would not have gotten away with the horse. This made Lone Chief angry and somehow the women came to discuss it. The issue was taken up between Lone Chief's mother, War Leader Woman, and the mother of Frank Leader, Lady Lucky Leader, and eventually it shifted to the relative social status of the two women. War Leader Woman cited her unimpeachable aristocratic descent, while Frank Leader's mother was heard to assert that it was no better than hers for she had charge of the Evening Star bundle. Word went around in the gossip channels, and finally Frank Leader got sick and died. Everyone was sure that War Leader Woman's witchcraft was the direct cause of his death. Frank Leader's mother began to curse War Leader Woman. She said, "That's the rottenest thing she could do. Even though her son is a great chief, she still practices witchcraft and kills a man." Some felt that since Lone Chief called Leader's mother, *itahi*, sister, and Frank Leader, therefore, *tiwat*, nephew, in view of the close classificatory kinship, this was really disgraceful. Others were saying, "One shouldn't pick a quarrel with Lone Chief's mother. She's a powerful witch!"

The services of witches were never for hire, but sometimes an old man could be induced by one of his close relatives to help him forward his fortunes by this means. Everyone knew Brave Chief as a poor boy who had raised himself by his own efforts and finally became a chief, although he had no hereditary status. On his deathbed, Pa-hukata-wa, "Hill-against-the-Bank," a famous chief of Village-in-the-Bottomlands, had designated him to take his place in the chiefs' council.

For many years before that time, Brave Chief had courted Pahukatawa's favor. He had served him and repeatedly gave him gifts. When he came home from the warpath, he would give his horses right to the chief instead of to his own father. He hoped that the chief would make him his official brave. But there was an obstacle to this. The chief's younger brother, Kills-the-Enemy (*Tiukauxki*) had many times expressed himself as being unfit to be a chief as he had a quick temper and was not gentle and judicious in his ways as would befit a chief. So he continued to hold the post of brave to his older brother, Pahukatawa, and Brave Chief was not able to get the post. His brother, continuing to disavow any interest in becoming chief, was not named to take a place in the chiefs' council by Pahukatawa. Rather Brave Chief was named by Pahukatawa on his death bed.

Not everyone was willing to accept the straightforward explanation of Brave Chief's rise to fame through his own industry and merit. Some attributed it to a well-laid plan involving witchcraft. In this view of the matter it was said that while he was still quite young, Brave Chief was very ambitious, and he made a plan with his old father Meat-Offering, to help him rise to power. The surmise was that he went to his father and proposed to him that it would be a good thing if he could become chief before the old man died, and that anyway people would cite it as a case of a poor boy who had raised himself from poverty and low degree, and never suspect their connivance. And so, the interpretation goes, the old man took out his doctor bundle and witched the chief and presently he got sick. Brave Chief stayed around and waited on him during his illness and finally when he was dying, Brave Chief sat down next to the chief's head. Many men were sitting around to hear the last words of Pahukatawa, among them Old Man Meat Offering, Brave Chief's father. Pahukatawa addressed the assembled company and said, "I want my son, Brave Chief, to have my place." "And so," said one of the partisans of this point of view, "this ambitious man became head chief of the village through his father's witchcraft!"

Suspicion of witchcraft was directed toward people known to be ambitious, envious, or frustrated. It was said of one old doctor, Angry Horse, that he was such a good man that he probably never used his witchcraft. "He never got sufficiently angry for that!"

Sexual affairs were a common cause of suspected witchcraft activity in both men and women. As witchcraft-prone situations, the following were cited:

Bringing Trophies was an old man married to a very young girl and he was very jealous of her. Joe E was an interpreter and had plenty of money and the girl made advances to him, inducing him to buy her some calico. As she sewed her dress, her husband became suspicious after she was unable to tell him how much the material had cost her. He investigated and finally confronted Joe E who told the old man that it was his business to watch his wife. Finally the young woman and Joe E went off together and although the old man came after them with his bow and arrows, they managed to stay hidden in the timber so that he was unable to get them. Finally the girl left her old husband and, after running around a bit, married a solid citizen of the community and had two children and settled down. If he were so inclined, the old man would be expected to direct an attack of witchcraft against Joe E.

Last-Man-in-the-Road (*Hatuxka*) was inclined to go after Pipe Offering's wife. They were all quite old, but Pipe Offering was the oldest. One day while he was sitting on top of the earth lodge he saw his wife coming home with a bucket of water. It was an accepted sign of consent in courtship when a man contrived to meet a woman on her way home from the creek carrying a bucket of water and requested a drink and was given one. The woman was in a position to signify her disinterest by not responding to his request and simply continue on her way. In this case when Last-Man-in-the-Road stopped Pipe Offering's wife and asked her for a drink, she gave it to him. When she got back to her lodge, Pipe Offering who had been watching, asked, "Who were you talking to?" "That was Last-Man-in-the-Road," she said. "What were you saying?" asked the old man. "He wanted a drink and I gave it to him. Nothing wrong. He said it was too hot." "But," said the suspicious husband, "he was on his way to the creek where he could get his own drink." "Oh, that's nothing," answered the wife. Under these circumstances, Pipe Offering might at some time feel impelled to bewitch Last-Man-in-the-Road and cause him to be sick or do him to death through witchcraft.

Old-Man-That-Chief was apparently a man who felt he had sufficient power to do whatever he wanted and he brooked no interference with his wishes. It was said of him, "He was a big witch!"

Once there was an old woman that he wanted. She refused him. So one night at midnight when everyone was asleep, he took his stick, as he was blind, and felt his way over to her lodge. He had his eagle-wing fan and some harmful material that he would "shoot" into her. He stood in front of her lodge waving his buffalo robe back and forth

until someone in the lodge happened to get up and see him. Then he
went home.

The next day the woman was sick in her stomach or her intestines.
It seemed she had ague. But the man who had been up the night before said, "I know who witched her. It isn't ague." When she was dying the woman said, "I see him. He has a fan before his face, but I
know him. It is That-Chief!"

Many other dark deeds were attributed to That-Chief, as he was the
most learned man in the tribe. He was the tribal historian, high priest of
the sacred bundles, outstanding elk doctor, and maker of chiefs in the
chiefs' council. One situation was rivalry with another old man, Horse
Finder (*Huras*), who was called in on a case of illness and then super-
seded by That-Chief who reversed the original treatment and substituted
some of his own. Horse Finder became angry and refused to continue his
treatment of the sick man.

Now each of these two men had to watch himself. Each would keep
careful track of the other to see if he were hovering near. He would
sleep with the covers over his head in fear that something would be put
down his throat by the other one. Even when they just took a walk,
they would have to watch carefully.

The fight was carried right into the Deer Dance. Horse Finder sat at
the northwest station and That-Chief at the northeast. After the spectators had gone a private performance was held after midnight. That-
Chief asked to be told where Horse Finder was (both men were blind),
and then he lit his pipe in the coals of the fireplace and gave it to Horse
Finder to smoke. Horse Finder took a couple of puffs and as in the
normal course of events, That-Chief tried to take back the pipe, the
bowl came off in his hand and the stem stuck between Horse Finder's
teeth. Then That-Chief stamped his feet, first one foot and then the
other. This was to stir up Horse Finder's stomach. Finally a lot of soft
white feathers came out of the end of the pipe stem, and in this way
That-Chief knew that he would not be able to harm Horse Finder by
projecting a magical pellet of sharp object into his stomach, for the
soft feathers he had inside would protect him.

Now Horse Finder got up to retaliate. He stood before That-Chief,
stamping twice with each foot in alternation so that he stepped four
times, saying "xi^n, xi^n, xi^n, xi^n (hee^n)," with a grunting tone. Then he
said to That-Chief, "What have you been doing to my fish?" Finally
everyone could see the tailbones of the fish's skeleton coming out of
That-Chief's mouth. Then Horse Finder began to pull it out and the
sharp rib bones of the fish cut That-Chief's mouth so that his whole

mouth and chest were covered with blood by the time he got it all out. Mainly old men were present at this particular session of the Deer Dance.

As can be seen from this account, the "fighting" in the Deer Dance was not mere formal ceremonial procedure but an expression of real hostilities between the performers. As the people watched, they understood all these interpersonal nuances and the effect of the "fighting" was something more to them than a mere show of sleight of hand, spectacular as this might be in itself at times.

Apparently despite their rivalry, the two old doctors, That-Chief and Horse Finder, were not above combining in a fee-splitting venture at the expense of a wealthy patient. Horse Finder would advise That-Chief that he intended to bewitch a Mr. A and that in a few days he would be sick. Mr. A got sick as expected and first his family would call in the most eminent physician they had, Big Doctor, for A was an important man. The messenger sent to get him would promise him horses, clothing, and food in payment if he would cure the patient. The doctor came in and, after hearing the symptoms, pronounced it a serious illness and very difficult to treat. He agreed to try it for two days and if there were no results he would have to leave the case to someone else. Possibly he thinks the fee offered is not generous enough. Another doctor is asked to come in, the family offering one horse, a chief's medal, blankets, and leggings. But apparently the fee is too small for this new man who feels he should get more if he is to treat an important man like Mr. A. Finally someone in the family says, "Why only one horse? After all if he dies we won't have anything!" Thus the fee is raised. The second man comes, but gives up in two days. Meanwhile the two schemers have been sitting there and stay all night with the sick man ostensibly as a friendly gesture. When the second man gives up, in desperation, the sick man's family looks about for help and their attention happens to fall on That-Chief who is right there, and they offer him three horses and a quantity of goods. After considerable maneuvers with the coaching of Horse Finder who has been the original witch, he gives the patient an emetic and there emerges one of the terrible poison pellets, the heelskin of a human corpse wrapped in buffalo wool, painted red, and tied around with horsehair. By this time, however, the parts have separated and the human skin has softened so that it has caused a lot of trouble to the victim. When this successful conclusion has been reached, That-Chief calls in four other doctors to sing and celebrate the cure. They all have a feast at midnight and go to their homes. The next night That-Chief sends his grandson, Might-Be-Chief, to call Horse Finder to his home and they discuss the final stages of the treatment, Horse Finder telling That-Chief that he should instruct the patient to have nothing but blue corn meal mush for a few days until his stomach is in order. Then the other four doctors who have sung with the patient are called in and perhaps one or two more, and they speak of the animals and their ways and have a ceremonial smoke and distribute the goods that That-Chief has received in payment. Of the three horses, That-Chief will give one to the owner of the earth lodge where he is living, one he will keep for himself and give one to Horse Finder. The other doctors will note his special generosity, but may explain it merely by the fact that they both have the same bundle powers. Even if they were to suspect, they would not reveal the secrets of their fellow professionals to the lay public.

The Pawnees were thus not immune to the common suspicion that comes to all people in the desperation of sickness, that the doctor is not doing everything possible to cure the patient and that somehow more could have been done if the doctor had willed it.

In view of some of these rather bizarre descriptions, I questioned my informant who was familiar with our methods of gathering evidence and attempting to establish reasonable proof, as to what evidence people had that witchcraft was at the bottom of so much death and sickness among the Pawnees. His reply in substance was that basically they just knew, no proof in our terms being possible. He said: "When men sit around talking, they would talk about these things. They would *know*, but they couldn't prove it."

Rarely would the Pawnees attribute a death to our type of "natural cause." With old people of little social importance, they wouldn't bother to press the question but with anyone of any social position, people were concerned to place the responsibility for the death on the hostility of someone in the community. It was thought that when the person was dying, the hostile person would appear to them as a witch who was hiding his face so that the dying man had to identify him by his body. The dying man or woman would then recognize and name the person. Then the news would get around but no further action would be taken.

The Pawnees recognized that anxiety and hostility were major causes of disease. From the Pawnee point of view, active witchcraft practices were the culmination of sustained, interpersonal hostility and the constant fear of witchcraft represented the anxiety felt in the face of such a threat.

People got sick to their stomach, or when something stuck them, got blood poisoning, or so the white people call it—but we say, "Someone witched you." Long afterwards if the man recovered, he would be sure to find out who witched him.

The reasoning here being that an important characteristic of his disease —and therefore cause—had been anxiety, and that this could be traced to some interpersonal hostility in the community whose source he would invariably find if he searched around for it.

The doctor on his part, helped restore a man's confidence while he was sick, by bringing him the friendship of the animals who were entirely outside the human community and to whom he could turn in his distress. This motivation can be seen in the vision of the poor boy, Small, whose position in the human community was threatening and insecure. It was in a council of the animals that he found justice for himself and understanding of his need. He also found, however, that some of his new-found animal friends had temperaments that were prevailingly vicious like the mole and the weasel, and this was a power from outside that he could turn against the human community at his desire. The doctor, therefore, in his knowledge of animals, had a kind of power for evil as well as for good that no one else possessed. "The doctors are all witches. Each one has a different way to witch as well as their other practices." Whether he used this evil power depended upon the temperament of the doctor. As cited in connection with old doctor Angry Horse, "He never got sufficiently angry for that!" and so would never be using this part of his power, but the people suspected that the majority of the doctors gave way to temptation at times, particularly the most ambitious ones. The old doctors were especially suspect, of course.

Interpersonal hostility represented a serious threat to the Pawnee community, particularly in its influential members. As there were no formally organized codes of behavior or courts of justice among the Pawnees, a person had no recourse in the face of personal threat except the expression of public opinion which was by no means readily forthcoming and also it was effective only within the existing social power structure. If possible, self-help was the wisest course. Behaille, in the face of the hostility of Old Bull toward his admission to the chiefs' council, used the method both of exposure and at the same time of mollification at a feast.

It was far more vital for the people of the Pawnee community to have a clear estimate of the range of personalities with which they had to deal in their daily lives than it is for those of us who live in larger polities. The pressures between individuals were far more potent than they are in groups where there is a larger and more complete political structure, for beyond the known range of personalities among the Pawnees, there was only the enemy. Interpersonal difficulties might or might not get some public reaction and beyond that there was no organized social machinery to which to appeal. In the social order, therefore, the attitudes, moods and inclinations of the individuals that composed it, were far more significant for the group well-being than in a larger polity, and people kept a closer watch on these personality factors than we are accustomed to doing. They knew where "the trouble spots" were likely to be in terms of interpersonal hostilities and the specific temper of the people involved. Only in these terms can we understand their sensitivity to these hostilities and the prevalent fear of their personal social consequences. The "witchcraft" atmosphere was a function of this situation. The doctors brought to bear the idea that a person could have unfailing personal allies in the animal community. Thus Old-Man-That-Chief in practicing his performance for the next day's session of the Deer Dance, addressed the bundle of chicken-hawk feathers that he was to make come alive in the ceremony. The bunch of feathers were lying tied up at the ends which pointed toward the fireplace, with the tips toward That-Chief. As he smoked he asked the feathers for their help, saying, "I want you to help me in every way. This is my son and my grandson," who were to assist him. By him sat his son, Herd-of-Horses, and his grandson, Might-Be-Chief, and he passed the pipe to them in turn and pointed the mouthpiece toward the feathers so that they might all smoke together.

Despite these psychological causes, the physical symptoms of illness were correlated by the Pawnees directly with physical objects that had been projected by sleight of hand into the body of the person. It was presumed that the doctor would hover about at night outside the dwelling of his intended victim and act as he did in the Doctor Lodge to send the object into the person. "In the old days people slept with the covers drawn up over their heads so that should they open their mouths, no witch could put anything down into them this way."

The different deadly witch-missiles were thought to produce varying physical symptoms. Uncomfortable and painful "movement" of the stomach was one important effect, and coughing up or vomiting was necessary for their cure.

The procedure for preparing such pellets was attested to by Roaming Leader who said that he had inadvertently been an eyewitness to such a process.

It was after sundown when one could barely see well and there stood That-Chief with his grandson, Might-Be-Chief, along with White Horse near a grave. They had dug it up and That-Chief was showing White Horse that one gets the tough skin of the heel of the corpse, lets it dry out flat, and then greases it with buffalo fat so that it can slide right in. Then it is wrapped up in buffalo wool and painted all over with red paint and tied up real tight and small with horse hair so that it approximates the size of a large capsule. "Then grease it well once more," he said. Now any time White Horse wanted to kill someone by witching, he knew what to do. He put the capsule in among the feathers of his eagle-wing fan, and while he was moving back and forth at the door after midnight doing his witching, he shook his fan so that the capsule flew through the air and into the victim's mouth.

Roaming Leader was standing right behind Might-Be-Chief he stated, but they were all so engrossed that no one saw him. That-Chief said, "It takes time for the capsule to have an effect. At first it just tickles and the person begins to cough and he thinks he must have eaten a piece of hard meat. Then as the bundle unwraps and the heel skin softens, the person gets very thin and dies, just as if he had tuberculosis. The skin gets rather black as if there were something the matter with the veins."

That-Chief was trading his information for White Horse's knowledge of how to make a bear claw enter a subject. White Horse told That-Chief that all he had to do was to cut it off to about a length of about two inches and grease it well and then it was ready for use.

The bear claw is the worst. When one tries to vomit, it just goes down again. When it enters the body, it begins to scratch in the stomach and the person coughs. Only once in a while could one get the bear claw to come out. If it lay crosswise, then it would never get out, and also if it was near the right side of the stomach. But if the doctor could press the stomach so that it would come up the middle, with the point up and outward, it might come out. When the doctor saw such a case, the patient would say, "It seems to come up, then go down again," and the doctor would know what it was. He would say, "It's a pretty hard case, but I'll try it." If he sees no sign that the claw is in the right position, he knows that the man is doomed to die.

The owl was "the worst witcher." It was especially common among the Wichitas. They are afraid of the owl but they use it. Among the Wichitas even today when they are camped, one can hear cackling and growling and they say this is a witches' meeting off somewhere in the moonlight. Big Doctor was eagle and owl doctor. He used the black owl, sending small owl claws into people's stomachs. They are sharp and no one can get them out of the stomach; they stay right there. When they try to bring them up, they can't come out. They choke a person. Big Doctor would also use a human toenail, which he would cut from himself or from anyone else. Victory Call was killed by Big Doctor through owl claws. He began to cough. As he was dying, Victory Call said he saw a person with an eagle-wing fan before his face and that person was Big Doctor who was the cause of his death.

The basis of this suspicion was the fact that Big Doctor was leader of the old established Doctor Lodge and Victory Call of the newer Deer Dance, which had grown to such proportions under his leadership that it was beginning to threaten the exclusive leadership of the Doctor Lodge and to vie with it for membership. Victory Call probably died in 1868 or 1869.

The course of treatment for That-Chief's pellet which followed a general pattern was as follows:

When the doctor was called in he would say, "You seem to have some kind of cold, but something else may be in your stomach. The doctor makes medicine in a big bucket of water. He tells the patient to drink and see if it can come up. (The witch may be in there while they are doctoring this person. He just sits there with his hand before his face as if he were thinking, but he knows what it is.) The patient has to drink a whole lot before he can throw up. Then when he says he has enough, they tickle his throat with a feather, telling him to stand up. Maybe it doesn't come up yet and the doctor tells him, "Take all the medicine." Then at last the person doubles up and the fragments of the witch-pellet come up. The doctor says, "Look, here, this is it. A bad person gave you this." The doctor will recognize that someone sitting there is the culprit, but he remains loyal to his profession and refrains from exposing his "brother-member of the Doctor Lodge." The doctor says, "Throw it (the poison pellet) into the fire," but the witch suggests they throw it outside where he can retrieve it. Someone who knows better finally induces them to burn it up.

Another method of witchcraft poisoning is to mix some material with the pipe tobacco that is offered to a person to smoke. Big Doctor, in addition to owl claws, had mole and weasel powers which were very bad. He had a tiny pipe that he mixed with the excrement of the ground hog, and when a person smokes this he gets sore on his thighs, back or elsewhere. With his weasel powers, Big Doctor would make a weasel skin drink and when anyone passes that he wants to witch he flicks water on him. The weasel causes the person to have night sweats and get weak.

In support of his assertion, in 1936 when we visited the Chicago Museum of Natural History, Mark Evarts showed us that in the bundle of Big Doctor was a package with a very small pipe inside a weasel skin, also a moleskin and a meteor for the warpath.

There were a few attempts at explanation of disease among the Pawnee that were not supernatural. In the old days it was said that people died when they were old because of injuries they had received while they were still young. When they got old, these injuries revived and killed them. Such diseases would be internal injuries from falling off horses (hemorrhage), smallpox, measles, typhus, and dysentery.

An old man got dysentery. It began with a sort of grabbing pains in the legs, then went up and choked you. When his legs began to grab, he said he could do nothing more about it and wanted to die. Then he got on his horse and tried to make it ride off the high bank, but the horse shied back. However, the rider was catapulted off into the water and when he came out, he was cured. So he found out the cure for this disease.

There was a great deal of faith in the virtue of bathing as a preventative and as a cure of disease. "In the old days people used to go and bathe in the creek and take sweat baths and there was no sickness."

Finally, it was thought that living on a high bluff was healthier than living in the lowlands.

They said that in the old days, there was no disease, for the villages were on top of a high bluff, and sickness follows along the creek. Whenever a sickness seemed to be coming, people would move up on top, for there the air was fresh and sickness would not come up there. It only stayed near the creek.

In more recent times it was said that many people died of rheumatism and stomach trouble. But from the Pawnee point of view, natural causation of disease and death was a relatively less important aspect of these basic human problems. The field of the emotions was considered the major element in the doctor's calling.

However, despite these other factors, when Otter was about twelve years old the doctors were able to save his life by direct physical therapy.

45

THE DOCTORS CURE
THE BOY OTTER

*Otter Breaks His Leg—the Doctors Consulted—
Their Remedies—the Boy's Instructions for Healing the Wound—Additional Treatments—the Release of the Boy from the Sickness—an Informal
Feast—the Gifts to the Doctors*

WHEN THE BOY OTTER was about twelve years old, his father Victory Call
had died and White Woman was remarried to Shot Arm, who under-
took to be a father to the boy. His uncle War Cry continued to take an
active interest in his welfare. One fall while they were in the village he
was riding on the east road when he fell off the horse and broke the small
bone (fibula) of his left leg near the ankle and near the knee. "It all
started," he said, "because I had stepped on the ground with that leg
where lightning had struck the earth. I thought I was smart!"

The leg was very painful throughout the fall and winter, and then in
the spring he was thrown off the horse again. In July his parents called in
Old-Man-That-Chief to try to cure him. The old man pressed his thumb
against the leg and took out a rock and he thought this was the cause of
the pain. But gave up trying to treat it as he didn't seem to be able to
do any more with it.

Now while they were out on the summer hunt, the boy stepped into a
gopher hole, but he thought nothing further of it. He just went on and
caught a bird in the creek and later in the day when he got home he was
covered with hives. He felt pretty bad and when his older "brother" Misery asked him what was the matter, he told him that his left leg hurt him.
Misery called in Wonderful Old Bull, one of the four leading doctors of
the Doctor Lodge, who arrived with four splints tied around with four
straps of tanned bison hide that he put around the leg and ankle. But this

did not help and Wonderful Old Bull gave up, saying that if he continued to try to doctor the boy, he would lose him. So Misery himself tried his own four splints, and because he had power from the deer they were fastened together with tanned deer hide straps. Meanwhile he spoke to the boy of old times and urged him to try to get well. But as soon as the leg would heal, the bone would start coming out again.

Now his uncle, War Cry, took a hand and told his adopted father that Old-Man-Good-Land was a good bone and leg doctor. Good Land was called in on the case and he came with his son-in-law, White Fox, who was his assistant. White Fox came in whistling about and saying, "Clean the room and fix a bed." Good-Land and White Fox sat down next to the boy, one one each side of him, blew some medicine on the leg and tied it up loosely with a clean cloth. When they left, they gave instructions that the boy was to be closely watched so that he did not handle any knives. But the boy had a wooden spool and he wanted to make a little top of it to spin on his hand. War Cry's wife was sitting nearby cutting out a moccasin pattern with a knife and the boy took it against the doctor's orders to make his top.

Now War Cry was considering cutting off the leg, but the boy said he would rather die with his leg than have a short one. He began to get angry and desperate and one day he saw the bone sticking out and he began to pull on it, but it hurt too much and he felt a choking in his throat and so he pushed it back.

When White Fox came back he sniffed about as if he smelled something bad and said something wrong must have happened. The boy confessed about handling the knife against his orders and when they unwrapped the leg it was all swollen. The doctor wanted to leave the case. But War Cry taunted him. Otter was classificatory son to White Fox and War Cry threw it up to him saying, "He's only your son, of course, and if he dies it really doesn't matter!"

Many of the people had gone off on the winter hunt and War Cry urged White Woman and her husband to go along, remaining behind in the village himself to keep the boy warm in the earth lodge and take care of him. When White Fox had gone, Otter confessed to War Cry how he had tried to pull out the bone. War Cry scolded him and accused him of not wanting to get well and of deliberately hindering the doctors. "Well," the boy answered, "My mother and father have gone off on the winter hunt and left me, so they don't care for me anyway." War Cry again scolded him and reminded him of the fact that it was he, War Cry, who had urged Otter's parents to go and that he had elected to stay home just because he wanted to nurse Otter and protect him. He said that the boy ought to get well before his parents got back and surprise them and that then they would be glad.

Next day old doctor Good-Land came in and War Cry told him the whole story. The old doctor gave him some plants to chew, saying, "You're a man and it won't hurt you. Just take the medicine." Then he told him to turn his head aside and pulled out the bone that was sticking out. He cooked some leaves in water and where the hole was in his left leg, he blew some of the water in. He blew it in again and again and each time he asked his assistant if the water was clear. Finally it was. The old doctor said to the boy, "Young man, your leg will be well in two weeks." Finally the boy did get well except that the leg was somewhat crippled and this distressed his mother, White Woman, very much. Shot Arm mixed some grease with red paint and other medicines and rubbed it well into the leg. In a week or so the leg was better and the boy could walk again. He had suffered a year and a half, falling twice off a horse and stepping into a gopher hole and he had been in danger of having his leg amputated or of losing his life. Now at last he was healed.

For his treatment, Good-Land had been promised a fee of two horses, one from his uncle War Cry and one from his stepfather, Shot Arm, and a quantity of other goods, i.e., three blankets, some squaw cloth to make ladies' dresses, and some red shawls such as were issued by the government at that time. Before he had begun his treatment War Cry had said to the doctor, "If you doctor him, there's a horse over here for you." And Shot Arm said, "If you doctor him, there's also a horse here for you, and some goods." It was a very good fee. One could compare a horse to an automobile in our terms.

One evening the doctor and his assistant announced to War Cry, "To-morrow sometime I'm going to quit the case. He's all right. He's getting well." As soon as he heard this, War Cry sent one of his wives to call in White Woman and Shot Arm. They would have to have the fee ready for payment next day. But before that, the doctor would release the boy psychologically from his illness. That evening four doctors would come in to sit down at the patient's bed and "sing to set him free." Big Doctor and Pipe Offering, the leaders of the Doctor Lodge were called in to join Good Land and White Fox who had treated the case.

The boy was wrapped in a tent skin and lain crosswise west of the fireplace, his head toward the south and his feet toward the north. The big doctors came in with their gourd rattles and sat at his feet ranged from west to east—Good Land westernmost, White Fox next to him, and then Big Doctor and Pipe Offering. At his head on the south side were his adopted father, Shot Arm, uncle War Cry, and White Woman. Ranged further along the north side were other doctors who had come to witness the ceremony. Good Land addressed Shot Arm, White Woman, and War Cry saying, "The songs that the animals have, these medicine bundles here, the gourd rattles and the eagle-wing fans, are all going to hear their songs through which Otter had been made to get up. Now he is going to get well. It is these songs that we are about to hear that made him well. Now we're going to start to sing." Together in unison the four doctors sing:

First song:	Here, here, they got him to get up.
Second song:	They got him up and going about.
Third song:	They (our forefathers) said, that they (the animals) could get him up.
Fourth song:	Now as they, the old doctors said, they have raised him up.

Now they pause and smoke and then take up their gourd rattles and sing again:

1. "When first I came, the bone was broken.
2. "I had to use the eagle wing (*kauk'tu,* "down").
3. "The bone was broken. Just as they told me to do when a bone is broken, one must use soft down feathers.
4. "I call you back now, old doctors of long long ago; when a bone is broken, you can heal it."

They sang three more songs, making eight in all and then they said, "Now we're through."

Now they would all be entertained at an informal meal prepared by War Cry's youngest wife, Bird Woman. While it was being served, War Cry and his wives took the host's position at the southeast of the lodge, while the others remained in their places. A woman carried one bowl of food to each of the doctors in succession and then to Shot Arm and White Woman at the west, and all the others, and finally the hosts. A little bread and coffee was at last given to the patient himself. While they were eating people told funny stories or recounted some familiar incidents. Then they went home.

The next evening Good-Land entertained the other doctors in his earth lodge at an informal feast upon the completion of his case and the receipt of his fee. A gift of a blanket was made to Big Doctor and a shawl to Pipe Offering by way of compensation for their participation in the previous night's ceremony. Either that morning or earlier in the evening White Woman had come to Good-Land's lodge, leading the two horses, while one of War Cry's wives was carrying the goods. They were greeted by a woman of the house who came outside, and White Woman said simply, "Here are the horses and the goods to pay for his cure" (*iri-wirawirata,* "that which he has earned or won"). White Woman and her companion turned around and left and the woman of the house tied up the horses and took the goods inside the lodge and piled it up to the east of the fireplace. When the doctors were assembled, Good-Land addressed them again mentioning the sacred objects symbolic of the animals and their curative power: "Now today we are here as doctors. The objects you see here, the animals (their medicine); they have consented to have him live. Now White Fox is going to get up and make the smoke offering." Now he lit the pipe and offered it to all the sacred objects and to the doctors themselves, and to the horses outside and the rest of the fee lying east of the fireplace, then to the cosmic "stations" and finally made his presentation of a blanket and a shawl to the two doctors, Big Doctor and Pipe Offering and the ceremony was complete. Good-Land had no wife but was staying with his daughter and he put the goods he had received on her bed. She served each of the doctors a dish of food and then sat down to eat with them. Each of the other doctors made some remarks and then Good-Land made the usual type of closing address: "Now Pipe Offering and Heavy Trophies, and son-in-law, White Fox, and brother Big Doctor, I have this to say: I had this medicine, and these animals have blessed me and they have given us this their goods and the horses that are outside and that are going to carry me about. You doctors have helped me. Now the animals have blessed us. Now we have smoked. Now we have eaten." At this, all got up and left.

The animals, the plants, man's ingenuity and devotion, and the love of his family had cured the boy of his sickness.

46

A TIME FOR STORYTELLING
AND FOR LEISURE

Old Men Invited to Talk of Old Times—the Storytelling Sessions—after Eating, the Stories—Eagle Chief Begins—War Cry Tells of a Fight with the Sioux—Storytelling Continues through the Night

THE SERIOUS BUSINESS of the season being over, the men would get together in one or another of the earth lodges to tell stories of the old times and to review past events. They had worked hard hunting the buffalo, making the harvest and performing their dances, and now it would be pleasant to sit around the fire and enjoy a little leisure before they set out again for the buffalo hunting grounds.

Old men especially are invited for they are going to talk of the Old Village, Kitahaxpakuxtu, and how things used to be and came to be. In the fall was the good time of year to be telling these stories when it's not too cold and not too hot, but just nice to have a fire—after the harvest. When people hear who is invited—old men, chiefs, warriors—they know there is going to be storytelling. These sessions would begin after supper about eight o'clock in the evening and continue on throughout the night. Refreshments would be served from time to time consisting of fried bread, cooked dried apples and coffee. The smell of the bread cooking would be wafted over the village if there was a wind blowing and someone would just follow his nose and come in. Or else he could see the smoke of the fire and would come in. As soon as he got inside they would all say, "Nawa, sit down on any side." The chiefs were ranged at the west, and on the east along both sides sat the old men. Casual guests sat in the spaces in between. People from the other villages would also hear about it and wander in. Sometimes quite a large group would be gathered there.

Once Victory Call served as temporary Agency policeman and when he got an extra sack of flour for his services, he decided to have a story-telling session in his lodge. He sent Horse Rider especially to invite a number of old men: Pipe Offering, That-Chief, Heavy Trophies, Arrived, Warrior (also known as Big Knife, a name also used to refer to white people—a lively raconteur), Know-His-Face, Good-Land, Wonderful Old Buffalo Bull, and Buffalo Ghost—nine in all. Then he was sent to call in some chiefs—Lone Chief of Village-across-a-Ridge and Eagle Chief of Pumpkin-Vine as well as Sitting Hawk and Good Pipe —and braves—War Cry and Bringing Horses. From Bottomlands and Wolf-in-Water villages they would wander in without being invited, knowing what sort of group it was to be. While White Woman was doing the cooking, the old men were telling each other how many different places were calling them in to tell stories. The women would say, "We're through cooking," and put the bread and coffee near Victory Call a little off to his right. Now all the women retired to their beds, and as they lay there they would hear the stories.

Victory Call addressed his guests by name and kin term and said, "We have a little something here for you to eat. I thought I'd invite you here tonight so that I could see you here. Now this meeting is called simply because I want you folks to tell some old-time stories." All said, "Nawa," and Victory Call then turned over the meeting to Lone Chief and Eagle Chief who directed the proceedings from then on. They directed the two errand men to serve the food and by the time they had finished eating it was ten o'clock.

Now Eagle Chief spoke, urging Old Man Warrior to begin. But Old Man Warrior parried his suggestion with, "We old men here know how things should be done and the custom is that the leader has to tell the first story. Isn't that right, That-Chief?" "That's right," said That-Chief, "the leader has to tell the story first." "Well," said Eagle Chief laughing, "I thought I could get you to do it, but I guess I'll have to." "You start it out and we'll follow," said the old men.

When Eagle Chief began, he opened with a discussion of what sort of a story it ought to be, a long or a short one. "I have stories, but if I tell a war story, it will be a pretty long one. If I tell a story of the Sioux coming on the warpath to attack the village, it will be sort of a short one. If I tell of my trip to Washington, it will be of medium length." The old men were thinking they would rather have old-time stories so that they could reminisce about the past, but someone finally spoke up in favor of a short story and said, "Let's hear stories about 'at home' [the Sioux attacking the village]. After a while we'll get away from the village and on the warpath." It was now understood that he would tell a story of attack on the village and that he would be followed by a story on the same theme by his brave, War Cry, after which the old men would begin. In both stories, the enemy was repulsed, not by main force alone, but by the power of the Peace Pipe, which is "beloved of Heaven."

"Now I'll tell a story," said Eagle Chief. "Now you all know when you first took me as a chief and when I was going to Washington, on the morning of the day that was set for us to go, I was all dressed up. I was wearing my government coat, and of course, my leggings and moccasins. I was wearing my government medal. Finally the delegation left the village and when we got about five miles east, all at once one of the men in the back said, 'Look back at the village. There must be a warpath coming!' We could see everyone standing on top of the earth lodges. 'Well boys,' I said, 'let's go back.' The Kitkehaxkis, Tsawis, Pitahawiratas and us Skidis all went back to our villages." As he told the story the old men sat smoking and they said, "That's the time. That's it."

"Well when I came to my earth lodge, I looked at my wives there and said, 'Dear wives, maybe Heaven doesn't want me to see the great government.' At the same time my horse was way out there and I had to get to it to go on the warpath. All I took was my bow and arrows. I walked over to the sacred bundle and there on top were the Pipe Dance sticks. I took the one with the black eagle feathers (the male pipestem). That was all I took with me. I said to my wives, 'Now if it's the will of Heaven, I'll come back. If not, I won't. I may not come back.' It was because I had heard old people say that Heaven loves these pipes, that I took it with me.

"I got on the horse and went to where the fighting was going on. 'Well, this is my last day,' I thought to myself. Because the pipestem has two soft feathers on it and I didn't want them to touch my horse, I raised it up out of the way. I rode right through where the Sioux were and to the fighting line. I arrived at the front line with a Sioux close on one side of me, one on the other side and one directly in front. When I arrived at the front line, the Sioux turned back their horses and started to flee. There I was facing the whole line of Sioux, holding my pipe up like this. As the retreating line was going, you could see the dust. But I still had my original Sioux escorts. Wedged in between them, they didn't dare to try and shoot me with their bow and arrow as they were likely to shoot each other in the attempt. I raised this pipe and hit the one that was riding in front of me right on the back of his head. I reined in my horse and they rode ahead. We had ridden way ahead of the fighting line. When I looked back all I could see of the Pawnee was the cloud of dust they were raising. Now that's what I did. Now you all know what I did.

The listeners said, "Nawa." Some said, "That's right, that's the time."

Now said Eagle Chief to his co-leader, Lone Chief, "Give it to War Cry!" Everyone laughed because they expected the story to be of a very different kind from that of Eagle Chief, since War Cry was a rough character. He didn't disappoint them. His story also concerned the power of the Peace Pipe to repulse an enemy attack upon the village, but the story had a quite different flavor from Eagle Chief's.

War Cry was a brave and his whole outlook was toward aggression and violence compared with a chief who was a man of peace and conciliation. To the stark combat realism of his story, Eagle Chief was moved to comment, "That War Cry is a wicked fellow!" War Cry's narrative was as follows:

"Now I'll tell a short story like he did. You all know that the Tsawis had come for a Pipe Dance to the Skidis. They had come to Pipe Dance on Lone Chief [the Tsawis coming as "fathers" with goods, clothing, etc.]. They had been dancing for three days and now on the fourth, they were to 'take the child out,' dancing outside. Lone Chief's daughter was all painted up and dressed as the 'queen.' She was seated at the west and ten or fifteen chiefs and braves were sitting inside to witness the proceedings. Man Chief of the visiting Tsawis was about to say, 'Now we're going to take her outside,' when someone cried out at the doorway, 'Warpath coming.' Some of the Skidis got up and ran out, but about half of them stopped. Man Chief said, 'You wait, you wait—' About eight of the Skidis sat still and waited.

"Man Chief walked up north of the fireplace where Lone Chief was and he said, 'Now child, I have heard this: That Heaven loves this Pipe Dance. Here's the child before you—your child. [Lone Chief's daughter is representing the "childhood" of the whole group of Skidis who are being visited]. 'If our faith is justified,' Man Chief continued, 'then when you go on the warpath, you are going to have good luck. Now we will see. It is as if I stood holding the child and the pipe, embracing them, and the Sioux came running over me. Now, my son, I don't want to talk too long, (some of the Tsawis had also slipped out), for I know you are all anxious to go. Now you're going on the warpath. If our faith is justified, then you're going to come back with success and conquer the enemy. Now you may go!'

"The Tsawi horses were far away and most of them had gone off. The Skidis tried to run for their horses. They had a lot of them tied up there nearby to present to the Tsawis after the ceremony. The horses were painted up with white clay across the eyes and at all the joints and down the backbone. Some were painted with red or black paint. Some had eagle feathers on the mane and some had feathers tied onto the tail. The Sioux just didn't realize that this pipe belongs to Heaven.

"Way off, the seven of us could see different bunches engaged in combat on the different hills. We began to set out in the direction of the enemy, when just then, the Sioux shone a mirror in our eyes as a farewell signal. We stopped in a bunch and all got off our horses. It was obviously too far to reach them in time.

"We were climbing a hill to the northeast of here near a place called Kira-rutsku while at the same time a young man of the South Bands was coming up on the opposite side. As soon as he got on top of the hill, instead of dismounting his horse, he just began to yell. In his hands he had two whips. He had seen a Sioux hiding in a trough nearby. The Sioux was running off thinking he had a chance to escape but all seven of us set out to attack him. At Kira-rutsku there is a kind of high bluff and right in the bend of it the Sioux was going up the high ridge and the South Band man was half way. Shot Arm and another fellow had horses that were good runners and they began to gain on him. Shot Arm called out to the South Band man to watch the Sioux and not let him get away. The Sioux rode his horse up the hill and as soon as he got to the top, Shot Arm and the other man shot at him. But they only succeeded in hitting the horse, which now began to buck. The Sioux jumped off onto his right leg and started coming toward them. The South Band man also jumped off his horse and he and the Sioux were face to face. The South Band man was brave and the rest of us just stood off to one side and watched. The Sioux's horse had remained at the top of the bluff, while the South Band man was standing next to his horse where he had dismounted. Shot Arm shouted a warning to the South Band man to look out or he would shoot his own horse. On the other hand, if the Sioux managed to get on it, they would never catch him.

"Now the South Band man and the Sioux started to fight. Both were jumping about like cats as they dodged each other's arrows. Shot Arm noticed that the South Band man was wearing a shirt and that the shirt sleeves diverted the arrow into a zigzag course so that it missed its mark. He called out to him, 'Undo your shirt sleeve.' After he had undone his sleeve and pulled it up he began to shoot straight. (We Skidis stood out of the way at a good distance where we would be wide of the mark.) At last the South Band man hit the Sioux with the arrow right in the stomach. He tried to pull the arrow out. He tried to go down the bluff. The Sioux was getting dizzy from his wound, and right near Lone Chief, he fell over.

"Everyone was thinking of making a strike on him and getting war honors. Lone Chief was especially anxious to make the first strike on this occasion. He ran toward him down the hill as fast as he could. As I turned around, the Sioux had gotten up and fallen over on his back. The South Band man also made a strike on him and ran down the hill as fast as he could."

The war honors consisted of touching the fallen enemy and before eye witnesses stating, *tat-i-ki*, "I-at him-strike." Two more could succeed the first strike, these being spoken of as *wi-taruh-hukita-sa*, "now-it is-on top-lying." If there were no witnesses around, one could put the dead Sioux in a sheltered place and bring witnesses afterward, or people who came could be shown the tracks of horses in the place and some blood to show there had been a skirmish. Even if such proof could not be made, the story was likely to come out later when the two tribes concerned were at peace and they talked over their past experiences.

At this point, the story was taken over by Shot Arm, who for its next episode, had been more directly in the thick of the fight. He said:

"The Sioux had two six shooters in his belt, one on each side. The Sioux now threw away his bow and arrows and took out his guns. But I was right next to him and before he had a chance to do anything I grabbed both his hands. Meanwhile Brave Shield took the second strike on him and rode away.

"While I was grappling with him you could hear someone coming grunting and panting. That was this fellow here, War Cry. [War Cry was heavily built.] When he arrived he said to the Sioux, 'You nearly killed my brother-in-law (meaning me) (*para-kaskur-rahux-kapakis*, almost-you mine-rotten-poor, viz., killed).' He put his hand to his left side and drew out his very sharp butcher knife. It was just as sharp as it could be. He cut off the whole scalp of that Sioux, ears and all. [The whole top and back of the headskin with the ears, viz., across the top of the forehead just under the hairline and way back to the base of the hair all around, including the ears.]

"All this time I was grappling with the Sioux for his guns. War Cry put his right knee up against the Sioux's shoulders and pulled off the entire scalp. Swoosh, it went! The skin of the forehead fell over his eyes and as War Cry put his knee against the Sioux's back, he cracked the backbone and the Sioux cried out i! i! i! i! and let go the rifles.

"Back at Lone Chief's lodge, all the time the fighting was going on Man Chief and two other Tsawis had remained. Man Chief sat without moving, his buffalo robe with the hair side out wrapped tight around him. He had asked the other two to remove the decorations from Lone Chief's daughter.

"Out at the scene of battle, the man who had shot at the Sioux horse was told to take it as it was simply injured in the shoulder and would recover. Dog Chief asked War Cry for a little piece of the scalp—just enough to put on a stick, but he refused saying, 'Wait till we get home.' It was nearly sundown and all the warriors had returned except we seven. People in the village were asking, 'Did you see those seven fellows?' 'Oh, they chased the Sioux way off to Kirarutsku.' Man Chief was worried by now, and all the Tsawis that were there wanted 'their sons' to come home. The Tsawis came outside and sat on the high bank along the bluff outside Lone Chief's lodge.

"We started back from Kirarutsku in a bunch with the South Band man leading his horse and the rest of us Skidis following. Between nine and ten in the evening the Tsawis along the bluff could see us coming on a ridge about half a mile away. We were shooting off the six-shooters to announce our good luck and they could see the sparks and hear the report of the guns. As soon as we came in sight, Brave Shield who has the loudest voice called out, 'Lone Chief struck the enemy!' Someone else called, 'Brave Shield struck second!' and then another, 'War Cry scalped the whole head!'

"Everyone took up the cry and began to shout, 'Lone Chief struck the enemy' and the old ladies began to sing and dance and everyone heard it for it was in his lodge that the Pipe Dance was going on and there his daughter was being made 'the child.' All the visiting Tsawis, young and old, all along the bluff, began to yell, 'Lone Chief struck the enemy. Brave Shield made second strike!'

"Someone at the door of Lone Chief's lodge called out 'Piirau (child), wi-ti-ki, now-he-make first strike!' Man Chief jumped up from where he had been sitting huddled in his robe and also some of the braves that were in there. They were saying, 'Cook right away. Get a bucket of water.' An old Tsawi man stood up and started to sing old war songs—victory songs. Some ladies began to sound the high shrill ululating victory cry.

"Man Chief selected one of his braves and said, 'Now you go and meet our sons and say to them, 'Sons, come right here to Lone Chief's lodge—all of you.' Halfway out the Tsawi brave called out, 'Children [pirau]' and they all answered, 'Father [atias].' 'Nawa, children, your father, Man Chief, has said that all of you are to come to Lone Chief's lodge. They are cooking now [witirakaruriku].' Now they followed on horseback after the Tsawi brave. Then as they got in, the returning warriors said, 'All right, we'll be there. But we must first take these horses home.'

"As Lone Chief was coming toward his lodge, a brave had been told to spread a buffalo robe on the ground outside. Man Chief embraced Lone Chief as he got off the horse and directed him to sit down on the buffalo robe. Then the braves got hold of the buffalo robe and carried him into the lodge, setting him down in his place near the door. Now all the Tsawis were singing—the old men and the old women, and when the rest of us seven arrived in a crowd, they gave us everything they were wearing—their blankets, leggings, and finally the Tsawis had almost nothing on.

"Now three old Skidi women came led by Grieves-the-Enemy. She was dressed to commemorate her war deed, when she had saved the village from the attacking Poncas by impersonating a medicine man. She had her hair all tied up in a knot at the front of her head to one side. She had black soot across her eyes. She was saying to the other two old women, 'Here's his lodge. I want you two old women to sing.' As soon as they sang and danced with their sticks, the Tsawis gave the three old ladies calico and other gifts."

This was the end of the story that War Cry had started and Shot Arm continued. The Pipe of Peace, beloved of Heaven, had brought them victory as they defended their village.

Now the real session that they had all been waiting for would begin and continue all night. First Old-Man-That-Chief and then the others told real old time stories. For the most part they described their experiences as they moved from place to place abroad in the land in times past. With vivid imagery and detail they described each location and its events. It was in just such a meeting right after they returned from the winter hunt, after the warriors and chiefs had told their stories that the old men would take up the question of the calendar and whether they needed to introduce the thirteenth intercalary month that year. Warrior would tell an old war story and also That-Chief and then Good-Land would begin to speak of what year it is. He would talk of the stars —of how when people are lost, they must find their way back by following them. Then he would say of the moon that when it is low, we must put on something warm for it might rain or snow at any time. If you are far off you will need something warm to weather the storm. And after the storm is over you look at the stars and find your way back. Now the conversation turned to specific stars—which ones are appearing now, and how one star that shines brightly in spring brings a big wind when it gets to a certain place. Also, that there are sometimes two or three stars that act together. Good-Land continued with some experiences that had taught him about these things. He told of how a man who went south to Oklahoma with a big party strayed off on the way back. In the day he was able to follow the sun and calculate the east and north, going by north and a little eastward. At night he walked right under the north star, and going a little to the east, even though it was night, he was able to overtake his companions. "This happened many times," he said.

Another old man would take up where he left off and tell more stories in the same vein. "Because the stars and the planets appear to be moving, the Indians believe the earth is still." Then they began to argue about the question of "the thirteenth month." Some said, "Not now," others thought this was the time. They spoke of the position of the constellations, "first one snake, then two ducks and then the real rattlesnakes (Scorpio). That marks the beginning of the year—the spring. The months should coincide with these constellations." Of the regular twelve months, nine were named for familiar activities—clearing, planting, cultivating, hunting, and harvest—while the tenth and eleventh were paired and named after the constellations—little duck (*kiwakski*) and big duck (*kiwaks-kutsu*). The twelfth month was called *kaata*, darkness. It was through the observation of the position of the constellations that the regular month names had to be set in their proper course for the various activities for which they were named. In the year when the intercalary month was introduced, the two duck months were thought of as being paired, and then *kaata*, darkness, paired with the introduced month; the rest of the months of the year being paired accordingly, with the fifth month, viz., the June 19–July 18 month "standing alone." This was the month when one went off on the summer hunt. The thirteenth or intercalary month, had a variety of names, the most usual being Entrance Passageway to the earth lodge, *Puhuweturukut*, or the Skidi version, *Puhuwaturukat*, the long 10- or 15-foot entranceway. Alternative names had various references: If it had thundered from the north (rather than the south) when they got back, they thought the cold weather would last late into the spring and they called the month, *Paruks-ti-taka*, Thunder or Storm-It-Is-White, for the snow they expected to have. Another name for this month was Hidden Child, *pira-paru*, "child-hidden," the Pawnee equivalent of our "illegitimate child." The reference was to abortion for it was said that the abandoned foetus was more conspicuous on the snow during that season than on the bare ground. A further name, *atatpiiwa*, is of unknown significance. From this example, it should be clear that the storytelling session was not a mere leisure pastime. Through it was transmitted history, climatology, theology, the logistics of war, topography, and many other important facets of Pawnee knowledge. Such a session was an invaluable preamble to setting out on the winter hunt.

47

EQUIPMENT AND
INDUSTRIAL MANUFACTURES

*The Fall of the Year, a Time for Manufacture—
Buffalo a Chief Source—History of Their Trad-
ing—Wood of Second Importance—Reeds and
Grasses Third in Importance—Clay and Stone
Scarce—History of Transition from Stone to
Metal—Crafts Highly Regarded but No Religious
Taboos—Learning to Make a Black Rope*

THE FALL OF THE YEAR was the time when the Pawnees made most of the
things they used. There was a plentiful supply of food and in the protected environment of the earth lodge, they could manufacture the various items of furnishings, clothing, and equipment they needed. Moreover, with the winter hunt and migration in prospect, they had to make
sure that everything was in order, as there would be little time in the
short daylight hours for more than setting up camp and processing the
meat and skins.

There were very few materials in the Pawnee environment that they
could use to make the things they needed. Their top resource for industry as well as for food was the buffalo. Hides, hair, horns, and bones
each found a number of essential uses. Hides made their all-important
tent cover, their blankets, curtains, containers, moccasin soles, and other
clothing. And even beyond their domestic needs, it gave them their major
item of external trade, the buffalo robe.

There is clear evidence that this was a leading trade item before the
Spaniards moved up into the Plains in 1540. Long before the advent of the
European on the continent, the settled villages were centers of trade for
the more nomadic peoples and there were seasonal trade fairs in recognized locations where peoples came to exchange their special products

and materials. European goods were first spread by itinerant traders who carried their wares to the different villages and centers and finally set up their own trade stores. Bishop and Matlock's was the favorite trade store for the Pawnees at this time, and the buffalo robe was the chief medium of exchange. The trade value of a well-tanned robe of ordinary quality was ten to fifteen dollars. For one of prime quality, expertly tanned, they might get thirty dollars worth of exchange goods. The national market of the trader justified him in paying these prices. In 1848, 100,000 robes were shipped out of St. Louis, and the American Civil War gave a special impetus to the buffalo leather trade for army needs. By 1874 even England was making use of the leather for its army. When supplies were running low in a Pawnee household, the man would point to an unworked buffalo hide and say to his wife, "Make up that buffalo robe so that we can get something at the store." In the past the same expedient probably served for trade with other tribes or villages.

The hair of the buffalo was intricately braided into a long rope known as Black Rope, which was used by the men to hold the buffalo robe in place as well as for other purposes. The horns provided the common eating and serving spoons and the bones were made into a number of important tools, notably the buffalo shoulder blade, which was the main spade or earth-digging tool as well as the hoe and the scythe. These bones also provided tools for skin working and for sizing and straightening the arrowshaft, as well as slivers for scraping and cutting. The sinews of the buffalo were used for sewing together the skins and for making bowstrings.

Second in importance as an industrial material was wood. In the open prairie plains, trees grew only along the streams. The supply was heavily drawn upon for fuel as well as for industry. Wood was used industrially for building and for equipment and utensils. Cottonwood and willow were the mainstay of the construction industries—the cottonwood because it was light for its strength and bulk and the willow for its flexibility. Elm was used for making the mortar and post oak for the pestle. They also used the post oak to make their common eating bowls. Dogwood was the material of the arrowshafts and ashwood for the bow as well as the gaming hoop and the pipestem. Wood was best gotten in the fall when the sap was running low.

Reeds and grasses were their third industrial resource. Grasses grew along the streams and reeds in the limited number of ponds to be found in the area. Since they matured about the same time as the cultivated crops, they had to be processed as soon as the harvest was over. The most important product they made from these materials was the large twined woven mat that they felt had to be spread on the dusty ground both in the earth lodge and in the tent while they were on the hunt. Next in terms of common use was porcupine grass for making stiff brushes to keep the hair in order.

The areas in which the villages were located were lacking in two essential materials that they needed, clay and stone—clay for pottery and stone chiefly for cutting implements. In the past, the materials must have been obtained by men going into outlying territories on the warpath or by international trade. The best clay was found to the southwest of their area. By 1867 these materials had been entirely replaced by metal made up into trade objects. Even in the late 1830's brass kettles for cooking and metal buckets for water were used. Moreover in 1833 the Pawnees were trading brass kettles in quantity to the Kiowas. By 1928, no one could remember how to make pottery. Even in 1899 in Oklahoma, Grinnell got an account from a fifty-year-old man who had never seen pottery in use and knew of it only from his grandmother. This would place it well before the 1830's. Grinnell's (1925, pp. 255-256) description follows:

> . . . They were accustomed to smooth off the end of a tree for a mould. A hot fire was then built, in which stones were roasted, which were afterward pounded into fine powder or sand. This pounded stone was mixed with fine clay, and when the material was of a proper consistency, they smeared it well over the rounded mould which was perhaps first well greased with buffalo tallow. After the clay had been made of even thickness throughout, and smoothed on the outside, they took a sharp stone and made marks on the outside to ornament it. When the material was sufficiently dry, they lifted it from the mould and burned it in the fire and while it was baking "put corn in the pot and stirred it about, and this made it as hard as iron." This may mean that it gave the pot a glaze on the inside. In these pots they boiled food of all kinds.

Pawnee pots are known to us from archaeological excavations. They have a characteristic shape with a well-rounded bottom and full globular body so that they could be set down on the ground. They have a thick "collar" around the rim and/or a number of loop handles. The broad collar was usually incised with slantline herringbone patterns. Boiling was the main method of cooking among the Pawnees and for the most part the pot was suspended over the fire from the wooden bracket. The rim and loops on the rim were no doubt used for tying on a handle. Pots were placed directly on the coals mainly for cooking in large quantities.

In the matter of transition from stone to metal cutting tools, we must also look to the archaeological record. By 1867, although the bow was entirely of native materials and the shaft was made of local wood, the arrow point was of sheet metal, mainly fragments of barrel hoops roughed out by the blacksmith and filed down with a trade-store file to the desired form and sharpness by the hunter himself. The first commercial metal to appear in this region was the Lower Loup sites of the 1600's where a few small fragments of sheet copper and bits of broken iron objects were found. In the protohistoric Pawnee villages of the 1700's, chipped-stone arrow points were plentiful and even in the 1830's in Old Village, they were fairly common. In the next thirty years they had gone out of use. A very characteristic Pawnee object is the diamond-shaped, bevel-edged knife of chipped flint known in archaeological circles as Harahey. By 1867 it had been entirely replaced with the metal knife bought from the trader. One of the early names for white people was "Big Knife."

Of the heavier objects of stone, the chipped, grooved stone mauls, axes, and polished celts of the protohistoric and historic archaeological sites had been replaced by the metal ax and hatchet. Two stone objects continued in use—sandstone buffers for smoothing the wooden arrow-shafts and the bowl of the pipe made of pipestone or Catlinite. The sandstone buffers came in pairs and were oval-shaped with a flat surface, each with a matching groove down the length, through which the shaft was pulled. Pipestone was a powdery red or black stone traded from southwest Minnesota where the quarry is located near the present town of Pipestone.

Most of the Pawnee crafts were highly specialized and their knowledge was confined to a limited number of people, who were reluctant to reveal their technical secrets. They were looked upon much as we regard electrical and mechanical skills in our present-day society.

The crafts had a respected place in the ceremonies and were part of ceremonial metaphor. In the ceremony of the Young Corn plant when the Young Mother Corn was being provided with her life, an expert arrowshaft maker was called in to fashion a shaft that would symbolize her body and particularly the windpipe, regarded by the Pawnees as the essence of life itself. When the arrow maker was cutting off the knots from the dogwood stick, they sang of "picking off the words" and when the shaft was drawn through the straightener, the squeaking noise was referred to as "rubbing the female voice." The process of fashioning the pipe stem for the calumet or peace pipe was also couched in poetic terms.

Nevertheless it is rather surprising that there were neither religious taboos nor ceremonial procedures connected with the actual practice of the crafts. Among the Polynesians strict taboos guard the conventional technical procedures against any variations. Among the Pueblos of the Southwest, basket making involves songs and taboos, while among the Plains-dwelling southern Cheyenne, there were organized craft guilds connected with many religious requirements. Sewing beadwork on skins was undertaken as a kind of religious vow—probably going back to older porcupine embroidery. If the work was not completed in the allotted time or not up to technical standards, or if the person failed to remain even-tempered during the work, direct consequences to the health and well-being of the craftswoman and her family would inevitably follow. The guild was in the charge of a woman who made sure that these conditions were met. The woman who supervised the fitting of the skins to make the tent—the tent architect—also belonged to a religious guild of a similar sort. The conventional character of Pawnee technical processes was just as firmly established as among these other peoples, most of them going back to very old practices, and their work was as fine and as precisely done but there were no religious connotations of any kind.

The mature women did most of the craft work that pertained to the domestic economy. The men made most of the things they used in hunting, war, and ceremonials. The crafts were not taught to the young people as a normal part of their education. A young man or a young woman had to be very eager to learn and only if an older person was willing to sponsor them were they able to do so. The teacher had to receive ample payment as well as a clear indication of a very real desire to learn. Both for the manufacture of a craft object and for teaching as well as other kinds of assistance, "payment" should provide the craftsman with "something to wear and something with which to feed the family." This consisted in skin clothing or commercial cloth, blankets or shawls, and the standard food stuffs, either native or trade.

The following is my informant's account of the circumstances of learning the craft of making a black rope of braided buffalo hair:

If a woman wanted to learn how to make a buffalo hair belt from Old Lady Lucky Leader, for example, one would go to her and put a necklace about her neck, and ask to be taught. She would certainly not consent at once. She might answer, "Some day I will teach you." This signified that if the applicant went quietly away and asked again another day, then repeated her request on subsequent occasions, she might finally give in. If she said, "I'll think about it," this meant she might capitulate if asked again. On the other hand, if she said, "I can't do it," this constituted an absolute refusal.

There were situations in which she would feel impelled to grant the request. This was particularly the case if the woman were a close and respected relative, especially an in-law. On the other hand, she might also feel impelled to teach a woman whose family fortunes were low and who needed to earn something to help out. Such a woman was the wife of Chief's-Road. Giving the old lady a gift she said, "I want you to take pity on me and teach me to make a buffalo hair belt. You know that I am poor and we can't seem to work out anything. What I want is for you to take pity on me so that it may earn something for us. My husband can't make much and my sister can't do anything."

Having consented, Old Lady Lucky Leader would say, "On so-and-so day I am going to make it. Come in then." When the wife of Chief's-Road came in, the old lady directed her to sit down to her left and watch everything. As the work progressed she paid close attention to the manner of braiding and after some of the work had been completed, the teacher asked the pupil to try her hand at it. At first she was very clumsy and was corrected by the teacher and finally she got the idea. When she got home, she tried to do it by herself and from time to time came in to see the old lady saying she didn't quite remember about this and this detail and asking to be shown.

She told no one that she had learned, but on an occasion when someone came to the old lady to have a belt made, she would say, "Go to the wife of Chief's-Road. She can make it. I taught her." The man now would go to the wife of Chief's-Road and tell her that he had been sent by the old lady because she had too much work. She would make the belt for the man and the entire fee would be hers, with no further financial obligation to her teacher. From now on others would hear of it and begin to apply to her and she would be able to earn something for her family.

Most mature women knew the techniques of skin working with a knowledge of mat making being somewhat less common but still widely known. Everyone could make buffalo-horn spoons. The weaving of the black rope and woven belts as well as the making of wooden bowls were known to a very limited number of craftswomen. In the men's crafts, the bow was made by everyone, but the extremely restricted number of arrowshaft makers has already been mentioned. The pipe makers were equally specialized and they made both the stem and the bowl. Next to the bow and arrow, the pipe was one of the most significant things the man needed. Only six or seven men among all the Skidi could make them. Skin shirts could only be worn by men who had an outstanding social or military status and these were made by a very limited number of specialists. These specialists were regarded like the village blacksmith of our early towns. They tried to have two or three of them in each village. But even the most common craft techniques could only be learned by a person who was sponsored by someone or had the wherewithal to pay for his instruction.

48

THE PROCESS OF MAKING

LEATHER AND FURS

〰〰〰〰〰〰〰〰〰〰〰〰〰〰〰〰〰〰

*Background Information of Indian Trading—the
Preparation of Hides—Rawhide and Tanning
Processes—Dressing the Deer—Saddle and Bridle
Making—Clothing of Women and Men—Moc-
casin—Special Clothing: Eagle Feathers, Braided
Belts*

〰〰〰〰〰〰〰〰〰〰〰〰〰〰〰〰〰〰

THERE IS REASON TO BELIEVE from archaeological and early historical evidence that formerly Indian trade involved a variety of regionally limited raw materials and items that were regarded as luxury foods and ornaments. In the archaeological Ohio Hopewell sites of a culture that flourished around the beginning of the Christian era there are raw materials from the Rockies to the Atlantic Coast and from the Gulf of Mexico and possibly even Middle America.

In 1738 the Mandans to the northeast of Pawnee territory, gave the Assiniboine middlemen painted buffalo robes, clusters of feathers, headdresses, garters, and girdles in exchange for muskets, axes, kettles, powder, bullets, knives, and bodkins which they had gotten from the British at Hudson's Bay.

In 1812, the Comanches chewed pieces of checker-plaited dried pumpkin mat as they rode, which they had received from the Pawnees and paid for in buffalo robes and horses.

From the accounts of first European contacts, the dressed buffalo hide was also an important item of native trade. The presumably Caddoan-speaking Tula who in 1541 were defeated by De Soto south of Hot Springs, Arkansas, were sent by their chiefs with tribute of "many cowhides as a gift which were useful because it was a cold land and they were serviceable for coverlets as they were very soft and the wool like that of sheep." It was further reported that to the north there were many "cat-tle." The reports of Coronado's expedition of about the same period in the Southwest describe the details of buffalo hunting with great accuracy and show that even in the 1860's they had survived substantially as they were then. In 1599, Oñate of New Mexico hoped the Spaniards could also develop a thriving trade in buffalo wool and hides, but the Spanish empire was already too decadent.

By the 1600's the big business in furs with Europe had been developed by France starting with the fateful beaver trade on the St. Lawrence. As we see from the present account, the Pawnees were still trapping the beaver with metal traps in 1867, in order to trade them for cash. By the end of the 1600's the Indians were no longer merely a source of raw materials for trade to Europe, but also a positive outlet for European manufactured goods. "The Indians were collecting sassafras, tanning buckskins, and building up a steady trade in buffalo wool." In 1702 seventeen Frenchmen left Tamaroa Mission near Cahokia, Illinois, east of St. Louis to ascend the Missouri about two hundred leagues to build a fort between the Pawnee and the Iowa. The French were attempting to control the inter-Indian trade to protect themselves from the encroach-ment upon the Indian trade by the Spaniards who were moving up from the Southwest. Their fears were not unfounded, for in 1706 the Spaniards were reported to have come to an Indian village to trade for buffalo hides with which to make harness for their mules.

At a somewhat later period, fur traders were sent out from Council Bluffs (Iowa) to live with the Pawnees at their earth lodges and follow them on their hunting expeditions.

Before he became mature, every man and woman had learned how to prepare hides. Most of all they needed the buffalo robe. As stated by the informant:

The wind blew through the blankets, the buffalo robe kept you warm. Almost everyone needed a new buffalo robe every winter. To-ward the summer, the hair would all wear off and by the late fall, there wouldn't be any wool on to keep a person warm. In Victory Call's family, they needed at least four robes in good condition for the winter —one for Victory Call himself, one for his wife, White Woman, one for Grandma and one for the boy, Otter. For the adults it took the skin of a whole buffalo. For children, the whole skin of a calf was used with the headskin and the two little horns left intact.

During the daytime, the robe was wrapped around the body hori-zontally with the head part overlapping at the left. At night, the same robe was used as a blanket the long way, with the hair against the body, the head part covering the head and the tail part the feet. One robe could keep a person warm in winter if it were well tucked in all around.

There were three stages by which the hide was prepared for its different uses—rawhide, tanned, or dyed.

Rawhide was the first stage. While they were on hunt, the fresh hide was pegged out with the hair side down and the flesh scraped off. The defleshing tool was made of a buffalo shinbone with the small end broken off and discarded. The broken edge was cut into a row of fine teeth with which to scrape the hide. The thick end of the bone had a hole drilled in it through which a buckskin strap was threaded to be worn around the wrist while the tool was in use. It took about half an hour to peg down and flesh a skin. After it was thoroughly dry, it was rolled up and carried home to the village where it was stored in the food pit or kept in the lodge to be dressed at the first opportunity. The largest number were worked in the fall. The skin was dressed as rawhide by simply removing the hair. The skin was unrolled and spread on the ground and the pieces of dried flesh picked off with a knife and boiled in the soup. Now the hide was turned over and the hair removed with an elbow-shaped scraper. This tool was like an adze with a handle of elkhorn and a cutting blade fastened to the bent end. In the old days the cutting blade was of chipped flint but at this time the women had the blades made by the blacksmith. To dehair it, the woman stood directly on the hide and bent over holding the elbow-scraper crosswise with her left hand on the handle end and her right hand on the elbow so that she could push it across the skin. She removed hair, chips and shavings, striking and pushing upon the skin and scraping with a sidewise motion toward the left. If the blade were not sharp, she would have to sit down while she worked and this would take a good deal longer. The hide of a big bison was used to make rawhide.

Rawhide was used for the large envelope in which the dried buffalo meat was contained, for moccasin soles, saddles, and for cutting into long continuous strips for ropes and whips. Half a bull hide was also used for making a baggage raft or water package.

Tanning the skin required many additional technical steps. All skins have three layers, a horny one on the outside, a soft fatty layer on the inside where the sweat and fat glands are embedded, and the middle layer, the corium, which is the true skin. The corium is made up of gelatinous fibers and it is the objective of the tanning process to enter into combination with these fibers so that they are preserved and still remain flexible. For this purpose the Pawnees used a decoction of elm bark and brains. The technical term for this mixture is *tann*, meaning "oak" in the old Celtic of Brittany. Besides brains, sour milk and various oils are alternative materials for improving the texture.

The skins were tanned either with or without the hair. The skins of old buffalo or with exceptionally thin wool had the hair removed and were kept on hand to wrap things in, for bedding, skin bags, moccasins, and occasionally, if they were light enough, for skirts. The heavier qualities were used especially for tent skins. Tanned hide with hair removed was used as a light wrap or blanket to be draped around the shoulders. When worn in this way it was often decorated with designs or colored.

In tanning the robe with the hair on, which was the main trade robe, the hide was unrolled the evening before. Next morning it was placed on the ground and scraped on the flesh side with the elbow-scraper. This was a more strenuous process than dehairing. The skin had to be thinned section by section and any irregularities removed. If no one interrupted and the work proceeded at top speed, it took three hours of back-breaking labor. After this, the skin was immediately sprinkled with water to keep it soft and by evening it was pliable enough to be folded up and put into a kettle with cold water poured over it and left to soak overnight.

The next morning after breakfast the woman prepared a stretching frame on which to fasten the skin so that she could apply the tanning mixture. The standing part of the frame was made of two pairs of tent poles, each pair being fastened together at the top, spread out at the bottom, and set apart at the proper distance to accommodate the length of the skin. The two sets of "bi-pods" were joined across the near arms by two additional tent poles, one above and one below to a distance of the width of the hide. The skin was bound onto this slanting rectangular frame by overcasting around the edges through the peg holes around the edge of the hide. The flesh surface was now uppermost and to this the tanning solution would be applied.

Some bark, used as a sort of sponge, was dipped into the tanning mixture, which was spilled and rubbed onto the hide until it was well soaked and the water was dripping down the surface. The solution was now pressed in and rubbed from the top downward with a special tool resembling the blade of an iron hoe. In this process of rubbing and scraping, a good deal of the excess water was removed. When the skin had dried somewhat, a pinch of flour was sprinkled on and rubbed all over the surface to make it white. While the skin remained on the stretcher to dry for about an hour, the equipment for the next step was prepared. The skin would be rubbed back and forth on a taut sinew rope in order to soften it. Two green sticks of uneven height, one 2 feet and one 5½ feet high, were set upright in the ground about 4½ feet apart. They were joined by a big sinew rope that was stretched between them and tied at each end. The skin was rubbed back and forth across the rope on the flesh side until it was softened. One woman could do this alone, but it was more convenient for two to work on it, one holding on to the hide at each end.

The stretching of the skin on the frame took all morning, the tanning the noon hour and the afternoon the rubbing and softening. By evening, although the skin was still quite wet it was taken indoors so that no one would appropriate it. It was beaten with a stick on the fur side to sprinkle out some of the water.

Next morning when the sun was quite high, the skin was again rubbed on the sinew and set on the ground with the hair side up to get completely dry. Then it was placed on a mat and the margin trimmed all around with a sharp knife to remove any peg holes or other irregularities. The robe was now complete and was rolled up ready for wear or sale.

The skins that were less prime were tanned without the hair on, as the tanning process differed somewhat from the fur robe. After the hair was scraped off with the elbow-scraper, the flesh side was scraped and thinned with the same tool. The hide was soaked over night and next morning, stretched on the frame to be treated with the tanning mixture. The skin was left on the frame until the flesh side was thoroughly dry and even though the dehaired surface remained a bit wet, the skin was removed from the frame and rubbed between the fingers to soften it, then twisted with a wringing motion as we twist our bedsheets. It was not necessary to rub the skin as violently as the fur robe as in the dehairing process the horny outer epidermis had been removed. Eight of these skins went into the construction of the tent cover; they were used for bedding, curtains, packages, and bags.

The skins to be worn as blankets were usually dyed. If a white blanket was desired, white clay was sprinkled on the wet surface while it was still stretched on the frame and allowed to dry in thoroughly before it was removed and twisted.

More commonly, for wear as blankets, the tanned hide was dyed black. The black dye was made by boiling sumach leaves in water, the dye being allowed to cool before being applied to the surface of the tanned hide. The dye was rubbed in with a rag, first on one surface and when this was dry, on the other. When both sides were thoroughly dry, the skin was rubbed between the fingers to soften it and hung across a horizontal pole and beaten with a stick to remove the excess dye that had dried onto the surface. Interspersed with the other housework of the fall season, it took four days to make a black-dyed blanket.

It was also possible to dye the tanned hide a light yellow. This was done by smoking it over a rotten log of any kind of wood. They dug a long rectangular trench in the ground and put the log into it with some hot coals. They built an archway of supple twigs over the trench by sticking a series of twigs in the ground along both sides and joining them at the top. A number of long sticks were fastened on top and on the long sides of the archway to strengthen the structure. The tanned hide was laid onto the framework and weighted down with earth or sticks on all sides to keep the air from reaching the inner surface. When they first removed the skin from the frame, the smoked surface was somewhat black, but when it was exposed to the air it quickly turned yellow. Any smoky patches that remained were rubbed with the fingers, and these promptly turned yellow, too. In the past these dyed skin blankets were the forerunners of the later trade blanket.

The skins of the deer and elk were used for clothing because they were considerably lighter and softer than the buffalo hide. In the fall particularly, when the doctor performances were in prospect, they made a critical inspection of their wardrobes to see if they had something suitable to wear for the occasion. The women thought about a new dress and the men considered whether their clothing wasn't too shabby to wear and what ceremonial costumes they would need. They had been on the march all summer and busy with the harvest and they had had no time to think about such matters. They also had to consider the forthcoming winter hunt.

In the Plains climate, clothing was a pressing necessity. The fresh deer and elk meat was a welcome addition to their staple diet of dried vegetables and buffalo meat, but it was consumed immediately and never preserved. Economically, the hides were of greater practical value.

There is some question whether it was the men or the women who dressed the deer and elkskins. Theoretically they both knew how, but the only accounts of the process I have seen or been able to collect refer to the work of the men. Apparently the hide was not treated with a tanning mixture but was simply dehaired and rubbed:

> The first step in dressing the deer hide was to get it wet. A stick was put slantwise in the ground and the hide draped over it hair side up and fastened at the top. The hair which slanted upward was scraped off with a sharpened horse rib that was pushed from the top down. The deer hair was used as a stuffing for pillows; the buffalo hair was always thrown away. The skin was now turned over with the flesh side uppermost and rubbed with a sharp rock as rough as a file. Next they continued to rub the flesh side with another rock that was gray and white and very porous. They kept rubbing the flesh side until the skin had dried.

A description of preparing a moose hide for a robe is somewhat simpler; allowing the skin to soak in water for a day and a night, removing the hair with a horse rib as it rested on a slanting cottonwood stick, and then simply spreading the skin on the ground to dry.

When needed, the men dressed bear or fox skins and those of some other animals, stretching them on frames and overcasting them all around the edges through a series of little holes. The beaver skins that they trapped for sale to the traders, were treated in the same way.

The men made their own saddles and horse trappings, some of deer and some of buffalo hide. All men made these for themselves and dressed the deer hides, even Eagle Chief himself. But buffalo hide was gotten from the women. They made saddles, bridles, stirrups, and saddle bags. For saddle bags, discarded buffalo robes were obtained from the women. The saddles were made either of deer and deer horns or wood and buffalo hide. The horn saddle took four or five days; the buffalo hide ten to fifteen. The men worked hard on their saddles and decorated them elaborately.

The basic clothing was cut out and sewn with an awl and sinew by the women. The women wore a wrap-around skirt, an overblouse, leggings fastened at the knee, and moccasins. The skirt, of tanned deer hide, reached just below the knee with the closing at the right side. It was fastened at the waist with a woven yarn belt. If no deer hide was available, they used a very soft buffalo hide.

The blouse was a simple sleeveless pullover extending down over the waist so that it covered the top of the skirt and the belt that held it in place. It was made of an oblong piece of skin folded in two and cut out for the neck and armholes so that it would not rub against the underarm. (See Figure 48-1.) It was sewn along the sides with sinew, the seams extending just a little below the waist. The bottom section that reached toward the hips was left unsewn on the two sides. Around the neck was a scarf about 4 inches wide sewn across the back and reaching over the shoulders so that it could be turned up in cold weather for protection. The neck was provided with a drawstring whose ends hung down in front unless they wanted to draw the blouse close together around the throat.

Until the age of five or six, the little girls ran around naked, but then they had to have a little wraparound skirt of buckskin with a drawstring at the top. They would always complain that it was too loose, for it was usually made to allow for growth; when the little girl complained her mother would say, "Oh, go on, you'll grow soon," or "After all, it might shrink."

Leggings of tanned deer or elk hide were worn by all the women, and these were tied around under the knee and turned down over the tie string at the top. For both men and women, they made two-piece moccasins with hard soles and softer uppers. Those of the Skidi were below the ankle and those of the South Bands a little above.

The clothing of the men, besides the basic garments, included a number of ceremonial trappings or some that signified special rank or achievement. The main clothes were a loincloth, leggings, and moccasins.

Around the waist they had an elkskin string. To it on each side they tied on the leggings which were of deer or elkskin, covering the whole leg and thigh. A strip of soft tanned deer hide was drawn between the legs and under the waist band so that the ends hung down in front and in back. One good deer skin made two pairs of leggings. Each legging took an hour to make—two hours for the pair. In warm weather a man might carry a tanned buffalo-hide blanket over the left shoulder when not in use. In winter they wore the furred buffalo robe for warmth.

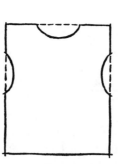

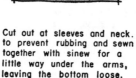

Cut out at sleeves and neck. to prevent rubbing and sewn together with sinew for a little way under the arms, leaving the bottom loose.

Rear view of shirt with scarf across shoulders. Blouse extended over the top of skirt, covering belted waistline.

Fold in two.

FIGURE 48-1. The pattern of a woman's skin shirt. A scarf about 4 inches wide was fastened to the neck and across the shoulders; it could be turned up against the back of the neck and head in cold weather. A string that went all around the neck with both ends hanging down in front could be tied at the neck to draw the shirt close around the throat. There was a wrap-around skin skirt closing at the right side and reaching just below the knee; this was fastened at the waist with a woven yarn belt. The costume was completed by leggings fastened at the knees and moccasins.

Keeping the family in moccasins was a constant problem for the women. During the migrations on the hunt, moccasins wore out all the time and the woman had to carry along some cutout moccasin leather all ready to be sewn up. A sewing bag with sinew, an awl, and moccasin patterns was an essential of the hunting equipment. A man going on a long journey over the country would take along a similar kit.

There were two kinds of moccasins in general use among North American tribes—one better adapted to rough open terrain, a hard-soled moccasin, the other with a soft sole suitable for forest dwellers. The hard-soled moccasin was the one the Pawnees used most, but in winter they sometimes made soft-soled moccasins out of buffalo hide with the hair turned inside for warmth. Sometimes they adapted the hard-soled moccasin to cold weather by wrapping the feet in hay or calico, changing the padding in the evening when it became damp.

The hard-soled moccasin was in two parts—a hard rawhide sole of buffalo leather with a softer top of deer skin sewn on. To make a soft-soled moccasin, one piece of hide was used folded over in the length, one section serving as the sole and the other as the upper.

Ordinarily, everyone had to have at least two pairs of moccasins at a time—one for everyday use and one for good wear. When the ordinary pair was worn out, the good ones were moved down and a new good pair made. Soles were patched when they wore through, and if the sole was entirely worn out and the top still good, the whole sole was replaced. On the summer and winter migrations, soles often had to be fixed en route. Children were not ordinarily provided with moccasins except in winter. The young boys who foraged about for bird's eggs in spring were the exception. Moccasins had to be made for them in order to protect them from snakebite. Winter moccasins were made large to accommodate the lining of hay or calico.

Each moccasin took about an hour and a half to sew—three hours for a pair. If they were decorated with beads it took five or six days of spare time. When a man was in a hurry for his moccasins, a woman would have to ask someone to help her out with the sewing. She would say, "My husband wants to go off and I'm making him one pair of moccasins. Would you help me out and sew up another one for me?" Sisters were likely to help out in this way or women married to two brothers. Other women would be given a small fee for their help—about five yards of calico, for example. In the spring, and again in the fall after the Doctor's Opera, men commonly went off on the warpath and then they would need at least three extra pairs of moccasins to take along. These would be filled with rations and placed in a "flat package" worn on the back.

There was a variety of supplementary clothing that was worn by men to denote rank and achievement. The skin shirt was one of the outstanding symbols of high status. Very few men were privileged to wear them. Among the chiefs only Eagle Chief and Lone Chief were eligible, while such able chiefs as White Eagle and Comanche Chief were not. Victory Call was "not high enough" as he was a cadet member of a chiefly family, while his older brother Sitting Hawk, who was the senior representative of the family, might well qualify. Big Doctor, although not a chief, could wear such a shirt. The man entitled to wear it would have to go to a specialist to have it made. He had to supply all the materials and pay the maker a pony for the labor alone. The shirt was decorated down the sleeves with enemy scalps with the hair on, and there was porcupine quill

work down the length of the shirt itself. The quill embroidery was done
by the wife of the maker. It took at least ten to twelve days to make such
a shirt.

The turban, while sometimes worn in winter to keep the head warm,
also indicated the warrior rank of the wearer. The highest warrior rank
was represented by a turban of wildcat skin. Second in rank was fox skin,
and third, a white or red handkerchief or any sort of calico. (Wolf skin
was never worn on the head.) Among the South Bands, the ranks differed
somewhat; wildcat was the highest, but the second was the big squirrel.

A Skidi brave wore a decorative knee band at the top of his leggings
just below the knees to show that he was an active warrior "going about
all the time." A leg band of raccoon denoted a comparable rank among
the South Bands.

A great warrior had the privilege of draping an otter skin like a necklace around his neck. While they were out on the summer hunt, a man
who had earned the right to wear it for a long time, could bring it
to the council tent and have it incorporated as a feature of a ceremony.

The particular skin that a man used to make a quiver was also a sign
of his rank. Otter skin could be used only by a chief. Only the bravest
men could use the skin of a panther—an animal that was seldom caught.
Should someone who was not privileged to use it manage to catch one,
the man who had the requisite rank would offer him a blanket and a pair
of leggings or some calico for it.

Bear and beaver skins were prepared only by the doctors for their
special ceremonies. The bear meat was considered inedible and was left
in the trees for the birds. It was thought that a person who ate it would
soon imitate the bear, and moreover, the bear ate humans and was therefore not considered fit for human food.

Eagles were a valuable commodity. Most of the time they made eagle-
wing fans from dead eagles. Only rarely did a man possess a good enough
eye to shoot one. Old Bull was such a good shot and should he manage
to shoot one while they were out on the summer hunt, he would bring
it to the council tent in the hope of getting good luck for himself and
others. They would divide it up as they saw fit—taking off the downy
feathers, the wings, the tail feathers, etc. Sometimes Old Bull would decide to keep the whole skin for himself. He would dry up the skin, giving one wing to a doctor as a gift so that he could make a fan. He made a
fan for himself out of the other one. Later when someone was going off
on a Peace Pipe trading expedition, he would ask Old Bull to give him
the skin and Old Bull would say, "I give it to you. I don't want anything
for it." However, should his enterprise prosper, he would remember the
generosity of his friend, Old Bull, and give him the best horse he had
gotten on the expedition.

Only one or two people were privileged to put eagle feathers around a shield. Some men could make themselves a war bonnet with eagle feathers (the traditional war bonnet of the plains symbolizing a comet). They would buy long white beads in the store and at the base of the throat, wear a big shiny disk about as large as a dollar made out of long black oyster shell.

An indispensable element of ceremonial costuming was the Black Rope made of buffalo hair. Only men could wear these. The process of braiding was very complicated and required great concentration. If a woman came around inclined to converse, the maker would excuse herself and say she had to get through and wasn't able to talk at this time. The work was done in the house and preferably in the fall when less interruptions were likely. Only a few women had the skill to do it. The hair of which the rope was made was from the mane or head of the buffalo. Four twisted strands were braided together into a long rope or belt. Each of the strands for braiding was wound onto a ball, and these balls were manipulated in order to form the braid. Some women did fine even work and some did it poorly and roughly. Working steadily at it, the work took about twelve days. If it had to be fitted in with other work, it would take more time. A woman would come to the belt maker on behalf of her husband and order one, bringing the materials. The maker would be paid well.

There were some few women who could make a colorful braided belt by interweaving five colors. They called it "red-woven." It was a wide flat belt that was made to order to fit the waist of the prospective wearer with long fringes hanging down to the ankles. A belt like this was usually made for boys and girls of good families and for young women. An older woman would not consider it proper to wear one although among the Osage, they were commonly worn by all women. A few men twisted these belts around their heads as a turban with the fringes hanging down on both sides of the face and eagle feathers at the back of the head. Most men regarded this as a "flashy" style of dressing.

The materials used were entirely commercial—wool for the body and cord for the concealed warps. A woman who wanted to have one made for her boy would ask her husband to buy the materials at the trade store so that she could take them to the weaver.

We do not know whether this skill is old or new among the Pawnee. In general, on the American continent, it goes back several thousand years as a fabric-producing technique. But the exclusive use of commercial materials and the reluctance of mature men and women to wear the belt suggests that its adoption is fairly new.

The work was usually done outdoors in the springtime for maximum visibility. It required great concentration and one mistake might compel the weaver to rip the whole thing. If a woman was making one on order, her family would do her spring planting to free her for the work. It took ten days to make a belt along with other housework and the pay was five or six yards of calico, half a sack of dried corn and a slab of dried buffalo meat.

Except for this one last item, all the rest of the Pawnee clothing was made of leather and fur.

49

THE CONSTRUCTION OF

THE TENT COVER

〜〜〜〜〜〜〜〜〜〜〜〜〜〜〜〜

Tents Made by Specialists—the Time Involved and the Payment—the Process of Making the Tent under Old Lady Lucky Leader's Direction

〜〜〜〜〜〜〜〜〜〜〜〜〜〜〜〜

THE BUFFALO-HIDE TENT COVER was a major family possession. It was made of at least eight tanned hides, with sinew from an equal number of buffalo to sew them together. The body of the tent was formed of seven skins and the eighth was cut up for gussets, loops for pegs around the bottom edge, and a double thickness on both sides of the doorway. Twelve years represented the life of a tent, and some of the skins wore out in the meantime and had to be replaced. About three years before the cover was worn out, they would have to think about acquiring the necessary tanned skins. It took at least two years to accumulate the eight skins—a summer and a winter hunt and then again a summer and a winter hunt and in each of the four hunts, two skins were saved for the tent.

In order to cut out the pattern of the skins and give directions for putting them together and sewing them, a specialist had to be called in by the family. Old Lady Lucky Leader, in addition to her many other accomplishments in the Doctor Lodge and as keeper of the Evening Star bundle, was also one of the outstanding tent architects. She would have to cut out the several buffalo skins and fit them together in the most economical way and direct the other women in sewing them together with sinew.

It took four days of steady work for the four women of Victory Call's household to complete the sewing of the cover under the old lady's direction.

But before she could be called in, in addition to having all the necessary materials prepared, they had to get ready the payment for the various services that would be involved. Lady Lucky Leader herself would get a good amount of flour, sugar, coffee, and some calico, and the other women of the household who helped with the sewing were given gifts of calico and special meals were prepared for entertaining them. These items had to be obtained at the trade store in exchange for a tanned buffalo robe. This was prepared by White Woman, and the day before the work was to begin Victory Call and she each mounted a horse and rode over to the store about two miles away, taking the robe with them. The two horses would be needed to bring home the supplies, otherwise White Woman would have walked, Victory Call ridden. At the trade store they got a sack of flour, some coffee, sugar, baking powder, prunes, dry apples, and about five yards of calico. At this time a hundred-pound sack of flour was worth $7.00 at the store. For the family alone without special events or guests, such a sack of flour lasted about two weeks (two double-handfuls for each meal). Amounts of the other items usually bought were fifty cents worth of coffee, fifty cents worth of sugar, twenty-five cents worth of baking powder. Five or six yards of calico were $1.00 so that, excluding the cost of the prunes and dry apples, the gift to Lady Lucky Leader would amount to about $9.25 worth of merchandise. An exceptionally well-tanned buffalo robe would bring $20-30 worth of value at the store. After providing payment for Lady Lucky Leader with the remaining value of the buffalo robe, they had to buy supplies for the special meals—an additional sack of flour, more sugar, coffee, baking powder, and some lard and prunes. Finally to each of the three women of the household that helped with the sewing— Grandma, No Corn, and Old-Lady-Grieves-the-Enemy—they would give five yards of calico to each (worth a dollar for the five yards), and some needles and thread. The buffalo robe would just about cover the labor costs for sewing together the tent.

About a week before the work was to begin, White Woman would have gone to see Lady Lucky Leader and have said to her, "Atira (my mother), I've come to ask you to make a new tent for me." "Well," she answered, "I have something to do right now, but I could do it a little later. Are you in a hurry?" "No, a week's time will be all right." "Well, then, have two good sharp knives ready," said the old lady.

At the appointed day, she arrived at Victory Call's lodge after breakfast. The skins and tools were taken outdoors, and while White Woman cleared up the breakfast dishes, the other three women went out with her and Lady Lucky Leader cut out the skins. She placed them in the most economical manner and then she assigned each of the women a particular seam to sew. Each woman had prepared herself with her own awl and a quantity of prepared sinew. Presently White Woman joined them and was also assigned a seam to sew. Before noon she had to retire to prepare the meal. They were served grease bread, coffee, and prunes. For supper she prepared boiled corn kernels, grease bread, and coffee. After supper, the old lady went home.

The second day the same procedure was followed. When White Woman retired to prepare the meal of grease bread, prunes, and coffee, War Cry and his brother Brave Shield heard that they were having a special meal in Victory Call's house and they proceeded to come in with the remark, "I see you're working here," and were promptly invited to join them for lunch. They would probably stay on talking to Victory Call and also stay for supper. This would make about eighteen people, including the guests for the evening meal. For this group they needed three double handfuls of dried corn kernels (one of these double handfuls represented eight ears of corn). For the eighteen large round disks of fried grease bread, it took three generous double handfuls of store flour (a meal for a family ordinarily required two). If meat were to be served instead of the corn they would need half a sheet of dry buffalo meat cut into long strips 7 inches long and 3½ inches wide. This meat would be boiled with a sheet of fat and served with the soup.

The third day was similar with the Old Lady going home after supper. By the evening of the fourth day the tent was completed. A process mentioned by another Pawnee informant, but not in this account, stated that before the cover was used, girls were sent inside to make a fire so that the skin would get permeated with soot, which would keep it from leaking in the rain or drying up in the sun.

Supper for the evening of the fourth and final day consisted of boiled corn kernels with boiled dried pumpkin strips mixed in. After the Old Lady Lucky Leader had gone home, a half-hour passed and then White Woman and Grandma took the food and goods for her payment. White Woman led the way and Grandma walked behind, carrying the gifts to her house. They set them down before her saying, "Here's flour, coffee, sugar, calico. You helped us with our tent." "Oh, I thank you for giving me this material. My spirit is glad for this food that we will eat," said the old lady. When the two women got home they reported to Victory Call, the old lady's appreciation. Victory Call again went to the store and got the three pieces of calico of five yards each and the needles and thread for the three women of his own household who have helped out—Grandma, Old-Lady-Grieves-the-Enemy, and No Corn.

The tent was now in good order for the winter hunt.

50

OBJECTS OF WOOD
FOR THE HOME

*Women Made the Wood Objects for Home Use
—Scarcity of Wood—Making the Wooden Bowl,
Ladles, Spoons, Mortar, Pestle, Digging Iron, Tent
Pegs, Bracket for Hanging Pots over Fire, Tipi
Poles*

WOMEN WERE THE MAIN MANUFACTURERS of objects made of wood. Not only did they gather the fuel and the building materials, but they also made all the objects of general utility in the household. The men were directly concerned only with those things that were for their own immediate use—their weapons and their ceremonial objects. In no other group that I know of, except among the Woodland Indians, are the women the woodsmen and the woodcrafters to the extent that they were among the Pawnees. Like other lumbermen in the world, Pawnee women would sometimes be killed while felling trees, and a story is told of a woman responsible for another woman's death in such an accident who grieved so deeply that she wandered off never to be seen again.

In the Pawnee prairie plains country, the only place that trees grow is along the streams, and in the distance one can readily identify the rivers and streams by the green belt of trees that grow along their banks. This limited distribution of the trees meant that the women often had to travel considerable distances to get the wood they needed. In 1867 they had to have military protection. How matters stood earlier is not known. They also had the advantage of horse transport. The likelihood is that in the past their dogs had this function and a good deal was packed on their backs, water-floated, or simply dragged over the country. When women went to the woods they took their pack ropes which they also made into a kind of lasso with a stick tied to the end as a weight for pulling down branches from the trees. They took with them their hatchets—the men usually working with axes—and from their present woodworking methods one can only speculate that in the past they felled the trees by a combination of burning, gouging, and scraping.

The utensils and equipment that the women made for the household were all-year round equipment, used both in the earth lodge and on the march. The wooden bowl and the wooden ladles for serving, along with the individual buffalo-horn spoon, were a necessity for every meal, and the mortar and pestle were carried along on the march as well as being in frequent use in the earth lodge for the preparation of meals. The wooden bracket and hook to suspend the pot over the fire were also common equipment in both domestic situations. The forked seven-foot-long *hiku* stick with the sharp fire-hardened point was primarily for making holes in the ground for the tent pegs and for the tipi poles, but it had many other domestic uses particularly as a carrying pole and as a digging iron in general.

The Wooden Bowl. The following are two different accounts, one given by Mark Evarts of the Skidi Band and one by Effie Blane of the Pitahawirata. Evarts gives an estimate of eight days that it took to make the bowl, while Effie Blane cites three days. The different estimate is probably between spare time and full-time work (Weltfish, 1937, pp. 47-48).

There were only six or seven old women among all the Skidi villages who knew how to make these bowls. In Victory Call's family, Grandma knew and in Old Bull's family on the south side of the lodge, Old-Lady-Blue-Calico who had come from Village-in-the-Bottomlands, also knew how. In order to get a bowl made, one had to have a knot ("wood knob") of cottonwood or black post oak that could be taken to the maker. The making took about eight days. Suitable payment for this work was either a combination of half a pumpkin mat and a bag of dried roasted corn kernels about six inches high, or some cutout skins for moccasins and leggings instead.

For a wooden bowl or *rakaraki*, one would select the knot according to the size of the bowl one wanted. After the knot is cut with a sharp hatchet, the woman would begin to chip it from the middle out, and finally while the wood was still damp and not hard she would make a hole on the inner surface of the requisite size. Next she trimmed it all over with a crooked knife, *retsi-pirus*, "knife-crooked," leaving a projection on the rim to be formed into a handle. When the surface was all smooth, she carved the handle called *rak-u-paks-tar-u-kita-ku*, "plate-with-head-plural-up-on top-sitting," the handle being toothed on top. After the carving was done, it was scraped and polished until it was a beautiful bowl. Then it was well greased. Several bowls were made at the same time. A bowl took at least three days to make.

The bowl for individual service at meals was estimated to be about 15 inches in diameter and 3 inches deep.

Ladles and Spoons. Larger wooden spoons or ladles were made for serving at feasts, and while I have no description, they were probably carved with the crooked knife like the bowl.

The spoons used for individual eating and the daily serving spoon were of buffalo horn. (See Figure 50-1.) The buffalo-horn spoon was called *taraha-ariki,* "buffalo-horn." Buffalo horns were kept on hand so that the spoons could be made at any time. Spring was the time most preferred as they all especially like to eat soup while on the summer hunt. Practically everyone knew how to make buffalo-horn spoons. In the period from nine o'clock in the morning until noon—three hours—one could make four spoons. The following is a free translation of the account of their manufacture by Effie Blane of the Pitahawirata Band (Weltfish, 1937, pp. 59-61).

FIGURE 50-1. Buffalo-horn spoon for ordinary use. When not being used the spoons were kept strung in sets. The ordinary eating spoons are 5 inches long with a bowl diameter of 3 inches. Large serving spoons are 8 inches long, the bowl being 4½ inches in diameter and 1½ inches in depth. (The dimensions and the drawings were supplied by informants.)

Buffalo horns were placed near the fire with the large ends extending into the coals. The heat softened the horn so that it could be more readily worked. The horn was expanded by pressing the foot on it. Then the small end was notched and scraped and the whole thing greased. When several were finished, holes were bored into the handles and they were strung on a buckskin string to be hung up when out of use.

The Mortar, kitutu. To make the mortar, they cut down an elm tree about a foot in diameter and cut off a section about 2 feet high. The small end was whittled to a point so that it could be stuck upright in the ground. In the broader end of the section, they formed a pit by charring the surface with hot coals and then scraping out the charred wood. The first step in this process was to coat the rim with wet clay so that it didn't burn. Then they put the hot coals in the center, turning the surface toward the direction from which the wind was coming to keep the coals glowing. Now they dumped out the coals and scraped away the charred wood with an oyster (?) shell (probably fresh-water clam). Again they put in hot coals, and again they scraped away the charred wood with the shell, and they repeated this process until the pit was deep enough. While the coals were inside, one had to keep them carefully scattered about so that they didn't burn the surface too unevenly. The pit was somewhat paraboloid in cross section, or a blunt-pointed V-shape. After the final scraping on the inside, "the foot" was scraped and the wet mud from around the rim removed. The mortar was now ready for use in pounding corn or, more occasionally, dry buffalo meat.

It took about five days to make a mortar along with the ordinary housework.

The Pestle, iks-ka-wi-itsa-ku, "hand-upon-sitting-on the end or point-sitting." When the mortar was completed, they would say, "Now the pestle." A search of the thicket was made to find a post oak with a large body. A tree with many limbs was preferred because then the top end of the pestle would be sturdy enough to stand the strain of the pounding. The tree was cut as close to the roots as possible so that the grain of the roots would be contained in the pounding end for toughness. The pestle was about 4 feet long. After the tree was felled, they smoothed it with an ax. The wood was seasoned in the fire and finished off by scraping with an oyster shell until it was very smooth.

Suitable pay for a woman's services in making a mortar was 5 yards of calico, and for the pestle, some dried corn; or alternatively, for the mortar a blanket and corn, or corn and some checker plaited strips of stomach lining (*pararitskusu*), and for the pestle, 5 yards of calico. "Something for the person to wear and something for the family to eat."

The Hiku Stick or "Digging iron." This was a stick 7 feet long and about 2½ inches in diameter, forked at one end and with a fire-hardened point at the other. It was grasped in the middle and thrust into the ground to make holes for the tent pegs and for the tipi poles. The fall was the time for making the *hiku* stick before setting out on the winter hunt. Every woman young or old knew how to prepare one, and it took about a day to do so. The wood was taken green, the bark removed with an ax, and the bottom end sharpened to a point. Then the stick was seasoned in the fire. A small fire was made outdoors and the stick passed through it, turning it over and over so that it was a little charred in places. These charred places were scraped off with another stick. The stick was now left leaning against the lodge outside for at least a week, so that it could dry out. Sometimes it was taken in and put out a second time. When it was finally ready for use, all the moisture had evaporated and it was light to carry but very strong.

The making of *tent pegs* of dogwood saplings has been described in connection with the rendezvous camp of the summer hunt. They might alternatively be made in the earth lodge before setting out, tied up in a set and carried along.

The Bracket for Hanging the Pot over the Fire. This was only needed in the earth lodge and on the winter hunt as its purpose was to suspend the pot over the hot flame of the fireplace. Such a hot flame was made for light and heat as well as for cooking only in the excavated circular basin-shaped fireplace, the earth lodge, and the pointed tipi. On the summer hunt with the open curve-roofed tent, a long rectangular fireplace was made outside to the north of the doorway and oriented north–south. In this long trenchlike arrangement, a log was kept smoldering and the pot was set directly on the coals, so that the bracket and hook were not needed. The bracket consisted of two parts—a more or less vertical post, forked at the top and pointed at the bottom so that it could be inserted in the ground, and a wooden hook suspended from one arm of the fork by a string of bison rawhide that could be wound around the arm so that the pot that was suspended from the hook could hang closer or further away from the flames. The vertical post was driven into the ground due east of the fireplace at a slant so that the hook hung directly over the fire, or else a trunk was chosen for the bracket that had a natural curvature. The process of treating and seasoning the vertical bracket was the same as for the *hiku* stick.

Tipi Poles. The conical pointed tent or tipi was used by the Pawnees only for their winter migration. The same tent skin was used as for the summer, but the wooden frame was different. The frame of the summer tent comprised a rack of two forked sticks at the front with a horizontal between, and, outlining a semiellipse, a series of flexible saplings stuck in the ground that were drawn down onto the rack and fastened there to form the characteristic curved roof. The Pawnee name for this summer tent was *kax-kata-sa,* "dwelling-upon-lying." The frame for the conical-pointed tipi was based on a tripod of rather heavy poles more than 15 feet long and made from trees 6 to 7 inches in diameter before removing the bark. Once the tripod was set up and a fourth stick added for the entrance, the other poles of equal thickness were leaned against it all around. The tipi was called *kax-ta-pe,* "dwelling-against-leaning," or *kar-rats-a-pe,* "dwelling-they-against-leaning." The tipi might be 18 feet in diameter, and the round excavated fireplace in the center and the shape and insulation of the walls made it warm in winter. The life of a set of tipi poles was five to seven years, and within that interval three or four of them were likely to bend or weaken and have to be replaced. They used cottonwood, which was light and easy to carry, and as an alternative, cedar, which was also rather light. The best supply was on Grand Island in the Platte and the best time to gather these was on the return journey from the winter hunt.

The first task was to select the trees which should be 6 to 7 inches in diameter as they stood with the bark on. From their encampment on the island, Victory Call, White Woman, and Horse Rider would go into the timber, and when Victory Call had selected his first tree he would start to cut it down with the ax. When Horse Rider would come up, he would say, "Let me do that," and take the ax and cut it down in his place. Victory Call now went further to select the other trees and Horse Rider followed cutting each one down in turn. Now White Woman got to work on the felled trees, cutting off the boughs and branches with her hatchet so that the bare trunk was left with the bark on.

Now Horse Rider began to drag in the bare trunks to camp, while Victory Call cut down the fourth tree that they needed and White Woman got to work lopping off the branches. Victory Call now pulled in the fourth trunk, returning to camp with White Woman. With a good sharp ax this operation had taken them a total of half an hour for all four trunks.

Back at camp, they removed the bark and this took a good deal longer. If one person worked at it alone, it took two to three hours to remove the bark from one trunk of this kind. Two people working together on one tree could do it in about an hour and a half. While White Woman worked from the bottom upward with the hatchet, the other person could work near the top end using a knife, because the bark is softer near the top. It sometimes happened that White Woman was able to make a convenient flap near the bottom, ripping off a strip of bark up the whole length. Horse Rider or Grandma might be free to give White Woman a hand at this work. After the bark was off, the whole stick had to be roasted. All four were first debarked and then all four roasted at the same time. A little fire was made outdoors and each stick turned around in it until the whole length was roasted. To roast the four sticks in this way took about an hour and a half. Now they were left to cool and the ashes and burnt places rubbed over with a stick to remove loose cinders. The next step was to even their length. The stub ends had been sharpened to points, and these were placed together and the heads all cut off to the same length to make them even.

The new tipi poles were now tied together and transported back to the earth lodge where, tied together tight, they were fastened to the ceiling to season until the next hunt. When they were in use, the thin ends of the poles would rest on the ground and the thicker end stand upward. Holes were drilled near the top in the thick end so that they could be tied together with rope, particularly for transport.

51

THINGS OF WOOD

MADE BY MAN

〰〰〰〰〰〰〰〰〰〰〰〰〰〰〰

The Bow—the Bowstring—the Arrow—the Pipe-stems—the Stone Bowl—the Individual Styles of Bowls

〰〰〰〰〰〰〰〰〰〰〰〰〰〰〰

THE MEN MADE THE BOWS, arrowshafts, pipestems, and cottonwood water drums.

The Bow. In the past the Osage Orange (*Toxylon pomiferum*) was the most highly valued wood for bows. At this time they used ash (*Fraxinus pennsylvanica*) known as *kirik-taka*, "eye-white." Every man made his own bow, though some were more and some less skilled. Little boys also made bows of ashwood to shoot birds. Ashwood was best gathered in the fall, generally in October before they left on the winter hunt. The ashwood saplings were left sticking among the willows in the ceiling to season, until they got back in the spring.

It took two days to make a bow. By splitting it in two down the length, two bows could be made from one sapling, unless it were not quite straight, when only one could be made. In each case, the outer surface of the tree became the outer surface of the bow.

The shaping was done by heating the stick in the coals until it was warm throughout and pliable. Putting the foot on the middle of the outside surface, the two ends were drawn very gently upward, and then each end was recurved with the foot so that the bow had a wide shallow dent in its back. The sinew bowstring was fastened to one end permanently, and at the other there was a series of notches in the bow so that the string could be tightened when in use and loosened at other times. (See Figure 51-1.)

Once, after Victory Call had died, Otter's adoptive father caught a panther and decided to honor the boy by making him a quiver of it. Not to be outdone, another man made him a sinew-backed bow. It was known as *atskats-tax-ka-sa*, "sinew-plural-between-lying." It was mentioned at times, but seldom actually made.

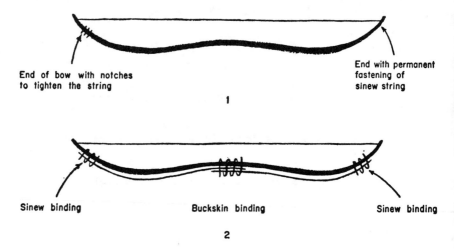

FIGURE 51-1. (1) A simple bow of ashwood. (2) A sinew-backed bow, *tskatstaxkasa*. Two pieces of sinew, crossed at the middle could be permanently pasted on when wet.

Two pieces of sinew, crossed at the middle were placed on the back of the bow when wet and could thus be pasted on permanently. The sinew was bound on in the middle by overcasting with buckskin and at both ends with a wrapping of sinew. Then the bow was colored black. It was easy to draw and could shoot far.

The Bowstring of Sinew. Every man made his own bowstring out of sinew. The first step was to soak the short pieces of sinew overnight. The next step was joining them, first by taking two of the short strands and overlapping their ends and giving them a preliminary twist between the fingers and then continuing the twist by rolling them on the thigh with the palm. Then they added the next piece in the same way, and so on until one long continuous string was formed.

Then they doubled over the string and began to twist it together, beginning with the loose ends, first between the fingers and then on the thigh. The twist was held by winding it on a stick a little thicker than a pencil—the string being wound on as the stick was turned in the direction away from the body. When one section of the string had been twisted and wound on the stick, they would proceed to twist and wind on the next section until the entire length was completed. The twisting of a bowstring took a morning and an afternoon.

When the entire string was wound onto the stick, the string would be stretched between two short stakes that were driven into the ground the requisite distance apart and the ends of the bowstring were fastened firmly to them. The string was left to dry for the rest of the afternoon until the dew came up in the evening. Then it had to be taken inside and again stretched outdoors the next day. It was well to fasten it up high out of the way of the dogs, who might eat it up.

The Making of Arrowshafts. Five arrow makers comprised the official body responsible for making all the arrowshafts used by the entire Skidi Band. They kept track of the needs of all the men and saw that they were met. None of the other technical industries, even those in which only a limited number of individuals were skilled, were of this public character. Just before leaving for the summer and for the winter hunts, they accelerated their activities. The arrow makers themselves saw to it that they had plenty of dogwood sticks on hand and kept on making the shafts, sometimes on special order, but often to have them on hand when called for. In almost all other crafts, the customer provided the materials and contracted only for the skilled services of the craftsman.

The following is paraphrased from an account given in my Caddoan Texts by Effie Blane:

The man making ready to fashion arrowshafts, will first get some needed materials together. He will assemble: a stick with a hide wound around it which has been boiled down to a gummy consistency to be used as a paste; two flat stones each with a long groove, used to abraid the stick by putting the stones together and pulling the stick back and forth in the groove (*rax-ka'is,* "going-between within," buffers); the bone shaft-straightener, *kis-kats,* "bone-very white"; also *rasats,* possibly pieces of split bone with the rough spongy inner surface exposed to smooth the surface (or a pulverized plant?).

These materials being ready, the man went into the timber and gathered some dogwood twigs. He then took them home and peeled off the bark (with a knife). Now he hung the debarked twigs over the fire from the bracket east of the fireplace on which the pot ordinarily hangs, so that the twigs could season and dry in the smoke of the fire. They were left there to smoke overnight and in the morning they were removed and each twig was "eyed up and down" to find any bumps or irregularities, which were removed with the *rasats* abrasive.

The next step was to attach the feathers to the blunt end. Turkey feathers were best because they tore straight, but turkey was hard to get, and if you didn't have them you used buzzard. While he was splitting the feather, he was chewing some sinew so that it would be soft enough to bind on the feathers. The three splints of feather were placed against the arrow and tied with the wet sinew. The feathered end of the arrow was then smeared with the gummy paste made of boiled hide and the feathers bent onto the stick and pasted down and tied in place with some more wet sinew at their lower end.

After the feathers were in place, the shafts were buffed by passing them between the two grooved sandstone buffers that were pressed together—the arrow being turned back and forth so that it was well rounded.

The next process was the use of the bone arrowshaft straightener that was a little bit like a fork. [Archaeological specimens from the Hill site of 1806 are pieces of bison rib with holes of different sizes drilled through them. In recent times, a tin can punched with holes was sometimes substituted.]

After straightening, downy feathers were fastened on at the lower end of the feathers that had already been attached.

The final step was to split the end for inserting the point. After the point was inserted, the end was bound with sinew to make it fast. Different kinds of shafts were called "black-lying-on," "red-lying-on," referring to the colors of the feathers.

The Pipestem. Next to the bow and arrow, the pipe was one of the most significant things the man used. The pipe was smoked both for relaxation and in every ceremony. The stem was symbolic of the human windpipe and the breath was considered the essence of life itself. *Tsiksu,* the word for "throat," was also the verb stem for "to think, to feel," *-atsiks-*. In the ceremony of the Peace Pipe, the main emblems were the two pipestems, a bowl from a sacred bundle being attached to one of them and smoked in the course of the ceremony. The pipestems were decorated with eagle feathers and other ceremonial insignia—one with the feathers of the brown eagle, signifying "night," "female," "fruitfulness" and known as *ra-hak-katitu,* "one-mouth-black"; and the other with feathers of the white eagle, signifying "day," "male," "defense," "war" and called *ra-hak-takaru,* "one-mouth-white." At various stages in the ceremony these were waved about so that they symbolized the flight of the eagles. The pipestems were ceremonially fashioned after instructions from the priests. He sent two men to bring in two sticks of ash, and as they sat east of the fireplace they prepared the sticks, warming them over the fire so that they could be straightened and cut to length, viz., four spans from thumb to third finger. The stems were peeled, scraped, and the pith removed by boring them from end to end with a reed so that the breath could pass through unobstructed. The pith was then burned out with a wire. The men cut a straight groove the entire length of each stick to represent the lifeline. Finally all scrapings and every particle of ashwood was placed carefully on the fire, and as the flame rose the two sticks were passed through the blaze so that the word of the fire might enter and be with them.

For personal use a man would go to one of the six or seven men who were the only ones that could make them among all the Skidi. An order for a pipe included both the wooden stem and the stone bowl. As usual, the materials had to be assembled by the man who wanted the pipe and taken to the maker. When he placed his order, he was sent to get the necessary ashwood stick. The stone for the bowl was Catlinite or red pipestone from the famous pipestone quarry in the extreme southwestern part of Minnesota, located northeast of Pawnee territory. When men went out on the warpath stealing horses in this vicinity, they were likely to get as much of the stone as they could carry. Nearer home there was a green rock (serpentine?) that could be used; it was soft and was blackened by the maker while the other kind was left red. A man who wanted to order a pipe made had to go to someone who had gotten it in this way:

He would say, "I want you to give me a stone for a pipe." When the warrior gave his consent, the man went home and waited and presently the warrior sent his wife with the block of stone to give to the man's wife. The wife of the warrior now returns home, having accomplished her mission. The man ordering the pipe, not wanting to take the stone for nothing, sends his wife to the home of the warrior with twenty arrows, a blanket and she adds some buffalo meat. She now sets out for the warrior's house and approaching his wife she says, "This is for your husband. He gave us that pipe." The warrior's wife demurs, saying, "Oh, don't do that." "Yes, keep it. It's for your husband." The warrior's family now enjoys eating the gift of dry meat and they put the arrows and the blanket up on the wall. Later on when the two men meet, the warrior says to the man who is ordering the pipe, "What did you do that for? I didn't want anything for the stone." "Oh, that's all right. I wanted you to have something for it." "Well, all right, thank you," says the warrior, "We ate it!"

With the stone in hand, the man would now go to the pipe maker whose work he considered best and speak to him about it. Each pipe maker had his own distinctive way of making a pipe and one would either come with his own specifications or simply accept the style of the pipe maker himself. The man would say, "With a horse on it," etc., or "I want just a plain pipe," in which case it would be made in the maker's style. Two alternative kinds were one with rings (like a windpipe) or one with a flat part on the half below the mouthpiece, then a thick ring of wood and the rest of the length round to the bowl end. Kind Warrior who was a leader of the Deer Dance, *Raris-ta*, had a pipestem with half the length from the bowl end to the middle flat, and three ridges from the middle up to the mouthpiece. This was something like the ridges on an arrow where the feathers were to be attached and may have had some symbolic reference connected with this. Some men ordered their stone pipe bowls to be made with five ridges to denote that they had sacrificed five buffalo, others three. A man who had a horse head carved on his pipe might do this to indicate that he gives away a lot of horses. On the other hand some people just had things put on their pipes "to be fancy."

To hollow out the wooden stem they burned out the pith with the same stiff weed used in making brooms, *kihax-piriwus*, "room-brusher," *Artemisia dracunculoides* Pursh., or fuzzy weed. The plant had a pleasant odor like sage which is also a variety of *Artemisia*. The weed was sharp and after the pith had been burned all the way through down the length,

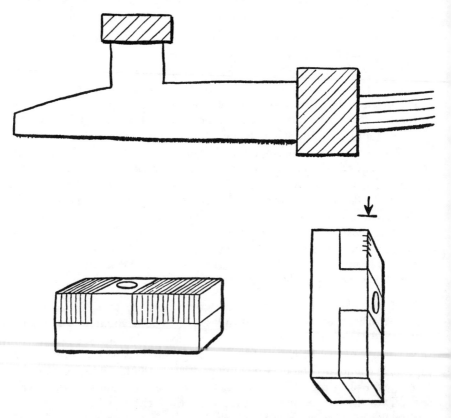

FIGURE 51-2. A pipe made by Brave Horse, *Asa-rahikutsu*, the bowl of red Catlinite or pipestone and the stem of ashwood. The first step of the pipemaker in fashioning the bowl was the marking off of the block with charcoal so that he could sculpt the bowl in the rough. Next the two blocks, one in front and one behind the bowl, were removed (hatched areas). In the old days this was a laborious task. There were no metal drills, files, or rasps; the two blocks of stone were chipped off from the outer edges inward piece by piece by sawing back and forth with a flint knife.

the same weed was used to scrape out the inside. Then the man blew through the stem to remove the small pieces from the inside.

Making the Stone Bowl of Catlinite or Red Pipestone. (See Figure 51-2.) A block of stone of the appropriate size was marked off with charcoal so that the bowl could be sculptured out in the rough. Two blocks of stone had to be removed, one in front and one behind the upward projecting bowl. The removal of these two blocks was a laborious task. When no metal drills, files, or rasps were available, each step took a long time and required a great deal of patience. In the old days to remove the two blocks of stone, the "pipe" was set up on end and a flint knife was sawed back and forth across the corner, making a shallow cut. Then a second cut was made underneath it until a series of three or four shallow cuts had been made one beneath the other. These "corners" were then chipped off from the top edge down. This operation of chiseling off small pieces was continued until the whole block had been removed. Then the second block on the other side of the bowl was removed. All red powder resulting from the sawing process was saved to be used as red paint.

The bore for the stem as well as for the bowl was begun by using a well-dried, fire-hardened stick. The stick was held stable pressed onto the surface where the hole was to be and the stone turned back and forth until a hole had been dug into it. The bowl was widened and deepened by using a sharp sliver of a buffalo femur in the same way, pressing it into the stone and twisting the stone itself until the bowl was the shape and size desired. The outer surfaces were shaped by rubbing with a rough stone.

After the bowl was shaped, the pipe was passed through the smoke of a small grass fire and the surface rubbed with grease. This data on making the stone bowl is condensed from a demonstration by Charles Allen at Pawnee, Oklahoma, in 1935. It took almost eight days, working the usual day of nine to five o'clock with an hour for lunch.

Each pipe maker introduced special features of his own. Rarawikita, Charles Allen's father, made them so that there was a hump on the bowl near where the stem was inserted and the pointed end of the bowl was five-sided. Chief's Road made pipes with three raised ridges around the head end of the bowl where the stem was to be inserted. Sometimes the pointed end was cut down at a downward slant, sometimes it was cut straight off. Good Bear made a pipe that was thick where the bowl was and tapered markedly at the point end and again at the end where the stem fitted. Brave Horse (*Asa-rahikuts*, "horse-brave") would make a wide ridge or collar around the mouth of the bowl and another one at the opening where the stem fitted in; on these "collars" he engraved diagonals trending upward toward the left. He was a left-handed man.

For the work of manufacturing the pipe, pay was expected though never stipulated. This might be tobacco or calico and a little food. For example about a quarter's worth or one block of tobacco, six yards of calico, and half a braided intestine mat were considered reasonable compensation. Sometimes a generous man would give a man who made a pipe for him a blanket that was used but not too old and still good enough to wear. This would be considered sufficient in itself. Or he might give some broadcloth along with a belt instead.

52

OBJECTS MADE
FOR RECREATION

〰〰〰〰〰〰〰〰〰〰〰〰〰〰〰

*Gambling among the Pawnees—the Hand Game
—the Religious Symbolism in the Games—the
Basic Equipment for the Game—the Game as
Played by Different Ages—the Plum Seed Game
of the Women*

〰〰〰〰〰〰〰〰〰〰〰〰〰〰〰

GAMBLING WAS A MAIN RECREATION for some Pawnees and an occasional one for others. It was recognized that habitual gambling was a compulsion that should be avoided as a psychologically destructive trait, and Old-Man-That-Chief could often be heard to give advice on how to regulate one's conduct to keep this impulse under control. He especially exhorted the chiefs to set a good example to the rest of the people. He would talk to the chiefs in the following way:

"You men are chiefs. It is a chief's place to talk to his people. You shouldn't gamble. You should set the people a good example. Having told the people that gambling is bad, if you gamble yourself, a boy of rough temperament will say to himself, 'There is my chief and he is gambling. There is no reason why I shouldn't gamble too.' Moreover, a gambling place is a fighting place and you might get involved in a fight and a man of low class might strike you. It would be a shame if some outsider were to hit you in the head and there would be blood all over your face. Then someone would say, 'Look at the chief with blood all over his face!' That would look bad.

"If you gamble you'll lose everything you have, perhaps even your wife's clothes. Then you'll have nothing. And another thing, if your wife sees you gambling she'll think, 'I can bet my clothes too,' and she'll go to the place where the women are playing the plum seed game.

397

Then if you're both gambling, who will cook for you? Who will take care of you?

"If you want to, go ahead. But at first you'll be lucky and then the sticks will try to draw you in. Then when they have you, you'll lose.

"If you want to, go ahead. But if you are lucky, just play for a month. Then leave it because your luck must change.

"If you have lost and want to retrieve your losses, do it and when you have won back what you lost, stop gambling."

The hand game was played by young men ranged along both sides of a trenchlike fireplace with a smoldering log in it. Facing each other on the opposite sides of the fire were "two opposing war parties." The crux of the game was the hiding of a white bead in the hands of a member of one party with the guesser from the other side trying to determine in which hand it was hidden. War songs were sung and in the motioning of the hands of the line in which the bead was hidden, the bead might be transferred by sleight of hand during the guessing. That-Chief also mentioned the hand game, addressing his remarks especially to Otter. Evarts observed that:

"At hand game you might bet your shirt and when the other fellow wins, you might not want to give up your shirt. Then he would get angry and tear at your shirt and he might even take a stick from the fire and burn your head. That would be the worst thing. Once I was in a game and I was the loser to Jim Murie. There I learned the real meaning of That-Chief's advice. Osborne was on the winning side and he began to brag saying, 'Look at those fellows. They can't do much.' Then he made disparaging remarks about my cousin, Sam Townsend, that I call child, *piirau*. Then I really got angry. I felt particularly sensitive as I had lost my leggings, my moccasins and many other things. I said, 'I can't stand all that talk,' and I took a stick from the fire and hit him. The coals flopped all over his head and I was about to hit him again, when they stopped me. To avoid further trouble, they sent Osborne home saying to him, 'You're the cause of the trouble. You talked too much.'"

However, there was quite a different aspect to these games that was implicit in their religious symbolism, with the gambling an extraneous feature. The rolling of the hoop along the long game grounds and aiming at it with the stick or "spear" was an act of sympathetic magic both for the increase of the buffalo and for the successful outcome of the buffalo hunt. Originally the game was played for the direct purpose of calling the buffalo, and when they were out on the summer buffalo hunt, wherever they could find a smooth patch of grass, they would set up a game. In the village, it was a major leisure-time preoccupation of men of all ages. Every village had one or two well-worn tracks. The gaming ground was the place where men would meet informally to transact most of their social, commercial, and political business. The formality of entertaining at home imposed more constraints and was commonly reserved for the more advanced stages of negotiations.

The basic paraphernalia for the game comprised a long "spear" and a hoop which was rolled down the long track and at which the spear was aimed as the men ran alongside.

The smallest boys began with a plain hoop, *tawirus*, "wheel," made for them by their grandmothers. The wheel was made of a peeled ashwood stick formed into a ring and tied at the ends. It was then entirely wrapped with a rawhide string and greased with buffalo fat so that it would not harden. It is not clear whether the boys shot at the wheel with arrows as told in a myth, or simply threw a pole or "lance" at it.

The second grade for young men was played with a wheel of small size—the *tawirus-pitku-sukita*, "wheel-two-upon." It is not clear whether the basis of this wheel was of wood or several coils of rawhide as for the succeeding grade. The base was completely wrapped with a strip of buckskin. The rings were supposed to represent a buffalo cow and were to be made of the skin of the vulva of the buffalo. The fore end of the stick was carved with a kind of knob to signify the penis of a buffalo. These aspects of the symbolism are recounted in a tale of how Coyote rescues a maiden who has been captured by the buffalo and taken to their village and turned into a gaming ring. In the course of the story, the play of the game is described:

Coyote is sitting in the buffalo village as a spectator of the game at the north end of the gaming ground. The two buffalo now arise, one of them taking the ring. (The ground is about 60 paces long, 15 wide and runs in a north–south direction in the length.) The players begin to run at the south end and when they get to about the middle, the one holding the ring rolls it toward the north, releasing it from between his thumb and forefinger and changing his spear from his left to his right hand. The two players now aim simultaneously at the rolling hoop so that the spears glide along the ground and overtake it, the best score being made by catching the ring with one of the small hooks near the hand end of the spear. Other points were gained by hooking with the end of the stick one of the cross pieces near the handle end or the large hook. It often happened that the spear did not catch the hoop at all and then points were calculated by the position of the spear with relation to the hoop—measurements being taken with a straw by someone who acted as umpire.

When the two players have reached the north end of the grounds, they picked up the ring and the sticks and started for the south end, rolling the ring as before and throwing the spears to score. Each set of players played the field once toward the north and once toward the south and then two other players got up and played their round.

The paraphernalia of *the mature men* differed from that of the youths in the size of the ring and in the complexity of the spear. The ring of the youths was about 8 inches in diameter, probably built on a wooden hoop wrapped in buckskin, while the mature men used a very small hoop, 4 inches in diameter, with strips of rawhide as a base, wrapped around with the buckskin string. The mature men's wheel was called, *ks-tats-awi-katus*, "hand-down-hanging-flat." The spear was about 5½ feet long. The pole was completely wound around with a strip of buckskin and at the hand end there was a large hook completely wrapped around with the same material. The shaft was slightly tapered from the hand end to the point. About three-eighths of the length in from the point the shaft was somewhat flattened and a cross piece was lashed onto it with a small hook fastened on top in the lashings. A similar cross piece with hook was fastened about one-eighth way in from the point end. It was with these small hooks that they aimed to catch onto the hoop or else with the ends of the cross pieces. The shaft used by the youths was plain wood with a knob on the end to represent the bison penis. At the hand end were fastened two hooks wrapped around with buckskin.

There was a game *played by old men* with a very large hoop (possibly 25 inches in diameter) with no spear. The hoop itself was rolled and aimed at one of the players of the opposing side as a kind of tag. The players lined up along both sides of the grounds and when the player had rolled the wheel and it struck one of the men standing on the opposing side to his, the man who was hit would spread his blanket and begin to run, while the other man pursued him. If he stumbled and tripped on his blanket, he would be caught and would then have to roll the hoop and try to tag a man of the other side. If the pursuer stumbled, he would have to roll the hoop again. The special play of the game was called *kiskiru'*.

The wheel itself was called *ka-huraru*, literally, inside-land or "land of inside" which in Pawnee referred to the universe. The circumference of the wheel represented the horizon and it was marked off into twelve sections with bunches of feathers that were fastened on at equal intervals. Each section represented a thirty-day lunar month of the twelve-month year. The four seasons of the year were marked off on the hoop by different colors for each quarter-arc. The winter quarter was white, the spring quarter light green, the summer quarter darker green, and the autumn, reddish-yellow. The universe was conceived as having a flat base and rotating around the motionless earth, the progression of the seasons resulting from this rotation. This had been inferred from the fact that the stars and the planets appear to have changed their positions with the seasons. Across the diameter was stretched a string of buckskin or sinew with a white bead in the middle. The string represented the Milky Way and the bead the earth. Certain men liked to play this game when they came in from buffalo hunting and each could make his own wheel. No gambling accompanied this game.

The large wheel took about two days to make. The hoop was made of a ·bent sapling, the ends being crossed over for a short distance where they joined. The buckskin thong was fastened from this joining to the opposite side of the diameter to represent the Milky Way with the white bead in the middle for the earth. A wrapping of otter fur was wrapped around the joining of the hoop and at the opposite side and also marking off the boundaries of the other two quarter-arcs. Twenty-four feathers and bunches of feathers were tied with thongs at equidistant intervals around the circumference, twelve on each half. Each sector carried one of the regular moon or month names. The men also made a water drum of a hollow cottonwood log.

The most popular game of the women was a game in which a series of marked dice made of plum seeds were tossed up in a shallow coiled basket made of willow. This too had cosmic significance, for the basket represented the container ordained by Heaven during the creation to carry the earth from which the world was created and contained the germs of life. In the spring time during the ground-breaking ceremony immediately preceding the planting known as *awari*, "vigorous movement" or "living," two coiled baskets were used that had been especially made by the wife or sister of the minister under his direction. The women moved the baskets gently back and forth through the air in the course of the ceremony. At the creation, Heaven caused this basket to move of itself through space.

There were only eight or ten women among all the Skidi Band who knew how to make these coiled gambling baskets. They were made of willow twigs, and a woman who wanted one made consulted with the craftswoman who told her what kind of willow twigs to get in such and such a condition at the edge of the creek. The making took from two or three days and the woman received the usual combination of something to wear and something to eat for her services—five yards of calico and some corn, or half an intestine mat and skin cut out and ready to be sewn into moccasins. The old ladies who made these baskets were usually the ones who liked to gamble. Some women expressed scruples about learning to make them as they felt they would be encouraging gambling. There were a number of inveterate gamblers among the women, and the betting was heavy. Others managed to keep their gaming to a casual pastime. The woman who made the basket was usually asked to make the plum seed dice although any woman could make them. She was asked to rub them and to hope that her customer had good luck.

When the woman had gathered the willow twigs, she took them to the craftswoman who left some of them to season for two days. The technique for the manufacture of the basket was coiling. The basket had a flat bottom with shallow walls. It was round and there were two basic elements used in the coiled sewing. There was a foundation element of a whole peeled willow twig that was carried around spirally for ten courses. These several courses of the spiral were overcast with flat strips of willow to hold them together. The awl was used in the sewing, the overcasting being done from the inner or convex surface. The stitches of the successive coils were made to interlock with one another. To make the flat sewing strips, the willow twig was split in the length, and an inner section bearing the pith was split away from each long section to make it flexible for the binding. Sometimes the bark was left on these strips and sometimes it was removed.

With all their equipment made and repaired, the Pawnees were ready to set out once more on their long migration to the buffalo hunting grounds.

53

PRODUCTS OF REEDS
AND GRASS

~~~~~~

*The Twined Woven Mats, Their Use and Manu-
facture—the Grass Brush for the Care of Hair*

~~~~~~

THE REEDS AND GRASSES matured about the same time as the cultivated
crops, and everyone knew that as soon as possible after completing the
harvest they would have to get to work gathering these materials before
they passed their prime.

The twined woven mat of reeds was one of the most important items
of Pawnee house furnishing. It was considered indispensable to cleanli-
ness, and only the poorest people or the most slovenly would use skins on
the ground instead. They were used both in the lodge and on the
march, and old mats were offered to people who had none. Every morning they were taken up and shaken to get the dust out; in the lodge the
house was well swept and the sweepings carried out on a skin to be
dumped at the base of the embankment before the mats would be replaced on the floor. When on the march, they were rolled up and tied
in the middle with a string fastened there for the purpose by the women.
When camp was set up, they were laid out to sit on; at night the beds
were made on them. In the lodge they were placed inside the central
pillars to sit on. Impromptu beds were made by putting them between
the pillars at night as a base for the bedding. Each mat was 5 feet wide
and 8 to 9 feet long. Ordinarily, there were two mats around the fireplace
on each side; if there were special guests, an additional one was placed at
the west. At a large feast, the mats were laid outside the house pillars
against the beds to enlarge the circle. Mats for gala occasions had special
decorations made by weaving in black or dark red-dyed wefts. These
were kept rolled up until guests came. For everyday use the family sat on
whatever mats happened to be around—the better ones being placed

nearer the west and those that were more worn, east toward the exit.

When a couple was newly married, they were always given a set of mats—two for each side of the house and one for the west. They were likely to get two from the girl's grandmother and two from the boy's. Except in such intimate circumstances, the mats were not ordinarily considered suitable gift items. They were regarded more as we look upon linens—particularly bedsheets and towels. Suitable gift items on the other hand were, from man to a man, a horse, and from a woman to a man, leggings, moccasins, material for moccasins, or dried buffalo meat.

The mats received the heaviest wear during the winter hunt, when they got all battered and broken up. In the fall, after the materials were gathered they were placed in the roof of the lodge to season all winter. In the spring, between planting and cultivating, they would feel they had to make some new mats to take along on the summer hunt. Old mats were left behind in the earth lodge.

The warp strands of the mat were of a three-sided prismatic grass that grew in ponds (not cattail?). The long blades were made into a double-twisted continuous rope of four strands.

The wefts were of bulrush (*Scirpus validus* Vahl.), a round tubular grass, spongy inside, 5 to 6 feet long. An alternative material was cattail (*Typha latifolia* L.). Both these reeds grew in the bottomlands of the streams, particularly along the Loup, but there were also a few patches along Beaver Creek. On the way home from the summer hunt, some people would gather the reeds on the Republican or the Loup and load the horses and bring them home. Or, noting good locations on the way home, they would return later.

Sometimes two old ladies would go out together and gather whatever small patches they could find on Beaver Creek, pulling up the reeds and piling them into two bundles about a foot in diameter. They would tie them up with ropes and each bring one in and go out again for more, obtaining about four bundles each in this way. The reeds were very heavy when green and a woman could not carry very much at a time. For larger supplies, the family would make up a combined expedition, since they had to go three to five miles from the village. A large party of men and women would ride out on their horses to the sources of supply they had spotted when returning from the hunt. The men went out to give the women protection. On the way back the horses were loaded with reeds. When one party went out, others would hear about it and be inspired to follow their example.

The weft or (crosswise) threads needed very little preparation to be ready for use. They had simply to be soaked in water overnight and then taken out and left to dry for about half an hour before weaving.

The long continuous lengthwise warp required considerably more preparation than the weft. The three-sided prismatic grass was soaked all night in water, and in the morning it was twisted into a continuous string which was wound onto a stick as the woman went along. When it was all wound on, it formed a cylindrical roll like a bale of wire. Each roll contained enough warp for one mat. The work was done by one woman working alone. For example, Grandma would put the stick between her toes while twisting the warp and then wrap it onto the stick as the string got longer. The roll was put away for a week or two to set before it was used for the weaving. It took an old woman a day and a half to twist the warp for one mat.

The weaving frame was set up at a slant, the far end being considerably higher than the near end. The warp beam at the far end was 2 to 2½ feet high, constructed of two forked sticks placed upright in the ground about 6 feet apart, with a horizontal stick resting in the forks. The cloth beam at the near side was set close to the ground and was controlled by pegs or pickets that could be adjusted to keep the warps taut. If the weather were good, they would work outdoors; if not, they would work in the lodge.

The first step was to carry the continuous bale of warp back and forth between the two beams in a simple under-and-over order. After the warping was complete, a long strip of elm bark was wrapped around each beam to include one warp thread in each wrapping so that all the warps lay on an even plane. No shedding would be required, as the weaving was twining of a pair of wefts.

The reeds for the wefts were used in whole strands 6 feet long and the finished mat was more than 5 feet wide. It was very awkward for one woman to try to weave a mat alone. It was best for two women to work together, one weaving from the middle out to the right edge of the mat and the other from the middle out to the left edge. The two women sat side by side in front of the low end at the cloth beam. Each row of weft was woven with a pair of bulrushes, the point end of one strand matching the stub end of the other. The woman on the right grasped the two wefts in the middle between her thumb and index finger and gave them a twist away from herself so that they crossed over at the center. She then placed the twist between the two central warp strands and proceeded to twine-weave rightward, the completed stitches leaning diagonally upward to the right. When she reached the right edge, she cut off the stub end of one of her wefts almost flush with the edge and the other she wove back into the warp for 1½ to 2½ inches, producing a thickened and reinforced edge. The woman at the left, beginning at the middle proceeded to twine leftward and at the left edge cut off one weft and wove the other back into the warps in the same way as the woman on the right. The woman on the left adjusts her weaving motions so that they are made in reverse in order to produce a consistent weave pattern across the entire mat—all stitches slanting upward to the right. This is a sophisticated adaptation for weaving a wide twined fabric, as the normal direction for the progress of twined weaving is from left to right, the woman on the left using a motor pattern equivalent in feeling to dancing the waltz in reverse, with a view to getting a visual effect in the texture.

When the mat had been woven about one third of the way, the women, who had been kneeling in front of the lower cloth beam, now moved up and knelt on the already finished fabric to work on the rest. As the work progressed, they continued to move up on the fabric so that the working edge would be within reach.

Two women could finish a mat in one day if they did nothing else. Beginning after breakfast, the weaving would be half done by noon. By a little after five in the evening, the work was complete.

Mat weaving was a household craft and the work would not ordinarily be contracted for outside, unless a woman were learning for the first time. Then she would call in an old woman and pay her to demonstrate the technique. During the demonstration, the young woman would try her hand at it from time to time. The finished mat would be hers. The teacher would receive four or five yards of calico and a layer of dried buffalo meat, or a sack of corn (about a foot high) and half a braided intestine mat.

In the household of Old Bull and Victory Call, each side took care of its own needs for mats. White Woman and Grandma would start one together, and when White Woman had to interrupt her work to prepare a meal, Old-Lady-Grieves-the-Enemy would take her place for a while, helping Grandma with the weaving. Any mats that Grandma made by herself were given to White Woman for the family. Old-Lady-Grieves-the-Enemy felt she should make at least one mat for herself and her grandson to use when they went on the hunt. No Corn also made one to take along, and, if Horse Rider was busy in the Doctor Lodge, the two old ladies would each contribute half the necessary materials, as she was too crippled to gather them for herself and under the circumstances Horse Rider was unable to get away. There was no question of compensation for this, as the old ladies felt that Horse Rider was helpful to the household at all times and No Corn also did what she could.

Carrying these mats on the march was very difficult for people with no horses. This was the case with poor people. When people noticed that they had no mats, someone would give them an old one and a man would carry it on his back with a baby perched on top and his wife would do the same. The occasional woman who was too lazy to make one, was also given an old mat. People who didn't have mats to put on the ground were considered poor indeed.

A brush made of stiff grass was indispensable to personal grooming. The brush was made out of Porcupine Grass or Spanish Needles (*Stipa spartea*) known to the Pawnee as *pitsuts*. It grew like oats about 3 feet high near the village, above the cemetary where the Skidi buried their dead. White Woman would ask Victory Call to go and gather it for her in the fall. It had long stiff branches and at the tip of each branch there was a sharp point fastened at a joint and surrounded with wooly fluff. The point was broken off at the joint and discarded and the fluff cleared off. The remaining bristle was very stiff and formed the working end of the brush. The stems were grouped into four little bunches, each bunch bent over at the top end and fastened down with a wrapping of buckskin. The four bunches were put together with the bent-over ends inward, and the whole bound around with buckskin to complete the brush. In addition to keeping the hair in order, doctors would rub the brush on top of the head to relieve headache or sleepiness. As generally with the Pawnee crafts, there was no ceremony involved in gathering the material or in the manufacture, but the grass appears metaphorically in the Peace Pipe ceremony as symbolic of vegetation in general and of grasses in particular.

Everyone went to a good deal of trouble to keep the hair in order and to dress it attractively. The women's hair styles were relatively uniform. It was parted in the middle and made into two braids hanging down over the shoulders in front. The end of the braid was wound around with buckskin. A relatively recent style was tying the braids together and flinging them to the back. The men's hair styles were more elaborate and varied. A great many of the men wore roaches, a ridge of hair standing up along the middle of the head with the hair removed on both sides and a braid hanging down at the back. Most writers refer to this hair style as characteristically Pawnee, but the Pawnees themselves speak of it as "like Osages." In the old days, each hair had to be pulled out one by one. Later they used scissors. In former times, face hairs were also pulled out one by one with the fingers, while more recently they used a close coil of brass with a stick through it so that it would be tied to the belt. The oldest son of Victory Call by a former marriage, Sun Chief, had long curly hair that he wore in two braids, one over each shoulder. He was known as Long Hair or "Head-Hanging-Down-From." Victory Call also wore two braids, but on the right side, in addition to the braid, he had his hair cut in terraces. He was called "like Arikara" on account of it. War Cry never seemed to comb his hair; he wore it loose and was always brushing it back off his forehead. His younger brother, Brave Shield, pushed his hair up so that it stood up stiff in back. People who were shabby or ill-groomed were regarded with considerable contempt by the Pawnees.

The industrial knowledge of the Pawnee transformed the meager materials of the plains environment into a setting that was worthy of their religious and conceptual achievements. They worked hard but were secure in the knowledge that their labors would bring them fulfillment. The hardships of the winter buffalo hunt would be intense in many ways as they traveled over the snow-covered prairie through the winter winds. But the buffalo they caught would give them food, clothing, housing, tools, and deep emotional value as well.

54

THE WINTER BUFFALO HUNT

The Second Hunting Expedition—Difficulties with Horses—Processing the Meat—the Care of Horses on the Hunt

FOR THE SECOND TIME within the year, the Pawnees would set out from their villages on the long journey to the buffalo hunting grounds. It was in early November and the trip lasted until the end of February or the beginning of March. This was the severest and most challenging period in the year's round. They traveled through slush and snow over hundreds of miles, braved the cold winds of the prairie plains, got their water by breaking through the ice of the river or by melting snow, and gathered their fuel from the scant supplies of timber along the streams.

The horses upon whom they depended for the chase and for transport suffered most of all, for they were unable to get food of their own. The buffaloes had small narrow feet and could push the snow aside to graze, but the horses' hooves were flat and broad and they were unable to get to the grass that lay under the cover of snow. Many of the horses died toward the end of the journey in January and February. It was hard to find enough food to give them, and the women had to gather the tenderer shoots and bark of the cottonwood for them to eat. At times they were compelled to feed them on corn.

Because of the cold, the women had to process their meat inside the tipi and often they would have to extend their working time beyond the short daylight hours, working by the light of the fire. They felt that, "At this time of year, things seemed to be pushing and pushing."

They moved over the land with the same order and precision as they had in summer, sending their messengers back and forth between the chiefs of the bands in order to coordinate their decisions, but their leave-taking of the villages was with less pageantry and pleasant anticipation. They knew it would be a hard and dangerous time.

The problem of the horses was especially acute and of major concern. From archaeology and written history we know that the Pawnees had acquired horses nearly two hundred years before this time. But apparently there were many essential techniques of horse care that they had not adopted from the European. For example, Lone Chief had only recently found out that they should store hay for their horses in the winter. There were no shoes for the horses. When a horse broke his hoof they tied on a "shoe" of hide.

If it snowed before they left the village or after they got back, the horses had to have special care. The young boys who took care of them in summer could not be utilized at this season for the purpose. Anyway, they were more interested in sliding on the ice. The women had to go a mile south to get whatever hay they could, and in the evening the horses were put in a corral near the lodge—a round structure of upright sticks with a gate that was closed across with five sticks. Inside there was a manger that was filled with hay when the horses were settled in for the night. They tried to economize on feed by taking them to graze at intervals during the day. In the morning, after being fed some more hay, they were taken from the corral to the bend of Beaver Creek where there was good grass. By noon they were brought back to the village and hobbled close by. Then toward evening, if snow were expected, they were again taken to Beaver Creek to graze in order to save the hay in the corral where they would have to be kept while it was snowing. If it got too cold, they would have to take the horses into the earth lodge and settle them near the wood pile. The long entrance passageway was quite large enough to accommodate them. While they were on the hunt, the horses had to be covered with an old tent skin during the night.

Some families tried to anticipate these problems by putting their horses in the best possible condition during the fall. Toward the end of September or the beginning of October, they would send them out to Grand Island for about six weeks under the care of a group of men and boys. On the island the horses could wander more or less freely, graze, rest, and water at will. Near the villages the grass was dry at this time, but here it was green and fresh and the horses would fatten. Allowed to run loose, they mated freely. No selective breeding was practiced. Some people had their horses gelded by one of the men who knew how. He tied up the horse and used certain medicines, tying up the wound with sticks which would fall off by themselves later. A buffalo robe and dry meat were paid for the operation. When he was about twelve, Otter was sent on such an expedition. He was told to take the mare, a colt, and a gray horse and join the others. They said to him, "If the Sioux overtake you, you must get on the gray horse and you will get away unless you are thrown off. Then, since you have no weapons, you will be killed." With this cheerful admonition, Otter set out about ten in the morning, taking half a sack of flour, some sugar, coffee, and baking powder as provisions. He went to the place on the Union Pacific Railroad known as Windmill and then across the sandhills on the north edge of the island, meeting the others at about two in the afternoon.

The men and boys had a good time of it on these expeditions. They built themselves dome-shaped grass houses, *kaharuut*, of big willow twigs. Their saddles served as pillows and the saddle blankets as bedding. If they wanted an especially soft bed, they put hay and willows underneath. The older men got up very early and looked around on the sandhills. Some of them cooked the bread and coffee that comprised their main diet. Otter had a cup and he shared a plate with another boy who had brought one along. Sometimes a white man, having killed a beef, would give them a chunk of it. They had great times!

Considering their dependence on the horses, the Pawnees were remarkably unsentimental about them. They never called them by name, only referring to them in conversation by such names as Spotted Horse, Spotted Black Horse, Spotted Red Horse, Black Face Horse, White Hoof, Spotted on the Side, Black Nose, White Horse, Yellow Horse, Roan Horse, Red Head, High Forehead. There was no personal identification with them.

55

ARRANGING THE
ADMINISTRATIVE LEADERSHIP

Meetings with the Interpreter, Behaille—Discussion of Arrangements with U.S. Government—Band Is Chosen to Lead Hunt—Final Preparations

THE TIME WHEN EVERYONE began to think in earnest about leaving for the hunt was between the tenth and fifteenth of November, when the wind got colder from the north. Men from the different bands would meet in the trade store and talk it over. They wanted to travel before the cold was too severe.

In September 1857 the Pawnees had signed a treaty with the United States Government agreeing to cease all hostilities between them, to cede some of their lands, and to move onto a restricted territory. The United States in return acknowledged its military responsibility to provide the Pawnees with protection and its financial obligation to pay an annuity for the ceded lands. By 1867 the military alliance was further solidified when a considerable number of Pawnees were organized into a U. S. Cavalry Battalion under Major Frank North to protect surveyors and tracklayers of the Union Pacific from attacks by other tribes.

Before leaving for the hunt, they would consult with the U. S. Indian Agent concerning their annuity payments and any military arrangements that had to be made. The mixed-blood interpreter, Behaille, went to visit his nephew, Lone Chief, to discuss with him the time and conditions of leaving. The annuity had not yet arrived and the question was whether or not to set out without it. There was in fact no question, as the time of its arrival was too uncertain to depend upon, and they could not afford to wait. Lone Chief called in Eagle Chief, and they agreed that the day after next the chiefs and important braves were to meet in council with the agent about it. Behaille would entertain them all at a simple outdoor lunch about noon at his home near the agency where they could discuss their strategy. Lone Chief sent his young nephew, Hawk Chief, to give the message to the leading chiefs of the three other bands, and in each case he was royally entertained as befitted his uncle's position. He returned loaded with gifts of dry meat, and from the chief of the Asking-for-Meat Band he received a new white blanket because of the Peace Pipe relationship between Lone Chief's village and their band. As he moved proudly through the South Bands villages sporting his new blanket, everyone realized that important matters had been discussed, and the more prominent personalities awaited further notification. The more curious among them would wander into the chief's lodge and find out what was discussed and then spread the gossip.

Next morning at about nine or ten, two chiefs from each of the bands with their braves and some of the outstanding "Boys" arrived and were seated on a large tent skin outdoors provided by Behaille's wife. There were four cushions at the west for the leading personalities. Man Chief of the Asking-for-Meat Band sat on the southwest pillow and his fellow chief next to him with their braves extending inward toward the south. At the west on the north side was Many Trophies of the Man-Going-Downstream Band and at his left, Curly Chief of the Little-Earth-Lodge, with the braves of the two bands indiscriminately ranged along the side. The "boys" of the various bands were scattered wherever places happened to be available. These arrangements have a particular interest, for this is the only record I have of the four bands meeting together in a council rather than sending emmisaries back and forth between them. Behaille as host simply stated that this was merely an informal meal and proceeded to select boys from each of the four bands who carried a wooden bowl for each two guests from the chiefs all the way down the line, each person receiving a round piece of grease bread, some prunes, and some coffee. After the meal, Behaille stated the questions at issue, and when all who wanted to had had a chance to speak and all had agreed on the decision, he instructed them as to how to proceed with the agent so as not to commit themselves to anything more than they intended. He said, "I want four to talk and say just what I say now—nothing else. Say only, 'It's not cold yet. We want to go, agent. You hold the money. That's what I want to tell you.' I want Man Chief to talk first," he said, "then Curly Chief, then Many Trophies and then our chief, Eagle Chief. Just say what I have said, and no more. That's the best thing for you to do."

With this sage advice, they all crowded into the agent's office, the Pawnees sitting on the floor, the agent in his chair. The agent said, "If you want to wait, I can write in to the department, but it will probably be at least a month before I hear." To this one of the chiefs remarked, "By then we could be halfway to the hunting grounds."

As agreed, Man Chief got up and shook the agent's hand and stood back, calling Behaille to interpret for him. He said, "I want you to tell

our grandfather that I think it would be best for me if he held the goods
and money until I come back. I want to go buffalo hunting first." "That's
all right," said the agent, "It's still warm enough to cross the rivers."
"That's why I want to go as soon as we can," said Man Chief. "Now that's
all I want to say." Then he went up and shook the agent's hand again and
went back to his seat and Curly Chief came up and went through the
same procedure saying, "I heard what he said and I agree with him entirely. We don't want to have to cross the rivers when the water is real
cold and there is ice floating in them." The other two chiefs did the
same and then one of the braves was moved to speak and he said, "Agent,
you have heard the chiefs of the different bands. I mean to say as they
did." Then the brave turned around to the rest of the assembled company and put it more or less to a voice vote by saying, "Nawa, ha'a?"
("How about it?") and they all replied, "Yes." The agent closed the
meeting saying, "I wanted to hear what you chiefs, braves, and boys
were going to do."

Back at the villages people were remarking with some sarcasm, "Well,
of course it's quite all right about not getting our goods. We can get our
own buffalo robes and leggings."

In the agent's office, Eagle Chief decided that this was a good opportunity to speed up the process of choosing which band was going to lead
the hunt. He named Man Chief, and, with due modesty, Man Chief rested
his head in his hands for a few minutes and then accepted. It was understood that from this point on Man Chief would make the final decisions
with regard to the joint hunt—the time of leaving the village, the place
of rendezvous, route to be traveled, scouting parties, religious observances, and that his messengers would carry his decisions to the chiefs of
the other bands as they went along.

When the chiefs got back to their respective bands, each one found a
conclave of his other chiefs and braves awaiting him in his lodge. His
wife served an informal meal while he told of the decisions that had been
reached. Ten days before leaving, Man Chief called his ritual chiefs' meeting, and the other bands called theirs concurrently with his. The errand
man went through the village while the meetings were in session announcing the decisions. He said, "Man Chief has given us ten days to get ready.
Whatever you have to do, get it ready before that time. If you have a
tent to sew, sew it up right now. If you have something to do with the
food pit, you have a chance to do it in these ten days. And you arrow
makers, try to make as many as you can. And womenfolks, try to look at
your husbands' feet to see if they have good moccasins. Prepare. We
must go as soon as Man Chief says so." As he was making his announcement, some women remembered that they had only two mats and had to
make another; others recalled that they had to make a buffalo robe to
trade at the store.

56

PLANS AND PROVISIONS

FOR THE HUNT

~~~~~~~~~~~~~~~~~~~~~~~~~~~~~~~~~~~~

*Plan of Journey—Provisions—Stay-at-Homes on
Grand Island—Special Foods Found There—List
of Food Taken for Journey—Allowances for Rain
and Enemy Attack*

~~~~~~~~~~~~~~~~~~~~~~~~~~~~~~~~~~~~

FOUR DAYS BEFORE LEAVING TIME, Man Chief would have a meeting to
draw up final plans. Eagle Chief would have been waiting in his lodge to
get word and others would have gathered there. Food was served to all
and the Tsawi errand man delivered his message giving the itinerary.
Their rendezvous camp was almost due south on the north bank of the
Platte. The next day they would cross the river and spend a whole day
waiting for any stragglers to catch up. The plan further was that all
would continue then to Fort Kearney on Grand Island, traveling along
the south bank of the Platte, then crossing the channel north onto the island. There a permanent camp could be set up for any "Stay-at-Homes,"
kaa-kusu ("at home-stay"), "who have very few or no horses." This plan
differed from the summer when the Stay-at-Homes had to remain near
their villages. In the summer, Grand Island was ridden with mosquitoes,
but now it was green and pleasant and sheltered from the worst winds.

The matter of provisioning this winter expedition was also somewhat
different from the summer, as certain favorite wild foods were ripe and
could be gathered in quantity. The two most important were Indian potatoes, *Glycine apios* L., and black-eye peas, *Falcata comosa* (L.) Kuntze,
popularly known to us as ground beans. The beans were hoarded by the
wood rat or vole and were gathered by raiding the hoards. The women
would find the track of the rat that led them to the beans. Our lima beans
were considered like them by the old Indian women. The plant bears two
types of beans, one on the upper leafy branches that are not used and the

large flat bean on leafless colorless branches that push into the earth. These are the ones garnered by the vole, their hoards amounting to a pint or more in each place. Only part of the store was appropriated by the women. Sometimes the beans had to be dug out with a shovel where they grew underground like peanuts. About half of them would be cooked immediately and half left simply to dry out like cultivated beans. Those that were dried were winnowed and then put in a sack for future use. For immediate use, the fresh beans were first washed, rubbed between the hands to remove the hulls, and then boiled and eaten. Their Pawnee name was *atik-uraru*, "bean-earth."

Artichokes (Jerusalem artichoke, *Helianthus tuberosus* L.) known as *kisusit*, were also gotten, but they could not be dried; they had to be eaten fresh. The most important wild crop was the potato, known as *its*. The Loup River was known in Pawnee as Many-Potatoes, *Its-kari*, "potato-many," from the abundance of this useful vegetable that flourished along its banks. These grew in the sand among the willows. A considerable number of these Indian potatoes were boiled, smoked, and dried for preservation and stored in skin bags. In addition to the larger-size potatoes, they gathered some small ones that were strung along the vine; these were called potato-many-tied-up, *its-kari-piru*, and were given to the small children to eat after boiling. They were bundled up and tied with a vine into little bunches and boiled in water, covered with a layer of grass along with the larger ones. The larger potatoes were then peeled, "strung" on a very thin willow twig, and placed across two forked sticks in the tipi so that the smoke would permeate them and improve their flavor. The potatoes prepared in this way could be eaten at any time without further preparation, and would not rot.

Quantities of potatoes were found on Grand Island and on both sides of the Republican River. Those who stayed on Grand Island, especially the old ladies, as well as any who went all the way out to the hunting grounds, would make sure to take a file along so that they could sharpen up their buffalo shoulder-blade "hoes" to dig up the potatoes.

These wild plant foods were a very important element of their provisions. The group that remained on Grand Island could be a kind of half-way station where they could leave extra baggage on the way out and where the people could be actively gathering and preparing the wild foods so that they would be sustained on the rest of the journey home. The men who remained on the island were actively trapping and could supply extra meat. Thus in the winter the Stay-at-Homes played a useful role, while in the summer they had no function in the enterprise.

In the family of Victory Call, Grandma planned to stay on Grand Island where she could do some useful work while the rest of the family went on. Those who proceeded all the way to the hunting grounds were Victory Call, White Woman, Horse Rider, and No Corn—viz., two couples—and the boy Otter. Of the dried and cultivated foods from White Woman's stores they took:

Roasted corn kernels (*rawaritu*)	2 small sacks (50-lb flour size)
Dried blue flour corn (*uraax-katit*)	1 small sack (50-lb flour size)
Dried spotted corn (*rikis-tipiku*)	1 sack
Beans	1 sack
Pumpkin mats	2 mats
Dried buffalo meat (*takaski*)	½ parfleche
Trade store goods	Flour (50-lb sack); coffee, sugar, baking powder; dried peaches and dried prunes

As on the previous occasion, Grandma contributed her specialty, pounded up sweet corn mixed with sugar, *rikis-karus-tapaxtu*, "corn-sweet-pounded-up," that she had pounded in the mortar before they left. She pounded as much of it as she could so that the family could carry it along. This was a valuable ready-to-eat food and there would be no time to prepare it while they were on the march without her, since she would remain on Grand Island. Particularly in winter, there would be little time to cook.

No Corn, wife of Horse Rider, took a similar array of foods to White Woman, but less in quantity. She took:

Roasted corn kernels (*rawaritu*)	1 sack
Dried blue flour corn (*uraax-katit*)	½ sack
Dried spotted corn (*rikis-tipiku*)	1 sack
Beans	1 sack
Pumpkin mats	1 mat
Dried buffalo meat (*takaski*)	½ parfleche
Trade store goods	Flour (50-lb sack); coffee, sugar, dried peaches and dried prunes

The roasted (*rawaritu*) corn was the quickest-cooking, while the dried blue flour corn (*urrax-katit*) had to soak and took much longer to cook. The spotted corn was parched in a pan with coals. For this winter expedition the main difference in the supplies was that they took half or less of the longer-cooking dried blue flour corn. Otherwise the supplies were substantially similar. However, they were out on their winter expedition about 3½ months rather than the summer period of only two.

While there is no way of getting a reliable estimate of how much these supplies amounted to in our terms, Samuel Allis who was missionary to the Skidi and traveled with them on their hunts in 1835–1836, stated that each parfleche that they carried with them contained four bushels of corn or eighty pounds of dried buffalo meat. The proportions of the dry meat he describes as 3 feet long and 2 feet wide per sheet.

It should be noted that some of the trade store supplies had their analogies in the native foods. Flour was analogous to finely pounded-up corn made into corn bread that was baked in the ashes, and the dried fruits with traditional dried wild plums and sand cherries, while sugar was obtained from the box elder.

The cache pit being in order and the provisions packed for travel, the horse gear was all gotten in order, the saddles and straps mended so that the goods could be securely packed on the horse. Finally the long-awaited announcement for leaving would come. The specific directions were from Man Chief of the Tsawi Band who was leading the hunt.

The night before it would be stated that rainy conditions would have to be taken account of. If they had a hard rain early in the morning, then they would have to delay their departure until the next day, but "If it rains only a little in the morning, as soon as the rain stops, we can go on." On the other hand, should it rain during the night, they would certainly go on next morning. If they had already started and it began to rain they would cover up the loaded horses with an old tent skin they carried along for the purpose and say, "It's on the way," and continue, unless it kept on raining hard all through the day, when they would have to un-load the horses, cover up the baggage with a tent skin, and all crawl under it until the rain was over. Then they would reload and go on.

Another cause for delay in their departure would be an enemy attack when they could do nothing else but stay and defend themselves. This would delay them for a day or two.

Meanwhile everyone was anxious to be on their way. On the appointed morning or the night before, Horse Rider tethered the horses right out-side the door of the lodge. They would be loaded as for the summer hunt, a place being arranged for No Corn to ride because of her arthritis.

57

THE JOURNEY TO
THE HUNTING GROUNDS

~~~~~~

*The Order of the Procession—Crossing the Loup
—Setting Up Camp—Hunting along the Way*

~~~~~~

FINALLY IT WAS THE MORNING for leaving. People everywhere got up well before dawn as they had a long journey of about 15 miles and they wanted to set up camp before sundown. Before they could get to their destination on the north bank of the Platte, they had to cross the Loup.

The formal procession started early. Man Chief of the Asking-for-Meat Band was in the lead, followed by his subchiefs and his people, then the other South Bands and the Skidis. The Skidis had gathered in Wolf-in-Water village and when Eagle Chief rode up he continued south with the crowd following. Just behind him, Lone Chief of Village-across-a-Ridge rode up with his family and Eagle Chief asked him to join him, the two riding side by side with Lone Chief to the west. Behind them came their subchiefs and then the rest of the people of their two villages, flanked by their braves. Next came the chiefs of the other two villages, Leading Chief of Bottomland and riding to his right, Feared-by-the-Enemy of Wolf-in-Water, then their subchiefs and the people, with their braves riding alongside.

When they got to the Loup, they crowded toward the bank as everyone tried to get across at once, but finally two parallel roads were established. Man Chief and his people were the first to cross, then Little-Earth-Lodge Band and the Man-Going-Downstream and then Eagle Chief and the Skidis, but in the confusion some Skidis got mixed up with the other two bands. When they got across the four bands had to realign themselves in the original order. The old ladies had gone ahead and by this time had arrived at the railroad station (Clarks? on the Union Pacific). Any of the people that felt inclined to go to the city of Columbus were

419

dissuaded and urged to come to Grand Island where they had a good chance of getting some buffalo meat.

By nightfall, they had set up their first rendezvous camp on the Platte. Stragglers would reach the camp at night and in the darkness they would call out, "Where are the Skidis camped?" Individuals who were joining a tipi called out, "Where is our tipi?" The hunters would not have been able to get any game that afternoon as the north side of the Platte was heavily populated with a railroad and a wagon trail and no animals ever came near. Only on the many islands in the Platte could one hope to get some deer or trap some beaver.

Next morning they all crossed over to the south bank of the Platte and set up their second rendezvous camp. Man Chief started the procession early that morning, and when he was about halfway across the river, the other bands followed. Having camped there the night before, they all had a good estimate of the conditions for crossing and each band took its own route, the Skidi furthest west as they had been encamped. From this encampment, some hunters crossed over to the islands and set their beaver traps and stalked deer while others rode south for antelope. Along the south side of the Platte there was an old trail that had long been followed, but still further south among the sand hills, the country was deserted and game was plentiful. A man looking for antelope might come across a lone buffalo bull. The lucky hunter who got a deer, antelope, and particularly a buffalo would invite the chiefs and other important men to his tent for a feast on ribs as was the usual practice.

Sporadic hunting continued as they traveled along the south bank of the Platte for the next five or six camps when they would reach Grand Island.

58

CAMP 6 ON GRAND ISLAND

~~~~~~

Problems with Stay-at-Homes—Rearrangement
of Groups for Hunt—the Journey South—the
Hunt

~~~~~~

TRAVELING ALONG THE SOUTH BANK of the Platte, when they arrived opposite the middle of Grand Island, they crossed the channel northward and
camped there. They set up a large encampment of all four bands with the
Skidi furthest west. Some people had planned to remain behind before
they left the village, but others, particularly old people, would decide
that it was too cold to go on and would seek a place in one of the tents of
those who were staying.

But sometimes the defections were more serious. A prominent man
like Misery, for example, would have a lapse of public spirit and secretly
plan to stay behind before they left the village. Misery was the son of
Sitting Hawk, Victory Call's oldest brother. He was married to three
daughters of a prominent chief of Bottomlands Village, Comanche
Chief, and lived in their household. As was the common situation in
such a lodge, there were a number of untitled "boys" who made their
home there. Four of them formed a small group together, their leader being Horse Finder who owned a number of horses while the others had
none. Horse Finder would ordinarily be the nucleus of a hunting group
with the other three to assist him. Misery had been able to induce him to
remain on the island with him along with his group. On the other hand,
he had not been successful in keeping another of the "boys" that lived
in the household, Jim Bear, from going along to the hunting grounds. Jim
Bear had two horses and a wife who could slice the buffalo meat. When
he got wind of the secret plans, he made arrangements to join the hunt
group of White Eagle. Misery's decision meant that his father, Sitting
Hawk, would also have to stay behind. There were a number of other
planned defections of this kind with the intention being to ride out as a

single group of hunters all the way due south to the Republican, get some buffalo meat, and bring it all the way back to the island where their families could process it in comfort. It would take them two days to get to the Republican and back and a number of short forays of this sort would yield them a good supply of meat and hides. Such a plan to anticipate the hunt on the Republican was decidedly antisocial.

Eagle Chief first became aware of the situation when the expedition was ready to leave for the main hunting grounds, but there was nothing he could do about it. In answer to his question, "What's the trouble that you're not going ahead?" Misery would try to make his decision appear spontaneous by remarking, "Oh, I don't feel like going this year anyway. I want to go trapping on this island. That's why I don't want to go." As the beaver skins could be sold for cash, this was intended to give the impression that he needed money. But Eagle Chief knew better.

In Victory Call's family, Grandma had made up her mind beforehand to stay behind and now she would join the camp of Misery in view of his close relationship to Victory Call. White Woman left enough food with her for her share in the household and some baggage to keep for them, along with their whole supply of roasted corn to be eaten on the way back, since No Corn had enough for the journey out. Grandma was diligent at gathering wild potatoes and ground beans, and after contributing some to Misery's household, would have a good supply for the family when they got back. She would also receive some dried buffalo meat for her help in the household.

None of the Stay-at-Home camps of the several bands had a formal leader, but the most prominent man among them would automatically assume the role. In the Skidi camp, Eagle Chief would remark to Misery, "I want you to look after these folks while we're away." The chiefs stopped off at Fort Kearney before leaving to receive army rations and when they held council with the army officers, Eagle Chief requested them to "Look after our people here," intending that they should keep an eye on the Stay-at-Homes and give them some food if necessary. Much to his surprise, however, they sent a troop of cavalry under Major North as an escort for the outgoing party. When they had gone a little way, it was discovered that Eagle Chief's remark had been misunderstood through a slight error of linguistic interpretation by the translator, and the cavalry turned back.

They left Grand Island from Fort Kearney and made four camps to Plum Creek near Lexington. They had sent out no forays from these camps to scout for buffalo to the south as they knew the Stay-at-Homes had gone before them. It was also unlikely that they would find any small buffalo herds in the neighborhood of the camp as they had in summer, since the buffalo of the Republican herd did not come that far north in the cold weather. Moreover they had to conserve the energy of their horses who were living on very short rations during this part of the journey getting only a little hay that they gathered for them. Should they want to undertake a special scouting expedition, the men would have had to stop to get some strips of cottonwood bark to give their horses extra strength.

In summer they were likely to stay at Plum Creek for several days before turning southward but, in view of the conditions, they spent only one night there and proceeded across the dry canyon-broken terrain the next morning until they found the head of Turkey Creek that would lead them to the Republican. They camped there at the head of the creek on the west bank. Meanwhile scouts had set out from the Platte that morning and came into the encampment with news of a small herd in the confluence of Turkey Creek and the Republican. That night Man Chief made plans for the attack on the herd next morning. His scouts went out way before dawn and climbed a hill to plan the strategy of attack and signal the hunters as they approached. At camp it was understood that everything should be packed in final order and the hunters all ready to ride off when they had gone half way down the west bank of the creek. The rest of the line was to proceed very cautiously south toward the confluence of Turkey Creek with the Republican, arriving in time for the hunt to be over and setting up the camp.

When the hunters reached the appointed place, they lined up at the base of the hill as directed by the scout. Their braves kept the line of hunters in order. Man Chief appointed a man as "hand-waver" to ask the ceremonial blessing, and then the hunters rode out on both sides to surround the herd. When they got to camp, they would leave the ribs of the killed buffaloes at the council tent and go home to rest, leaving the meat and hides before returning to make their report.

59

THE POINTED SKIN TIPI

~~~~~~

Transporting the Tipi—the Women Set Up the Tipi with Help from the Men—the Arrangements in the Tipi

~~~~~~

ONE OF THE MOST IMPORTANT TECHNICAL achievements that made this trip possible across the open prairie in the cold of winter was the pointed skin tipi. With its fire burning in the middle, its skin cover tight and its poles firmly set on the ground, it was a warm shelter against wind and weather. It was named for its framework of poles, viz., *kax-ta-pe,* "house-against-leaning," or the Against-Leaning House. An alternative name was *kar-rat-sa-pe,* the infix *-rat-* referring to the plurality of the poles, viz., They-against-Leaning House. For transportation, the poles were divided into two equal groups, laced through the thick end with rawhide rope and placed one on each side of the horse and tied to the saddle horn. The thinner ends dragged on the ground. The two groups of poles were fastened together across the lower part with cross sticks and the space covered over with skin placed underneath with the edges lapped over on top. This made a convenient carryall where they placed extra packages and sometimes the baby on top. In former times dogs were similarly packed and they were still in active use for this purpose in the late 1830's —a usage reminiscent of a time before they had horses and the women and the dogs did most of the packing. This is vividly shown by the painter Alfred Jacob Miller in 1837 and described by the missionary to the Skidi, Allis, on the winter hunt of 1835, who claims that the dog carried seventy to a hundred pounds of meat. For the time before horses, we have an account of the use of the dog travois in the report of the Coronado expedition across the Plains in 1541.

When the line of march would set out in the morning after breakfast, the common routine was for the hunters to leave the line of march and go on their individual hunts or the mass attack on the buffalo herd and for the rest of the party to continue to the appointed place and set up camp. They tried to have it ready by around noon so that the men could have a place to rest when they came in and the meat could be treated. In summer the mass attack on the herd usually took place about eleven o'clock in the morning when the herd had returned from the water to the pasture; in winter it was somewhat earlier.

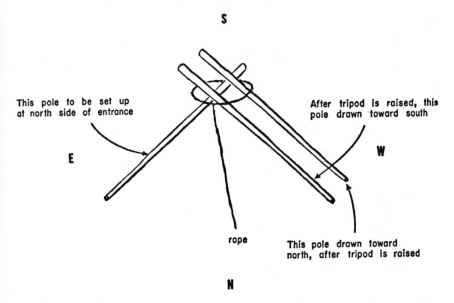

FIGURE 59-1. Erecting the framework of the pointed tipi. Three poles were laid on the ground as shown, the east pole first and the two west poles on top of it. The rope was tied around the poles at the crossing toward the top. Someone at the south end pushed up the frame while an assistant at the north end pulled the rope. The thick ends of the poles were near the top, tapering to the base. The poles were about 15 feet long, the trees being 6 to 7 inches in diameter before the bark was removed. The west was the rear of the tent, and these two poles were set 2 to 3 feet apart. A fourth pole that matched the one at the north was rested in the crossing at the apex of the tripod to form the south post of the doorway. Now other poles were placed all around, also resting in the tripod, and the woman grasped the end of the rope that was hanging down in the middle and carried it around from the south by west by north until she had made four circuits. She tossed it up from time to time and jerked it in place to make sure it was tight around the apex. She fastened the rope at the south doorway pole by winding it three or four times around the pole and tying it at the bottom.

At the campsite that had been agreed upon, the woman of the house would select a place for her tipi and begin by excavating a circular fireplace with the earth banked up all around it. She then proceeded to erect over it the pointed skin tipi. This could be set up by one person if necessary, but two made it more convenient and four still better. As was usual with the Pawnees, the back of the tent would be placed toward the west and the opening to the east. In our current way of drawing maps, we think of the top of the paper as the north, the bottom south, the west toward the left edge and the east toward the right. The beginning of the installation was the construction of a tripod of tall poles fastened together at the top. The first step was to lay these three poles parallel on the ground with their thin ends pointing north and the thick ends at which they were fastened, pointing south. From the place at the south where the three poles were fastened, a long rope extended with its free end pointing northward. In forming the tripod, the thick ends of the poles were to be elevated for the apex and the thin ends rested on the ground. They now drew the thin ends of the poles apart, two of them toward the west and one toward the east to form an acute angle. The long rope still pointed due north between them.

No Corn stood at the free end of the rope at the north, and her husband Horse Rider at the south where the thick ends of the sticks were tied. Now White Woman gave the instruction, "We've got to raise them up," and Horse Rider lifted the tied end of the poles while No Corn who stood opposite him, pulled at her end of the rope. Victory Call was standing at the east pole which was to be the entrance, while White Woman was stationed at the west where the two poles for the back had been placed. As the frame was elevated, Victory Call steadied the east pole with his foot and White Woman called out, "Hold steady and try to part the two poles at the west!" Horse Rider then ran over to the west to assist her, and they drew the two rear poles about 3 feet apart. The tripod now stood firm. There were now two poles for the back of the tent, but only one for the entranceway at the northeast. White Woman now selected a pole to match it and rested it in the tripod to form the southeast door pole.

The rest of the poles, four along the north side and four along the south, were now leaned in the tripod. A space at the west was left free of poles. Meanwhile, the long rope was hanging down the middle from the apex with a weight on the end of it. White Woman took it up now and carried it all around in a clockwise circuit beginning at the southeast, through south, west, etc., to bind the sticks in place at the apex. Tossing the rope upward toward the apex, she would pull it tight from time to time, making four circuits and then fastening the end of the rope at the southeast doorway pole, winding it three or four times around the pole and then tying it at the bottom.

Now the skin cover was put on the frame. The skin cover had been carried folded in two down the length and rolled up (see pp.179-180, Figure 19-1). It was unrolled and opened out with the inner surface uppermost and a long pole placed upon it which was tied to the cover with two rawhide strips found near the top end and two more near the bottom. This pole was to act as a kind of "backbone" when the skin cover was elevated onto the frame. It was lifted with the cover attached and rested in the tripod at the west. The cover was carried first around the south side, then around the north until they met at the front where they were either laced together with thin sticks above the doorway or with strips of rawhide. If the cover was a little loose, White Woman now straightened it up at the top.

The next step was to tighten up the frame again. This she did by driving holes in the ground into which each individual tent pole could rest. First at the northeast entrance pole she took her seven-foot-long *hiku* stick with its fire-hardened point and punched it down into the ground before her, putting the pole in the hole. Next she did the same for the southeast entrance pole, then the one due west with the cover attached to it, then the one due north and the one due south. She fixed up the rest of the poles in any order that was convenient. She tried to make a nice even circle.

The final step was to tighten the cover by pegging it down with the tent pegs. All around the tent cover there were strap loops of rawhide through which she drove the tent pegs. The pegs were of dogwood, each about a foot long, with the thick end sharpened to a point. They were driven into the ground with the ax head in the same order used in stabilizing the poles, viz., northeast, southeast, west, north, south.

Two more poles, *tsuxtsakatawisu*, were used to hold the flaps around the smokehole open at the top. These were placed on the outside, one on each side of the entrance and hooked into the holes of the smokehole flaps so that they could be adjusted to make the smokehole more or less open, depending on the wind. Sometimes they forgot to get these two sticks beforehand, and Horse Rider had to go out into the woods to get some for current use. Either inside or outside, over the door, a blanket was hung.

While the tent was being pegged down, Horse Rider would have been reminded by his wife that they had no wood. He would have brought a supply of water before that. Now with wood and water available and the whole tent firmly in order, the inside was furnished. First the parfleches were taken in and placed around the walls in piles of two from west to east. Then the twined woven rush mats were laid down to the north and south of the fireplace. The proportions of the tent given by Allis in 1835 are 18 feet in diameter and 14 feet high.

Victory Call's family occupied the south side of the tipi, and Horse Rider and his wife, No Corn, the north side. At meals, White Woman sat due south and did the cooking and serving, while Victory Call occupied the southwest position on her left and little Otter, the southeast position on her right. On the north side, the northwest position was vacant, leaving room for piling kettles, mortars, and other things—Horse Rider sitting in the due north position and No Corn at the northeast position. They sat close enough around the fire to simply pass the food around at mealtimes.

60

PROCESSING THE MEAT

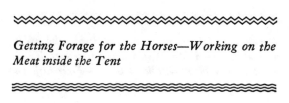

Getting Forage for the Horses—Working on the Meat inside the Tent

AFTER THE TENT WAS SET UP, White Woman and No Corn got some cottonwood tops and bark for the horses to eat when the men got in from the chase. They went out and cut down a few trees and dragged them in two loads, taking one at a time into the tent, cutting off the tops and making a number of cuts with the ax along the trunk to loosen the bark. Most of the time the bark could then be struck off easily, but if it was too tough, it was macerated a bit with the ax head. They also gathered whatever hay they could find and got wood and water for their cooking. High over the fire, they built a grate to warm the meat through after slicing, as in winter the meat had to be treated inside the tent before it was finally dried outdoors.

When the hunters got in they immediately brought the meat inside lest it freeze so that it could not be sliced. The horses were tethered outside the tent, each one covered over with a skin spread so that he would not catch cold, and left out all night to eat their cottonwood tops and bark that had been placed before them on a hide. Sometimes if the horses did not have enough, the Pawnees had to feed them corn. When the meal was over, the men went to the council tent and the women began to slice the meat.

They made a low fire, and after the meat was sliced they put it on the grate to warm through. Outside they built another rack of a different form. This had an elliptical ridge pole and withes along one side on which the meat rested under which they placed hot coals in order to dry the meat thoroughly.

Sometimes they built another grate similar to the one indoors so that the meat could finally be exposed to the sun and wind. In this condition the meat was thoroughly cooked and could be eaten without further cooking as well as being preserved for storage.

61

THE COUNCIL TENT

Ceremonial Observances of the Hunt—the Meat
Is Delivered—a More Informal Procedure Than
the Summer Hunt—Police Chosen—Four Official
Scouts Chosen Also—the Hunt

EVERYONE KNEW THAT the council tent would be set up at Turkey Creek while the men were out attacking the herd, and that that evening the special police would be appointed to take charge during the subsequent attacks. During the summer, with White Eagle in the lead, the hunt had been conducted under the religious sponsorship of his left hand bundle, whose tradition was a special form of the creation legend. The present hunt was being carried on under the auspices of the Evening Star and its sacred bundle, which was also known as Yellow Calf. Its tradition was the official creation legend of the Skidi Federation. The "keeper" of this bundle was Old Lady Lucky Leader of Pumpkin-Vine Village and she was assisted by her son, Frank Leader (also known as Dog-at-the-West), and her son-in-law, Roaming Leader. The old lady had built a particularly large tent but even then only about thirty could gather in there at a time.

As soon as the tent was set up and while the men were still off chasing the herd, the five priests came in and sat down at the west. Due west was Heavy Trophies, the head priest. To his left on the north side were Pipe Offering and Bringing Horses. To his right on the south side were Angry Horse and then Wonderful Old Bull.

On this occasion, Bringing Horses was sitting as an apprentice priest. From time to time the head priest would say, "If there is anyone in this room who wants to learn, he should come closer and sit with us. It is necessary that someone should do this as we are likely to die at any time. We are old and after we die, the world will go on and on and this is the word of Heaven and should be carried on after we are gone. Anyone who is willing should come and sit closer and observe and listen to the way these things should be done." This was considered a major public service and no payment was involved nor considerations of kin relationship. Bringing Horses was a brave and apparently had had a call to carry out this mission.

The five priests sat smoking and talking together informally. They were old men and had traveled over this same ground many times. They knew just how far apart the rivers were and which were the quickest routes to follow. Now they were reminiscing about the past. One would say, "One summertime we camped way down there in this and this direction from here and so and so happened," for example a warpath came or some other notable event. Meanwhile Old Lady Lucky Leader was taking care of the practical affairs since the menfolks of her family were still out on the hunt. She was a vigorous old woman and a good manager. One of the men coming in early from the hunt reined in his horse outside her tent and called out, "Lady Lucky Leader, here are ribs!" throwing down the ribs as his contribution to the forthcoming council meeting and riding off home to his own tent. The old lady went out and got them at once and put them inside the tent on the north side near the entrance so that they wouldn't freeze. Now she decided to get the meal under way for the council. The boy Might-Be-Chief was passing by and she called him in and asked him to get the chief's errand man Know-His-Face, who came in and, after exchanging greetings with the priests, began to roast the ribs to the northeast of the fireplace as directed by the old lady. She asked her daughter to sit down to the south and fry some bread so that the men would have something to eat as soon as they got in before the council began.

Now the men could be heard coming and the meat creaking a little as it was packed on the horse since it was a bit frozen. The two men of the family knew they had better get in early and Frank Leader called out to his mother, "Atira [my mother], spread something out here for the meat." The old lady came out and put a skin spread on the snow in front of the tent and her son tethered his horse to a stake nearby. She covered the horse and put down another spread with cottonwood tops and bark on it for the horse to eat. She saved some of the cottonwood for her son-in-law's horse and he arrived soon after. As soon as the two men entered the tent they asked their mother for some water to wash their hands with, and Frank tied his quiver and bow to the southwest post while Roaming Leader tied his at the northwest. Then they sat down on either side of the entrance. The men talked about how they had killed the buffalo that day and how there had been good herds north of the river. The family had its meal of bread and ribs and then the boy Might-Be-Chief was sent around to call in the other members of the council. He also called in Horse Rider to help the errand man Know-His-Face to cook for the feast.

They decided to build a fire outside and proceed with it there. The contributions of ribs were apt to be light at this time, possibly only four sets.

The guests at the council were representatives of each of the four Skidi villages. They included the leading chief and a subchief from each and their respective braves. The head chiefs of each of the villages sat in their usual semicardinal positions with their subchiefs and braves ranged inward toward the north and south. This made sixteen official delegates from the villages.

The head priest now addressed the assembled company, mentioning each of the chiefs and villages and stating that they were to make this tent their administrative headquarters. He also pointed out that while in summer they selected their hunt police from the military societies, during the winter the societies were suspended and they would simply choose the police from among the braves present without benefit of the symbolic lances and belt of the societies. He mentioned that the hunt was under the aegis of the "Yellow Tent," still another name for the Evening Star bundle.

Lone Chief took over greeting the priests and others and stating he was going to choose the police from among the braves. He now chose War Cry (of Pumpkin-Vine Village) to be head policeman, and then from the other three villages, Shot Arm, Strikes-the-Enemy and Leading-Downhill. Each of these would choose his own deputy. The head priest now officially assigned the conduct of the rest of the meeting to Lone Chief. The ribs were served under his direction and when a second helping was carried around, a number of the men gave theirs to the boy Might-Be-Chief, who went home with his arms loaded with buffalo ribs.

The meal over, the official police belt was hung up tied to the south pole of the tent, south of the Evening Star bundle, and the head policeman War Cry would wear it when he was on duty. There were sleigh bells for each of the other three official policemen so that they could make themselves heard as they went through the camp warning people to be quiet. Everyone knew that they should not linger as the family of Old Lady Lucky Leader had to get their meat sliced in the tent, and so as soon as they had eaten, Lone Chief said the customary "Now we have eaten," and everyone got up directly and left.

Women were not permitted at council meetings or ceremonies, and the old lady and her daughter had gone elsewhere as soon as the council was in session. Now they came back in and the two women and Frank and Roaming Leader got to work slicing and drying their meat as fast as they could. They might have to work a good part of the night.

The priests had appointed four official scouts and they were out very early the next morning going west along the north side of the Republican. When they looked across to the south bank, they saw a certain kind of calf with a long body that they called "Calf-That-Has-a-Rope" signifying that it was a calf around whom the herd gathers like a circular rope. They believed that when this calf was killed, all the buffalo were impelled to come seeking it. On the other hand, if they did not succeed in killing it, the herd would turn back when attacked. It took an exceptionally fast horse to kill this calf and Jim Bear (also known as In-the-Front-Line) managed to overtake it and kill it because, as he said with characteristic modesty, "the calf got tired running in the deep snow." Now the buffalo were running eastward in a vast herd along the south side of the river. They knew they wouldn't have to go any further for this hunting expedition, but could set up a permanent encampment at a place called Many Deer to the west of Turkey Creek, for the herd were sure to continue coming in this direction. When they set up camp at Many Deer they could hear the roar of the herd. The skin of the special calf who had been herd leader was donated to Wolf-Standing-in-Water Village as a wrap for its sacred bundle.

Meanwhile, at Turkey Creek, after the Skidi scouts had gone out, Man Chief of the Asking-for-Meat Band announced his plan to go to a place to the south that the South Bands preferred. Eagle Chief sent back a message that they were unable to join him as his scouts had already killed some buffalo to the west. It was then understood that the four bands would part, and no rancor whatever was involved. The Man-Going-Downstream Band joined Man Chief, while the Little-Earth-Lodge Band had a place they liked to camp they called, "Where-the-Cane-Plants-Are-Sitting-up-Against." This was located on the south side of the Republican just about opposite the Skidi camp of Many Deer that was on the north bank of the river. They all stayed at Turkey Creek for an extra day to give the women a chance to cure the meat and prepare the hides, and then the bands went to their several destinations.

62

THE MAIN HUNT

~~~~~~

Handling the Meat after the Hunt—Winter Problems—Storytelling—Camp Moves to Many Deer—Dismantling the Tent—Meeting in Council Tent—the Hunt at Many Deer—Donations to the Sacred Bundles—Scouts Return to Grand Island to Report

~~~~~~

VERY EARLY THAT MORNING after the scouts had ridden west, most of the other men rode out after them, leaving the women in camp to finish drying the meat with only a few men to protect them. The men took only the horses they rode to the chase; the rest were left to the care of the women. In warmer weather, a boy might ride an extra horse so that it would be ready for packing after the chase, but at this time the weather was too bad. In Victory Call's camp, White Woman, No Corn, and the boy remained and the two men rode west.

At Many Deer, Eagle Chief had decided that they would stake out a camping place on the north shore, sheltered by timber and big hills from the cold winds, and lead their horses over the ice to the south bank for the chase. After the buffalo had been killed and butchered, the meat was loaded on the horses and carried to the south bank of the Republican. There the meat was unloaded and the horses tethered. Then the men made "hand travois," *raku-rarahu-kita-hukhu*, in order to-pack of buffalo meat-upon-water or ice-carry. This was a dead cottonwood with a fork at the top. Sticks were fastened across the fork and upon this the meat was loaded and tied with the man pulling the travois across the ice by the trunk. (In summer they made a "water package" raft of half the rawhide of a bison to float across the water in a similar situation.) When a man had pulled all his meat across the ice, someone on the north shore would ask him for his travois. He would say, "All right, that's a good horse!"

The horses were still tethered on the south bank, and when all the meat was over, Eagle Chief would ask "the boys" to sprinkle soil or earth on the ice so that the horses could be led over. They would organize into two parties, one from each shore, each man with a supply of earth in his buffalo robe or blanket to sprinkle on the ice. The two parties would meet in the middle of the river and then the horses could be led across. The next day the earth would have melted into the ice and the crossing would be easier. Even though they were not loaded, the horses had a hard time to keep from slipping as they had no shoes. When the horses arrived on the north shore they were again loaded with the meat and led to the place selected for the encampment. Each man chose a site for his family's camp and cleared it of snow and gathered plenty of wood. The meat was put on the hide and bundled up in it. As soon as the meat was unloaded, Eagle Chief called out that the horses better be sent back to the camp at Turkey Creek so that the people could join them early next morning. Victory Call sent Horse Rider back with the two horses for the family, while he stayed at Many Deer, going on with the work of preparing the camping place and looking after the meat.

After the hunters at Many Deer had completed their duties, they made five big fires, one for each of the four Skidi villages, and an extra one. The men of each village sat around them wrapped up well in their buffalo robes and stayed up all night smoking and talking. If one should doze off, his neighbor awakened him. They were accustomed to staying up like this on the warpath as much as three days and nights to get out of range of the enemy with the booty and horses. The next morning while the line of march was on the way from the camp on Turkey Creek, some of the men like War Cry, Victory Call, and Eagle Chief would decide to begin to slice and dry the buffalo meat so that no time would be lost. At some of the other fires, when they saw War Cry with his meat drying, they would tease him with, "Look at that War Cry. He has his *takaski*. He's just like an old woman." But he was totally impervious to such remarks.

As soon as Frank Leader and his brother-in-law Roaming Leader had decided where they were going to set up the council tent, Eagle Chief said, "Don't wait. As soon as the council tent is set up, come in any time. We have a home there. This is where we come to tell stories and make reports." As the returning hunters had come in, they donated ribs for the Council that evening by hanging them on a nearby tree. Old Lady Lucky Leader realized that she and her family would have to be up all night again slicing meat, and she decided that when she got to Many Deer she would build herself a grass house beside their large tipi with the help of the two men, so that she could carry on her work while they were in the council tent. A grass house, *haharutu*, was made by sticking supple withes upright in the ground in a circle and tying them together at the top, then carrying the rope all around the frame spirally from top to bottom. The frame was then entirely covered over with buffalo grass and a large smokehole left at the top and an opening at the east for an entrance. Over the central fireplace a wooden grate or drying rack like the one in the tipi would be built high up so that the meat could dry. Donations for the council tent could also be kept in there to keep them from freezing. When the tipis were all set up, the chiefs, braves, and boys would meet in the council tent in the evening to discuss tactics and have a feast on ribs. Eagle Chief had sent out two scouts to climb a high hill now covered with snow to look far to the west up the river and determine where the herds were. They would report that night at the council tent.

Meanwhile, when the men arrived back at Camp 11 with the horses so that they could move the encampment from Turkey Creek westward to Many Deer, at Eagle Chief's direction, the errand man, Know-His-Face went announcing through the camp:

They killed many buffalo up there and Eagle Chief says we must move from here to there. The meat is sleeping up there and they have a camping place all prepared. People do not need to wait for one another in the morning but can start out any time they are ready as the trail has already been broken by the men coming over here with the horses.

When Horse Rider got into camp where White Woman, No Corn, and the boy were, he tethered the horses outside the tipi and the women covered them and gave them cottonwood tops and bark to eat, leaving them there for the night. Horse Rider told of what a good camping place they had at Many Deer, the problem of how they had to transport the meat across the ice from the south of the river, and how much wood Victory Call had gathered for them. In the morning, right after breakfast, the horses were saddled up and loaded by Horse Rider while the two women dismantled the tent. Some of the meat was still moist (*kiparu*) and he bundled this up in an extra package and piled it on top of the saddle. It would not spoil because the weather was so cold. The two parfleches of meat that were completely dried were fastened one on each side of the saddle.

Meanwhile White Woman was shaking the tent pegs loose and pulling them out. No Corn was inside rolling up the mats and tying them and whatever blankets they had. The two sticks from outside the smokehole were removed. Next they removed the pegs laced over the door flap, rolling them up with it for further use. Now they could remove the tent cover. First the south half was pulled to the back and folded over, then the north half was carried around and also folded over at the back. They now pulled down the "backbone" pole at the west so that it lay on the ground with the partially folded cover underneath it. The pole was untied at the top and bottom ends and removed and the cover folded down the length in two. The shape of the cover was something of an equilateral triangle with broad squat arms and a point at the top and two extra flanges with a hole in each for the smokehole. After the cover had been folded once in the length, the two broad ends near the base were folded in, and then the cover was folded in the length once more and tightly rolled from the bottom up toward the point when it was tied with two attached straps around the middle. It was now tied around and across each end with extra ropes.

The frame was still standing and they had to be careful not to break the poles in taking them down. First they unwound the rope that bound them at the top: it was untied at the bottom of the south doorway pole, unwound four times and then left hanging in the middle. After the other poles were removed from the sides and south doorway, the three poles of the tripod were left standing with the rope hanging from the top. The two poles at the west were gently drawn together while someone stood at the north and held the end of the rope, slowly letting the three poles down. They were now untied and the poles bound together six for one side and six for the other side of the horse to be ready after the loading. With the tipi dismantled, the parfleches were still on the ground and the horses were backed up nearby and loaded with them and then they set out for Many Deer.

As soon as the tipis were up at Many Deer, the men got together in the council tent. The two scouts sent out by Eagle Chief to locate the herd were now ready with their report. They said that the buffalo were coming from the west along the south side of the river very slowly. Nevertheless they thought they would get there that night. This meant that the police had to get into action and keep the camp quiet. War Cry as chief of police sent his deputy Roaming Scout to notify the people. He walked quietly through the encampment, stopping now at this tipi, now at that, telling them that on that evening the dogs had to be muzzled and the children cautioned not to make too much noise as the buffalo would be passing near that night. "That's the order of the chief of police," he said. "Don't try to cut wood with an ax. Break it or use what you have already cut. Don't let the baby cry too long. You must nurse it right away." Then he returned to the council tent reporting that his message had been delivered. Now War Cry gave further directions. He said, "I want Shot Arm and Leading Downhill to go out early tomorrow morning and see where the herd is. We must chase them tomorrow morning about nine or ten o'clock so that we can have the meat ready to be thinned all afternoon. Some of the women have been having to thin meat during the night. When we come across the river with the meat, we ought to put more dirt on the ice because I think we'll be staying here for the rest of our hunt."

The business over, it was time to serve the feast of donated boiled buffalo ribs which were served without delay. As no corn had been donated, no offering was made to the sacred bundle that night. The guests made haste to go home so that the family could prepare their dry meat. However, the police had to remain until after midnight to see that there were no infractions of the antinoise rules. Every now and then one of their number was sent out to see that no one happened to forget and was laughing too loud. The policeman put on his belt with the sleigh bells and taking his stick walked cautiously through the camp. One could hear the snow cracking under his feet. As he arrived where the noise was, he tapped the tent with his stick. Then the noise would stop. He had been holding his sleigh bells so that they would not sound, but now he released them so that everyone would know that he was passing through.

The next day the antinoise injunction continued. Some women went out toward evening to cut wood and although they were supposed to chop very gently, the echo could be heard by the police in the council tent. Two officers were sent out to punish them. They made each woman forfeit one of her moccasins and whatever else the policeman could get. He carried the forfeits up to the council tent and waited there for the women to come and redeem them. It was very cold and each woman had to wrap something around the foot from which the moccasin had been taken. Then she came limping into camp and when she got home, she made some bread and coffee and took it over to the council tent to the police. "All right," said War Cry, "Give her her moccasin." Other women would bring calico or a little tobacco to redeem their things. "Give them to her," said War Cry, "but next time watch out!"

During the day, Know-His-Face had gone through the camp remarking that they could use some corn and coffee at the council tent. With this gentle reminder, they were likely to receive at least two buckets of corn for the evening. As the men came in from the hunt, they donated ribs as usual for the evening council and Old Lady Lucky Leader put them in her grass house. Some men were particularly fond of ribs with an unborn calf inside, and when one of these was donated they would ask to have them served right away. As the men left the ribs at the council tent they were told that special invitations would not be issued but that they were to come right back when they had attended to their business at home. Sometimes men waited at home to get a supper of fried bread and coffee before going to the council if their wives had any, since these supplies were pretty well depleted throughout the camp.

At the council everyone was talking of the buffalo chase that day—of how deep the snow was that they had to go through in some places, etc.

They had made two killings already and still the buffalo were coming. Eagle Chief stated that the next day they would not go out, but simply keep an eye on the herd as there was so much meat in the camp that they had to give it a chance to dry. He also mentioned that the hides should be treated and thinned down. Some of the old men remarked that this was a good time to make bone grease by boiling the bones and skimming off the fat as there were lots of bones about at this time and the grease would harden easily in the cold weather. Almost all the old women in camp would busy themselves with this work, storing the grease in a paunch. Some would make dried intestines and dried and braided strips of stomach (*pararitskusu*).

They made five killings while they were camped at Many Deer and along with the killing at Turkey Creek, they felt that this was enough and they should turn toward home. They had made killings almost every other day and stayed about fifteen days. Victory Call killed six in all and Horse Rider five.

Now that they were considering turning back, they must decide what donations of buffalo meat were to be pledged for the sacred bundle ceremonies in the spring. Each sacred bundle must have at least one *rarahuru*, a parfleche containing the dried meat of a whole buffalo. The different doctor cults also needed pledges of meat for their spring renewal rites, but they simply needed backbone steaks. For example, the two leaders of the Bear Cult reserved two steaks for their cult. Victory Call set aside one steak for his Deer or Whistle Dance and one for the Bear Cult.

There were twelve major sacred bundles, each of which had to be provided for with a parfleche of dried meat. The Evening Star bundle owned by Old Lady Lucky Leader would be provided for by her son Frank Leader in some years, and by her son-in-law Roaming Leader in others, according to the circumstances of the kill on a particular hunt. Lone Chief and Shot Arm alternated in this way for the Morning Star bundle. War Cry and his younger brother Brave Shield alternated in supplying the meat for War Cry's war bundle (*karaxkata karusu*) that had been derived from the Evening Star bundle, etc.

Everyone was interested in the news of how the donations had gone and Eagle Chief sent out his errand man Know-His-Face to find out at the different tipis where the sacred bundles were kept.

Sometimes a man couldn't manage to get a good buffalo for his bundle. He approached a man who had just killed a fat cow and said, "I want you to take pity on me. I have a sacred bundle and I want to make *rarahuru* [a parfleche of meat]." "Go ahead, take it," said the hunter, and went off, leaving the bundle owner to butcher the sacred buffalo himself. When he got home with the meat he told his wife, "*ra-waruksti-ti*" ("one that is-sacred-it is"). Then she would know that it is to be preserved, but not eaten by the family—except possibly only some very inferior part like the leg.

One of the main sacred bundles was owned by Misery—the Elk (*Arikariki*) bundle—and some of his friends were concerned since he had remained on Grand Island and they thought he might not get the necessary buffalo meat to hold the ceremony. There were three of them and Bringing Horses who had a good horse agreed to get the necessary buffalo for the purpose. He and the two other friends, Running Scout and Blue Hawk, made up their minds to ride together back to Grand Island as soon as possible to reassure Misery that his Elk bundle was taken care of. Such a group of three men could arrive at Grand Island in a day from their camp on the Republican while it took the pack train at least seven days to get there. The men would take a diagonal course across the country and avoid stopping at Fort Kearney, but it was still a strenuous journey and took a whole day of hard fast riding until evening. When they came to ride downhill crossing the hills, they had to proceed cautiously as the ground was slippery.

Hearing of their plans, Eagle Chief wanted to send a message to Sitting Hawk, one of the main chiefs who had remained on the island. He delegated Running Scout who was one of the three men, to carry back the news. He especially stated that "with the consecrated meat, it is this way: there are twelve parfleches, one for each sacred bundle." When the three men arrived at Grand Island that night they went straight to Sitting Hawk's tipi. As the three men came in one after another, Misery, Sitting Hawk's son, was surprised. He said, "Kira, what's up?" "Well, we started from this side of Many Deer early this morning and just got here tonight." As soon as he heard this, Advance Scout went through the camp calling out, "The three hunters (*parisu*) are here. There is lots of meat. There are twelve consecrated parfleches for the sacred bundles."

63

THE RETURN FROM THE HUNT

Stories Told of the Hunt—Rest of Skidis Arrive at Grand Island—Bands Go Their Separate Ways —Arrival Home to Earth Lodges—the New Year About to Begin

THE THREE HUNTERS on their return to Grand Island told Sitting Hawk and Misery the rest of the news. They told of how Bringing Horses had obtained some sacred meat for the Elk bundle that Misery owns and he thanked them. Then they told all about the hunt and how they had come to stay at Many Deer. "The buffalo came so close they practically touched us," they said, "and Bear killed the calf-that-has-a-rope." "Well," said Sitting Hawk, "No wonder the buffalo were coming. They must have been looking for the calf." The men continued with their storytelling that they had given the hide of the calf for the Wolf-Standing-in-Water bundle. "That's good," said Sitting Hawk. They told of how the cavalry had accompanied the line of march on the way out through a linguistic error, but how at the Republican River it had been straightened out and the cavalry rode back. "The Stay-at-Homes knew about that," they said, for Fox Chief, Victory Call's older son was a member of the cavalry and had come in to tell them. Then the Stay-at-Homes told their news.

In five or six days, the Skidis arrived at the island. As soon as they turned back from Many Deer, they suspended all formality and there was no longer a council tent and the errand man no longer went through the village announcing further plans. Word on these matters went informally by word of mouth through the camp. If word had not reached anyone, they would inquire of Eagle Chief and upon being told, set out directly for the next camp, not waiting to move in any special order. When they finally arrived at Grand Island, they camped there for five or six days before setting out for the final lap of their journey to the village. It was relatively warm and pleasant there and they could well use the rest.

Victory Call and the others of the family were glad to see Grandma who now moved in with them from the tent of Misery where she had been staying. She showed them the nice sack of dried potatoes and one of dried beans that she had accumulated and she said, "I'm not the only one. Everyone in camp went looking for potatoes." They also had the roasted corn that she had been keeping for them. The vegetable food tasted good as their supplies had given out by this time. White Woman was busy cooking the dry meat and bread and Grandma made her potatoes to go with the soup.

By the time they got to the island it was February and one could hear the ice cracking from time to time in the river. It sounded like a shot. Because of this, Eagle Chief thought they had better try to cross over right away and get home before the ice cracked up. A small minority in the different bands felt like lingering, but most of the people wanted to get back to the village. Some wanted to see their children that they had left at school.

Eagle Chief announced, "Day after tomorrow we'll go. We must cross where the white people have already roughened the ice when they carried their wood and ice across." When the tents were all down, those who were staying behind said, "I hope you folks have good luck on your way back." "I hope you get along well here too," said Eagle Chief. "If anything happens, see the officer at Fort Kearney." Others were saying to the Stay-Behinds, "You make us lonesome, letting us return like this without you." Then they set off for home.

From Grand Island to the railroad station (Clarks?) where they would turn north, it took four days. Then it took another day to reach the village.

We walked right through water and snow. Sometimes women took off their moccasins to go through the water and we never caught cold. When we got to the railroad station, everyone was happy. We would soon be home. We would feel glad at the very sight of the schoolhouse. The waterways were all frozen at this time about a foot to a foot and a half thick. Earth had to be sprinkled on the ice to get across.

The Loup River was awfully slippery and smooth and we had to get the boys to go to the other side and begin making a roadway by sprinkling earth. "Hold the horses steady. Go slow. Throw some more dirt," people would be saying when the first horse went over. Old ladies slipped on the ice and slipped around before they could get up.

As soon as they got home they moved into the earth lodge. There were no fleas or vermin there such as they had gotten during the summer.

After their travels over the snow and ice, they were glad to return to the warmth of their homes.

Soon the thunder would sound from the south. Then the priests would call down the gods from the heavens to re-create the earth and Wonderful would come down from his home in the western skies and walk the land that the gods had made—in all his aspects as the lightning, the thunder, the storm—going on the hill, the plain, the prairie—in the bottomlands, across the water, in the village and back to his home in the western skies where he would rest.

The new year would begin—the house, the food pit, the hunt, the harvest and again the winter hunting time. But there came a time when the year would not begin for the Pawnee. For beyond the Pawnee universe was the outer world and from it would come its destruction after six hundred years, and a new world would be born.

64

POSTSCRIPT INTO THE PRESENT

~~~~~~

*The Modern Pawnee—Otter's Later Life—the
Arrival in Oklahoma—the Fate of Otter's Family
and Friends—His Marriage—the Modern Day
Pawnee Powwow*

~~~~~~

SOME MIGHT WONDER how the modern Pawnees came into being, seeing that they are thoroughly integrated citizens of the present United States, many of them living as residents of various urban centers. The Pawnees count among their numbers teachers, artisans, business managers, engineers, journalists, artists, nurses, social workers, professional entertainers, and one former Big League baseball player.

Perhaps the fate of some of the principal characters I have mentioned offers a good means of illustrating the process of transition. The boy, Otter, is a good case in point. When he was about seven years old his father, Victory Call, died. He felt he had been bewitched by his anxious rival in the religious field, Big Doctor, leader of the Doctor Association, whose hegemony the success of Victory Call's Deer Dance cult was challenging. In his dying vision, Victory Call saw a man with an eagle-wing fan before his face that he positively identified as Big Doctor.

White Woman, Grandma, and the boy were given a home by Uncle War Cry in whose house they settled, taking a subordinate position near its eastern end. The old house was left to the other inhabitants. The boy was warned to break off all relationships with his old friends who might insult him with mention of the fact that he had no father. His mother kept him close to the house. He tried to get acquainted with some of the children nearby, but he found it hard.

Two years later, Shot Arm, a brave of Lone Chief's Village-across-a-Ridge, came and sued for his mother's hand. Shot Arm approached War Cry and said, "Victory Call was my uncle and he has a son here. He is as my own son and I'd like to raise him." Finally he was told to speak to

White Woman and after pleading his cause with her, Shot Arm came to live with them. The boy was told that "his father" had come. When he demurred and said that he thought Victory Call was his father, he was quieted. Shot Arm gave him gifts and did his best to father him. White Woman had had some reservations as Shot Arm already had a wife, but he convinced her that he was determined to part from the other woman in any event. Later there were recriminations from this quarter.

Once on the winter hunt, Shot Arm was invited to bring his new family to live in the household of White Eagle. He had been formally invited by "his two old mothers" who were the official owners of the house. In their new home the family occupied a place at the west and had status and Otter had new friends—David Gillingham, son of White Eagle, and the two brothers, Luther and Andy Coons.

In the Sioux massacre of 1873 during the summer hunt, when from 60 to 120 Pawnees lost their lives while butchering their kill in a canyon near Trenton, Nebraska, Otter and White Woman were guided to safety through the Sioux lines by a young warrior at the request of Mad Bear.

Finally the Pawnees moved to Oklahoma in three contingents. White Eagle went with the first group, while Shot Arm and his family were true to the faction of Lone Chief who wanted to remain on their old land and stayed to the last. The two old ladies who owned White Eagle's earth lodge gave over the pillars and materials to Shot Arm who set up a hexagonal frame of six forked pillars and no outer sod collar or wall, so that they had a high pointed lodge to live in.

When the last group decided to go, the government assigned them ten wagons for the poor people who had no horses for transport, and some beeves to be killed every Saturday for their food.

In Oklahoma, the three contingents had set up three earth-lodge villages in different locations. Lone Chief set up one on the Arkansas River three or four miles this side of Ralston where there was a ferryboat. White Eagle built a log house on top of a hill near the big pond west of the present town of Pawnee, with the earth lodges of his following on the east side of the hill toward the pond. Half a mile east of the agency, Misery and his father-in-law Comanche Chief, along with War Cry, were the leading spirits of another log-house village.

Shot Arm, who had become agency policeman, settled his family in a tent near the school. All winter they lived in the tent. Then in spring, April 1876, without any outward sign of illness, White Woman died. She asked to have her grandchild brought to her and then spoke to its mother, telling her that she was bidding them farewell and that she should take good care of the child. And so she fell asleep and never awakened.

Victory Call's former retainer, Horse Rider and his wife, No Corn, were living in a frame house with No Corn's oldest daughter. The girl had married a man of the Little-Earth-Lodge Band known as Abraham

Lincoln who was the government blacksmith. They invited Shot Arm
and the boy to come and live with them. They stayed there for six years
and then Shot Arm's sister, Woman White Star, invited them to come and
live with her. One winter both Shot Arm and the boy were very ill with
a high fever. Fox Chief, his older half brother, came and took the boy to
live with him. From there the boy moved from one house to the other,
sometimes with Misery, then with War Cry and others. Because of his
wandering about, he did not know that his father, Shot Arm, had died.
The relatives suspected that his death was due to witchcraft by a member
of the family of their old rival, Big Doctor. The feeling was so strong
that the agent had an autopsy performed, which showed that Shot Arm
had died of an old gunshot wound that had affected his lungs. But the
Pawnees were not convinced. And neither was Mark Evarts when he told
of it in 1928. During the first five years in Oklahoma, 800 Pawnees died.

Otter's old playmates, David Gillingham and the Coons brothers, had
gone to Carlisle School in Pennsylvania and they induced him to come
along. After his schooling he worked at harness making in Harrisburg,
Newark, and Philadelphia. He experienced such wonders as climbing
into the arm of the Statue of Liberty in New York Harbor and playing
baseball for a period with the Cuban Giants, a colored team. While he
was with them in the South, he was questioned by the authorities "about
the grandfather clause." His right hand was permanently broken in baseball, for in those days they played without benefit of a catcher's mitt. He
was very lonesome and went home. As he says,

> When I got home from Carlisle, I had no home. My older brother,
> Fox Chief, War Cry, and Misery had all died. It was cold weather and
> Behaille (the interpreter) met me on the road and took me in his
> buggy and gave me a swig of whisky. He offered me a home at his
> house where Brave Chief, Frank Leader, and Peter Wood were living.

An older woman in Behaille's house befriended him and established a
relationship with him. Finally the agency took a hand in his life. The
agent said he had made a good record at school and he should settle
down. He was trained as a blacksmith and given a position. At last the
Riding-In family gave him their daughter, Hannah, in marriage and they
set up a farm together and had a daughter. Then Hannah died of tuberculosis and shortly afterward, at the age of twelve, their daughter followed. The farm was lost to the bank as the result of a crop failure and
an unpaid loan. This was in 1924. In 1928 this record of old Pawnee life
was made with Mark Evarts' help.

When he returned to Pawnee from the east, Mark Evarts had a severe
emotional crisis and finally an important religious experience. He returned home permanently in 1897–1898. The Pawnee version of the re-

vivalist Ghost Dance religion was in full force. Through it the people hoped that the new would be swept away and old conditions return. It was invested with many of the old and rich Pawnee ceremonial constructs that were vividly recalled in memory and in visions. As one of their fond remembrances, they thought of the old Hand Game, and this became the framework for a new and elaborate ceremonial synthesis of old religious patterns. With the beginning of the twentieth century, the religious elements diminished in importance.

In World War I and again in World War II, the Pawnees for whom defense of country had always been a leitmotif enlisted generously, and their war veterans became an important element of modern Pawnee life. Following World War II and their extensive contacts abroad, a considerable number of Pawnees availed themselves of the educational benefits of the G.I. Bill of Rights, acquiring college degrees and specialized professional training.

The Pawnee powwow held in the beginning of July, when the Pawnees used to leave on their summer buffalo hunt, takes place at Pawnee, Oklahoma. It is a colorful combination of traditional and adapted Indian dances and music under the auspices of the Pawnee war veterans. The Pawnees, from wherever their lives have taken them, come by car, train, or plane to this their homecoming, where there is a brief period of camping in tents and cooking over an open fire or a charcoal grill, renewing social contacts and kin reminiscences. The rest of the year's round is in another place and in the present, just as the old people had envisioned their future.

65

THE UNIVERSE REGAINED

IDEAS AND FORECAST

IN THE WORLD SCENE the Pawnees were a small group of people on a small piece of land, but as a nation and as a people their lives were of remarkable complexity and order withal, proving that the human dimension is never simple. Their lives moved in cycle upon cycle in a never-ending interplay of influences. These cycles and epicycles reached always into the community instead of being turned in upon themselves in a small household group.

During World War II those of us who lived in city apartments and who had always professed a desire for absolute privacy found ourselves forced into a kind of cooperative life because of the curtailment of many kinds of services. The house I lived in near Columbia University was six stories high and on each floor there was a small rectangular hallway onto which the five surrounding apartments opened. Because it was almost impossible to obtain a private telephone, the management installed a pay telephone in the hallway downstairs on the ground floor. Most of the people in the house had to receive their calls through this phone, and the messages were received by the grace of whoever happened to be passing the phone when it was ringing and was willing to answer and to call the party downstairs to the phone.

One day I heard a little boy wailing pitifully in one of the apartments on my floor. I spoke to him through the closed door and he said his mother had gone down to answer the phone. We kept up our conversation on opposite sides of the door until his mother returned and then I pointed out to her that like many children I thought he was afraid she was leaving him inside the apartment and alone in the world. We tried a little practical experiment. We instructed the boy to ring the doorbell of the lady across the hall to see what would happen, while we watched from inside. There were four elderly sisters who lived in that apartment, and one of them answered and said, "Come in, come in," and straightway gave him a cookie. He bid her goodbye and part two of the experiment began. He rang the doorbell of the woman who had the apartment right next door to his. As he rang, she came to the door. She had two little girls of about his age and she invited him to play. After a while he returned home with a second cookie, and his mother went to explain to her neighbor what had happened. A very pleasant friendship began from that day on between the two young women as well as the children. The mother in the house that the boy had visited was of Armenian extraction and the father of the family was Irish. The mother of the frightened little boy was originally from New England and earned some money as a part-time fashion model. The two young women began exchanging recipes and other relevant data about life, and mostly the doors of the two apartments were left open and the children ran back and forth as they wished and sometimes set up little games in the hall. Some of the rest of us began to leave our front doors open from time to time too, and we might come out in less than formal dress to take a look at the children at play and we managed to say a word to one another as well.

In recent years our newspapers have been full of the tragedy of apartment isolation. Children burned to death in an apartment as a result of playing with matches while their mother was out buying a few needed groceries. Children with keys around their necks coming home after school to an empty apartment or staying in the streets for want of company at home, or even for hours in the movies. In 1961 there were 7½ million women with children under eighteen in the labor force, the number having doubled in ten years. There were half a million latch-key children under twelve alone during their mother's working hours. For a majority of these women their work outside the home was an economic necessity. A considerable number of apartments contain a partially disabled person who may be either totally incapacitated or cannot properly be left alone. A figure of one out of four apartments containing a person of this description was cited to me in the past, although I have no way at this time of checking the statistics. These are the most drastic situations in which apartment isolation is a severe handicap. There are others of a less drastic nature, such as the lonesomeness of a young person temporarily living in an apartment or a single person living alone temporarily or permanently. The young couple find it impossible to go out of an evening into a social environment so that they can cement their relationship a little more pleasantly than over the dishes and other repetitive household chores, unless they hire someone hourly to reign over their home and their children. There are more or less adequate members of this baby-sitting profession, but this is hardly the most desirable way of taking care of the problem as the procedure is exceedingly haphazard. This is necessarily the case, as the pay for this work must be marginal and the people who work in it transient.

This situation is typical of our present social adjustment. The apartment household is provided with many material conveniences, probably as many as ever appeared in a household in the world's history—but in its social form we have been remarkably uncreative. Our household retains the isolation of the Roman patriarchal domain but lacks its slaves and even a single servant. It is the fortified castle of the Middle Ages without serfs or retainers. It is the family farm without farmhands, servant girls, or maiden aunts. We moan about the intransigence of those who refuse to make themselves into domestic servants. We think they should, while we prefer industrial and office jobs. We call this "the servant problem." It is not the by now hypothetical servant, but the person with a frozen pattern that is at fault. There is no reason why anyone should possess such an all-purpose servant. It is a type of division of labor that will no longer be feasible as educational patterns on many levels reach out to everyone. In this situation, the full isolation of the apartment dweller becomes more and more universal. The good neighbor with little else to do, the elevator operator, the superintendent and his family—all of them resources of the past—are also no longer available. Apartment houses with rentals running to $550 a month and more have found it of value in attracting tenants to hire a corps of private police. These police patrol halls and basements where washing machines and other conveniences are located, check up on baby-sitters, regulate the use of garbage pails, feed goldfish in addition to providing patrol service that is roughly "on a scale with that of Fort Knox." This material is as reported in the New York Daily News, August 6, 1963. As stated in the newspaper article, some of the security aspects stem from the close proximity of these fancy dwellings to poor ones, but just as interesting for the problem I am raising are the multifarious tasks that still remain to be done for the apartment dweller even when he can afford to pay these high rentals.

What desperate circumstances bring the police to the very doors of our apartments and inside the house as well? This is surely the medieval castle without retainers, serfs, or servants with the invader lurking near. We now need protection from neighborhood hostility, neighborhood unconcern, and the inadequacies of the household arrangements themselves. We have looked at the past with nostalgia and deplored the loss of "neighborhood," but we cannot restore the old functions of old institutions when new institutions have evolved demanding new adjustments. Policing is hardly the best kind of adjustment where protecting property must supersede human interrelationships. In the course of our urban evolution, we have developed beyond neighborhood protection and neighborhood concern to unconcern, as a corollary of the maximum mobility that has become a primary need of our style of life. Instead of coping with the changing functions of our changing institutions, we try to "make do" and we fare very badly. We cannot turn back and immobilize people in a nostalgic flashback to "neighborhood." We are in the Jet Age. Mobility is our privilege as the fruit of the larger horizons of communication that we have achieved on a social level as well as on a physical. American society with its breakdown of the rigid class lines of the Old World has made an important contribution to human society.

The next steps in our combined physical and social revolution must be taken in uncharted territory. We are pioneers of plenty, for no other people has equaled us in the food we can produce and the things we can make or in the consequent freedom and mobility of our people. Our ability to move does not mean that we should move for the sake of moving, nor our ability to develop variety that we should vary for the sake of varying.

Real problems, however, do confront us and it is in the light of these that we should begin to make our departure from the rigidities of the past. As 70 per cent of our population now live in urban centers and a growing proportion are trending toward them, it is in the urban setting that many of our most pressing needs appear. These needs cluster around three foci—family, home, and work. In the family we can see that there will be greater mobility of the woman on all levels. The woman is now being invited to keep up and improve her occupational skills, to broaden her intellectual and cultural horizons, and to participate more actively in the democratic politics of our nation if only in the form of a more knowledgeable use of her franchise. These influences can only draw the woman from her household, and how and when is this to be if the household demands she be stationed there twenty-four hours a day? There is no letup in family duties. During the day, children and household maintenance have maximum claim; during the evening, a tired husband wants a meal and social comfort. These needs certainly cannot be dismissed, but they can be better rationalized than we have done so far. The household maintenance can be developed through group service approaches toward (a) furniture and plant, (b) clothing, and (c) food. The children need warmth and maximum concern, but they can receive some watch-care at times from another person than their mother. Our hopes for our family unit are based on the idea that the sentiments of the sex pair for each other is the keystone of the affection that will extend to the children.

I will not here try to deal with the many problems and nuances of this hypothesis, but granting it for the moment, the twenty-four-hour household duty of the woman allows the couple little opportunity to seek social recreation together if there are children or even one child. Even when they stay at home together, they have little time to themselves, as the children leave them little chance for uninterrupted communication. It would also be possible for the childless couple, the grandparent, or the

single person to entertain children in their homes if temporary watch-
care were available when they needed to go out.* As matters now stand,
the child is fully justified in clinging desperately to his adult guardian.
The child should have some alternative to this. I have many times
mulled over these problems in the light of my experience in the Columbia
University apartment, and of my knowledge of Pawnee life in which
parents and children enjoyed a mobility in the community impossible to
us. Once while I was visiting in Oklahoma I opened one of the national
magazines and there saw just what I was looking for—the Pawnee house
in modern form. In this case, the specific model was a picture of a round
hospital connected with the famous Mayo Clinic in Rochester, Minnesota. The round hospital was 60 feet in diameter and all around the
periphery, except for the entryway, were separate rooms for the patients.
In the middle was the station for one or more nurses, who could turn
on their heels and maintain eye to eye contact with each of the twelve
patients around the outside of the circle, and the patients with them,
while the several patients did not see into one another's rooms. A relatively short walk could take the nurse to any one of the rooms where she
was needed. I began to work on the adaptation of such a structure to
the problem of the mobility of the apartment dweller along with the
maintenance of reasonable privacy.

That year, by good fortune, the American Anthropological Association held its annual meeting in Minneapolis, and I determined to go and
see the round hospital for myself. Mr. Harold Mickey, director of the
hospital, was kind enough to give me of his time and show me through,
and we had a long talk about my problem and the evolution of the round
hospital as a social as well as a physical project. He commended me to
the architects of the building, Ellerbe and Company of St. Paul, where
Mr. Dawson of that firm was persuaded by phone to "make a contribution to social science" by seeing me about the problem. I received many
major insights from this talk of well over an hour of a busy morning
from this practical and imaginative architect. I subsequently consulted
Christopher Tunnard, City Planner of Yale, and I. Irving Rouse, Profes-

* Compare this item from the *New York Times,* Saturday, August 17, 1963:

HOUSEKEEPING SERVICE AIDS SUMMER BACHELORS IN PARIS

Paris (Reuters)—A Paris department store has begun a new service called S.O.S.
Lonely Husbands.

Men living alone in the city while their families bask on seaside beaches now need
only call a telephone number to have a cleaner come to tidy the apartment, wash
linen, cook meals and sew on shirt buttons.

The same service will have shoes resoled, buy the groceries and clean suits.

If the summer bachelor wants to have a dinner party, the service will offer "instant
menus," prepare the one selected, serve it, and clean up afterward.

One of the first applicants to the service was a woman.

sor of Anthropology of the same university, Karl Koch, of Karl Koch Associates, designer of Tech Built Houses, of Cambridge, Massachusetts, Joseph Monteserrat, Director of the Migration Division of the Commonwealth of Puerto Rico, Department of Labor, and other close friends and associates, including Dr. Vera Rubin, Director of the Research Institute for the Study of Man, and Mrs. Florence Goldin of the Grey Advertising Company, Prof. Charles Wagley of Columbia, Prof. David Riesman of Harvard, and others, particularly concerning the social problems. The concept of the house is shown in the accompanying illustration, which gives some of the additional practical details.

Newly Delevoping Needs That Make the Family-oriented House Necessary

Before a house is to be built a very important element in the planning should be the question, "What human needs should it serve?" Our lives have changed radically in the recent past, and new needs have arisen that make our older type of housing inadequate. As I have pointed out, mobility has become a prime need as well as a privilege in our modern life. As a consequence, certain important dislocations have developed between our new needs and our old style of life. We have lost neighborly and neighborhood guardianship and have developed isolation to the point of danger—not only of the trauma of simple loneliness, but of actual physical attack and unavailability of assistance in case of unforeseen illness or incapacity. Bring in however many people we may on a transient basis, these factors cannot be compensated for in this way. It is essential that someone be obliquely aware of us at all times and that we should be able to count on this awareness. At the same time we want to be able to withdraw from attention except in case of need. These conditions were met by and large in the urban neighborhood of the past.

It has been thought that the disappearance of the neighborhood is a consequence of the huge housing complexes that have recently been built, but it is not the buildings in themselves but rather the social factors behind their building which are accountable. Of these, the need and desire for ready mobility is an essential one. Because the need for mobility will increase, our next question is, "How do we live in our urban houses and fulfill our needs that were inherently satisfied in the old neighborhood?

The family-oriented house diagrammed in Figure 65-1 concentrates this need in single individuals who are stationed outside the apartments but within easy reach of them. The plan groups eight apartments around a central hall, in the middle of which a floor host or hostess is stationed, with an occupational category that bears some analogy to an airplane steward or hostess, though not exactly with the same set of duties. As a structure, the house itself is feasible and the successful New York builder Aaron Diamond has been kind enough to consider with me possible costs of land and building. It would appear that the plot might be about 150 feet square. The land costs would be augmented by the fact that while normally a city house takes up about 66 per cent of the land leaving 33 per cent free, this house would occupy 33 per cent and require that 66 per cent of the land be free.

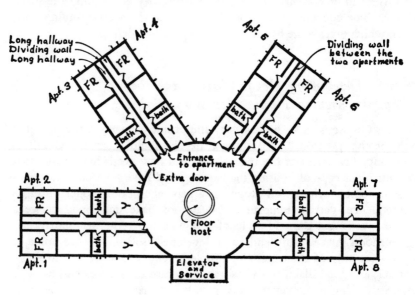

FIGURE 65-1. The family-oriented house with eight apartments, two in each arm. (Scale, approx. ½ inch = 10 feet.)

This would mean that it would. have to be built in parts of the city where land areas were less expensive than in the center of town. Some of the costs could be ameliorated by erecting the building twenty stories high, so that the rentals would then be in a median category. In terms of cost, the real problem centers on the floor host. This still remains both the crux of the idea and the problem. The person on the night shift would need little technical training except for a fund of good will, dependability, and alertness. At least two people would be needed on the day shifts with a fill-in for absences, holidays, lunch hours, etc. A supervisor would be needed to coordinate the operation and the personnel. The day people would need more specialized briefing than those of the night. As matters now stand, this work could be supplied only by more or less volunteer help or through public subsidy. Such sources as possible social science interns who are receiving college or university training in these fields, or the proposed Domestic Peace Corps are possible sources, with minimum fees paid from the public coffers. Some of the occupants of the apartments might be a party to such arrangements at stated times. All occupants of the surrounding apartments would be beneficiaries of the "neighborhood guardianship" function. Those with children or with disabled persons would receive special benefits in terms of baby-sitting requirements. The plan is such that the room fronting on the central hall would have an extra door to that room alone which could be left open or shut as required (Y, open and closed room). The apartment itself would have its main entrance into the long corridor which runs along one side of the rooms. In the case of small children, the internal rooms (Y) could be closed off should the parents go away, leaving the child in its own room, opening onto the central area. Chronically ill, feeble, or old persons could be left in this room when the woman or regular caretaker of the house had to leave temporarily. The number and kind of supplementary functions that the floor host could encompass in these cases is something to be determined in practice. Clearly this does not include some of the functions that have been grafted onto the baby-sitting function such as putting children to bed, washing dishes, serving children meals, etc. A drink of water or a dose of medicine might possibly be included, for the old, the disabled, or children. Instructions for emergency with referral to the responsible parties would certainly be part of the floor host's mission.

For the rest of the people in the apartments, the possible services would vary from receiving packages, taking messages, admitting repair men, feeding pets when the occupants are away, to small talk with a teen-ager alone in an apartment who would like to wander out and say a word or two, or even someone of more mature years who may be alone. To my mind, the common circle onto which the apartments open should in no sense be a ballroom-type lobby or its equivalent. The occupants can reserve this type of affect for their front rooms (FR) if they have a desire for it. I would think the lobby should be a somewhat familiar working area—neat, but a place for traffic to move in and out or to stay. It is not beyond the bounds of possibility that each apartment could have a locker there and possibly an ironing board, sewing machine, cupboard for materials, workbench, tools, to be necessarily put away when not in use. There is no reason why people would have to do this, but some might want to. One common washer-drier machine located in this region might also be a good thing instead of one in each apartment or many lined up in the basement.

I feel that through these or similar arrangements, certain tragedies of our present typical apartment living could be mitigated, and some problems lightened even though admittedly new ones would arise which could be coped with when they do. The freer mobility of mother, child, and parents as couples would carry them beyond *a feeling of entrapment* which is all too common in our present arrangements. The adult with an aged parent or disabled relative could move about, and this might make all the difference between placing such persons in institutions and nursing homes or not doing so. Orphan children or others that need foster care could be taken care of by a greater variety of persons. Even a teenager with a sympathetic ear available to him at all times might find his current life crises less of a strain. On another level, with the acceleration of automation, people are going to have reduced working hours and a good deal more leisure, as well as periods of job transition or occupational reconversion. There is no reason why a "do-it-yourself" trend should not occupy some of this time for some of these people. I can envision a mass-production industry which packages materials and patterns and explores creative principles which allows the individual to produce some of the things he wants to use to his individual taste, taking his time about it because he has the time. The floor lobby area would be a possible location for doing such things. If he wanted to practice music, for example, he could do it in his front room, far from the center, which might even be soundproofed to some degree. Through these activities a certain degree of casual association to the individual taste could occur between people of various ages instead of *total segregation of age levels*. Social centers for segregating people of special interests would certainly also be available for specialized associations away from home. I feel that as the need for eight-hour full-time employment becomes less pressing, some people might chose the occupation of floor host for its human interest. New kinds of occupations of this service type may be welcome as new categories of work, with creative possibilities in the area of human relations.

A series of such buildings built roughly to a common pattern in various parts of the nation and in different neighborhoods of the cities would make *transplanting oneself from one to another location* less difficult than having to transpose one's life to an entirely different physical plant and different community. In our need for mobility we might find an accustomed home in many locations.

Roughly, these are some of the thoughts that have come to my mind over the years as I have contemplated Pawnee life and thought of our own.

The Problem of Work in an Automated Age

Historically most of our modes of work were developed to pressure people into working toward goals devised by others. This process became the more efficient as we were able to substitute internalized guilt for the lash. Pawnee impetus to work came not from this type of pressures but from a sense of community. The internalized process was a search by each individual for his own goals, as we see in the naming process and in the vision that he deliberately sought. Our present circumstances of overproduction and automation call for drastic revisions in our age-old motivations. The Pawnee way is now actually more suitable for us than our own.

Ironically, just at this time when gross human labor becomes unnecessary we are also faced with the population explosion, when rather than producing and raising as many children as possible in order to provide a labor force and an army, women are called upon to limit these traditional activities and to supplement them with other kinds of work. As the traditional work categories dwindle, youth also finds itself hard-pressed to find a place in the only activities in the community that can really mark them as adults—for however mature a level school activities may reach, the school student is still immature in our community. Only the breadwinner can enjoy full dignity. On the other end of the age spectrum, people are being pressed to retire earlier and earlier, and here again they face the loss of social dignity as they give over their status as full breadwinners.

The permanence of this problem has not been faced. I know of only one major breakthrough by social scientists in our approach to the logistics of work in recent times, i.e., that of Herbert R. Shepherd of the Case Institute of Cleveland and Robert R. Blake of Texas ("Changing Behavior through Cognitive Change," *Human Organization*, special issue, summer, 1962, pp. 88-96; *Human Organization* is the publication of the Society for Applied Anthropology). Describing our present type of bureaucratic management structure the authors state that:

> . . . they can learn only at the top where control is centralized and . . . they demand passive conformity of most of their members. . . . Conflict is normally resolved by automatic suppression of the less powerful party to the conflict.

On the grounds of its actual inefficiency as a work form, the authors tried a social experiment within the Esso organization, consisting of the withdrawal of a group of workers from the prevailing management structure and development of a new type of interpersonal coordination among them. Although this experiment was conducted within a limited setting, it has an important relevance to the larger questions of work patterns in general that we must necessarily face at this stage of our social development.

Each person within himself will have a hard time getting beyond the built-in acceptance of our traditional work attitudes as inevitable or at least as indispensable to survival. It is significant for us that the Pawnees with a direct confrontation of the survival problem, succeeded, with a very different attitude toward work and its motivation. The detailed account of their interpersonal operations while at work offers us a natural social laboratory for the consideration of this question.

The problem of the reorientation of our work goals as we progress from a mercantilist to a humanist society will require extensive study. Occupational reconversion will be required of all of us. As we cultivate individual goals, this may be a continuing process throughout our lives. I would suggest that we develop an Adult College of Continuing Education as a locus of this process. The present adult college trains for the traditional vocations, academic degrees, or fragments of the traditional intellectual disciplines for mild personal uplift. Some revision in this regime will be called for. The goals will have to be at the same time more long-range and more fluid. These institutions will have to develop a new and imaginative kind of student counselor who will have to do a great deal more individual counseling on the educational problems of each person. In our present hurried tempo, there has been little precedent for such counseling. The Pawnee individual was encouraged to seek his own individual vision, and he had an imaginative priest or medicine man to give him an active outlet for his vision when he achieved it. He got to work providing food and other materials and participated in an elaborate performance. We need an analogous mode in the organization of our lives. There is no reason why, in addition to the traditional intellectual and aesthetic disciplines, an Adult College could not include in its academic curriculum such occupationally oriented fields as the history (over a long period of time), the wide-ranging sociology, the mathematics, philosophy, or methodology of such fields or areas as insurance, or banking, or the meat industry, or agricultural production, storing and marketing, the transportation industry, the communications industries, lumbering industries, ceramics and plastics industries, metallurgical industries, textiles, recreation, construction and buildings, administration, and many others—each *viewed as an intellectual challenge rather than a mercantile occupation.* The social, intellectual, historical, philosophical, and even aesthetic implications of these foci might well lead the student from these into the other disciplines, contributing to them a new perspective, and in this cross-cutting of fields we might also bring new dimensions to the applied categories, tending to reorient them toward a more human and humane functionalism.

In our present world mood and outlook, the first question that will be asked is "Who will pay?" and "Who will do the world's work?" I can only answer that I am sure we will do it better as far as human values are concerned and find ways to pay that are less destructive to the human personality than our present modes. A second question must inevitably be, "Why bother now? Such questions will not be relevant in the next hundred years—or two hundred, five hundred, a thousand." I think it is a matter of decades, not centuries. There is a compelling acceleration of multiple factors that we have no power to arrest. We have had a good example of this phenomenon in the field of civil rights. The events themselves are not sudden; the suddenness is due to our refusal to face the trends, and the chaotic results are due to the all-too-common idea that we had best not look ahead, but "muddle through" instead. We have a profound need of a genuine social science that faces major issues and long-range trends.

Some recent newspaper items help us to look into the future:

Frank L. Whitney, industrial designer and president of Walter Kidde Construction Inc., gives us a prediction on the July 15, 1963 financial page of the *New York World Telegram* of widely dispersed, almost totally unmanned factories in such distant areas as San Francisco, California, Birmingham, Alabama, and Hartford, Connecticut, operated out of a central control center in Chicago with raw materials brought in by conveyor, pipeline, or some other automatic method and deposited on the assembly line. It should be a short step to conveying the finished products in similar automatic manner. The present oil- and gas-pipeline systems cover our country over such distances that it should not be too long a step to adapt them to many types of use.

The McLouth Steel Corporation of Detroit, Trenton, and Gibraltar, Michigan, advertises that it has "the first fully automated hot-strip steel mill in the world." This is operated by an electronic computer. "We just feed it 19-ton slabs of steel, and a job description. The electronic brain gives the orders, monitors the steel, controls the mill rolls—even adjusts its thinking for unexpected developments. In $3\frac{1}{2}$ minutes, orange-hot, foot-thick steel comes out as thin as $\frac{1}{16}$ of an inch and 3,200 feet long— precisely to specifications." (*Newsweek*, July 20, 1963.)

Recently announced is the fact that the U.S.S.R. has a cable that can carry electric power as much as 2,000 miles.

Another headline in the *New York Times* to an article dated June 9, 1963, "An Automation Center in Detroit Urged for Use by World Industry." Mr. Ross, president of Federal Department Stores of that city, suggested that application of "Detroit type automation" not only in the United States but also throughout the world offered the city "its golden opportunity in the second half of the 20th century." "Detroit automation," Mr. Ross added, "must become a byword like Swiss watches, sterling silver, Sheffield cutlery, French champagne and Brazilian coffee."

Another item describes a process of freeze-drying foods so that they retain their shape, color, flavor, and cellular structure, become very light in weight, and when properly packaged can be stored as much as two years without refrigeration. Such items as chicken and beef stews, scrambled eggs, ham slices, pork chops, shrimp, crab meat, and coffee—all to be restored almost as good as new by adding water or other liquid. A United States Department of Agriculture economist reports that the Quartermaster Corps will purchase about 1,750,000 pounds of freeze-dry foods this year for use by the Armed Forces. (A pound of beefsteak is reduced to four ounces—two pounds of chicken stew to six and a half ounces.) "The United States Department of Agriculture has forecast that freeze drying will develop into a billion dollar a year industry by 1970. . . . The freeze-dry process was first used in the drug and medical fields, with freeze-dry blood plasma an important example."

Only a few months before his tragic assassination President Kennedy had a special commission on automation which was "to report to him by the end of [1964] on the impact of technological change over the next ten years and what steps should be taken by management labor and state, local and federal governments to soften its impact on workers" (*New York Times*, July 24, 1963). In a subsequent article (*New York Times*, July 22, 1964, p. 36, cols. 3, 4), it is noted that the issue was pursued by President Johnson, who forwarded draft legislations to Congress, and that the bill approved by the House on July 21 would establish a national commission on technology, automation, and economic progress. It would have fourteen members, selected from outside the government by the President, and the nominations would be subject to Senate confirmation. The commission would be required to report to the President and Congress by January 1, 1966, but could issue interim reports at any time. It would expire with the filing of its final report. Its tasks encompass an investigation of economic, technical, human, and social questions.

It should be clear that this kind of automation will not be contained within this country alone. The idea that nonindustrialized nations will now enter the road to well-being by industrializing through the same past historic stages of the highly industrialized nations is an oversimplification. Newly industrializing nations will soon find themselves confronted with processes of advanced automation imported as the current industrial know-how rather than the more antique methods. The new hypothesized "Detroit Automation Center" will probably see to that. Many people in the world will suffer idleness before they have ever had a commercial job. For example, with the finding of oil in the desert interior of the North African nation of Libya, commercial development has brought in the most modern automated equipment so that only 3,000 of its one-million population can be employed in the industry. Moreoever, in the new Mediterranean capital city, Beira, Texas oil millionaires and others of similar means have imported by air, all modern conveniences for their own living. Meanwhile the Libyan peasant, who has scratched a starvation subsistence out of the dry ground with a digging stick, clusters about the outskirts of the city and cannot be driven back to his dry acres. Even should he benefit from the increased national income, he may very well be workless for some time. When he is eventually offered schooling, will we be able to tell him what its ultimate purpose is? The city of Beira is not without its analogies in Caracas, or Mexico City or, for that matter, almost any large city in the rapidly developing nations, with their ring of spontaneously growing and deeply depressed slums. They tend to count on industrialization with little vision of what it may actually be like.

The most important fact of all is the inevitable disorganization of the human being as he faces the rapid tempo of our transition into an entirely new human dimension. We are approaching a "Postindustrial Era." Our great need is for human wisdom. I have sought some insight into the human possibilities of Postindustrial Man in the life of a people who, through the accidents of history, were spared certain distortions of the human personality that have accompanied our mass industrialization. While we are waiting with hope and fear of finding the superman on other planets or in other universes, we have within ourselves a new and expanding universe of our own to explore—one that is here, for us to grasp. It is within the individual that the universe will be regained.

NOTES AND COMMENTS

3   The Pawnees and other Caddoan peoples were an integral part of European trading plans. The Wichita played the part of middlemen in the trade between the Spaniards in the Southwest and the French to the east along the Mississippi. By 1777 the Wichita were so heavily depleted in numbers by disease and war that the Spanish authorities induced a considerable contingent of Skidi Pawnees to come and live permanently in the territory and join the Wichitas so that they could defend themselves against the tribes to the east who were aligned with the British. The fact that they have "kin" among the Wichita is remembered among the Pawnees today, and gift-giving relations are maintained among them along with formal intergroup visiting. See Weltfish, 1959, pp. 332-333; Hodge, 1912, p. 706.

3   Both the Pawnees and the Wichitas changed the locations of their villages at intervals of from twelve to fifteen years; this was considered a necessary sanitary measure. The direction of these movements was determined by a variety of social and political causes, but military and trade reasons were the most common ones. My informants gave me a list of the successive Pawnee villages in recent times and the contemporary locations of the Wichita villages. I have added, in parenthesis, Wichita locations cited in Wedel, 1959, pp. 67-68, for approximately these time periods:

Wichita	Pawnee
Rio Grande in Texas (Wedel, north fork of Red River, Kiowa County, Oklahoma)	Old Village or Kitkehax-Pakuxtu before 1842
Chickasaw on the Washita River east of Anadarko (Wedel, the Washita drainage, Leeper Creek)	Willows-along-a-Stream or Kitapatuat, near Fullerton, Nebraska 1842–1846
	Hill-in-Water-Sitting or Pahaku, near Fremont, Nebraska 1851
Wichita, Kansas (also Wedel, 1863)	Reservation Village near Genoa, Nebraska October 1859
Anadarko, Oklahoma (also Wedel, 1867)	

5, 79   James R. Murie, 1914, pp. 550-551, lists the names of thirteen
villages, each of which he states had a sacred bundle, excepting
the thirteenth, *Turawiu*, which was part of a village. The village
names are:

1) *Turikaku* (Center Village), Evening Star bundle
2) *Kitkehaxpakuxtu* (Old Village), the four semicardinal direction bundles
3) *Tuhitspiat* (Stretching-Out-in-the-Bottomlands)
4) *Tukitskita* (Village-on-Branch-of-a-River)
5) *Tuwahukasa* (Village-Stretching-across-a-Hill), the
   Morning Star bundle (This bundle was divided into
   two.)
6) *Arikararikutsu* (Big-Antlered-Elk-Standing)
7) *Arikarariki* (Small-Antlered-Elk-Standing)
8) *Tuhutsaku* (Village-in-a-Ravine), the left hand bundle
   (All use left hands in the ceremony.)
9) *Tuwarakaku* (Village-in-Thick-Timber)
10) *Akapaxtsawa* (Buffalo-Skull-Painted-on-Tipi), Black Star
    bundle
11) *Tskisarikus* (Fish-Hawk) (Bundle buried with White
    Hawk.)
12) *Tstiks-kaatit* (Black-Ear-of-Corn), meaning corn-black
13) *Turawiu*, part of a village.

These were the known member villages of the Skidi political federation. According to tradition, two villages did not join—
Pahukstatu (Pumpkin-Vine) and Tskirirara (Wolf-Standing-in-
Water). These two villages survived into the time of our narrative together with only two of the other thirteen, numbers 3 and
5, Tuhitspiat and Tuwahukasa. Tu- is the prefix signifying village or settlement; eight of Murie's thirteen are village names,
seven of them beginning with this prefix and indicating a location, the eighth, number 2, meaning Old-Earth-Lodge Village.
Four are animal names, and one, a corn name.

5   In the article by Levy and Fallers, 1959, the authors comment
on departures from our working model of the "nuclear" or "biological" family, questioning whether it is in fact as basic as we
assume. I suggest that our working model of family life stems
from the Adam and Eve story and that of the Pawnee from their
interpretation of the cosmos and the nature of human life which
derives from it. This fundamental difference in our viewpoints
does not depend on an ignorance on the part of the Pawnees of
the basic fact of physiological paternity. They believed that conception took place as a result of the combination of a male and
a female substance similar to egg white in consistency—red in the
case of the female and white in that of the male.

52   The "worm" love song adapted from Dunbar, 1881, p. 745

65   Pawnee text version of making "beans-inside" bread, Weltfish, 1937, pp. 37-38.

21, 62   In the settlement near Fremont, Nebraska (Pahaku), the oldest brother of the three, Rotten House, and Sitting Hawk, the second oldest, and Victory Call, the youngest, established a huge earth lodge, 90 feet in diameter with two sets of central pillars, concentrically arranged. In it he assembled a large group of "brothers," most of them doctors.

14-15   The integrity of the account of Pawnee life obtained from informants by the field ethnologist is clearly validated by the account of an eyewitness, the missionary Samuel Allis, 1887, who lived with the Skidi in Old Village more than a hundred years before this record was made. He comments on the efficiency with which the domestic arrangements operate:

> [H]e lives with her in her father's lodge. It is customary for a young man to marry in a family, and if there is more than one daughter, he takes the oldest and so on as fast as they mature and gives a horse for each additional wife. In this way one sometimes gets as many as six or seven wives. They are like the Mormons in some ways. The oldest wife is "Sister Young" or "Sister Kimball" and so on and is mistress of the lodge. Each woman, however, has her own bundle of meat, corn, etc. and takes her turn in cooking; and the lord sleeps by turns in different parts of the lodge to avoid jealousy. Some of them have their women in different lodges and own a share in each lodge. In this way they fare better. *They have so much system in cooking, dressing robes, cornfields and other work that they get along better than one would suppose.**

This outlook on the fluidity of the division of labor was not confined to the Pawnees. Wolf Chief, an old man of the Hidatsa tribe, a Siouan group of North Dakota, stated in 1910, "In my tribe in old times, some men helped their wives in their gardens. Others did not. Those who did not help their wives talked against those who did saying, 'That man's wife makes him her servant!' And others retorted, 'Look, that man puts all the hard work on his wife!'" "Men were not all alike; some did not like to work in the garden at all, and cared for nothing but to go around visiting or to be off on a hunt. My father Small Ankle liked to garden and often helped his wives. He told me that was the best way to do. 'Whatever you do,' he said, 'help your wife in all things!' He taught me to clean the garden, to help gather the corn, to hoe and to rake. My father said that that man lived best and had plenty to eat who helped his wife. One who did

* Italics mine.

not help his wife was likely to have scanty stores of food." (Wilson, 1917, p. 115, footnote 1.)

On the winter hunt, Uncle War Cry, head brave of the Skidis, considered the most aggressive personality in the tribe, did not hesitate to thin and dry the buffalo meat pending the arrival of the women of his family. The taunts of the other men did not affect him (see p. 435). The desirability of helping one's wife was also stated in connection with harvesting (see pp. 242, 244). Taking all of the Americas, in the more highly developed civilizations—Peru, Mexico, and Central America and the southwestern Pueblos—men did the gardening; basketry was made by the men among some of the Amazon tribes; and among the southwestern Pueblo peoples, some were made by men some by women.

57   On the Comanche version of the "kick" game, see Wallace and Hoebel, 1952, general account pp. 8-14, specific reference p. 9.

63-64 On the analogy between the cosmic universe outside and the inside of the earth lodge, see Fletcher, 1904, pp. 325-326, "The sun's ray has walked around the lodge and touched all within, then climbs out and rests upon the tops of the hills that stand as a wall and inclose as a lodge the abode of the people."

64   On the kindness and closeness of the cosmic gods see the song sung by Effie Blane—"The Thunder Spoke Quietly" (Densmore, 1929, p. 61). "A certain young man was afraid of the storm and wept when he heard the thunder, but in a dream the thunder spoke softly and said, 'Do not be afraid, your father is coming.'" He heard the thunder sing a song and learned it and sang it when he went to war. His name was Eagle, and he lived to be one of the old warriors of the tribe. (See McDermott, 1940, for Tixier's account.) Tixier remarks on the Osage report of the courage of the Pawnee warrior (p. 223): "Dark stormy nights are the ones the Pawnee choose by preference to attack." In 1954 on a visit to Pawnee, Oklahoma, I was watching television with my old friend, Mrs. Blanche Matlock, when a thunderstorm broke. She remarked that the Pawnees were not afraid of the storm," on the contrary they were part of it and went out into it.

68, 238, 268- On the European Neolithic food pit, see Burkitt, 1924, p. 7. On
270   archaeological examples of Pawnee food pits, see Wedel, 1936, pp. 53-54. An early Linwood site has a pit 11 feet deep and 10 feet across the bottom. "All (historic and protohistoric examples) are of the usual bell shape . . . with smooth beaten walls, curving evenly downward and outward from the mouth, a slightly depressed, usually bark-covered floor. Sand was present beneath the bark in at least four of the caches opened at the Hill site." See also Hodge, 1912, Vol. I, pp. 178-179; Vol. II, pp. 643-644.

80 On the ownership of the sacred bundles: The Evening Star bundle is in the American Museum of Natural History, New York City; also the Skull bundle. At the Chicago Museum of Natural History is the Big Black Meteoric Star bundle, the Northeast Four-Direction bundle with the star chart (*riwirutsaku*, round-package) attached to it; also in the Chicago Museum is the Elk bundle, *arikarariki*. The Morning Star bundle is privately owned.

80 Dorsey, 1904a, p. 331, note 24, makes the distinction between dream and vision. Vision is to "learn by being touched when the individual is awake or is in a trance, brought about by fasting or self-imposed hypnotism. Thus in a group of priests sitting in silence in a ceremony, one of them may in a vision see clearly some god or supernatural being and hold converse with it, while the other priests present are not aware of the presence of supernatural beings." The Pawnee made a clear distinction between hysteria as a source of vision and a vision of creative imagination. An example is the young man, Yellow Calf, who saw a deer woman whose charms he was unable to resist although his vision had dissolved. His problem was resolved by his marriage to an older medicine woman, Old Lady Tsitawa, leader of the Deer Medicine Lodge in the Doctor Association. In general it was prescribed that when someone is seen wildly coming out of the woods, they be immersed in water to bring them out of it.

80 The spirits of the dead priests are thought to be contained within the gourd rattles, symbolized particularly by the pebbles they contained.

83 Compare in Whorf, 1929, p. 670, the five suns listed—water, jaguar, rain, wind, and ollin—and the remarks on each with the Pawnee creation story in view of the tradition of the four direction villages, their leadership in ceremonialism, the star chart attached to one of the bundles, and other cosmic references. Note in the Whorf reference that it is stated that in the year 752, the Toltecs set up King Mixcoatmazatzin who began the Toltec kingdom. In Ceacatl 843 Quetzalcoatl was born. In five house the Toltec retain him in the country and make him their king and priest. Quetzalcoatl built a fourfold group of buildings where he and others prayed and fasted, conducted skilled work in precious stones and held religious rites. It was a celestial and astronomical cult with stellar and solar deities. Far-fetched as it may seem, Pawnee ideology appears to embody a faint echo of such conceptions. Certain elements in J. Eric Thompson's, *The Rise and Fall of Maya Civilization* (1956) contain some tantalizing parallels. For example: "The sky was sustained by four

80-81 Bacabs who stood at four sides of the world. More general, of course, is the association of the colors with the directions. In Pawnee mythology, the storm that accomplishes the creation through its four elements, clouds, winds, lightning and thunder, is personified into a single gigantic personality, Paruksti, who makes a tour of the newly created world for the gods, his footsteps being carefully noted in the most minute detail." In

81, 127 Thompson, p. 171, the world is created in terms of a personified First Day who makes an extensive journey afoot over the land.

82 Toothed vagina "like the mouth of a rattlesnake," Dorsey, 1906, p. 41. See Bogoras, 1902, p. 667, for wider distribution of this theme.

83, 152, 154- Buckstaff, 1927, is well illustrated with diagrams and a photo-
155 graph of the Pawnee Star Chart in the Chicago Museum. He states (p. 285): "The Indians recognized the constellations as we do, also the important stars, drawing them according to their magnitude." Double stars were also shown as well as constellations. Astronomical analysis is included in the article.

84, 117 On the sacrifice of Haxti, the Oglala Sioux girl, see de Smet, 1905, pp. 974-987; Thwaites, Vol. 27, pp. 209-210; George E. Hyde, 1951, p. 164, based largely on Schoolcraft, *Indian Tribes*, Vol. V, p. 77, footnote, also Vol. IV, p. 50. See also, Von Hagen, 1958, p. 98, where it is noted that after the seventeenth month,
   "they repaired to Cuauhtitlan, where the prisoners of war were
111 lashed to scaffolds, after the manner of the Pawnee of the western plains and killed with arrows." Note Grinnell's, 1925, pp. 363-369, description of such a prisoner sacrifice. Wissler and Spinden,
117 1916, p. 54, show one of the drawings in the *Codex Porfirio Diaz* representing scaffold sacrifice, the manuscript preserved in the National Museum of Mexico City and attributed to the Cuicatecan
319 tribe of the State of Guerrero. They estimate that the time must have been between 1506 and 1519—1506 when it appears in the Aztec codices for the first time and 1519 when the arrival of the Spaniards 'cut off abruptly the ancient religious rites of the
330 Mexicans . . ." (p. 55). See Irving's, 1955, pp. 184-188, account of sacrifice of a Cheyenne woman captive, especially the annotated footnotes.

84 Murie-Wissler manuscript, pp. 442-428, claims that after the new corn plant (*kurahus*, priest) was gathered in the spring, a new-fire ceremony was held and that the people let their fire die out and cleared out the ashes. The people are said to have gone off to a place where they made a new fire ceremony (p. 431). They state it was connected with a scalp ritual. I have no record of such a ceremony.

97 The only explanation of the use of loon necks and deer heads as hoeing implements in the *Awari* or Ground-breaking ceremony is possibly the statement of Will and Hyde, 1917, p. 269, that

97   Maximillian reports that in the spring corn ceremony among the Mandan, wild goose signified maize, swans represented the gourds and the duck, the beans. It may well be that the deer and the loon represented the squash and beans respectively among the Pawnees at some time. There was no known symbolism connected with these essential food plants at the time of my report, the concentration being entirely on the maize.

100   The *Awari* songs are from the Murie-Wissler manuscript, in my retranscription and translation as it appears there.

102   Oehler and Smith, 1914. On May 8th, 1851: "Early in the morning we were awakened by the shrill voices of the Pawnee women, who were engaged in cleaning up the lodge and collecting their hoes, previous to going out to the fields to prepare the ground for planting corn."

105   Weltfish, 1937. From the Pawnee texts; old man speaks to the women (pp. 29-30); a little girl goes into the fields with her mother (p. 30); Pawnee women as horticulturists (pp. 27-28).

106   Adapted from Murie-Wissler, pp. 308-325, as well as from other
107   sources. The foot painted on the warrior's forehead represented the Pawnee astronomical constellation known as bird, *rikutski*, which was said to be on the Milky Way itself, but is otherwise unidentified. The Tsawi Band calls Cassiopeia, turkey foot, but the Skidi Band calls it rabbit, *parus*. See Dunbar, 1881, p. 744.

113-114   Von Hagen, 1958, p. 98.

106   See Drucker, Heizer, and Squier, 1959, for the time depth of elaborate formal religion in Mexico at La Venta, Tabasco, southeastern Mexico near the Gulf. The structures have been radiocarbon dated at 800–400 B.C. and show a high degree of religious organization and complex symbolism that can be clearly inferred from the archaeological remains.

122   It took milennia to evolve the current uses of maize among the Pawnees. At La Perra cave where some of the earliest examples of North American domesticated corn have been found (radio-
121   carbon dated 4445 ± 180 B.C.) some steps in patterns of utilization indicated in the finds are: (a) chewing young ears husks and all shortly after pollination—wasteful, but quick and simple way of getting a little sugar; (b) roasting the ears of green corn; (c) making parched corn; (d) removing kernels from cob, shown with glumes battered and broken as though the ears were forced across a rough surface or beaten with a stick; (e) maize apparently pounded, inferred from the finding of stone mortars. (Mangelsdorf, MacNeish, Galinat, 1956, pp. 145-146).

121   Mangelsdorf, 1958; Mangelsdorf, 1964.

122   Walster, 1956.

122   Will, 1930; Will and Hyde, 1917.

126   *Pa-hu-kata-wa* was said to be a famous warrior. Dunbar, 1881, p. 736, translates the term as "kneeprint-by-the-water," explaining that the warrior once left the print of his knee by the side of a stream when he hurriedly kneeled to take a drink of water. Pahukatawa is also identified by Grinnell as a constellation (1925, pp. 142-161).

127, 138, 391   See Weltfish, 1937 pp. 98-100, 106, for an account in Pawnee texts of Pawnee arrow-shaft making.

140   While horses were highly valued as wealth, they were not genuinely personified. They were never addressed by name, descriptive names being applied to them for reference in conversation. Names were: Spotted Horse, *Asa-waki*; Red Spotted Horse, *Asa-waki-pahat*; Black Face Horse, *Paks-takax-katit*; White Hoof, *Askats*; Spotted on Side, *Karaxkats-kataku*; Black Nose, *Tsus-katit*; White Horse, *Asa-taka*; Yellow Horse, *Asa-raxkata*; Red Head, *Paks-pahat*; High Forehead, *Rika-patsa*. Horses were never buried in separate graves or mourned. When a man died who had been very fond of a particular horse, they would sometimes kill the horse in his honor, but considerable opposition would often be raised to this by the people who might inherit the horse.

140   Dog's names, on the other hand, were used to call them. They were: Wide Feet, *As-katarihu'*; White Spotted, *Paras-taka*; Bear Head, *Kuruks-paksu*; Red Puppy, *Kirax-pahat*; Hate-His-Tail, *Pits-tatur-ritku*; Gray-Headed-Female, *Ts-paks-kats*; Wooly, *Pararus*; Snub Nose, *Tsus-kataku*; Red-Sore-Eyes, *Kirki-itsparus*. Victory Call did not want dogs in his house. He said they barked when people came in and that this was not cordial. Dogs were never allowed in the earth lodge. They were kept outside all the time. Some people kept them as watchdogs, and in some cases, the puppies were used to supply the ceremonial meal of the Dog Society. Lone Chief and his brother, Shot Arm, used dogs for hunting and for dog fights. Women disliked dogs because they tended to snatch the meat. Dunbar and Allis, 1918, give a very vivid description of the use of the dogs and Jacob Miller (Ross, 1951) painted them in his picture of the Pawnees on the march pulling the travois in 1834-1836. The Pawnees were able to identify themselves with wild animals and had great respect for them, but did not accord a similar value to the domestic varieties.

140   The Pawnees lost the hard-won horses they had gained through trade and war through constant Sioux raids. Murray, 1839, Vol. I, pp. 243-245, an English sportsman and naturalist who accompanied the Pawnees on their summer hunt in 1834, experienced a stampede while in camp of "several thousands" of Pawnee

140 horses over the prairie, "trampling over skins, dried meat and some of the smaller tents." At the same time Murray's host had only five or six horses of the poorest kind for he had been robbed of his many good horses by the Sioux. He reports that another chief had "at least thirty, among which some were wild, some Spanish and three of American breed." Pike found the Pawnee horses far superior to those of the Osages. In 1829 an American

141 horseman among the Osages on the Verdigris River in Oklahoma reported a most beautiful iron gray stallion captured from the Pawnees (*American Turf Register and Sporting Magazine*, Baltimore, 1833, 501-503). In 1778–1779, Patrick Henry, Governor of Virginia, was avid to acquire Spanish horses from the west. He wrote to Colonel George Rogers Clark, who had been sent by Virginia to the Northwest Territory, that without valuing "the cost of the horses or the expense of sending them in," Patrick Henry wanted "two Horses" and "Eight Mares" of "the true Spanish Blood." He wrote that Clark was not to "lose a moment in agreeing for them, for vast numbers of people are about to go out after them from here and will soon pick them all up and raise the price very high." He asked that he be quick and suggests that the horses might be obtained from either Indian tribes or Spanish settlements. After months Clark replied, "you have conceived a greater opinion of the Horses in this country than I have." True he had an excellent stallion from New Mexico a thousand miles to the west and south, but could not at the time send him across the drowned lands of the Wabash. The Pawnees six hundred miles away had superior horses. Maybe later he could get some of them. Of Illiniois mares he writes that he had seen some good ones, but hard usage from their barbarous horse masters had ruined them (Clark, 1912, pp. 75-78, 88-89, 303-304).

In 1724, De Bourgmond, an established Illinois trader, was commissioned by the French government to induce the Skidi Pawnees, Otos, and Padoucas (Comanche or Apache?) to set up working relations so that the French could use them as intermediaries for obtaining Spanish horses. He called a meeting at Doniphan Kansas on the Missouri and such a peace was concluded:

> One of the chiefs spoke, stating that the women and little girls of his tribe were broken down from carrying heavy loads on their backs when the tribe went on its semi-annual hunts, and that he was willing to make peace with the Padoucas, solely to obtain horses in trade so that his women would not have to walk and carry heavy burdens. The other chiefs seemed to have approved of this view of the matter; one by one they gave their assent. The peace pipe was filled and passed around the circle and peace with the Padoucas was concluded. (Hyde, 1951, note 35, p. 48, p. 44.)

141   By 1746 the Pawnee had become emissaries for establishing friendly relations of the French with the Comanche: "About 1746 friendly relations of the French with the Comanche were greatly facilitated through the peace which the latter tribe made with the Jumano of the Arkansas country and the Pawnee of the Platte. Now French traders, hunters and deserters, guided by Jumano and Pawnee, began to make their way to the Comanche in considerable numbers, some of them even going to Santa Fe." (Bolton, 1914, Vol. I, p. 58.) And finally, from Murray, 1839, of his visit to the Tsawi in 1834, states that the horse-poor chief he was with was waiting anxiously for the return of his son from a trading expedition among the Ute to the west for horses. "I learned distinctly from the Pawnees that many of their horses had come from the Haitans (Ute); and as certainly that a great proportion of the guns and other articles annually distributed among the Pawnees find their way to this rambling tribe in payment for their horses." (Murray, 1939, p. 365.)

Many Pawnee horses were also acquired on the warpath. Tixier (McDermott, 1940, p. 225) states that "The Maha (Skidi Pawnees) do not lose courage; their warlike virtues are so great that one brave is often seen setting out by himself to go five or six hundred miles away to steal horses at the hazard of his life, for all the nations are at war with this tribe." The name *rarip-akusu*, warrior, was sometimes translated for me as explorer. Tixier contrasts the Osage practice of war raiding with the Pawnees in the following terms: "The Osage do not make war like the Pawnee; their aims are more noble; they want scalps. Horse stealing is far less important in their eyes. The Osage sometimes go out on a war expedition on foot; but usually their troops are on horseback and always rather numerous—seldom less than twenty-five men strong."

> The Panee-Maha who live on the banks of the Nebraska or Platte River, are today the greatest enemies of the Osage. They do esteem the stealing of horses more highly than bringing back scalps. The purpose of their expeditions is to bring back the horses of the other nations. They risk their lives by going through the huge desert which separates them from the villages, and hunting where other nations spend part of the year. The war parties of the Pawnees are not numerous; six, eight, fifteen men at most, armed with knives, arrows, axes, seldom with guns, set out without any provision. They expect Oua-Kondah to provide them daily with a buffalo, and they prepare ambushes for bison and shoot them with their bows and arrows. . . . Hardship, hunger, heat, do not discourage them. Some young men die without seeing the enemy during their first expedition." (Tixier, pp. 221-224.)

141   The surround on foot was called *tut-kawi-pitahaku*," it-to-them-inside-moving-round-and-round." In summer the buffalo tended to be scattered in smaller bunches. In winter the buffalo traveled in closer formation. They also would try to drive them over the ice during the winter: *situks-ukita-hai-iwarit*, "they-used-to-upon-water-or-ice-aim-or-direct." In winter, in the deep snow, one could chase the buffalo into a hollow where the snow was deep and some of them got their feet stuck in the snow and could readily be killed. The north wind was called Lucky Wind because it chased the buffalo to them. When the second party was going to Oklahoma (1876), old man Frost, *Huriru'us*, held a doctor dance. Then Lucky Wind began to blow and a lot of buffalo came close to the camp. At one time, east of the Missouri River, a bit east of Omaha, Nebraska, there were villages of Pumpkin-Vine people and further eastward the village of Bones-Sticking-Up, *Kis-karaxwa*, of the Tsawi Band. Buffalo came into these villages.

Even in Oklahoma in the 1920's women continued to pack heavy loads on their backs. In 1928 I met an old Pawnee grandmother of delicate build trudging along the road out of the town of Pawnee one Saturday afternoon with a huge load of groceries—a sack of flour, a lard pail full, and other sundries—done up in a blanket, the ends tied across her forehead and the weight of the bundle resting on her protruded buttocks and backbone. She refused an offer of a lift in a Ford Car, preferring to continue with her moccasined walk for the two miles to the house.

145, 363   In Lower Loup archaeological villages sheet metal was found for the first time (about 1600), possibly for arrow points (Dunlevy, 1936, p. 201).

138   Dunbar, 1918, p. 632, gives an estimate of the number of males and females among the Skidi (1840): total 1906; males over 10 years, 469; females over 10 years, 598; children, males under 10 years, 367, females under 10 years, 472.

145, 363-364   Although pottery was still in use in Old Village (Allis, 1887, p. 140) the Pawnees had for some time been carrying on a trade in brass buckets with other tribes. Mooney, 1898, pp. 257-259, describes a gruesome incident when the Osage attacked the unprotected Kiowa camp, cutting off the heads of their dead victims and placing them one each in a brass kettle, "which had been obtained by the Kiowa from the Pawnee, who procured them on the Missouri and traded them to the southern tribes." This was the year 1833 "Summer They Cut Off Their Heads." During the attack "A party of women was saved by a brave Pawnee living in the camp, who succeeded in fighting off the pursuers long enough to enable the women to reach a place of safety" (p. 258).

145, 363-364	Trade was carried on by the Pawnees with the Kiowas through the Calumet or Pipe Dance. (See Fletcher, 1904, pp. 280-281, where the purpose of the ritual is described.)
149	In an informal conversation with Prof. John L. Champe, he pointed out that in the neighborhood where the Stay-at-Homes set up their impromptu village near Columbus where the Loup River empties into the Platte was the area of some old archaeological sites: Bellwood, occupied by the Tsawi Band about 1800, overlapping and overlaying an older protohistoric site of the Burkett type (Lower Loup) (see Wedel, 1936, p. 40). The Pawnees claimed that this was an old Pawnee home. They claimed that about five miles west of Columbus was *Kitkeharawits-a-ku,* "Earth-Lodge-Village-Adjacent-to-a-Spring-Sitting."
159	Hyde, 1951, pp. 96-97, feels that the tobacco of the northern Indians might have been an attractive trade item for the southern tribes. He feels that trade with the Arikara in this item may go back to 1680 and cites Tabeau for such trade c. 1802, southern Indians coming north to trade horses for tobacco with the Arikara.
159	Gilmore, 1919, pp. 113-114, states that Pawnee tobacco was *Nicotiana quadrivalus* Pursh. and was cultivated by all the tribes of Nebraska. "Since the advent of the Europeans, tobacco is one of the crops whose culture has been abandoned by these tribes, and they have all lost the seed of it, so that the oldest living Omaha have never seen it growing; but they sometimes receive presents of the prepared tobacco from other tribes to the north who are still growing it." Gilmore obtained seeds from an old Hidatsa man in 1908 which he succeeded in growing. Gilmore, 1919, plate 27, pictures an old Arikara man gathering his tobacco.

> A Pawnee informant said that his people in old time prepared the ground for planting this tobacco by gathering a quantity of dried grass, which was burned where the patch was to be sown. This kept the ground clear of weeds so that nothing grew except the tobacco which was planted. The crop was allowed to grow thick, and then the whole plant— leaves, unripe fruit capsules, and the tender small parts of the stems—was dried for smoking. The unripe seed capsules, dried separately were specially prized for smoking on account of the flavor, pronounced by the Indians to be like the flavor now found in the imported Turkish tobacco." (Gilmore, 1919, p. 114.)

359-360	The need for a good knowledge of the stars and constellations on the Plains as well as at sea and the possibility of getting lost is indicated by a modern incident reported in the *Sunday World*

359-360   *Herald*, Omaha, Nebraska, October 13, 1957. A man was driving into the sandhills of western Nebraska to meet his wife who was teaching at a school 35 miles north of the town of Ashby. Riding to the end of a vague road onto the land, he ran out of gasoline and, leaving his car, got lost for three days. He had to live on rose buds and frog legs until he was found. A good knowledge of the stars and constellations would have helped him.

175   The Pipe Dance among the Caddo, 1687, was reported by Joutel, companion of La Salle, as witnessed by him in July 1687 (Swanton, 1942, pp. 179-180).

175-176, 199,   Calumet ceremony current in the Mississippi region as observed
223, 354-355   by the French explorer Marquette in 1672:

> He says of this "calumet" that it is "the most mysterious thing in the world. The scepters of our kings are not so much respected, for the Indians have such a reverence for it that one may call it the god of peace and war, and the arbiter of life and death. . . . One with this calumet may venture among his enemies, and in the hottest battles, they lay down their arms before the sacred pipe. The Illinois presented me with one of them which was very useful to us in our voyage." (Fletcher, 1904, p. 279.)

354   In one of their story telling sessions, Eagle Chief told of how he had carried the calumet right into the Sioux line of battle and when the Sioux saw the pipe, the whole line of battle turned back and rode off.

141-142   The buffalo jump was a primitive device for attacking the herd by lining up in a V-formation and chasing the herd over a cliff. At the base of these old buffalo jumps, archaeological excavation reveals large heaps of buffalo bones, giving some indication that numbers of the animals died in vain. The Pawnee method of surround made it possible to include all the animals and utilize all the meat of those killed. Frank North, a participant observer of a hunt in the fall of 1859, states (1859, p. 20):

> 4-500 of the Indians strung out in a long line single file. They rode up as close to the herd as possible without being seen and got as near to them as they could without frightening them. The leader of the surround gave a signal, until which time no one has the right to make noise or leave the line, and they instantly wheeled their horses, one half heading in one direction and the other half facing in the opposite way. Each party then started off on the gallop, riding in a semicircle until they met, and had made a complete surround of the immense herd. In this instance they had surrounded about 500 of the buffaloes and closing in on them, killed every one."

141-142   On the buffalo jump, see Forbis, 1958; Lowie, 1954, pp. 14-15, Fig. 3, Assiniboin buffalo pound at the foot of the bluffs or cut bank.

209   "The lances could never be taken out in private war parties or raids, but only used to repel or meet a general attack." (Murie, 1914, p. 560.)

209   One of the five Skidi military societies had no war functions at all, but was specialized in the role of hunt police. It was known as *Raris arusa*, "Society Horse," and was also referred to as "Two Lance." While most of the decorated lances had crooks on their tops, this one was unique in lacking this feature. Among the three South Bands, there was also a military society with a similarly specialized function. It was the *Raris pahat*, "society red." This society was said to have been derived from and sanctioned from the main sacred bundle of the *Pitahawirata*, where only the descendants of chiefs could belong. (Murie, 1914, p. 569.)

223   The Skidi, Tsawi, and Kitkehaxki, each had a society with combined war-hunt functions, and each band had several exclusively for war. Every spring when the decorations on the official lances were renewed, the lances were put outside the door on a pole where the people could see them. In the course of the several society ceremonies, the people were told that the lances were to bring the buffalo and to protect the lives of the people (Murie, 1914, p. 559). The hunt police were appointed after the first big kill on the Republican River when the encampment on Turkey Creek was set up right within the path of buffalo migration.

176, 227-228   For a description of Massacre Canyon and the dangers of the Western territory see Hyde, 1951, pp. 244-248; Williamson, 1925; *Massacre Canyon Number*, 1936 (Nebraska History Magazine).

241   On the roasting pit for corn, see the Pawnee texts, Weltfish, 1937, p. 34.

243-244   Among the Hidatsa, a man would request one of the young men's military societies (Fox or Dog Society) to come to his fields to husk the corn. One of the society's officials would announce from the roof of the lodge and the members would line up and go singing to the designated field. The young men would hope their sweethearts would hear them and that perhaps they would get a chance to see them working in an adjacent field. They marched to the fields carrying guns for fear the Sioux would attack. "If a society went early, they got through just after midday. By early I mean nine o'clock in the morning." "We worked late, by moonlight even." (Wilson, 1917, p. 43, footnote.)

272   An intensive "twenty-day" doctors' ceremony was also held in the other three South Bands at this time, although they apparently did not model the figure of the water monster. It was called by them *tawaru-kutsu*, "sleight-of-hand-big." (Murie, 1914, p. 602).

273   See Murie, 1914, pp. 600-616, on private doctor cults as distinct from those with tribal or social functions.

241   The Iruska or War Dance was performed in spring in May, but preparations had to be made for it in the fall in order to get the necessary buffalo meat for the banquets and more especially in order to raise a puppy for sacrifice. Murie has a long and detailed account of the vision of Crow Feather who directed the ceremony (pp. 606-616). According to Murie, this was an important ceremony of the Tsawi and Pitahawirata bands, the two collaborating—the Tsawi taking the north position, the Pitahawirata, the south. This ceremony was especially to shield a person from fire and to give knowledge of how to cure burns. Apparently the people were at times trapped in the earth lodges which were burned by the enemy. Interestingly, the first instigation of the vision was the handling of the hot ears of corn as they were roasting in the fire at harvest time.

277   On the possible identity of the plant snake shot, *rut-patsat*, we have no data. Gilmore, 1919, pp. 110-111 mentions the dodder or love vine, *Cuscuta Paradoxa* Raf. A Mexican living at Pine Ridge, North Dakota mentioned that his people call it rattlesnake food and say that rattlesnakes take it into their dens for food. Another plant connected with snakes mentioned in this source as "snake food" is bittersweet, *Celastrus scandens* L., known to the Dakota as *zuzecha-to-wote*," snake-genitive-food." An Omaha called it snake food and held the notion that it was poisonous (Gilmore, 1919, p. 102).

280, 290   Pearl Caesar, Fox Indian of Tama, Iowa, gives the following estimates on wood for fuel: for ¼ cord of wood, about 2 cubic feet, which was a back load according to Mark Evarts, according to Pearl Caesar, the cubic foot referred to would be one armload. Two armloads could be carried on the back. Four armloads would last 24 hours from breakfast to breakfast, plus two big logs. Thus, according to Mark Evarts' reckoning, eight armloads would equal one cord of wood. Evarts: In the fall, 6-7 cords would last about a month if it was still rather warm. In two haulings, they would get about 10 lengths of thicker logs of cottonwood about 5 inches in diameter, 4 ft. long. In coldest winter, thicker logs were taken, about 20 days' supply in the coldest weather. They would get small stuff when it was warmer.

305   Incident described in North, 1859, pp. 39-58, the scalping taking place during the Sioux raid as the women were coming home

305   from the fields, June 1, 1861. The woman was found alive, buried up to the neck in an old Mormon cellar with a straw matting over her head and face and left to die. North further states, that having been rescued and nursed back to health by the school teacher, Mrs. Platt, on her return to the tribe, she may have been dispatched with a tomahawk and sunk in a deep eddy in Beaver Creek. There is no way to verify this incident, but the manner in which the young woman was found by the school teacher indicates the horror the Pawnees felt for a scalped person.

276-278   Luther North describes (Pauline Bilon, *Nebraska Farmer*, Lincoln, March 21, 1931) the experience he and Grinnell had trying to learn to perform magic. An old medicine man was contacted by his nephew, an educated Indian, on their behalf and he stated that, "Tomorrow morning you get together the young men and I will teach them." The next morning six young men ranging in age from 20-25 were brought to him by the investigators. He picked up a small ax and cut off a little tree. . . . Next he found a large flat stone which he placed in front of him. He took the small sapling and placed the end which he had cut next to the stone. Holding it firmly in place he began reciting in the Indian language, "Father the Great Spirit, you are the ruler; you see me; my mind is poor; I can do nothing without your help, etc. etc. . . . He requested them to hold the sapling. They did so, expecting to pick it right off the stone, but the sapling was firmly rooted into the stone. They pulled but it was no use. Then the medicine man turned to his young Indian pupils. He told them to do exactly what he had done. This they did, following out his previous actions to the letter. Before they knelt to begin their chants, he said to them, "Make your mind strong. Believe what you say." After the young man had finished the ceremony, they released their hold on the small trees. Over fell the trees. The results were the same for all the young men. They all looked at the old man. "I can't teach you anything" he said and walked away. And so once more Grinnell shook his head and said, "It simply cannot be explained." Luther North reports that some of his scouts would practice their illusionist feats while they were out on campaigns with him. One man hid among the tall grass and appeared as a deer, then the next moment was a man. Another would simply take up a handful of mud and rubbing his hands together produce a live turtle, reconverting it into mud again. North asked him what would happen if he released the turtle and let him go. The man said he would die. North returned to the spot after such an episode and found the dead turtle there.

293, 296, 302-   See Frank North's (1959) description of the Big Dance, Chap-
304   ter 4.

357-358   Like other Plains tribes, the Pawnee had the tradition of honor-
               ing a warrior for touching a fallen enemy. In anthropological
               literature, this has come to be known as "counting coup." The
               first one to touch the fallen enemy among the Pawnees as among
               the other Plains tribes, got the greatest honor. It was said of
               him, *wi-ti-ki*, "now-he-strikes." The second to touch the fallen
               enemy got a secondary honor and the third was the final strike
               that could count. Taking the scalp could count as a "strike." As
               the strike is being made, the warrior must call out "I strike" at
               the scene of battle itself if possible with witnesses to the deed.
               Otherwise, only if there were some concrete evidence, could the
               deed be counted. For example, if one struck a dead Sioux, one
               would put him in a sheltered place until you could bring wit-
               nesses or people who came to see tracks of horses in the place
               where the exploit occurred and some blood to show there had
               been a skirmish. However, even if such proof could not be made,
               later when peace was made and the erstwhile enemies were sit-
               ting together at peace, they might recount their former war ex-
               ploits and the deeds of the brave would be confirmed by the
               enemy so that the warrior's own people would know.

363   On polished stone axes, celts, etc. see Wedel, 1936, pp. 77-78: In
               the archaeological Pawnee and proto-Pawnee sites, polished
               stone axes and celts are rare, and there seems to be a preponder-
               ance of crude stone mauls. Also see Strong, 1935, pp. 59-60,
               66-67.

375-376   The comet of 1882, *upirik-kiskuxka*, "feather headdress," was so
               named to indicate the identification of the traditional Plains war
               bonnet with a comet.

403-406   See Weltfish, 1937, Caddoan texts, on the making of a bulrush
               mat, pp. 151-152.

382, 385   See Weltfish, 1937, Caddoan texts, on the making of wooden
               bowls, pp. 47-51, and the mortar and pestle.

   As this book went to press, there appeared in *Science* (July 10, 1964, 145,
No. 3610, 117-136) a definitive article, "Economics and the Quality of Life" by
the outstanding economist, John Kenneth Galbraith, that so closely parallels
the general viewpoint that I have tried to express here that I feel it should be
especially mentioned.
   In the *New York Times* (July 12, 1964), an article appeared which was entitled "Landlord to Hire Social Worker to Help His Tenants Live Better."
The realtor referred to is Mr. Howard Offit, one of Baltimore's largest land-
lords, who owns about 1,000 red-brick-row or attached houses. The social
worker hired by Mr. Offit will work in a West Baltimore neighborhood.
Harold C. Edelston, executive director of Baltimore's Health and Welfare
Council, who is one of the program's advisers, states its purpose: "to have the
social worker provide brief counseling service for tenants with personal family

problems. If necessary, the worker will get them to the right agency for the type of help they need." The relevance to my suggestion is that the landlord feels that it is worthwhile to pay for such a service. He feels that it will improve his rent collections and maintenance of the building and the kind of tenants he attracts.

BIBLIOGRAPHY

THE BULK OF THE MATERIAL presented in this book is based on the original field data I collected from Pawnee informants in Oklahoma. It is the only material on the Pawnees that was gathered with a full knowledge of the nature of the Pawnee language. The Pawnee language cannot be readily translated into English. Structurally it is one of the most complex of the American Indian languages. In place of single discrete words, a structural form known as polysynthesis was developed to an unusual degree. In normal discourse there are long composite word units comprising a wide range of functional elements—verbal, prepositional, adjectival, pronominal, and modal—each capable of a range of modifications, the whole complex being phonetically integrated so that a single word of inseparable elements contains the meaning of a long phrase or sentence in English commonly only translatable into five or six separate English words. Although a single word phrase of this sort may have ten or eleven syllables, it is not possible to assign an equivalent English word under each syllable. The meaning can only be stated as a whole. By careful comparison of a large number of these phrases, it is possible to find the various locations within the phrase that have different functions and to extract elements with generalized meanings. Those interested may refer to my Pawnee text with its grammatical analysis: "The Vision Story of Fox Boy," *International Journal of American Linguistics*, IX No. 1 (1936), 44-75.

In the last decade of the nineteenth century, an educated half-blood Pawnee, James R. Murie, made it his life purpose to present the religious rituals and ceremonies of his people. He carried forward this work under the stimulation and direction of a number of anthropologists, continuing through the first and second decades of the twentieth century. He spanned both cultures—the Pawnee and the American. To some extent this was a major advantage, while in other ways it was an important obstacle to the accomplishment of his true purpose. The most obvious advantage was his direct entrée to the religious leaders of his people. The disadvantage lay in the fact that he had a preconceived idea of how the material should be presented to the American reader and scholar in order to place it before them in the best possible light. There was little need for such a self-conscious effort as Pawnee religion and ceremony would do credit to any people ideologically and aesthetically as a system of thought and practice. Secondly, because Murie had shared in both cultures before he came to the decision to embrace his Pawnee identity, he never fully shared in its systems of belief. In his later years he attempted to obtain a religious vision and to enter more fully into Pawnee religious life, but he failed and remained by and large a participant observer, not a full participant. His preconceived idea of the nature of translation, particularly of the interlinear variety, stood in the way of his making an authentic translation of the Pawnee materials he wrote down in the phonetic alphabet which he acquired in the course of his contact with anthropologists. He divided his recorded texts into single syllables, each comprising a consonant and a vowel and each syllable separated from the next by a hyphen and then placed an English word under each of these syllables. As I have already indicated, the Pawnee language cannot be translated into English in that manner. Any material will suffer some distortion when it is translated from one language to another, but the nuances of religious ideology are even more strongly effected by this process.

Murie's crowning effort to systematize the religion of his people was carried out under the direction and editorship of the late Clark Wissler, curator of anthropology at the American Museum of Natural History in New York City. Together Wissler and Murie produced a voluminous manuscript of some 1560 pages. In view of the recognized inadequacies of Murie's Pawnee transcription and translation, in 1930 Matthew W. Stirling, then Chief of the Bureau of American Ethnology in Washington, D.C., where the manuscript had been deposited some years before, commissioned me to retranscribe all the Pawnee texts contained there with the help of my Pawnee linguistic informants and to obtain a linguistically adequate translation. The texts were reviewed with my informants and translated with the help of my interpreter, Henry Chapman, in 1930–1931 in Pawnee, Oklahoma. The manuscript is now on deposit in the archives of the bureau. It is titled "The Ceremonies of the Pawnee," by James R. Murie, arranged and edited by Clark Wissler, 1921. Phonetic texts revised and translated by Gene Weltfish, 1930–1931.

The second most important source on Pawnee ceremonialism is: "The Hako: A Pawnee Ceremony," by Alice C. Fletcher, assisted by James R. Murie. This was published in the *Twenty-second Annual Report of the Bureau of American Ethnology*. The author, Alice Fletcher, is listed in the publication as Holder of Thaw Fellowship, Peabody Museum, Harvard University. Miss Fletcher was a trained ethnologist who went into the field to work with the Omaha and Ponca Indians in Nebraska in 1881 when she was in her forties. She several times witnessed the ceremony of the peace pipe or calumet among these tribes and others in the area, but as a result of the death of the only man who could furnish her with an authentic account of the ceremony she searched among other tribes and found that an account of a comparable ceremony would be obtainable among the Pawnees. She then went to Oklahoma where she contacted Mr. James Murie and began the work which was done over a period of four years. The term Hako which appears as the title of this work is not the Pawnee name for this ceremony. The term means mouth, *aka'u*, and is the comprehensive term used to designate all the articles that belong to the ceremony. A number of other terms are used for the ceremony itself. The author decided to use this title as a convenient designation that could readily be pronounced by the English reader. The beauty of patterning and the intricacy of the structure of the ceremony are well represented, but the translation of the Pawnee texts is ludicrous. The bulk of the linguistic texts are the words of ritual songs. A great deal of this material consists of rhythmic syllables that have no semantic significance whatever with one or two simple words included among them. Often the successive stanzas consist in a repetition of these rhythmic syllables, the single words being replaced by one or two others. The author translates these Pawnee texts into florid mid-Victorian-style English poetry, every meaningless rhythmic syllable receiving her attention with a new flight of fancy. It appears that she must have zealously pressed James R. Murie for translations of each syllable and no doubt liberally interpreted the terms he did give her. On his part, Murie must also have felt the need to press these texts into acceptable English poetry of the period. In any case because of these circumstances, The *Hako* can only be used very critically as a source.

The second anthropologist to work extensively with James R. Murie was George A. Dorsey, who did this work as part of a more ambitious project. Pawnee is one member of a language family, the Caddoan stock, of which there are three other major members—Arikara, Wichita, and Caddo. Dorsey procured mythology from the four different member groups of the Caddoan stock. Dorsey was Curator of Anthropology of the Field Museum of Natural History in Chicago under whose auspices the work was begun and then continued with the support of the Carnegie Institution of Washington, D.C. He produced two book length publications on the Pawnee, *Traditions of the Skidi Pawnee* ("American Folklore Society Memoirs," Vol. VIII), Boston and New York, 1904, and *The Pawnee, Mythology*, published by the ("Carnegie Institution of Washington Publications," No. 59), Washington, 1906. A body of unpublished material supplied to Dorsey by Murie remains in the archives of the Chicago Museum of Natural History. Subsequent curators at that institution have published from this source.

A series of pamphlets by Ralph Linton: *The Thunder Ceremony of the Pawnee* (Field Museum of Natural History Anthropological Leaflets," No. 5), Chicago, 1922; *The Sacrifice to the Morning Star* (Field Museum of Natural History Anthropological Leaflets," No. 6), Chicago, 1922; *Purification of the Sacred Bundles, A Ceremony of the Pawnee* (Field Museum of Natural History Anthropological Leaflets," No. 7), Chicago, 1923; *Annual Ceremony of the Pawnee Medicine Men* (Field Museum of Natural History Anthropological Leaflets," No. 8), Chicago, 1923.

Alexander Spoehr: *Notes on Skidi Pawnee Society* (Field Museum of Natural History Anthropological Series," Vol. XXVII, No. 2), Chicago, 1949.

While Murie was working in New York, he prepared under Clark Wissler's direction, *Pawnee Indian Societies* ("American Museum of Natural History Anthropological Papers," Vol. XI, Part VII), New York, 1914, pp. 545-644. Wissler very generously inhibited his identity from his publication, appearing simply as "the editor." He states that the work "was prepared by James R. Murie, a member of the Skidi division, under the direction of the editor who is in the main responsible for its form and limitations. Mr. Murie's method was to collect and write out in full such information on the several topics as could be secured. These notes were then made the subject of several conferences with the editor during which the present manuscript was prepared." The large manuscript on the ceremonies of the Pawnee as well as the manuscript material in the Chicago Museum of Natural History must have been prepared in a similar fashion. My own work with my informants on the manuscript, "The Ceremonies of the Pawnee," made it possible for me to limit the amount of material I had to gather on the formal aspects of Pawnee religion and ceremony and permitted me to concentrate on the personalities involved and the way they functioned within the pattern. Death claimed James R. Murie before my work began, and I never had the good fortune of meeting him.

In the years since the late 1930's I have read a great deal of material on the Pawnees. I visited the archaeological sites, read the literature, and consulted with the outstanding archaeologists in the field. I also worked with historical sources at the Nebraska Historical Society in Lincoln, Nebraska. In addition I have given considerable thought to a number of expanded horizons for our own future that are suggested through a consideration of the Pawnee way of life. I have listed a number of bibliographic items that refer to these different facets of interest, listing them under four categories—archaeological material, ethnology, historical sources, related subjects and theoretical questions. I will not make specific references to my text in connection with these publications as the presentation in this book represents a synthesis of all these sources along with my own.

Archaeology (A) Ethnology (E) History (H) Theoretical Subjects (T)

(H) ADAMS, JAMES TRUSLOW. 1943. *Atlas of American History*. New York: Scribners.

(H) ALLIS, SAMUEL. 1887. "Forty Years among the Indians and on the Eastern Borders of Nebraska," *Proceedings and Collections of the Nebraska State Historical Society*, Vol. 2, 133-196.

(H) ———. 1918. See Dunbar, John B.

(H) *American Turf Register and Sporting Magazine*. 1823. Pp. 501-503. Baltimore.

(E) BOGORAS, WALDEMAR. 1902. "The Folklore of Northeastern Asia Compared with That of Northwestern America," *American Anthropologist*, n.s., IV, 577-683.

(E) BENEDICT, RUTH F. 1923. *The Concept of the Guardian Spirit in North America*. ("Memoirs of the American Anthropological Association," 29.) Lancaster.

(H) BOLTON, HERBERT E. 1911. "The Jumano Indians in Texas, 1650–1771," *Texas Historical Association Quarterly*, 15, No. 1, 66-84.

(H) ———. 1914. *Athanase de Mezieres and the Louisiana-Texas Frontier, 1768–1780*, Vol. I. Cleveland: A. H. Clark Company.

(H) ———. 1915. *Texas in the Middle Eighteenth Century*. ("Studies in Spanish Colonial History and Administration, University of California Publications in History," Vol. III.) Berkeley.

(H) ———. 1916. *Spanish Exploration in the Southwest, 1542–1706*. New York: Scribners.

(H) ———. 1949. *Coronado: Knight of the Pueblos and Plains*. Albuquerque: Whittlesey House and University of New Mexico Press.

(H) BRANCH, EDWARD DOUGLAS. 1929. *The Hunting of the Buffalo*. New York and London: D. Appleton and Company.

(H) BREBNER, JOHN B. 1933. *Explorers of North America, 1492–1806*. London: A. & C. Black, Ltd.

(H) BRUCE, ROBERT. 1932. *The Fighting Norths and Pawnee Scouts*. New York: Privately Printed, 1932.

(E) BUCKSTAFF, RALPH N. 1927. "Stars and Constellations of a Pawnee Sky Map," *American Anthropologist*, 29, 279–285.

(A) BURKITT, MILES C. 1924. *Our Early Ancestors*. Cambridge, Eng.: University Press.

(H) BURTON, O. 1935. Communication from O. Burton of Friend, Nebraska, a pioneer, on the Pawnee buffalo-hunting encampment at Turkey Creek. *Nebraska History Magazine*, XVI, No. 2, 81.

(H) CARLETON, JOHN HENRY. 1943. *The Prairie Logbooks*, "Dragoon Campaigns to the Pawnee Villages in 1844 and to the Rocky Mountains in 1845," ed. Louis Pelzer. Chicago: Caxton Club.

(A) CHAMPE, JOHN L. 1946. *Ash Hollow Cave*. ("University of Nebraska Studies," No. 1.) Lincoln.

(H) CHITTENDEN, H. M., and RICHARDSON, A. T. (eds.) 1905. *Life, Letters, and Travels of Father Pierre Jean de Smet, S.J., 1801–1873*. Vol. III, pp. 974-988. New York: F. P. Harper.

(H) CLARK, GEORGE ROGERS. 1912. *George Rogers Clark Papers, 1771–1781*. ("Collections of the Illinois State Historical Library," Vol. VIII, pp. 75-78, 88-89, 303-304.) Springfield.

(A) CUTLER, HUGH C. 1957. See Whitaker, Thomas W.

(E) DENSMORE, FRANCES. 1929. *Pawnee Music*. (Bureau of American Ethnology Bull. 93.) Washington, D.C.

(H) DOBIE, J. FRANK. 1952. *The Mustangs*. Boston: Little Brown.

(E) DORSEY, GEORGE A. 1904a. *Traditions of the Arikara*. Washington, D.C.: Carnegie Institution.

(E) ———. 1904b. *The Mythology of the Wichita*. Washington, D.C.: Carnegie Institution.

(E) ———. 1905. *Traditions of the Caddo*. Washington, D.C.: Carnegie Institution.

(E) ———. 1906. *The Pawnee, Mythology*. Washington, D.C.: Carnegie Institution.

(H) DE SMET, PIERRE-JEAN. See Chittenden, H. M.

(A) DRUCKER, PHILIP, HEIZER, ROBERT F., and SQUIER, ROBERT J. 1959. *Excavations at La Venta, Tabasco, 1944*. (Bureau of American Ethnology Bull. 170.) Washington, D.C.

(H) DUNBAR, JOHN B. 1881. "The Pawnee Indians," *Magazine of American History*, 8, 738-741.

(H) ———. 1911. Material copied verbatim from a manuscript of Rev. John B. Dunbar. *Nebraska State Historical Society Proceedings and Collections*. Lincoln. Vol. 16, p. 276.

(H) ———, and ALLIS, SAMUEL. 1918. *Letters Concerning the Presbyterian Mission in the Pawnee Country near Bellevue, Nebraska, 1831–1849*. ("Collections of the Kansas State Historical Society," XIV, pp. 570-689, 690-741.) Topeka.

(A) DUNLEVY, MARION LUCILLE. 1936. "A Comparison of the Cultural Manifestations of the Burkett and Gray-Wolfe Sites," chapters in *Nebraska Archaeology*, ed. Earl H. Bell, Vol. I, 149-247. Lincoln: University of Nebraska.

(E) EWERS, JOHN C. 1955. *The Horse in Blackfoot Indian Culture*. (Bureau of American Ethnology Bull. 159.) Washington, D.C.

(T) FALLERS, L. A. 1959. See Levy, M. J., Jr.

(E) FLETCHER, ALICE C. 1904. "The Hako: A Pawnee Ceremony," *Twenty-second Annual Report of the Bureau of American Ethnology*, Part 2. Washington, D.C.: Government Printing Office.

(A) FORBIS, RICHARD G. 1958. *The Old Woman's Buffalo Jump*. Sixteenth Plains Conference for Archaeology, November 29, 1958, Norman, Oklahoma.

(T) GALBRAITH, JOHN KENNETH. 1958. *The Affluent Society*. New York: Houghton Mifflin.

(T) ———. 1964. "Economics and the Quality of Life," *Science*, CXLVI, No. 3628, 117-123.

(A) GALINAT, WALTON C. 1956. See Mangelsdorf, Paul C.

(E) GILMORE, MELVIN R. 1919. "Uses of Plants by the Indians of the Missouri River Region," *Thirty-third Annual Report of the Bureau of American Ethnology, 1911–1912*, pp. 43-154. Washington, D.C.

(E) GRINNELL, GEORGE BIRD. 1925. *Pawnee Hero Stories and Folk Tales*. New York: Scribners.

(H) HAZEN, R. W. 1893. *History of the Pawnee Indians*. Fremont, Nebraska

(E-H) HODGE, FREDERICK WEBB, ed. 1912. *Handbook of American Indians North of Mexico*. (Bureau of American Ethnology Bull. 30, Vol. I, 178-179; Vol. II, 643-644; 706 Tawehash.) Washington, D.C.

(E) HOFFMAN, W. J. 1891. "The Midewiwin or Grand Medicine Society of the Ojibway," *Seventh Annual Report of the Bureau of American Ethnology*, pp. 143-300. Washington.

(E) HYDE, GEORGE E. 1917. See Will, George F.

(H) ———. 1951. *Pawnee Indians*. Denver: University of Denver Press.

(H) ———. 1959. "Ancestry of Latakuts Kalahar (Fancy Eagle)" (written by George H. Roberts, annotated by George E. Hyde), *Nebraska History*, 40, No. 1, 47-75.

(H) INMAN, HENRY. 1897. *The Old Santa Fe Trail*. New York: Macmillan.

(H) IRVING, JOHN TREAT, JR. 1955. *Indian Sketches*, ed. John Francis McDermott. Norman: University of Oklahoma Press.

(A) KIVETT, MARVIN F. 1952. *Woodland Sites in Nebraska*. ("Nebraska State Historical Society Publications in Anthropology," No. 1.) Lincoln.

(T) KOHN, HANS. 1961. *The Idea of Nationalism*. New York: Macmillan.

(A) KRIEGER, ALEX. 1947. "The Eastward Extension of Puebloan Datings toward Cultures of the Mississippi Valley," *American Antiquity*, XII, No. 3, Pt. 1, 141-148.

(T) "Landlord to Hire Social Worker to Help His Tenants Live Better," *New York Times*, July 12, 1964, Sec. 8, p. 1:7, 8, p. 6:7.

(T) LANTIS, MARGARET. 1960. "Vernacular Culture," *American Anthropologist*, 62, No. 3, 292-296.

(E) LESSER, ALEXANDER. 1933. *The Pawnee Ghost Dance Handgame*. ("Columbia University Contributions to Anthropology.") New York.

(T) LEVY, M. J., JR., and FALLERS, L. A. 1959. "The Family: Some Comparative Considerations," *American Anthropologist*, 61, No. 4, 647-651.

(E) LINTON, RALPH. 1926. "The Origin of the Skidi Pawnee Sacrifice to the Morning Star," *American Anthropologist*, n.s., 28, No. 3, 457-466.

(H) LONG, MAJOR STEPHEN H. 1823. Account of an Expedition from Pittsburgh to the Rocky Mountains performed in the years 1819 and 1820. Edwin James edition, 2 vols. Vol. I, pp. 445-446. A. H. Carey and I. Lea, Philadelphia.

(E) LOWIE, ROBERT H. 1935. *The Crow Indians*. New York: Farrar and Rinehart, Inc.

(E) ———. 1954. *Indians of the Plains*. New York: McGraw-Hill.

(A) MACNEISH, RICHARD C. 1956. See Mangelsdorf, Paul C.

(A) ———. 1957. See Whitaker, Thomas W.

(A) ———. 1964. "Ancient Mesoamerican Civilization," *Science*, 143, No. 3606, 531-534.

(A) MANGELSDORF, PAUL C. 1958. "Ancestor of Corn," *Science*, 128, No. 335, 13-15.

(A) ———. 1964. "Domestication of Corn," *Science*, 143, No. 3606, 538-545.

(A) ———, MACNEISH, RICHARD C., and BALINAT, WALTON C. 1956. *Archaeological Evidence on the Diffusion and Evolution of Maize in Northeastern Mexico* ("Botanical Museum Leaflets 17," No. 5, p. 130.) Cambridge: Harvard University Press.

(E) MARRIOTT, ALICE. n.d. *The Trade Guild of the Southern Cheyenne Women*. ("Oklahoma Anthropological Society Publication.")

(H) Massacre Canyon Number. 1936. *Nebraska History Magazine*, July-September 1935. Lincoln.

(H) McDERMOTT, JOHN FRANCIS, ed. 1940. *Tixier's Travels on the Osage Prairies*. Translated from the French by Albert J. Salvan. Norman: University of Oklahoma Press. Pp. 221-224, 225.

(H) McKenney, Thomas L., and Hall, James. 1842. *History of the Indian Tribes of North America,* "With Biographical Sketches and Anecdotes of the Principal Chiefs." Vol. I, pp. 101-106. Philadelphia: Daniel Rice and James G. Clark.

(T) Merton, Robert C. 1959. *Sociology Today.* New York: Basic Books.

(E) Mooney, James R. 1898. "Calendar History of the Kiowa," *Seventeenth Annual Report of the Bureau of American Ethnology,* Part I, 1895–1896. Washington, D.C., pp. 334-335.

(H) Murray, Charles Augustus. 1839. *Travels in North America during the Years 1834, 1835, 1836.* 2 vols. London: R. Bentley.

(H) Nasatir, A. P., ed. 1952. *Before Lewis and Clark.* "Documents Illustrating the History of the Missouri 1785–1804." 2 vols. ("St. Louis Historical Documentary Foundation.") St. Louis.

(A) *Newsletter of the Museum of the Plains Indian.* 1959. 3, No. 1. Report of a buffalo jump at Cut Bank Creek site north of Browning, Wyoming. Browning, Montana.

(H) *New York Times.* 1960. Note on the Calendar. January 1.

(H) North, Frank. 1859? *The Adventures of Major Frank North the "White Chief" of the Pawnees,* A Quarter of a Century on the Frontier (the story of his life as told by himself and written by Alfred Sorenson). Manuscript in the Nebraska Historical Society, Lincoln.

(H) North, Luther. 1920. Letter from Luther North to A. E. Sheldon, February 9, 1920. Manuscript in Nebraska Historical Society, Lincoln.

(H) ———. 1928. Letter from Luther North to George Bird Grinnell, June 1, 1928, from Columbus, Nebraska. Manuscript in Nebraska Historical Society, Lincoln.

(H) ———. 1931. Eyewitness account of a Pawnee medicine man's performance involving George Bird Grinnell and Luther North in Oklahoma as told to Pauline Bilon by Luther North. Article in the newspaper, *The Nebraska Farmer,* March 21, 1931.

(H) ———. n.d. Recollections of Luther North, ed. George Bird Grinnell. Manuscript in Nebraska Historical Society, Lincoln.

(H) Oehler, Gottlieb F., and Smith, David Z. 1914. *Moravian Church Miscellany of 1851–1852,* p. 19. Description of a journey and visit to the Pawnee Indians who live on the Platte River, tributary of the Missouri, 70 miles from its mouth, April 22–May 18, 1851. New York.

(H) Olson, James C. 1955. *History of Nebraska.* Lincoln: University of Nebraska Press.

(E) Parker, Arthur C. 1910. *Iroquois Uses of Maize and Other Food Plants.* (New York State Museum Bull. 144). Albany.

(E) Parsons, Elsie Clews. 1929. "Ritual Parallels in Pueblo and Plains Cultures with special reference to the Pawnee," *American Anthropologist,* 31, No. 4, 642-654.

(H) Pike, Zebulon Montgomery. 1895. *The Expeditions of Zebulon Mont-*

gomery Pike, ed. Elliott Coues. Vol. II, pp. 533, 542. New York: F. P. Harper.

(H) RICH, EDSON P. 1887. *Slavery in Nebraska* ("Transactions and Reports [Publications] of the Nebraska State Historical Society," Vol. II.) Lincoln.

(H) ROE, FRANK G. 1951. *The North American Buffalo*. Toronto: University of Toronto Press.

(H) ———. 1955. *The Indian and the Horse*. Norman: University of Oklahoma Press.

(H) ROOSEVELT, THEODORE. 1955. *The Hunting and Exploring Adventures of Theodore Roosevelt*, ed. Donald Day. New York: Dail Press.

(H) ROSS, MARVIN C. 1951. *The West of Alfred Jacob Miller (1837)*, notes by M. C. Ross. Norman: University of Oklahoma Press.

(H) SANDOZ, MARI. 1954. *The Buffalo Hunters*. New York: Hastings House.

(H) SECOY, FRANK R. 1953. *Changing Military Patterns on the Great Plains*. ("American Ethnological Society Monographs," No. XXI.) New York.

(A) SKINNER, MORRIS F., and KAISEN, OVE C. 1947. *The Fossil Bison of Alaska and Preliminary Revision of the Genus*. (American Museum of Natural History Bull. 89, Article 3, pp. 127-256.) New York.

(E) SPINDLER, G. D. 1955. *Socio-cultural and Psychological Processes in Menomini Acculturation*. Berkeley: University of California Press.

(A) SMITH, CARLYLE S. 1949. "Fieldwork in Kansas, 1949," *Plains Archaeological Conference Newsletter*, II, No. 4, 5-6.

(A) ———. 1950. "European Trade Material from the Kansas Monument Site," *Plains Archaeological Conference Newsletter*, 3, No. 2, 2-9.

(A) SMITH, E. C. 1950. *Prehistoric Plant Remains from Bat Cave*. ("Bontanical Museum Leaflets 14," No. 3, 157-180. Cambridge: Harvard University Press.

(E) SPINDEN, HERBERT J. 1906. See Will, George F.

(E) ———. 1916. See Wissler, Clark.

(A) STRONG, WILLIAM DUNCAN. 1935. An Introduction to Nebraska Archaeology. ("Smithsonian Miscellaneous Collections," 93, No. 10.) Washington, D.C.

(H) *Sunday World Herald of Omaha, Nebraska*. 1957. October 13. A man lost in the sandhills of western Nebraska for three days.

(E) SWANTON, JOHN R. 1942. *Source Material on the History and Ethnology of the Caddo Indians*. (Bureau of American Ethnology Bull. 132.) Washington, D.C.

(E) ———. 1946. *The Indians of the Southeastern United States*. (Bureau of American Ethnology Bull. 137.) Washington, D.C.

(A) THOMPSON, J. ERIC. 1956. *The Rise and Fall of Maya Civilization*. 3rd ed. Norman: University of Oklahoma Press. Pp. 171, 225.

(H) THWAITES, R. G. 1748-1846. *Early Western Travels*. Vol. 27, 209-210. Cleveland: A. H. Clark.

(H)   TIBBLES, THOMAS HENRY. 1957. *Buckskin and Blanket Days.* (Written in 1905 by Thomas Henry Tibbles.) Garden City: Doubleday and Company Inc.

(H)   TIXIER, VICTOR. See McDermott, John Francis, ed.

(H)   TURNER, FREDERICK J. 1891. *The Character and Influence of the Indian Trade in Wisconsin* "A Study of the Trading Post as an Institution." ("Johns Hopkins Studies in Historical and Political Science," ninth series, Nos. XI, XII.) Baltimore.

(A)   VON HAGEN, VICTOR W. 1958. *The Aztec,* "Man and Tribe." New York: Mentor Books.

(H)   WALKER, EDWIN F. 1953. *World Crops Derived from the Indians.* ("The Southwest Museum Leaflets," No. 17.) Los Angeles.

(E)   WALLACE, ERNEST, and HOEBEL, E. A. 1952. *The Comanches.* Norman: University of Oklahoma Press.

(H)   WALSTER, HARLOW LESLIE. 1956. "George Francis Will 1884–1955, a Biography," *North Dakota History,* 23, No. 1, 4-25.

(A)   WATSON, VIRGINIA. 1950. *The Optima Focus of the Panhandle Aspect,* "Description and Analysis." ("Bulletin of the Texas Archaeological and Paleontological Society," No. 21.) Lubbock, Texas.

(A)   WEDEL, WALDO. 1936. *Introduction to Pawnee Archaeology.* (Bureau of American Ethnology Bull. 122.) Washington, D.C.

(A)   ———. 1938. *The Direct-Historical Approach in Pawnee Archaeology.* ("Smithsonian Miscellaneous Collections," 97, No. 7.) Washington, D.C.

(A)   ———. 1940. *Culture Sequence in the Central Great Plains.* ("Smithsonian Miscellaneous Collections," Vol. 100, 291-352. Washington, D.C.

(A)   ———. 1947. "Culture Chronology in the Central Great Plains," *American Antiquity,* XII, No. 3, Part 1, 148-156.

(A)   ———. 1949. "Some Provisional Correlations in Missouri Basin Archaeology," *American Antiquity,* XIV, No. 4, Part 1, 328-340.

(A)   ———. 1959. An Introduction to Kansas Archaeology. (Bureau of American Ethnology Bull. 174.) Washington, D.C.

(A)   WELTFISH, GENE. 1930a. "Prehistoric North American Basketry Techniques and Modern Distributions," *American Anthropologist,* vol. 32, 435-495.

(E)   ———. 1930b. "Coiled Gambling Baskets of the Pawnee and Other Plains Tribes." *Indian Notes,* VIII, No. 3, 277-295.

(A)   ———. 1932. "Problems in the Study of Ancient and Modern Basket-Makers," *American Anthropologist,* XXXIV, 108-117.

(E)   ———. 1936. "The Vision Story of Fox Boy, a South Pawnee Text with translation and grammatical analysis," *International Journal of American Linguistics,* IX, No. 1, 44-75.

(E) ———. 1937. *Caddoan Texts, Pawnee, South Band Dialect.* ("Publications of the American Ethnological Society," XVII.) New York.

(T) ———. 1956. "The Perspective for Fundamental Research in Anthropology," *The Philosophy of Science*, 23, No. 1, 63-73.

(T) ———. 1958a. "The Linguistic Study of Material Culture," *International Journal of American Linguistics*, XXIV, No. 4, 301-311.

(T) ———. 1958b. "The Anthropologist and the Question of the Fifth Dimension," in *Culture in History (Radin Festschrift)*, ed. Stanley Diamond. New York: Columbia University Press.

(T) ———. 1959. "The Question of Ethnic Identity, an Ethnohistorical Approach," *Ethnohistory*, 6, No. 4, 321-346.

(T) ———. 1960. "The Ethnic Dimension of Human History: Pattern or Patterns of Culture?" in *Selected Papers, Fifth International Congress of Anthropological and Ethnological Sciences*, ed. Anthony F. C. Wallace. Philadelphia.

(E) ———, and LESSER, ALEXANDER. 1932. *Composition of the Caddoan Linguistic Stock.* ("Smithsonian Miscellaneous Collections," Vol. 87, No. 6.) Washington, D.C.

(A) WHITAKER, THOMAS W., CUTLER HUGH C., and MACNEISH, RICHARD S. 1957. Curcurbit Materials from Three Caves near Ocampo, Tamaulipas (northeast Mexico). *American Antiquity*, 22, No. 4, 357.

(A) WHORF, BENJAMIN L. 1929. "The Reign of Huemac." Translated from the Aztec Text of "The Annals of Quauhtitlan." *American Anthropologist*, n.s., 31, 668-670.

(E) WILSON, GILBERT L. 1917. *Agriculture of the Hidatsa Indians.* ("University of Minnesota Studies in the Social Sciences," No. 9.) Minneapolis.

(H) WILL, GEORGE F. 1930. *Corn for the Northwest.* St. Paul: Webb Book Publishing Company.

(E) ———, and HYDE, GEORGE E. 1917. *Corn among the Indians of the Upper Missouri* ("Little Histories of North American Indians," No. 5.) St. Louis: William Harvey Miner.

(E) ———, and SPINDEN, HERBERT J. 1906. *The Mandans.* ("Papers of the Peabody Museum of American Archaeology and Ethnology, Harvard University," Vol. 3, No. 4.) Cambridge.

(H) WILLIAMSON, JOHN, and others. 1925. "Contemporary Report of Massacre by Sioux at Massacre Canyon (near Trenton, Neb.) in 1873," *Nebraska History Magazine*, XVI, No. 3.

(E) WISSLER, CLARK. 1917. Comparative Study of Pawnee and Blackfoot Rituals. XIX International Congress of Americanists of 1915. Washington, D.C.

(E) ———, 1914. "The Influence of the Horse in the Development of Plains Culture," *American Anthropologist*, n.s., 16, No. 1, 1-25.

(E, H) ———. 1936. *Population Changes among the Northern Plains Indians.*

("Yale University Publications in Anthropology," No. 1.) New Haven.

(E) ———, and Spinden, Herbert J. "The Pawnee Human Sacrifice to the Morning Star," *American Museum Journal*, XVI, No. 1. New York: American Museum of Natural History.

(A) Witthoft, John. 1953. "The American Indian as Hunter," *Pennsylvania Game News*, 24, Nos. 2, 3, 4.

(A) Wolf, Alvin W. 1950. "A Study of Lower Loup Pottery." Manuscript. University of Nebraska Laboratory of Anthropology.

(H) Yanovsky, Elias. 1936. *Food Plants of the North American Indians*. ("U. S. Department of Agriculture Miscellaneous Publications," No. 237.) Washington, D.C.

(T) Zweig, Stefan. 1942. *Amerigo*. Translated by Andrew St. James. New York: Viking Press.

INDEX

493